MERGERS
AND
ACQUISITIONS

THE IVEY CASEBOOK SERIES
A SAGE Publications Series

Series Editor
Paul W. Beamish
Richard Ivey School of Business
The University of Western Ontario

Books in This Series

CASES IN ALLIANCE MANAGEMENT
Building Successful Alliances
Edited by Jean-Louis Schaan and Micheál J. Kelly

CASES IN BUSINESS ETHICS
Edited by David J. Sharp

CASES IN ENTREPRENEURSHIP
The Venture Creation Process
Edited by Eric A. Morse and Ronald K. Mitchell

CASES IN GENDER AND DIVERSITY IN ORGANIZATIONS
Edited by Alison M. Konrad

CASES IN OPERATIONS MANAGEMENT
Building Customer Value Through World-Class Operations
Edited by Robert D. Klassen and Larry J. Menor

CASES IN ORGANIZATIONAL BEHAVIOR
Edited by Gerard H. Seijts

CASES IN THE ENVIRONMENT OF BUSINESS
International Perspectives
Edited by David W. Conklin

MERGERS AND ACQUISITIONS
Text and Cases
Edited by Kevin K. Boeh and Paul W. Beamish

KEVIN K. BOEH
PAUL W. BEAMISH
University of Western Ontario, London, Canada

MERGERS AND ACQUISITIONS

Text and Cases

SAGE Publications
Thousand Oaks ▪ London ▪ New Delhi

For information:

Sage Publications, Inc.
2455 Teller Road
Thousand Oaks, California 91320
E-mail: order@sagepub.com

Sage Publications Ltd.
1 Oliver's Yard
55 City Road
London EC1Y 1SP
United Kingdom

Sage Publications India Pvt. Ltd.
B-42, Panchsheel Enclave
Post Box 4109
New Delhi 110 017 India

Printed in the United States of America

Library of Congress Cataloging-in-Publication Data

Boeh, Kevin K.
Mergers and acquisitions : text and cases / Kevin K. Boeh, Paul W. Beamish.
    p. cm. — (The Ivey Casebook Series)
Includes bibliographical references.
ISBN 1-4129-4104-0 or 978-1-4129-4104-4 (pbk.)
  1. Consolidation and merger of corporations. 2. Consolidation and merger of corporations—Case studies. I. Beamish, Paul W., 1953- II. Title.
HD2746.5.B64 2007
658.1′62—dc22   2006019605

This book is printed on acid-free paper.

06   07   08   09   10   10   9   8   7   6   5   4   3   2   1

Acquisitions Editor:	Al Bruckner
Editorial Assistant:	MaryAnn Vail
Production Editor:	Libby Larson
Copy Editor:	Gillian Dickens
Typesetter:	C&M Digitals (P) Ltd.
Proofreader:	Theresa Kay
Cover Designer:	Candice Harman

CONTENTS

Introduction to the Ivey Casebook Series

As the title of this series suggests, these books all draw from the Ivey Business School's case collection. Ivey has long had the world's second largest collection of decision-oriented field-based business cases. Well more than a million copies of Ivey cases are studied every year. There are more than 2,000 cases in Ivey's current collection, with more than 6,000 in the total collection. Each year approximately 200 new titles are registered at Ivey Publishing (www.ivey.uwo.ca/cases), and a similar number are retired. Nearly all Ivey cases have teaching notes available to qualified instructors. The cases included in this volume are all from the current collection.

The vision for the series was a result of conversations I had with Sage's Senior Editor, Al Bruckner, starting in September 2002. Over the subsequent months, we were able to shape a model for the books in the series that we felt would meet a market need.

Each volume in the series contains text and cases. "Some" text was deemed essential in order to provide a basic overview of the particular field and to place the selected cases in an appropriate context. We made a conscious decision to not include hundreds of pages of text material in each volume in recognition of the fact that many professors prefer to supplement basic text material with readings or lectures customized to their interests and to those of their students.

The editors of the books in this series are all highly qualified experts in their respective fields. I was delighted when each agreed to prepare a volume. We very much welcome your comments on this casebook.

—Paul W. Beamish
Series Editor

PREFACE

This book benefits from both practitioner and academic inputs, as one author has extensive practitioner experience working on Wall Street as an investment banker, while the other author has a 25-year record of teaching and publishing and is highly respected and experienced in both academic and practitioner circles.

This case-oriented book provides guiding frameworks and information on mergers and acquisitions (M&A), complemented by a set of well-matched cases. The purpose is not to rehash the existing set of M&A books but to provide real-world examples of situations that allow the reader to use the core concepts and processes in M&A. The book may be used on a stand-alone basis, yet is also an ideal complement to an existing text or set of course materials that give an in-depth treatment to the core concepts of M&A.

The format is conducive to the case method of teaching and learning. Each chapter begins with a concise treatment of key topics within an overarching framework of M&A offered through the 10 chapters. Each chapter then includes real-world business cases that allow the reader to put the key concepts into practice. As well, this version includes an integrated series of five cases concerning a proposed deal to combine certain operations of CIBC and Barclays into the FirstCaribbean Bank. The five cases allow the student to address deal issues from numerous perspectives to gain a fuller understanding of the complexities of the deal life cycle.

This book can be used as the basis for a stand-alone course or executive programs on M&A. The book adopts a cross-enterprise perspective, one that bridges all the traditional functions, and is of major relevance to the senior leadership of every organization. Along with our general management area colleague, Professor Jean-Louis Schaan, as well as colleagues with three other disciplinary perspectives, we taught such a course for the first time in the fall of 2005.

Finally, we explicitly put forward the disclaimer that we offer no legal, financial, or other type of advice to any party; rather, we help the reader become more knowledgeable about M&A through the use of text and cases. As such, we suggest you hire professional advisors to guide you rather than rely on anything written here.

INTRODUCTION

Mergers and acquisitions (M&A) are a tremendously important phenomenon in business both because of their prevalence and because of the value involved. Among the largest firms in the world whose deals are large enough to be captured in international deal databases, tens of thousands of deals occur each year. These figures do not include the deals that occur among smaller and many nonpublic firms. The value of the deals represented is in the trillions of U.S. dollars each year. Over the past 10 years, the peak year for M&A was the year 2000, in which roughly $3.5 trillion U.S. dollars worth of deals were consummated.[1] As such, both the volume of deals and value at stake make M&A an important phenomenon.

While M&A are important, generally, they are also important in relation to other well-studied phenomena such as initial public offerings (IPOs). The ratio of M&A to IPOs is typically over 10 to 1, even among the venture capital–backed firms that we expect to be the darlings of the IPO market. As well, within the M&A phenomenon, cross-border M&A represent roughly one third of the total number of deals and value. Given this and the rate of globalization of business generally, it is important to study the unique characteristics and complexities of these deals. We devote a chapter to these deals specifically but note that there are numerous other international deals and firms represented among the cases to help the reader gain a more international perspective.

One aim of this book is to present an integrated view toward doing deals that extends beyond the pure finance-based elements of deal making. As such, we use a process-based perspective of deal making that begins with firm strategy formulation, continues through the execution and implementation phases, and then gets into the operational aspects of postdeal operations. We have seen too many deals approved by their boards and stockholders with little more strategic insight than an accretion-dilution model (i.e., a purely financial model that yields little more than an indication of how the deal will affect the earnings per share of the firm over the next few quarters). Successful deals rely on more than simple financial models. By presenting our process-based view of M&A, outlining a few frameworks for analysis, and presenting these along with real-world cases, the reader can gain a more complete understanding of how to succeed at M&A.

The M&A Process—A Basic Framework

Throughout the book, we use a three-step M&A process framework in which the firm should first strategize about a deal, execute the deal, and then realize the value.

We organized the book around this process. Chapters 1 through 7 take the reader through this process flow and present cases that have issues specific to the steps in the process. We would like to first acknowledge that no two M&A deals are alike and that the process flow of any given deal may or may not look like this. Because of this, we leave the process flow diagram at a high level in order to present perhaps a "normal" deal flow. We would recommend the reader refer back to this diagram to better understand how the deal flows and how each chapter fits into the overall deal process.

Chapters 8 through 10 consider specific issues that will be important to most readers who plan to be involved in M&A. Chapter 8 examines how firms can avoid M&A (e.g., a hostile deal) and what alternatives a firm might choose to doing a "standard" merger. In Chapter 9, we hope to shed some light on a perhaps overlooked topic, that of recovery

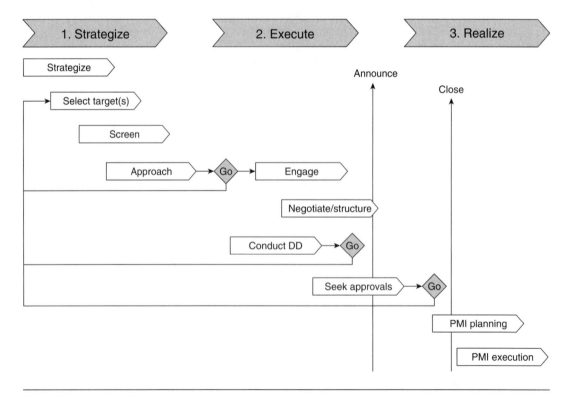

Figure 0.1   The M&A Process

Note: PMI = postmerger integration; DD = due diligence.

and/or exits when deals fail. We see no shortage of books that deal with the how-tos and key success factors in M&A but much less attention to what to do when things fail. The final chapter is specifically focused on the issues of cross-border M&A. While much of the expertise needed to do both domestic and cross-border deals is similar, we use this chapter to lay out a framework that allows the reader to begin thinking about the intricacies and complexities specific to cross-border deals.

We specifically suggest that the reader view M&A as a cross-functional phenomenon. The same M&A process we use to organize this book can be used to map the varying levels of input and involvement of all parts of the organization.

In our experience, failed M&A deals are often the result of overemphasizing certain parts of the organization or not properly coordinating and involving the various constituencies in the organization appropriately. As such, while the involvement of the various functional groups will certainly differ by deal and by firm, the critical point is that the reader takes a broader view of the organization while progressing through the text and cases. To that end, we also have amassed a list of the areas of emphasis, key success factors, and characteristics of successful M&A deals. As with other "key success factor" lists, ours has many items, but we add that these factors should be considered across an organization's functional groups.

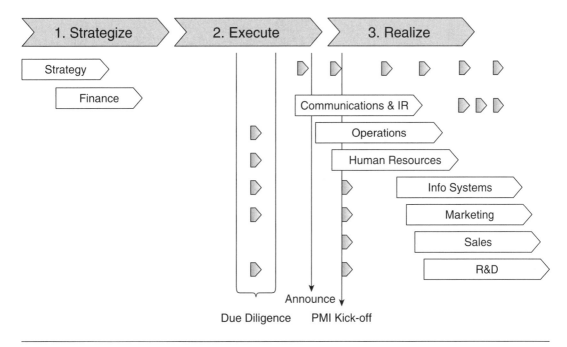

Figure 0.2   The M&A Process: A Cross-Enterprise View

Note: PMI = postmerger integration.

CONSIDERATIONS

AREA OF FOCUS

- Fit – Strategic, operational, etc.
- Contingency plans – Exit mechanisms
- Discontinuous opportunity – A chance to create value
- Implications – Plans for consequences/reactions to your actions
- Due diligence – Careful and complete
- Synergy identification – Rigorous and realistic
- Viability – Ability to finance, and ROI
- Governance – Mechanisms, and proper use
- Risk management – Financial, operational, strategic, etc.
- Cultural challenges – Awareness and management
- Expertise – Appropriate knowledge leveraged
- People – Personnel focus, motivation peaks/troughs
- Customers – Retention, sales enhancement
- Organization – Structure, responsibility, authority alignment
- Realization – Management by objective; incentive alignment
- Leadership – Experience, time sufficiency, commitment
- Action-orientation – Decision → implementation on key issues
- Creativity – Non-standard approaches
- Prioritization – Focus on critical drivers of value

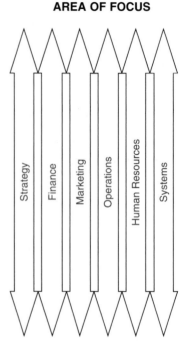

Figure 0.3   Cross-Enterprise Considerations for Successful M&A

Note: ROI = return on investment.

THE IMPORTANCE OF M&A

While M&A are important in the global economy, these deals can make or break the firms that do them. Most research on M&A shows that a majority of deals fail to create value for firm owners. This opens the basic question of "value to whom?" The existence of deals themselves may actually create value for the economy by increasing the velocity of spending in the economy. Deals may also increase efficiencies through synergies. However, when deal "failure" is researched and cited, the topic of study is typically value from the perspective of the stockholders of the buying firm. Too often, these firms do destroy value for their stockholders. However, they create value for the selling stockholders because they often overpay for the deals. As such, even failed M&A can be quite a good thing for certain selling stockholders. We point this out to ensure that the reader is careful to distinguish value creation/destruction from value transfer. Both of these can be present in a deal, and the "successful" M&A practitioners will aim to achieve both in favor of their own stockholders.

Finally, while these deals have a couple of moving value measures for the firms involved, an important piece of that value gets paid to the professional advisors to deals. The investment bankers, lawyers, accountants, and other professionals get their cut, and often a sizable one. A little simple math brings this to light. According to Thomson's SDC database, 2005 worldwide M&A were valued at U.S.$2.7 trillion. Assume that investment bankers get paid an average of .75% to advise each party in a two-party deal. Also assume that 75% of deals use advisors. This would yield worldwide fees to M&A bankers of about U.S.$30.4 billion for 2005. Thomson reports M&A fees to financial advisors of U.S.$31 billion. Given these numbers, if investment bankers were their own country, their gross domestic product (GDP) would make them the 94th largest country in the world when compared to the 232 countries and territories listed in the *CIA World Factbook* GDP rankings.[2]

NOTES

1. Thomson Financial Securities Data Corporation (SDC) database, 2006.

2. *CIA World Factbook* (www.cia.gov/cia/publications/factbook/index.html), GDP rankings by country, as accessed March 1, 2006.

To my wife, Kim—Kevin K. Boeh
To my wife, Maureen—Paul W. Beamish

1

M&A Responsibilities, Roles, Duties, Governance

Mergers and acquisitions (M&A) are complex transactions that involve teams of lawyers, bankers, consultants, boards, accountants, internal personnel, stockholders, creditors, customers, regulatory authorities, and numerous others and ultimately affect many beyond these. Each party plays a role in the process, whether a complex or simple one. While volumes are written to guide parties through the legal, financial, fiduciary, and other intricacies, we briefly describe the most typical roles of each, given a typical deal.

The deal team itself can be quite small at the beginning of the process and grows larger as the deal progresses. In the initial phase, the deal team may be just a handful of individuals with an idea. Upon analysis, inspection, reflection, approvals, and so on, the idea may then progress into execution and eventually be realized. That said, the numerous checkpoints and processes kill most deals well before they are ever executed. Because of this, M&A at the firm level are very iterative in nature, and the process flow perspective is useful in considering the roles various parties play in M&A.

INTERNAL ROLES

Executive Officers

The chief executive officer (CEO), chief financial officer (CFO), and several others from the top management team (TMT) are typically heavily involved in the M&A process. This group is responsible for strategy development and execution and thus often develops or at least delegates and approves M&A plans. A handful of these key executives manage the entire M&A process (typically) alongside their advisors and, at appropriate points, seek various approvals to move forward. Often, it is the CFO that is most heavily involved on a daily basis in executing a deal, negotiating the deal terms, and putting together the packages required to seek approvals. However, other executives and expertise across functional groups are often needed to conduct due diligence and orchestrate the deal, especially in a postmerger phase when the deal team broadens. While not all TMT members have fiduciary duties (alongside the board of directors) to stockholders, certainly the executive officers do.

Board of Directors

The board, or at least a subset or committee of the board, is typically aware of merger or acquisition plans when the firm is considering buying another firm (hereafter, the *buy-side*) as well as when considering selling to another party (hereafter, the *sell-side*). The board or its members are not typically involved in the day-to-day execution of a merger deal unless there is some specific expertise that the firm hopes to use. This, of course, varies by firm and by deal. The primary role of the board is to give (or not give) its approval to the execution of deals. Depending on the size and importance of a given deal, the board may or may not be involved in the planning of a deal but, again dependent on size, is typically involved when the TMT executing a potential deal seeks the board's approval. Often, one of the pivotal board functions is to consider a "fairness opinion" from an investment bank as to the financial fairness of the deal terms. Using this information, the board then votes on whether to move forward with a deal. Importantly, the board may often be the subject of litigation in the aftermath of M&A, especially when the deals do not turn out well. As such, boards of directors are well advised to seek professional (legal) counsel when involved in M&A.

Execution Teams

Many larger firms employ a dedicated internal corporate development group to execute deals (e.g., alliances, investments, joint ventures), including M&A deals. These teams may be staffed by ex-investment bankers, attorneys, and experienced deal makers and thus can avoid the expense of outside legal and financial advisors altogether. These teams typically report to the TMT directly, and are often used to manage the day-to-day relationship with outside advisors, instead of having to take the CEO, CFO, and others away from their daily duties. As a deal moves from idea to reality, these teams enlist the support of other internal personnel for their expertise in conducting due diligence and in planning and executing the postmerger integration. Part of the difficulty of an internal team is that the cost of employing the team is fixed to the firm, whereas with outside advisors, the firm need only pay when deals are done. Given that the preponderance of research on M&A finds that M&A deals, on average, destroy value, it is critical for a firm to examine whether to employ such an internal capability, whose primary mission is to seek and conduct M&A deals.

OWNER-STAKEHOLDERS

Stockholders

The stockholders own the firm. On the sell-side, they are often asked to vote on whether to approve a merger or are given a tender offer by the buyer to purchase their shares. In a typical merger, the individual stockholder has little say in M&A decisions. In a tender offer, the stockholder can decide whether to tender and, if enough stockholders feel the same way, can affect the outcome of a merger. However, while these minority stockholders have plenty of legal rights, they can eventually be squeezed out and forced to accept the buyer's offer. The terms of the agreement with preferred stockholders must also be considered. These parties may have differential voting rights and an ability to convert their shares into common shares that affect the viability of a deal.

Debt Holders

While debt holders do not own the firm and thus do not vote, the terms of the debt and credit instruments of the firm may restrict the firm's actions. For example, a firm might agree to a minimum interest coverage ratio with a creditor. To finance a contemplated M&A transaction, a firm may be put into a situation where it is unable to remain with its agreed-upon covenants and restrictions and thus cannot move forward. When other instruments such as convertible debentures are in place, these terms may have other restrictions on a firm whereby, for example, the debenture holders have the right to convert their debt into stock at a dilutive price or to demand immediate repayment of their notes. The terms and structure of the entire set of debt holders (broadly defined) need to be considered.

NONOWNER STAKEHOLDERS

Employees

Clearly, the employees are a key stakeholder group that is often affected in M&A. Employees, unless they are stockholders, have little ability to affect the M&A decision but are critical to the success of a deal, especially in the postmerger phases. One of the most common reasons for the failure of M&A is employee departure and the inability to integrate employees sufficiently to get them to work together. Of the most common justifications for doing M&A, "synergies" often involves cutting redundant personnel. The legal rights of employees differ by location. For example, in certain jurisdictions, the purchase of a firm (e.g., a "stock" purchase) includes the employees, but when the deal is structured as a "sale of assets," the employees are not included. That means that by structuring an asset deal, the buyer need not take on the employees. Of course, many labor laws exist to avoid this and many other scenarios that might adversely affect employees.

Unions

When organized labor exists at either a buy-side or sell-side firm, they must typically be considered and involved. Unions are typically fierce supporters of their members and are not likely to support M&A plans that would result in personnel reductions. Depending on the country, the legal rights of unions also differ. For example, in certain countries, unions are given the right to be involved at the negotiating table and must, by law, be informed of M&A talks, even if informal. As well, certain jurisdictions allow the union status of a firm to carry over to the new owners, although in other jurisdictions, the legal change of hands officially removes the union. These are the stories we often read about in the press.

Customers

While individual consumers may be mostly unaffected and uninterested, many customers may be linked into the firm's processes, products, and services. The customers of a firm will weigh the potential for better products/services and/or lower prices with the potential disruptions of having one of their suppliers involved in an M&A deal. Customers may choose to buy elsewhere to avoid the inconvenience of such disruption or may have some objection to the potential new owners. In concentrated markets, certain customers may oppose a deal and complain to regulatory authorities that the deal will make their supply markets less competitive.

Competitors

While no decision-making authority exists, competitors may take both offensive and defensive steps in response to M&A. When focused on executing an M&A deal, a firm's current and potential customers and key employees may be at risk of being poached by competitors. As well, when a deal is announced, competitors may move quickly to respond by pursuing other M&A targets.

Suppliers

Those that sell to firms involved in M&A are also interested in the deal outcome. They likely compete with others to supply these firms and are at risk of being replaced by the current suppliers to the other M&A party. As such, suppliers are likely to be keenly interested in the outcome of M&A, including which management team is in control afterwards, such that they can improve their odds of retaining the combined firm as a customer.

ADVISORS

Financial

Investment bankers are typically the key advisors to firms in the execution of M&A. They are often the source of the idea, whether on the buy- or sell-side, and play the primary deal orchestration role on behalf of the firm. They often manage both the M&A process and many of the other service providers (e.g., tender agents, lenders). As well, they conduct most of the financial analyses, valuation work, and due diligence and negotiate the terms of the deal itself. The bankers also advise their clients as to the various alternatives open to them at various points in the process. These include alternative buyers, targets, deal structures, legal structures, tax structures, financing alternatives, defenses to hostile bids, and so on. Finally, bankers are also often asked to perform what is called a *fairness opinion*. In this formal process, the bankers opine as to the financial fairness of a particular deal and present this to the board of directors of their client firm. Interestingly, the investment bank that has advised on the deal up to that point (and whose fee is contingent upon deal completion) may also be asked to provide this opinion. In many other cases, it is more advisable to have an outside investment bank provide the opinion. In all cases, this is one of several steps a board takes to ensure it is in step with its fiduciary duties.

Legal

Several sets of lawyers may be involved in a deal, especially when the deal is complex. Each side (buyer, seller) or party will have legal representation, as may the investment bankers to a deal, especially when the deal involves the issuance of debt or equity to aid in the financing of a deal. As well, when the firms are in different locations, the firms may seek additional representation in the local jurisdictions. When the deal involves regulatory approvals, firms may also employ specialized counsel to interact with these agencies. Legal counsel may also be employed to settle or move forward other complaints that arise as a consequence of the deal itself. Legal fees can be quite sizable in M&A.

Accounting

The legal and tax structures of a deal have critical impacts on whether taxes become due and affect the resulting organization's accounting going forward. As well, accountants provide audited financial statements that are used to value the companies and are typically instrumental in the due diligence processes, during which they inspect and assess certain financial and operational aspects of the firms.

Business Advisors

Oftentimes, firms will employ business consultants to provide strategic counsel that sometimes leads to M&A or to the selection of M&A partners. This input is most relevant in the preexecution phases of M&A. As well, business consultants are sometimes employed during the execution phases of M&A to conduct due diligence and to begin preplanning the postmerger integration (PMI). Finally, consultants are quite often employed during the PMI process to help integrate the merged firms. The PMI process is often a long and arduous process during which many of the synergies of the deal are realized. Most research on M&A points to the PMI process as the most critical of all in determining the success or failure of a deal. As such, numerous consultancies specialize in helping firms through PMI.

Technical Services

Depending on the nature of the firms involved and the type of deal contemplated, other specialized professional service providers may play a role. For example, when a tender offer is used, a tender agent (bank) is a third party that accepts the tenders of stockholders. For public firms, an outside investor or public relations firm may be used to help position the deal in the minds of investors and analysts, especially when the complexity and importance of the deal exceeds the capabilities of internal personnel. When a deal is done across a border, the firm may hire local translation experts and advisors who can provide local business knowledge and appropriate due diligence guidance. When complexities exist that are beyond the capability of internal personnel, outside experts are typically used.

REGULATORY BODIES

Securities Regulation

In the United States, bodies such as the Securities and Exchange Commission (SEC) and state securities regulators require certain procedures, filings, and disclosures to conduct M&A. Similar regulatory bodies exist in most countries around the world.

Exchanges

When at least one of the parties is a publicly traded company, the exchange(s) on which the firm(s) trade needs to be involved, although typically this is only a minor issue. This is more of an issue when one of the stocks will be delisted.

Merger Review/Antitrust

Various antitrust authorities exist around the globe to review deals and ensure that the deals meet regulatory hurdles and ensure the deals will not create an anticompetitive business environment. In much of Europe, the European Commission is the regulatory enforcement body of the European Union. In the United States, deals that meet certain tests are subject to the Hart-Scott-Rodino Act, and documents must be filed to be reviewed and approved by the Federal Trade Commission before the deal can occur. When deals involve multiple jurisdictions (i.e., cross-border deals), this is especially important because the home-country regulatory bodies may both consider themselves to have jurisdiction.

Foreign Issues

In addition to the antitrust bodies around the world, many countries are also concerned with specific issues related to intellectual property and to national security and thus review deals with these issues in mind. For example, deals that involve the foreign purchase of a U.S. corporation may be subject to an Exon-Florio review by the Department of the Treasury. Similar reviews are conducted by most countries, and rules and processes differ by country.

Industry Reviews

M&A deals in certain industries, especially regulated industries, may be subject to specific reviews. Industries such as telecommunications, banking, and airlines are industries in which merger reviews are commonly in the news.

Tax Authorities

While tax authorities may not play an approval role in M&A, they are critical. It is not uncommon to seek specific advanced rulings from tax authorities as to whether certain tax strategies and treatments of M&A will be allowed by the tax authorities. Depending on how the tax authorities decide to treat a particular deal, the deal itself may become unfeasible, and so the parties to a deal may terminate it.

BOARD DUTIES AND GOVERNANCE

The legal duties of the board differ by jurisdiction, but in the United States, the Delaware Court of Chancery has taken a lead position as a source of legal decisions regarding

M&A and corporate governance. This is a result of the large number of U.S. corporations that are legally headquartered in Delaware and, as such, are often sued in the Delaware courts. The decisions in these suits have set much of what is now considered to be the standards by which boards should act in M&A. The basic fiduciary duties of the board include the duties of care, loyalty, and obedience (or good faith). The definitions of these duties have evolved through various court cases and are the subject of many other texts. Concisely, unless a director breaches one of these duties, the courts will not second-guess the judgments of a board. This doctrine is called the *business judgment rule* and was originally defined in the landmark governance case, *Smith v. Van Gorkum* (1985). In M&A, directors must apply these same duties throughout the planning, execution, and integration phases. The board must ensure that the strategic decision to pursue an M&A deal is in line with the best interests of the stockholders, as is the deal itself. As such, the board plays a critical oversight role in M&A when the deals have significant strategic or financial impact on a firm. When deals are small, boards may simply rely on the judgment of the executive officers. The definitions and legality of board and governance-related concepts in M&A are the topics of several high-profile court cases and are likely to continue to evolve.

CASES

Husky Energy Incorporated

Two large oil and gas companies agree to merge to form Husky Energy Incorporated. An individual investor has received the information circular with respect to the transaction and has gathered some other information about the merger. She must decide whether the offer is attractive enough for her to vote her proxy in favor of the transaction and tender her shares. The case provides an opportunity for students to evaluate the acquisition from the unique perspective of an individual investor holding shares of the target company. Extensive data are provided on comparable firms and transactions allowing for ratio-based valuation of the transaction. This valuation is complicated by the fact that payment to shareholders consists of both cash and shares. Information is also provided that allows for a general discussion of the takeover process as well as the pros and cons of using a takeover as a means of going public (a reverse takeover).

Issues: Valuation, financial strategy, financial analysis, proxies, role of the shareholder

ConAgra, Inc.

The vice president of corporate finance with Bunting Warburg, Inc. had just received a directors' circular issued by the Canada Malting Co. Limited (CMCL). The circular had been issued the previous day and recommended the rejection of an offer by Bunting Warburg's client to purchase the shares of CMCL. One week earlier, the client, ConAgra, Inc. of Omaha, Nebraska, the second largest food processor in the United States, offered to acquire all of the outstanding common shares of CMCL at a price of CA$20.00 per share. Now that the offer had been rejected, the vice president's challenge was to advise ConAgra on how to proceed from this point.

Issues: Tender offer, strategic planning, valuation, role of the financial advisor

A Guide for Directors: How Directors Can Navigate the Potential Problems of M&As

Although deeply experienced in running a business, members of boards of directors are often less knowledgeable about—and vulnerable to—their legal responsibilities as a director of a target company. In this article, a senior partner at the law firm of Torys outlines a director's liability in the event of a takeover, particularly a hostile one, and how that director should conduct himself or herself. Among the recommendations? Act on an informed basis with the advice of outside experts and consider any and all conflicts of interest. These and other questions are important, for there are no clear answers to the hardest decisions.

Issues: Corporate governance, role of the board of directors

Husky Energy Incorporated[1]

Prepared by Paul Asmundson
under the supervision of Professor Craig Dunbar

 Version: (A) 2002-07-22

Introduction

On August 2, 2000, Krista Melnick sat down at her desk with a cup of coffee and opened the rather large package she had received in the mail. On June 19, Renaissance Energy Ltd. (Renaissance) and Husky Oil Limited (Husky Oil) had announced that they had agreed to merge to form Husky Energy Inc. (Husky Energy) (henceforth referred to as the transaction). Since the announcement of the transaction, Melnick had anticipated receiving the information circular that would provide her, as a shareholder of Renaissance, with the information she would need to decide whether or not to vote her proxy in favor of the transaction and tender her shares. As she flipped through the first few pages of the information circular, she found the first piece of information she needed: "Your proxy must be received by 3 p.m. on August 18." Melnick knew that figuring out whether the offer was attractive enough for her to vote her proxy in favor of the transaction and tender her shares would not be an easy task—she had heard that this was not a straightforward transaction.

Oil and Gas Industry Overview

The oil and gas industry was enjoying a very good year. Driven by renewed global demand, low production inventories, limited unused OPEC capacity and limited non-OPEC supply, crude oil markets had continued to show considerable strength. Given the current strength of the industry fundamentals, analysts believed that oil prices would continue to trade above their historical range of US$18 to US$22. Recently, however, prices had fallen from approximately US$35 to US$28, amid speculation that OPEC may increase crude oil production. Natural gas prices were also strong, driven by compelling fundamentals, including the growth of gas-fuelled electric power generation needs. Analysts expected prices to continue to rise as the market took stock of increasing evidence of tightening supply in the face of a very robust demand forecast. Exhibit 1 reports recent oil and gas commodity market prices.

Companies in the oil and gas industry were benefiting from the rise in commodity prices and were expected to post strong earnings in 2000.

OIL FUTURES PRICES (AUGUST 2, 1999–AUGUST 1, 2000)

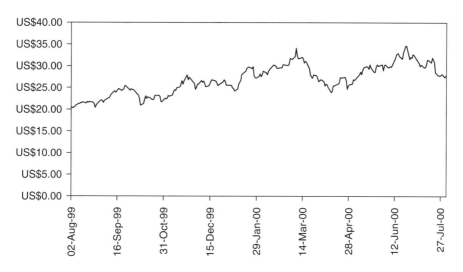

Note: Based on the near term crude oil and natural gas futures contracts traded on NYMEX.

NATURAL GAS FUTURES PRICES (AUGUST 2, 1999–AUGUST 1, 2000)

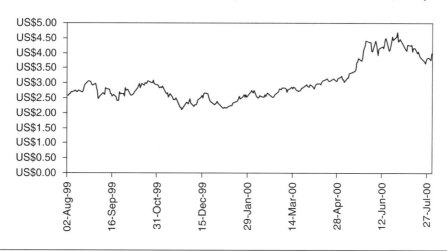

Exhibit 1   Commodity Price History

The TSE Oil & Gas Sub-Index had outperformed the TSE 300 Index until June, posting returns of approximately 35 per cent versus the broader index returns of approximately 16 per cent. However, the oil and gas sector had slipped somewhat in June and July, at the same time as the TSE 300 benefited from its exposure to the technology sector. Exhibit 2 provides information on the performance of the TSE 300 Index and the TSE Oil & Gas Sub-Index.

Equity analysts were bullish on the integrated oil companies (Integrateds), as valuations continued to be attractive, despite strong operating and financial trends. Rising production, strong commodity prices and firm product margins were expected to result in significant earnings growth. Exploration and production (E&P) companies were also viewed very favorably by equity analysts and were expected to benefit from high crude oil prices. Attractive market valuations and rising cash flows for E&P companies had led to a flurry of merger and acquisition activity, a trend that was expected to continue.

OVERVIEW OF RENAISSANCE ENERGY

Compared to the rest of the oil and gas sector, the performance of Renaissance shares was less than spectacular over the past year. Production problems had prevented the company from taking advantage of the rising oil prices that its peers had capitalized on. In the last 12 months, shares of Renaissance had fallen approximately 30 per cent, while the TSE Oil & Gas Sub-Index had gained 12 per cent. From August 1999 until January 2000, Renaissance shares were on a steady fall from approximately $25 to $13. On the advice of her broker, Melnick had purchased her shares in January 2000 at a price of $13.75. She subsequently watched as the shares fell further to near the $10 level in March. Since March, however, the shares had risen almost 50 per cent amid speculation of a strategic transaction. On June 16, 2000, the last trading day prior to the announcement of the transaction, Renaissance shares closed at $16.60. The day before that, Renaissance shares had closed at $14.90, suggesting that perhaps there had been some market speculation of a pending announcement. More recently, on August 1, 2000, Renaissance shares closed at $15.05. Exhibit 2 provides information on Renaissance's recent market performance.

As an E&P company, Renaissance's business was the acquisition of petroleum and natural gas rights and the exploration, development, production and marketing of crude oil and natural gas.

Renaissance's 1999 results had shown significant improvement over 1998. Driven by improved commodity prices in the last half of the year, and with continued focus on cost control, profitability had been restored and cash flow had increased substantially. The positive trends in earnings and cash flow continued into the first quarter of 2000. Record cash flows of $208 million and earnings of $59 million had positioned Renaissance to have one of the most successful years in its 17-year history. A summary of the results of Renaissance's operations for the past two years and the first quarter of 2000 is presented in Exhibit 3. Despite the recent improvement in financial results, the market remained concerned about the company's longer-term prospects because of an absence of major growth projects.

OVERVIEW OF THE TRANSACTION

In March 2000, Renaissance began implementing a new strategic plan that called for a diverse and balanced asset base to allow for more stable and sustainable growth for its shareholders. Renaissance intended to utilize a large part of its cash flows and strong balance sheet to enter into property acquisitions, corporate acquisitions or corporate mergers to rebalance its portfolio. As part of this process, in the first few months of 2000, Renaissance management reviewed over 30 companies in Canada and the United States, identifying five as potential strategic partners. Renaissance subsequently entered into further discussions with three of these companies, including Husky Oil. As a result of these discussions, the other two companies indicated that they were not interested in proceeding with a strategic transaction. In May, financial advisors were retained and Renaissance and Husky Oil commenced discussions about the basis upon which they each would be willing to proceed with a transaction. On June 14, they agreed upon the basic parameters of the deal, and on June 18, the boards of directors of each of the companies approved the transaction.

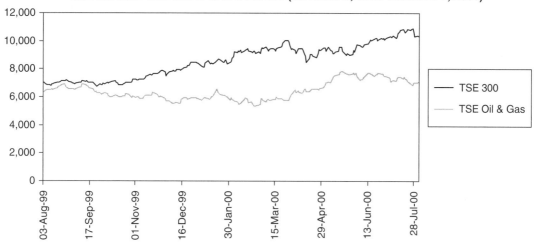

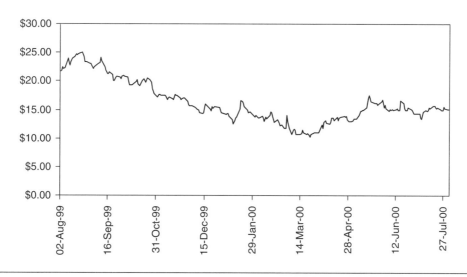

Exhibit 2   Oil & Gas Company Stock Price Performance

Source: Company files.

On June 19, Husky Oil and Renaissance announced that they had entered into a definitive agreement to merge, forming Husky Energy, a publicly traded company listed on the TSE. According to management, Husky Energy would be one of Canada's largest integrated oil and gas companies with an exceptional growth profile, a strong cash-generating asset base and the financial flexibility to pursue strategic projects. The transaction was essentially structured as a

	3 months ended Mar. 31, 2000	3 months ended Mar. 31, 1999	Years ending Dec. 31	
			1999	1998
Total assets	4,745	4,731	4,438	4,691
Net debt	1,352	1,466	1,102	1,423
Shareholders' equity	2,647	2,686	2,588	2,697
Net revenue	302	182	901	689
EBITDA	228	117	637	447
Cash flow	208	94	548	372
Earnings	59	(9)	69	(10)
Shares outstanding (mm)				
Basic[2]	144	144	144	144
Fully-diluted	155	154	156	154
Average production				
Oil and liquids (bbl/d)	96,906	92,167	91,534	87,891
Gas (mmcf/d)	378	495	465	468
Total (boe/d)[2]	134,706	141,667	138,034	134,691
Proven and probable reserves[3]				
Oil and liquids (mmbbls)	505	n.a.	475	561
Gas (bcf)	1,871	n.a.	1,710	2,535
Total (mmboe)[2]	692	n.a.	646	815
Net undeveloped land (000s acres)	7,955	n.a.	8,639	11,981

Exhibit 3   Renaissance Energy Financial Performance (Cdn$ millions, unless otherwise noted)

Source: Information circular, RBC DS fairness opinion, and Renaissance Annual and Quarterly Report.

1. As of the date of the transaction, there were approximately 150.5 million shares outstanding.
2. Converted on a 10:1 basis.
3. Q1 2000 reserves as per management estimates.
4. bbl/d = barrels of oil per day: mmcf/d = one million cubic feet per day; boe/d = barrels of oil equivalent per day; mmbbls = one million barrels of oil; bcf = one billion cubic feet; mmboe = one million barrels of oil equivalent.

reverse takeover[2] whereby Husky Oil shareholders would end up owning approximately 65 per cent to 71 per cent of Husky Energy. As part of the transaction, each share of Renaissance would be exchanged for one Husky Energy share, plus a cash payment of $2.50. Husky Oil's shareholders would then acquire up to 27.8 million shares of Husky Energy from former Renaissance shareholders at $18 cash per share, to a maximum of $500 million (the cash option).

The transaction was targeted to be completed by August 25. A more detailed description of the transaction is provided Exhibit 4.

The day of the announcement, Renaissance shares closed down 2.7 per cent, falling $0.45 to close at $16.15. However, the TSE 300 Oil & Gas Sub-Index was also down 2.5 per cent on the day, making it difficult to separate the market and company-specific factors of the price decline. However, the day after the

The transaction can be broken down into two steps:

Step 1: Merger of Husky Oil and Renaissance

- Each of Renaissance and Husky Oil will contribute their assets into Husky Energy.
- Based on an agreed ownership split (see below), a total of 431.4 million Husky Energy shares will be outstanding after the transaction.
- Husky Oil shareholders will receive 65 per cent (280.4 million) of the common shares of Husky Energy.
- Renaissance shareholders will receive 35 per cent (151.0 million) of the common shares of Husky Energy by exchanging each Renaissance share for a Husky Energy share on a one-for-one basis.
- In addition, all Renaissance shareholders will receive a special return of capital of $2.50 per Renaissance share.
- Management believes that Husky Energy shares should trade at approximately $16.65 post closing, representing a 15.0 × P/E multiple on 2001E EPS.
- As such, management believes that the total value per Renaissance share is $19.15.

1 Renaissance Share	=	$2.50 Cash	+	1 Husky Energy Share ($16.65)	=	$19.15

Husky Energy Share Valuation:

2001E EPS	2001 P/E	Husky Energy Share Value
$1.11[1]	15.0 ×[1]	$16.65

(1) Using actual Q1 2000 pro forma annualized earnings as a proxy and assuming a 15.0 × P/E multiple.

Step 2: $500 million share repurchase (by Husky Oil shareholders)

- Renaissance shareholders will have the option to sell their Husky Energy shares to the original Husky Oil shareholders for $18.00 per Husky Energy share in cash (the cash option), subject to a maximum of $500 million (27.8 million shares).
- Assuming $500 million of Husky Energy shares are tendered, the ownership position of the current Husky Oil shareholders would increase to approximately 71 per cent (308.2 million shares), and the ownership of the current Renaissance shareholders would drop to approximately 29 per cent (123.2 million shares).
- Assuming the maximum number of shares are tendered under the cash option, each Renaissance holder will receive $3.31 cash and 0.816 Husky Energy shares, in addition to the $2.50 special return of capital.

1 Renaissance Share	=	$2.50 Cash	+	$3.31 Cash	+	0.816 Husky Energy Share ($13.59)	=	$19.40

Exhibit 4   Transaction Details

announcement (June 20), Renaissance shares closed down another 5.7 per cent, falling $0.90 to close at $15.25, while the TSE 300 Oil & Gas Sub-Index actually gained 0.3 per cent.

Melnick was confused. This certainly was not a straightforward transaction. After reading over the details a number of times, she knew that figuring out the total value of the offer was going to be even harder than she originally thought. If she elected the cash option, it was simple enough—she would receive the $2.50 cash special return of capital plus $18 cash for each share she tendered, for a total value of $20.50 per share. However, if all shareholders chose the cash option, the maximum of $500 million would be reached and all shareholders would be pro-rated,[3] meaning that each shareholder would instead receive $3.31 cash plus 0.816 Husky Energy shares for each Renaissance share, in addition to the $2.50 cash special return of capital. In this case, the total value of the offer was uncertain, since the value of Husky Energy shares was not yet known. Melnick would have to figure out the value of the Husky Energy share portion of the offer in order to determine the total value. As a first step, she wanted to familiarize herself with Husky Oil, the company with which Renaissance was combining, and Husky Energy, the resulting new entity.

OVERVIEW OF HUSKY OIL

Husky Oil was a privately held, integrated oil and gas company headquartered in Calgary, Alberta, and operating throughout Canada and internationally. Prior to 1987, Husky Oil had been publicly traded. In 1987, it reorganized into a privately held company (95 per cent owned by Hong Kong billionaire Li Ka-Shing) and had remained so until now. With assets of approximately $5 billion, Husky Oil ranked among Canada's top producers of crude oil and natural gas. As an integrated company, Husky Oil engaged in the upstream, midstream and downstream sectors of the oil and gas business. Upstream operations included exploration for, development and production of crude oil, natural gas, natural gas liquids and sulphur, primarily in Canada, with some interests outside of Canada. Midstream operations included upgrading of heavy crude oil feedstock into synthetic crude oil; marketing of the company's and other

producers' crude oil, natural gas, natural gas liquids, sulphur and petroleum coke; and pipeline transportation and processing of heavy crude oil, storage of crude oil and natural gas, and cogeneration of electrical and thermal energy. Downstream operations included refining of crude oil and marketing of refined petroleum products including gasoline, alternative fuels and asphalt.

Husky Oil had benefited from the increase in oil prices in late 1999 and early 2000. Revenues in 1999 had increased almost 38 per cent compared to 1998, and operating profit had increased almost 48 per cent. These positive trends continued into the first quarter of 2000, with revenues and operating profits up dramatically as compared to the first quarter of 1999. If first quarter conditions persisted, Husky Oil was on track for another year of revenue growth in the mid-30 per cent range, and operating profit growth in excess of 50 per cent. A summary of the results of Husky Oil's operations for the past two years and the first quarter of 2000 is presented in Exhibit 5.

OVERVIEW OF HUSKY ENERGY

According to management, Husky Energy would be a pre-eminent Canadian integrated oil and gas company, ranked as Canada's second largest in terms of production, third largest in terms of reserves, and fourth largest downstream retailer in terms of retail outlets. The company would have an attractive portfolio composed of Western Canadian production, significant exploration and development opportunities (Canadian East Coast offshore and Western Canadian heavy oil and oil sands), as well as a meaningful participation in the midstream and downstream oil and gas business.

The transaction would significantly increase oil and gas production and reserves. Total annual production would be approximately 245,000 barrels of oil equivalent[4] per day (boe/d) and total

	3 months ended Mar. 31, 2000	Years ending Dec. 31	
		1999	1998
Total assets	4,989	4,816	4,194
Net debt	1,326	1,382	1,129
Shareholders' equity[1]	280	252	226
Net revenue	951	2,794	2,029
EBITDA	219	567	502
Cash flow	191	517	449
Earnings[2]	71	161	132
Average production			
Conventional oil (bbl/d)	34,600	26,500	27,600
Heavy oil (bbl/d)	50,000	42,100	42,000
Gas (mmcf/d)	257	251	233
Total (boe/d)[3]	110,300	93,700	92,900
Proven and probable reserves			
Oil and liquids (mmbbls)	n.a.	650	492
Gas (bcf)	n.a.	1,348	1,440
Total (mmboe)[3]	n.a.	785	635
Net undeveloped land (000s acres)	2,438	2,373	2,307
Refining throughput (mbbls/d)	32	28	32

Exhibit 5   Husky Oil Financial Performance (Cdn$ millions, unless otherwise noted)

Source: Information circular and RBC DS fairness opinion.

1. Before giving effect to the Husky Oil recapitalization.
2. Earnings before ownership charges.
3. Converted on a 10:1 basis.
4. Does not include 416,718 acres in the federal Arctic and Northwest Territories.
5. bbl/d = barrels of oil per day; mmcf/d = one million cubic feet per day; boe/d = barrels of oil equivalent per day; mmbbls = one million barrels of oil; bcf = one billion cubic feet; mmboe = one million barrels of oil equivalent; mbbls/d = 1,000 barrels of oil per day.
6. n.a. = information not available.

proven and probable reserves would be in excess of 1.43 billion barrels of oil equivalent (boe). Husky Energy was expected to have superior earnings and cash flow growth. Based on annualized first quarter 2000 pro forma[5] results, the company was projected to generate revenues in excess of $5.0 billion, net earnings of approximately $500 million, and cash flow from operations of approximately $1.6 billion. A summary

of the pro forma results of Husky Energy's operations for 1999 and the first quarter of 2000 is presented in Exhibit 6.

The management of Renaissance believed that the transaction was in the best interests of shareholders for a number of reasons:

- Renaissance shareholders would participate in one of Canada's largest energy companies.

	3 months ended Mar. 31, 2000			Year ended Dec. 31, 1999		
	Husky Oil	Renaissance	Pro Forma Combined[1]	Husky Oil	Renaissance	Pro Forma Combined[1]
Total assets	4,989	4,745	8,877	4,816	4,438	8,397
Net debt	1,326	1,352	3,179	1,382	1,102	2,783
Shareholders' equity	280	2,647	3,742	252	2,588	3,623
Net revenue	951	302	1,253	2,794	901	3,695
EBITDA	219	228	444	567	637	1,189
Cash flow	191	208	390	517	548	1,029
Earnings	71	59	127	161	69	207
Average production						
Oil and liquids (bbl/d)	84,600	96,906	181,506	68,600	91,534	160,134
Gas (mmcf/d)	257	378	635	251	465	716
Total (boe/d)[2]	110,300	134,706	245,006	93,700	138,034	231,734
Proven and probable reserves						
Oil and liquids (mmbbls)	n.a.	505	n.a.	650	475	1,125
Gas (bcf)	n.a.	1,871	n.a.	1,348	1,710	3,058
Total (mmboe)[2]	n.a.	692	n.a.	785	646	1,431
Net undeveloped land (000s acres)	2,438	7,955	10,393	2,373	8,639	11,012

Exhibit 6   Pro-Forma Financial Performance (Cdn$ millions, unless otherwise noted)

Source: Press releases, Information circular and RBC DS fairness opinion.

1. Pro Forma Combined is not a straight sum of Husky Oil and Renaissance due to adjustments.
2. Converted on a 10:1 basis.
3. bbl/d = barrels of oil per day; mmcf/d = one million cubic feet per day; boe/d = barrels of oil equivalent per day; mmbbls = one million barrels of oil; bcf = one billion cubic feet; mmboe = one million barrels of oil equivalent.

- The transaction would accelerate Renaissance's strategic plan to increase its exposure to high quality, long-life assets.
- Husky Energy would have a much more balanced asset mix than Renaissance would as an independent company.
- Husky Energy would have greater financial capacity to fund future growth and capitalize on future opportunities than Renaissance or Husky Oil would on their own.
- Husky Energy would benefit from the leadership of a combination of the senior management from each of Renaissance and Husky Oil.

The transaction would result in the shares of Husky Energy being publicly traded on the TSE, something that Husky Oil had been considering for years. As such, this was a way for Li Ka-Shing to take the company public without the scrutiny of regulators that accompanies an initial public offering.

From watching the business news and reading the financial press, Melnick had learned that, in general, the market had a positive view on the prospects for the new company. Analysts viewed the companies as an excellent fit. They commented that the transaction enhanced Husky Oil's short- and medium-term growth profile while providing Renaissance strategic direction and much-improved prospects for sustained long-term growth. The consensus seemed to be that production growth would drive growth in earnings and would result in strong cash flow generation for capital expenditures and debt repayment. Despite these positive sentiments, some skepticism remained because the company and its management were not well known by the investment community.

Valuing Husky Energy

Management and analysts agreed that the market would value Husky Energy as an integrated. Traditional oil and gas companies engaged in exploration and production are valued on P/CF[6] multiples as well as on reserves and production. However, because it would be considered an integrated with value-added downstream operations in addition to exploration and production operations, Husky Energy was expected to be valued primarily off of P/E[7] multiples, with some market participants also looking at EV/EBITDA[8] and P/CF multiples.

Husky Energy's peer group of companies would include the four major Canadian integrateds: Imperial Oil, Petro-Canada, Shell Canada and Suncor Energy. The Canadian integrateds were currently looked upon very favorably by equity analysts, and had performed very well recently. Melnick turned to a recent research report that she had received from her broker. In it, she found a comparable company analysis, similar to that contained in Exhibit 7.

Melnick knew that one way to estimate the value of Husky Energy shares would be to apply a P/E multiple to an estimate of Husky Energy's EPS. In materials distributed in relation to the transaction, the management of Husky Energy

had suggested that the company should be valued at $15.0 \times$ forward earnings, based on the trading ranges of its peers at the time of the transaction. According to these assumptions, each share of Husky Energy would be worth $16.65 and the pro forma market capitalization would be $7.2 billion. Including approximately $3.2 billion of pro forma net debt[9] resulted in an enterprise value of $10.4 billion. Under these assumptions, the total value of the offer was $19.40, consisting of $5.81 cash ($2.50 special return of capital and $3.31 pro-rated cash) and $13.59 value in Husky Energy shares (0.816 shares at $16.65 each). Melnick wanted to explore the sensitivity of the share price to the P/E multiple applied, so she completed the analysis contained in Exhibit 8.

Her broker had told Melnick that there was another way to look at the value of Husky Energy shares. Given the terms of the transaction and the price that Renaissance was currently trading at in the market, it was possible to determine what the market viewed as the implied value of a Husky Energy share, along with the implied multiples. Melnick completed this type of analysis (see Exhibit 9) for a range of Renaissance share prices. Renaissance shares had been trading in a range of approximately $13.50 to $16.50 since the announcement of the transaction. This indicated that the market believed that the value of a Husky Energy share was lower than what management had suggested, and that lower multiples may be more appropriate. At the current Renaissance share price of $15.05, the implied value of each Husky Energy share was $11.32, and the implied multiples were $10.2 \times$ 2001E EPS, $4.3 \times$ 2001E EBITDA, and $3.1 \times$ 2001E CFPS. The market consensus seemed to be that Husky Energy shares would initially trade at the lower end of the range of multiples for the Canadian integrateds for a number of possible reasons, including the lack of market knowledge regarding the company's assets, performance and management, and the complicated nature of the transaction structure.

Company	52-Week High	52-Week Low	Current Price 31-Jul-00	Shares O/S (millions)	Market Cap.	LT Debt	Pref. Shares	Work. Cap.	Enterprise Value[1]	EPS 1999	EPS 2000E	EPS 2001E	CFPS 1999	CFPS 2000E	CFPS 2001E	EBITDA[2] 1999	EBITDA[2] 2000E	EBITDA[2] 2001E
Canadian Integrateds																		
Imperial Oil (IMO)	$39.55	$26.50	$36.30	418	15,173	1,254	0	406	16,021	$1.31	$2.78	$2.68	$2.70	$4.19	$4.71	1,818	2,877	2,766
Petro-Canada (PCA)	$31.15	$19.00	$28.60	271	7,751	1,747	0	833	8,665	$0.86	$2.23	$2.21	$3.45	$5.19	$5.34	1,199	1,910	1,994
Shell Canada (SHC)	$37.50	$25.00	$32.75	283	9,268	22	0	851	8,439	$1.21	$2.49	$2.49	$2.75	$3.79	$4.44	1,020	1,591	1,587
Suncor Energy (SU)	$36.90	$26.00	$31.00	220	6,820	1,741	514	(116)	9,191	$0.72	$1.59	$1.58	$2.47	$3.59	$3.81	681	1,046	1,130
Canadian Exploration & Production (Seniors)																		
Alberta Energy (AEC)	$61.75	$37.75	$53.75	138	7,434	3,565	641	426	11,214	$1.26	$3.69	$4.38	$6.68	$12.04	$12.66	1,062	1,987	2,222
Anderson Exploration (AXL)	$29.40	$14.75	$25.00	130	3,245	1,353	0	(100)	4,698	$0.56	$1.94	$2.01	$3.03	$5.53	$6.48	448	876	1,009
Baytex Energy (BTE)	$15.50	$8.10	$12.20	46	556	108	0	(17)	681	$0.39	$1.62	$1.76	$1.67	$4.38	$5.28	72	217	282
Berkley (BKP)	$17.75	$7.80	$9.05	100	904	315	0	(62)	1,281	$0.14	$0.71	$0.74	$1.02	$2.27	$2.43	114	256	277
Canadian Hunter (HTR)	$35.25	$19.50	$29.90	60	1,782	261	0	20	2,023	$1.12	$2.45	$2.88	$3.81	$7.17	$7.63	261	465	514
Canadian Natural (CNQ)	$49.45	$29.80	$41.70	121	5,033	3,100	120	(40)	8,293	$1.93	$5.60	$5.34	$6.49	$14.11	$14.46	830	1,934	2,190

Exhibit 7   Comparable Trading Statistics

Company	52-Week		Current Price	Shares O/S	Market Cap.	LT Debt	Pref. Shares	Work. Cap.	Enterprise Value[1]	EPS			CFPS			EBITDA[2]		
	High	Low	31-Jul-00	(millions)						1999	2000E	2001E	1999	2000E	2001E	1999	2000E	2001E
Canadian Occidental (CXY)	$44.65	$25.80	$37.00	118	4,366	1,906	724	750	6,246	$0.46	$3.88	$3.15	$5.02	$10.35	$10.63	995	1,742	1,667
Crestar (CRS)	$25.00	$17.00	$21.40	55	1,168	685	0	(1)	1,854	$0.92	$3.40	$3.15	$5.28	$9.66	$9.32	436	796	773
Encal (ENL)	$10.50	$5.30	$8.80	109	960	422	0	11	1,371	$0.23	$0.77	$0.92	$1.10	$2.17	$2.41	165	341	404
Gulf Canada (GOU)	$7.80	$4.41	$6.70	352	2,358	2,035	577	132	4,838	($0.58)	$0.29	$0.54	$1.35	$2.24	$2.41	723	1,067	1,135
PanCanadian (PCP)	$34.50	$19.50	$29.00	252	7,299	910	126	54	8,281	$1.38	$2.81	$2.79	$4.16	$6.99	$6.76	1,193	1,962	1,998
Paramount (POU)	$26.00	$10.50	$13.25	60	788	299	0	(24)	1,111	$0.50	$1.15	$1.36	$1.84	$3.47	$4.09	124	225	261
Penn West (PWT)	$41.50	$26.50	$32.55	51	1,667	615	0	(132)	2,414	$1.57	$3.31	$3.69	$4.60	$8.42	$9.44	255	510	571
Rio Alto (RAX)	$31.20	$16.30	$26.10	74	1,929	644	0	(80)	2,653	$0.95	$2.25	$2.74	$2.98	$5.56	$6.79	256	465	574
Talisman Energy (TLM)	$54.50	$33.50	$44.10	138	6,099	2,036	431	118	8,448	$1.31	$5.25	$4.00	$8.04	$15.06	$15.18	1,270	2,624	2,646

(Continued)

Source: CIBC WM Research.

1. Enterprise Value is defined as Market Cap. + LT Debt + Pref. Shares – Work. Cap.
2. EBITDA is defined as earnings before interest, taxes, depreciation and amortization.

Exhibit 7 (Continued)

Company	P/E			P/CFPS			EV/EBITDA			Proven Reserves		1999 Oil Production	Gas Production
	1999	2000E	2001E	1999	2000E	2001E	1999	2000E	2001E	Oil	Gas		
										(mmbbls)	(bcf)	(mbbls/d)	(mmcf/d)
Canadian Integrateds													
Imperial Oil (IMO)	27.7 ×	13.1 ×	13.5 ×	13.4 ×	8.7 ×	7.7 ×	8.8 ×	5.6 ×	5.8 ×	1,928	1,964	284	393
Petro-Canada (PCA)	33.3 ×	12.8 ×	12.9 ×	8.3 ×	5.5 ×	5.4 ×	7.2 ×	4.5 ×	4.3 ×	476	2,481	95	719
Shell Canada (SHC)	27.1 ×	13.2 ×	13.2 ×	11.9 ×	8.6 ×	7.4 ×	8.3 ×	5.3 ×	5.3 ×	897	3,119	74	552
Suncor Energy (SU)	43.1 ×	19.5 ×	19.6 ×	12.6 ×	8.6 ×	8.1 ×	13.5 ×	8.8 ×	8.1 ×	527	1,013	116	226
Average	**32.8×**	**14.6×**	**14.8×**	**11.5×**	**7.9×**	**7.1×**	**9.5×**	**6.0×**	**5.9×**				
Canadian Exploration & Production (Seniors)													
Alberta Energy (AEC)	42.7 ×	14.6 ×	12.3 ×	8.0 ×	4.5 ×	4.2 ×	10.6 ×	5.6 ×	5.0 ×	859	3,613	96	904
Anderson Exploration (AXL)	44.6 ×	12.9 ×	12.4 ×	8.3 ×	4.5 ×	3.9 ×	10.5 ×	5.4 ×	4.7 ×	194	2,276	34	568
Baytex Energy (BTE)	31.3 ×	7.5 ×	6.9 ×	7.3 ×	2.8 ×	2.3 ×	9.5 ×	3.1 ×	2.4 ×	94	114	10	56
Berkley (BKP)	64.6 ×	12.7 ×	12.2 ×	8.9 ×	4.0 ×	3.7 ×	11.2 ×	5.0 ×	4.6 ×	41	594	11	147
Canadian Hunter (HTR)	26.7 ×	12.2 ×	10.4 ×	7.8 ×	4.2 ×	3.9 ×	7.8 ×	4.4 ×	3.9 ×	20	1,077	8	357
Canadian Natural (CNQ)	21.6 ×	7.4 ×	7.8 ×	6.4 ×	3.0 ×	2.9 ×	10.0 ×	4.3 ×	3.8 ×	702	2,574	87	721
Canadian Occidental (CXY)	80.4 ×	9.5 ×	11.7 ×	7.4 ×	3.6 ×	3.5 ×	6.3 ×	3.6 ×	3.7 ×	655	726	193	278
Crestar (CRS)	23.3 ×	6.3 ×	6.8 ×	4.1 ×	2.2 ×	2.3 ×	4.3 ×	2.3 ×	2.4 ×	155	1,030	43	351
Encal (ENL)	38.3 ×	11.4 ×	9.6 ×	8.0 ×	4.1 ×	3.7 ×	8.3 ×	4.0 ×	3.4 ×	39	569	14	153
Gulf Canada (GOU)	n.m.	23.1 ×	12.4 ×	5.0 ×	3.0 ×	2.8 ×	6.7 ×	4.5 ×	4.3 ×	431	2,296	101	554
PanCanadian (PCP)	21.0 ×	10.3 ×	10.4 ×	7.0 ×	4.1 ×	4.3 ×	6.9 ×	4.2 ×	4.1 ×	417	3,314	114	821
Paramount (POU)	26.5 ×	11.5 ×	9.7 ×	7.2 ×	3.8 ×	3.2 ×	9.0 ×	4.9 ×	4.3 ×	6	595	2	220
Penn West (PWT)	20.7 ×	9.8 ×	8.8 ×	7.1 ×	3.9 ×	3.4 ×	9.5 ×	4.7 ×	4.2 ×	124	876	21	245
Rio Alto (RAX)	27.5 ×	11.6 ×	9.5 ×	8.8 ×	4.7 ×	3.8 ×	10.4 ×	5.7 ×	4.6 ×	43	1,341	8	365
Talisman Energy (TLM)	33.7 ×	8.4 ×	11.0 ×	5.5 ×	2.9 ×	2.9 ×	6.7 ×	3.2 ×	3.2 ×	590	3,221	158	904
Average	**35.9×**	**11.3×**	**10.1×**	**7.1×**	**3.7×**	**3.4×**	**8.5×**	**4.3×**	**3.9×**				

Source: CIBC WM Research.

1. mmbbls = one million barrels of oil; bcf = one billion cubic feet; mmboe = one million barrels of oil equivalent.

	P/E Multiple Applied			
	12.0 ×	**13.0 ×**	**14.0×**	**15.0 ×**
Husky Energy 2001E EPS[1]	$1.11	$1.11	$1.11	$1.11
P/E multiple applied	12.0 ×	13.0 ×	14.0 ×	15.0 ×
Trading value of one Husky Energy share	$13.32	$14.43	$15.54	$16.65
To equate to pro rata Husky Energy share[2]	0.816	0.816	0.816	0.816
Pro rata value of one Husky Energy share	$10.87	$11.77	$12.68	$13.59
Pro rata Cash Option value per share[2]	$3.31	$3.31	$3.31	$3.31
Blended value per share	$14.18	$15.08	$15.99	$16.90
Return of capital per share	$2.50	$2.50	$2.50	$2.50
Total value per share	$16.68	$17.58	$18.49	$19.40

Exhibit 8   Transaction Value Per Share for Renaissance Energy Shareholders (Cdn$, unless otherwise noted)

Source: Information circular and other material distributed associated with the transaction.

1. Management estimate, using Q1 2000 pro forma annualized earnings as a proxy.
2. Assuming the maximum under the cash option, on a pro rata basis, each shareholder will receive 0.816 Husky Energy shares and $3.31 cash for each Renaissance share tendered.

ASSESSING THE OFFER

Based on her analysis, Melnick had to choose an appropriate range for the value of the Husky Energy shares she would receive. She then could determine the total value of the offer and consider whether it was lucrative enough for her to tender her shares and vote her proxy in favor of the transaction.

Melnick knew that in assessing the fairness of an offer, investors often looked to a number of indicators. These included: (i) an analysis of the multiples of comparable companies currently trading in the public market; (ii) an analysis of the multiples paid in recent comparable transactions in the sector; and (iii) a comparison of the total consideration to recent market prices. Melnick again looked to the comparable companies analysis she had (see Exhibit 7) for the multiples of publicly traded companies. Since there had been an abundance of merger and acquisition activity in the oil and gas sector to date in 2000, there were many "precedent transactions" to which Melnick could compare the transaction (see Exhibit 10). Melnick could see that a number of parameters were used in this analysis, including multiples of forecasted financial results (P/CF, EV/EBITDA) and production and reserves (EV/Production, EV/Reserves). Finally, in comparing the total value of the consideration to recent market trading prices, Melnick knew that she essentially wanted to calculate the "premium" that was being paid. She also knew that there were a number of benchmarks she could use, including the closing price the day prior to the announcement and the 30-day average ending the day prior to the announcement, among others. Exhibit 11 contains price information for Renaissance for a period of time around the announcement of the transaction.

In addition to her "number crunching," there were other factors for Melnick to consider.

	Renaissance Share Price				Current	Suggested[1]
	$14.00	$15.00	$16.00	$17.00	$15.05	$19.40
Renaissance share price Less: Cash rec'd by Renaissance shareholders	$14.00 5.81	$15.00 5.81	$16.00 5.81	$17.00 5.81	$15.05 5.81	$19.40 5.81
To equate to a full Husky Energy share	8.19 0.816	9.19 0.816	10.19 0.816	11.19 0.816	9.24 0.816	13.59 0.816
Implied value of one Husky Energy share	10.04	11.26	12.49	13.71	11.32	16.65
Husky Energy 2001E EPS[2]	1.11	1.11	1.11	1.11	1.11	1.11
Implied 2001E P/E multiple Implied value of one Husky Energy share	9.0 × 10.04	10.1 × 11.26	11.3 × 12.49	12.4 × 13.71	10.2 × 11.32	15.0 × 16.65
Husky Energy 2001E CFPS[2]	3.62	3.62	3.62	3.62	3.62	3.62
Implied 2001E P/CF multiple Husky Energy shares outstanding Implied market capitalization Husky Energy net debt	2.8 × 431.4 4,329.9 3,179.3	3.1 × 431.4 4,858.5 3,179.3	3.4 × 431.4 5,387.2 3,179.3	3.8 × 431.4 5,915.9 3,179.3	3.1 × 431.4 4,885.0 3,179.3	4.6 × 431.4 7,184.7 3,179.3
Implied enterprise value Husky Energy 2001E EBITDA[3]	7,509.2 1,868.5	8,037.8 1,868.5	8,566.5 1,868.5	9,095.2 1,868.5	8,064.3 1,868.5	10,364.0 1,868.5
Implied 2001E EV/EBITDA multiple	4.0 ×	4.3 ×	4.6 ×	4.9 ×	4.3 ×	5.5 ×

Exhibit 9   Valuation Implied by Renaissance Energy Market Share Price (Cdn$ millions, unless otherwise noted)

Source: Information circular and other material distributed associated with the transaction.

1. "Suggested" is the original value proposed by management.
2. Based on 2001E EPS estimate of $1.11 and CFPS estimate of $3.62, provided in materials distributed with transaction.
3. Based on 2001E EBITDA estimate of $1,868.5, provided in materials distributed with transaction.

Based on a fairness opinion provided by its financial advisors, the board of directors of Renaissance had concluded that the transaction was financially fair to Renaissance shareholders. As such, the board of directors had unanimously recommended that shareholders vote to approve the transaction and had agreed to a "break-up" fee[10] of $82 million if the deal was not consummated.

DECISION

With a sigh of relief, Melnick put her pen down and sat back in her chair after working the afternoon away. She looked at the materials in front of her—an information circular covered with highlighter marks, an analyst report covered with red underlines and circles and some scrap paper covered with calculations. All that was left to do

Date	Acquiror	Target	Implied Equity Value ($mm)	Implied Enterprise Value ($mm)	Bid Price/Forecasted DCF [1] 1 Yr.[2] (times)	2 Yr.[2] (times)	Bid Enterprise/Forecasted EBITDA 1 Yr.[2] (times)	2 Yr.[2] (times)	Bid Adj. Enterprise Value[3] Proven ($/boe)	Proven + Probable ($/boe)	Bid Adj. Enterprise Value[3] 1 Yr. Prod.[2] ($/boe/d)	2 Yr. Prod.[2] ($/boe/d)	Premium 30-day (%)	60-day (%)
Pending	Canadian Natural Res.	Ranger Oil	1,081.6	1,588.0	3.6 ×	3.4 ×	3.9 ×	4.5 ×	$5.83	$4.25	20,059	19,487	9.0%	18.3%
Pending	Unocal	Northrock Resources	104.2	133.9	3.5 ×	3.2 ×	5.0 ×	4.5 ×	$7.27	$5.53	23,769	21,857	44.0%	44.0%
Jun-00	Rio Alto Exploration	Renata Resources	221.6	381.6	5.1 ×	4.8 ×	n.a.	n.a.	$10.35	$7.98	24,927	22,484	32.8%	48.1%
Jun-00	National Fuel Gas	Tri Link Resources	182.1	352.6	3.1 ×	3.5 ×	4.2 ×	4.6 ×	$4.54	$2.97	18,657	17,685	n.a.	n.a.
Jun-00	Alberta Energy	Westpoint Energy	37.2	62.9	3.2 ×	1.8 ×	4.6 ×	2.6 ×	$11.63	$9.31	28,615	19,076	n.a.	n.a.
Jun-00	Samson Canada	Calahoo Petroleum	85.3	140.1	3.2 ×	2.7 ×	5.2 ×	4.4 ×	$9.49	$7.31	36,868	31,900	77.9%	85.9%
May-00	Anderson Exploration	Ulster Petroleums	645.1	950.4	4.4 ×	4.4 ×	5.7 ×	5.7 ×	$9.45	$7.81	33,604	31,246	66.6%	44.5%
Mar-00	Baytex Energy	Bellator Energy	145.2	198.5	2.8 ×	2.1 ×	n.a.	n.a.	$5.05	$3.94	21,594	n.a.	64.5%	68.5%
Mar-00	Kaiser-Francis/ Taurus	Petrorep	122.7	129.4	3.7 ×	3.4 ×	3.9 ×	3.5 ×	$9.90	$7.65	20,201	17,566	31.0%	41.6%
Feb-00	Enermark Income Fund	Pursuit Resources	79.5	115.2	3.2 ×	n.a.	n.a.	n.a.	$7.83	$6.38	19,668	n.a.	18.7%	19.7%
Median					*3.4 ×*	*3.4 ×*	*4.6 ×*	*4.5 ×*	*$8.64*	*$6.85*	*22,682*	*20,672*	*38.4%*	*44.3%*
Mean					*3.6 ×*	*3.3 ×*	*4.6 ×*	*4.3 ×*	*$8.13*	*$6.31*	*24,796*	*22,663*	*43.1%*	*46.3%*

Exhibit 10   Comparable Transactions

Source: Information circular and RBC DS fairness opinion, except premium information, which is from CIBC WM Research.

1. DCF is discretionary cash flow, which is essentially cash flow from potations less debt service requirements.
2. 1 Yr. is the current year's (2000) forecast; 2 Yr. is next year's (2001) forecast.
3. Adj. Enterprise Value is Enterprise Value less value of undeveloped land at Cdn$50/acre.
4. n.a. = information not available.

Date	Price	Date	Price	Date	Price
23-Mar-00	$10.20	05-May-00	$13.40	19-Jun-00	$16.15
24-Mar-00	$10.65	08-May-00	$14.00	20-Jun-00	$15.25
27-Mar-00	$11.00	09-May-00	$14.75	21-Jun-00	$15.00
28-Mar-00	$11.00	10-May-00	$14.75	22-Jun-00	$14.90
29-Mar-00	$11.05	11-May-00	$14.95	23-Jun-00	$15.40
30-Mar-00	$10.95	12-May-00	$14.90	26-Jun-00	$15.15
31-Mar-00	$11.05	15-May-00	$15.35	27-Jun-00	$15.00
03-Apr-00	$12.35	16-May-00	$17.00	28-Jun-00	$14.65
04-Apr-00	$11.80	17-May-00	$17.50	29-Jun-00	$14.35
05-Apr-00	$12.80	18-May-00	$17.10	30-Jun-00	$14.35
06-Apr-00	$13.15	19-May-00	$16.40	04-Jul-00	$14.25
07-Apr-00	$12.60	23-May-00	$16.10	05-Jul-00	$13.50
10-Apr-00	$12.50	24-May-00	$16.15	06-Jul-00	$13.45
11-Apr-00	$12.80	25-May-00	$15.90	07-Jul-00	$14.60
12-Apr-00	$13.50	26-May-00	$15.95	10-Jul-00	$14.85
13-Apr-00	$13.55	29-May-00	$16.40	11-Jul-00	$14.75
14-Apr-00	$13.10	30-May-00	$16.70	12-Jul-00	$14.85
17-Apr-00	$13.65	31-May-00	$15.35	13-Jul-00	$15.35
18-Apr-00	$13.15	01-Jun-00	$15.85	14-Jul-00	$15.30
19-Apr-00	$13.50	02-Jun-00	$15.30	17-Jul-00	$15.70
20-Apr-00	$13.65	05-Jun-00	$14.80	18-Jul-00	$15.65
24-Apr-00	$13.80	06-Jun-00	$15.05	19-Jul-00	$15.40
25-Apr-00	$13.75	07-Jun-00	$15.00	20-Jul-00	$15.20
26-Apr-00	$13.90	08-Jun-00	$15.10	21-Jul-00	$15.40
27-Apr-00	$13.25	09-Jun-00	$14.95	24-Jul-00	$15.05
28-Apr-00	$12.95	12-Jun-00	$15.05	25-Jul-00	$15.00
01-May-00	$12.90	13-Jun-00	$15.30	26-Jul-00	$14.90
02-May-00	$13.10	14-Jun-00	$15.00	27-Jul-00	$15.55
03-May-00	$13.40	15-Jun-00	$14.90	28-Jul-00	$15.25
04-May-00	$13.40	16-Jun-00	$16.60	31-Jul-00	$15.15
				01-Aug-00	$15.05

Exhibit 11   Renaissance Energy Stock Price Performance

Source: Company files.

Note: Data from Bloomberg.

was to fill out the form of proxy and letter of transmittal. Should she vote her proxy in favor of the transaction and tender her shares? Melnick began to fill out the form.

NOTES

1. This case has been written on the basis of published sources only. Consequently, the interpretation and

perspectives presented in this case are not necessarily those of Husky Oil Limited or any of its employees.

2. A reverse takeover is a transaction in which a private company purchases a public company as a means of obtaining a listing on a stock exchange.

3. Pro-ration occurs when the maximum cash available under the offer is not sufficient to satisfy all the claims on it as a result of shares being tendered under the cash option. For example, if all Husky Energy shares held by Renaissance shareholders (151.0 million) were tendered under the cash option

($18 per share), $2.7 billion of cash (151.0 million × $18) would be required in order to fully satisfy all claims. Since only $500 million is available, it is divided equally among all shares tendered, with a resulting cash payment of $3.31 per share ($500 million / 151.0 million). Since there is only enough cash to satisfy the purchase of 27.8 million shares ($500 million / $18), the remaining 123.2 million shares (151.0 million—27.8 million) are returned to the shareholders, resulting in a return of 0.816 shares (123.2 million / 151.0 million) for each share tendered.

4. Barrels of oil equivalent (boe) is a measure of combined volumes of oil, including natural gas liquids and natural gas. Most commonly, natural gas is converted to a barrel of oil equivalent on the basis of: (i) 10,000 cubic feet of natural gas to one boe, referred to as 10:1; or (ii) 6,000 cubic feet of natural gas to one boe, referred to as 6:1.

5. Pro forma financial statements are designed to show what results might have been if an enterprise had been structured in the past as it will be structured in the future.

6. P/CF is calculated by dividing the current market price of the company's shares by an estimate of cash flow per share.

7. P/E is calculated by dividing the current market price of the company's shares by an estimate of earnings per share.

8. EV/EBITDA is calculated by dividing the enterprise value (market value of equity plus net debt) of the company by an estimate of the earnings before interest, taxes, depreciation and amortization.

9. Net debt includes all permanent debt and debt-like financing (e.g., capital leases, etc.), less cash and cash equivalents (e.g., marketable securities, etc.).

10. A "break-up" fee is a fee paid by the seller to a potential acquirer of a business in the event that the transaction contemplated fails to be consummated and certain criteria in the purchase agreement are not met.

ConAgra, Inc.

Prepared by Rob Barbara and Lisa Newey
under the supervision of Professor Robert White

Version: (A) 2003-01-07

Ann Watson, Vice President, Corporate Finance with Bunting Warburg Inc., had just received a Directors' Circular issued by the Canada Malting Co. Limited (CMCL). The circular, dated October 6, 1995, had been issued the previous day and recommended the rejection of an offer by Bunting Warburg's client to purchase the shares of CMCL. One week earlier, the client, ConAgra, Inc. (ConAgra) of Omaha, Nebraska, the second largest food processor in the United States, offered to acquire all of the outstanding common shares of CMCL at a price of Cdn$20.00 per share. She, along with David Macdonald, head of Corporate Finance in Toronto and Brian Hanson of S.G. Warburg[1] in New York, had worked on structuring the offer.

Now that the offer had been rejected, Ann's challenge was to advise ConAgra on how to proceed from this point.

Canada Malting Co. Limited

CMCL, established in 1902, was the largest producer of malted barley in the world. Through its 10 plants in five countries, including Canada, the United States, the United Kingdom, Uruguay and Argentina, CMCL had captured approximately eight per cent of the world market for malted barley. In addition to its malting operations, CMCL's Leaver Mushrooms Co. Ltd., a wholly owned subsidiary, was Canada's largest producer of mushrooms. Leaver grew and packaged mushrooms under the Leaver and Dixie brand names.

The brewing industry was the primary consumer of malted barley, purchasing about 95 per cent of the world's production in 1994. The major purchasers of production included CMCL's domestic markets in Canada, the United States and the United Kingdom. While these markets, which consumed 68 per cent of CMCL's consolidated malt shipments, were maturing, the industry participants believed that there was substantial growth potential in Latin America and Asia. In response to this potential opportunity, CMCL stated in its 1994 annual report to shareholders that it intended to increase its 20 per cent share in its Argentinean joint venture to 33 1/3 per cent.

In addition to its successful domestic operations, CMCL reported a 16 per cent increase in its export sales. Because of the maturity of North American and Western European beer markets, in 1994 brewers were rapidly consolidating and expanding their international presence in an effort to develop new markets and attract higher sales. CMCL's exports to these developing markets was, therefore, expected to increase also.

On May 3, 1995, CMCL issued a press release reporting that first quarter total revenues were higher than any quarter in the company's history. Fiscal 1994 results were also impressive, showing a steady increase in earnings per share over the past five years. Financial statements for the company are presented in Exhibits 1, 2 and 3. Interim financial results for the six months ending June 30, 1995 were sales of $213.5 million, and EBIT of $25.859 million. On October 22, 1993, CMCL sold 800 debenture warrants granting the holders thereof the right, but not the obligation, to purchase in the aggregate US$80 million 7.65 per cent debentures due July 15, 1999 to be issued by the corporation upon the exercise of the warrants (the yields on Canadian and U.S. five-year Treasury bonds were six per cent and 4.76 per cent, respectively). The issue price per warrant was $6,124.00. The warrants were all exercised on April 15, 1994 and the debentures were issued, at PAR, on that date.

CMCL Ownership

As of October 6, 1995, approximately 40 per cent of CMCL was owned by two major Canadian brewing companies, The Molson Companies Limited (Molson) and Labatt Brewing Company Limited (Labatt), each of which owned 19.8 per cent of the company. The remaining 60 per cent of the shares in CMCL were widely held. The combined sales of these two brewers dominated the Canadian brewing market. Molson and Labatt had originally purchased large shares of CMCL in an effort to secure a source of raw materials for their brewing processes.

Under an agreement dated November 1964, CMCL's two controlling shareholders each agreed to purchase a minimum of 90 per cent of their annual malt requirements from CMCL. The agreement was to be automatically renewed annually unless terminated by either Labatt or Molson. Sales to the two shareholders were made on the same terms as sales to unrelated customers.

In mid-1995, Labatt was purchased by Interbrew S.A./N.V., the white knight in a hostile takeover attempt by Onex Corporation. As part of the acquisition, Interbrew, a Belgian brewery, assumed ownership of John Labatt's 19.8 per cent share in CMCL. Interbrew stated that it was mainly interested in Labatt's brewing assets and would put all non-core assets up for sale following the Labatt purchase.

In its 1995 annual report, issued on March 31, 1995, Molson stated that "Our plan is to exit from non-core businesses in an orderly manner." Labatt, in its last annual report prior to the Interbrew takeover, made a similar comment: "The strategic realignment of Labatt during the past five years has been predicated on its desire to become larger in its two core businesses of brewing and broadcast." For Molson and Labatt's new owner, Interbrew, intended divestitures included, among other businesses, their interests in CMCL.

	December 31	
	1994	**1993**
Current assets		
Cash	$29,691	$21,896
Accounts receivable	54,858	39,975
Inventories	64,785	61,919
Income taxes recoverable	—	1,063
	149,334	124,853
Fixed assets	343,860	310,526
Investment in affiliate	20,139	19,236
Goodwill	8,387	7,617
	$521,720	**$462,232**
Current Liabilities		
Short-term borrowings	$ 14,794	$ 68,911
Accounts payable and accrued liabilities	44,867	43,214
Income taxes payable	13,198	—
Current portion of long-term debt	—	41,120
	72,859	153,245
Long-term debt	129,661	23,133
Deferred warrant proceeds	7,052	8,217
Deferred income taxes	38,628	38,749
Shareholders' Equity		
Common shares	70,727	69,724
Retained earnings	184,425	165,556
Unrealized foreign currency translation adjustments	18,368	3,608
	273,520	238,888
	$521,720	**$462,232**

Exhibit 1   Canada Malting Co. Limited Consolidated Balance Sheet (in thousands of dollars)

CONAGRA, INC.

ConAgra was the second largest food processor in the United States. As of its fiscal year end on May 28, 1995, ConAgra operated in 27 countries and had in excess of 90,000 employees. ConAgra's principal businesses were each related to the food industry with divisions that included: Refrigerated Foods, Grocery/Diversified Products and Food Input and Ingredients. In fiscal[2] 1995, ConAgra had sales of US$24.1 billion, net income of US$495.6 million, a capital structure comprised of 50 per cent long-term debt and

50 per cent common equity, a common equity beta of 1.0 and an EBIT interest coverage of four times. ConAgra's 1995 average annual price-earnings multiple was 15.4 times.

ConAgra had a history of growth through acquisitions. Previous major acquisitions included: United Agri Products, Banquet Foods, Country Pride Foods, Peavey Company, Monfort of Colorado, the Morton, Chun King and Patio frozen foods businesses, SIPCO, Pillsbury's grain merchandising business and many others. The acquisition of CMCL would complement its Food Inputs & Ingredients

	Year ended December 31	
	1994	**1993**
Net sales	$367,074	$375,200
Cost of products sold and all expenses, except items shown below	305,000	317,213
Depreciation and amortization	17,825	12,960
	322,825	330,173
Earnings from operations	44,249	45,027
Foreign exchange gain	4,890	—
Reorganization expense	—	(1,500)
Interest expense, net	(10,234)	(7,756)
Earnings before income taxes	38,905	35,771
Income taxes[a]		
Current	14,583	1,746
Deferred	(1,814)	10,224
	12,769	11,970
Earnings before loss from affiliate	26,136	23,801
Loss from affiliate	(339)	—
Net earnings for the year	**$25,797**	**$23,801**
Earnings per share		
Basic and fully diluted	**$1.34**	**$1.24**

a. The corporation's effective income tax rate is determined as follows:

	1994	**1993**
Canadian Statutory Rate	44.5%	44.5%
Increase (decrease) in income tax rate resulting from		
Manufacturing and processing profits deduction	(2.4)	(2.1)
Lower rates in other countries	(9.0)	(9.2)
Other	(0.3)	0.3
Effective tax rate	32.8%	33.5%

Exhibit 2 Canada Malting Co. Limited Consolidated Statement of Earnings (in thousands of dollars, except per share amounts)

segment and make ConAgra the world's largest malted barley producer.

THE MALT INDUSTRY

A 1991 Canadian government *Industry Profile* publication[3] made the following comments regarding growth in the malting industry:

The future of the Canadian malting industry will continue to be shaped by the developments in the brewing industry and the continued ability of that industry to compete in domestic and export markets . . . the Canadian market, as in many developed countries, is one of static consumption. Growth prospects for Canadian-based maltsters . . . lie in the export market. After two or three years of strong growth, driven largely by Japanese consumer interest in dry beers, that market can be

| | Year ended December 31 | |
	1994	1993
Funds provided by (used in) operating activities		
Net earnings for the year	$25,797	$23,801
Non-cash items		
Depreciation and amortization	17,825	12,960
Amortization of deferred warrant proceeds, net	(986)	—
Deferred income taxes	(1,814)	10,224
Unrealized foreign exchange gain	(6,696)	(6,751)
Loss from affiliate	339	—
Change in non-cash working capital	(1,835)	50,745
	32,630	90,979
Funds used in investing activities		
Additions to fixed assets, net	(35,269)	(44,870)
Investment in affiliate	—	(19,236)
Other	(85)	(1,401)
	(35,354)	(65,507)
Funds provided by (used in) financing activities		
Common shares issued	1,003	449
Dividends paid	(6,928)	(6,900)
Issue of 7.65% debentures due July 15, 1999	110,634	—
Repayment of long-term debt	(83,710)	(10,065)
Realized foreign exchange gain	36,986	—
Debenture warrant proceeds	—	8,217
	57,985	(8,299)
Effect of exchange rate changes on cash and short-term borrowings	6,651	(256)
Increase in funds during the year	61,912	16,917
Short-term borrowings, net of cash, beginning of year	(47,015)	(63,932)
Cash, net of short-term borrowings (short-term borrowings, net of cash), end of year	**$14,897**	**$(47,015)**

Exhibit 3   Canada Malting Co. Limited Consolidated Statement of Changes in Financial Position
(in thousands of dollars)

expected to stabilize at current levels of demand for the next two years. Over the longer run, demand should continue to increase at one to two per cent a year . . .

The article also stated that the Canada/U.S. Free Trade Agreement was expected to have little or no effect on the Canadian malt industry. In summary, most growth prospects, at the time of the article and continuing into late 1995, were expected to be a result of export demand.

Surplus capacity and low prices continued to pressure the industry worldwide for the most of 1994. In addition, the poor quality of much of the 1993 North American barley crop resulted in increased processing costs (Canadian barley is considered to be the best in the world). The world's brewing industry was becoming more concentrated every year, and its major players were becoming increasingly international in scope. In 1994, over 50 per cent of worldwide demand for malt was accounted for by only 20 brewing groups, 16 of which operated in more than one country. The maturity of developed markets in North America and Western Europe was galvanizing the world's major brewers into an intense search for new opportunities, and inevitably their focus turned to Asia and South America. Economic growth in these areas fuelled robust consumer spending, which, in turn, was expected to increase demand for malt by 1.5 million tonnes within the next five years.

THE OFFER

ConAgra was approached in July 1995 by Lazard Freres & Co. (Lazard), who were advisors to Interbrew in connection with the divestiture of certain non-core assets. Interbrew wished to sell Labatt's 19.8 per cent interest in CMCL and Lazard inquired about ConAgra's interest in purchasing the shares. Lazard indicated to ConAgra management that Molson might also be prepared to sell its interest in CMCL.

ConAgra followed up this initial contact with letters to both Molson and Labatt. ConAgra expressed its interest in purchasing the shares of both principal shareholders. Meanwhile, Ronald Eden, President and CEO of CMCL, called ConAgra to inquire about information he had received concerning the company's interest in CMCL.

On August 7, 1995, ConAgra, Molson and Labatt, accompanied by their respective investment bankers, met in Toronto to discuss the principal terms of a proposal. On August 18, 1995, the CMCL board of directors formed a special committee to make recommendations regarding ConAgra's offer. ConAgra, Molson and Labatt continued to meet over the following five weeks. Meanwhile, on August 22, 1995, CMCL retained

the services of Wood Gundy Inc., another Toronto investment dealer, to advise its special committee. The special committee was successful in obtaining a guarantee from Molson and Labatt that they would tender their shares as long as the bid period was greater than 30 days. CMCL was informed of the progress of private meetings between the other parties.

Molson and Labatt entered into an agreement with ConAgra on September 17, 1995 to offer their common shares in CMCL for sale at $20.00 per share. On September 30, 1995, Bunting Warburg and S.G. Warburg, acting on behalf of ConAgra, presented the minority shareholders of CMCL with an offer to purchase all of the remaining common shares of CMCL for the same price of $20.00 per common share. See Exhibit 4 for an outline of the offer.

ConAgra had a logical interest in CMCL. ConAgra's specialty grain business, which processed oats, barley and corn, diversified into barley malting in 1991 with the acquisition of Australia-based Elders Brewing Materials Group. Ever since, barley malting had been a significant driver of growth for ConAgra. With the acquisition of CMCL, ConAgra would double the size of its sales (to US$550 million) and add to its holdings 10 plants in Canada, the United States and the United Kingdom, as well as joint ventures in China, Argentina and Uruguay.

The offer was valid until midnight on October 31, 1995 and stipulated that:

(1) at least 66 2/3 per cent of the common shares[4] be offered for sale and;

(2) secondly, that not less than 50 per cent of the common shares plus one share that were owned by individuals other than principal shareholders (Molson and Labatt) be offered for sale.

Molson and Labatt had previously agreed to deposit their combined 39.6 per cent of CMCL shares at the offering price of $20.00 per share. This agreement to offer their common shares was under the condition that a competing cash offer greater than $20.00 per share not be received. If

This document is important and requires your immediate attention. If you are in doubt as to how to deal with it, you should consult your investment dealer, broker, bank manager, lawyer or other professional advisor.

September 30, 1995

OFFER TO PURCHASE FOR CASH
all of the common shares of
CANADA MALTING CO. LIMITED
at a price of
Cdn. $20.00 per Common Share
by
CONAGRA INVESTMENTS (CMA) LIMITED
a wholly-owned indirect subsidiary of
CONAGRA, INC.

The Offer by ConAgra Investments (CMA) Limited (the "Offeror") to purchase all of the issued and outstanding common shares ("Common Shares") of Canada Malting Co. Limited ("Canada Malting") will be open for acceptance until 12:00 midnight (Toronto time) on October 31, 1995 (the "Expiry Time"), unless withdrawn or extended.

The Offer is conditional upon, among other things, there being validly deposited under the Offer and not withdrawn at the Expiry Time (i) not less than 66 2/3% of the Common Shares (on a fully-diluted basis); and (ii) more than 50% of the Common Shares (on a fully-diluted basis) exclusive of the Common Shares which are beneficially owned by the Principal Shareholders referred to below. This condition and the other conditions to the Offer are described in Section 3 of the Offer, "Conditions of the Offer."

ConAgra, Inc. ("ConAgra") has entered into a deposit agreement (the "Deposit Agreement") with Labatt Brewing Company Limited and The Molson Companies Limited (together, the "Principal Shareholders") pursuant to which each of the Principal Shareholders has severally agreed, subject to certain terms and conditions, to deposit or cause to be deposited under the Offer all of the Common Shares it beneficially owns. As of September 17, 1995, each Principal Shareholder held 3,793,062 Common Shares, for a total of 7,586,124 Common Shares, representing, in the aggregate, approximately 39% of the outstanding Common Shares. See Section 4 of the Circular, "Agreement with Principal Shareholders."

Holders of Common Shares who wish to accept the Offer must properly complete and duly execute the accompanying Letter of Transmittal (which is printed on yellow paper) or a manually executed facsimile thereof and deposit it, together with certificates representing their Common Shares, at one of the offices of Montreal Trust Company of Canada (the "Depositary") or The Bank of Nova Scotia Trust Company of New York (the "U.S. Forwarding Agent") shown on the Letter of Transmittal in accordance with the instructions in the Letter of Transmittal. Alternatively, a holder of Common Shares who desires to deposit Common Shares and whose certificates for such Common Share are not immediately available may deposit certificates representing such Common Shares by following the procedures for guaranteed delivery set forth in Section 2 of the Offer, "Manner and Time of Acceptance."

Questions and requests for assistance may be directed to Bunting Warburg Inc., in Canada, and S.G. Warburg & Co. Inc., in the United States (collectively, the "Dealer Manager"), the Depositary or the U.S. Forwarding Agent and additional copies of this document, the Letter of Transmittal and the Notice of Guaranteed Delivery (which is printed on blue paper) may be obtained, without charge, on request from those persons at their respective offices shown on the Letter of Transmittal.

Persons whose Common Shares are registered in the name of a nominee should contact their broker, investment dealer, bank, trust company or other nominee for assistance.

Members of the Soliciting Dealer Group will be paid the fees described in Section 20 of the Circular, "Soliciting Dealer Arrangements."

The Dealer Manager for the Offer is:

Bunting Warburg Inc.
in Canada
(416) 364–3293

S.G. Warburg & Co. Inc.
in the United States
(212) 224–7000

Exhibit 4   Offer to Purchase for Cash

a competing non-cash offer was received by Molson and Labatt, that offer could not be accepted unless it was at least (the equivalent of) $21.00 per share.

REASONS TO ACCEPT THE OFFER

Bunting Warburg's sales force contacted shareholders of CMCL with the suggestion that there were five key reasons to accept ConAgra's offer. First, Molson and Labatt had agreed to the offer in the absence of a more attractive bid.[5] Second, Molson and Labatt had disclosed that, if the offer was not successful, they still intended to divest their shares. This divestment could be completed through a private transaction which would not be available to all shareholders.

Third, the offer treated all shareholders equally, guaranteeing that they all received the same price. Historically, CMCL's stock had been relatively illiquid.[6] Fourth, CMCL had actively been seeking a white knight with the aid of its investment advisor.

Wood Gundy had approached several agriculture-related companies in Australia, Japan, Europe, the United States and some Asian countries in pursuit of a more attractive bid from an alternate purchaser. One otherwise-interested party, Archer-Daniels-Midland Co (ADM) of Illinois, already owned between seven and eight per cent of CMCL, but was not able to enter a bid for the shares. The company's management was embroiled in defending itself against a price-fixing investigation brought against it by the U.S. Justice Department. ADM's management attention was devoted to dealing with that issue at the time.

ADM is in the business of procuring, transporting, storing, processing and merchandising agricultural commodities and products. In fiscal[7] 1995, ADM had sales of US$12.672 billion, a capital structure comprised of 25 per cent long-term debt and 75 per cent common equity, a common equity beta of 1.0 and an EBIT interest coverage of six times. ADM's 1995 average annual price-earnings multiple was 11.9 times.

On September 20, 1995, the *Globe and Mail* newspaper reported that Wood Gundy remained optimistic about its efforts to locate a white knight. The Wood Gundy team had presented information packages to all potential buyers, who were required to sign confidentiality agreements before pursuing the issue.[8] To date, CMCL had not received a competitive tender.

The final reason for accepting the offer, as stated by Bunting Warburg, was that the offer price exceeded previous trading levels. The share price rose dramatically during 1995, in part due to market speculation on take-over rumours if a financially leveraged company acquired Labatt. The offer represented a 43 per cent premium over the December 30, 1994 closing price of $14.00 and a 33 per cent premium on the February 24, 1995 closing price, the day prior to the first public speculation that Onex might offer to acquire Labatt.

MARKET REACTION

Some Canadian Business Service analysts recommended, in their October 1995 report on CMCL,[9] that shareholders tender[10] their shares. The analysts cited both impressive results and exciting developments for the company, but still felt that a $20.00 bid was a good price. Historical share prices and trading activity for CMCL and the TSE300 Total Return Index[11] are presented in Exhibit 5.

CMCL REJECTS OFFER

The Board of Directors of CMCL issued a Directors' Circular on October 6th, 1995 recommending a rejection of the offer by ConAgra and that shareholders not tender their shares. The circular stated that the special Independent Committee of the Board, assisted by its financial and legal advisors, had carefully considered the offer and recommended rejection based on five

Date	Canada Malting Co. Limited				TSE 300 Total Return Index
	Daily Price High	Daily Price Low	Number of Transactions	Volume Traded	
950808	18.500	18.500	3	300	9,120.50
950809	18.625	18.500	4	6,500	9,125.33
950810	19.000	18.625	18	109,600	9,096.97
950811	20.500	19.000	35	435,670	9,056.45
950814	21.000	20.000	32	414,750	9,076.92
950815	20.750	20.000	23	9,650	9,068.00
950816	20.625	20.375	35	16,645	9,098.21
950817	20.500	20.375	9	115,435	9,122.85
950818	20.500	20.375	22	6,397	9,122.40
950821	20.500	20.500	9	2,098	9,099.59
950822	20.625	20.500	21	5,603	9,086.95
950823	20.500	20.500	5	7,069	9,101.15
950824	20.500	19.750	11	3,350	9,078.42
950825	19.500	19.375	4	1,000	9,067.70
950828	19.875	19.375	8	2,300	9,040.60
950829	19.500	19.500	2	1,300	8,991.49
950830	19.500	19.375	18	8,000	8,955.04
950831	19.500	19.125	9	17,300	8,926.86
950901	19.625	19.250	3	900	8,945.00
950905	20.000	19.250	7	2,350	9,012.99
950906	20.000	19.375	14	2,540	9,038.70
950907	19.500	19.250	11	3,350	9,029.41
950908	19.250	19.250	2	1,500	9,037.93
950911	19.750	19.500	15	3,990	9,080.12
950912	19.625	19.375	10	2,687	9,122.63
950913	19.500	19.250	6	2,800	9,080.53
950914	19.625	19.500	6	1,300	9,072.55
950915	20.000	19.500	10	9,200	9,029.13
950918	21.750	21.000	105	1,070,975	9,006.92
950919	21.875	21.500	128	387,083	8,985.32
950920	21.625	21.375	69	332,761	9,009.99
950921	21.875	21.250	70	161,776	8,993.67
950922	21.750	21.625	34	47,211	8,955.32
950925	21.750	21.625	21	27,400	8,953.56
950926	21.625	21.500	26	99,549	8,953.22
950927	21.625	21.500	38	98,950	8,916.67
950928	21.625	21.500	6	4,400	8,959.17
950929	21.625	21.500	26	136,734	8,977.74
951002	21.625	21.500	24	24,817	8,908.65
951003	21.625	21.500	41	111,462	8,917.77
951004	21.500	21.375	45	106,977	8,904.61
951005	21.625	21.500	29	20,230	8,918.78
951006	21.500	21.125	60	252,600	8,910.20

Exhibit 5   Historical Share Prices and Daily Trading Activity

WOOD GUNDY INC.
BCE Place, P.O. Box 500, Toronto, Ontario M5J 2S8
Telephone (416) 594–7000
SCHEDULE A

October 6, 1995

Independent Committee of the Board of Directors
Canada Malting Co. Limited
10 Four Seasons Place
Suite 600
Toronto, Ontario
M9B 6H7

To the Members of the Independent Committee:

We understand that ConAgra Investments (CMA) Limited (the "Bidder"), a corporation indirectly owned by ConAgra, Inc., has made an offer (the "Offer") to purchase all of the issued and outstanding common shares ("Common Shares") of Canada Malting Co. Limited ("CMCL"). The consideration under the Offer is $20.00 in cash per Common Share (the "Consideration"). The terms and the conditions of the Offer are set out in an Offer to Purchase and Circular dated September 30, 1995 (the "Offering Circular").

The Independent Committee of the Board of Directors of CMCL (the "Board") has retained Wood Gundy Inc. ("Wood Gundy") to provide financial advice to the Board and our opinion ("Opinion") as to the adequacy, from a financial point of view, of the Offer to the holders of Common Shares other than either the Bidder or ConAgra, Inc.

Opinion

It is our opinion that the consideration offered pursuant to the Offer is inadequate, from a financial point of view, to the holders of the Common Shares other than either the Bidder or ConAgra, Inc.

We base our opinion that the Offer is inadequate and does not recognize the inherent value of CMCL's operating assets on a variety of factors, including, amongst others, the business' leading market position, historical and current profitability and cash flow characteristics, and prospects for growth.

Credentials of Wood Gundy

Wood Gundy is one of Canada's largest investment banking firms with operations in all facets of corporate and government finance, mergers and acquisitions, equity and fixed income sales and trading and investment research. The Opinion expressed herein is the opinion of Wood Gundy and the form and content herein have been approved for release by a committee of its directors, each of whom is experienced in merger, acquisition, divestiture and valuation matters.

Scope of Review

In connection with rendering our Opinion, we have reviewed and relied upon, or carried out, among other things, the following:

i) the Offering circular and the CMCL Directors' Circular approved by the Board today;
ii) all financial information that has been disclosed publicly by CMCL in the last five years;
Independent Committee of the Board of Directors
Canada Malting Co. Limited
iii) certain internal information, primarily financial in nature (including forecasts, business plans, estimates, and analyses prepared by CMCL), concerning the business, assets, liabilities and prospects of CMCL;
iv) discussions with various members of senior management of CMCL concerning CMCL's current business operations, financial condition and results, and prospects and potential alternatives to the Offer;

Exhibit 6   Wood Gundy Recommendation to Canada Malting Board of Directors

v) a certificate as to certain factual matters dated the date hereof by CMCL and addressed to us;

vi) and such other information, discussions and analysis as we considered necessary or appropriate in the circumstances.

Assumptions and Limitations

This Opinion is subject to the assumptions, explanations and limitations set forth below.

We have not been asked to prepare and have not prepared a valuation of CMCL or any of its material assets and our Opinion should not be construed as such.

We have relied upon, and have assumed the completeness, accuracy and fair presentation of all financial and other information, data, advice, opinions and representations obtained by us from public sources or the Offering Circular and provided to us by CMCL and its affiliates or advisors or otherwise pursuant to our engagement, and the Opinion is conditional upon such completeness, accuracy and fairness. We have not attempted to verify independently the accuracy or completeness of any such information, data, advice, opinions and representations. Senior management has represented to us, in a certificate delivered at the date hereof, amongst other things, that the information, opinions and other materials (the "Information") provided to us by or on behalf of CMCL are complete and correct at the date the Information was provided to us and that since the date of the Information, there has been no material change, financial or otherwise, in the position of CMCL, or in its assets, liabilities (contingent or otherwise), business or operations and there has been no change of any material fact which is of a nature as to render the Information untrue or misleading in any material respect.

We have acted as financial advisor to CMCL in connection with the Offer and will be paid a fee for our services as financial advisor, including fees that are contingent on a change of control or certain other events.

The Opinion is rendered on the basis of securities markets, economic and general business and financial conditions prevailing as at the date hereof and the conditions and prospects, financial and otherwise, of CMCL as they are reflected in the information and documents reviewed by us and as they were represented to us in our discussions with management of CMCL. In our analyses and in connection with the preparation of the Opinion, we made numerous assumptions with respect to industry performance, general business, market and economic conditions and other matters, many of which are beyond the control of any party involved in the Offer.

Yours very truly,

factors. First, Wood Gundy, CMCL's financial advisor, sent a letter (Exhibit 6) stating that, in their opinion, the offer was inadequate. This opinion was based primarily on CMCL's leading market position, the company's historic and current profitability, the quality of their cash flow and their favourable prospects for growth.

Second, the Board felt that the price neglected the recent completion of a $250 million six-year expansion and modernization program. This program increased capacity, upgraded facilities and enhanced cost efficiencies, positioning the company for strong improvement in revenue, cost containment and cash flow in 1996 without large capital expenditure requirements. Likewise, the price was thought to neglect the fact that CMCL was beginning to capitalize

on growth opportunities in the rapidly growing markets of Asia and Latin America. Currently, the company had a 20 per cent stake in Malteria Pampa S.A. of Argentina and had experienced increased sales to Brazil from its Canadian operation. In 1995, CMCL was also exporting to Japan, South Korea and other Asian markets.

Third, several other "superior" prospects existed for CMCL. These prospects stemmed from its market leadership, geographic diversity, close proximity to many of the world's largest brewers, its excellent source of raw material supply (Canada was the world's largest producer of barley) and strong relationships with leading international beer producers. The company was also well configured to take advantage of export opportunities. This configuration included a malt-container loading facility in Vancouver, B.C. and Pampa's proximity to Argentina's largest marine grain-handling facility.

The fourth reason for the committee's rejection recommendation was a concern that the investment objectives of Molson and Labatt may have differed from those of the other common shareholders. While Molson and Labatt had not discounted the opportunity for a competing bid to emerge, they were willing to expedite the sale to achieve their objective to divest non-core assets.

Fifth, during the several trading days prior to the offer, the market price of CMCL's shares consistently exceeded the offer price, ranging from $21.00 to $21 7/8. The premium over the $20.00 offer price indicated that the market viewed the value of the shares, in the context of a change in control, in excess of the current offer.

The CMCL Director's Circular went on to assure shareholders that they were continuing to actively pursue alternative bids. The independent committee was currently involved in discussions with other buyers and had recently entered into confidentiality agreements with numerous parties. The terms of the agreements allowed potential buyers access to non-public information relating to the company for the purpose of evaluating the possibility of acquiring 100 per cent of CMCL. The Director's Circular concluded with the following comment:

> There is no advantage to be gained and holders of common shares may in fact be prejudiced if they tendered to the offer early. The Board recommends that the holders of common shares intending to tender their shares under the offer not do so until shortly before the expiry to offer.

THE DECISION

The rejection of ConAgra's offer by the independent committee of CMCL's board of directors posed a new challenge for Watson. She realized that her client was extremely interested in acquiring CMCL but was unwilling to pay excessively for this opportunity. The Board's claim that they would be able to find a "white knight" might never materialize. If this were the case, ConAgra could still acquire the company without raising its bid price. However, if it were to encounter competition, ConAgra would need to establish the maximum price that it would be willing to pay for CMCL (see Exhibit 7 for financial market data). Watson wondered what the next move should be.

	Canadian Yields	U.S. Yields
T-Bills		
1-month	6.10%	5.31%
2-month	6.24	5.30
3-month	6.40	5.35
1-year	6.41	5.28
Bonds		
2-years	6.60	5.73
5-years	7.20	5.89
7-years	7.40	5.98
10-years	7.62	6.07
30-years	8.04	6.42

Source: Financial Post, October 7, 1995.

Canadian Equity Market Risk Premiums January 1950 to December 1994

Estimated Long-Term Canadian Market Risk Premium, Arithmetic Means	= 11.80—6.61	= 5.19%
Estimated Long-Term Canadian Market Risk Premium, Geometric Means	= 10.52—6.14	= 4.38%
Estimated Medium-Term Canadian Market Risk Premium, Arithmetic Means	= 11.80—6.98	= 4.82%
Estimated Medium-Term Canadian Market Risk Premium, Geometric Means	= 10.52—6.67	= 3.85%
Estimated Short-Term Canadian Market Risk Premium, Arithmetic Means	= 11.80—6.41	= 5.39%
Estimated Short-Term Canadian Market Risk Premium, Geometric Means	= 10.52—6.33	= 4.19%

Canada Malting Co. Limited Beta

Five-year monthly beta for period ending Dec. 1991	= 0.531
Five-year monthly beta for period ending Dec. 1992	= 0.662
Five-year monthly beta for period ending Dec. 1993	= 0.608
Five-year monthly beta for period ending Dec. 1994	= 0.466
Five-year monthly beta for period ending Sept. 1995	= 0.216

Source: TSE Common Equities CD-ROM, 1996

Canada Malting Co. Limited Book Value

Canada Malting common equity book value/share: $14.18

Source: The Stock Guide, Stock Guide Publications Inc., October 1995

Exhibit 7   Financial Markets Data Interest Rates for October 6, 1995   *(Continued)*

Comparable Canadian Companies	Debt/ Equity	P/E Ratio	CashFlow/ Share	Price/ Book Value	Oct. 2, 1995 Market Price	Avg. Shares Outstanding (000s)
Canada Malting	0.53	10.5	1.79	0.99	21.50	19,250
Cobi Foods Inc.[a]	negative	loss for 1995	0.00	neg. book	0.36	26,125
Corporate Foods Limited[b]	0.27	13.8	1.66	1.88	17.50	20,975
Fishery Products International[c]	0.61	8.5	1.45	0.81	6.00	16,418
MRRM Inc.[d]	no debt	7.7	9.83	0.85	75.00	253
National Sea Products Limited[e]	8.35	11.8	0.92	neg. book	4.50	7,213
Schneider Corporation[f]	1.00	9.3	2.85	0.83	13.50	5,950
XL Foods Ltd.[g]	1.24	2.9	0.53	0.61	1.40	7,500

	EARNINGS PER SHARE					
	1995	1994	1993	1992	1991	
Canada Malting		1.34	1.24	0.8	1.19	
Cobi Foods Inc.	−0.05	−0.43	−0.21	0.02	−0.6	
Corporate Foods Limited		1.06	1.02	0.8	0.94	
Fishery Products International		0.85	−0.94	−4.1	−0.02	
MRRM Inc.	9.06	6.84	4.74	6.16	7.11	
National Sea Products		0.68	−6.08	−4.72	−6.88	
Schneider Corporation		1.35	1.31	1.12	0.93	
XL Foods Ltd.		0.27	−0.18	0.04	−0.49	

Exhibit 7 (Continued)

a. Cobi Foods Inc. purchases, stores, packages and markets canned and frozen fruits and vegetables. The company also produces and sells "Honeydew" brand frozen fruit-flavoured beverage concentrates.

b. Corporate Foods Limited manufactures and distributes bakery products. The products are sold under the company's own brands names and private label brands to the retail and food service industries.

c. FPI is an international seafood company. The company, through its subsidiaries, markets and distributes products made from various types of seafood including cod, redfish, shrimp, scallops, Alaskan king crab and farmed salmon. Fishery Products' customers are located in Canada, the United States, Europe and Japan.

d. Formerly Mount Royal Rice Mills Limited, MRRM Inc. is a food processor with operations that include rice milling, grocery products brokerages and a ship agency.

e. Limited NSP processes and markets seafood products mainly in Canada and, to a lesser degree, in the United States under the "Fisher Boy," "Treasure Island," and "High Line" names.

f. Schneider is one of Canada's largest producers of premium food products. Divisions include meat products, baked goods operations, poultry processing, and dairy goods. Schneider has major distribution centres in Surrey, Calgary, Winnipeg and Kitchener.

g. XL Foods is a vertically integrated beef producer with operations encompassing feedlot operations, slaughtering and hide processing as well as beef, pork, veal and lamb processing, packaging and marketing.

NOTES

1. Bunting Warburg was a subsidiary of S.G. Warburg.

2. Fiscal year ends last Sunday in May.

3. Industry, Science and Technology Canada and International Trade Canada Industry Profile: Malting 1990–1991.

4. On a fully diluted basis.

5. An all cash bid greater than $20.00 or a part-paper bid of greater than $21.00 would qualify for this condition.

6. During 1994, the average daily trading volume was 8,186 shares compared with 222,491 shares per day for Labatt and 442,697 shares per day for ConAgra.

7. Fiscal year ends June 30.

8. *The Globe and Mail*, September 20, 1995, page B3.

9. Canadian Business Service's Blue Book, October 1995.

10. Within days of (or prior to) the public announcement of a tender offer, a significant proportion of the widely held shares end up in the hands of risk arbitrageurs. The typical profit for risk arbitrageurs is $0.50 a share.

11. Market value weighted portfolio of the 300 largest securities, excluding control blocks, listed on The Toronto Stock Exchange. The index assumes that dividends are re-invested.

A GUIDE FOR DIRECTORS: HOW DIRECTORS CAN NAVIGATE THE POTENTIAL PROBLEMS OF M&AS

Prepared by James E. A. Turner

Business people acting as directors of public companies are increasingly finding themselves embroiled in merger and acquisition transactions whether their company is the object of a hostile bid, puts itself up for sale or is a willing participant in a negotiated merger. While many corporate directors are experienced in this area and understand their legal responsibilities, other directors are uncertain. The potential for personal liability concerns them.

This article attempts to dispel some of that concern. I will address primarily the position of the directors of a company which is the subject of a hostile bid, because that transaction will illustrate the basic principles, but I will also discuss the situation where a public company puts itself up for sale or is a willing merger participant. The principles identified can be readily applied to other situations.

THE ROLE OF DIRECTORS

It is only through the decision-making of directors that a corporation can act. As a result of this role, directors are so-called fiduciaries. That means that they have a duty to act honestly and in good faith for the benefit of the corporation and its shareholders. In practical terms, this means that directors must avoid circumstances in which there is a conflict (actual or potential) between their personal interests and the interests of the corporation. A director does not have a conflict of interest, however, simply because he or she is a director of a company which is the subject of a takeover bid. The requirement that directors act in the best interests of the corporation means that they must act in the best interests of the shareholders as a whole, in the sense that the shareholders are the ultimate owners of the corporation. Directors do not, however, owe duties directly to shareholders as such. They owe their duties to the corporation.

In addition to the duty discussed above, directors also have a duty of care. A director's duty of care means just that: A director must take reasonable care in reaching decisions on behalf of the corporation. Inherent in taking care is an obligation of the director to inform him or herself of the issues relevant to the decisions he or she is making and to take sufficient time to consider them. This entails no more than identifying what a prudent business person would want to know before making a particular decision.

THE BUSINESS JUDGMENT RULE

The decisions which get made in the takeover bid context, whether of process or of substance, are ultimately business decisions. Canadian courts will not second-guess a business decision made on an informed basis where there is at least some reasonable justification for the decision. Conversely, "if there are no reasonable grounds to support an assertion by the directors that they have acted in the best interests of the Company," a court will feel justified in intervening (Maple Leaf Foods v. Schneider Corp.).

In the result, a Canadian court may not agree with a particular business decision but it will not interfere unless it concludes that the directors did not proceed on an informed basis or that no reasonable person could have come to the decision in the circumstances. This judicial deference to business decisions is well established and provides directors a very broad discretion in exercising their business judgment. This deference of the courts is sometimes referred to as the "business judgment rule" (although that term has a more technical meaning under U.S. law and is not used with the same meaning in Canada). Courts don't make business decisions; directors make business decisions.

As a result, someone attacking a business decision made by the directors of a corporation has a difficult task. The most productive line of attack is to allege not that the decision was wrong but that the decision was not made on an informed basis. Thus, the attack is often focused on the process followed in making the decision because courts are more inclined to interfere where that process has been defective. Directors should recognize that, from a legal perspective, the actual decisions they make are often less important than ensuring that all of the relevant questions were canvassed in making those decisions.

DIRECTOR LIABILITY FOR FAILURE TO TAKE CARE

We have not had a legal decision in Canada in which directors of a public company have been held liable for damages as a result of a lack of care. In fact, modern Canadian corporations statutes (such as the Canada Business Corporations Act and the Ontario Business Corporations Act) permit a corporation to indemnify a director provided he or she acted honestly and in good faith with a view to the best interests of the corporation. That is not a high standard. Thus, a director can be negligent by, for example, making decisions on a precipitous and uninformed basis, and thereby breaching his or her duty to take care, and yet be fully indemnified by the corporation for any claims resulting from such negligence. A director cannot, however, be indemnified by the corporation for breach of his or her duty to act honestly, in good faith with a view to the best interests of the corporation.

RELIANCE ON EXPERTS

A director is also expressly protected from liability when relying in good faith upon financial statements of the corporation passed upon by an officer of the corporation or by its auditor or in relying upon a report of a lawyer, accountant or other professional adviser. As a result, where difficult judgments are being made in the heat of a hostile takeover bid, directors of the target company are well advised to protect themselves by acting with the advice of experts. The advice does not have to be right; it must simply be given by a person whose profession lends credibility to his or her statements.

INVESTMENT BANKERS

That takes us to the role of investment bankers. Occasionally clients ask whether they need to retain an investment dealer in connection with a merger or acquisition transaction, particularly given the large fees most dealers charge. Clearly, there is no legal requirement to retain an investment banker. But advice from an investment banker is the most effective way to demonstrate that a board has acted on an informed basis and to establish the defence of reliance on the advice of an expert. Investment bankers provide opinions as to the adequacy of an offer and as to whether a transaction is fair from a financial point of view to shareholders (referred to as a "fairness opinion"). They bring expertise and experience from numerous other transactions and they provide key strategic advice. The fairness opinion that an investment dealer delivers is usually the centrepiece for the analysis and deliberations of the board.

When a board is grappling with the many difficult issues which arise in the takeover bid process, I always ensure that the investment bankers (and other advisers) make recommendations to the board for resolution of those issues. It does not matter whether the advice is related to matters squarely within the expertise of the adviser or not. Courts will give the directors the benefit of the doubt. And the reality is that in making most of the strategic decisions that get made in a takeover bid context, there is no one right answer.

QUALIFICATIONS IN RELYING ON EXPERTS

Two additional points. First, in order to rely on expert advice, a director must understand the advice given and the basis for it. That is why an investment banker should review in detail with a board the analysis forming the basis for its

fairness opinion. An investment banker is entitled to make assumptions, but the directors should know what those assumptions are and decide if they make business sense in the circumstances.

Second, while obtaining the advice of experts is important, directors should maintain control of the process and should make the key business decisions. It is their judgments that have the benefit of the business judgment rule. Advisers should advise, not decide.

RESPONDING TO AN APPROACH

A good starting point for our discussion is the question of how a company should respond to a casual inquiry (the so-called "casual pass") as to whether it would be prepared to engage in discussions about being acquired. A U.S. lawyer's stock and invariable response is "the company is not for sale." One of his or her concerns under U.S. law is that if a company decides that it is "up for sale," it may trigger on obligation of the directors to initiate an auction and maximize short-team value to shareholders (this obligation of directors is referred to as their "Revlon" duty, based on a U.S. case involving Revlon Inc.). In considering this principle, you should note that the U.S. cases where the duty has been held to apply were often circumstances in which the board unfairly skewed a sale process in favour of one bidder or opted for a transaction with a clearly lower value for its shareholders. It is not surprising that the U.S. courts rejected those actions. Even where an auction is called for under U.S. law, "directors are not required . . . to conduct an auction according to some standard formula, only that they observe the significant requirement of fairness for the purpose of enhancing general shareholder interests" (Mills Acquisition Co. v. MacMillan Inc. 1989). A Canadian court would likely come to a similar conclusion but probably by a slightly different route.

In Canada, the legal framework is different but the U.S. response to the casual pass is probably the right one. Directors in Canada do not have a Revlon duty (in the sense that the concept is used in the U.S.). I will discuss the obligation to "maximize value" later. But on the narrower question here, there is no legal obligation on a company to engage in discussions with any third party and a company can appropriately indicate that it is not interested. At the same time, if a company in Canada wishes to engage in discussions, it can do so without concern that it has crossed some critical legal line that now requires an auction.

The dynamic shifts a little if the company receives a written (although non-binding) proposal for a specific change-of-control transaction involving a credible third party which on its face appears to provide value to shareholders. Generally, such proposals are communicated by management to the board. Even when such a proposal is received, however, the board is under no legal obligation to engage in discussions with the potential acquirer. Usually, the board will review the proposal and conclude that it is not prepared to pursue it further based on a relatively cursory assessment of the proposal and the target's existing business plan and objectives. The target may respond in this way without receiving the advice of outside advisers; on the other hand, such an approach may be a precursor to a hostile bid and so would usually trigger the company's defence response plan (involving meetings with advisers and a more comprehensive review of the proposal and the circumstances of the corporation).

In terms of the initial decision to be made by the board, the practical reality is that an insistent suitor can go directly to shareholders by launching a hostile bid without the support or concurrence of the board. It is extremely unlikely that directors would ever incur liability for simply deciding not to engage in merger discussions with a third party. Engaging in discussions creates expectations; it is always preferable not to begin creating those expectations unless there is strong support for a transaction.

THE HOSTILE BID

So, let's assume the initial approach has been rebuffed and a hostile bid is publicly announced. One certain consequence of a formal bid is that it creates a legal obligation on the part of the board of the target company to communicate with its shareholders (through mailing a so-called directors' circular) and to make a meaningful recommendation to shareholders with respect to the bid (or provide detailed reasons why it is not doing so). The board must now put itself into a position to make an informed recommendation to its shareholders.

JUST SAY NO

Assume at this point that the directors have concluded, based in part on expert advice, that the offer is inadequate and not in the best interests of the company or its shareholders. Now the debate begins: Can the board "just say no" to the bid or does it have a duty to take positive steps to "maximize value" to its shareholders? A board is entitled to reject a bid (assuming it has taken care in coming to its decision and there is some reasonable basis for its position) and to stay the course with its existing business plans. But it doesn't much matter. There is relatively little the board of a target company can do in Canada to prevent shareholders from ultimately accepting a bid if that is what they want to do (and it usually is). Experience has shown that shareholders are likely to accept a bid made at a premium to market if no other higher-value transaction comes along. Canadian companies have generally not been successful in simply convincing shareholders not to tender because the bid is "inadequate" or because the company's strategic plan will provide more long-term value.

OPPRESSION

But if by "just saying no" we mean that a board is entitled to take unilateral action to prevent shareholders from accepting a bid, that is a completely different question. In the U.S., defensive responses must be reasonable and not coerce shareholders to accept a particular transaction. Canadian securities regulators and courts have stated clearly that shareholders must ultimately be permitted to decide whether to accept or reject a takeover bid. I have no doubt that directors who simply interfere with that choice, without providing an alternative, will be viewed by Canadian courts as having acted in a manner that unfairly prejudices or disregards the interests of shareholders. In that circumstance, shareholders can assert an action against the corporation and its directors under the so-called oppression remedy available under most modern Canadian corporations statutes. The oppression remedy gives courts an extremely broad jurisdiction to intervene even where directors have acted in good faith on an informed basis. The remedy gives legal effect to the "reasonable expectations" of shareholders as to how directors and the company will conduct themselves in the circumstances. One court has stated in the takeover bid context that ". . . in Canada protection of shareholders is best achieved through the application of the oppression remedy provisions (including the analysis of reasonable shareholder expectations)" (Pente Investment Management Ltd. v. Schneider Corp. 1998). Where a board ultimately prevents shareholders from being able to sell their shares pursuant to a bid, the "business judgment rule" is unlikely to be a viable defence to shareholder action.

We have, however, not had a definitive legal decision in Canada dealing with the situation where a board simply prevents its shareholders from being able to sell their shares pursuant to a bid, probably because responsible (or litigation-averse) boards recognize that the position is untenable.

Note that I am not saying that a target board has to "roll over and play dead" in the face of a hostile bid. Directors are entitled, as discussed below, to take action to delay a bid in order to give them time to respond. But if they take other business actions in the face of a bid, those actions should be justifiable either as a bona fide attempt to enhance value to shareholders or on the basis of legitimate business objectives unrelated to the bid. At the end of the day, if shareholders want to sell their shares, the board had better not get in their way unless it provides some tangible value-enhancing alternative. Where a board is attempting to provide such an alternative, Canadian courts have given directors broad discretion in responding to a bid.

MAXIMIZING VALUE

Where a hostile bid has been made, does the board have a special duty under Canadian law to "maximize value" to shareholders? I would argue that this concept is often misunderstood and misused. Notwithstanding statements in some Canadian legal decisions, there is, I submit, no special duty imposed on Canadian directors to maximize value. Rather, directors continue to be obligated to act in the best interests of the corporation and its shareholders. But this is a legal debate which doesn't have much practical impact. If a takeover bid is made which the board of the target concludes is inadequate, what should a responsible board of directors do? It should attempt to delay or frustrate the bid in order to give itself time to induce or implement a higher-value alternative for its shareholders. No director should be concerned, however, that if he or she fails to induce or initiate a higher-value competing transaction, that as a result he or she incurs some liability to shareholders. If directors take reasonable steps to induce a higher-value transaction but fail to do so, they are not going to have any legal liability to shareholders who voluntarily tender to a bid which the board has advised is inadequate.

Similarly, if the directors take steps to increase value to shareholders and the actions taken are ones which a reasonable person could conclude would do so, no Canadian court is going to second-guess that decision. But if you as a director are in doubt or are concerned as to what the likely consequences of a proposed response would be, my advice is not to take the action; you have no legal obligation to take any such action and by failing to do so you will incur no liability.

OTHER DEFENCES

There is another aspect of responding to a hostile bid that I should mention. It is almost always in the best interests of shareholders for a board to delay a bid (even where there is a risk that the bid will go away) in order to give the board more time to develop alternatives. If a bid is illegal or does not comply with securities laws, no one can fairly criticize a board of directors for having established that point through litigation. And if the only effect of litigation is delay, that's not bad either.

CONSIDERING OTHER INTERESTS

There is one other legal principle you need to know as a director in considering responses to a bid. You shouldn't be influenced in making decisions by any consideration other than the interests of your shareholders. As a legal matter, what may be in the best interests of employees of the target or of the communities in which the target operates aren't relevant considerations. Your only concern should be the financial interests of your shareholders. A qualified exception to this principle arises in a share-for-share bid where your shareholders will have a continuing equity interest in the combined company. In that situation, the effect of the transaction on other "stakeholders" can be considered to the extent that the transaction could prejudice the continuing business of the combined entity. Where shareholders have the option of being completely cashed out as a result of a transaction, such considerations should not be given much weight.

In contrast to the narrow focus a director must have on shareholder interests, a shareholder (who has extremely limited legal obligations to any other shareholder) can sell to whomever he or she chooses for whatever reasons he or she likes. That's what the Schneider family did in selling to Smithfields Foods at a price below that offered by Maple Leaf; and that sale forced the public to accept the same lower price.

SPECIAL COMMITTEES

One of the initial questions which faces directors of a company that is the subject of a takeover bid or is considering a sale transaction is whether a special committee of directors should be constituted to supervise the process. There is no legal obligation to appoint such a committee except in the limited circumstances noted below. Special

committees are, however, an accepted mechanism for managing conflicts of interest, including those which may arise in the context of a bid or a sale of control of the company. Special committees are most often used where a director of the target is the nominee of a person making a bid or of a controlling shareholder of the target, or is a member of management. A special committee is used in such circumstances as a mechanism to ensure that the decision-making process of the board is not influenced by persons who may have an interest which is at odds with the interests of the corporation and its shareholder. "If a board of directors has acted on the advice of a committee comprised of persons having no conflict of interest, and that committee has acted independently, in good faith, and made an informed recommendation as to the best available transaction for the shareholders in the circumstances, the business judgment rule applies" (Maple Leaf).

There are no hard and fast legal rules as to whether a special committee should be constituted. A judgment must be made in the circumstances whether supervision or review by such a committee would be desirable. I have been involved in a number of change-of-control transactions where no special committee was struck. In one case, no one had any doubt that the CEO's motivation was to obtain the highest offer for shareholders (the CEO was the only management representative on the board). In another case, independent directors met after board meetings to discuss separately any issues of concern to them. Often the main motivation for having a special committee is to have a smaller group than the full board charged with more active involvement in what is often an intensive and time-consuming process.

WHERE A SPECIAL COMMITTEE IS APPOINTED

However, securities rules do require the use of an independent committee of directors where a bid is made by an insider of the corporation and such rules encourage the use of a special committee where a related-party transaction is involved. As a result of the practice with respect to such committees, if a special committee is constituted, both courts and regulators expect that its members will not include nominees of a controlling shareholder or members of management; and they expect that such persons will not participate in the deliberations of the committee. Where these practices are not followed, however, it does not necessarily mean that the decisions of the special committee will be invalidated.

With respect to the activities of management, I have been involved in deals which range from circumstances where management was driving the response to a bid with a special committee simply looking over its shoulder, to circumstances where a special committee was running the process to the virtual exclusion of management. Generally, responding to a bid requires the involvement of management to provide resources, assistance and guidance. In addition, potential third-party bidders will want to carry out due diligence and management will be a key component of that process.

Directors should be sensitive to the potential for conflict in the position of members of management, particularly where management is involved in discussions with an existing bidder or other potential bidders. Most hostile takeover bids are rife with allegations by the bidder of "management entrenchment" and the board should take appropriate steps to blunt that attack.

So why wouldn't I recommend a special committee in all cases? Simply because it isn't always necessary and I don't believe in automatically adopting a mechanism that may not be necessary or desirable in the particular circumstances involved. Potential conflicts can be managed in a number of different ways; the important point is that directors must identify the issue and make a judgment in the circumstances as to how to deal with it.

THE FIDUCIARY-OUT

One additional legal principle you need to know is that, as a fiduciary, you cannot agree with a potential acquirer to restrict the future exercise of your responsibilities to the corporation and its shareholders. You can agree to recommend a particular transaction but you can't agree to continue to recommend it if a higher-value transaction comes along; you can agree to take steps to support and implement a transaction but you can't agree to continue to do so if it becomes clear that it is no longer in the best interests of your shareholders. In these circumstances, as a fiduciary, you need the ability to get out of the deal when that deal is no longer in the best interests of your shareholders (this right to get out of a deal is called a "fiduciary-out," for obvious reasons). And, of course, if you want that right, the other party will want to be compensated if you exercise it (i.e., to be paid a so-called break fee).

There may be situations in which a company has bargained for a fiduciary-out but where the other party refuses to agree to it. What do you do then? You take the action which in your business judgment will result in the most desirable transaction being available to your shareholders. Where shareholders must ultimately approve a transaction, the directors may be influenced by that fact in agreeing to a transaction without a fiduciary-out. But this difficult decision will not often arise since the inclusion of a fiduciary-out is now accepted practice in Canada in virtually all merger and acquisition transactions.

AUCTION/MARKET CANVASSES

One of the important decisions for the board in a consensual transaction is whether to carry out an auction process or some "market canvass" before locking into a transaction with a particular party. There is no legal obligation to do either and there are a number of reasons why a board might decide not to: the uncertainty for the business of the company and its employees if it is publicly known that the company is up for sale; the negative consequences of a public process if no transaction is successfully completed; and the possibility that the prime candidate for a transaction (to whom you are talking) is not prepared to participate in an auction or engage in or continue discussions if you are going to "shop its offer" by approaching other parties. There is no general rule, however. Clearly, there may be transactions where these concerns are not as important as establishing a price through an auction or market canvass, but that is not always the case.

In this context, you should know that the financial advice of an investment banker or other adviser is not necessarily a substitute for determining the value of a company by canvassing the market for alternative purchasers or transactions. As one U.S. court has said, "a decent respect for reality forces one to admit that . . . advice [of an investment banker] is frequently a pale substitute for the dependable information that a canvass of the relevant market can provide" (Barkan v. Amsted Industries Inc., Del. 1989). While this comment somewhat overstates the point, clearly one of the important business judgments that directors must make in connection with a consensual merger or acquisition transaction is whether an auction or market canvass should be carried out.

Most consensual Canadian transactions are, however, entered into without an auction or market canvass and the directors take comfort from the fact that there is a fiduciary-out contained in the relevant support agreement.

STOCK-FOR-STOCK MERGERS

In Canada, a board of directors can approve a consensual merger if it considers the transaction to be in the best interests of the corporation and its shareholders. It would be unusual for a company to approach other third parties or to conduct even a limited market canvass in connection with a consensual merger. Generally, doing so results in a termination of discussions with the party who is likely the most desirable merger candidate. The question of whether there will be a controlling shareholder after the transaction is completed is not as sensitive an issue in Canada

as it is in the U.S. It is simply one element of the transaction which must be considered by the directors. Many Canadian mergers are carried out on a consensual basis after exclusive negotiations where there is a controlling shareholder after the transaction.

SHAREHOLDER APPROVAL

It is difficult to conceive of circumstances in which directors would have any liability to shareholders where those shareholders have, after full disclosure to them, approved a transaction either by an actual vote or by tendering to a bid. If no such approval is an element of a transaction, directors should recognize that this puts more pressure on their decisions. Even then, directors are not at risk in making informed decisions applying the principles discussed in this article. It would only be in the most unusual circumstances that I would recommend that shareholder approval be obtained where it is not legally required as a result of concerns for director liability. The converse of directors taking comfort from shareholder approval of a transaction is that directors should take particular care where the transaction they are facilitating is a "done deal" because of a shareholder lock-up. That aspect of the transaction should figure prominently in the directors' deliberations and business judgments.

You now know all of the legal principles you need to know as a director in considering a merger or acquisition transaction. Act on an informed basis with the advice of outside experts. Consider any conflicts of interest you or any member of management may have. Focus on the interests of your shareholders and recognize that there is no blueprint for either the process to be followed or the substantive terms of a transaction. The hardest decisions are difficult because there are no clear answers, and that's when directors are most protected in exercising their business judgment.

2

M&A Strategy Formulation

Measuring Success in M&A

In order to justify M&A, there should be some benefit to the firm, whether it is financial or strategic. If the justification is strategic, in the end, that too should result in some financial benefit. The studies on the success and failure of M&A are plentiful, although the measures of "success" vary. This brings to light the question of whether M&A deals do create value, for whom, and over what timeframe. All good questions.

While all of the parties described in the previous chapter stand to gain or lose from M&A, some of these parties have direct, measurable financial impacts. Bearing in mind that board and executive fiduciary duties are solely to the stockholders of a firm (and not to the other parties), many studies of M&A measure the impacts on equity prices alone. However, the cash flows that a firm generates are owned by both the debt holders and stockholders. Both the debt and equity of many public companies are traded openly on public exchanges and, as such, have market values. While equity is an obvious measure, debt values change when the credit quality of the postdeal firm differs or when the prospect of a deal changes the likelihood that certain types of debt securities will be called, exchanged, or converted into shares.

Because of the direct and measurable financial impact on both debt and equity holders, both should be considered. Many factors affect the market values of both debt and equity holders, including interest rates, the risk of the firm itself, and the stock market. However, the underlying driver of both measures is the cash flow of the firm. Therefore, it may be more important to measure whether the combined entity generates more cash flow than what the stand-alone firms would have on their own. While cash flow is telling, it is also important to understand the amount of capital that must be invested to generate these cash flows and at what cost of capital (risk). Important measures of the stand-alone versus postdeal firm may thus include the overall riskiness of the cash flows, the cash flows themselves, and the amount of investment capital needed. Based on these measures, one can begin to understand whether value is created or destroyed in M&A and how that value and/or risk is transferred among these parties.

A second critical question concerns the time period of measurement. While an efficient market should immediately reflect all information, these values do change over time. The strategic and tactical decisions that drive executives to do M&A may have short- or long-term plans underlying them. Because of this, the returns themselves may perhaps be best measured over the time periods of the strategic intent behind them. For example, imagine that Sony Corporation has a 10-year strategic plan to enter a particular product market and makes an acquisition today as a part of that plan. Shall we measure the success or failure of that plan on the basis of a three-day abnormal stock return as is commonly done in the academic finance literature? Thirty-day? While in an efficient market the stock should reflect the present value of all foreseen future benefits, the investor's ability to value and foresee such benefits will make it difficult to accurately measure the future value until the future benefits, if any, are actually realized.

Finally, it may be important to measure the impacts of M&A on competitors and the broader economy. Because value (for stockholders) is often destroyed in M&A, do competitors gain? Interestingly, while value may be destroyed for stockholders, M&A may also bring efficiencies to the economy overall. The postdeal firm may produce the same products or services but do so with less overhead, less total capital deployed, and at a lower cost of capital. That is good from an economic perspective (less inputs, more output) but arrives at the expense of losing jobs at the firm level and decreasing competition at the industry level. These are the trade-offs that make M&A both good and bad, at various levels, and to various interests. Because this book is not a political economy, political science, or economics text and instead is a management text focused on creating value for the firm, it is this strategy-value linkage that is critical here.

WHY DO M&A? STRATEGY AND TACTICS

Many good and bad strategic (and nonstrategic) reasons exist for doing M&A. One succinct framework for such reasons comes from the Brealey and Myers[1] finance text in which the authors detail "Sensible" and "Dubious" motives for mergers. Using this framework, with a few additions, we can begin to understand the linkage back to the strategic intent of the firm.

Sensible Motives for Deals

Economies of Scale

Simply, the same productive output may be possible with a lower average overhead or cost per unit of production. This is one of the most commonly stated strategic reasons for doing deals—"synergies."

Economies of Vertical Integration

When a firm purchases up or down the value chain, either its suppliers or customers, it may be able to reduce or remove its reliance on either. A firm may be able to increase its market power and thus benefit its strategic position.

Risk Reduction

Instead of actually increasing cash flows, a firm may simply be able to reduce its strategic risk by M&A. This is not to say that the firm can reduce its cost of capital per se but that the reduced underlying risk of the assets of the firm may simply increase the value of the same cash flows.

Complementary Resources

The assets and resources of many firms may be complementary and thus synergistic. One firm may have great research and development capabilities, while another has a vast distribution network. These firms may have complementary assets, resources, or capabilities that create value in a combined entity.

Unused Tax Shields

Oftentimes, firms have accumulated losses against which a buyer with profits can offset its gains and reduce its tax burden. The gain from reducing taxes payable is wealth transferred to the combined firm. Because of this, the tax authorities have severely limited the ability to use accumulated losses in an acquisition. While the limitations are complex, one critical rule forbids offsetting acquired accumulated losses against unrelated gains in the acquiring firm. That is, an unrelated firm cannot purchase a firm purely for its tax benefits. Being in the same industry (a subject typically debated in a court) is a minimum requirement.

Surplus Funds

A firm may have excess funds in search of positive net present value investments. When a firm has no more good internal investment ideas, rather than give the money back to stockholders in the form of a dividend, it may "invest" in other firms by doing M&A. Dividend policies differ by jurisdiction, but there used to be a double taxation issue in the United States that disadvantaged dividends; oftentimes, M&A was a better use of funds.

Eliminating Inefficiencies

When the assets or resources of another firm are being underutilized or poorly managed, a firm may have the opportunity to purchase it and improve things. When the premium the buyer pays for the target firm is less than the values of the efficiencies gained, value can be created for the buying firm.

Dubious Reasons for Deals

Diversification

This is one of the more commonly stated justifications for doing M&A. The basic argument from finance is that if an individual stockholder wants to be diversified, he or she can do it more cheaply than can the firm. As such, the firm should not diversify but rather give the money back to the stockholders and let them diversify, if they wish to do so.

Earnings Per Share

The argument here is that if the selling firm has higher earnings per share than the buyer (assuming the number of shares exchanged and the exchange ratio allow this), the buyer increases its earnings per share and thus its value. The fallacy is that while earnings per share will rise, the price-to-earnings ratio will also adjust to reflect the price to earnings previously paid for the other firm, as well as the earnings growth expected for each. In the end, the adjustments may affect earnings per share, but either the earnings quality or earnings growth expected will counteract this, and there will likely be no net gain.

Lower Financing Costs

This argument relies on a firm hoping to reduce its cost of capital by buying another firm with lower financing costs. There may be some scale economies to issuing equity or debt together (by having lower fees), but the costs of the equity or debt will be a blend of the two sets of underlying assets. While the combined firms may be able to slightly lower their costs of borrowing, each set of stockholders must now guarantee the debt of the other firm. Any gain from lower financing costs is likely offset by financial guarantees provided.

Management Preferences and Hubris

Plenty of research has shown that executive pay is linked to the size of the organization, and as such, it may be in the personal financial interest of the executives to pursue deals, although the benefits to the firm may be questionable. Richard Roll[2] coined the "hubris hypothesis" to explain how some executives are overconfident that they can better run another firm and so end up deciding to pursue M&A.

M&A STRATEGY: BUY-SIDE VERSUS SELL-SIDE

While both good and bad reasons may exist for M&A, the specific decisions regarding M&A may also differ depending on which side of the transaction a firm may be. Under the assumption that buyers tend to overpay (i.e., a transfer of wealth to the sellers), being on the selling side of a deal may make great sense for a set of stockholders. While a deal may destroy net value (i.e., value of the whole is less than the parts), the wealth transfer may still make the set of selling stockholders better off than before. That said, certain factors and characteristics of a firm may increase its likelihood of becoming a target. As well, with fluctuations in the stock markets, there may be opportunities that drive a firm to sell itself. On the buy-side, the same timing and opportunism is important. There may be more opportune times to consider pursuing M&A and certain conditions that improve the odds of success. The combination of all of these considerations begins to highlight the strategic importance and complexity of M&A strategy and of measuring "success."

CASES

Hewlett-Packard in 2001

Hewlett-Packard (HP) hired a new chief executive officer in 1999 to lead it into the future. The company, despite a strong legacy of success, had been faltering since the late 1990s, with slow sales growth and declining profitability. Industry observers felt that HP was not responding appropriately to competitive threats in its server, printer, and personal computer markets. Industry conditions were also worsening, suggesting hard times ahead. The CEO felt a dramatic move was required to improve HP's position in the market. An attempt to expand HP's information technology (IT) services business through the acquisition of PriceWaterhouseCoopers was unsuccessful. The CEO was considering a merger between HP and Compaq.

Issues: Competition, strategic positioning, buy-side/merger

Newell Company: The Rubbermaid Opportunity

The Newell Company, a multi-billion-dollar company dealing in hardware and home furnishings, office products, and housewares, was contemplating a merger with Rubbermaid, a renowned manufacturer of plastic products. Newell had a remarkable record of success in growth by acquisition. Rubbermaid would mark a quantum step in this program but equally would pose a formidable challenge to Newell's capacity to integrate and strengthen acquisitions. Corporate strategy and advantage is studied, particularly through the Collis and Montgomery[3] framework, to determine if the proposed merger is a step too far.

Issues: Corporate strategy, M&A strategy, merger

MapQuest

MapQuest is a leading provider of mapping services and destination information as well as a publisher of maps, atlases, and other guides. On the Internet, it provides these products and services both to consumers directly and to other businesses, enabling these businesses to provide location, mapping, and destination information to their own customers. The company completed a successful initial public offering 5 years before and was in a strong competitive position. However, the markets were allowing competitors to quickly get funding in both private and public deals. As well, there were perceptions that a general stock market bubble existed for technology companies. The chief executive officer had several options available and wanted to consider those options and present a recommendation to the board. Possible options included splitting the firm's old- and new-line business units, raising capital to fund an acquisition strategy, forging a set of alliances, focusing on organic growth, and pursuing the sale of the firm.

Issues: Corporate strategy, competitive advantage, strategic alternatives, sell-side M&A

CIBC-Barclays: Should Their Caribbean Operations Be Merged?

At the end of 2001, the Canadian Imperial Bank of Commerce (CIBC) and Barclays Bank PLC were in advanced negotiations regarding the potential merger of their respective retail, corporate, and offshore banking operations in the Caribbean. Some members of each board wondered whether this was the best direction to take. Would the combined company be able to deliver superior returns? Would it be possible to integrate, within budget, companies that had competed with each other in the region for decades? Would either firm be better off divesting regional operations instead? Should the two firms just continue to go-it-alone, with emphasis on continual improvement? A decision needed to be made within the coming week.

Issues: Cross-border M&A, corporate strategy, integration, emerging markets, cultural differences

NOTES

1. R. Brealey and S. Myers, *Principles of Corporate Finance,* 7th ed. (Boston: McGraw-Hill/Irwin, 2003).
2. Richard Roll, "The Hubris Hypothesis of Corporate Takeovers," *Journal of Business* 59, no. 2 (1986): 197–216.
3. David J. Collis and Cynthia A. Montgomery, "Creating Corporate Advantage," *Harvard Business Review* 76, no. 3 (May-June 1998): 70–83.

HEWLETT-PACKARD IN 2001[1]

*Prepared by Ken Mark and Jordan Mitchell
under the supervision of Professor Charlene Zietsma*

Version: (A) 2005-01-11

To remain static is to lose ground.[2]

David Packard, co-founder of HP

INTRODUCTION

Carly Fiorina, president and chief executive officer of Hewlett-Packard (HP), was considering a proposed merger of HP and one of its main rivals, Compaq Computer Corporation (Compaq). The idea of a merger was developed when Fiorina, attending an industry seminar in late 2000, met Michael Capellas, chief executive officer of Compaq. HP insiders estimated that the final purchase price would be $25 billion.[3] Sensing that there was interest in collaboration from both sides, Fiorina wanted to continue her dialogue with Capellas as soon as possible.

It was early February 2001, and Fiorina believed that the combined entity would position HP well for the anticipated resurgence in industry demand. However, a merger was fraught with business risk, and there would be no promises that HP's many stakeholders would endorse the bid. Fiorina wondered whether other options, including joint ventures, division spin-offs or divestitures, could be considered. Furthermore, was Compaq the right target?

HEWLETT-PACKARD

In early 2001, HP's 600 sales and support offices were located in more than 120 countries. HP employed 88,500 people and generated profits of $3.7 billion on revenues of $48.8 billion. Sales and profit growth were slowing and negative, respectively, and HP's January 2001 stock price was trading below October 1999 levels. In January 2001, HP was valued at $71.1 billion.

David Packard and Bill Hewlett founded Hewlett-Packard in 1938 with the mission of creating first-class instruments. In a speech to young engineers, Packard once stated: "You're not here to make the average instrument. You're going to make a breakthrough in the art of instrumentation—or we're not going to put it in the catalogue."

Instead of the typical office layout where executives were located on higher floors, Hewlett and Packard created open-plan seating where employees of all levels worked next to each other. In addition, employees, even the founders, were known to each other by their first names. The goal for pretax earnings was 20 per cent of sales. New businesses were evaluated based on whether they could produce profits from the beginning. Once these businesses were developed and incubated by engineers, they would be handed over to managers to be run as if they were independent companies. These little differences in operations (as compared to norms in many technology firms in the 1950s) became known, collectively, as the "HP Way."

HP's first foray into computers occurred in the 1960s despite hesitancy on the part of both Hewlett and Packard. In the late 1970s, its printer division emerged as a result of a key manager breaking many of HP's rules: licensing printer technology from Canon and using HP's own distribution and sales staff to sell the products. But by the 1990s, HP seemed to be stagnating. It became known less for its products and services and more for its employee programs such as diversity and telecommuting (which gave employees the option of working from their homes). The organization developed an aversion to risk. For example, executives found it difficult to carry out bold moves without consensus from multiple stakeholders (who were reluctant to challenge the status quo).

In the late 1990s, even as the technology boom was driving up growth rates at most companies, HP missed analysts' expectations for nine consecutive quarters. Employees at HP argued that their company did not have a strategy for the Internet, and worse, did not understand it. In order to focus its energies on the computer and printing divisions, HP's instruments division was spunoff as Agilent Technologies in 1999.

With the mandate to find "an incredible leader," HP's board of directors hired Fiorina.

Carly Fiorina at Hewlett-Packard

Fiorina joined HP in July 1999 after having spent 20 years at AT&T and Lucent Technologies. At Lucent, Fiorina held several senior leadership positions and directed Lucent's initial public offering and subsequent spin-off from AT&T. She had a bachelor's degree in medieval history and philosophy from Stanford University, an MBA from the Robert H. Smith School of Business (University of Maryland at College Park, Maryland), and a master of science degree from MIT's Sloan School.

Fiorina's first year was considered by many to have been a success. She had injected new energy into the firm by reinterpreting its longstanding values, and she had set the company on track towards an Internet-centric strategy. During her first 12 months, year-over-year revenues rose by 15 per cent and net income by 14 per cent. However, in mid- to late-2000, the overall computing industry was experiencing the beginnings of a recession. Revenue and profit growth at HP fell. Industry observers opined that HP was not responding satisfactorily to competitive threats, notably from IBM and Sun Microsystems (Sun) in the server market, Lexmark in the printer market and Dell in personal computers.

In late 2000, HP was unsuccessful in its attempt to take over PriceWaterhouseCoopers (PWC), a consulting partnership. The deal was aimed at increasing HP's depth in the IT services market. The fact that it failed (and that PWC was subsequently absorbed by IBM's global services division) was not entirely a negative result: some observers strongly felt that the deal was ill-advised—the terms were expensive and integration was considered to be an issue—and, if it had succeeded, would have put Fiorina's job at risk.

In 2001, after a year and a half of service at HP, Fiorina voluntarily handed back her second-half bonus of $625,000 because HP's financial performance did not pass muster.[4] Fiorina was accustomed to pressure. A few years previously, while she was deputy president at Lucent, she became known as Lucent's informal chief executive officer (CEO), with the company turning to her to figure out how to make quarterly financial results.[5] She was certain that Wall Street's pressure on HP would not abate.

Attempting to look beyond HP's current declining performance and the general malaise in the industry, Fiorina wondered whether there existed a great opportunity, with her proposed merger with Compaq, to effect significant and lasting change.

Products and Services

HP had three principal operating areas: imaging and printing systems, computer systems and information technology (IT) services. In addition, the company also offered financing to customers entering into HP service agreements.

Imaging and printing systems made up 41 per cent of the company's revenues and 64.8 per cent of its operating profits. HP divided their activities into printer hardware, imaging, printing supplies and commercial printing. The printer hardware division included black and white and color laser and inkjet printers. During 2001, HP released the lowest priced printer of its family, the LaserJet 1000, as well as printers with capabilities to print from wireless devices and from mobile devices using the Bluetooth technology. In imaging, HP offered scanners, digital cameras, copiers, faxes and other imaging products. Printing supplies included ink and LaserJet cartridges, paper and related products. Commercial printing involved solutions in storing, managing and producing digital solutions for printing presses.

Computing systems made up 42.2 per cent of the company's revenues and 22.7 per cent of the company's operating profit. The division included home and commercial PCs, workstations, Unix and PC servers, storage and software products. HP developed their PCs and laptops to complement Microsoft's latest XP operating system. HP produced the Pavilion and Vectra desktop series and OmniBook and Pavilion laptop series. Servers ranged from platforms such as Unix, HP-UX to Linux and Microsoft Windows. A major initiative in the server business was using Intel's new Itanium processor (developed in conjunction with HP). By focusing on the Itanium processor market, HP had already garnered a 12 per cent share of this small-but-growing market. (Incidentally, HP also had a 12 per cent share of the Unix market.) HP believed in offering multiple platforms allowing customers to choose the best solution for their environment. However, some industry observers felt that HP's real strength in servers was still based in Unix (where competitor Sun Microsystems had a 51 per cent share in that segment).

IT services generated over 14.3 per cent of the company's revenues and made 15 per cent of the company's operating profit. The IT services division was involved the planning, implementation, support and ongoing operations of IT solutions. The company offered breadth from infrastructure, storage, supply chain management, e-services, business intelligence, CRM, portals, Internet, networking and mobile communications. HP saw its advantage was its knowledge of infrastructure and its ability to provide strong outsourcing services to clients.

See Exhibit 1 for HP's performance by division.

THE COMPUTING INDUSTRY

Global spending in the computing industry was estimated at $950 billion in 2000, and growing to $1 trillion in 2003. The computing industry could be broken out into the following categories:

- Computer hardware, including personal computers, servers and storage devices
- Printers and imaging devices
- IT consulting services
- Computer software

For a breakdown of the segments by revenues and estimated future growth, see Exhibit 2. According to industry and stock analysts, competition in each segment was intensifying because of the sudden slowdown in demand. The major players, such as HP, IBM, Compaq, Dell, Lexmark, and Sun Microsystems (to name a few who competed in the overall industry), had different product and service line-ups—no two firms had exactly the same menu to offer to their customers. Product and service overlap, between one major player and the next, ranged from high (consider Toshiba and Gateway, both of whom sold personal computers) and low (consider Dell [personal computing hardware] and IBM [business services and hardware]). As a result, any two major firms could be potential partners in one segment and fierce competitors in another. One factor contributing to this diversity in offerings was the sheer number of segments in the industry; another factor was the ongoing stream of mergers and acquisitions between firms in related segments.

	1998	1999	2000
Printing Systems			
Net Revenue	**16,709**	**18,550**	**20,476**
% of Total	*41.3%*	*42.6%*	*41.0%*
Earnings (loss) from Operations	2,043	2,335	2,746
Earnings % to Revenue	12.2%	12.6%	13.4%
% of Total	*62.6%*	*63.3%*	*64.8%*
Computing Systems			
Net Revenue	**17,315**	**17,814**	**21,095**
% of Total	*42.8%*	*40.9%*	*42.2%*
Earnings (loss) from Operations	480	850	960
Earnings % to Revenue	2.8%	4.8%	4.6%
% of Total	*14.7%*	*23.0%*	*22.7%*
IT Services			
Net Revenue	**5,685**	**6,255**	**7,129**
% of Total	*14.0%*	*14.4%*	*14.3%*
Earnings (loss) from Operations	748	575	634
Earnings % to Revenue	13.2%	9.2%	8.9%
% of Total	*22.9%*	*15.6%*	*15.0%*
All Other			
Net Revenue	**773**	**886**	**1,299**
% of Total	*1.9%*	*2.0%*	*2.6%*
Earnings (loss) from Operations	(5)	(71)	(103)
Earnings % to Revenue	−0.6%	−8.0%	−7.9%
% of Total	*−0.2%*	*−1.9%*	*−2.4%*
TOTAL SEGMENTS			
Net Revenue	**40,482**	**43,505**	**49,999**
% of Total	*100.0%*	*100.0%*	*100.0%*
Earnings (loss) from Operations	3,266	3,689	4,237
Earnings % to Revenue	8.1%	8.5%	8.5%
% of Total	*100.0%*	*100.0%*	*100.0%*

Exhibit 1   HP Performance by Division (in millions of dollars)

Source: "HP Annual Report," www.sec.gov, October 31, 2000, p. 57.

Note: Total Segments do not equal overall company.

Despite the differences, firms competed in similar ways across all segments, i.e., product or service innovation and performance, perception of quality and reliability, service and support, perception of brand value, and strength of value-added reseller (VAR) relationships.

In early 2000, as a result of the current economic malaise, analysts predicted that the computing industry would experience a new wave of consolidation.

Industry Segments in More Detail

The following discussion focuses on four segments in the computing industry: personal

Market Size (US$ millions)	2000	Growth Prospects for next few years
Personal Computers 　*Desktop PCs* 　*Notebook PCs*	$152,185 $105,011 $47,174	Optimistic: 5-10% per year; Pessimistic: Flat to negative growth Expected to grow significantly faster than Desktop PCs
Printing and Imaging 　*Inkjet Printers* 　*Monochrome Laser Printers* 　*Desktop Color Laser Printers*	$40,000 $33,851 $5,824 $325	 Low growth (under 10% per year) Low growth (under 10% per year) High growth (over 15% per year)
Servers	$40,677	Low growth (under 10% per year)
Storage 　*Open Systems SAN* 　*Unix Disk Storage Systems*	$19,549 $4,793 $14,756	 Low growth (under 10% per year) Low growth (under 10% per year)
IT Services	$395,000	About 10% per year

Exhibit 2　　Selected Computing Industry Segments by Revenue and Growth Prospects

computers, printing and imaging, servers and storage, and IT services.

The Personal Computer (PC) Segment

The total PC market was estimated at $174 billion for 2000, of which $122 billion were desktop PC sales and $52 billion were laptop sales.[6] Gross margins in the industry ranged from about 10 per cent to 18 per cent. Key competitors in this industry included Compaq, Dell, IBM, HP and Fujitsu Siemens. For the market shares (dollar shares) of key competitors, see Exhibit 3.

Growth in the PC segment had been high in the late 1990s, with industry revenues in 1999 rising 25 per cent over the previous year. The sudden downturn in 2000, with global PC shipments dropping 3.6 per cent from the third to fourth quarter of 2000, prompted one observer to note: "This is the worst it's been in the history of

Market Share (2000)	HP	Compaq	Dell	IBM	Lexmark	Sun
Personal Computers	13.9%	13.6%	12.8%	7.3%	0.0%	0.0%
Printing and Imaging	51.2%	5.6%	0.0%	2.5%	9.5%	0.0%
Servers	16.3%	16.6%	7.0%	15.7%	0.0%	23.9%
Storage						
Open Systems SAN	8.8%	16.1%	3.9%	8.9%	0.0%	13.6%
Unix Disk Storage Systems	11.4%	8.2%	0.0%	10.8%	0.0%	21.9%
IT Services	1.9%	1.7%	0.0%	8.4%	0.0%	0.7%

Exhibit 3　　Global Market Shares by Competitor

the industry."[7] Looking ahead, industry growth prospects in 2001 and beyond were uncertain, with revenue growth estimates ranging from five per cent to 15 per cent.

PCs were generally sold through VARs and retail outlets, with the exception of Dell, which sold direct to consumers and businesses. The other major firms, including IBM, HP and Compaq, had largely failed to transition over to a direct-to-consumer model. One explanation was that they underestimated the challenges posed by the sophisticated supply chain logistics of the direct model.[8]

In 2001, competition based on price was increasing, with Dell (and its 10 percentage point cost advantage over the major firms) leading the charge. A Gartner Group analyst suggested, "We anticipate a price war in the United States in 2001, as direct vendors [like] Dell . . . endeavor to gain market share from Compaq, Hewlett-Packard and IBM."[9]

Another analyst suggested,

The PC industry is at a critical juncture. Managements and investors need to recognize that the problem is not the end of the PC, but slower growth and overcapacity. It is time for bold moves. It is time to do it before it is done to you. We believe investors should stay on the sidelines until they see concrete steps toward consolidation.[10]

Printing and Imaging

The total printing and imaging market was estimated at $40 billion in 2000. This segment experienced growth similar to that of the PC segment. Printers typically had gross margins ranging from five to 15 per cent. In the last few years, many printer manufacturers had begun selling printers at cost or at a negative margin of five to 10 per cent in order to benefit from future printer cartridge sales; printer cartridges generated gross margins of approximately 70 per cent.[11] The dominant players in printers and printer supplies included Hewlett-Packard, Lexmark, Canon and Seiko-Epson.

Industry observers felt that the printer market would flatten out because of the declining consumer demand for PCs. While the printer market had suffered in the downturn, sales of cartridges had remained steady and continued to grow in line with PC shipments. Like PCs, printers were generally sold through VARs and retailers, with the former relying on cartridge sales to generate repeat visits from consumers.

Significant innovation had occurred in the printer industry in the last five years, with HP leading the way by being one of the first firms to introduce a sub-$100 printer. The effects of HP's subsequent market share gain (in the inkjet market) on its competitors were mitigated by strong overall segment growth. It was not clear how competitors would react now that growth was slowing.

Servers and Storage

The word *server* was used to denote both the physical piece of hardware such as mainframes, minicomputers or personal computers, as well as software that ran applications for a number of users. *Storage* referred to any device that was used to save information apart from an actual PC, work terminal or server.

In 2000, the total server market was estimated at $40.7 billion. The server market had posted a growth rate of 30.9 per cent in 2000. By early 2001, however, the slowdown in the rest of the industry had led to a decrease in the demand for servers. Gross margins on servers were estimated to be between 20 and 40 per cent. The top five vendors of servers held 79.4 per cent of market share (measured on revenues) in 2000.

Most servers were purchased by businesses and sold through VARs and by a firm's direct sales force (typically in combination with a consulting and hardware installation package).

In 2000, the total storage market was worth $29 billion and gross margins were estimated to be between 15 and 30 per cent.[12] Storage was divided into either disk storage or tape storage, with such solutions like storage area networks (SANs) being common links between disk array controllers and servers. The major players in storage were EMC, Compaq and Sun.

The majority of storage devices were purchased by businesses through VARs and a firm's direct sales force. Like the rest of the computing industry, storage sales were expected to slow, with 2001 growth rates projected between 15 per cent and 20 per cent.

IT Services

IT services were defined as any range of consulting, education, design, installation, implementation, ongoing support and maintenance and outsourcing services provided to other companies.[13] The size of the IT services market in 2000 was estimated at $395 billion with an average growth of nine per cent over the last three years. Some industry observers predicted that IT services would continue to enjoy consistent growth rates of eight per cent to 10 per cent over the next three years. Gross margins on IT services ranged from 10 per cent to 200 per cent, depending on many variables including personnel cost and ability to meet standards and deadlines. Additional products and services were often sold to IT clients.

The industry for IT services was highly fragmented, with the top 10 providers accounting for roughly 30 per cent of the market. The key players were IBM with Electronic Data Systems (EDS), Fujitsu, Accenture, and Computer Sciences Corporation (CSC).

COMPAQ

Compaq was founded in 1982 and competed in the following markets: consumer and corporate PCs, handheld devices, workstations and servers. In 1995, Compaq was the global leader in PCs with a strong position in the PC server business. In 1996, it moved into the enterprise segments of the computing market with servers and powerful workstations, placing it in direct competition with IBM and HP. In order to penetrate the enterprise segment against the strong sales and field service and support organizations of IBM and HP, Compaq developed alliances with systems integrators such as Andersen Consulting, and with SAP, the leading enterprise resource-planning software vendor.

As part of its growth strategy, Compaq had made two major acquisitions: Tandem Corporation in 1997 for $3 billion, and Digital Equipment Corporation (DEC) in 1998 for $9.6 billion. The acquisitions were aimed at strengthening their position in the enterprise market. With Tandem, Compaq acquired the Himalaya server, giving the company greater strength in high-end computing. With DEC, Compaq inherited its proprietary Unix server platform, some important storage technology and access to its NT service organization. This meant that Compaq had the largest channel structure, delivering 80 per cent of its products and services through its channel partners. The merger between DEC and Compaq was viewed as being difficult and uneven as it involved combining DEC's 50,000 employees and Compaq's 33,000 employees and the company's two distinct cultures.[14] Observers noted that Compaq continued to be a company with at least three distinct cultural environments cobbled together. For example, employees from the original companies—Compaq, Tandem, and DEC—continued to identify with their previous pre-merger organizations.

By the fall of 1999, Compaq was organized into three large business units: enterprise solutions and services, commercial personal computing (small and mid-sized businesses) and consumer. A significant proportion of the revenues in the enterprise solutions and services segment came from professional and support services, an important result of the Tandem and DEC acquisitions. The business critical server business was largely a legacy of the Tandem acquisition.

Operating in over 200 countries with 94,600 employees, Compaq had increased revenues by 10 per cent from 1999 to $42.4 billion in 2000. For the same period, net income had stayed flat. Refer to Exhibit 4 for Compaq's performance by division. For financial comparisons between selected competitors, see Exhibit 5. Compaq's market capitalization had suffered a major decline, falling 42.7 per cent from early 2000 to $25.9 billion in early 2001.[15]

	1998	1999	2000
Enterprise Computing			
Revenue	10,498	12,974	14,316
% of TOTAL	*33.7%*	*33.7%*	*33.8%*
Operating Income	948	1,201	2,140
Operating Income %	9.0%	9.3%	14.9%
% of TOTAL	*54.3%*	*63.8%*	*59.9%*
Compaq Global Services			
Revenue	3,990	7,162	6,993
% of TOTAL	*12.8%*	*18.6%*	*16.5%*
Operating Income	776	1,148	944
Operating Income %	19.4%	16.0%	13.5%
% of TOTAL	*44.4%*	*61.0%*	*26.4%*
Commercial Personal Computing			
Revenue	11,846	12,185	13,136
% of TOTAL	*38.0%*	*31.6%*	*31.0%*
Operating Income	(46)	(448)	289
Operating Income %	−0.4%	−3.7%	2.2%
% of TOTAL	*−2.6%*	*−23.8%*	*8.1%*
Consumer			
Revenue	4,932	5,994	7,586
% of TOTAL	*15.8%*	*15.6%*	*17.9%*
Operating Income	183	262	170
Operating Income %	3.7%	4.4%	2.2%
% of TOTAL	*10.5%*	*13.9%*	*4.8%*
Other			
Revenue	(97)	210	352
% of TOTAL	*−0.3%*	*0.5%*	*0.8%*
Operating Income	(115)	(281)	27
Operating Income %	118.6%	−133.8%	7.7%
% of TOTAL	*−6.6%*	*−14.9%*	*0.8%*
TOTAL			
Revenue	31,169	38,525	42,383
% of TOTAL	*100.0%*	*100.0%*	*100.0%*
Operating Income	1,746	1,882	3,570
Operating Income %	5.6%	4.9%	8.4%
% of TOTAL	*100.0%*	*100.0%*	*100.0%*

Exhibit 4   Compaq Revenues by Division (in millions of dollars)

Source: "Compaq Annual Report," www.sec.gov, December 31, 2000, p. 12.

Revenues (US$ millions)	1997	1998	1999	2000
Hewlett-Packard Co.	42,895	47,061	42,370	48,782
Compaq Computer Corp.	24,584	31,169	38,525	42,383
International Business Machines Corp.	78,508	81,667	87,548	88,396
Sun Microsystems Inc.	8,598	9,791	11,726	15,721
Dell Inc.	12,327	18,243	25,265	31,888
Lexmark International Inc.	2,494	3,021	3,452	3,807
Operating Margin (before depreciation)	**1997**	**1998**	**1999**	**2000**
Hewlett-Packard Co.	13.7%	12.7%	11.8%	10.3%
Compaq Computer Corp.	14.0%	5.6%	5.5%	9.1%
International Business Machines Corp.	16.7%	16.7%	18.5%	18.3%
Sun Microsystems Inc.	16.2%	17.8%	19.4%	20.2%
Dell Inc.	11.2%	11.8%	10.3%	9.4%
Lexmark International Inc.	14.1%	15.2%	16.1%	14.4%
Net Profit Margin	**1997**	**1998**	**1999**	**2000**
Hewlett-Packard Co.	7.3%	6.3%	7.3%	7.3%
Compaq Computer Corp.	7.5%	−8.8%	1.5%	1.4%
International Business Machines Corp.	7.8%	7.7%	8.8%	9.2%
Sun Microsystems Inc.	8.9%	7.8%	8.8%	11.8%
Dell Inc.	7.7%	8.0%	6.6%	7.0%
Lexmark International Inc.	6.5%	8.0%	9.2%	7.5%
Current Assets (US$ millions)	**1997**	**1998**	**1999**	**2000**
Hewlett-Packard Co.	20,947	21,584	21,642	23,244
Compaq Computer Corp.	12,017	15,167	13,849	15,111
International Business Machines Corp.	40,418	42,360	43,155	43,880
Sun Microsystems Inc.	3,728	4,148	6,116	6,877
Dell Inc.	3,912	6,339	7,681	9,491
Lexmark International Inc.	776	1,020	1,089	1,244
Total Assets	**1997**	**1998**	**1999**	**2000**
Hewlett-Packard Co.	31,749	33,673	35,297	34,009
Compaq Computer Corp.	14,631	23,051	27,277	24,856
International Business Machines Corp.	81,499	86,100	87,495	88,349
Sun Microsystems Inc.	4,697	5,711	8,420	14,152
Dell Inc.	4,268	6,877	11,471	13,435
Lexmark International Inc.	1,208	1,483	1,703	2,073
Common Equity	**1997**	**1998**	**1999**	**2000**
Hewlett-Packard Co.	16,155	16,919	18,295	14,209
Compaq Computer Corp.	9,429	11,351	14,834	12,080
International Business Machines Corp.	19,564	19,186	20,264	20,377
Sun Microsystems Inc.	2,742	3,514	4,812	7,309
Dell Inc.	1,293	2,321	5,308	5,622
Lexmark International Inc.	501	578	659	777
Free Cash Flow	**1997**	**1998**	**1999**	**2000**
Hewlett-Packard Co.	1,451	2,820	1,250	2,050
Compaq Computer Corp.	2,959	(51)	(160)	(738)
International Business Machines Corp.	1,289	1,919	3,273	2,729
Sun Microsystems Inc.	551	696	1,734	2,772
Dell Inc.	1,600	2,140	3,529	3,713
Lexmark International Inc.	205	187	180	180

Exhibit 5   Financial Comparisons (Selected Items From the Income Statement and the Balance Sheet)

Source: Compustat Database.

Compaq aimed to be the leading global provider of information technology products, services and solutions. Compaq sold its goods through dealers, VARs (value added resellers) and system integrators. With direct sales increasing, pressure was mounting on VAR margins, estimated to be approximately four per cent to five per cent in 2000. Its customers included large and medium-sized businesses as well as government and educational facilities. Compaq employed a direct sales force and offered its products on its Internet site and by telephone—a reaction to Dell's success with its direct model. Compaq used a variety of channels to sell its products. It sold to large and medium-sized business and government customers through dealers, value-added resellers and system integrators. Small business and home customers were reached through dealer and consumer channels. Compaq also had a direct sales force and sold its product on an Internet site and by telephone.

When Compaq attempted to bypass its 44,000 resellers by touting its direct-to-consumer sales, resellers responded by steering their customers to other brand-name manufacturers such as HP or to their own "white label" PCs. At the end of 2000, Capellas still had not resolved the channel issues, particularly in the important commercial personal computing segment. In this segment of the business, more than 85 per cent of Compaq's sales were still generated by the traditional, indirect channel, and less than 10 per cent of sales came from Compaq's new direct-to-consumer channel. Yet Capellas persisted with the latter option, most likely because it was the model used by Dell, Compaq's fiercest competitor.

Although Capellas had estimated Compaq revenue growth for 2001 to be between six per cent and eight per cent, Compaq cut its revenue forecasts for 2001 a few days into the fiscal year, citing the unexpectedly sharp slowdown in the desktop PC market.

In early 2001, Compaq Computer Corp.'s (Compaq) chairman and chief executive officer, Michael D. Capellas, was answering questions about his firm's future. After a confident presentation about his company's global prospects,

Capellas added, "I think the fact that we have a global business protects us reasonably well, but some U.S. companies will be hammered and will have to make dramatic changes. Are we concerned about economic slowdown? Yes, these are uncertain times."

An accountant by training, Capellas worked in steel and oil before joining Compaq in 1998, coming from Oracle Corporation. When he arrived at Compaq, Capellas received a three-year contract that more than doubled his pay after he became chairman in September 2000. Just two weeks later, he received an $850,000 one-time bonus, base pay of $1.6 million a year and an annual bonus of twice his base pay. Capellas also had performance-based stock options and incentive awards that were targeted to a range of seven to 10 times his salary.

In addition, Capellas received options for close to one million shares of Compaq stock. About half the options vested at various dates, based on Capellas's employment through 2004. The remainder vested according to a schedule of stock-price targets or if increases in earnings per share matched or exceeded those of major rivals. As an incentive to raise the company's stock price, 250,000, or a quarter of Capellas's options, would vest if shares stayed above a stair-stepped schedule of stock-price targets for 15 days in a row.

CONCLUSION

Many onlookers predicted that the economic situation would worsen, inevitably hurting the entire computing industry. In addition, competitive actions were hard to predict. Dell and Lexmark could continue their aggressive pricing in PCs and printers, respectively. On the other hand, there were rumors that IBM would end its involvement in the PC market in the next year. As for smaller competitors—see Exhibit 6 for a partial list—it was difficult to predict what they would do.

In light of all the issues facing her industry, and the scrutiny on her company, Fiorina wanted to know what she should do to position her

Apple

Apple had had success with innovative hardware such as the iMac and iBook, which had revived its mid-90s struggling business performance. Apple was relatively small in comparison to other PC manufacturers, with $8.0 billion in sales, but had carved a niche with innovative products and releases, such as the iPod.[1]

EMC

EMC was the world leader within the storage sector and was dedicated to automated networked storage. The company slogan, "where information lives," demonstrated EMC's commitment to storage and server resources. EMC had revenues of $8.9 billion and profits of $1.8 billion in 2000.[2] In 2001, it was expected that the company would sign a deal with Dell, allowing the resale of its storage system under a co-branded name.

Gateway

Gateway posted revenues of $9.7 billion in 2000 and was a supplier of PCs, sold mostly through the company's own distribution network and owned a chain of approximately 200 "Country Stores." In 2001, Gateway slowed retail expansion and decided to focus on the U.S. market by exiting its international business.[3] Gateway also supplied TVs and was known for its direct-to-consumer touch and warranty programs.[4]

IT Services

There were several firms that competed in IT services. Besides the leader, IBM, other major companies included EDS (Electronic Data Systems) with revenues of $21 billion, Accenture with revenues of $10 billion and Computer Sciences Corporation with revenues of $10 billion.

Japanese Competitors

NEC (marketing Packard Bell PCs) and Fujitsu Siemens had a stronghold of the western European market with prominence in Japan. Sony was a leader in its many divisions, ranging from audio, video and communications to information technology. It had worldwide sales of $62 billion; $20 billion was accounted for by U.S. sales. Sony was leveraging its other divisions and was trying to make headway into the PC market.[5] Toshiba had U.S. sales of $5.5 billion and worldwide sales of $41 billion; it was also a major player within the laptop computer segment.[6] Seiko Epson, a Japanese-based company, began in 1942 and had experienced steady increases in sales over 10 per cent in the last three years. Seiko Epson aimed to deliver cutting-edge imaging solutions on paper, screen and glass (such as mobile displays). Canon was founded in 1937, originally as a camera company, but grew as a major force within the printer market. By 2001, computer peripherals, which included printers, made up nearly half of Canon's revenues; 20 per cent of sales were from cameras.

PDA Manufacturers

Palm, Handspring, Research in Motion and Sony all fought against HP and Compaq for market share in the PDA market. Palm was the leader in the market and had sales of over $1 billion, in comparison to Handspring with sales of $371 million and Research in Motion with sales of $220 million.

Notes

1. "Apple Company Capsule," hoovers.com, August 27, 2003.
2. "EMC Company Capsule," hoovers.com, August 23, 2003.
3. "Credit Suisse First Boston Equity Analyst Report," January 9, 2002, p.18.
4. "Gateway Corporate Website," gateway.com, August 20, 2003.
5. "Sony Corporate Website," sony.com, August 20, 2003.
6. "Toshiba Corporate Website," toshiba.com, August 20, 2003.

Exhibit 6   Other Competition

company for the next few years. She knew that, aside from short-term pressures to meet forecasts, a more dramatic move was needed in the longer term to get HP back on track.

NOTES

1. This case has been written on the basis of published sources only. Consequently, the interpretation and perspectives presented in this case are not necessarily those of Hewlett-Packard or any of its employees.

2. "HP fires back . . . ," *ITworld.com*, December 31, 2001.

3. All figures in U.S. dollars.

4. "HP Chief Gave Back Her Bonus," *The Wall Street Journal*, January 9, 2001, p.C16.

5. George Anders, "Perfect Enough," *Penguin Book*, 2003.

6. "Hewlett Packard Analyst Report," *CIBC World Markets*, July 10, 2003, p. 26.

7. "Dataquest and IDC: PC Shipments," *Purchasing*, February 22, 2001.

8. Charles Wolf, "PC Hardware: PC Industry Overview—Perception vs. Reality," *Needham Analyst Report*, January 2001, p. 5.

9. James Connell, "Tech Brief: PC Price War," *International Herald Tribune*, March 27, 2001.

10. "PC Industry Manifesto," *Bear Stearns Analyst Report*, January 2001, p. 3.

11. "Print Prevue," *Credit Suisse First Boston Analyst Report*, March 13, 2001, p. 4.

12. "Hewlett Packard Analyst Report," *CIBC World Markets*, July 10, 2003, p. 26.

13. "Hewlett Packard Annual Report," www.sec.gov, October 31, 2000, p. 2.

14. "ABN-AMRO Analyst Report," *Compaq Computer*, December 19, 2001.

15. "Compaq Company Capsule," www.hoovers.com, accessed August 10, 2004.

NEWELL COMPANY: THE RUBBERMAID OPPORTUNITY[1]

Prepared by Professor Joseph N. Fry

Copyright © 2000, Ivey Management Services

Version: (A) 2001-01-19

In October 1998, the board of directors of the Newell Company was considering a proposed merger with Rubbermaid Incorporated to form a new company, Newell Rubbermaid Inc. The transaction would be accomplished through a tax-free exchange of shares under which Rubbermaid shareholders would receive Newell shares valued at approximately $5.8 billion at a ratio which represented a 49 per cent premium on Rubbermaid's current stock price. At the time of the transaction the annual revenues of Newell and Rubbermaid were, respectively, about $3.2 billion and $2.4 billion. If approved, the agreement would mark a quantum step in Newell's growth, but, equally, it would pose a formidable challenge to the company's demonstrated capacity to integrate and strengthen its acquisitions.

NEWELL: RIDING THE ACQUISITION TIGER

In 1998, the Newell Company had revenues of $3.7 billion distributed across three major product groupings: Hardware and Home Furnishings ($1.8 billion), Office Products ($1.0 billion), and Housewares ($.9 billion). Over the past ten years the company had achieved a compound sales growth rate of 13 per cent, an earnings per share growth rate of 16 per cent and an average annual return on beginning shareholder equity of 21 per cent. These results were consistent with Newell's formal goals of achieving earnings per share growth of 15 per cent per year and maintaining a return on beginning equity of 20 per cent or above. Further financial details on Newell are given in Exhibit 1.

	To End Q3/98	12/31/97	To End Q3/97	12/31/96
Net sales	**$2,650,263**	**$3,336,233**	**$2,395,037**	**$2,972,839**
Cost of products sold	1,786,640	2,259,551	1,631,253	2,020,116
Selling, general and administrative expenses	404,882	497,739	365,123	461,802
Goodwill amortization and other	40,502	31,882	22,872	23,554
Operating Income	418,239	547,061	375,789	467,367
Interest expense	43,966	76,413	54,363	58,541
Other, non-operating, net	(213,373)*	(14,686)	(12,862)	(19,474)
Profit before tax	587,546	485,334	334,288	428,300
Income taxes	250,740	192,187	132,373	169,258
Net Income	**$336,806**	**$293,147**	**$201,915**	**$259,042**
Current assets	1,767,370	1,433,694		1,148,464
Property, plant and equipment	834,486	711,325		567,880
Trade names, goodwill, other	2,001,862	1,559,594		1,342,086
Total Assets	**4,603,718**	**4,011,314**		**3,058,430**
Current liabilities	1,061,675	714,479		665,884
Long-term debt	912,650	786,793		685,608
Other non-current liabilities	243,862	285,241		206,916
Convertible preferred securities	500,000	500,000		
Shareholders' equity	1,885,531	1,725,221		1,500,022
Total Liabilities and Shareholders' Equity	**4,603,718**	**4,011,314**		**3,058,430**
Approximate common shares outstanding (000)	173,000	163,300		162,000
Earnings per share (fully diluted)		$1.80		$1.60
Stock Price $High/Low	$54/37	$43/30		$33/25

Exhibit 1   Selected Financial Information for Newell Company, 1996-1998 ($000)

Source: Company Financial Reports.

*Primarily gain from sale of Black & Decker holdings.

Acquisitions

Acquisitions were the foundation of Newell's growth strategy. Given the relatively slow growth of the product markets in which it chose to operate, Newell's corporate goal for internal growth was only three per cent to five per cent per annum—with internal growth being defined as the growth of businesses that Newell had owned for over two years. Actual internal growth in the past five years had averaged about five per cent per annum. This put a premium on acquisitions if Newell was to meet its aggressive growth targets. Indeed, over $2 billion of its current sales were the result of over 20 acquisitions made since 1990.

Newell's approach to acquisition was both aggressive and disciplined. Its targeted acquisition candidates were generally mature businesses with "unrealized profit potential" which further passed a number of screening criteria, including having a:

- strategic fit with existing businesses—which implied product lines that were low in technology, fashion and seasonal content and were sold through mass distribution channels.
- number one or two position in their served markets and established shelf space with major retailers.
- long product life cycle.
- potential to reach Newell's standard of profitability, which included goals for operating margins of 15 per cent, and Sales, General and Administrative costs at a maximum of 15 per cent.

The size of the acquisitions varied. In 1996, Newell made one acquisition for $46 million cash, in 1997, three material acquisitions for $762 million cash and in 1998 to date, four material acquisitions for about $413 million cash. Once acquired, the new companies were integrated into the Newell organization by means of an established process that had come to be called "newellization."

Newellization

Newellization was the profit improvement and productivity enhancement process employed to bring a newly acquired business up to Newell's high standards of productivity and profit. The Newellization process was pursued through a number of broadly applicable steps, including the:

- transfer of experienced Newell managers into the acquired company.
- simplification and focusing of the acquired business's strategy and the implementation of Newell's established manufacturing and marketing know-how and programs.
- centralization of key administrative functions including data processing, accounting, EDI, and capital expenditure approval.
- inauguration of Newell's rigorous, multi-measure, divisional operating control system.

Newell management claimed that the process of newellization was usually completed in two or three years.

Continuing Operations

A summary of Newell's product groups and major lines is outlined in Table 1. These products were, for the most part, sold through mass merchandisers. In 1997, Wal-Mart accounted for 15 per cent of Newell's sales; the other top ten Newell customers (each with less than 10 per cent of Newell sales) were Kmart, Home Depot, Office Depot, Target, J.C. Penney, United Stationers, Hechtinger, Office Max and Lowe's. International sales had increased from eight per cent of total sales in 1992 to an expected 22 per cent in 1998 as Newell followed customers and opportunities into Mexico, Europe and the Americas.

Newell's fundamental competitive strategy, which applied to all of its operations, was to differentiate on the basis of superior service to its mass merchandise customers. For Newell, superior service included industry-leading quick response and on-time, in-full delivery, the ability to implement sophisticated EDI tie-ins with its customers extending to vendor-managed inventories, and the provision of marketing and merchandising programs for product categories that encompassed good, better and best lines.

Table 1   Newell Product Lines, 1998

Housewares	Hardware and Home Furnishings	Office Products
Aluminum Cookware and Bakeware	Window Treatments Home Storage	Markers and Writing Products
Glassware	Picture Frames	Office Storage
Hair Accessories	Hardware	

Organization

Newell centralized certain key administrative functions such as data management (including order-fulfillment-invoice activities), divisional coordination and control, and financial management. Otherwise, the presidents of the company's 18 product divisions were responsible for the full scope of manufacturing, marketing and sales activities for their product lines and for the performance of their businesses.

Divisional coordination and control were facilitated by the fundamental similarities of the Newell businesses. These similarities made it possible for corporate level management to develop a common pool of managers and know-how that could be transferred relatively easily from one division to another. The business similarities also made it possible for corporate management to apply a common set of detailed operating standards and controls across the businesses, and to play a knowledgeable role in reviewing divisional progress and plans. Corporate management held monthly reviews (called brackets meetings) with divisional presidents to track multiple operating and financial measures and to ensure that appropriate attention was given to items that were off budget. As a result, divisional management operated in a goldfish bowl under high pressure, but they were paid very well for meeting their targets.

Outlook

In Newell's view, the company's adherence to a highly focused strategy had established a sustainable competitive advantage for the corporation and this, coupled with abundant acquisition opportunities and internal growth momentum, would support the continuing achievement of its financial goals.

RUBBERMAID: A FALLEN ICON

Rubbermaid was a well known, and, for several decades, a renowned manufacturer of a wide range of plastic products ranging from children's toys through housewares to commercial items. From 1986 through 1995 Rubbermaid was ranked among the top 10 in *Fortune*'s list of America's most admired companies, including the No. 1 spot in 1993 and 1994. But by March 1998 Rubbermaid had fallen to No. 100. After a wonderful run of growth and profitability, extending as far back as the 1960s, the company had clearly hit a rough patch.

Rubbermaid earned its early reputation by setting aggressive goals for 15 per cent growth in revenues and profits and then, by and large, meeting its targets. Under the intense and very personal management of Stanley Gault, an ex-senior executive at General Electric and CEO and chairman of Rubbermaid from 1980 to 1991, the company was pressed to broaden its product line through development and acquisition and to meet demanding operating targets. From propitious beginnings Rubbermaid became an ubiquitous brand and a Wall Street darling—with sales and profits, respectively, at the end of Gault's tenure of $1.7 billion and $162 million.

Rubbermaid's earnings momentum continued into the early years of Gault's successor, Wolfgang Schmidt, but the good times were to be short-lived. In 1994 Rubbermaid was hit by a doubling of plastic resin prices.[2] The company's clumsy reactions to this shock revealed a number of accumulating problems. *Fortune* enumerated them in a 1995 article[3]:

- Customer relations: Rubbermaid angered its most important retail buyers with the heavy-handed way it has passed along its ballooning costs. Some are so angry that they have given more shelf space to competitors . . .
- Operations: Although it excels in creativity, product quality, and merchandising, Rubbermaid is showing itself to be a laggard in more mundane areas such as modernizing machinery, eliminating unnecessary jobs, and making deliveries on time . . .
- Competition: It has been slow to recognize that other housewares makers—once a bunch of no-names who peddled junk—have greatly improved over the past half dozen years. The premium prices that Rubbermaid charges over its rivals have grown too large, and customers are turning away.
- Culture: The company's extraordinary financial targets . . . seem unrealistic—and straining to reach them is proving increasingly troublesome. Some of the friction between Rubbermaid and its customers can be traced to Rubbermaid's voracious appetite for growth.

Rubbermaid's profits peaked in 1994 at $228 million. In 1995 sales were up eight per cent but the company took a restructuring charge of $158 million pre-tax and net earnings fell to $60 million. The restructuring charges were taken in anticipation of a two-year program designed to reduce costs, improve operating efficiencies and accelerate growth. In 1997, Rubbermaid reported[4] that the realignment activities were substantially complete and that the company "has or initiated closure of all nine locations slated for closure in the plan, completed the associated reductions, and achieved the estimated annual savings of $50 million anticipated in the 1995 program." Unfortunately, this action did not have a material effect on sales, which remained essentially flat, and operating profits, which dipped somewhat, as detailed in the financial summary given in Exhibit 2. Thus, early in 1998, Rubbermaid announced another restructuring charge, which it estimated would reach at least $200 million pretax, to fund a program that would include centralizing global procurement and consolidating manufacturing and distribution worldwide.

Rubbermaid Lines of Business

In 1998, Rubbermaid manufactured and sold over 5,000 products[5] under four key brand names:

- Rubbermaid: a wide range of household utility products encompassing five categories (Kitchen, Home Organization, Health Care, Cleaning, and Hardware/Seasonal) and 23 product lines.
- Graco: children's products in six product lines focusing on baby strollers and related items.
- Little Tikes: juvenile products, with 11 product lines focusing on toys and furniture.
- Curver: a European-based home products business with revenues of $180 million, acquired at the beginning of 1998.

Rubbermaid's international sales and operations had been growing in recent years as it followed its customers abroad. The Curver acquisition increased foreign sales, including exports from the United States, to about 25 per cent of total revenues, helping the firm along the path to its goal of 30 per cent by 2000.

Rubbermaid Strategy

Rubbermaid's strategy reflected an uneasy balance of not necessarily consistent ambitions. The 15 per cent growth goals of the past had disappeared from public statements, but there was no question that the company remained aggressive in its goals and optimistic about its

	To End Q3/98	12/31/97	To End Q3/97	12/31/96	12/31/95
Net sales	**$1,936,829**	**$2,399,710**	**$1,825,416**	**$2,354,980**	**$2,344,170**
Cost of products sold	1,383,564	1,748,424	1,327,990	1,649,520	1,673,232
Selling, general and administrative expenses	353,805	416,641	314,229	432,063	402,586
Operating Income	199,460	234,645	183,197	273,397	268,352
Interest expense	27,795	35,762	28,463	24,348	10,260
Restructuring costs	73,740	16,000	16,000		158,000
Other, non-operating, net	(23,749)	(51,032)	(49,729)	4,046	4,457
Income taxes	42,586	91,370	77,717	92,614	35,863
Net Income	**$79,088**	**$142,536**	**$110,746**	**$152,398**	**$59,772**
Current assets	952,841	816,204		856,720	
Other assets	445,995	399,716		475,346	
Property, plant and equipment	784,228	707,974		721,914	
Total Assets	**2,183,064**	**1,923,984**		**2,053,980**	
Current liabilities	802,231	567,084		742,841	
Long-term debt	152,556	153,163		154,467	
Other non-current liabilities	171,302	153,385		142,992	
Shareholders' equity	1,056,885	1,050,262		1,013,700	
Total Liabilities and Shareholders' Equity	**2,183,064**	**1,923,984**		**2,053,980**	
Approximate common shares outstanding (000)		149,900		151,000	158,800
Earnings per share (fully diluted)		$0.95		$1.01	$0.38
Stock Price $High/Low		$30/22		$30/22	$34/25

Exhibit 2   Selected Financial Information for Rubbermaid, 1995-1998 ($000)

Source: Company Financial Reports.

prospects. To achieve its aims Rubbermaid relied on a multi-faceted competitive strategy. It wanted, at once, to be a company with a:

- strong consumer franchise based on unique product features, quality and rapid innovation, and on brand recognition and aggressive advertising. Rubbermaid had, for example, set a goal that 10 per cent of each year's sales should come from new, high value products and it had reduced new product time to market from 20 plus months in the 1980s to six months currently, with a goal of four months by 2000.
- low-cost sourcing, production, and fulfillment base. The company was in the process, for example, of cutting product variations by 45 per cent and consolidating its supplier base from 9,000 to less than 2,000 vendors.
- reliable and efficient supplier to mass merchandisers. Rubbermaid was moving, for example, to scheduling manufacturing by customer order and to just-in-time service and continuous replenishment of its best selling items.

There was a tension at work behind these aims. In its 1996 Annual Report Rubbermaid noted that its market was at a point of inflection, in which the control of information was shifting from mass marketers to individual consumers. In this context Rubbermaid claimed that it would strike a new balance in its strategies, to continue to lead in innovation while becoming a low cost producer. Similarly, in its 1997 Annual Report, the company noted that in a squeeze of higher costs and lower retail prices it was making bold moves to become the low-cost producer, while retaining world-class quality and innovation. Finally, another "point of inflection": in his 1997 Letter to Shareholders, Wolfgang Schmidt promised that, "with the initiatives of the past two years and the opportunities ahead, we are at the inflection point from which we can combine our financial strength and innovation capabilities with a more favorable cost climate to generate stronger shareholder returns."

THE OUTLINE OF A DEAL

Newell's appetite for all of Rubbermaid might have been whetted with its $247 million acquisition of Rubbermaid's Office products division in 1977, adding about $160 million of annualized revenues to Newell's developing office products line of business. Whatever the stimulus, talks soon began on a total combination of the two firms.

Negotiations led to a provisional agreement under which Rubbermaid shareholders would receive 0.7883 shares of Newell common stock for each share of Rubbermaid common stock that they owned. Based on Newell's closing price of $49.07 on October 20, 1998, this represented $38.68 per Rubbermaid share or a premium on 49 per cent over Rubbermaid's closing price of $25.88. Under this arrangement Newell would issue approximately 118 million shares of common stock to Rubbermaid shareholders. Rubbermaid shareholders would end up holding approximately 40 per cent of the combined company. The transaction represented a tax-free exchange of shares and would be accounted for as a pooling of interests. A simple pro forma of the results, the transaction is given in Exhibit 3.

Newell management forecast[6] that, as soon as the transaction was completed, they would begin the "newellization" process and improve Rubbermaid's operating efficiencies to achieve 98 per cent on-time and line-fill performance and a minimum 15 per cent pretax margin. They also expected revenue and operating synergies through the leveraging of Newell Rubbermaid's brands, innovative product development, improved service performance, stronger combined presence in dealing with common customers, broader acquisition opportunities, and an increased ability to serve European markets. They forecast that by 2000 these efforts and opportunities would produce increases over anticipated 1998 results of $300 million to $350 million in operating income for the combined company.

	Newell	Rubbermaid	NewellRubbermaid
	Q3/97-Q3/98	Q3/97-Q3/98	Q3/97-Q3/98
Net sales	3,591,459	2,511,123	6,102,582
Cost of products sold	2,414,938	1,803,998	4,218,936
Selling, general and administrative expenses	537,498	456,217	993,715
Goodwill amortization and other	49,512		49,512
Operating Income	589,511	250,908	840,419
Interest expense	66,016	35,094	101,110
Other, non-operating, net	(215,197)*	48,688	(166,509)
Profit before tax	738,692	167,126	905,818
Income taxes	310,554	56,239	366,793
Net Income	428,138	110,887	539,025
Balance Sheet as of End Q3/98			
Current assets	1,767,370	952,841	2,720,211
Property, plant and equipment	834,486	784,228	1,618,714
Trade names, goodwill, other	2,001,862	445,995	2,447,857
Total Assets	4,603,718	2,183,064	6,786,782
Current liabilities	1,061,675	802,231	1,863,906
Long-term debt	912,650	152,556	1,065,206
Other non-current liabilities	243,862	171,302	415,164
Convertible preferred securities	500,000		500,000
Shareholders' equity	1,885,531	1,056,885	2,942,416
Total Liabilities and Shareholders' Equity	4,603,718	2,183,064	6,786,782
Approximate common shares outstanding (000)	173,000	150,000	291,000
Earnings per share (fully diluted)	$2.47	$0.74	$1.85

Exhibit 3   Simple Pro Forma Financial Information for Newell Rubbermaid, End Q3-1998 ($000)

Source: Estimates based on Company Financial Reports.

*Primarily gain from sale of Black & Decker holdings.

NOTES

1. This case has been written on the basis of published sources only. Consequently, the interpretation and perspectives presented in this case are not necessarily those of Newell Company or any of its employees.

2. Materials accounted for between 45 and 50 per cent of Rubbermaid's net sales.

3. Lee Smith, "Rubbermaid Goes Thump," *Fortune*, October 2, 1995.

4. Rubbermaid Annual Report, 1997.

5. In 1997 Rubbermaid had sold its Office Product business to Newell for a $134 million pretax gain, which it promptly offset by a one-time charge of $81 million for asset impairment related to acquisitions.

6. Newell Press release, October 21, 1998.

MAPQUEST

Prepared by Kevin K. Boeh
under the supervision of Professor Paul W. Beamish

Version: (A) 2004-08-25

On October 1, 1999, Chief Executive Officer (CEO) Mike Mulligan's team at MapQuest closed the third quarter books. Revenue was strong and the company's cash position was good. During the past year, Mulligan had led the firm through a successful initial public offering (IPO) and record growth. However, Mulligan questioned being able to sustain the growth rate and the market value of the firm, which many called irrational. He wondered how he could take advantage of the stock price and continue to sustain growth (see Exhibits 1 and 2) and value going forward. Mulligan planned to lay out a course of action for the board later that month.

INDUSTRY BACKGROUND

Growth of the Internet

The Internet had become an increasingly significant global medium for distributing and collecting information, conducting commerce and communicating. Internet growth was being fuelled by increased use of personal computers, improvements in network infrastructure, more readily available and lower cost Internet access, an increased acceptance of conducting transactions online and the proliferation of compelling available content.

MapQuest and many of its competitors had been in the mapping, printing and location information businesses for years and were now faced with the prospects of this dynamic digital business environment. Many of the existing offline companies and many start ups that were focused on the space, some very well funded with growth capital, saw the opportunity to leverage their offline assets online.

Convergence of Traditional and Digital Mapping

Geospatial information had traditionally been provided through reference materials including atlases, maps, travel guides, telephone directories and textbooks. According to the International Map Trade Association, the annual market for such publications in the United States alone would exceed $1.6 billion. Advances in technology allowed companies to put their geospatial information into computer applications and to place their databases onto CD-ROMs and the Internet. MapQuest had followed just such a path and was using its extensive databases of geographically relevant information to provide online services.

	1996	1997	1998	1999e	2000e	2001e	2002e
Revenue							
Internet Business	$7.0	$4.8	$6.5	$12.8	$20.6	$42.6	$63.3
Internet Consumer	0.1	1.3	1.4	6.4	13.9	26.4	44.4
Traditional DMS	12.4	15.4	16.8	14.7	20.0	24.0	28.0
TOTAL	**19.6**	**21.4**	**24.7**	**33.9**	**54.5**	**93.0**	**135.7**
Cost of Revenue							
Internet	4.3	4.5	4.8	9.7	13.2	18.5	24.4
Traditional DMS	8.0	10.8	12.8	11.4	14.7	17.6	21.0
TOTAL	**12.3**	**15.3**	**17.6**	**21.1**	**27.9**	**36.1**	**45.4**
Gross Profit	7.3	6.1	7.1	12.8	26.6	56.9	90.3
Sales & Marketing	4.5	7.3	5.2	19.0	25.1	30.0	40.0
General & Admin	1.9	1.8	2.3	4.8	6.4	8.0	11.5
Product Development	2.6	5.0	3.0	5.6	7.5	11.0	15.0
TOTAL OPEX	**9.0**	**14.1**	**10.5**	**29.4**	**39.0**	**49.0**	**66.5**
Operating Income	**(1.7)**	**(8.0)**	**(3.5)**	**(16.6)**	**(12.4)**	**7.9**	**23.8**
Interest Income (Expense)	0.2	0.1	0.1	1.6	1.0	—	—
Other Income (Expense)	0.2	0.3	0.2	0.3	0.4	—	—
Pretax Income	**(1.3)**	**(7.6)**	**(3.2)**	**(14.7)**	**(11.1)**	**7.9**	**23.8**
Tax Expense	0.0	0.0	0.0	0.0	0.0	0.0	0.0
EPS			$(0.12)	$(0.47)	$(0.33)	$0.21	$0.66
Total Shares Outstanding			27.6	31.4	33.8	36.9	36.2

Exhibit 1 MapQuest—Income Statement and Projections (all amounts in millions, except per share amounts)

Note: e = estimates.

Online Destination Information for Business and Consumers

Businesses had traditionally communicated their existence and location to customers using print media including newspapers and the Yellow Pages, which targeted only a narrow geographic audience and had limited ability to provide updated information. MapQuest gave businesses the opportunity to provide customized driving directions and real-time physical location information. As well, MapQuest provided businesses with an additional set of information and tools that online sites used to enrich and differentiate their own offerings. Very few of these companies

had the personnel or technical resources to cost effectively develop the services in-house that MapQuest provided to them.

Consumers and travellers had traditionally located businesses and other points of interest using maps and telephone inquiries, among other methods. As the Internet was growing, consumers were increasingly turning to the Internet for such information.

Geographically Targeted Online Advertising

Forrester Research estimated that online advertising of approximately $1.0 billion in 1998

Assets	Dec. 31, 1998	Sep. 31, 1999
Current assets		
Cash and cash equivalents	$564	$29,685
Short term investments	—	17,940
Accounts receivable, net of allowances	6,647	9,840
Accounts receivable - affiliates	128	707
Inventories	1,365	1,126
Contracts works in progress	147	231
Prepaid expenses and other current assets	482	1,684
Total current assets	9,333	61,213
Property and equipment, net of accumulated depreciation (1998 - $3,433; 1999 - $4,455)	1,844	4,488
Goodwill, net	178	155
Other assets	95	825
Total assets	**$11,450**	**$66,681**
Liabilities and stockholders' equity (deficit)		
Current liabilities		
Accounts payable	$1,715	$2,719
Current portion of note payable	48	5
Accrued personnel costs	562	1,231
Advance billings on contracts	498	686
Deferred revenue	1,208	2,434
Other accrued liabilities	1,001	2,411
Total current liabilities	5,032	9,486
Stockholders' equity (deficit)		
Convertible Preferred Stock, Ser. A, B and C	26,477	—
Notes receivable from issuance of preferred stock	(291)	—
Preferred stock, $01 par; 5 million authorized	—	—
Common stock, $.001 par; 100 million authorized; 336,038 o/s in 1998; 33,572,562 o/s in 1999		
Notes receivable for common stock	—	—
Additional paid in capital	140	88,246
Retained deficit	(19,908)	(30,861)
Total stockholders' equity (deficit)	(19,768)	57,195
Total liabilities and SE (deficit)	**$11,450**	**$66,681**

Exhibit 2   MapQuest—Balance Sheet (all amounts in thousands, except share counts)

would grow to over $8.1 billion over the next four years. While online advertising was growing, it was primarily national or international advertising. That is, the products and services offered were not location-specific, yet most actual consumer expenditure was indeed local. While figures varied, it was estimated that as much as 80 per cent of a consumer's expenditure, net of housing, occurred within five miles of the primary residence. As well, of the offline advertising market, nearly 80 per cent of the total expenditure was for local businesses, using location-specific advertising media. The opportunity to allow online advertising to be location-specific had yet to be realized.

COMPANY BACKGROUND

History and Transformation

R.R. Donnelley & Sons, a media and printing company, founded MapQuest, originally called GeoSystems Global Corporation, in Lancaster, Pennsylvania, in the late 1960s as a cartographic services division responsible for creating free road maps for gas station customers. In the 1970s, MapQuest became a leading supplier of custom maps to reference, travel, textbook and directory publishers. The company grew in the mapping industry as a high-quality custom map-maker and expanded its client base to include American Express, Bertelsmann, Langenscheidt, Reader's Digest, Houghton Mifflin, Reed Elsevier, The National Geographic Society, and World Book.

In 1991, R.R. Donnelley combined its mapping expertise with technology to pioneer electronic publishing software for interactive mapping applications. MapQuest developed electronic applications for call centres, kiosks, client-server environments and wireless devices, as well as packaged software applications for travel, directory, reference and street mapping. In 1994, MapQuest created travel titles for the first handheld devices brought to market by Apple Computer. MapQuest produced travel titles that allowed Fodor's, TimeOut and Michelin to bring top international city guides, tour information and directory mapping to consumers. In this same year, MapQuest was split into a separate entity from its corporate parent, R.R. Donnelley & Sons, to management and certain investors, including R.R. Donnelley.

In 1996, MapQuest launched the first consumer-focused interactive mapping site on the Web. The company began to offer business solutions to map-enable other websites. This innovative business model captured the attention of the Internet consumer and the business market.

In April 1997, The National Geographic Society entered into a cartographic product development, publishing, marketing and distribution agreement with the firm. The agreement was for five years, ending in May 2002. National Geographic took a seat on the board and received warrants to purchase 954,147 shares at $1.04 per share.

In July of 1997, outside venture investors, including Highland Capital, Weston Presidio Capital and Trident Capital, invested in the firm, taking 3.4 million shares for $12 million. In November of that year, insiders, including the chief financial officer and senior vice-president, also purchased stock, largely funded using interest-bearing notes from the firm.

In May 1998, R.R. Donnelley & Sons and 77 Capital Corporation, two of the original investors from the spin-off, sold their equity positions to Highland Capital, Weston Presidio Capital and Trident Capital for an additional $7 million. In June of this same year, Chief Executive Officer Barry Glick took a voluntary termination of employment as, whereby MapQuest agreed to pay Glick $43 thousand representing separation and salary. In August, Michael Mulligan was hired from American Express Travel as CEO and chairman of the board. At American Express, Mulligan had been responsible for Corporate Services Interactive, an American Express Travel offering. Prior to American Express, Mulligan was the chief operating officer (COO) of OAG, the Official Airlines Guide, and was thus a very fitting candidate to lead the company.

The Initial Public Offering

In late 1998, the board of directors selected underwriters to lead an initial public offering. The company officially changed its name to MapQuest.com, established its corporate head-quarters in New York City, along with its development facilities in Mountville, Pennsylvania, and Denver, Colorado. The investment banks drafted the IPO prospectus in January 1999, and filed an initial registration statement (S-1) on February 19 to sell up to $50 million of stock. On April 12, an amended S-1 was refiled with an offer to sell 4.6 million shares in the range of $10 to $12 per share with an over-allotment option to the underwriters to increase the number of shares by up to 15 per cent (see Exhibit 3).

Date	Nasdaq Index	MQST
7-May-99	2,503.62	$22.19
14-May-99	2,527.86	21.38
21-May-99	2,520.14	17.56
28-May-99	2,470.52	16.75
4-Jun-99	2,478.34	16.38
11-Jun-99	2,447.88	15.69
18-Jun-99	2,563.44	15.00
25-Jun-99	2,552.65	15.69
2-Jul-99	2,741.02	18.13
9-Jul-99	2,793.07	19.63
16-Jul-99	2,864.48	20.13
23-Jul-99	2,692.40	17.00
30-Jul-99	2,638.49	14.94
6-Aug-99	2,547.97	10.13
13-Aug-99	2,637.81	10.31
20-Aug-99	2,648.33	13.94
27-Aug-99	2,758.90	12.38
3-Sep-99	2,843.11	12.00
10-Sep-99	2,887.06	12.88
17-Sep-99	2,869.62	13.50
24-Sep-99	2,740.41	12.50
30-Sep-99	2,746.16	$11.88

Exhibit 3   Closing Stock Prices—Weekly

The IPO roadshow was held during the last two weeks of April, continuing into the first few days of May. On May 3, 1999, the pricing range was increased to $12 to $14 per share to allow flexibility of pricing to meet the hot market demand. The shares were priced after the close of Nasdaq trading on May 3 at $15 per share, and began trading on Tuesday, May 4. Shares debuted late in the morning at $28 per share, an 87 per cent gain from the pricing to IPO buyers. The stock price made the market capitalization of the firm approach $1 billion in its first day of trading.

MAPQUEST—THE BUSINESS

The Solution

MapQuest was a leading online provider of mapping and destination information for businesses and consumers. MapQuest's online products and services enabled businesses to:

- Provide customized maps, destination information and driving directions to potential customers;
- Expand the service offerings of their websites to attract and retain users;
- Use outside sources to meet their map-generating and destination information needs, thereby avoiding a significant portion of the expenses normally associated with establishing and maintaining a map-generating personnel and technology organization; and
- Provide potential customers with information regarding which of a business's multiple locations was closest to the potential customer.

MapQuest's online products and services enabled consumers to:

- Receive maps and destination information on a real-time basis based on specific location parameters provided by the customer;
- Generate detailed, door-to-door driving directions at any time; and
- Create and retrieve customized maps based on the consumer's preferences.

MapQuest was also a leading provider of traditional and digital mapping products and services to the educational, reference, directory, travel and governmental markets in the United States. In addition, companies that incorporated call centres, CD-ROMs or driving direction kiosks into their information delivery strategy required non-Internet customized mapping solutions. MapQuest had adapted its map-generating software to promote the rapid development of mapping applications in these environments.

MapQuest Strategy

MapQuest's objective was to be the leading online provider of destination solutions for businesses and consumers. Key elements of MapQuest's strategy, as put forth in the IPO prospectus, included their intention to:

• *Build Brand Awareness:* In addition to branding on its website, MapQuest co-branded its products and services on each of its business customer's websites. MapQuest intended to expand its use of advertising, public relations and other marketing programs designed to promote its global brand and build loyalty among its customers. In the future, MapQuest planned to expand both its online and offline marketing programs.

• *Expand and Enhance the MapQuest Service:* The company planned to continue to broaden and deepen its services by providing comprehensive, cost-effective, accurate and easily accessible information and value-added tools and features. The company was developing product and service enhancements aimed at its business customers, including enhancing their opportunity to offer geographically targeted advertising programs on their websites. MapQuest's planned enhancements to its consumer service included introducing greater personalization features to mapquest.com.

• *Grow Sales Channels Aggressively:* The company hoped to build its sales capabilities in order to broaden penetration of its products and services and increase revenue. The company planned to build its direct field sales force to target United States and international markets, and it sought to develop strategic relationships in the value-added-reseller channels. The company also intended to build its own advertising sales force in order to augment the current third-party representative sales force it had engaged to sell advertisements on mapquest.com.

• *Develop Additional Advertising Opportunities:* The company intended to increase and expand its advertising revenue opportunities by offering new methods of targeted advertising based on a consumer's geographic information. The company planned to use consumer-provided information to provide advertisers the ability to base their advertising and promotions on a consumer's geographic information.

• *Use Existing Integrated Geographic Data as a Platform:* The company wanted to develop new products and services by effectively employing the comprehensive integrated geographic databases it had been developing since 1967. The company had utilized proprietary editing software tools to create its geographic data from multiple content providers in a variety of data formats.

• *Pursue International Opportunities:* The company believed that significant opportunities existed to expand MapQuest's products and services internationally. As of December 1998, approximately 10.8 per cent of the maps that MapQuest generated from its own website represented international locations. The company intended to expand its international marketing efforts to gain access to additional business customers seeking to improve the service offerings of their websites and consumers seeking online map-related information.

MapQuest Products and Services—Internet and Traditional

Internet—Business Products/Services

Connect	Enabled businesses to display requested maps based on any combination of city, state, street address and ZIP code.
InterConnect	Enhanced MapQuest Connect. Enabled consumers who visited a business's website to find the closest location to a user's location.
Locator	Enhanced MapQuest InterConnect. Enabled more advanced searching by integrating MapQuest with specific geographic search parameters contained in its business customer's database, such as "find closest gas station with a car wash."
TripConnect	Enabled businesses to provide consumers with door-to-door driving instructions, including a route-highlighted map, trip mileage and estimated driving time.
Enterprise Service	Provided mapping and routing capability designed primarily for high-volume websites. Enabled business customers to integrate generated map pages into their websites.
Enterprise Server	Non-hosted. Provided mapping and routing capability designed primarily for high-volume websites. Enabled business customers to integrate generated map pages into their websites.
Server for NT	Non-hosted. Provided mapping and routing capability designed primarily for low-volume websites. Enabled business customers to customize their own mapping solutions.

Internet—Consumer Products/Services

The mapquest.com website offered several menu options for consumers:

- Maps—enabled map generation either based on detailed supplied information or a more general location request;
- Driving Directions—provided the most direct route from a point of origin to a destination using a variety of options and formats, including door-to-door, city-to-city, overview map with text, text only or turn-by-turn;
- Travel Guide—provided access to lodging, dining, city and weather information for most consumer-requested destinations, all of which could be tailored by the consumer to fit his or her particular information needs;
- Buy A Map—provided access to the MapStore to buy United States and international maps,

road atlases, travel guides and other map and travel-related products; and
- Membership—by becoming a member, the consumer could save generated maps, place personalized icons on generated maps that could be stored for future use, receive advance notice of new MapQuest features and enhancements and become eligible for promotional offers.

Digital Mapping (Traditional) Products/Services (DMS)

MapQuest published or provided the relevant geographic data for printed road maps, atlases, travel guides, hotel and telephone directories, maps used in textbooks and reference books, and CD-ROMs. In addition, MapQuest's products and services included software applications incorporating customized mapping solutions for publishers and producers of CD-ROMs. MapQuest also provided extensive cartography, geographic database development, comprehensive map data maintenance, advanced mapping technology and consultation services to a wide variety of customers on a fee-for-service basis. MapQuest's traditional and digital mapping customers included National Geographic, Galileo International, Ryder, Exxon, Best Western and the Alamo and National Car Rental (Republic).

Future Product and Service Directions

The technology team had integrated MapQuest services, including driving directions, into the Palm Pilot 7, the first full-time Internet-connected handheld, using an advertising-based business model. The firm planned and budgeted for a nationwide rollout later in the year. The firm also considered opportunities for products and services to be supplied to and bundled with competing Internet appliances, including the latest cell phones with LCD screens. Finally, the team foresaw the integration of its products and services into the digital mapping capabilities and GPS in autos and other forms of transportation.

Sales and Marketing

MapQuest sold its Internet business products and services in the United States through a sales organization of 17 employees as of January 31, 1999. This sales organization consisted of 12 direct field salespeople based throughout the United States and five telemarketers located at MapQuest's Denver office. In addition, MapQuest sold its Internet products and services through indirect sales channels, including value-added resellers such as Moore Data and SABRE BTS.

Sales of advertisements on mapquest.com were generated by third-party advertising sales representatives and, to a lesser extent, by MapQuest's internal advertising sales force, which consisted of two persons as of January 31, 1999.

MapQuest sold its traditional and digital mapping products through a direct sales force of 11 field salespersons and telemarketers. MapQuest marketed its products and services online by placing advertisements on third-party websites. In addition, MapQuest advertised through traditional offline media and utilized public relations campaigns, trade shows and ongoing customer communications programs.

MapQuest Customers

MapQuest had licensed its products and services to over 380 business customers. No one customer accounted for over 10 per cent of MapQuest's overall revenues (see Exhibit 4).

MapQuest Suppliers— Geographic Data

MapQuest licensed a significant portion of its primary geographic data from a limited number of sources through non-exclusive, short-term contractual arrangements. MapQuest relied on U.S. street level data drawn from the U.S. government and through agreements with NavTech and Geographic Data Technologies (GDT). Data covering Canada were supplied by Desktop Mapping Technologies Inc. MapQuest obtained Western European street and major road data from TeleAtlas, NavTech and Mapping NV. Major road data for the rest of the world was obtained from AND Mapping NV. MapQuest relied on these sources of third-party data, and if any were to change, MapQuest would have needed to substitute alternative sources of data or attempt to develop substitute sources of data internally.

MapQuest's own proprietary data assets also supported its online and traditional and digital mapping products and services. MapQuest had spent approximately six years developing a U.S.

Content Providers:	Telecoms/Directories:	Travel/Entertainment:
• Excite • Infoseek • Lycos • TicketMaster Citysearch • Yahoo!	• Ameritech • APIL (Don Tech) • GTE • Pacific Bell • Southwestern Bell • US West	• American Auto Assoc • American Express • Avis • Best Western • Budget • Galileo International • Hertz • Republic Industries • Ryder • Sabre Group (Travelocity)
Media:	**Publishers/Ad Agencies:**	**Retail/Services:**
• *LA Times* • *National Geographic*	• Classical Atlas • DDB Needham • Harte Hanks • McGraw-Hill • Modem Media-Poppe Tyson • RR Donnelley	• Blockbuster • Border's • Home Depot • Kinko's • Sears
Real Estate:		
• Cendant • Moore Data		
Other:		
• Citgo • Exxon		

Exhibit 4   MapQuest Customers

major road database. MapQuest also maintained a graphical image database that contained over 190,000 archived files to serve as an internal reference library. In addition, MapQuest had developed a suite of international city map data that included over 300 metropolitan maps and over 500 downtown maps of most major international tourist and business destinations.

THE CAPITAL MARKETS

The capital markets for Internet and technology companies were doing well (see Exhibit 5), and

had experienced one of the greatest run-ups in history (see Exhibit 6).

Initial Public Offerings and Venture Capital

The number of venture-backed companies was increasing as well, which made Mulligan feel that more potential customers would get funded, but might also allow more competitors to emerge (see Exhibit 7).

As more and more companies were funded in the private markets and had the capital to fuel growth, more companies drove quickly to the public markets and created a heated market for initial public offerings (see Exhibit 8).

Company	Ticker	Stock Price (Sep 3, 1999)	Shares O/S	Market Cap (M)	Trailing Quarter Rev (M)	Enterprise Value (EV) (M)	Unique Visitors Jul-99
About	BOUT	$39.50	12.1	$478	$3.7	$416.5	8.3
America Online	AOL	97.06	1,207.0	117,151	1,377.0	113,927.4	42.2
Ask Jeeves	ASKJ	33.75	24.9	840	2.7	777.1	4.2
CNET	CNET	41.50	80.1	3,324	25.6	3,083.0	8.2
EarthWeb	EWBX	35.88	9.1	327	7.2	293.9	0.6
Excite@Home	ATHM	40.94	361.0	14,779	100.4	14,654.0	16.4
Go2Net	GNET	66.81	41.1	2,746	5.7	2,475.1	11.2
GoTo	GOTO	37.56	35.8	1,345	3.6	1,217.8	7.3
Infoseek	SEEK	31.00	62.0	1,922	36.1	1,838.6	21.1
LookSmart	LOOK	27.50	84.1	2,313	10.5	2,214.4	10.1
Lycos	LCOS	44.75	89.4	4,001	45.1	3,850.2	30.2
MapQuest	**MQST**	**12.00**	**33.0**	**396**	**7.4**	**366.3**	**5.4**
The Globe	TGLO	10.63	24.4	259	4.1	187.1	3.7
Ticketmaster CitySearch	TMCS	25.63	72.9	1,868	25.5	1,779.6	4.0
VerticalNet	VERT	33.94	16.8	570	3.6	540.2	n/a
Xoom	XMCX	37.63	16.8	632	6.5	421.4	8.7
Yahoo!	YHOO	155.00	300.0	46,500	128.6	45,707.0	38.9
ZDNet	ZDZ	15.69	80.9	$1,269	$22.9	$1,268.9	8.0

Exhibit 5   Market Valuations and Statistics

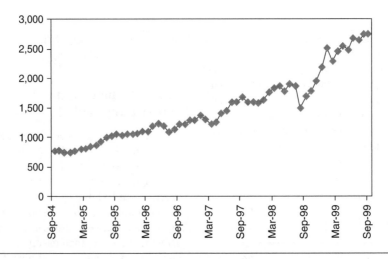

Exhibit 6   NASDAQ Index, September 1994 to September 1999

Year	Deals	US$ Total (Millions)
1994	1,207	$4,143.9
1995	1,870	7,630.8
1996	2,609	11,506.8
1997	3,181	12,772.3
1998	3,691	$21,244.3

Exhibit 7   Venture Capital Funding—United States

Source: NVCA.

Mergers and Acquisitions

The mergers and acquisitions market had picked up tremendously as new capital flowed into the hands of IPO- and venture-backed companies. Inflated stock valuations were driving many companies to use their own stock as acquisition consideration. These factors helped drive the market for the acquisition of venture-backed companies (see Exhibit 9). However, there was fear that the Financial Accounting Standards Board (FASB) in the United States would rule to make the use of pooling-of-interests more difficult in a merger, if not impossible altogether. Such a move would require acquirers to use the

Period	Number of IPO's	Avg. Offer Amount US$ (Million)	Avg Valuation US$ (Million)
YTD 1999	180	$72.4	$435.6
1998	78	49.2	229.1
1997	138	35.9	164.3
1996	280	43.6	209.3
1995	204	$40.6	$163.0

Exhibit 8   Initial Public Offering Markets—United States

Source: NVCA, as of October 1, 1999.

Period	Total # of Companies	Total US$ (Billions)	Avg Price US$ (Millions)
1999 (1st half)	91	$7.2	$119.9
1998	195	8.4	72.8
1997	161	7.6	66.4
1996	103	5.4	82.4
1995	99	3.7	65.6
1994	104	$3.2	$49.5

Exhibit 9   Mergers of Venture-Backed Companies—United States

purchase accounting method, likely slowing acquisition activity, since acquirers would have to immediately take a full write-off of goodwill rather than write it off over an extended period.

(Internet traffic), stickiness (how long users used a site), and wallet-share (how much of a consumers total expenditure could be influenced) when touting the merits of a particular business model or offering (see Exhibits 10 and 11).

THE COMPETITIVE LANDSCAPE

The market itself was still shaping, and new players, new technologies and new offerings were rapidly emerging. Stock analysts and venture capitalists frequently spoke of "eyeballs"

Data and Map Data Vendors

There were two sources of data used in the industry. First, there were numerous data vendors that sold demographic and business information such as white pages listings, business

Company	Reach % (Home & Work)	Avg Daily Unique Pages Per Visitor (home & work) (millions)	Unique Visitors (home & work) (millions)	Home/ Work	Home	Work
City Search-TicketMaster Online	7.8	12.5	3,112	9.7	9.1	9.9
MapQuest	**4.8**	**8.9**	**3,062**	**10.9**	**9.2**	**10.1**
Expedia	1.9	9.8	4,140	11.0	10.1	9.9
Travelocity	5.5	16.5	3,498	16.2	14.2	15.2
CheapTickets.com	1.6	7.3	1,002	9.5	9.6	8.7
Delta-Air.com	1.9	6.3	1,219	9.7	8.1	10.4
LowestFare.com	2.2	4.7	1,382	3.6	3.2	3.6
MapBlast.com	1.1	10.9	707	n/a	n/a	n/a
MapsOnUs.com	1.3	2.0	831	0.9	0.9	0.8
PreviewTravel	4.5	11.4	2,826	11.7	10.5	10.3
TicketMaster	4.0	13.1	2,514	9.1	9.2	8.0
Trip.com On Line	1.6	5.5	1,015	9.9	7.4	10.3
USAirways	1.5	7.4	961	7.1	6.1	6.4
1travel.com	0.7	8.5	287	8.2	7.2	9.7
AA.com	2.3	6.7	1,442	11.6	8.5	12.6
Travelscape	1.0	6.7	481	7.2	8.0	4.4
Tickets.com	0.5	7.5	311	6.7	6.9	n/a
UAL.com	2.1	5.6	1,317	11.5	9.7	9.9
NWA.com	1.9	7.0	1,175	6.2	5.8	5.3
Domain Category						
Travel/Tourism	31.3	21.2	19,857	22.7	17.2	22.5
Airline Sites	9.7	12.8	6,170	16.2	12.7	15.2
Shopping	66.1	72.2	41,869	70.2	55.7	56.5

Exhibit 10   Internet Traffic Statistics—September, 1999

MapQuest—Recent News

Mapquest.com Licenses Routing Software To Onstar Communications

NEW YORK, N.Y. (Dow Jones)—Sept 22, 1999 MapQuest formed an alliance with OnStar Communications, an in-vehicle safety, security and information service used in GM vehicles.

Nokia Selects MapQuest.com to Provide Driving Directions to Nokia's New Media Phones; MapQuest.com Expands Its Wireless Reach With Addition

NEW YORK—(BUSINESS WIRE)—Sept. 22, 1999—MapQuest announced an agreement with Nokia (NYSE:NOK) to provide MapQuest.com driving directions and travel information.

AOL's Digital City, Inc. Expands Relationship With OnHealth Network Company

SEATTLE, Sept. 21/PRNewswire/—OnHealth Network Company (Nasdaq: ONHN), a leading online health and wellness destination, today announced the expansion of its strategic relationship with AOL's Digital City, Inc.

Getting Local Online Knight Ridder draws from its newspapers to build a national network of local portal sites

Network World Fusion, 20 September 1999, From job portals to music portals to personal portals, it's hard to keep track. Here's another growing category to add to the list: local portals.

infoUSA.com Announces 5 New Partners for Free Internet White and Yellow Page Services

SILICON VALLEY—(BUSINESS WIRE)-Sept. 20, 1999 – The leading provider of proprietary business and consumer databases and Internet white and yellow page directory services . . .

MapQuest.com Teams With Adace to Provide Small Businesses With Geographically Targeted Advertising

NEW YORK-(BUSINESS WIRE)-Sept. 14, 1999. MapQuest strengthens position as leader in Geo-targeted web advertising by announcing a partnership with AdAce, a nationwide ad firm.

MapQuest Selects SpeechWorks Tech For Phone Svc >MQST

NEW YORK (Dow Jones)—Sept 13, 1999—MapQuest selected SpeechWorks International Inc., to develop speech recognition technology for a MapQuest service that will provide driving directions over the telephone.

SPRINT PCS, MAPQUEST PARTNER ON DRIVING DIRECTIONS

NEW YORK—Sept 13, 1999—MapQuest announced a new partnership with Sprint PCS to provide driving directions to Sprint PCS Wireless Web phone users.

Mapquest.com Seeks Agency Partner

NEW YORK—Aug 30, 1999—MapQuest is looking for a medium to large-size agency to handle its estimated $10 million to $15 million account.

MapQuest.com Selected to Provide Enhanced Mapping Technology for Sabre Inc., Including the Travelocity.com Web Site

NEW YORK—(BUSINESS WIRE)—August 23, 1999—Sabre Inc., Including Travelocity.com, Upgrades Agreement With MapQuest.

MapQuest.com Partners With Metro Networks, Adding Real-Time Traffic to MapQuest.com and Its Partner Sites

NEW YORK—(BUSINESS WIRE)—August 18, 1999 MapQuest.com Now Offers Exclusive Package of State-of-the-Art Digital Traffic Information, Maps and Driving Directions.

Exhibit 11   MapQuest—Recent News

listings, demographic and address data. Players included:

- InfoSpace—(Nasdaq: INSP) A data and content provider to sites and online information providers, the company was also very focused on its consumer site. InfoSpace relied heavily on InfoUSA as a data source.
- InfoUSA—(Nasdaq: IUSA) A long-time data directory and demographic information provider. InfoUSA was a source of primary data to most white pages and directory publishers in the United States. The company's online site offering such information had little traffic.

A second group of data providers included mapping specialized data vendors. These vendors collected and created specific mapping information from primary sources, including governments and survey data, as well as from secondary sources. While there was some competition, these companies tended to offer coverage of specific locations or types of data. Major players included:

- Nav-Tech—(Private) Founded in 1985, based in Chicago, the company offered digital mapping data and technologies, including GPS systems.
- GDT—(Private) Founding in 1980, the company was a major supplier of data to both Vicinity and MapQuest, the first use of its data on the web.
- TeleAtlas—(Private) Founded in 1984, the company had broad data coverage of Europe.

See Exhibit 12.

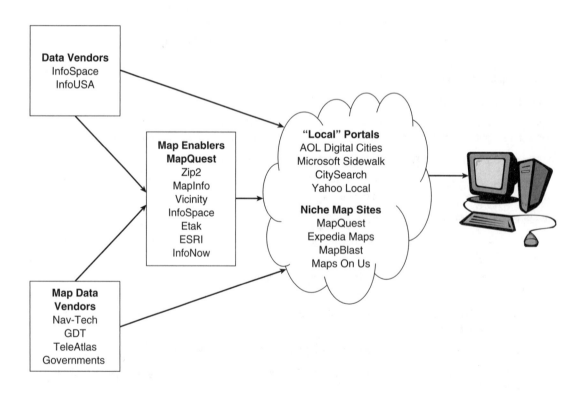

Exhibit 12   Geospatial Data and Mapping—Industry Structure

Map Enablers

These companies offered products and services that enabled businesses and portals to offer richer, better content and services on their own sites. Since growth capital was plentiful among their customers (e.g., the Portals), revenue growth was rapid. Key players included:

- Zip2—(Owned by Alta Vista, owned by CMGI, Nasdaq: CMGI) A pioneer in local content and city guides, the firm sold in February 1999 for $347 million to Alta Vista.
- MapInfo—(Nasdaq: MAPS) A software provider focused on location enabling services for businesses.
- Vicinity—(Private, owned partly by CMGI, Nasdaq: CMGI) An information services provider to businesses, it also owned MapBlast, the consumer-focused mapping site. CMGI, the part owner, was a holding company that invested in pre-IPO companies.
- Etak—(Owned by Sony) Sony had purchased Etak from NewsCorp. Etak was a provider of mapping software and technologies.
- ESRI—(Private) Primarily a software provider for GIS applications for locating telecom and pipeline infrastructure, as well as consumer application software.

"Local" Portals

The Internet mega-portals had realized the "local" opportunity and had each begun to offer localized content. These large players had abundant capital and were eagerly spending to gain market share. Major local offerings included:

- AOL Digital Cities—(NYSE: AOL) AOL was the world's largest Internet service provider with a portal specifically for its subscribers.
- Microsoft Sidewalk—(Nasdaq: MSFT) Microsoft offered a competing set of local sites. In July of 1999, it sold its Sidewalk business to TicketMaster CitySearch in a deal that included providing local information and content back to Microsoft under the Sidewalk brand.
- CitySearch (TicketMaster)—(Nasdaq: TMCS) A comprehensive set of city/local guides and information, including local event ticket sales, from the world's largest event ticketing company.

- Yahoo Local—(Nasdaq: YHOO) A set of localized sub-sites tailed to specific cities.
- Alta Vista—(owned by CMGI, Nasdaq: CMGI) Purchased in August 1999 from Compaq, the firm announced its plans for an IPO. Alta Vista owned Zip2.

Competition—MapQuest Business Offering

Of the approximately 764 websites that were currently map-enabled, MapQuest had roughly a 50 per cent market share (see Exhibit 13). The largest historical competitors were Vicinity and Zip2, but MapQuest was taking share and was by far the largest provider in the market. MapQuest also faced potential competition from "one-stop shop" content suppliers such as InfoSpace, which offered a wide range of services and had broad distribution for many of its products but with no current focus on a competing product or service offering.

MapQuest	49%
Zip2	21%
Vicinity	11%
ESRI	10%
InfoNow	4%
MapInfo	3%
Etak	1%
InfoSpace	1%

Exhibit 13   Market Share of 764 Map-Enabled Websites

Source: MediaMetrix.

Competition—MapQuest Consumer Offering

MapQuest was the leading travel/mapping site on the Internet (see Exhibit 14). Traffic data

MapQuest	64%
Expedia Maps	18%
MapBlast	12%
MapsOnUs	3%
All others	3%

Exhibit 14　　Market Share of Site Page Traffic

Source: MediaMetrix.

showed MapQuest gaining share against competitors even while little was spent on marketing and promotion. After the IPO, the launch of a $2 million promotional campaign accelerated share gains.

Competition—MapQuest Digital Mapping (Traditional)

The company faced a wide range of competitors including Rand McNally, Langenscheidt (American Map), Universal, Magellan, ESRI and DeLorme. However, MapQuest management had planned to shift focus away from the DMS business to the high growth, higher margin Internet mapping opportunity.

THE MEETING OF THE BOARD

Mulligan and his executive team planned to present strategic alternatives to the board of directors. Recently, MapQuest stock traded around $12 per share. This price was below the IPO price of $15, while the Nasdaq index was up about 10 per cent during the same period. Still, the $12 price made the firm worth around $400 million in market cap. However, other "pure-play" software and content providers were trading at higher multiples. Mulligan wondered whether the traditional DMS business was anchoring the firm value. Investors were hungry for Internet businesses. Or, given that the market valued revenue, how could he grow the revenue streams? If nothing else, Mulligan wondered whether to believe pundits in the market suggesting an overall market bubble. If this *was* a bubble, Mulligan wondered what he could do to take advantage of it.

CIBC–BARCLAYS: SHOULD THEIR CARIBBEAN OPERATIONS BE MERGED?

Prepared by Don Wood and Professor Paul W. Beamish

Version: (A) 2004-09-30

At the end of 2001, the Canadian Imperial Bank of Commerce (CIBC) and Barclays Bank PLC were in advanced negotiations regarding the potential merger of their respective retail, corporate and offshore banking operations in the Caribbean. Motivated in part by a mutual desire to achieve greater economies of scale, the negotiations had gained momentum ever since the possibility had been raised a year earlier.

Notwithstanding the progress to date, some members of each board could not help but wonder whether this was the best direction to take. Would the combined company be able to deliver superior returns? Would it be possible to integrate, within budget, companies that had competed with each other in the region for decades? Would either firm be better off divesting regional operations instead? Should the two firms just continue to go-it-alone with an emphasis on continual improvement? These and other issues and options continued to be discussed by the executives at CIBC, and their counterparts at Barclays.

Decision time was fast approaching. Both executive teams knew that to prolong discussion further would increase employee, investor and customer anxieties and perhaps do serious harm to both firms. A decision needed to be made within the coming week; there was little time for additional research.

AN OVERVIEW OF BANKING IN THE CARIBBEAN

Banking in the Caribbean can best be described as complex and dynamic. Most of the Caribbean countries are islands, with the consequent natural isolation from each other and the main continental world (see Exhibit 1).

Most Caribbean countries were colonies until the latter half of the 20th century. Caribbean banks were originally largely a convenience for the colonial governments and their representatives, and focused on savings, some lending and financing trade. In colonial times, branches of international banks such as Barclays were set up in the region to finance the production and export of commodities such as bananas, sugar, rum, bauxite and petroleum. These banks viewed the Caribbean as a small part of their global operations, and they typically focused on maximizing profits and shareholder returns. They were an oligopoly, involving a small number of players with limited government control. Consequently, the banks

Exhibit 1   Map of the West Indies

Source: CIA World Factbook, 2004.

co-operated in setting interest rates and terms of credit and were able to make significant profits.

In the post-colonial period, there was an effort by governments in the region to exert greater control over the economies, and some governments nationalized a number of industries, including the banking sector. By the 1980s, the limitations of state ownership had become evident, and many state-owned banks were privatized. The most significant result was increased competition and an improvement in customer service and product innovation.

The Caribbean banking industry is currently undergoing structural change characterized by mergers and strategic alliances. These mergers and alliances have been driven by the need for economies of scale and scope and the need to be more competitive in the light globalization in the overall industry. Mergers are complicated, however, because of the many central banks and different currencies—many countries have individual central banks and their own currency, the exception being the Organization of Eastern Caribbean Countries (OECS), comprising eight countries,[1] which share a central bank and currency.

CURRENT OPERATIONS IN THE CARIBBEAN

Barclays PLC (total assets of US$500 billion) and CIBC (total assets of US$200 billion) have extensive operations throughout the Caribbean. Although neither has branches in all countries, between the two, they cover most of the English-speaking Caribbean, as illustrated in Exhibit 2.

Country	Population	GDP/Capita (US$)	CIBC	Barclays
Anguilla	10,000	4,000		•
Antigua and Barbuda	70,000	8,419	•	•
The Bahamas	280,000	13,847	•	•
Barbados	270,000	7,750	•	•
Belize	230,000	2,688		•
British Virgin Islands	20,000	12,000		•
The Cayman Islands	30,000	24,000	•	•
Dominica	70,000	3,233		•
Grenada	100,000	877		•
Jamaica	2,570,000	1,756	•	
St. Kitts and Nevis	40,000	5,761		•
St. Lucia	160,000	3,581	•	•
Netherlands Antilles	200,000	N/A		•
St. Vincent and the Grenadines	110,000	•	•	•
Turks and Caicos Islands	20,000	6,000	•	•

Exhibit 2   Caribbean Presence

Source: CIBC Economics, World Fact Book, Americas Review 1999—Economic Indicators.

CIBC CARIBBEAN OPERATIONS

CIBC Canada is one of North America's leading financial institutions, measured by assets, with more than eight million personal banking and business customers worldwide. It has provided banking services in the West Indies[2] since 1920 and employs approximately 1,600 staff serving 350,000 retail and commercial clients at 42 branches and four commercial banking centres.

The West Indies comprises 29 countries with four major language groups. The countries in which CIBC operates represent nine per cent of the total population of the Caribbean, and 57 per cent of the English-speaking population.

Although the West Indies is a small market, it is growing faster than North America on a population basis. Economic measures, such as GDP per capita, unemployment and inflation, vary widely across the region.

CIBC is the only major bank serving the Caribbean as a separate, integrated unit, CIBC West Indies Holdings Limited (WIHL). Exhibit 3 displays WIHL and its subsidiaries.

CIBC's Caribbean operations showed net income of US$67.8 million, and total assets were US$4.6 billion for the year ended October 31, 2001. The Company is listed on three regional stock exchanges: the Jamaica Stock Exchange, the Barbados Stock Exchange and the Trinidad and

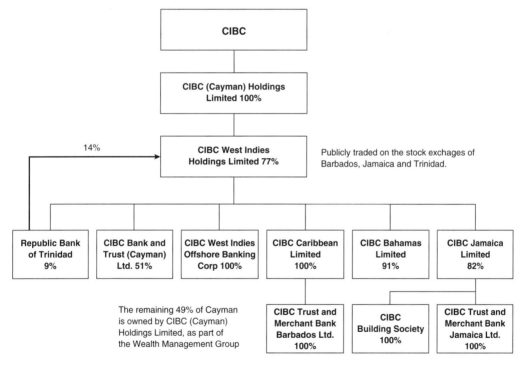

Operating Units:

1. Bahamas — CIBC Bahamas Limited
2. Jamaica — consists of CIBC Jamaica Limited, CIBC Building Society and CIBC Trust and Merchant Bank Jamaica Limited.
3. Barbados — consists of CIBC Caribbean Limited and CIBC Trust and Merchant Bank Barbados Limited, which includes our operations in Barbados, Antigua, St. Lucia, St. Vincent and Turks & Caicos.
4. Cayman — Fifty-one per cent of operations of CIBC Bank and Trust (Cayman) Ltd., which relate to the Retail and Commercial Operations in Cayman.

Exhibit 3 Current Situation—CIBC West Indies Holdings Limited (WIHL) and Subsidiaries

Source: Company files.

Tobago Stock Exchange. In addition, two subsidiaries, CIBC Bahamas Limited and CIBC Jamaica Limited, are also listed on their local stock exchanges. Caribbean headquarters for CIBC is in Barbados.

During 1999 through 2001, CIBC had invested US$48 million in a new banking system, FISERV's International Banking System (ICBS), and related technology and operational improvements. While the conversion to the new system had created operational and customer service problems in the 1999 through 2001 period, the system and its operational platform were now stable and working effectively. The capacity of the ICBS system, however, was built for a bank roughly twice the size of CIBC WI, and full efficiencies would not be realized at the current size of the bank.

CIBC views its strengths and weaknesses in Exhibit 4.

BARCLAYS BANK PLC— CARIBBEAN OPERATIONS

Barclays Caribbean Banking Operations had a net income of US$72.6 million and total assets of US$5.2 billion for the year ended December 31, 2001. Barclays Caribbean branch network employed 1,584 staff: 157 were management staff, 738 were in front office functions and 846 were in back office functions. Staff were unionized in six countries: Antigua & Barbuda, Barbados, Dominica, Grenada, St. Lucia, and St. Vincent & the Grenadines. Apart from salaries and a fully funded pension scheme, local staff received benefits in the form of a medical scheme, loans at preferential rates, 20 to 30 days annual leave, uniforms and profit sharing. Management grades also participated in a bonus scheme, received the use of bank cars, and many had club memberships provided.

Corporate and business services are offered in all 14 countries (see Exhibit 5), and offshore banking services are offered in the Bahamas, Barbados, Cayman, the British Virgin Islands (BVI), and Turks & Caicos. Corporate banking accounts for 45 per cent of corporate income, personal banking 27 per cent and offshore banking 28 per cent.

Barclays' current Caribbean strategy has been rationalization, alongside focused development of the onshore business, together with controlled development of offshore business. Increasing focus has been placed on managing the level of operational risk. Specifically this has meant:

- Organic growth of the corporate and retail presences in existing countries;
- Focus on increased share of existing customers through improvement of consumer lending propositions;
- Limited investment to rationalize the operating model through centralization initiatives and closure of marginal branches.

Barclays' view of current competitive conditions and their strengths and vulnerabilities can be summarized as follows:

Competition is increasing. For example:

- Traditional Canadian bank competitors are marketing aggressively;
- Regional indigenous banks are expanding their footprints;
- Competitors with new business models (e.g., niche players like CitiGroup) are increasingly entering Barclays' markets;
- In the onshore and retail and corporate businesses, competition comes from large Canadian banks (principally CIBC, Royal Bank of Canada and Scotiabank) and from regional indigenous banks (e.g., Republic Bank of Trinidad);
- Barclays' strong customer relationships have been key to maintaining the bank's market position and have helped to maintain margins;
- Price and convenience are becoming increasingly important as buying factors; as markets become more crowded, price erosion can be expected to reduce currently relatively high margins;
- Barclays sees its delivery channel "gaps" of real-time electronic banking for corporate accounts and full telephone and Internet offerings for retail customers as becoming increasingly significant.

STRENGTHS

CIBC Ownership
- Strong brand and public image
- Expertise in retail banking
- Effective mix of delivery channels
- High loyalty ratings
- Excellent relationships with governments, important business players and the public
- Enormous value in WIHL franchise on local equity markets – currently selling at 26 X earnings

Management
- New leadership with strong management support from CIBC in Canada
- Extensive knowledge of the region (economic and political)
- Important relationships with business and political leaders

Products and Delivery Channels
- An established strength in product lines currently experiencing tremendous growth in the region (mortgages, cards, ABMs)
- Ability to leverage expertise in all products and services from the Canadian organization

Operations
- Co-ordinated regional operations strengthened by strong linkages to CIBC
- Established branch network with 40 branches in eight countries
- Ability to leverage CIBC Canadian operations expertise from Intria Items Inc., O&T and National Operations Support

Technology
- An integrated banking system (ICBS) that will enable consistent and efficient operations in the WI and will allow new channels such as Internet banking
- An extended wide area network (EWAN) will provide a dependable robust real-time environment
- Ability to leverage CIBC Canadian technology expertise from Intria Corporation and O&T

WEAKNESSES—Issues (all of which were being resolved)

Credit Risk Management
- During the conversion period, Retail Loan losses have increased substantially.
- Recent audits have revealed weaknesses in lending practices.
- There was not a consistent view on credit risk appetite between local management and the credit risk group, which is largely seconded from CIBC Canada.

Items Processing
- Three item processing centres have been found to be inefficient and lacking in reliable processes.

Systems and Technology
- Two years ago, systems were antiquated and not Y2K compliant; however, the new platform is stable and operating effectively.
- The investment in technology exceeds the scale of the current operations.

Organization
- Until recently the West Indies operations were organized geographically.
- Inefficiencies and overlaps.

Jamaica
- Very inefficient operations with high NIX ratios and low returns.
- Poor credit risk management.

Exhibit 4   CIBC Internal Analysis

Country	Operating Income — 1999 (US$ millions)	No. of Accounts ('000)			No. of Outlets*
		Personal	Business	Total	
Anguilla	2	4.3	0.1	4.4	1
Antigua and Barbuda	8	28.5	0.7	29.2	1
The Bahamas	49	50.1	2.4	52.5	9
Barbados	42	101.0	2.9	103.9	6
Belize	8	16.9	3.1	19.9	4
British Virgin Islands	16	17.6	1.6	19.2	3
The Cayman Islands	34	11.9	3.4	15.3	2
Dominica	4	20.0	0.7	20.7	2
Grenada	6	23.6	1.3	24.9	4
St. Kitts and Nevis	5	14.1	0.4	14.5	2
St. Lucia	12	43.1	1.1	44.2	4
Netherlands Antilles	3	5.7	0.6	6.3	3
St. Vincent and the Grenadines	4	20.8	0.4	21.1	1
Turks and Caicos Islands	12	11.0	2.3	13.2	3
Totals	**205**	**368.6**	**21.0**	**389.3**	**45**

Exhibit 5   Barclays Caribbean Business Base

*In addition, there is a Card & Mortgage Centre and a Regional Processing Centre in the Bahamas, as well as a Card and Operations Centre in Barbados.

With no player having an obvious opportunity to develop a sustainable competitive advantage, Barclays believes that the player that achieves the best productivity (and can match the best customer service) is likely to succeed in the medium term. This has led Barclays to increase its focus on how to maximize the cost effectiveness of its operating model.

Barclays' information technology (IT) approach focuses on its Caribbean Regional Data Processing Centre (RPC), located in Nassau,

Bahamas. One reason for locating the centre in the Bahamas is the strong Bahamian secrecy laws, which protect confidential client data from being disclosed to third parties. The RPC operates the core banking applications for 13 of the 14 countries in the region.[3] It performs the following:

- BRAINS (Barclays Retail Accounting and Information System), the retail banking software package, which is also used by Barclays Africa;

- Interlink connection for the ATM network (55 units);
- Gateways to the MasterCard and VISA networks;
- BusinessMaster, online access to information and customer service for corporate and offshore customers; and
- BarclayCall, online access to information and customer service for retail customers (available only in the Bahamas and Barbados).

All the applications above are run on stand-alone Caribbean systems, with no dependency on the United Kingdom except for contingency arrangements.

The BRAINS system had been installed about 10 years previously and lacked the ability to consolidate projects by customer as to facilitate Internet and telephone banking. Barclays operations in both Africa and the Caribbean were faced with a costly decision on whether to replace BRAINS with a more modern banking system. Moreover, Barclays operations tended to be more manually intensive and costly than those of its competitors, Royal, BNS and CIBC, who had installed more modern technology.

The Competition

The four major international players identified in Exhibit 6 have each developed a different market niche in which to compete successfully in the retail and commercial markets in the West Indies. The Royal Bank is considered the best performer across the region. CIBC summarized its competitive niches as shown in Exhibit 6.

Banking oligopolies existed across the West Indies, with the five largest banks in each country controlling more than 80 per cent market share. CIBC estimated market shares in the various national markets it serves as shown in Exhibit 7.

In addition to the retail and commercial services, major banks in the Caribbean also serve the US$1.1 billion capital markets in the region. The capital markets business in the West Indies is composed mainly of debt financing arrangements. It is considered a new and emerging sector comprising eight players in this marketplace (see Exhibit 8).

The capital market segment began to develop in the 1980s and is expected to grow at about 10 per cent annually for the next few years. The majority of debt financing is government borrowing, government divestitures of banks, hotels and utilities, and large multinational corporations' projects. More recently, the resource sector has brought more sophisticated arrangements to the West Indies capital markets sector. The market is driven mainly by the large economies of Jamaica and Trinidad & Tobago. Revenue in this sector is generated by a typical one per cent fee and a 3.5 per cent lending spread. In 2000, the total size of all CIBC WI Capital Markets deals was estimated at US$118 million generating about US$3 million of revenue and US$1.5 million in profits.

A few large competitors like CS First Boston, Citibank and ABN AMRO have entered the market and basically manage the region through local relationships with business and government leaders, augmented by head office expertise to complete the transactions. These key relationships are important to gaining business, and many other large competitors like DLJ, Merrill Lynch, and Smith Barney have not been able to enter the market successfully. Exhibit 8 summarizes the main players in the West Indies Capital Markets.

Both CIBC and Barclays now need to assess their options, evaluate the factors and select the best strategy for their respective firms. They must consider whether to merge or not, and determine the implications for merging in this complex environment. Exhibits 9 and 10 provide financial information on the two firms' Caribbean operations.

Each of the four major international players has developed a different market niche in which to compete successfully in the retail and commercial market in the West Indies. Royal Bank is considered the best performer across the Region.

Player	Operations	How They Compete in West Indies
CIBC	• 40 branches in eight countries serving 350,000 retail and commercial customers • Core business is retail banking with trust, offshore and capital market activities as other lines of business	• Strong in Retail and Small Business and Merchant services across the West Indies Region, particularly in Bahamas which has a sizeable market share • Market leader in credit card sales in Barbados but lags behind in Bahamas and Jamaica • Good reputation for corporate and capital markets activities • Newest technology in the region • Only major competitor to manage the West Indies as a separate, integrated unit
ScotiaBank	• 158 branches in 24 countries with a balance sheet of Cdn$6.9 billion built primarily on consumer products, hospitality financing and loans to government • Very efficient at managing expenses • In 1998, Bank of Nova Scotia Jamaica earned $73 million, five per cent of total BNS profit • In 1999, international retail operations were larger than domestic operations—the West Indies accounts for the majority of international operations.	• Leader in consumer loans, particularly vehicle loans • Competitive advantage by having hard currency lending operations maintained out of Puerto Rico, giving them access to inexpensive government funding, which they have leveraged throughout the West Indies Region • Focus on product offering and strong marketing efforts • Very successful operations in Jamaica • Good development of local staff using secondments to Canada, consistent
Royal Bank	• 33 branches in nine countries with the most comprehensive convenience delivery channels in those countries and are leaders in the offshore industry	• Active high value strategy and a leader amongst high value clients • Considered best performer of retail banks • Significant offshore and international presence in Barbados and Bahamas • Dominating in certain products in each country
Barclays PLC	• 45 branches in 17 countries and have recently invested US$30 million in new technology for the region	• Strong remittance and offshore business • Strong corporate banking connections • Good Cards business run by Barclaycard US • Offers telephone banking • Strong client relationship building system, (Premiere Service), targeted to its working professional client base

Exhibit 6 External Analysis—Retail and Commercial

	Measure	CIBC	Barclays	Scotiabank	Royal Bank	NCB*	Others
Antigua	% total assets						
	% deposits	12		14	10	24	40
	% loans	11	9	22	7	20	31
	No. branches	1	3	4	3		15
	No. ATMs	1	3	4	2		10
Barbados	% total assets						
	% deposits	18	22	13	21	17	9
	% loans	19	21	21	10	18	11
	No. branches	10	6	8	7		15
	No. ATMs	11	8	8	13		14
Jamaica	% total assets						
	% deposits	7		41		36	16
	% loans	9		50		27	14
	No. branches	13		45			100
	No. ATMs	8		31			55
St. Lucia	% total assets						
	% deposits	10	23	16	10	24	19
	% loans	12	24	17	10	21	17
	No. branches	2	4	4	4		10
	No. ATMs	3	4	7	3		12
St. Vincent	% total assets	14	14	13			59
	% deposits						
	% loans						
	No. branches	1	1	1			10
	No. ATMs	1	1	1			5
The Bahamas	% total assets	19		15	21		45
	% deposits						
	% loans						
	No. branches	8	10	17	21		27
	No. ATMs	9	11	21	21		18
The Cayman Islands	% total assets	25	25	15			35
	% deposits						
	% loans						
	No. branches	2	2	4	2		10
	No. ATMs	4	3	3	2		16
Turks & Caicos	% total assets		70	16			14
	% deposits						
	% loans						
	No. branches	1	2	2			
	No. ATMs	1	2	1			

Exhibit 7   Selected Market Share Measures

*National Commercial Banks.

The West Indies Capital Markets business is dominated by a small number of players. Citibank is the dominant competitor in the Region and is estimated to have earned profits of US$20 million in the Capital Markets sector in each of the last five years.

Financial Services Company	Industry Focus[1]	Product Focus[2]	Level of relationship with foreign Parent/ Partner[3]	Level of Physical Caribbean Presence	Market Share (approx)	Level of Offshore Booking (approx)
CIBC	E&P, H&R,A, Cong. PS	Bnd U/W, PF, LS	Medium	High	10%	100%
Citibank	E&P, PS, A	Bnd U/W, D, CBF, LS, S	High	Low	50%	80%
Royal Merchant Bank (Trinidad)	E&P, H&R,A, Cong. PS	Bnd U/W, E U/W, S. PF	Medium	High	15%	50%
Republic Bank (Fincor)	E&P, H&R, A, Cong. PS	PF, Bnd U/W, E U/W, LS	Low	Medium	10%	60%
Scotia Bank	E&P, H&R, A, Cong. PS	Bnd U/W, LS	High	High	5%	70%
Credit Swiss First Boston	E&P, PS	Bnd U/W, LS	High	None	5%	100%
ABN Ambro	E&P	LS	High	None	4%	100%
Chase	E&P, PS	Bnd U/W, LS	High	None	1%	100%

Exhibit 8   External Analysis—Capital Markets

1. Energy and Petrochemicals (E&P), Hotel and Resorts (H&R), Agriculture (A), Conglomerates (Cong), Public Sector (PS).
2. Bond Underwriting (Bnd UW), Project Financing (PF), Equity Underwriting (E U/W), Derivatives (D), Commodity Based Financing (CBF), Loan Syndication (LS), Securatization (S), Advisory Services (AS).
3. This variable measures the relationship with the foreign partner in terms of advisory assistance on financial products structuring.

Condensed Consolidated Balance Sheets (as of October 31) (Bds '000s)					
	2001	2000	1999	1998	1997
Assets					
Cash resources	2,743,877	1,849,630	1,961,285	813,025	772,552
Securities	2,417,865	2,249,992	1,578,942	458,508	450,235
Loans	3,760,574	3,411,184	3,162,052	2,424,544	2,030,889
Customer's liability under acceptances	11,587	42,880	1,651	1,600	4,532
Net Investment in leases	3,055	4,221	5,396	6,817	6,061
Fixed assets	138,114	123,427	120,401	75,175	62,281
Other assets	113,982	127,393	127,179	118,460	67,039
	9,189,054	7,808,727	6,956,906	3,898,129	3,393,589
Liabilities and Shareholders' Equity					
Deposits	8,191,737	6,716,869	6,016,367	3,285,774	2,895,778
Acceptances	11,587	42,880	1,651	1,600	4,532
Other liabilities	101,172	303,874	279,636	173,236	97,697
Minority interests	232,282	195,375	170,298	39,829	37,321
Shareholders' equity common shares	316,380	316,380	316,380	274,980	274,980
Retained earnings	335,896	233,349	172,574	122,710	83,281
	9,189,054	7,808,727	6,956,906	3,898,129	3,393,589

Consolidated Statements of Income (as of October 31) (Bds '000s)					
	2001	2000	1999	1998	1997
Interest income	601,309	594,914	497,534	348,231	317,178
Interest expense	(316,737)	(313,945)	(252,750)	(149,632)	(147,423)
Net interest income	284,572	280,969	244,784	198,599	169,755
Non-interest income	128,378	126,846	120,286	71,640	63,020
Total income	412,950	407,815	365,070	270,239	232,775
Non-interest expenses	218,519	224,891	210,402	159,211	136,167
Provision for credit losses	10,287	28,602	23,908	15,342	10,277
Total Expenses	228,806	253,493	234,310	174,553	146,444
Net income before income taxes	184,144	154,322	130,760	95,686	86,331
Income taxes	8,616	7,038	4,027	12,980	15,228
Net income before exception/ extraordinary items and minority interests	175,528	147,284	126,731	82,706	71,103
Exceptional/extraordinary items	—	—	(2,171)	—	583
Minority interests	(39,919)	(29,702)	(29,536)	(7,690)	(4,563)
Net income	135,609	117,582	95,024	75,016	67,123

Exhibit 9   Five Year Statistical Review—CIBC West Indies Holdings

Profit and Loss/Balance Sheets (for years ending December 31) (US$ millions)					
	1995	**1996**	**1997**	**1998**	**1999**
Net interest income	103	107	116	134	153
Commission income	41	42	46	51	54
Total operating income	**144**	**149**	**162**	**185**	**207**
Staff Costs	(53)	(57)	(58)	(61)	(66)
Property, equipment and other expenses	(36)	(34)	(42)	(48)	(50)
Depreciation/amortisation	—	(6)	(8)	(8)	(10)
Operating costs	**(89)**	**(97)**	**(108)**	**(117)**	**(126)**
Net operating income	**55**	**52**	**54**	**68**	**80**
Provisions	**(8)**	**(11)**	**(2)**	**(1)**	**(9)**
Profit before Tax	**47**	**41**	**52**	**67**	**71**
	1,995	1,996	1,997	1,998	1,999
ASSETS					
Loans to banks	54	50	168	55	87
Loans to customers	1,141	1,240	1,360	1,618	1,884
Other assets	255	572	593	752	860
Accruals and prepayments	—	3	14	21	23
Due from BBPLC	2,270	2,017	2,188	2,897	2,855
Property & Equipment	54	62	61	60	79
Total assets	**3,774**	**3,944**	**4,384**	**5,403**	**5,788**
LIABILITIES AND CAPITAL					
Customer deposits	3,469	3,513	3,836	4,654	4,972
Other liabilites	108	206	279	161	180
Due to BBPLC	166	194	235	549	580
Revenue reserve	31	31	34	39	56
Total liabilities	**3,774**	**3,944**	**4,384**	**5,403**	**5,788**

2000 FULL YEAR FORECAST (US$ millions)		
	H1 2000 **Actual**	**H2 2000** **Forecast**	**2000** **Forecast**
Net interest income	91	91	182
Fees and commission	30	29	59
Total operating income	**121**	**120**	**241**
Staff Costs	(32)	(30)	(62)
Property and equipment	(11)	(11)	(22)
Other expenses	(14)	(11)	(25)
Depreciation/amortisation	(4)	(5)	(9)
Operating costs	**(61)**	**(57)**	**(118)**
Net Operating Income	**60**	**63**	**123**
Provisions	**(4)**	**(4)**	**(8)**
Profit before Tax	**56**	**59**	**115**

Exhibit 10   Financial Information—Barclays

*Income analysed between net interest, fees and commissions and other.

NOTES

1. The Eastern Caribbean comprises Anguilla, Antigua and Barbuda, the Commonwealth of Dominica, Grenada, Montserrat, St. Kitts and Nevis, St. Lucia, and St. Vincent and the Grenadines.

2. For the purpose of this case, the terms "West Indies" and "the Caribbean" are used interchangeably.

3. The remaining country is British Virgin Islands, which, for historic reasons, uses a stand-alone accounting system.

3

M&A VALUATION
AND EVALUATION

While most research finds that M&A tend to destroy value, to not return their cost of capital, to rarely achieve their planned synergies, and so on, in reality, these can all be linked back to saying that the buyer overpaid. At a low enough price, most any deal can be justified and make financial sense. However, even paying a great price for a target in M&A can go wrong if either the strategy underlying it is not well thought-out or if the buyer is not buying what it thinks it is buying. While much attention is paid to the clearly important art of valuation, attention also needs to be paid to both the underlying strategy and due diligence aspects. We include an overview of these three topics below.

THE ART OF VALUATION

Numerous methods exist to financially value a proposed deal. Depending on the industry, type of company, stage of company growth, structure of deal proposed, strategic plans for the target, private or public status, and other considerations, different valuation techniques, or combinations thereof, will be used. While we may think of finance and valuation techniques as scientific and precise, doing valuation is a highly subjective exercise, and as such, it is as much an art as a science. Because the best method of valuation differs by situation, numerous methods are typically used to provide a range of valuations, after which the parties often rationalize the choice of analysis that supports their intended objectives (and valuations). We discuss many of the typical methods used.

Contribution Analysis

When two firms are to be combined (often a merger rather than an acquisition), this is a technique to measure the relative contribution (e.g., 40%/60% versus 50%/50%) of each party to the combined, pro forma financials. Typically, several financial measures are used but often include revenue, cash flows, earnings, profits, and assets and liabilities. The relative contribution of each party will likely vary somewhat among the different measures, giving a range of possible splits among the firms. After negotiation and deliberation, the parties may choose to keep or drop certain measures and perhaps weight the remaining measures to come to a proposed weighted average contribution. This technique works best when the firms are of somewhat equal size, are in the same business, have similar trading multiples, and have decent insight into their financial projections.

Comparables

While the public market valuations of a firm's equity and debt are meant to reflect a true market value, it is common to revalue a firm based on the trading multiples of a group of similar firms. Underlying this technique is the presumption that the markets can misperceive the value of a firm and that, by looking at its competitors, you can find a more appropriate valuation. It is critical to find a peer group of firms that are direct competitors, or in closely related industries, and of comparable sizes and growth stages. The numbers often need to be adjusted for capital structures, growth rates, firm sizes, different fiscal year ends, and perhaps seasonality to make an apples-to-apples comparison group. Common comparison metrics include market capitalization and enterprise value multiples of revenue and cash flow, plus measures of price-to-earnings and price-to-earnings to growth rate ratios. Each of these ratios would typically be calculated for the last 12 months and the next 2 or 3 years going forward. By using all of the ratios of the comparable companies (if needed, weighted by the "most" comparable), you then value the actual and projected figures of the target firm by the comparable company multiples to see what you think the true value is. This is an especially useful technique when a buyer plans to reposition or refocus the target firm into a new industry or as a different business model, where valuations may differ.

Precedent Acquisition

This technique is used to value a firm based on the other similar acquisitions that have recently occurred. A unique quality of this technique is that it includes any acquisition premiums paid. The more comparable, the better. That is, deals in the same industry and of the same size, same business model, same stage of growth, same capital structure, more recent, and so on are the most closely related and often the best to use. However, it is typically very difficult to find exact matches, and so instead you review numerous deals and analyze how the deal values (multiples of revenues, cash flows, profits, premiums paid) vary by size of target, by industry, and by deal type. This gives the firm several directional pointers as to the most appropriate valuation to use. This technique may also help the firm develop strategic insights into what its competitors are doing by way of deals. Oftentimes, revealing patterns of deals and consolidations emerge that are of strategic importance.

Discounted Cash Flow

This is likely the most common valuation technique. The basic theory is that the value of the firm is the discounted value of the cash it generates over time. The mechanics of the technique are well detailed in other texts, but a few mistakes are common. In the calculation of free cash flow, it is not uncommon to forget to remove all noncash expenses, including, for example, deferred taxes. When calculating the cost of equity for a firm, analysts often forget to unlever the beta. Market betas are calculated as the levered (based on the existing capital structure of firm, including the debt) betas and, as such, must be unlevered to reflect a pure equity beta in order to calculate a true weighted average cost of capital. In calculating the cost of debt, common mistakes are to use the face coupon of debt, or the marginal rates of debt. The cost of debt (and return on debt) fluctuates for many firms, as can be witnessed by the fluctuating value of publicly traded notes and debt. The cost of debt is what it would cost to recapitalize the debt across the firm at the then-current cost of debt in the market, yielding an average cost of debt. While face values are often used to calculate an average, at a minimum, adjustments for changes in interest rates and firm credit quality since the issuance of the debt should be applied. This same mistake can occur in the equity value calculation; while it is important to use the market (rather than book) value of debt, the same applies to equity. However, with equity, it is also important to correctly calculate the number of shares outstanding and to consider how to adjust the debt and equity when excess cash exists. Finally, when conducting discounted cash flow (DCF), attention needs to be paid to the proportion of the value that comes from the terminal value and how that is affected by the sensitivity of the analysis to discount rates and terminal value multiples. Small changes in either input can drastically affect the DCF valuation results. The subjective nature of determining these inputs is proof of the valuation as an art.

Liquidation/Break-Up

Sometimes, a firm is viewed as a set of assets that may be worth more separate than together. This is often the case when a firm is losing money and has seen a decrease in its market value. Each asset (e.g., division, plant, subsidiary, product line, asset) is valued separately based on the tactical decision for each—that is, whether to keep it, sell it, or shut it down. When valuing a firm this way, it is important to bear in mind all the costs of dispositions and to consider the probabilities of outcomes within certain timeframes. That is, you need to both accurately predict market values and account for the uncertainty regarding the ability to sell them in a timely manner.

Leveraged-Buyout Model

While the leveraged-buyout (LBO) model is not used to value the firm per se, it is a model used to determine whether an equity investor should attempt to purchase a firm using the LBO method. The equity investors in an LBO typically require a very high rate of return on their equity investment because of the high risk in having such a highly leveraged firm. The basic structure of the analysis is to figure out if the target being considered produces sufficient cash flow to support the debt payments and equity returns required by the purchaser. As such, assumptions regarding the cash costs of debt and the financial projections for free cash flow are critical. Because of the high debt servicing requirements (debt is often 60%–90% of the purchase consideration paid for the firm), equity holders often require rates of return of 30% or more.

Business Metrics Analysis

Financial projections for firms are often suspect. Internal numbers may be skewed to favor the insiders. The numbers created by outside analysts may be based only on public information and may not fully reflect the true value. As well, high-quality research coverage may not exist for all public firms and certainly does not exist for private firms. Because of this, another valuation technique is to measure the value of nonfinancial business metrics. This is especially useful in a merger of similar firms when a comparables analysis is done. Examples might be to include the number of customers, new products, Web site visitors, subscribers, or headcount or may include comparison of operating ratios such as inventory turnover. These metrics can provide valuable information about the value of a firm.

Other Considerations in Analysis Choice

These techniques vary in applicability by deal. The quality of the financial projections and operating history, as well as whether the firm is public or private, can greatly affect the utility of each. It is not uncommon to have to separately value a nonreporting subsidiary of a larger reporting firm. When this is the case, there are no external market values and no separate financial statements. Because of these factors, valuation is often done in several ways to zero in on an appropriate value.

NONFINANCIAL EVALUATION—STRATEGIC FIT AND THE M&A DECISION

While the financial valuation analyses may make a deal look good, either a bad strategic fit or the incorrect tactical choice of M&A as a deal type can ruin a deal. On the strategic front, there must both be a good strategic justification and the absence of any of the dubious reasons for doing a deal. When firms conduct M&A without duly considering their own strategic intent, not only can the deal go wrong, but it can also end up destroying the whole firm. The strategic fit and the choice of deal type (e.g., M&A versus joint venture, or alliance) will vary by target and need to be considered in the evaluation of potential partners. As such, the search for an M&A partner often begins with a strategic decision to pursue a deal, which reduces the pool of potential candidates to a smaller group of possible companies. Financial analyses are done on each of these firms, and those without sufficient returns or accretion are often removed. For the remaining firms, a strategic analysis needs to be added in to each financial analysis, leading to better decisions. A deal requires a rationale beyond a financial return to make sense.

DUE DILIGENCE—WHAT ARE YOU BUYING?

The due diligence process is critical to ensuring that you are getting what you think you are getting. Firms considering deals put their best foot forward. Based on this alone, many firms look to be on the right track. In the due diligence process, bankers, lawyers, accountants, R&D personnel, and many other experts inspect the actual operations and question the personnel of the other firm to ensure they discover both the good and the bad aspects of a potential partner.

The process of due diligence in M&A deals requires care in ensuring what information is exchanged/conveyed and when. Consider the case of two competitors considering a merger that exchange confidential, inside information before the deal is approved by antitrust authorities. If regulatory approval is not granted, the firms will not be able to simply "roll back" the information exchange. As such, strict timing regarding what information is allowed to be conveyed, and when, must be followed. Of course, this presents difficulties for those trying to value another firm but with perhaps partial, incomplete, or uncertain information. The firms will typically set up a "data room," perhaps at the offices of their attorneys, where such confidential information is kept. The due diligence personnel from the other side of the deal will have access to the information in this physical room. This procedure keeps the information and knowledge of the deal itself confidential and privy only to the authorized deal team. This also allows controlled access to such information on a gradual basis—often called "peeling back the onion"—as layers of information are revealed as the certainty of deal closure increases over time. As the deal progresses, these due diligence checks and meetings may move on-premise, especially after the deal itself is announced to the public.

The content of due diligence includes both financial and nonfinancial checks on the firm. Financial information typically includes financial statements and projections, including very detailed schedules, breakdowns, and explanations of procedures and policies, including, for example, communications with tax authorities and firm policies on recognition. Nonfinancial information includes detailed product information and internal information on market and competitive information and plans. When technology is important, detailed technological descriptions, patents, tests, software code, testing results, and other key data are made available. Complete lists of customers and sales data by channel, customer, product, and geography are needed to get a complete picture. Information and backgrounds on management and key personnel are also needed, especially when certain personnel are critical to the value (e.g., in R&D, the scientists) of a firm. Finally, it is important to review past, current, or threatened legal actions, including other potential risks or liabilities, including insurance-related, environmental, or other material matters that may affect the value of the firm. Because of the comprehensive and technical nature of the due diligence process, legal, technical, and other specialists are typically engaged to guide the firm. Despite the care in due diligence, firms typically ask their partner firm to provide representations and warranties as to the veracity and completeness of the disclosures. However, despite such careful due diligence, representations, and warranties, firms often still find that they did not get what they thought they had purchased. Buyer beware.

CASES

The Empire Company Limited—The Oshawa Group Limited Proposal

An associate director at Scotia Capital Markets must make a recommendation to his client, Empire Company Limited (Empire), regarding a possible bid for rival Oshawa Group Limited (Oshawa). Both companies are in the food retail and wholesale business. Empire was based in Atlantic Canada, with an expanding presence in Ontario and Quebec, while Oshawa competes on a national basis. There were increasing public signals and rumors that suggested that Oshawa's controlling shareholders (the Wolfe family) might be willing to entertain an offer for the company. To get a clearer picture of the value of the company, the associate director performed a discounted cash flow analysis and comparable analyses to determine the stand-alone and synergy values of the acquisition target. He also had to consider the methods of financing the acquisition and examine the effect of the ownership structure on the market for corporate control.

Issues: Valuation, M&A strategy, financial analysis

The Gillette Company's Acquisition of Duracell International Inc.—Cost of Capital

Following a 5-year search for a profitable, technologically driven branded consumer products business with international growth potential, The Gillette Company announced its intended acquisition of Duracell. The focus of the case is on assessing the risk of Duracell and the measurement of a discount rate for valuation. The case is particularly rich because of the changing risk profile of Duracell.

Issues: Cost of capital, valuation, strategic planning

FirstCaribbean: The Proposed Merger

This case provides students with an abridged version of the offering circular provided to investors for the proposed merger of the Caribbean operations of two international banks. Taking the perspective of an investment advisor, students are asked to evaluate the proposed merger and make a recommendation to the existing shareholders regarding how they should manage this investment going forward (i.e., sell or hold the shares in the new company). Students will discuss several of the issues involved in valuing international companies, using somewhat limited data and putting them in the position of assessing the value of the proposal to existing shareholders.

Issues: Valuation, investment analysis, offering circulars, role of investment banker

---

THE EMPIRE COMPANY LIMITED— THE OSHAWA GROUP LIMITED PROPOSAL

Prepared by Chris Lounds under the supervision of Professors Tom Bates, Craig Dunbar, and Steve Foerster

Version: (A) 2001-03-29

INTRODUCTION

On Monday, September 8, 1998, Greg Rudka, managing director at Scotia Capital, called James Vaux, associate director, into his office. The purpose of the meeting was to discuss a story that had appeared in the newspaper that morning. The Oshawa Group Limited (Oshawa), a food retail, wholesale and distribution firm, had just announced the hiring of John Lacey as president and chief executive officer, with a mandate to enhance shareholder value. This was surprising as it meant the resignation of former president and chief operating officer, Jonathan Wolfe, a member of the family of controlling shareholders of the company. Rudka had long considered Oshawa an attractive acquisition target for the Empire Company Limited (Empire), a client interested in expanding beyond their Atlantic Canada roots. He wondered if this latest development was a signal that the Wolfe family, who controlled 100 per cent of the voting securities of the company, might consider a takeover offer. They discussed some of the key issues such as valuing Oshawa, identifying potential synergies and deal financing. Consolidation in the grocery business had been rampant in the United States and was likely to spread to Canada. They would have to act fast if Empire was to take advantage of any potential opportunity.

EMPIRE

Empire was founded in 1907 when J.W. Sobey opened a butcher shop in Stellarton, Nova Scotia. Over the years, the company grew into a diversified holding company, with interests in food distribution, real estate and corporate investment activities. The main thrust of the company was the support and operation of the Sobeys retail grocery business. Empire earned $88 million on revenues of $3.3 billion in fiscal 1998 (see Exhibits 1 and 2 for selected Empire financial data).

Food Distribution

The food distribution business, which made up 95 per cent of the company's 1998 revenue (but only 37 per cent of operating income), was comprised of five operating groups: retail, wholesale, foodservice, drug and industries.

The retail group operated 112 stores under the Sobeys name. Sobeys was the largest food retail and distribution company in Atlantic Canada and had begun to expand into Ontario and Quebec. By April 1998, 34 per cent of Sobeys retail square footage was located in these two provinces. Each Sobeys location offered national

and regional brand-name products, as well as private label products under the brand names Our Best and Signal. The retail group also operated corporate, franchised and associated stores under the Foodland, Lofood, Price Check Foods, Needs, Green Gables, Kwik-Way, Clover Farm and Riteway names.

The wholesale division consisted of three companies: TRA Maritimes and TRA Newfoundland in Atlantic Canada and Lumsden Brothers in Ontario. The wholesale group supplied all of the Sobeys and other stores operated by the retail division, as well as over 2,000 independent outlets, both directly and through cash and carry outlets. The wholesale division operated seven distribution outlets throughout the Atlantic provinces and one each in Ontario and Quebec.

The Sobeys Group was the largest food-service operator in Atlantic Canada. It operated 11 distribution centres and serviced institutional clients, as well as independent and chain restaurant businesses. It also supplied fresh produce to Sobeys grocery stores in Atlantic Canada. Key operating units included The Clover Group and Judson Foods in Atlantic Canada and Burgess Wholesale in Ontario. The foodservice group also provided value-added services to clients, including access to a buying group, online ordering, menu planning and costing and nutritional education programs.

The drug group consisted of the Lawton's Drugs chain. The drug group operated both stand-alone pharmacies and assisted with the development of the Sobeys combined food and drug store format.

The industry group provided ancillary services primarily to the food distribution group. The main businesses included a private label soft-drink maker (Big 8), a printing company (Eastern Sign-Print) and a video distribution business (Downeast Video).

Real Estate

The main focus of the real estate group was the acquisition, development and management of property portfolios, which supported or complemented

CONSOLIDATED BALANCE SHEET April 30 (in thousands of dollars)		
	1998	**1997**
Assets		
Current Assets		
Cash	$28,268	$32,185
Receivables	89,153	78,701
Inventories	197,650	194,126
Prepaid Expenses	15,319	14,100
Investments, at cost (quoted market value $246,418; 1997 $211,468)	156,388	148,746
	486,778	467,858
Investments, at equity (quoted market value $800,436; 1997 $575,133)	325,579	300,447
Current assets and marketable investments	812,357	768,305
Fixed assets	1,069,026	1,001,873
Other assets	25,850	27,193
	$1,907,233	$1,797,371
Liabilities and Shareholders' Equity		
Current Liabilities		
Bank loans and notes payable	$286,532	$239,757
Payables and accruals	338,774	298,550
Income taxes payable	9,712	11,462
Long term debts due within one year	24,222	89,702
	659,240	639,471
Long term debt	616,571	606,843
Minority interest	—	171
Deferred income taxes	73,083	71,336
	1,348,894	1,317,821
Shareholders' Equity		
Capital stock	229,889	234,130
Retained earnings	305,422	228,254
Foreign currency translation	23,028	17,166
	558,339	479,550
	$1,907,233	$1,797,371

Exhibit 1   Empire Company Ltd. Financial Statements

CONSOLIDATED BALANCE SHEET April 30 (in thousands of dollars)		
	1998	**1997**
Revenue	$3,320,000	$3,149,773
Cost of sales, selling and administrative expenses	3,127,112	2,971,925
	192,888	177,848
Depreciation	70,404	65,433
	122,484	112,415
Investment income	41,253	35,568
Operating income	163,737	147,983
Interest expense		
Long term debt	64,340	70,512
Short term debt	12,328	8,746
	76,668	79,258
	87,069	68,725
Gain on sale of investments and properties	6,524	1,447
	93,593	70,172
Gain on sale of investment in Jannock Limited	35,868	—
Share of asset impairment provision by equity accounted investment	(8,788)	—
	120,673	70,172
Income taxes		
Sale of investment in Jannock Limited	7,792	—
Other operations	25,092	16,930
	32,884	16,930
Minority interest	7	363
	$32,891	$17,293
Net earnings	$87,782	$52,879

Source: Empire Company Limited Annual Report, 1998.

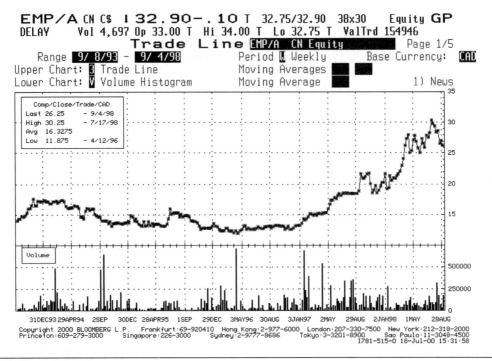

Exhibit 2   Five-Year Stock Price of Empire

Source: Bloomberg.

Empire's retail operations. The group was further divided into Atlantic Shopping Centres, which consisted primarily of enclosed shopping centres and mixed-use office and retail developments, and Sobeys Leased Properties, which consisted mainly of free-standing food stores and attached shopping plazas. In total, the real estate group owned and managed 11.3 million square feet, of which 83 per cent was retail space and 17 per cent was office space.

Investments

The investments group consisted of equity investments in other companies, both long and short term. The goal of the investments group was to provide both geographic and industry diversification to Empire. Long-term investments, which comprised 76 per cent of the total investment portfolio, consisted of a 25 per cent ownership interest in Hannaford Brothers Company and a 43 per cent interest in Wajax Limited.

Hannaford

Hannaford was a U.S. based food retailer with operations in Maine, New Hampshire, Vermont, Massachusetts, New York, Virginia, North Carolina and South Carolina. The company operated 148 supermarkets under the Shop 'n Save and Hannaford names and 100 pharmacy operations within certain Hannaford locations. Earnings from continuing operations were US$84.4 million on revenues of US$3.2 billion for the year ended January 3, 1998. As of September 8, 1998, Empire's holdings of Hannaford was valued at approximately US$450 million.

Wajax Limited

Wajax was a distribution company engaged in the sale and service of mobile equipment, diesel engines and industrial components through a network of 100 distribution outlets throughout the United States and Canada. Industries served by Wajax include natural resources, construction, transportation, manufacturing, industrial processing and utilities. Wajax earned $21 million on revenues of $947 million. As of September 8, 1998, Empire's holdings of Wajax was valued at approximately $60 million.

Other

In addition to these core operations, Empire also ran Atlantic Canada's largest chain of movie theatres, with more than 100 screens under the Empire Theatre name.

Share Capital

Empire had 17.4 million Class B common shares and 19.5 million Class A non-voting shares outstanding. The Class B common shares were not publicly traded, and were held entirely by members of the Sobey family. The two share classes ranked equally, except that Class A had no voting rights, and directors could declare dividends for Class A without being obligated to declare equal or any dividends for the Class B shares. Class B shares were convertible at any time to Class A shares on a one-for-one basis. Under certain circumstances, if an offer was made to purchase the Class B shares, Class A shareholders had the right to receive a follow up offer at the highest per share price paid to Class B shareholders. This type of arrangement was known as a "coattail provision." The company also had several series of preferred shares outstanding.

OSHAWA

Oshawa was a food retail, wholesale and distribution company. It directly operated some grocery stores, but the majority (82 per cent) of their 845 stores were franchised operations. Earnings after tax from continuing operations before unusual items were $40.1 million on revenue of $6.8 billion in fiscal 1998. In 1997, after tax earnings from continuing operations were $54.6 million on revenue of $6.0 billion (see Exhibits 3 and 4 for selected Oshawa financial data).

The company was formed in 1951 when Ray Wolfe first brought the Independent Grocers Alliance to Canada. The Wolfe family remained relatively active in the operation of the company, retaining all of the voting equity in the firm, as well as occupying senior management positions and five of the 12 board seats (see Exhibit 5). The company was divided into a grocery division, Agora Food Merchants and a food service division, SERCA Foodservice.

Agora Food Merchants

Agora was Canada's second largest food retailer and was responsible for 82 per cent of Oshawa's revenues in 1998. It operated in all provinces of Canada, except British Columbia, primarily as a supplier of products and marketing programs to independent grocers under the IGA, Knechtel, Omni and Bonchoix banners. While the majority of the stores it served were franchised operations, Agora also owned corporate stores under the IGA and Price Chopper banners.

SERCA Foodservice

SERCA Foodservice was Canada's largest foodservice business and distributed a full line of grocery and perishable products to the institutional, health care, hotel and restaurant trades. It operated in all 10 Canadian provinces, but the majority of its revenue came from the western provinces.

Oshawa Strategy

Oshawa management felt that returns on shareholder equity had traditionally been insufficient and, as a result, had recently considered

CONSOLIDATED BALANCE SHEETS
January 24, 1998 and January 25, 1997
(in millions of dollars)

	1998	1997
Assets		
Current Assets		
Cash and short-term investments	$65.0	$20.1
Accounts receivable	318.5	294.8
Income taxes receivable	5.6	0.8
Inventories	302.6	274.2
Prepaid expenses	17.4	16.9
Net assets of discontinued operations	—	99.7
	709.1	706.5
Fixed assets	501.8	509.7
Other assets	294.7	219.2
	$1,505.6	$1,435.4
Liabilities and Shareholders' Equity		
Current Liabilities		
Bank indebtedness	$17.1	$36.0
Accounts payable and accrued liabilities	429.5	379.0
	446.6	415.0
Long-term debt	128.6	120.0
Deferred income taxes	36.2	53.9
Unearned revenue	36.4	24.6
	647.8	613.5
Shareholders' equity		
Capital stock	255.9	252.9
Retained earnings	601.9	569.0
	857.8	821.9
	$1,505.6	$1,435.4
Sales and other revenues - continuing operations	$6,813.1	$5,987.6
Cost of sales and expenses	6,651.7	5,837.5
Depreciation and amortization	66.2	59.7
Earnings from continuing operations	95.2	90.4
Interest	(7.9)	(6.5)
Unusual items	(20.3)	8.8
Earnings before income taxes	67.0	92.7
Income taxes	(26.9)	(38.1)
Net earnings from continuing operations	40.1	54.6
Discontinued operations	13.9	0.6
Net earnings	$54.0	$55.2

Exhibit 3   Oshawa Group Ltd. Financial Statements

Source: Oshawa Group Limited Annual Report, 1998.

Exhibit 4   Five-Year Stock Price of Oshawa

Donald Carr, Q.C.	Partner, Goodman and Carr
Allister P. Graham	Chairman, Oshawa Group
Stanley H. Hart, O.C. Q.C.	Charman, Salomon Brothers Canada Inc.
Peter C. Maurice	Vice-Chairman, CT Financial Services Inc.
Charles Perrault, C.M. M.Eng.	President, Schroder Investment Canada Limited
Lawrence Stevenson	President and CEO, Chapter Inc.
Charles Winograd	Deputy Chairman, RBC Dominion Securities Inc.
Harold J. Wolfe	Vice-President Real Estate, Oshawa Group Ltd.
Harvey S. Wolfe	President, Boatwright Investments Limited
Jonathon Wolfe	[Former] President and COO, Oshawa Group Ltd.
Myron J. Wolfe	Group Vice President, Foodservice and Produce, Oshawa Group Ltd.
Richard J. Wolfe	President, Codville Distributors (a division of Oshawa)

Exhibit 5   Oshawa Group Limited Board of Directors

Source: Oshawa Group Limited Annual Report, 1998.

	1997	Two Year	Three Year	Five Year
TSE Food Stores Index	63.2%	32.6%	31.3%	17.6%
Empire	64.2%	29.4%	16.5%	15.7%
Loblaws	83.0%	58.6%	48.2%	31.9%
Metro-Richelieu	42.9%	26.5%	38.7%	26.2%
Provigo	55.9%	2.4%	20.1%	2.2%
Average	61.8%	29.9%	30.6%	18.7%
Oshawa	23.5%	2.1%	10.3%	1.9%

Exhibit 6   Share Price Appreciation of Canadian Grocery Companies

Source: Scotia Capital Markets as of December 31, 1997.

various options designed to enhance shareholder value (see Exhibit 6 for the relative performance of Oshawa shares). Fiscal 1998 was a year of major restructuring which involved, among other things, the sale of non-core holdings, including the divestitures of its drug store operation (Pharma Plus), its cold storage facilities (Langs Cold Storage) and non-strategic real estate, and the expansion of its retail and foodservice businesses. During the year, Oshawa expanded its food businesses through the acquisition of Scott National, a food service distributor operating in Alberta, Saskatchewan, Manitoba and Northern Ontario, and the assets of six grocery stores in the province of Quebec. The company had previously acquired Neptune Foods of British Columbia in fiscal 1997. In fiscal 1999, Penner Foods of Manitoba was acquired.

Share Capital

The Oshawa Group had two classes of common shares outstanding, common and Class A. There were 685,504 common shares outstanding, distributed (substantially) equally amongst five members of the Wolfe family. The common shares were not publicly traded. As well, there were 37,894,905 Class A shares outstanding.

The Class A shares were non-voting, participating and entitled to a $0.10 non-cumulative annual dividend in priority to common.[1] Most importantly, there was not a coattail provision for Class A shares. This implied that, at least in theory, voting control of the company could be acquired by purchasing the common shares privately, with no obligation to make a bid for Class A shares, or in the event that a bid was made to provide the same consideration offered for the common shares. Class A shares were mostly held by a limited number of large financial institutions, although members of the Wolfe family were believed to hold, in the aggregate, approximately 10 per cent to 15 per cent of the issued Class A shares (see Exhibit 7 for a breakdown of share ownership).

THE GROCERY BUSINESS

The grocery business was a mature industry. In 1998 grocers faced increasing competition not only from other grocers, but also increasingly from various non-traditional vendors including drug stores, discount retailers, wholesale clubs and internet-based operations. On the revenue side, growth occurred primarily through

Shareholder*	Shares Held	% of Total
Trimark	6,775,300	17.9%
Templeton	4,556,159	12.0%
Investors Group	3,634,550	9.6%
		39.5%
Gryphon	1,021,822	2.7%
Caisse de Depot	853,074	2.3%
Mackenzie	600,000	1.6%
C.A. Delaney	561,600	1.5%
	18,002,505	47.5%
Total Shares Outstanding	37,894,905	

Exhibit 7   Ownership Blocks of Oshawa Class A Shares

Source: Scotia Capital Markets.

*It was also estimated that the Wolfe family members held approximately 15% of the outstanding Class A shares.

(Based on 1997 Revenue, in millions of dollars)		
	Sales ($)	Share
Loblaw Companies Ltd.	$11,008	20.5%
The Oshawa Group Ltd.	6,813	12.7%
Provigo Inc.	5,956	11.1%
Canada Safeway Ltd.	4,720	8.8%
Metro-Richelieu Inc.	3,432	6.4%
Empire Co. Ltd.*	2,978	5.6%
Great Atlantic & Pacific Co. of Canada	2,458	4.6%
Federated Co-ops Ltd.	2,411	4.5%
Southland Canada Inc.	830	1.5%
Silcorp Ltd.	743	1.4%
Calgary Co-operative Association Ltd.	592	1.1%
Alimentation-Couche Tard	390	0.7%
Interprovincial Co-op	218	0.4%
Total Industry Sales	$53,578	

Exhibit 8   Share of Grocery Dollars

Source: Financial Post, Canadian Grocer, Empire Company Annual Report 1998.

*Food distribution revenue from Empire Company. Includes revenue from drug and foodservice.

horizontal merger and acquisition activity. Consolidation had increased substantially across North America in recent years for several reasons. First, it was generally cheaper to acquire a competitor than to open new stores. Acquisition also mitigated risks associated with entering a new market including lack of local knowledge, difficulty of attracting a qualified work force and the threat and intensity of competitive response. Horizontal acquisition activity also generated the economies of scale in marketing, procurement, distribution, technology, corporate overhead and private-label development.

The Competitive Landscape

Vaux knew that in order to gauge the potential success of an acquisition, an analysis of the competitive landscape would need to be done (see Exhibit 8 and Exhibit 9 for market share and financial performance comparisons of selected Canadian grocery store operators). It was also essential to assess the potential of rival bidders. Empire did not want to overpay for any

acquisition and it was, therefore, essential that any transaction not escalate into a bidding war.

Loblaws

Loblaws was a subsidiary of George Weston Co., and was Canada's largest food retailer, with 20 per cent of the national market. In western Canada, it operated under The Real Canadian Superstore, Extra Foods, Real Canadian Wholesale Club, SuperValu, Shop Easy and Lucky Dollar banners. In the east, it operated under the Loblaws, Zehrs, Atlantic Superstore, Dominion (in Newfoundland only), Your Independent Grocer, no frills, Fortino's and valu-mart names. Loblaws was the only company that competed on a national basis. In fiscal 1997, Loblaws earned $213 million on revenues of $11 billion.

(in millions of dollars)	Empire	Oshawa	Loblaws	Metro-Richelieu	Provigo
Market Value of Equity (as of 2/13/98)	776	951	6,735	850	990
Total Debt	918	135	876	77	327
Enterprise Value*	1,695	1,086	7,629	927	1,317
Revenues	3,208	7,052	10,554	3,432	5,859
EBITDA	219	165	534	155	232
EBITDA Margin	6.8%	2.4%	5.1%	4.5%	4.0%
Net Income	59	49	199	66	90
Net Margin	1.8%	0.7%	1.9%	1.9%	1.5%
Beta**	0.74	0.77	0.55	0.59	1.20
Credit Rating***	A	AA	A	n/a	BBB

Exhibit 9   Canadian Food Store Company Comparison

Source: Bloomberg, Scotia Capital Markets.

All information based on latest twelve months
* Market value of equity, plus market value of debt, less cash
** Beta based on weekly returns over two years
*** Canadian Bond Rating Service Rating of Senior Unsecured Debt
    Risk premiums over government yields were currently around 75 basis points for
    AAA-rated firms, 100 for AA and 125 for A, and 150 for BBB

Loblaws was also seen as the greatest competitive risk for a rival bid for Oshawa. They had the financial capacity to make a rival bid and may have been able to capture high synergistic strategic gains. By acquiring Oshawa, Loblaws would be far and away the dominant player in the Canadian grocery business. The only mitigating factor in considering Loblaws as a potential competitor in an acquisition was speculation that there may be increased scrutiny from the Competition Bureau.[2]

Canada Safeway

Canada Safeway was based in Calgary and was a private, wholly-owned subsidiary of Safeway Inc. of California. Despite damaging labor disputes in 1996, Canada Safeway remained the dominant grocery store chain across Western Canada. Income before taxes and extraordinary items from Canadian operations was US$97.9 million on revenues of US$3.4 billion.

Although they had ample financial capacity to make a competing bid for Oshawa, it was not expected that they would do so. They had not yet shown any interest in expanding into the competitive Ontario market, or further east.

Metro-Richelieu

Metro-Richelieu was the largest food retailer in Quebec. It operated Metro supermarkets, Super C discount stores and Marché Richelieu neighborhood stores. It also ran an extensive wholesale distribution business. Net income in fiscal 1997 was $66.2 million on revenues of $3.4 billion.

Metro-Richelieu was seen as a potential rival for the acquisition of Oshawa. If successful, it would solidify their position as the largest grocer in Quebec, as well as giving them national scope.

Provigo

Provigo was the largest food distributor in Quebec and had a growing presence in Ontario. It operated under the banners Provigo, Loeb and Maxi & Co. Until 1997, it had also operated convenience store chains under its C-Corp subsidiary, but this division was sold to Alimentation Couche-Tard. Net income in fiscal 1998 was $68.7 million on revenues of $5.9 billion.

If Provigo were to acquire Oshawa, they would become the largest grocer in Quebec, improve Ontario penetration and extend their reach nationally. While Provigo also operated franchised stores, their preferred method of expansion was by building their own corporate network.

Overwaitea Food Group

The Overwaitea Food Group was based in Langley, B.C. and was privately owned by the Pattison Group. It operated supermarkets under the Overwaitea and Save-On-Foods & Drug Stores and the wholesale operation Associated Grocers. The Pattison Group also operated Buy-Low Foods, a smaller chain with its own wholesale operation. Because it was a privately held company, results of operations were not known.

A potential rival bid from the Pattison Group was seen as possible. While Oshawa had only a small presence in British Columbia, the acquisition would provide national exposure.

The Great Atlantic & Pacific Company of Canada Ltd.

The Great Atlantic & Pacific Company of Canada was a private, wholly-owned subsidiary of The Great Atlantic & Pacific Tea Company of New Jersey. It operated under the A&P and Dominion banners. Income from Canadian operations were US$895,000 on sales of US$1.5 billion in fiscal 1998.

A & P was not seen as a potential rival bidder, despite the fact that the Canadian operation was outperforming the U.S. counterpart. The parent company had never before expressed any interest in expanding their Canadian operations.

Canadian Economy

The most significant events of 1998 were the Asian and Russian economic crises. Both had resulted from defaults on corporate and government debt, which led to massive currency devaluations. These events had left the Russian and most major Asian economies in turmoil, significantly lowering world demand for most commodities and reducing Canadian corporate profit expectations.

The Bank of Canada had lowered interest rates nine times since 1996 to boost the economy and lower unemployment. The low interest rates were also having the effect of devaluing the Canadian dollar against most world currencies. By August, the Canadian dollar was worth slightly less than US$0.65. This devaluation initially helped alleviate some of the effects of the global crisis. To restore confidence in the dollar, the Bank of Canada increased the bank rate by a full percentage point on August 27, 1998. This action halted the slide of the dollar, but did not reverse it. It was currently trading at US$0.6474 compared to US$0.7207 one year before. The current yield for 91-day treasury bills was 5.6 per cent and the 10-year government bond yield was 5.8 per cent.

Real Gross Domestic Product (GDP) growth had increased substantially since 1992 and was 1.2 per cent in 1996, and 3.7 per cent in 1997. Real GDP was forecast to grow by 3.4 per cent in 1998 and 2.4 per cent in 1999. There were significant risks that, because of global economic conditions, this growth would not be achieved.

Despite the world economic crises, unemployment in Canada had actually decreased over the year. Unemployment currently stood at 8.3 per cent, as opposed to 9.0 per cent a year earlier. The decrease in unemployment had not yet had any effect on inflation. The Consumer Price Index had increased only 1.6 per cent in both 1996 and 1997. Forecasts called for inflation to slow to 1.2 per cent in 1998 and 1.3 per cent in 1999.

VALUATION OF OSHAWA

Oshawa stock was currently at $26, but had traded as high as $29.25 six weeks earlier (average price over the last 20 trading days was $26.46). With just over 38 million shares outstanding, this implied an equity market value of approximately $1 billion. Vaux knew, however, that the Wolfe family was unlikely to sell their shares unless they were offered a significant premium to market. Further, in the event that Empire wanted to make a pre-emptive offer for the company and avoid a bidding war, Vaux understood that an attractive offer would be necessary. He began by gathering information on food industry mergers that had taken place in the United States, as no similar transactions had taken place in Canada (see Exhibit 10). He also examined the relative value of comparable firms (see Exhibit 11).

In order to get a clearer picture of the value of the company, Vaux elected to do a discounted cash flow (DCF) analysis of Oshawa. He decided to perform two separate DCF analyses. The first would be based on Oshawa as a stand-alone entity with a specific cash flows forecast five years into the future (see Exhibits 11 and 12 for some information gathered). This analysis would assist in determining the intrinsic value of Oshawa, relative to its current market value. The second would be a separate DCF of the potential synergies with Empire. Vaux knew that revenue growth, EBITDA margins and capital expenditures would be the key drivers of the analysis. Examining historical data, he saw that revenue growth had averaged approximately six per cent over the past 10 years. He believed that it would be reasonable to assume this growth was

sustainable for the next five years. Beyond that, he thought that a growth rate in line with long-term GDP growth was reasonable. As of September, he estimated sales for the previous twelve months to be $7 billion. Based on discussions with Empire management, Vaux believed that EBITDA margins at Oshawa would increase over the near term to 2.6 per cent, still far below the industry average given their heavy concentration in the food service business. Recent years had seen increases in capital expenditures by Oshawa, relative to sales. Vaux believed that this was because store improvements had traditionally been low, which might mean that some of the stores would be in very poor condition and would require substantial investment. As a result, he believed that capital expenditures as a percentage of sales would remain at or near two per cent of sales for the first year following the merger, but could fall to approximately one per cent by year five.

Vaux also wanted to derive the value of any potential synergies through a separate DCF analysis. He considered two kinds of potential synergies: those related to margin enhancements and those related to cost reductions. In conversations with Empire management, he received the following "best case" information. In terms of the EBITDA margin, Empire management believed that annual EBITDA savings could be generated through stronger and more coordinated buying power. While Empire management believed that no improvement in margins was possible in the first year, they estimated that a 0.15 per cent improvement could be realized in the second year, as well as 0.25 per cent in the third year and 0.50 per cent in all subsequent years. Further cost synergies based on elimination of duplicate administration, merchandising, buying, pricing and accounting were estimated to be $39.5 million per year. Distribution and divisional management costs savings were estimated at $4.1 million per year and reflected the rationalization of direct operating and warehouse wages in Ontario and Quebec. Advertising savings were estimated at $2 million per year, based on the ability to

| Target | Acquirer | Announcement Date | Transaction Size | | | Premium to 20 Day Avg | Enterprise Value to | | | | Price to | |
| | | | Equity | Enterprise | Consideration | | Revenue | EBITDA | EBIT | Earnings | Earnings | Book |
							(Latest twelve months)				(LTM)	
Carr-Gottstein	Safeway Inc.	06-Aug-98	$113	$319	cash	56.3%	0.55 ×	6.9 ×	10.8 ×	n/a	n/a	4.4 ×
American Stores Co.	Albertson's	03-Aug-98	$8,939	$11,930	shares	25.8%	0.62 ×	9.5 ×	15.4 ×	26.8 ×	26.8 ×	3.8 ×
Delchamps . Inc	Jitney-Jungle Stores	08-Jul-97	$227	$240	cash	0.4%	0.22 ×	5.8 ×	13.5 ×	26.8 ×	26.8 ×	3.1 ×
Riser Foods	Giant Eagle	14-May-97	$426	$480	cash	15.3%	0.36 ×	8.5 ×	13.0 ×	17.2 ×	17.2 ×	4.9 ×
Vons Companies	Safeway Inc.	30-Oct-96	$2,498	$3,025	shares	25.1%	0.56 ×	8.8 ×	13.7 ×	26.9 ×	26.9 ×	0.9 ×
Kash 'n' Karry Food Stores	Food Lion	31-Oct-96	$126	$347	cash	14.5%	0.34 ×	6.3 ×	11.7 ×	n/a	n/a	6.5 ×
Stop & Shop	Royal Ahold NV	28-Mar-96	$1,682	$2,795	cash	20.6%	0.68 ×	8.9 ×	12.4 ×	22.3 ×	22.3 ×	1.2 ×
National Convenience Stores	Diamond Shamrock	08-Nov-95	$186	$250	cash	9.9%	0.28 ×	6.8 ×	10.9 ×	19.6 ×	19.6 ×	3.8 ×
Super Rite	Richfood Holdings	26-Jun-95	$212	$327	shares	29.4%	0.22 ×	6.6 ×	8.9 ×	15.9 ×	15.9 ×	5.3 ×
Bruno's	KKR	20-Apr-95	$947	$1,167	97% cash, 3% shares	29.7%	0.41 ×	9.3 ×	15.9 ×	27.9 ×	27.9 ×	2.2 ×

Exhibit 10   Historical Transaction Data

Source: Scotia Capital Markets.

119

	Year End	Enterprise Value to EBITDA			Price to Earnings	
		1997	1998E	1999E	1998E	1999E
Empire	April	9.5 ×	7.8 ×	7.1 ×	14.6 ×	11.8 ×
Loblaws	December	15.9 ×	13.6 ×	11.4 ×	31.4 ×	27.0 ×
Metro-Richelieu	September	6.5 ×	6.0 ×	5.5 ×	12.4 ×	11.4 ×
Provigo	January	6.0 ×	5.8 ×	5.5 ×	14.8 ×	12.3 ×
Oshawa	January	6.8 ×	6.7 ×	5.7 ×	17.9 ×	14.6 ×

Exhibit 11   Trading Ratios of Selected Canadian Grocery Retailers

Source: Scotia Capital Markets.

merge retail banners. Vaux had observed that the full value of potential synergies was rarely fully realized, and that in any event, given the risk of achieving the synergies, Empire would be unwilling to pay for their full value in the transaction. Therefore, in order to be conservative, Vaux estimated that no cost synergies would occur in the first year, 37.5 per cent of potential cost synergies would occur in the second year, then 75 per cent of potential cost synergies would occur in year three and beyond.

Partially offsetting the synergy benefits, Vaux recognized that some up-front merger costs would arise. He estimated that a merger would result in one-time charges of approximately $80 million consisting of items including severance packages, and the costs associated with closing and converting existing retail spaces. All up-front merger costs were tax deductible.

DEAL FINANCING AND STRUCTURE

If the deal were to be viable, Vaux would also need to recommend a financing package. Empire carried a substantial investment portfolio, the sale of which could generate more than $1 billion at market prices and perhaps more, assuming a premium for control blocks

of Hannaford and Wajax. However, the Sobey family viewed the investment portfolio, especially the long-term portion, as part of a diversified asset base essential to the long-term viability of the company.

Empire already carried a substantial debt load relative to its competitors (due in part to its extensive real estate operations) and, therefore, any additional debt could be relatively expensive and threaten their A debt rating.

Empire was a publicly traded company and, therefore, additional equity could be issued to finance an acquisition. However, the Sobey family wanted to retain control over Empire and they felt the stock was trading at a substantial discount to its true value. Another option would be to spin off the food business into a separate entity. Oshawa shareholders would receive equity in the new company as consideration in the transaction. However, if this option were to be pursued, a value needed to be determined for the new shares. Vaux believed that the easiest way to value equity in a new company would be to use trading multiples of similar companies (see Exhibit 11). This alternative posed risks as well, as the new shares would not trade publicly until after the transaction was completed. There was a chance that Oshawa shareholders would not react well to receiving something with no observable value. The advantage of the spin-off

	1998	1997	1996	1995	1994	1993
Empire						
Sales	3,320.0	3,149.7	2,915.2	2,699.5	2,577.4	
Dep. & Amort.	70.4	65.4	60.0	57.5	50.7	
Working Capital	153.1	128.8	178.5	183.6	204.3	
Capital Expend.	137.5	82.7	125.7	120.1	98.1	
Oshawa						
Sales	6,813.0	5,988.0	5,765.0	5,650.0	5,305.0	
Dep. & Amort.	66.0	60.0	57.0	55.0	50.0	
Working Capital	262.0	292.0	193.0	223.0	201.0	
Capital Expend.	130.0	135.0	106.0	60.0	59.0	
Loblaws						
Sales		11,008.0	9,848.0	9,854.0	10,000.0	9,356.0
Dep. & Amort.		147.0	122.0	129.0	138.0	126.0
Working Capital		202.0	154.0	179.0	29.0	148.0
Capital Expend.		517.0	389.0	302.0	339.0	315.0
Metro-Richelieu						
Sales		3,432.3	3,266.0	3,145.6	2,909.0	2,772.7
Dep. & Amort.		39.2	37.0	38.7	40.4	37.1
Working Capital		4.6	1.0	3.8	(4.7)	(8.7)
Capital Expend.		79.1	57.1	38.0	40.5	19.5
Provigo						
Sales	5,956.2	5,832.5	5,725.2	5,542.5	5,433.4	
Dep. & Amort.	77.6	70.9	62.1	61.0	59.7	
Working Capital	(45.0)	(104.9)	(104.3)	(24.5)	(209.9)	
Capital Expend.	184.0	171.4	95.3	37.5	41.9	
Safeway						
Sales		22,483.8	17,269.0	16,397.5	15,626.6	15,214.5
Dep. & Amort.		455.8	338.5	329.7	326.4	330.2
Working Capital		n/a	n/a	n/a	n/a	n/a
Capex		829.4	620.3	503.2	352.2	290.2
A&P						
Sales		10,179.4	10,262.2	10,089.0	10,101.4	10,332.0
Dep. & Amort.		233.7	234.2	230.7	225.4	235.4
Working Capital		90.0	262.1	215.4	191.0	92.3
Capex		438.3	267.6	296.9	236.1	214.9

Exhibit 12   Five Year Selected Historical Financial Information

Source: Annual reports of listed companies.

alternative was that it would create a "pure-play" stock, which would be easier for the market to understand, likely leading to a higher valuation.

Using some form of equity to (at least partially) finance the deal would be attractive to the Wolfe family, as well, as it would allow them to defer some capital gains taxes. Whatever the final structure, it was absolutely essential that Empire retain majority equity interest and voting control over all its businesses.

SUMMARY

Vaux and Rudka knew they had an enormous task ahead of them. There were many questions that needed answers and they did not feel that they had much time to find them. They had to find a way to approach the Wolfe family and secure their support. They needed to derive a value for both classes of shares that was both reasonable for Empire to pay and that would be enough to appease the Wolfe family and other Oshawa equity holders. They also had to develop a strategy that would dissuade others from entering into a bidding war. Last, but definitely not least, they needed to find a way to finance the deal. As Vaux left the office, he knew he would be busy, but was eager to get started on what was to be, at the very least, an exciting transaction.

NOTES

1. Participating means that if certain criteria are met, participating shareholders will receive an additional dividend payment beyond the pre-determined amount.

2. The Competition Bureau was an agency of the Canadian Government. Part of its mandate was to review merger transactions to ensure that, if completed, they would not result in a lessening or prevention of competition in the marketplace.

THE GILLETTE COMPANY'S ACQUISITION OF DURACELL INTERNATIONAL INC.—COST OF CAPITAL

Prepared by Anna Garcia (Malveena)
under the supervision of Professor Robert W. White

Version: (A) 2002-11-18

On September 15, 1996, Donald Green, a new analyst at Cromwell Financial, puzzled over the financial markets and industry data he had collected in order to estimate the cost of capital for Duracell International Inc. (Duracell). Three days prior, on September 12, following a five-year search for a profitable, technologically-driven branded consumer products business with international growth potential, The Gillette Company (Gillette) announced its intended acquisition of Duracell. Duracell was valued at approximately $7 billion or 0.904 of Gillette share for each Duracell share owned. Shares in Duracell rose $9 to $58.125, and shares in Gillette rose $0.875 to $66, on the New York Stock Exchange. Subsequent to that, one of Cromwell's larger clients, who held a significant position in Duracell at the time of the announcement, requested an evaluation of the fairness of Gillette's offer, and Green received his new assignment.

Green knew that there were three generic approaches to valuing a firm: market capitalization, comparable transactions and discounted cash flows. While the first two methods were fairly straightforward, the discounted cash flow approach presented a number of important issues concerning the appropriate discount rate to use in the calculations. First of all, should he be estimating the weighted average cost of capital (WACC) of Gillette, the acquiring firm, or of Duracell, the target? Secondly, what specific techniques and inputs for estimating the WACC component costs were most appropriate under the circumstances? Lastly, should he base his calculations on Gillette's, Duracell's or some other target capital structure?

THE GILLETTE COMPANY

Gillette was a leading manufacturer of inexpensive grooming aids and household products, with 1995 worldwide revenue of $6.8 billion. Razors accounted for over one-third of the firm's sales, while 70 per cent of its revenue came from international operations. See Exhibit 1 for the composition of Gillette's sales by business segment and geography. The company's major brands included Sensor razors; Right Guard, Soft and Dry toiletries; Paper Mate, Liquid Paper stationery products; Parker pens; Braun appliances; and Oral-B oral care products.

Source of 1995 Sales by Business Segment

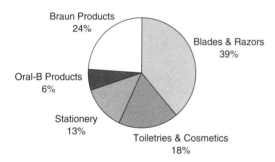

Source of 1995 Sales by Geography

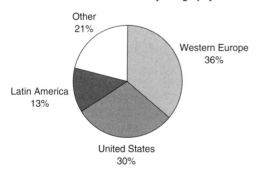

Exhibit 1   The Gillette Company

Source: Gillette's 1995 Annual Report.

The markets in the United States and Western Europe for inexpensive grooming aids were firmly established and demand was advancing roughly in line with the population growth. Products were generally price sensitive due to little room for differentiation, as well as to fierce competition for the limited shelf space and for the time-pressed shopper's attention. Competitive pressures came mainly from three sources. First of all, shoppers, who were becoming much more sophisticated, were able to recognize and were determined to receive good value for their money. Secondly, technological advances had narrowed the quality spread between premium-priced and cheaper products. Lastly, retailer order patterns had become irregular and were based on the consumer buying behavior trends instead of systematic replenishment. Just-in-time deliveries, which had become the norm, shifted inventory holding costs from retailers to manufacturers.

Gillette's lead in the universal blade market was insurmountable due to its global strength in distribution and marketing, high brand recognition, and established expertise in its international businesses. Consumers were still willing to pay for the quality associated with the well-recognized brand name, which allowed Gillette some flexibility in setting prices. Nevertheless, competitive pressures and limited growth in demand forced the firm to actively seek a strategic acquisition of a growing complementary business to boost its sales volume growth. In recent years, Gillette's sales had been growing by nine percentage points per year, while net income had grown at twice that rate but only by improving profit margins (see Exhibit 2 consolidated financial statements).

Gillette was a consistently profitable firm with a stable dividend stream. By September 1996, the company had reported 24 consecutive quarters of double-digit growth in operating earnings (see Exhibit 3). Gillette had been one of the growth stocks of the 1990s: the shares were up 26 percentage points in 1996 and 88 percentage points in the past two years. Gillette's debt level was within the industry

CONSOLIDATED STATEMENT OF INCOME
(Millions of dollars, except per share amounts)

	12/1995	12/1994	12/1993
Net Sales	$6,794.7	$6,070.2	$5,410.8
Cost of Sales	2,540.2	2,221.9	2,044.3
Gross Profit	4,254.5	3,848.3	3,366.5
Selling, General and Administrative Expenses	2,883.2	2,621.6	2,279.2
Realignment Expense	—	—	262.6
Profit from Operations	1,371.3	1,226.7	824.7
Nonoperating Charges (Income)			
Interest Income	(9.9)	(19.0)	(27.3)
Interest expense	59.0	61.1	59.8
Other charges - net	25.3	80.5	109.5
	74.4	122.6	142.0
Income before Income Taxes and Cumulative Effect of Accounting Changes	1,296.9	1,104.1	682.7
Income Taxes	473.4	405.8	255.8
Income before Cumulative Effect of Accounting Changes	823.5	698.3	426.9
Cumulative Effect of Accounting Changes	—	—	(138.6)
Net Income	823.5	698.3	288.3
Preferred Stock dividends, net of tax benefit	4.7	4.7	4.7
Net Income Available to Common Stockholders	818.8	693.6	283.6
Earnings Reinvested in the Business at beginning of year	2,830.2	2,357.9	2,259.6
	3,649.0	3,051.5	2,543.2
Common stock dividends declared	266.3	221.3	185.3
Earnings Reinvested in the Business at end of year	$3,382.7	$2,830.2	$2,357.9
Income per Common Share before Cumulative Effect of Accounting Changes	$1.85	$1.57	$0.96
Cumulative Effect of Accounting Changes	—	—	(0.32)
Net Income per Common Share	$1.85	$1.57	$0.64
Dividends declared per common share	$0.60	$0.50	$0.42
Weighted average number of common shares outstanding (millions)	443.5	442.3	440.9

CONSOLIDATED BALANCE SHEET

	12/1995	12/1994
Assets		
Current Assets		
Cash and cash equivalents	$47.9	$43.8
Short-term investments, at cost, which approximates market value	1.6	2.3
Receivables, less allowances: 1995 - $59.2; 1994 - $52.1	1,695.5	1,379.5
Inventories	1,035.1	941.2

Exhibit 2   The Gillette Company Financial Statements

Deferred income taxes	220.2	220.6
Prepaid expenses	140.2	113.0
Total Current Assets	3,104.5	2,700.4
Property, Plant and Equipment, at cost less accumulated depreciation	1,636.9	1,411.0
Intangible Asserts, less accumulated amortization	1,221.4	887.4
Other Assets	377.5	314.6
	$6,340.3	$5,313.4
Liabilities and Stockholders' Equity		
Current Liabilities		
Loans payable	$576.2	$344.4
Current portion of long-term debt	26.5	28.1
Accounts payable and accrued liabilities	1,273.3	1,178.2
Income taxes	248.0	185.5
Total Current Liabilities	2,124.0	1,736.2
Long-Term Debt	691.1	715.1
Deferred Income Taxes	72.7	53.1
Other Long-Term Liabilities	919.2	774.3
Minority Interest	20.0	17.4
Stockholders' Equity		
8.0% Cumulative Series C ESOP Convertible Preferred, without pV,		
Issued: 1995 - 160,701 shs; 1994 - 162,928 shs	96.9	98.2
Unearned ESOP compensation		
Common stock, par value $1 per share - Authorized 1,160,000,000 shares	(34.3)	(44.2)
Issued: 1995 - 559,718,438 shares; 1994 - 558,242,410 shares	559.7	558.2
Additional paid-in capital	31.1	(1.4)
Earnings reinvested in the business	3,382.7	2,830.2
Cumulative foreign currency translation adjustments	(477.0)	(377.1)
Treasury stock, at cost: Shs 1995 - 115,254,353; 1994 - 115,343,404	(1,045.8)	(1,046.6)
Total Stockholders' Equity	2,513.3	2,017.3
	$6,340.3	$5,313.4

Source: Gillette's 1995 Annual Report.

	Past 10 Years	Past 5 Years	Estimated 1993–1995 to 2000–2002
Sales	11.5%	6.5%	12.0%
Cash Flow	16.0%	13.0%	17.5%
Earnings	17.5%	18.0%	19.0%
Dividends	12.5%	16.0%	19.0%

Exhibit 3   The Gillette Company Selected Statistics, Compound Annual Growth Rates per Share

Source: Value Line Investment Survey.

norm. The company's capital structure (book) as of December 31, 1995, included 22 per cent long-term debt and 78 per cent equity. Annual dividends increased from $0.16 per share in 1985 to $0.60 per share in 1995. Gillette's quarterly dividends in 1996 were $0.18 per share (annualized $0.72), projected earnings per share for 1996 were $2.22, and published beta[1] was 1.15. The average beta for the high quality consumer global growth franchise stocks[2] was 1.05 (the betas are tightly grouped with a maximum of 1.15 and a minimum of 1.0). Based on market values, the average debt to equity ratio for the global growth franchise stocks was less than 10 per cent (Wm. Wrigley, for example, had zero debt).

DURACELL INTERNATIONAL INC.

Duracell had been purchased by the New York buyout firm Kohlberg, Kravis Roberts & Co. (KKR) in 1988 for $1.8 billion, or the equivalent of $5 per share, in a leveraged buyout from Kraft, Inc.[3] The lending institutions put stiff covenants on the debt to protect Henry Kravis from himself. To finance the deal, KKR raised $350 million in equity through the sale of limited partnerships and borrowed $725 million in senior debt term loans from a consortium of banks. Following the acquisition, Kravis refinanced the bridge loans to subordinated junk paper as KKR issued $400 million in 13 1/2 per cent straight coupon notes due in 2000 and $670 million in 13 1/8 per cent zero-coupon bonds due in 1998. Proceeds from the zeros totalled $386 million, which was used to pay down the bridge loans and to take $188 million off the bank debt. In 1991, KKR took Duracell public in an initial public offering at $15 a share, raising new equity. Soon after, KKR began selling its shares in secondary offerings. As of September 12, 1996, KKR still held a 34 per cent stake in Duracell, and had four seats on the company's 11-member board. KKR was shedding investments in 1996. Officials there wouldn't comment.

In a worldwide market of 20 billion battery sales annually, Duracell sold about three billion in 1995, somewhat less than Eveready. In 1996, Duracell was the largest producer of alkaline batteries worldwide with annual revenue of $2.3 billion. Duracell's primary market was the United States, with less than half of the company's sales coming from international sales (see Exhibit 4 for geographic segmentation of Duracell's sales). In fiscal 1994, Duracell formed joint venture companies in both China and India, large markets offering significant growth opportunities, to manufacture and distribute Duracell brand alkaline batteries. Duracell held controlling interest in each of these companies. The company also manufactured lithium, zinc air, zinc carbon and nickel metal hydride rechargeable batteries. Alkaline batteries produced a far greater amount of energy within any given battery size than was possible in zinc carbon batteries, the dominant battery type throughout the world until the 1980s. This performance superiority resulted in alkaline batteries steadily displacing zinc carbon batteries.

The worldwide battery market was highly competitive, particularly as to price and product performance. The overall demand for the product was growing quickly as the society was becoming more portable. The global battery market in 1996 was about $9 billion, with projected annual growth of 11 per cent for the following five years to $15 billion by the year 2000. A high growth rate of 10 per cent was expected in the subsequent years. The alkaline battery segment was the largest—$4 billion—with the best growth prospects. In the United States, where 87 per cent of battery sales were alkaline, Duracell had a 48.6 per cent market share by revenue in 1995; Eveready, its major competitor, had 35.8 per cent; Rayovac had 8.3 per cent and private labels and others had 7.3 per cent. (Eveready was owned by the St. Louis-based conglomerate Ralston Purina, which in turn, was owned by the British conglomerate Gand Metropolitan PLC. Rayovac was closely held and was being largely acquired by Boston buyout firm Thomas Lee Co.) Duracell attributed most of its future growth

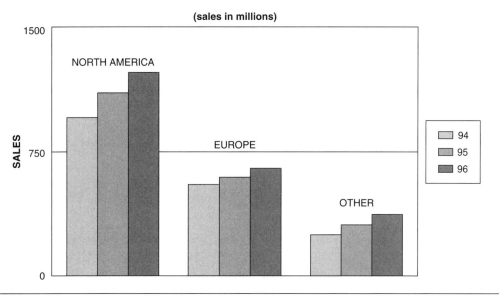

(sales in millions)

Exhibit 4   Duracell International Inc., Geographic Segmentation of Sales

to unit sales growth; its profit margin was not growing as quickly.

Although Duracell was continuously profitable, the firm had disappointed investors over the past few years with weaker than expected earnings growth and stock lagging significantly behind the overall market. Duracell's financial statements are presented in Exhibit 5. Sluggish earnings growth was explained primarily by the firm's difficulty in growing European volume and shrinking profit margins in the United States under pressures from private-label batteries; additional factors were losses on high powered batteries and costs associated with expansion. Duracell had, however, shown commitment to improving its earnings situation by rolling out new products such as PowerCheck battery with a fuel-gauge tester and investing heavily in rechargeable batteries for cellular phones and computers.

Duracell, which was at the forefront of primary lithium battery development, was a leading lithium battery manufacturer for consumer devices. These batteries had performance advantages over conventional consumer batteries in certain applications, with their extremely high energy density and long shelf life being the most notable. Duracell's line of zinc air batteries, most of which were "button cells," were used principally in hearing aids and medical equipment. Over the past several years, Duracell, Toshiba Battery Co. Ltd. of Japan and Varta Batterie AG of Germany had engaged in joint research and development of nickel hydride rechargeable cells. By 1996, nickel metal hydride rechargeable batteries were becoming the battery of choice for use in devices having high power requirements, such as portable computers. They were also an environmentally attractive substitute for the nickel-cadmium batteries currently being used to power many such devices. During fiscal 1995, affiliates of the three companies formed a joint venture for the purpose of constructing and operating a manufacturing facility in the United States to produce nickel metal hydride cells for use in rechargeable batteries sold by the three companies. Duracell had a 40 per cent interest

CONSOLIDATED INCOME FOR THE YEARS ENDED JUNE 30				
	1996	**1995**	**1994**	**1993**
Revenue	$2,289.6	$2,079.0	$1,871.3	$1,742.2
Cost of Products Sold	841.6	727.3	647.6	640.4
Gross Profit	1,448.0	1,351.7	1,223.7	1,101.8
Selling, General and Admin. Expense	1,003.0	942.0	867.5	795.2
Restructuring Expense	0.0	0.0	0.0	65.0
Operating Income	445.0	409.7	356.2	241.6
Interest Expense	24.5	27.0	29.6	45.6
Other Income (Expense)	20.2	5.4	(6.4)	(13.2)
Income Bef. Accting. Change & Inc. Taxes	400.3	388.1	320.2	182.8
Provision for Income Taxes	155.6	152.3	120.0	58.7
Income Bef. Accounting Change	244.7	235.8	200.2	123.9
Cumulative Effect of Accounting Change	0.0	0.0	0.0	(75.4)
Net Income	$244.7	$235.8	$200.2	$48.5
EPS Before Extraordinary Items	$2.02	$1.95	$1.68	$1.04

CONSOLIDATED BALANCE SHEET

	6/1996	**6/1995**	**6/1994**
Cash and Cash Equivalents	$43.6	$35.0	$36.1
Net Accounts Receivable	429.5	390.0	322.8
Inventories	341.0	284.4	229.9
Deferred Income Taxes	42.0	41.1	80.3
Prepaid and Other Current Assets	69.9	61.3	51.4
Total Current Assets	**926.0**	**811.8**	**720.5**
Property Plant and Equipment	492.1	378.3	313.2
Intangible Assets, Net	1,289.6	1,208.9	1,235.4
Other Assets	20.8	20.8	17.2

CONSOLIDATED BALANCE SHEET

	6/1996	**6/1995**	**6/1994**
Total Assets	**2,728.5**	**2,419.8**	**2,286.3**
Accounts Payable	136.3	117.8	107.3
Short-term Borrowings	47.1	59.0	51.0
Accrued Liabilities	202.8	195.6	183.2
Total Current Liabilities	**386.2**	**372.4**	**341.5**
Long-term Debt	428.5	364.5	355.0
Post Retirement Benefits Other Than Pensions	98.4	98.4	95.3
Deferred Income Taxes	352.2	269.1	280.9
Other Non-Current Liabilities	60.0	52.0	60.1
Total Liabilities	**1,325.3**	**1,156.4**	**1,132.8**
Common Equity	1,109.2	1,095.8	1,070.9
Retained Earnings	349.4	221.7	98.7
Accumulated Translation Adjustment	(14.2)	(12.9)	(16.1)
Treasury Stock	(41.2)	(41.2)	0.0
Total Equity	**1,403.2**	**1,263.4**	**1,153.5**
Total Liabilities and Equity	**$2,728.5**	**$2,419.8**	**$2,286.3**

Exhibit 5   Duracell International Inc. Financial Statements (millions)

Source: Bloomberg.

in the joint venture, with Toshiba and Varta holding the remaining 40 per cent and 20 per cent, respectively. In fiscal 1995, Duracell continued its efforts to convince the leading manufacturers of portable computers and cellular telephones to design-in standardized nickel hydride rechargeable batteries as the power source for their devices. Duracell made its initial shipments of Duracell brand nickel metal hydride rechargeable batteries to original equipment manufacturers in fiscal 1993. Consumer sales of rechargeable batteries were initiated during fiscal 1994. Duracell planned to begin manufacturing lithium ion high power rechargeable batteries in the United States during fiscal 1997.

The market for these expensive rechargeable batteries was expected to grow from $2 billion in 1995 to $5 billion in 2000, because of battery use in cellular phones and laptop personal computers, along with personal communication systems (PCS) and personal digital assistants (PDA). And the number of cell phones and PCSs was expected to double, to 69.6 million by the year 2000. In addition, the number of laptops and PDAs could grow from 11.9 million to 32.9 million.

RATIONALE BEHIND THE ACQUISITION

Cost savings could be realized by eliminating duplicative functions. Gillette expected to realize $80 million to $120 million in cost savings over two years, reaching the full run rate in 1999. Additionally, Gillette believed it could achieve $25 million in savings by bringing Duracell's 39 per cent tax rate down to the 36.4 per cent Gillette corporate average.

As the most sophisticated and efficient consumer non-durable manufacturer, Gillette's number-one core competency was its world-class manufacturing. While Duracell was also good in this area, there was still room for improvement. For example, Gillette's manufacturing was

truly global, with worldwide supplier standards and movable parts. As such, it could optimize its capacity utilization on a worldwide basis and ensure better consistency and quality control. Duracell's manufacturing was still characterized as a multinational operation, without the flexibility to shift supply sources to meet demand. Gillette's long-time experience in building new plants in developing regions might also help Duracell in India and China, where the joint ventures had consistently missed deadlines due to operating and administrative challenges. Duracell's manufacturing process could benefit from Gillette's value-added engineering strategy.

The acquisition presented an opportunity for both companies to leverage each other's international sales channels. Duracell's main products, batteries, were homogeneous, small in size, easily distributed, and could be marketed across many different markets. The firm, therefore, had the potential to grow its market share outside the United States in conjunction with a worldwide marketing organization such as Gillette by using the partner's wide overseas network and strong foothold in developing markets. Duracell made less than half its sales outside the United States. In many big markets, such as Germany, Poland, India and Indonesia, Gillette had 10 times more sales than Duracell; as a result, it already had the warehousing and merchandising capabilities to expand Duracell's market quickly. In Brazil, for instance, Duracell had only the Sao Paulo and Rio de Janeiro areas, but Gillette had salespeople dealing with tiny stores in even the remote reaches of the Amazon.

Conversely, through Duracell, Gillette would gain access to outlets it was not as familiar with, such as home centers and toy stores. The acquisition would also allow Gillette to strengthen its already strong line of household products, diversify out of its traditional base in shaving products and take advantage of Duracell's high unit sales growth potential. Benefits were also anticipated from the use of complementary research and development in forming metal and

	Actual		Estimated					
	1994	**1995**	**1996**	**1997**	**1998**	**1999**	**2000**	**2001**
Sales Growth %								
Gillette	12.2	11.9	9.3	10.9	11.0	10.0	10.0	10.0
Duracell	9.3	10.6	13.7	12.7	12.1	11.4	10.9	10.7
Total	11.5	11.6	10.4	11.4	11.3	10.4	10.2	10.2
Gross Margins %								
Gillette	63.4	62.4	62.9	63.0	63.0	63.6	64.0	64.4
Duracell	65.2	64.1	62.3	62.0	63.0	63.5	64.0	64.2
Total	63.8	63.0	62.7	62.7	63.0	63.6	64.0	64.3
Operating Income Growth %								
Gillette	12.8	11.8	16.0	10.0	12.4	13.5	13.8	12.4
Duracell	15.6	11.6	11.0	29.7	28.4	20.5	15.5	11.1
Total	13.5	11.7	14.8	14.5	16.6	15.5	14.3	12.0
Shares Outstanding								
Total (millions)	553.1	554.3	556.0	544.9	531.3	518.0	505.0	492.4
% Change	0.3	0.2	0.3	−2.0	−2.5	−2.5	−2.5	−2.5
EPS	$1.65	$1.93	$2.22	$2.65	$3.18	$3.78	$4.45	$5.12
% Growth	17.4	16.4	15.2	19.3	20.0	19.0	17.7	15.2

Exhibit 6   The Gillette Company With Duracell International Inc. Common Year-End, December 30, Summary Financials

Source: Smith Barney, Inc.

plastics and machine engineering. As a result of this move, Gillette was likely to approach growth of 19 percentage points in annual earnings over the years leading up to 2001; see Exhibit 6.

THE DECISION

After reviewing the information he had collected on Gillette and Duracell, Green was unsure whether the business risks for the target and the acquirer were significantly different and whether it really mattered whose cost of capital he used in his calculations. Gillette and Duracell both produced small, inexpensive consumer products, and had similar debt levels and promising combined growth prospects.

The second difficulty concerned the specific methods and inputs he could use in the cost of capital calculations. Relevant financial markets data is presented in Exhibit 7. He could estimate the cost of equity using the Infinite Growth Model or the Capital Asset Pricing Model (CAPM). Estimating the cost of equity through the CAPM required decisions on the risk-free rate of the appropriate maturity and the expected

INTEREST RATES AS OF SEPTEMBER 12, 1996			
U.S. Treasury Bills		**U.S. Government Bond Yields**	
1-month	4.95%	2-year	6.33%
3-month	5.15%	5-year	6.69%
6-month	5.29%	7-year	6.83%
1-year	5.57%	10-year	6.88%
		30-year	7.11%

Source: Financial Post, September 13, 1996.

HISTORICAL MEAN ANNUAL RATES OF RETURN FOR THE PERIOD 1926-1996		
	Geometric Mean	**Arithmetic Mean**
Large Corporations Common Equity	10.7%	12.7%
Long-term Government	5.1	5.4
Intermediate-term Government	5.2	5.4
U.S. Treasury Bills	3.7	3.8

Source: Ibbotson Associates, Stocks, Bonds, Bills and Inflation.

Exhibit 7   Financial Markets Data

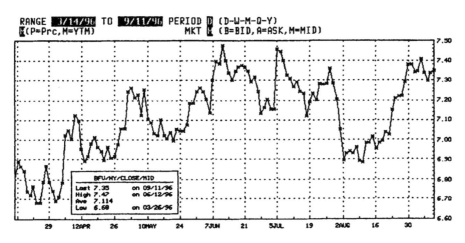

5.75 Per Cent Coupon 10-Year Bond's Credit Ratings:		The Gillette Company's Credit Rating:	
Moody	Aa3	Moody	Aa3
S&P	AA-		

Exhibit 8   The Gillette Company Yield on 5.75 Per Cent Coupon 10-Year Bond

Source: Bloomberg.

market risk premium. Exhibit 8 shows the yield on Gillette's 5.75 per cent-coupon 10-year bond. The flotation costs for raising additional debt and equity were estimated to be one per cent and three per cent, respectively. Duracell's reported[4] beta was 0.93.

As Donald Green reflected on all the issues involved in estimating the cost of capital for Duracell, he knew that Cromwell's client needed an evaluation of Gillette's response quickly.

NOTES

1. Source: Value Line Investment Survey; based on five years of weekly data.

2. Avon Products, Coca Cola, Colgate Palmolive, Gillette, McDonald's, Procter & Gamble, Rubbermaid, and Wm. Wrigley.

3. Gillette was one of the firms bidding for Duracell in 1988.

4. Source: Standard & Poor's Inc. Compustat Service; based on two years of weekly data.

FirstCaribbean: The Proposed Merger[1]

Prepared by Professor Stephen Sapp

    Version: (A) 2005-11-25

It was August 27, 2002, and John Midas, a new associate at Confederation Bank's Barbados office, was sitting in his office enjoying his morning coffee. As he was getting ready to check the state of international equity markets, his manager walked into his office to give him the offering circular for CIBC West Indies Holdings Limited (CIBC WI). It had arrived the previous day, and Midas was asked to read through the entire circular and prepare a report on the proposed deal for Confederation Bank's clients. Specifically, his manager wanted to know whether the Confederation Bank should advise its clients to accept shares in the new company, FirstCaribbean, in exchange for their shares in CIBC WI or whether they should sell their shares.

THE MERGER

Although it had been relatively well-known by investors that CIBC was negotiating with Barclays Bank PLC to merge their respective retail banking businesses in the Caribbean, investors were unclear of the status of the negotiations until the announcement was made on August 26. Investors appeared to believe that the merger was a smart strategic move for both firms. The Caribbean banking industry was undergoing structural change characterized by an increasing number of mergers and strategic alliances, which had been driven by the need for economies of scale and scope to take advantage of the growing local market and the increased globalization in the overall financial services industry.

As a result, it was believed that it would make sense for CIBC to combine its Caribbean operations with those of Barclays Bank PLC. Both organizations had a strong presence in the region but neither was large enough to take advantage of the growing market. For CIBC, it was consistent with the bank's overall goal to increase its involvement in the retail banking sector. For Barclays, it would help increase the efficiency of its operations in the region, a key factor it believed was necessary for any player to succeed in this market. A combination of these firms also made sense as they were both mid-size players in this market, but felt they needed to be larger to effectively compete in the growing Caribbean market. Between the two of them, they covered most of the English-speaking countries in the Caribbean.

Other banks located in the region, as well as banks from the United States, had been increasing their marketing efforts and therefore their presence, so CIBC and Barclays felt pressure to grow. The proposed merger was one of the most effective means of increasing their customer base, regional coverage and therefore increasing

their ability to sell financial products to a larger market. This merger would allow both banks to more directly compete with many of the new entrants into the market.

Despite the logic of the merger from a strategic perspective, Midas realized that a smart strategic deal must also be done under the right financial terms—"no deal" is better than "a deal at any price"—which was what his clients wanted him to evaluate. Its main priority was to make sure that the deal made sense for the clients as CIBC West Indies shareholders. The first step in the process was to wade through the significant offerings circular and pull out the most relevant financial data so that he could value each of

	2001	2000	1999	1998	1997
Assets					
Cash resources	$1,371,939	$924,815	$980,643	$406,513	$386,276
Securities	1,208,933	1,124,996	789,471	229,254	225,118
Loans	1,880,287	1,705,592	1,581,026	1,212,272	1,015,445
Acceptances	5,794	21,440	826	800	2,266
Net investment in leases	1,527	2,111	2,698	3,409	3,031
Property and equipment	69,057	61,714	60,201	37,588	31,141
Other assets	56,990	63,696	63,588	59,229	33,518
Total assets	$4,594,527	$3,904,364	$3,478,453	$1,949,065	$1,696,795
Liabilities and Shareholders' Equity					
Deposits	$4,095,869	$3,358,435	$3,008,184	$1,642,887	$1,447,889
Acceptances	5,794	21,440	826	800	2,266
Other liabilities	50,585	151,936	139,817	86,618	48,848
Minority interests	116,141	97,688	85,149	19,915	18,661
Common shares	158,190	158,190	158,190	137,490	137,490
Retained earnings	167,948	116,675	86,287	61,355	41,641
Total liabilities and shareholders' equity	$4,594,527	$3,904,364	$3,478,453	$1,949,065	$1,696,795

Exhibit 1   CIBC West Indies Holding Company, Five-year Statistical Review, Condensed Consolidated Balance Sheet for Years Ending October 31 (in US$000s)

Source: CIBC West Indies Holding Company Offering Circular, August 26, 2002, http://www.firstcaribbeanbank.com/WIHL-OFFERING.pdf.

	2001	2000	1999	1998	1997
Interest income	$300,655	$297,457	$248,767	$174,116	$158,589
Interest expense	(158,369)	(156,973)	(126,375)	(74,816)	(73,711)
Net interest income	142,286	140,484	122,392	99,300	84,878
Non-interest income	64,189	63,423	60,143	35,820	31,510
Total income	$206,475	$203,907	$182,535	$135,120	$116,388
Non-interest expenses	$109,260	$112,446	$105,201	$79,606	$68,084
Provision for credit losses	5,144	14,301	11,954	7,671	5,139
Total expenses	$114,404	$126,747	$117,155	$87,277	$73,223
Income Taxes	$4,308	$3,519	$2,014	$6,490	$7,614
Exceptional/extraordinary items	—	(1,085)	—	293	—
Minority interests	(19,959)	(14,851)	(14,768)	(3,845)	(2,282)
Net Income	$67,804	$58,790	$47,513	$37,508	$33,562

Exhibit 2   CIBC West Indies Holding Company, Five-year Statistical Review, Consolidated Statement of Income for Years Ending October 31 (in US$000s)

Source: CIBC West Indies Holding Company Offering Circular, August 26, 2002, http://www.firstcaribbeanbank.com/WIHL-OFFERING.pdf.

	2001	2000
Cash flows from operating activities		
Income before taxation and minority interests	$93,002	$77,940
Provision for credit losses	5,195	14,445
Depreciation and Amortization	11,671	8,965
Operating income before changes in operations	$109,868	$101,351
Increase in securities, net of disposal	(37,633)	(314,292)
Increase in loans and leases, net	(181,066)	(149,887)
(Decrease)/increase in other assets and liabilities	(59,792)	31,684
Increase in deposits, net of withdrawals	744,883	329,314
Cash generated from (used in) operating activities	$576,260	$(1,830)
Corporate taxes paid	(8,542)	(6,410)
Net cash from/(used in operating activities)	$567,717	$(8,240)
Cash flows used in financing activities		
Dividends paid	(30,899)	(24,719)
Net cash used in financing activities	(30,899)	(24,719)
Cash flows used in investing activities		
Purchase of subsidiaries	$(47,152)	$—
Increase in property, plant and equipment	(20,584)	(7,780)
Net cash used in investing activities	(67,735)	(7,780)
Effects of exchange rate changes on	(8,408)	(14,486)
Net increase/(decrease) in cash	460,675	(55,225)
Cash and cash equivalents beginning of period	934,118	989,343
Cash and cash equivalents end of period	1,394,793	934,118
Cash resources	1,385,796	934,157
Cheques and other items in transit	8,996	(38)
Cash and cash equivalents end of year	$1,394,793	$934,118

Exhibit 3   CIBC West Indies Holding Company, Consolidated Statement of Cash Flows

Source: CIBC West Indies Holding Company Offering Circular, August 26, 2002, http://www.firstcaribbeanbank.com/WIHL-OFFERING.pdf.

	2001	2000	1999	1998	1997
Profitability					
Return on equity	23.40%	23.30%	22.30%	19.50%	19.60%
Assets					
Net interest income on average assets	3.21%	3.70%	3.62%	5.48%	5.02%
Net income before minority interest return on assets	2.06%	1.96%	2.07%	2.28%	2.12%
Capital and Related					
Average common shareholders' equity	319,889	268,123	230,440	192,473	171,210
Average assets	4,426,634	3,745,300	3,377,496	1,810,761	1,689,642
Average assets to average common equity	13.80%	14.00%	14.70%	9.40%	9.90%
Regulatory total capital ratio	19.40%	17.70%	17.80%	18.20%	16.90%
Productivity and related					
Non-interest expenses to revenue ratio	52.90%	55.20%	58.20%	58.90%	58.50%
Full-time equivalent employees	1,676	1,666	1,679	1,577	1,411
Number of branches	43	43	40	38	32
Number of automated banking machines	49	45	38	36	34
Common Shares					
Average number outstanding	611,810	611,810	568,935	440,310	440,310
Earnings per share	0.11	0.10	0.08	0.85	0.76
Price close	1.63	1.48	1.83	2.00	1.10
Dividends per share[1]	0.03	0.05	0.04	0.04	0.04
Dividend yield	1.50%	3.10%	2.20%	2.00%	3.20%
Payout ratio[1]	22.50%	46.80%	44.30%	47.00%	45.90%
Price to earnings ratio	14.60	15.30	21.80	23.50	14.40
Book value	0.54	0.45	0.40	0.45	0.41
Price to book ratio	3.05	3.31	4.57	4.43	2.70

Exhibit 4   CIBC West Indies Holding Company, Key Ratios

Source: CIBC West Indies Holding Company Offering Circular, August 26, 2002, http://www.firstcaribbeanbank.com/WIHL-OFFERING.pdf.

1. For year 2001, the dividend is to be increased to $0.06 per share. These values do not reflect the change.

the entities separately. Using this information Midas hoped to be able to evaluate the terms of the proposed merger and how the synergies and cost-savings from the merger could be split among the CIBC WI shareholders and Barclays PLC shareholders.

Valuation

Midas knew that a variety of methods were available to value the shares of financial services firms. Although CIBC WI was publicly traded, he wanted to use a consistent method to value the

	Years to Maturity					
	Within 1	**1 to 5**	**5 to 10**	**10+**	**2001**	**2000**
SECURITIES						
Governments						
Treasury bills	$83,314	$—	$—	$—	$83,314	$95,693
Debentures	11,276	7,591	35,000	28,865	82,732	237,601
Debt securities	41,006	37,522	77,647	55,688	211,863	84,477
Other						
Debt securities	934,342	24,000	20,000	—	978,342	1,011,193
Equity securities	820,439	—	—	241,175	1,061,614	821,028
	$1,890,377	$69,113	$132,647	$325,728	$2,417,865	$2,249,992
Estimated market value					$2,551,309	$2,359,234
LOANS						
Mortgages	$62,437	$46,578	$173,293	$804,334	$1,086,642	$975,068
Personal loans	161,946	228,285	184,443	91,809	666,483	663,475
Business loans	852,269	509,687	450,277	154,939	1,967,172	1,767,434
Government securities						
Purchased	67,019	—	—	—	67,019	28,904
Agreements	$1,143,671	$784,550	$808,013	$1,051,082	$3,787,316	$3,434,881
Less: Allowance for credit losses					$(26,742)	$(23,697)
Estimated market value					$3,760,574	$3,411,184

Exhibit 5   CIBC West Indies Holding Company, Securities and Loans

Source: CIBC West Indies Holding Company Offering Circular, August 26, 2002, http://www.firstcaribbeanbank.com/WIHL-OFFERING.pdf.

equity for both firms since Barclays' operations were not part of a stand-alone firm. The most common methods for valuing financial services firms were the book value of the equity, a premium over the book value, pricing earnings (P/E) multiples and discounted cashflow techniques.

To perform this task, Midas looked through the offerings circular and found that it provided most of the necessary information for each of these companies (see Exhibits 1 to 9). To obtain information on comparable companies, Midas went to his Bloomberg terminal and pulled down information he thought may be useful on several Canadian, U.S. and international banks (see Exhibits 10 to 12). Midas started by focusing on the valuation of each of the companies separately. Subsequently, he knew that he would have to determine how the value of the combined

	2001	2000
Interest Income		
Loans	$343,895	$357,896
Securities	225,221	111,125
Lease financing	619	736
Other	31,574	125,157
	$601,309	$594,914
Non-interest Income		
Fees and commissions	$85,885	$91,080
Foreign exchange	30,489	34,213
Other	12,004	1,553
	$128,378	$126,846
Non-interest expenses		
Staff costs	$110,876	$114,694
Depreciation and amortisation	23,108	17,751
Property (excluding depreciation and amortization)	40,202	32,401
Other	44,333	60,045
	$218,519	$224,891

Exhibit 6   CIBC West Indies Holding Company, Interest and Non-interest Income and Non-interest Expenses

Source: CIBC West Indies Holding Company Offering Circular, August 26, 2002, http://www.firstcaribbeanbank.com/WIHL-OFFERING.pdf.

	2001	2000
ASSETS		
Cash and balances at Central Banks	$134,700	$108,450
Due from other banks	2,785,583	2,976,261
Investments	203,841	164,834
Loans and advances	1,969,628	2,119,213
Other assets	54,442	92,871
Property and equipment	51,532	55,101
Pension asset	40,337	43,958
Total assets	$5,240,063	$5,560,688
Liabilities and Shareholders' Equity		
Deposits	$5,029,332	$5,329,873
Other liabilities	90,347	126,280
	$5,119,679	$5,456,153
Head Office accounts:		
Share capital	$2,924	$2,924
Assigned capital	5,593	5,593
Reserve fund	10,347	8,671
Retained earnings	37,946	21,032
Due to head office	63,574	66,315
Total	120,384	104,535
Total Liabilities and Shareholders' Equity	5,240,063	5,560,688

Exhibit 7   Barclays Bank PLC, Combined Balance Sheet (in US$000s)

Source: CIBC West Indies Holding Company Offering Circular, August 26, 2002, http://www.firstcaribbeanbank.com/WIHL-OFFERING.pdf.

entity and its increased growth potential over that of either of the individual firms and the cost savings. Although Midas knew that there was no "right" valuation method, he felt it would be best to obtain several different estimates to evaluate these firms.

Midas started with a valuation method, which attempts to value a firm based on its growth potential. To estimate how investors value growth potential, Midas decided to apply a reasonable price-earnings (P/E) multiple to the current year's earnings per share. Because of the thin trading in CIBC WI shares and the lack of shares in Barclays' Caribbean operations, Midas considered both the price-earnings multiples for banks in Canada, the United States and the United Kingdom (see Exhibit 10). From Exhibit 4, he

	2001	2000
Interest Income		
Interest income	$334,118	$409,411
Interest expense	164,682	226,954
Net interest income	$169,436	$182,457
Other Income		
Commission income	$33,418	$36,401
Foreign exchange income	21,853	23,940
Rental and other income	1,626	1,535
	$56,897	$61,876
Total Income	$226,333	$244,333
Operating expenses		
Staff costs	$65,577	$64,574
Other operating expenses	34,404	30,091
Property and equipment expenses	18,093	19,067
Depreciation	8,242	8,377
Foreign exchange loss on translation of pension assets	1,893	3,735
	$128,209	$125,844
Charge for bad and doubtful debts	$15,353	$16,966
	$143,562	$142,810
Income before taxation	$82,771	$101,523
Taxation	$10,181	$10,275
Net income for the year	$72,590	$91,248

Exhibit 8 Barclays Bank PLC, Combined Statement of Income (in US$000s)

Source: CIBC West Indies Holding Company Offering Circular, August 26, 2002, http://www.firstcaribbeanbank.com/WIHL-OFFERING.pdf.

knew that CIBC WI's earnings per share for 2001 were $0.11[2] resulting from overall earnings for the firm of $67.8 million (see Exhibit 2) and thus a value for the firm of between $888 million and $1.400 million depending on whether the P/E multiple was used for Canadian banks or International banks. For Barclays Bank, the overall earnings for its Caribbean operations in 2001 was $72.6 million leading to a value for the firm of between $958 million and $1.510 million.

Another multiple that had been used in recent bank mergers and acquisitions was a premium over the book market of equity. As a result, Midas looked at the book value of the equity for both banks. For CIBC WI, he found the book value of equity was $326.1 million (see Exhibit 1) and $120.4 million (see Exhibit 7). Although Midas had some concerns about the calculation for Barclays' operations, he used the average price/book multiples to get values for the firms of between $597 million and $776 million for CIBC WI and $220 million and $286 million for Barclays Caribbean operations. Because of the disparity across these values, Midas also calculated valuations using the price to sales ratio and other ratios.

The final form of valuation Midas wanted to consider was the discounted cashflow (DCF) technique, which was the way that Midas was always told one should value a project—evaluate each firm as if one were valuing it as a capital investment decision. In this way he could compare the value obtained using his projections of the value that each firm would bring to the investors based on the present value of all future cash flows discounted at the appropriate discount rate to the values he just obtained using multiples. Although Midas realized that there were many short-comings of this method for valuing a financial services firm, he thought that it would allow an easier baseline to which to add the value of the potential synergies. Further, Midas remembered reading some recent research that the dividend discount model had worked remarkably well at pricing bank stocks in Canada over the past century.

To use a standard DCF valuation, Midas carefully considered what types of modifications he would have to make to the free cashflows because a bank makes its money from borrowing or lending. As a result he decided to focus on the free cashflows (FCFs) that would go to equity

	2001	2000
Cash flows from operating activities		
Income before taxation	$82,771	$101,523
Charge for bad and doubtful debts	15,353	16,966
Depreciation	8,242	8,377
Foreign exchange loss on translation of pension assets	1,893	3,735
Pension charge	1,728	337
Gain on disposal of property, plant and equipment	(80)	(729)
Operating income before changes in operating assets and liabilities	109,907	130,209
Decrease in due from other banks	190,678	64,046
Decrease (increase) in loans and advances	134,232	(273,345)
Decrease in other assets	38,429	8,547
Decrease in deposits, current accounts and other borrowings	(300,541)	(139,735)
Decrease in other liabilities and accruals	(26,850)	(13,778)
Net taxation paid	(12,620)	(12,487)
Net cash from (used in) operating	$133,235	$(236,543)
Cash flows from investing activities		
(Increase) decrease in investments	$(39,007)	$306,636
Purchase of property, plant and equipment	(5,201)	(5,280)
Proceeds of disposal of property, plant and equipment	608	2,240
Net cash (used in) from investing activities	$(43,600)	$303,596
Cash flows from financing activities		
Dividends paid	$(1,907)	$(4,381)
Remittance to Head Office	$(61,478)	$(58,427)
Net cash used in financing activities		
Net increase in cash and balances at Central Banks	$(63,385)	$(62,808)
Cash and balances at CB—beginning of year	26,250	4,245
Cash and balances at CB—end of year	108,450	104,205
	$134,700	$108,450

Exhibit 9   Barclays Bank PLC, Combined Statement of Cash Flows (in US$000s)

Source: CIBC West Indies Holding Company Offering Circular, August 26, 2002, http://www.firstcaribbeanbank.com/WIHL-OFFERING.pdf.

holders. The resulting FCFs that he decided upon are presented in Exhibit 14. The relationship he used to get these numbers was:

FCF = Net Income (profit after taxes) + Depreciation–Capex (change in fixed assets)

To do the valuation, Midas used the cost of equity for CIBC and Barclays to estimate the cost of equity for the investors in each of their Caribbean operations (see Exhibit 12). Making some assumptions about future growth in two stages, the next five years and from then onward, he obtained estimates for the value of

	P/E		Price/Book		Price/Sales	
	2001	**2000**	**2001**	**2000**	**2001**	**2000**
Canadian Banks						
Bank of Montreal	13.65	11.99	1.72	1.80	1.01	1.02
Bank of Nova Scotia	10.83	12.39	1.72	1.93	1.04	1.13
CIBC	10.75	12.35	1.85	1.92	13.96	—
Royal Bank	14.81	13.76	1.95	2.53	1.18	1.28
Toronto Dominion	15.76	13.28	1.90	2.35	1.08	1.30
U.S. Banks						
Bank of America	12.72	9.72	2.03	1.56	1.89	1.31
Citigroup	18.13	17.33	3.03	3.70	2.38	2.11
JP Morgan-Chase	22.03	15.35	1.79	2.15	1.42	1.45
International Banks						
Barclays	15.47	12.69	2.62	2.61	1.98	1.90
HSBC	21.70	19.40	2.36	2.99	2.24	2.58
Royal Bank of Scotland	24.73	17.58	2.15	2.22	2.09	1.57
UBS	21.32	13.68	2.39	2.51	1.26	1.31

	Return on Assets		Return on Common Equity		Earnings per Share	
Canadian Banks						
Bank of Montreal	0.59	0.76	13.99	17.94	2.72	3.31
Bank of Nova Scotia	0.77	0.76	17.15	17.45	2.06	1.84
CIBC	0.56	0.75	16.39	20.75	4.19	4.97
Royal Bank	0.70	0.76	16.47	19.36	3.55	3.53
Toronto Dominion	0.47	0.40	11.30	8.89	2.07	1.56
U.S. Banks						
Bank of America	1.07	1.18	14.14	16.34	2.72	3.31
Citigroup	1.43	1.58	19.44	22.18	2.79	2.69
JP Morgan-Chase	0.23	0.81	4.02	15.17	0.83	2.99
International Banks						
Barclays	0.73	0.87	17.68	22.82	0.37	0.41
HSBC	0.75	1.09	11.11	17.08	0.54	0.76
Royal Bank of Scotland	0.54	0.90	8.92	16.84	0.68	0.90
UBS	0.42	0.75	11.26	20.75	2.33	3.81

Exhibit 10   Ratios for Canadian, United States and International Banks, 2000 to 2001

Source: Bloomberg.

	Dividend Yield (past year)		Net Income		Dividend Payout	
	2001	2000	2001	2000	2001	2000
Canadian Banks						
Bank of Montreal	$4.05	$2.79	$1,471	$1,857	$41	$30
Bank of Nova Scotia	2.83	2.30	2,169	1,926	30.13	27.28
CIBC	2.95	2.67	1,686	2,060	34.25	25.93
Royal Bank	2.95	2.36	2,411	2,274	39.41	32.20
Toronto Dominion	3.03	2.19	1,383	1,025	52.57	59.03
U.S. Banks						
Bank of America	$2.63	$3.20	$9,249	$6,792	$53	$45
Citigroup	1.28	1.09	14,126	13,519	23.44	18.92
JP Morgan-Chase	2.23	1.32	1,694	5,727	165.21	41.80
International Banks						
Barclays	$2.98	$2.82	$2,446	$2,473	$45	$37
HSBC	4.52	2.60	4,992	6,613	89.48	60.50
Royal Bank of Scotland	2.29	0.67	2,625	2,169	58.81	47.92
UBS	2.05	3.78	2,947	—	—	22.64

	Market Value of Equity		Number of Shares Outstanding		Book Value of Equity (per share)	
Canadian Banks						
Bank of Montreal	$16,560	$18,421	508	522	$20	$20
Bank of Nova Scotia	22,091	21,661	1,004	993	13	11
CIBC	17,731	18,254	373	390	26	25
Royal Bank	31,544	29,096	683	602	24	19
Toronto Dominion	22,587	26,119	628	622	19	18
U.S. Banks						
Bank of America	$98,158	$74,025	3,147	3,255	$16	$15
Citigroup	241,742	238,526	5,145	5,033	15	13
JP Morgan-Chase	71,733	87,626	1,973	160	20	21
International Banks						
Barclays	$37,947	$34,437	6,628	6,628	$2	$2
HSBC	109,644	136,363	9,332	9,229	5	5
Royal Bank of Scotland	47,811	42,370	2,849	2,671	8	7
UBS	62,630	69,766	1,264	1,273	21	—

Exhibit 11   Dividend Yield, Income and Payout for Canadian, U.S. and International Banks, 2000 to 2001

Source: Bloomberg.

	Cost of Debt	Cost of Preferred	Cost of Equity	WACC
Canadian Banks				
Bank of Montreal	2.28	8.67	8.33	4.75
Bank of Nova Scotia	2.83	4.00	8.50	5.70
CIBC	1.34	4.55	8.73	4.44
Royal Bank	2.25	3.71	7.99	4.72
Toronto Dominion	2.76	5.95	8.67	5.62
U.S. Banks				
Bank of America	2.82	7.01	8.12	4.33
Citigroup	2.99	6.04	9.24	4.66
JP Morgan-Chase	3.12	24.46	9.80	4.70
International Banks				
Barclays	4.22	—	10.20	4.83
HSBC	3.51	—	9.12	5.54
Royal Bank of Scotland	3.13	5.66	10.02	4.53
UBS	1.22	—	10.27	2.13

Exhibit 12   Cost of Capital Calculations for Canadian, U.S. and International Banks, 2001

Source: Bloomberg.

WACC = Weighted Average Cost of Capital

the equity for both firms of $1.513 million and $1.145 million for CIBC WI and Barclays operations respectively (see Exhibit 13). Using just the dividends (they are the actual value that the equity holders would receive), Midas estimated the values in Exhibit 14 and valued the equity for the firms at $777 million and $654 million respectively.

Because of the sensitivity of these values to the many assumptions he was required to make, Midas considered what factors could impact the ability of the operations from each bank to maintain the cashflows estimated in Exhibits 13 and 14. He was especially concerned about the values from Barclays where there was such high variability in the free cashflows and the dividend payments (assuming the remittances to head office are a form of dividend) are so large relative to the net income.

THE DECISION

Although the offering circular provided pro forma financial statements for the merged entity, Midas did not know how to allocate them to the firms. Since the firm sizes based on the number of employees and total assets were similar, Midas decided to simply split the value of the synergies and cost savings on a pro rata basis. That just left the final stage of the analysis—to determine whether the existing offer was a good investment for his clients who currently held shares in CIBC WI.

Specifically, were the terms of the deal where the owners of Barclays and the owners of CIBC WI obtain equal ownership in the new entity, FirstCaribbean, fair for the owners of CIBC WI stock? When Midas's manager was leaving his office she said that she wanted a preliminary

			Forecasts					
	2000	2001	2002	2003	2004	2005	2006	Terminal value
CIBC WI								
Net Income	58,790	67,804						
Depreciation and Amortization	8,965	11,671						
Capital Expenditures	1,621	637						
Free Cashflow	66,134	78,838	83,568	88,582	93,897	99,531	105,503	1,896,470
Present Value			76,858	74,928	73,047	71,213	69,425	1,147,756
Actual Growth Rate 2000-2001		19.20%						
Projected Growth Rate '02-'06		6.00%						
Terminal Growth Rate		3.00%						
Cost of Equity	8.70%							
Equity Value	1,513,228							

			Forecasts					
	2000	2001		2003	2004	2005	2006	Terminal value
BARCLAYS								
Net Income	91,248	72,590						
Depreciation and Amortization	8,377	8,242						
Capital Expenditures	5,280	5,201						
Free Cashflow	94,345	75,631	80,169	84,979	90,078	95,482	101,211	1,447,884
Present Value			72,749	69,976	67,309	64,744	62,276	808,434
Actual Growth Rate 2000-2001		−19.80%						
Projected Growth Rate '02-'06		6.00%						
Terminal Growth Rate		3.00%						
Cost of Equity	10.20%							
Equity Value	1,145,487							

Exhibit 13 Forecasted Free Cashflows

Source: Casewriter's estimates.

			Forecasts					
	2000	2001	2002	2003	2004	2005	2006	Terminal value
CIBC WI								
Dividends	24,719	30,899	34,761	39,107	43,995	49,494	55,681	1,000,898
Present Value			31,970	33,079	34,226	35,413	36,640	605,750
Actual Growth Rate 2000-2001		25.00%						
Projected Growth Rate '02-'06		12.50%						
Terminal Growth Rate		3.00%						
Cost of Equity	8.70%							
Equity Value (000s)	$777,078							

			Forecasts					
	2000	2001	2002	2003	2004	2005	2006	Terminal value
BARCLAYS								
Dividends	62,808	63,385	64,019	64,659	65,306	65,959	66,618	731,353
Present Value			58,093	53,243	48,798	44,725	40,991	408,354
Actual Growth Rate 2000-2001		0.90%						
Projected Growth Rate '02-'06		1.00%						
Terminal Growth Rate		1.00%						
Cost of Equity	10.20%							
Equity Value (000s)	$654,205							

Exhibit 14   Forecasted Dividend Payments

Source: Casewriter's estimates.

discussion of the value of this proposal on her desk the next morning and it was already getting late.

NOTES

1. This case has been written on the basis of published sources only. Consequently, the interpretation and perspectives presented in this case are not necessarily those of CIBC and Barclays Bank PLC or any of its employees.

2. All currencies in US$ unless otherwise specified.

4

M&A Approach
and Structuring

Once a deal passes the initial screens of strategic fit and valuation, the buyer needs to decide how to approach the target entity. In an acquisition and in certain types of mergers, the approach involves methods of gaining control of the target entity. The three basic ways to gain control of a firm are by controlling its assets, stock, or board of directors. In a negotiated deal, a buyer can gain control of the assets of the firm by way of a negotiated agreement with the seller. A buyer can gain control of the stock of a firm with or without the participation of the selling firm by way of a tender offer directly to the selling firm's stockholders. Finally, a buyer may use a proxy to gain board seats on a target's board of directors and have its slate of directors elected. Using any one or a combination of these three basic approaches, a buyer can gain control of a target entity, although certainly the level of cooperation of the target firm's board and management will vary by approach.

This chapter deals more specifically with the negotiated deal approach, although the structuring considerations are relevant to any type of deal. After an approach is chosen, although typically before the deal price itself is negotiated, the bankers, lawyers, and accountants need to consider the deal structure or structures that may be most suitable. Three key decisions to be made concern the legal, accounting, and tax structures of the deal. These decisions are made to maximize the benefits from the deal and to minimize negative consequences of the deal by considering how to, for example, minimize the taxes due, limit any undue legal liability, remove potential obstacles to deal closure, and send appropriate signals about which entity will remain. Based on the deal structuring decisions, various types of consideration and consideration structures can be used to pay the sellers for their stakes. Finally, buyers must decide how they will finance the purchase, as there are many ways to raise the necessary consideration. These decisions are fairly technical and are affected by ongoing changes to generally accepted accounting principles (GAAP), tax codes, and laws and so typically require the expertise of specialized bankers, lawyers, and accountants.

DEAL LEGAL STRUCTURE

There are numerous legal structures that a potential deal may take, and we cannot cover them all here, nor can we cover any of them in detail. The structure chosen depends on several strategic and financial choices, including whether control is desired, which entity or entities are intended to survive, and what is for sale (e.g., assets, the firm, the stock, parts of the firm). When a firm wishes only to take a stake in another firm, a minority (< 50%) investment is made. When a new jointly held, jointly managed entity is sought, a joint venture may be created where both parties contribute some assets, cash, or both. More standard mergers and acquisitions (M&A) oftentimes take the form of different types of mergers or acquisitions. Several of the more common forms are detailed here.

Forward Merger

This is the typical legal structure of a deal. The acquirer is the buying and surviving entity. It buys and subsumes the target into its own legal structure, although it is also possible that the target is left as a wholly owned but separate legal entity. Many options are then possible, including that the subsidiary may have its own publicly traded tracking stock, a different class of the parent stock to separately recognize the performance of the subsidiary.

Reverse Merger

Another structure is the reverse merger, in which the acquirer is the larger party but the smaller target is the surviving entity. The acquirer merges itself into the smaller target but then owns a majority of the surviving entity. Some firms do this as a way to immediately go public into an already public target entity, oftentimes a "shell" company that is a fully legal entity with no real operations.

Merger of Equals

These are transactions in which neither party truly relinquishes control, and the pro forma entity is jointly owned and run. Ownership of both parties typically ranges from 45% to 55% and is set to reflect the relative contribution of the two parties. Often, an exchange ratio is set that determines the number of shares of each firm that are equal to those of the other firm. These deals may allow a firm to realize synergies and to increase scale without having to pay a high acquisition premium to a target. Certain tax advantages may also exist.

Triangular Merger

These deals involve three parties: an acquirer, a target, and an acquisition subsidiary. Within the triangular mergers, there are both forward triangular deals, in which the subsidiary survives, and reverse triangular deals, in which the target survives. The acquisition subsidiary may be set up in a particular locale to facilitate the acquisition and keep the assets and liabilities separate from the target.

Asset Purchase

In these deals, the acquirer buys only the assets of the target and not the liabilities. The target uses the proceeds from the sale of its asset to first satisfy the claims of its creditors, then distributes the rest to its stockholders. These deals are commonly used when the acquirer does not want to assume ownership of potential legal claims of an entity, or perhaps as a mechanism to remove a union from an operation (this is legal in some jurisdictions and not in others), since employees may or may not be part of an asset deal, depending on the jurisdiction.

Stock Purchase

The acquirer buys the stock of the target and thus owns some portion of the entity, including both its assets and liabilities, in relation to the percentage of stock purchases.

Deal Accounting Structure

The possible accounting structures for a deal depend on the tax jurisdictions in which the entities exist. Two basic accounting methods for acquisitions are the pooling and purchase methods. The pooling method is an advantageous (to firms and owners) method that was popular in the United States but was made inaccessible by several accounting board decisions over the 1999–2001 timeframe. However, it still exists in various forms around the world, including those countries that use the International Accounting Standards (IAS). Its rules allow for a "uniting of interests" method that is similar to a merger of equals. Under pooling, the carrying amounts on the books of the firms are carried forward (they do not become realized or taxable), the two entities basically combine their financial statements as if they had always been a single firm, and there is no goodwill to be recognized. Very basically, goodwill is the price paid for a set of assets that exceeds the cost. Using the purchase method of accounting, the amount that the price paid exceeds the cost is called goodwill and may have tax consequences for the target party that gained, and thus it is written off on the books of the acquirer. There are complex and important allowable periods of time over which the underlying assets become "impaired" and thus over which the write-downs may occur. Importantly, these write-downs affect the earnings and taxes of the acquirers.

A second, albeit related, set of accounting considerations involves how the acquiring party accounts for the investment on its own books. Generally, the treatment varies based on the percentage of the target entity that is held. Noninfluence investments (0%–20%) use what is called a *cost method* that treats the investment as an asset on the balance sheet, applying the lower of the cost or the then current market value. Gains and losses from the sale of these securities are only shown on the income statement when realized. Stakes that allow influence, but not control (20%–50%), use what is called the *equity method* of accounting. With this, the stake is shown on the balance sheet at the cost of the investment plus the share of the target's net income, less any dividends received since the purchase. The "owned" share of the target's net income is recognized on the acquirer's income statement as earned. When a controlling stake (> 50%) exists, the assets and liabilities of the target are reflected on the balance sheet of the acquirer, except that minority interest, if any, in the target's net assets is shown in the equity portion of the balance sheet, typically called *minority interests*. The revenue and expenses of the target are fully included in the acquirer's income statement, except that a minority interest, if any, in the target's net income is shown as a subtraction from the acquirer's net income. While the reporting and tax rules differ by jurisdiction and will surely change over time, it is important to recognize that these choices will affect the financial statements.

DEAL TAX STRUCTURE

The legal and accounting structures used, as well as certain tax elections and judgments made by the tax authorities, can have tax consequences for the parties to a deal. The details of the tax consequences of each method are beyond the scope of this text, but a few key concepts are important. The most basic intention of the choice of structures is to minimize taxes or to defer such payment until later. One critical impact of the tax choice involves whether the acquirer will inherit the target's basis or will be adjusted to reflect the purchase price. The difference in basis is critical to the amount of capital gains taxes due. Another question concerns whether the sellers can defer their gain or be forced to recognize a gain and, if so, how it will be calculated (what is the basis, and at what level(s) is tax applied) and whether the gain will be treated as a capital or ordinary gain. Finally, the structures chosen may affect the future tax liability of the entity based on the transferability of net operating losses under different structures.

CONSIDERATION

The acquirer must offer some type of consideration in exchange for the stock or assets received. The choice of consideration is a function of what is available to the acquirer (e.g., some acquirers may not have enough cash readily available), what the target is willing to accept, and what the intentions for the deal may be. As well, the choice of consideration has an impact on the tax, legal, and accounting mechanisms and so is important. The basic choices are cash, stock, notes (any form of debt), earnouts, and potentially other types, such as assets, but this is less common. While cash is easily valued, stock may not be, and so the use of stock may require a value premium be paid. Certain stock may not be as liquid as a target may hope, and so, again, a premium may need to be paid to compensate for the illiquidity. However, the receipt of cash is typically a taxable event for a seller, whereas the receipt of stock may not be. As such, receiving stock may allow a seller to defer taxes, perhaps indefinitely. Earnouts are a mechanism whereby the acquirer agrees to pay the target or, more commonly, its managers additional consideration based on certain performance measures over time. This is a tool used to both retain managers and to ensure that the target performs at or above the promised level to receive the fully negotiated price.

FINANCING THE DEAL

How do acquirers pay for mergers? Obviously, this depends on the type of consideration chosen. For a stock deal, the acquirer simply needs to go through its requisite approvals to issue more stock. If the consideration is a note, the firm is merely agreeing to pay the target some amount at some later date. The acquirer must therefore integrate this future cash need into its strategic and financial operating plans going forward. Earnouts are much the same. At some point in the future, the acquirer is likely to be required to pay some additional amounts based on the performance of the entity. However, those future amounts may be either stock or cash. If the purchase consideration is cash, however, the acquirer may not simply have sufficient cash readily available. As such, an acquiring firm may choose to raise general proceeds by conducting a follow-on stock offering whereby it offers newly issued shares into the market and raises cash. It may also choose some sort of debt or convertible debenture-type of instrument or use some unused credit facility to raise the cash. These methods are all useful when the firm raises cash on its own accord, with plans to use it for a deal. Firm also may raise cash with a specific deal in mind and may in fact pledge the cash flows or assets of the target to raise the cash. These deals may be leveraged buyouts in which the acquirer actually highly leverages the target's cash flows. A final common cash source is what is called *acquisition financing*. Oftentimes, investment banks or investment funds will provide temporary access to capital that is used to conduct the transaction with the expectation that the acquirer will recapitalize the purchase or raise other funds later to pay off these interim sources. Of course, experienced acquirers with successful track records have more options available to them and at more favorable terms. Suffice it to say, firms considering M&A may have many sources of capital available to them, despite the fact that so many deals continue to fail.

CASES

Bluewater Foods Corporation

The chief financial officer of Bluewater Foods Corporation has just returned from a meeting with management of County Chickens Ltd., Bluewater's largest supplier of chicken breast meat and current acquisition target. The chief financial officer must put together a recommendation as to how a purchase of County might be structured and how it would affect Bluewater's financial statement.

Issues: Accounting methods, deal structuring

Merger of NOVA Corporation and TransCanada Pipelines Limited

Several large Canadian public companies announced their intent to merge and use the "pooling of interests" method rather than the traditional "purchase method." Pooling had been rarely used to account for business combinations in Canada. The case focus is on an analyst who wanted to ensure that she understood the differential impact of both methods so that she could more fully represent her clients' interests. She decided to use an analysis of the recent merger of TransCanada Pipelines and NOVA Corporation to help her better understand and evaluate the two alternative accounting methods and their impact on the financial statements.

Issues: Financial reporting and disclosure, accounting principles, financial analysis

Accounting for Acquisitions at JDS Uniphase Corporation

JDS Uniphase Corporation is a high-technology company that designs and manufactures fiber-optic components for the telecommunications and cable television industries. The company announces a record-high year-end loss; it attributes the losses primarily to the write-down of goodwill. Using accounting for acquisitions and goodwill, the company must reassess the value of its past acquisitions.

Issues: Accounting methods, valuation, assets

BLUEWATER FOODS CORPORATION

Prepared by Janet Carter under the supervision of Professor Mary Heisz

Version: (A) 2005-02-17

Andrea Carson, the chief financial officer (CFO) of Bluewater Foods Corporation (Bluewater), a publicly traded company, placed her briefcase and laptop on her desk and poured herself a large cup of coffee. She had just returned from a meeting with management of County Chickens Ltd. (County), Bluewater's largest supplier of chicken breast meat and current acquisition target. Carson was to put together a recommendation as to how a purchase of County might be structured and how it would affect Bluewater's financial statements. The recommendation had to be ready in time for the next negotiation session tomorrow morning.

THE CHICKEN INDUSTRY

Canada was one of the top 10 producers, importers and exporters of chicken in the world. The $1.3 billion industry employed over 20,000 people on chicken farms and in processing plants across Canada and supported many spin-off jobs in trucking, hatcheries, feed mills, equipment manufacturing, food service and retail.

The chicken industry was one of several farm products industries in Canada where supply was managed through a marketing agency in order to control production and prices. The Chicken Farmers of Canada (CFC), formed in December of 1978, was a farmer-run organization that represented over 2,800 chicken farmers and approved processors. CFC was primarily in place to protect the producer by guaranteeing a price for 12 months. The organization set chicken prices for producers and processors, considering current inventory levels and the effects of imports and exports, thereby protecting those in the chicken industry from the effects of price volatility.

Through the use of a quota system, the CFC also controlled who was allowed to produce and process chicken in Canada. The CFC allocated quota to provincial boards, which then sold the quota to chicken producers in their respective provinces. Chicken producers, in turn, were able to sell their excess quota to other chicken producers on the open market. In Ontario in 2004, one unit of quota represented a right to produce 27 pounds of chicken per year and was worth approximately $52 to $54. Since quotas were expensive to obtain and were mandatory, they provided a high barrier to entry in the industry.

The chicken industry was highly vertically integrated with many processors owning large stakes in chicken farms and other smaller processors. This integration was often needed to ensure future supply, given that there were no long-term supply agreements in the industry. Good working relationships and ownership were often the only means to ensure consistent supply in the future.

BLUEWATER FOODS CORPORATION

Bluewater Foods Corporation was one of Canada's largest producers of quality food products and a chicken processor approved by the CFC. The company produced more than 1,500 products, including hot dogs, deli meat, sausage, bacon, chicken and breaded chicken strips. These products were sold throughout Canada and the United States under the Bluewater brand through retail stores, restaurants and delicatessens. As a result of continued strategic growth and a continually increasing portfolio of products, Bluewater had become one of the leading food production companies in the North American market. In 2003, Bluewater received

ASSETS	
Current Assets	
Cash and cash equivalents	$22,256
Accounts receivable	139,124
Inventory	127,158
Other current assets	30,731
	319,269
Property, plant and equipment	302,771
Investments	104,565
Goodwill	83,907
	491,243
Total assets	$810,512
LIABILITIES	
Current Liabilities	
Bank advances	$33,113
Accounts payable and accrued liabilities	117,506
Current portion of long-term debt	51,414
	202,033
Long-term debt	241,505
Other long-term liabilities	88,067
Total liabilities	531,605
Minority Interest	38,771
SHAREHOLDERS' EQUITY	
Share capital	52,895
Retained earnings	187,241
	240,136
Total liabilities and shareholders' equity	$810,512

Exhibit 1   Bluewater Foods Corporation, Consolidated Balance Sheet, (as at July 31, 2004) ($000s)

Source: Company Annual Report.

over 80 per cent of its breast meat supply from County. Without County's sure supply of chicken breast meat, Bluewater would have to obtain supply from other competitors in the industry, which would be difficult, if not impossible.

Note 6: Debentures and Loans	
Bankers' acceptances	$22,400
8% Debentures, maturing November 2019	97,545
5.25% to 10%, Term loans, maturing up to January 2017	55,241
7.5% Loan payable, April 2016	43,497
9.85% Sinking fund debentures, maturing September 2011	23,849
4.65% to 9.5%, Capital lease obligations, maturing up to May 2007	18,216
8.81% Sinking fund debentures, maturing September 2003	13,074
Other	19,098
	292,919
Principal included in current liabilities	51,414
	$241,505

Exhibit 2   Bluewater Foods Corporation, Excerpts from Notes to Financial Statement (2004) ($000s)

Source: Company Annual Report.

Note: The debentures are secured with property, plant, and equipment and a floating charge against all other accounts receivable and inventory. The Corporation is required to maintain equity of $200 million. In addition, the Corporation is required to maintain certain financial ratios, including debt to equity of under 2.5:1.[1]

1. Per the Corporation's bank agreement, debt is defined as total liabilities including minority interest divided by total equity.

Although highly leveraged, Bluewater had an impressive financial position. In 2004, the company had sales of over $1.8 billion, a positive cash flow from operations and a net income of $150 million. Despite this strong financial position, the company was restricted by several debt covenants by its bankers, including maintaining certain financial ratios. Exhibits 1 and 2 include excerpts from Bluewater's financial statements.

COUNTY CHICKEN LTD.

County Chicken Ltd. operated out of Brantford, Ontario, and was an exclusive processor of premium chicken. County was a privately owned, fully integrated processor. The company supplied chicken feed from its feedmill operation and converted chicken manure into fertilizer for its crop production. Like Bluewater, County was approved by the CFC and supplied the retail and food service industries. Three individuals each owned 23 per cent of the company, and approximately 40 individuals owned the remaining 31 per cent of the company.

In 2003, County was one of the largest holders of chicken quota in the industry, owning quota to produce 24 million pounds of chicken. The quota was purchased at the company's inception for $6 million. County had fully depreciated its quota on a straight line basis over a six-year period, due to speculation that the quota system would be eliminated and, as a result, quotas would have no book value. In fact, since County's purchase of quota, the opposite had occurred, with the quotas gaining value. Based on current market prices for quotas, County's quotas were worth over $46 million. As of 2004, there was no indication that the quota system of supply management would be terminated in the near future. Exhibits 3 and 4 include excerpts from County's financial statements.

Like Bluewater, County was a highly leveraged company. In addition to debt in the form of a demand loan from the bank, County also had non-retractable preference shares that were classified as debt due to their dividend payment terms. The large amount of debt on the balance sheet meant that obtaining any additional financing from the bank without a guarantor was out of the question. For this reason, County was interested in restructuring its balance sheet through changes to equity.

In addition to finding additional financing, County's management wanted to ensure that the company was kept intact. County's management was concerned that although the company

ASSETS	
Current Assets	
Accounts receivable	$13,583
Inventory	39,587
Other current assets	1,473
Total current assets	54,643
Property, plant and equipment	42,596
Other long term assets	62,792
Quota	—
	105,388
Total assets	$160,031
LIABILITIES	
Current Liabilities	
Bank indebtedness	$19,286
Accounts payable and accrued liabilities	15,111
Current portion of long-term debt	8,373
	42,770
Long-term debt	55,488
Other long-term liabilities	25,213
Total liabilities	123,471
SHAREHOLDERS' EQUITY	
Share capital	6,170
Retained earnings	30,390
	36,560
Total liabilities and shareholders' equity	$160,031

Exhibit 3　County Chicken Ltd., Consolidated Balance Sheet (as at July 31, 2004) ($000s)

Source: Company Annual Report.

was an attractive takeover target, it may be more attractive in pieces rather than as a whole. If acquired, County's management preferred that the acquirer be a company with which County had a strong history and an ongoing positive relationship. Bluewater was one of County's largest

Note 4: Other Assets			
	Cost	Accumulated Amortization	Net Book Value
Goodwill	$2,772	$402	$2,370
Quota	6,000	6,000	—
Deferred restructuring costs	180	68	112
Other	295	186	109
	$9,247	$6,656	$2,591

Exhibit 4   County Chicken Ltd., Notes to
Financial Statements
(2004) ($000s)

Source: Company Annual Report.

Note: The company holds 888,889 kilograms of
commercial chicken quota. Each quota has a fair market
value of $52.

customers and their business would be difficult,
but not impossible, to replace.

THE ACQUISITION

Bluewater's management approached County in
the fall of 2003 with the idea of acquiring
between 40 per cent and 60 per cent of County's
equity. County was receptive to this idea
since both the equity infusion and the possibility
for additional long-term debt financing from
Bluewater would allow the company to restructure its balance sheet, provide much needed
cash and help to meet current bank covenants.
Carson knew that a major food processing company, also a customer of County and a competitor of Bluewater, had also expressed an interest
in acquiring County.

The valuation of the business was based on
a multiple of earnings before interest, taxes,
depreciation and amortization (EBITDA). At the

outset, Bluewater was interested in paying
County a maximum multiple of three times
EBITDA as they argued that County's recognition was limited to Ontario with no national
brand recognition. At the same time, County's
management, with the help of a financial consultant, put together a valuation analysis of
their business. (See Exhibit 5 for excerpts
from the valuation analysis.) County's valuation
supported a multiple of approximately seven
times EBITDA, with chicken production assets
valued at over $106 million. County also felt
that the stability of the chicken industry with
its steady production and prices posed an additional argument for a higher multiple.

Land	$8,609
Quota	46,222
Working capital	20,250
Office	4,200
Compost facilities	1,800
Buildings	11,850
Equipment	9,300
Mill	4,200
County Chicken assets at fair value	$106,431

Exhibit 5   County Chicken Ltd., Valuation
Analysis based on Market Values
(as at July 31, 2004) ($000s)

Source: Company Purchase Agreement.

The current proposal was for Bluewater to
purchase 49 per cent of the common shares
for $27 million. In addition, the agreement
provided the opportunity for County common
shareholders to sell their remaining 51 per cent
ownership to Bluewater over a three-year
period at a price of $49 per share. At July 31,
2004, there were 1,307,971 common shares
outstanding in County. Carson knew that the
$49 price for the remaining common shares was

likely an attractive price and, therefore, Bluewater may eventually own 100 per cent of the company. Regardless, Carson was confident that 49 per cent ownership would be sufficient to allow Bluewater to effectively manage County and to ensure the continued supply of chicken. She wondered whether Bluewater should attempt to immediately purchase 51 per cent of the company in order to guarantee its controlling position. Carson was unsure of what the premium would be, if any, for a controlling position.

If the acquisition went through at 49 per cent, the new County board would consist of three people: the current president of Bluewater, the current president of County and one of County's current majority shareholders. Although, in form, this composition suggested County would control the board, Carson realized that there was some debate over how the current president of County would vote. On the one hand, the County president may feel some ongoing loyalty to County's original shareholders; on the other hand, he may feel an allegiance to Bluewater, as the likely future controlling shareholder and his boss.

As Carson sat at her desk, she wondered how this acquisition would benefit Bluewater and what impact it would have on the company's financial position going forward. She finished her coffee and started up her laptop to begin her analysis.

MERGER OF NOVA CORPORATION AND TRANSCANADA PIPELINES LIMITED

Prepared by Jacqui Murphy
under the supervision of Professor Claude Lanfranconi

Version: (A) 2001-04-03

INTRODUCTION

On Friday, October 2, 1998, Bev McCune, an oil and gas pipeline investment analyst, sat down to review the NOVA Corporation (NOVA) and TransCanada Pipelines Limited (TransCanada) merger. In January, when the companies had first announced their intent to merge, she had briefly questioned in her mind their use of the pooling of interests (pooling) method rather than the standard purchase method to account for the merger. At that time, McCune had wanted to make sure that she would be able to evaluate the return that her clients were getting on the investment and be able to compare the merged company to its competitors. She had put her concerns aside and decided not to do a lot of immediate substantive analysis because of her other more pressing deadlines. Since July, she had been very busy due to the decline of oil and gas prices and the significant decrease in the value of the entire market (see Exhibits 1 to 3 for charts of values over the past year).

A controversial statement made by Arthur Levitt, the Securities and Exchange Commission Chairman, had prompted her current review of the method that was used to account for the merger. He had said:

> Increasingly, I have become concerned that the motivation to meet Wall Street earnings expectations may be overriding common sense business practices. Too many corporate managers, auditors, and analysts are participants in a game of nods and winks. In the zeal to satisfy consensus earnings estimates and project a smooth earnings path, wishful thinking may be winning the day over faithful representation.[1]

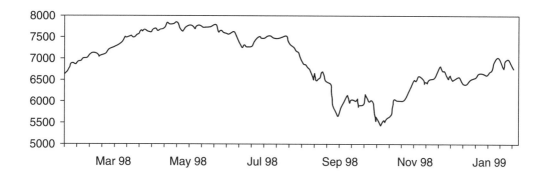

Exhibit 1   Toronto Composite 300 Index

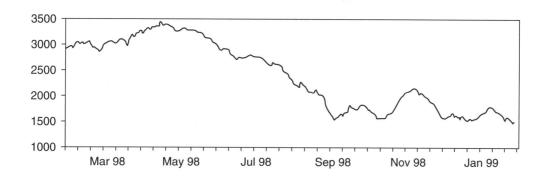

Exhibit 2   Toronto Oil & Gas Service

He had specifically mentioned "creative acquisition accounting" as one of the accounting practices that was problematic.

Also, in reviewing an issue of *Accounting Horizons*, McCune had read a commentary written by Robert C. Lipe, who worked as Academic Accounting Fellow in the Office of the Chief Accountant (OCA) in the U.S. Securities and Exchange Commission (SEC). He had mentioned that "the OCA team responsible for business combination issues (referred to as the 'pooling' team) meets twice per week on a regular basis due to the large volume of mergers in which registrants want to use the pooling-of-interest method."[2] He had also written that he believed that these "meetings are likely to continue until either U.S. GAAP is modified to eliminate pooling-of-interest accounting or the

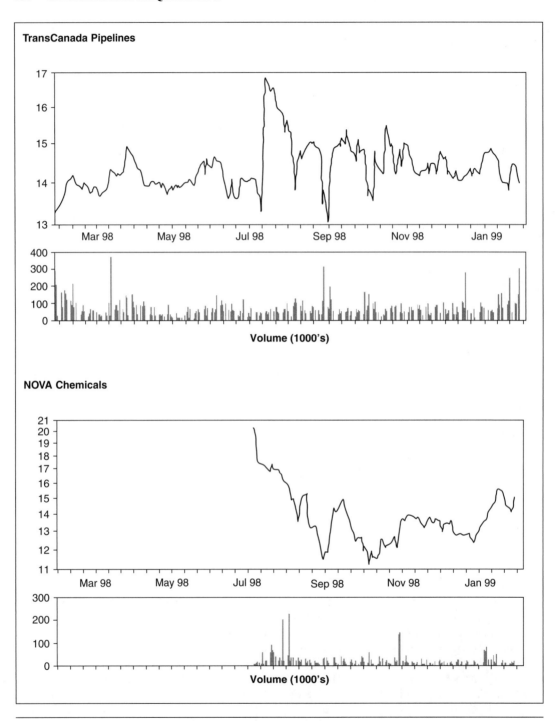

Exhibit 3   Charts of Share Values Over the Past Year (US dollars)

merger boom ends, neither of which appears likely in the near future."[3] McCune wanted to determine in her own mind whether or not the NOVA/TransCanada merger had been appropriately measured and reflected on the company's financial statements.

McCune decided that it was time for her to review her understanding of the different methods of accounting for mergers. Besides NOVA and TransCanada, other companies were indicating the use of the controversial pooling method and to fully represent her clients' interests, she needed to understand the differences. She had learned the methods in university, but it had been awhile since she had had to actually use the information. The NOVA/TransCanada merger was a good opportunity for her to relearn the methods of accounting for mergers and determine the impact that the different methods would have on the consolidated financial statements and her analysis.

McCune had been collecting information related to the merger since it had been announced on January 26, 1998. These materials included: The "Joint Management Information Circular with Respect to an Arrangement Involving NOVA Corporation and TransCanada Pipelines Limited"; The CICA Handbook—Section 1580 (Business Combinations); a book called "Financial Reporting in Canada 1998" which surveyed the annual reports of 200 Canadian public companies; and various newspaper articles discussing the merger.

OVERVIEW OF THE TWO COMPANIES

NOVA and TransCanada were both large Canadian corporations with headquarters in Calgary, Alberta. NOVA had a virtual monopoly on the transmission of natural gas in Alberta, and TransCanada owned and operated a natural gas pipeline system that extended from the Alberta/Saskatchewan border into the Province of Quebec. NOVA supplied 90 per cent of TransCanada's natural gas at the Alberta border.

According to Robert Hastings, an analyst at Goepel Shields and Partners Inc. in Vancouver, the merger was a good fit. "If you look at every side it's a really good fit. You've got a stronger, more diverse company, with pretty solid earnings and an attractive dividend yield."[4] "There is very little duplication. There could be a lot of cost-savers."[5]

McCune had found an article that described how the president of TransCanada had been trying to bring the two companies together for years. It stated that ". . . over the years, the president and chief executive of TransCanada Pipelines Ltd. kept tripping over the same idea—a union with petrochemical and pipeline giant NOVA Corp. It was just that he couldn't come up with a way to sell his board, or his shareholders, on how to deal with what he calls 'the pickle'—NOVA's chemical division. The division was a small player ($4 billion in assets) and its cyclical fortunes in the volatile commodity chemicals business routinely caused problems for its parent."[6] Apparently, the two companies had found a way to deal with "the pickle." McCune made a note to herself to take a look at how the companies had accounted for this division.

The two companies had approximately the same book values and market values. This similarity made them financially compatible to be classified as a merger rather than an acquisition. On the date of the merger announcement, NOVA had a net book value of $3.8 billion (assets minus liabilities) and TransCanada had a net book value of $3.5 billion. Their market values were $7.2 billion and $7.1 billion, respectively. NOVA had approximately twice as many shares outstanding and the company's share price was half of that of TransCanada's.

McCune had researched the stock values for both companies at various points in time over the past year (see below for table of share values over the past year):

Key milestone	Date	TransCanada/ EnergyCo	NOVA/NOVA Chemicals
Before announcement	Dec. 2/97	30.80	13.40
Day after announcement	Jan. 27/98	30.30	15.05
Day after first ¼ of the year	Apr. 1/98	33.45	16.75
Day before merger	July 1/98	32.60	16.85
Day after merger	July 3/98	32.40	16.80
Day shares exchanged	July 4/98	27.05	30.75
Today	Oct. 2/98	21.50	18.95

She had also pulled some relevant financial information out of the Information Circular document that the two companies had prepared.

NOVA

December 31			
Common Shares Issued and Outstanding 1997	1996	Book Value of Retained Earnings* 1997	1996
(number of shares)		(millions of dollars)	
448,903,784	465,294,809	$3,836	$3,875

TransCanada

December 31			
Common Shares Issued and Outstanding 1997	1996	Book Value of Retained Earnings* 1997	1996
Number of shares (thousands)		(millions of dollars)	
222,420	217,536	$3,482.3	$3,219.9

*Numbers calculated by subtracting liabilities and preferred shares from assets.

For consolidated financial statements of both companies see Exhibits 4 and 5.

PRO FORMA CONSOLIDATED STATEMENT OF INCOME FOR THE YEAR ENDED DECEMBER 31, 1997
(unaudited) (millions of dollars except per share amount)

	NOVA	TransCanada	Reclassifications	Pro Forma Adjustments	Notes	Pro Forma Combined	Pro Forma NOVA Chemicals	Pro Forma EnergyCo.
			(Note 6)				(Note 3(c))	
Revenues	4,840	14,242.8	1,324.0	(240.0)	3(e)	20,166.8	3,360	16,806.8
Cost of Sales	3,429	11,157.0	716.0	(240.0)	3(e)	15,062.0	2,782	12,280.0
Other Costs and Expenses		1,433.6	624.0			2,057.6		2,057.6
Depreciation	469	424.8	28.0			921.8	235	686.8
	3,898	13,015.4				18,041.4	3,017	15,024.4
Operating Income	942	1,227.4				2,125.4	343	1,782.4
Other Expense/(Income)								
Financial charges	384	567.6	1.0			952.6	79	873.6
Financial charges of joint ventures		97.5	17.0			114.5		114.5
Allowance for funds used during construction	(12)	(27.4)				(39.4)		(39.4)
Equity earnings	(105)		21.0			(84.0)	(84)	
General and corporate	12		(3.0)			9.0	9	
Other losses	122		(65.0)			57.0	57	
Interest and other income		(28.6)	(15.0)			(43.6)		(43.6)
	401	609.1				966.1	61	905.1
Income before Income Taxes	541	618.3				1,159.3	282	877.3
Income Taxes	216	161.3				377.3	114	263.3
Net Income	325	457.0				782.0	168	614.0
Preferred Securities Charges		13.1				13.1		13.1
Preferred Share Dividends	9	36.3				45.3		45.3
Net Income Applicable to Common Shares	316	407.6				723.6	168	555.6
Pro Forma Net Income per Share	.70	1.85					1.85	1.22
Pro Forma Average Shares Outstanding (millions)	456	220					90.81	453.7

Exhibit 4   ENERGYCO[1]

1. Joint Management Information Circular with Respect to an Arrangement Involving NOVA Corporation and TransCanada Pipelines Limited, May 19, 1998, p. J-3.

PRO FORMA CONSOLIDATED BALANCE SHEET FOR THE YEAR ENDED DECEMBER 31, 1997
(unaudited)
(millions of dollars)

	NOVA	TransCanada	Reclassifications	Pro Forma Adjustments	Notes	Pro Forma Combined	Pro Forma NOVA Chemicals	Pro Forma EnergyCo.
			(Note 6)				(Note 3(c))	
ASSETS								
Current Assets	12	115.2	84.4			211.6	175	36.6
Cash and short-term investments	821	1,513.4	(33.9)			2,300.5	443	1,857.5
Accounts receivable	389	352.5	(35.1)			706.4	304	402.4
Inventories		34.2				34.2	—	34.2
Other	1,222	2,015.3				3,252.7	922	2,330.7
	1,667	274.8	(222.0)			1,719.8	1,051	668.8
Long-Term Investments	7,685	12072.9	35.1			19,793.0	1,817	17,976.0
Plant, Property and Equipment		208.6	222.0			430.6		430.6
Other Assets	10,574	14,571.6				25,196.1	3,790	21,406.1
LIABILITIES AND SHAREHOLDERS' EQUITY								
Current Liabilities								
Notes payable	362	668.0	84.4			1,114.4	84	1,030.4
Accounts payable	936	1,447.7		230.0	3(d)	2,613.7	576	2,037.7
Accrued interest		178.7				178.7		178.7
Long-term debt due within 1 year	136	282.3				418.3	53	365.3
		51.0				51.0		51.0
Non-recourse debt of joint ventures due within 1 year	1,434	2,627.7				4,376.1	713	3,663.1
	393	113.1	(59.9)			446.2	346	100.2
Deferred Amounts	4,711	6,020.6	(237.0)			10,494.6	1,015	9,479.6
Long-Term Debt		982.8	237.0			1,219.8		1,219.8
Deferred Income Taxes		232.5	26.0			258.5		258.5
		223.9				223.9		223.9
			96.1			96.1		96.1

Exhibit 5 ENERGYCO[1]

PRO FORMA CONSOLIDATED BALANCE SHEET FOR THE YEAR ENDED DECEMBER 31, 1997
(unaudited)
(millions of dollars)

	NOVA	TransCanada	Reclassifications	Pro Forma Adjustments	Notes	Pro Forma Combined	Pro Forma NOVA Chemicals	Pro Forma EnergyCo.
			(Note 6)				(Note 3(c))	
Non-Recourse Debt of Joint Ventures								
Junior Subordinated Debentures								
Non-Controlling Interests								
Shareholders' Equity								
Preferred securities		263.1				263.1		263.1
Preferred shares		280.0				280.0		280.0
Common shares	200	512.6				712.6		712.6
Contributed surplus	2,486	1,660.5				4,146.5	751	3,395.5
Retained earnings	1,293	1,530.4		(230.0)	3(d)	2,593.4	905	1,688.4
Foreign exchange adjustment	57	28.3				85.3	60	25.3
	4,036	4,274.9				8,080.9	1,716	6,364.9
	10,574	14,571.6				25,196.1	3,790	21,406.1

SELECTED NOTES TO PRO FORMA CONSOLIDATED FINANCIAL STATEMENTS

3. Pro Forma Assumptions and Adjustments

3 (b) The number of common shares used in the calculation of net income per share is based on the issued and outstanding common shares of NOVA at December 31, 1997 multiplied by the exchange ratio of 0.52 plus the weighted average common shares of TransCanada for the year ended December 31, 1997.

3 (c) Pursuant to the Arrangement, after the combination of NOVA and TransCanada, the commodity chemicals business is split off by the distribution of the shares of NOVA Chemicals, which will continue as a separate, publicly traded corporation. This information represents the unaudited pro forma financial statements of NOVA Chemicals which are included elsewhere in this Joint Circular.

3 (d) Costs related to the transaction are estimated to be $230.0 million. Energy Co.'s share of such costs is estimated to be $195.0 million. These costs include investment banking, legal and accounting fees, as well as certain income tax costs incurred as part of the corporate reorganizations required to complete the Arrangement. The transaction costs are charged to retained earnings.

3 (e) Intercompany transactions between the energy services businesses of NOVA and TransCanada are eliminated.

6. Reclassifications
Certain figures have been reclassified so that the presentation of information is consistent between the combining companies.

---

1. Joint Management Information Circular with Respect to an Arrangement Involving NOVA Corporation and TransCanada Pipelines Limited, May 19, 1998, p. J-4.

REASONS FOR THE ARRANGEMENT

NOVA and TransCanada were two of Canada's largest companies. The merger was designed to streamline each company's operations and eliminate the duplication in the services that they each provided. The two companies stated that they had "complementary energy services businesses, corporate objectives and growth strategies."[7]

The merging of the two companies would create North America's fourth largest energy services company with approximately $16.8 billion in annual revenues,[8] $21.4 billion in book value assets[9] and a stronger competitive position. The companies stated that as a result of the merger, they would realize operating cost savings of approximately $100 million and annual capital cost savings of approximately $50 million (realized within three years).[10] Revenues would also be enhanced through energy transmission, energy marketing, energy processing and international markets.

THE ARRANGEMENT

See diagrams in Exhibit 6 for a visual representation of the merger.

NOVA and TransCanada agreed to a merger of equals that would become effective on or about 1800 hours (Mountain Daylight Savings Time) on the effective date of the Arrangement expected to be July 2, 1998. One unusual component of the merger was that immediately after merging, NOVA's commodity chemicals business ("the pickle") would be spun off as a separate public company. The companies would be divided so that TransCanada would conduct the energy services businesses and NOVA Chemicals would conduct the commodity chemicals business.

Typically, when companies used the pooling method to account for mergers, shares were exchanged. In the case of the NOVA/TransCanada merger, shareholders of both of the companies would exchange their current shares for new shares in NOVA Chemicals and EnergyCo. The Information Circular detailed the values:

i. each NOVA Common Share will be exchanged for 0.52 of a TransCanada Common Share;

ii. each NOVA Preferred Share will be exchanged for 0.5 of an EnergyCo. Preferred Share; and

iii. each TransCanada Common Share (including TransCanada Common Shares acquired in exchange for NOVA Common Shares pursuant to (i) above) will be exchanged for 0.2 of a NOVA Chemicals Common Share and one EnergyCo. Common Share.

The circular also mentioned that no fractional shares would be issued and that shareholders would receive cash in lieu of fractional shares. All outstanding TransCanada Preferred Shares would remain preferred shares of EnergyCo. without any amendment to their terms.

The management of both companies wanted to account for the Arrangement using the pooling method under Canadian generally accepted accounting principles. The boards of directors for both companies sought the advice of their auditors regarding the use of this method and all auditors concurred with managements' decision. Interestingly, this approach was reinforced by a covenant which was added to the agreement that the Arrangement was "subject to the reaffirmation at the Effective Date of the opinions of each of the auditors of NOVA and TransCanada regarding the expected use of the pooling of interests method to account for the Arrangement."[11]

McCune was curious about why management would have been so concerned about the accounting method since "efficient markets" should be able to detect the difference in reporting method and adjust the companies' valuations appropriately no matter what accounting method was used to account for the business combination. She investigated this thought further and found a study presented by the Canadian Bankers' Association in 1996—"*The Competitive Impact Arising from the Inconsistency of Canadian Accounting for Acquisitions with International Practices.*" This study stated that "the market provides higher market premiums to banks using pooling of interest versus the purchase accounting. This is contrary to the opposite expectation

1. NOVA and TransCanada Before the Arrangement

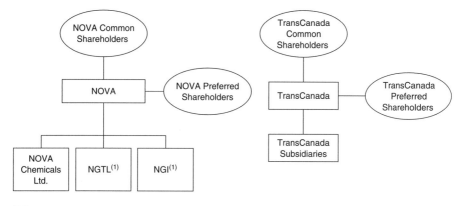

Note:

• NGTL and NGI will be indirect subsidiaries of NOVA.

2. NOVA and TransCanada as Merged Pursuant to the Arrangement[1]

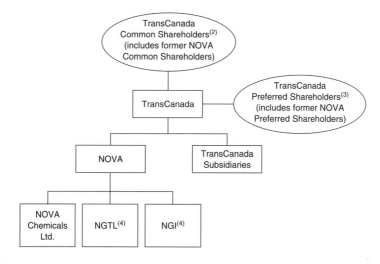

Notes:

1. At this step under the Plan of Arrangement, TransCanada will indirectly hold NOVA's entire interest in its energy services and chemicals businesses. At the conclusion of the Plan of Arrangement, there will be a separation of the aggregated energy services businesses of TransCanada and NOVA under EnergyCo., from the chemicals business of NOVA under NOVA Chemicals, as illustrated in Schematic III.
2. Each NOVA Common Share is exchanged for 0.52 of a TransCanada Common Share, hereafter referred to as EnergyCo. Common Shares.
3. Each NOVA Preferred Share is exchanged for 0.5 of a TransCanada Preferred Share, Series S, hereafter referred to as EnergyCo. Preferred Shares.
4. NGTL and NGI will be indirect subsidiaries of NOVA.
   Split off of NOVA Chemicals from EnergyCo. pursuant to the arrangement

---

Exhibit 6   Schematic Representations of the Arrangement Process[1]   *(Continued)*

1. Joint Management Information Circular with Respect to an Arrangement Involving NOVA Corporation and TransCanada Pipelines Limited, May 19, 1998, p. 20.

3. Post-Arrangement Structure

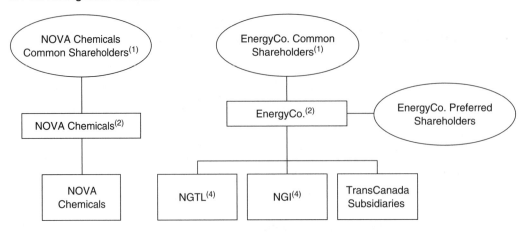

Notes:

1. Formerly TransCanada Common Shareholders and NOVA Common Shareholders.
2. For ease of reference, NOVA, after the Effective Date, is referred to as "NOVA Chemicals" in this Joint Circular (except in Appendices G and I). Also, for ease of reference, TransCanada, after the Effective Date, is referred to as "EnergyCo." in this Joint Circular.
3. After the Arrangement, the holders of EnergyCo. preferred shares will consist of the TransCanada Preferred Shareholders and the former NOVA Preferred Shareholders.
4. NGTL and NGI will be indirect subsidiaries of EnergyCo.

Exhibit 6 (Continued)

which would occur if the market was seeing through differences in accounting." The study also compared the price/earnings and Market to Book ratios of banks using the two methods and found that "both the multiples (P/E ratio and Market to Book) are consistently higher for banks that use pooling of interest accounting versus purchase accounting." McCune found the study interesting but realized that it should not have much impact on her analysis since the sample size was relatively small. Only 12 banks had been included in the study (four that used purchase, six that used pooling, and two that used a mix and were not included in the final analysis). She figured that there might be other specific factors related to these transactions that would account for the differences.

Purchase vs. Pooling of Interest Methods

After reading the CICA Handbook and reviewing the various articles that she had collected, McCune was able to summarize the two most popular methods for accounting for mergers. She also discovered that there was a third method that was not used called the new entity method. This method assumed that a brand new company had been created from the two merged companies and that all assets and liabilities of both companies would be accounted for on the new company's statements at fair market value.

McCune was primarily interested in the differences between the pooling and purchase methods because these were actually being proposed and used by public companies. Both Canadian and U.S. accounting standard setters enforced strict regulations governing the use of the pooling method. In Canada, the rules were relatively simple. The CICA Handbook stated that this method could only be used in those rare business combinations in which it is not possible to identify one of the parties as the acquirer.

Although the Canadian regulations seemed fairly straightforward, in practice, regulators would not accept the use of the pooling method unless two companies were virtually equal. According to *Financial Reporting in Canada 1998*, 86 of the 200 companies surveyed had been involved in business combination transactions in 1998. However, only two of these companies had used the pooling method to account for their combinations. Prior to 1998, there were even fewer.

In the past couple of years the Canadian banks that were also contemplating mergers indicated to the regulators that they planned on using the pooling method. Other companies in other industries had also begun structuring their mergers to be able to use this method.

In the U.S., companies had to meet twelve conditions before they were permitted to use the pooling method (see Exhibit 7). These detailed guidelines, which clearly spelled out the conditions, allowed companies to structure their mergers so that they complied with the guidelines of their preferred method.

Many believed that the CICA and the FASB wanted to eliminate the pooling method since there was general concern that the method did not accurately represent the merger or transaction that had taken place. The accounting method chosen had a significant effect on the consolidated

1. Autonomous—Has not been a subsidiary or division of another company within two years before the plan of combination is initiated

2. Independent—The other combining companies in total own no more than 10 per cent of the voting stock of any combining company

3. Single transaction—The business combination must take place in one transaction or be completed in accordance with a specific plan within one year after initiation

4. Exchange of common stock—One of the companies must offer and issue only common stock for substantially all (90 per cent or more) of the outstanding voting stock of another company

5. No changes in equity interest of the voting common stock in contemplation of combination (two-year rule)

6. Shares reacquired only for purposes other than combination

7. No change in proportionate equity interests—Each individual common shareholder in each of the combining companies retains the same proportionate interest

8. Voting rights immediately exercisable

9. Combination resolved at consummation (no pending provisions)

10. Issuing company does not agree to reacquire shares

11. Issuing company does not make deals to benefit former stockholders

12. Issuing company does not plan to dispose of significant part of assets within two years after combination

Exhibit 7   Twelve Conditions for Pooling in the United States[1]

1. APB Opinion No. 16

financial statements of the merged company because the two methods could show significantly different financial results for the same company.

PURCHASE METHOD

According to the CICA Handbook, "The purchase method should be used to account for all business combinations, except for those rare transactions where an acquirer cannot be identified."[12]

McCune summarized her understanding of the purchase method:

- Assets and liabilities of the acquired company were adjusted to their market values. The excess of the purchase price over the market value of the company's identifiable assets and liabilities was allocated to goodwill.
- The financial statements of the merged company reflected the market values of the acquired company's assets and, if necessary, goodwill.
- Goodwill was written off over a period not to exceed 40 years. Any existing goodwill carried by the acquisition was not transferred to the acquirer because it was assumed that this amount was included in the new goodwill amount.
- Income generated by the acquired company was recorded from the date of acquisition only.

POOLING OF INTERESTS METHODS

Very few Canadian companies were using the pooling method for recording mergers. The merger had to be structured so that neither of the companies could be identified as the acquirer and the transaction was completed through an exchange of voting shares.

"Where an acquirer cannot be specifically identified, the combination may represent either:

1. the uniting of resources, talents and risks of two or more businesses to carry on in combination their previous operations (the pooling of interests concept); or

2. the formation of a new entity which acquires the assets and assumes the liabilities of the previous businesses (the new entity concept)."[13]

The CICA recommended that "the pooling of interests method should be used to account for those rare business combinations in which it is not possible to identify one of the parties as the acquirer."[14]

Some possible ways of identifying the acquirer included:

- If one company offered cash or assets, or assumed liabilities to acquire the assets or voting shares of another, it was considered the acquirer;
- If voting shares were issued or exchanged and one company's shareholders held more than 50 per cent of the voting shares of the combined company, it was considered the acquirer;
- If the first two ways failed to identify an acquirer, regulators looked at the composition of the board of directors, the number of voting shares held, the companies' participation in management of the merged company, and the voting trusts to determine the acquirer.

McCune summarized her understanding of the pooling method:

- The assets and liabilities of both companies were recorded in the combined companies' financial statements at their book values on the date of the merger, which meant that assets were recorded at their depreciated values. Essentially, the two pre-existing balance sheets were added together.
- No adjustments to the financial statements were needed and, therefore, no goodwill was created.
- The income of the merged company included the income of both companies for the entire fiscal period.
- All previous financial statements were restated as if the two companies had always been consolidated (including retained earnings).

REASONS FOR THE TWO REPORTING METHODS

Canadian accounting standard setters were expending considerable effort to develop reporting procedures that were close to those used in the U.S. Based on the articles that McCune had read, it seemed that the U.S. regulators were planning to move towards the exclusive use of the purchase method to account for mergers. This anticipated change was causing frustration among standard setters because Canadian companies wanted to use the pooling method so that their financial statements could be prepared in a manner similar to their U.S. counterparts. The term "operating on a level playing field" was sometimes used as an argument in requests to permit the use of the pooling method in Canada. Recently, other Canadian reporting standards had been modified to bring them closer to the U.S. standards (accounting for pensions, segmented reporting and accounting for corporate taxes). McCune understood why Canadian companies wanted to use the pooling method but realized the difficulty that this might cause for analysts. Extra time and money would have to be spent on information processing to identify the accounting method that was used and on adjustments that had to be made to ensure that the statements of various companies were comparable.

McCune's main concern was whether or not she would be able to assess, or more specifically compare, pooling companies with companies that used the purchase method. The two methods would result in different measurements of asset bases, equity revenues and expenses. Adjustments would have to be made to ensure that the financial statements of different companies were comparable. To make these adjustments, additional data would need to be used, and therefore disclosed, in the financial statements. Also, McCune was a proponent of transparent reporting and it seemed that the pooling method omitted some key pieces of information.

Analysis of the TransCanada and Nova Merger

McCune tried to calculate how the merged consolidated statements would be different if the purchase method had been used. She knew now that the surplus of market value of the company over its book value would have to be allocated to an increase in assets or as goodwill and also as

higher equity. She would then need to depreciate this amount over a maximum of 40 years to determine its effect on income.

McCune needed to decide how she would approach this issue. In the end she wanted to understand more clearly the two alternatives and their impact on the financial reports she used to assess and compare companies. Further, she believed that it would be useful for her to reach her own conclusions as to the appropriateness of the two accounting methods and determine why managers might choose to use one method over the other.

Notes

1. Press Release, Chairman Levitt Announces Action Plan to Improve Quality of Corporate Financial Reporting, Securities Exchange Commission, September 28, 1998, Washington, D.C.

2. Lipe, Robert C., Accounting Horizons, Vol. 12, No. 4, December 1998, American Accounting Association, p. 420.

3. Ibid., p. 420.

4. Carol Howes, analysts like new-look TransCanada, *Financial Post*, v.91 (26) June 27/29, 1998, p. 27.

5. Carol Howes and Claudia Cattaneo, NOVA confirms TCPL talks: analysts believe merger is a good fit, with little duplication, *Financial Post Daily*, v.20 (201) January 23, 1998, p. 3.

6. Claudia Cattaneo, George Watson's pipe dream: the CEO of TransCanada Pipelines has more than a few big deals to his credit, but his company's pending merger with NOVA Corp. could produce the biggest rewards of all, *Financial Post*, v.91 (10) March 7/9, 1998 p. 9.

7. Joint Management Information Circular with Respect to an Arrangement Involving NOVA Corporation and TransCanada Pipelines Limited, May 19, 1998, p. 2.

8. Ibid., p. 6.

9. Ibid., p. 7.

10. Ibid., p. 21.

11. Joint Management Information Circular with Respect to an Arrangement Involving NOVA Corporation and TransCanada Pipelines Limited, May 19, 1998, p.31.

12. CICA Handbook, 1580.18.

13. CICA Handbook, 1580.20.

14. CICA Handbook, 1580.21.

ACCOUNTING FOR ACQUISITIONS AT JDS UNIPHASE CORPORATION

Prepared by Aly Alidina
under the supervision of Professor Christine Wiedman

    Version: (A) 2002-03-19

JDS Uniphase Corporation (JDSU) had just released its fourth quarter earnings and consolidated results for fiscal 2001. The networking and telecommunications sector was amidst a major downturn, which had precipitated from the reversal of the technology market that began in April 2000. The company was declaring $51 billion[1] in losses—a record amount in the history of publicly traded companies. Although other companies such as Cisco Systems, Lucent Technologies and Nortel Networks were also reporting dismal earnings, the losses of JDSU were the most staggering.

JDSU CORPORATION

JDSU was a high-technology company that designed, developed, manufactured and distributed advanced fibre-optic components and modules for the telecommunications and cable television industries. JDSU's products allowed telecom, cable television and subsystem providers (original equipment manufacturers) to build advanced optical networks to deliver their services to end users.

JDSU was formed in June 1999 as a result of the merger between Uniphase Corporation and JDS FITEL Inc. In February 2001, JDSU acquired its primary competitor, SDL Inc. (SDL), which became a wholly owned subsidiary of JDSU. SDL's products enabled faster transmission of voice, data, video and Internet information over fibre-optic networks. Due to rapidly accelerated growth of the Internet in 1999 and early 2000, telecom and television providers were struggling to satisfy customer demands for greater

bandwidth. Conventional electronic and optical technologies no longer sufficed, since Internet traffic was jamming existing telecommunications networks, resulting in sluggish and inefficient data transmission. Given the widely held view that Internet growth rates would continue to soar, the merger between JDSU and SDL seemed like a natural combination.

As stated in the merger press release of July 26, 2001, Jozef Straus, co-chairman and chief executive officer (CEO) of JDSU, commented,

> JDS Uniphase and SDL share a common vision to provide customers with the most innovative and technologically advanced products that enhance their ability to deliver next-generation optical systems.

Don Scifres, SDL chairman, president and CEO added,

> This combination brings together world-class technical and manufacturing teams that promise to deliver best-in-class products at increased volumes for today's systems while developing solutions for tomorrow. We also expect to enable the migration from today's hybrid integration and module level products to tomorrow's truly integrated system on a chip.

JDSU FINANCIAL RESULTS: FISCAL 2000/01

On July 26, 2001, JDSU announced a whopping $50.6 billion in losses, or $46.30 per share, on revenues of $3.2 billion for the fiscal year ended

June 30, 2001. JDSU reported a 35 per cent sequential decline from the third quarter to the fourth quarter, with sales falling from $920 million to $641 million, respectively.

In response to the severe industry downturn, JDSU began implementing a "global realignment program" aimed at reducing annual expenses by $700 million through reductions in manufacturing capacity, employment reductions, product rationalization and decreased discretionary spending. At the time of the announcement, JDSU was in the process of reducing the company's total office and manufacturing space by 30 per cent, or two million square feet. By the end of fiscal 2001, JDSU had eliminated 9,000 jobs and expected to cut another 6,000 jobs during the first quarter, ended September 30, 2001. The global realignment program (GRP) had generated $500 million in charges for fiscal 2000/01 including: $264 million in restructuring charges, $220 million in charges to cost of goods sold, and $16 million in operating expenses.

Due to lowered sales forecasts, JDSU incurred charges related to various write-downs, which were substantially greater than the costs associated with the GRP. These write-downs included $270 million in excess inventory; however, the majority of JDSU's losses came from write-downs of goodwill. JDSU revised third-quarter results for fiscal 2001 to include a $38.7 billion reduction in goodwill. The fourth quarter also included a goodwill-related charge of $6.1 billion. Hence, JDSU incurred $44.8 billion in goodwill write-downs for fiscal 2000/01.

The reductions in goodwill of JDSU were related to three main acquisitions—Optical Coating Labs, E-TEK, and SDL—which, combined, represent $56 billion in purchased goodwill. As shown in the table below, the combined value of three transactions was $58.8 billion.

All three transactions were all-stock deals whereby JDSU purchased the companies by issuing new shares rather than paying cash. At first glance, it would appear that JDSU substantially overpaid for its acquisitions. However, others felt that the acquisitions were made using "overvalued currency."

As Bill Mann of The Motley Fool wrote, ". . . it's like offsetting sins. Sure they paid too much, but at least they paid with grossly overvalued stock."

In his article "What did JDS Uniphase Really Lose?" (see Exhibit 1), Mann went on to argue that the write-downs represent a logical adjustment to the "currency value" of JDSU's acquisitions. The notion of "currency value" relates goodwill to the market capitalization of JDSU. As required by Generally Accepted Accounting Principles (GAAP), the majority of goodwill should be recorded based on stock prices at the time merger agreements are executed and announced. If a significant decline in value occurs after the acquisition, a company is required to write-down the goodwill to its net recoverable amount.

Acquisition	Total Value Announced	JDS Price (billions)	Shares Issued (split-adjusted)	(millions)
OCLI	November 4, 1999	$2.8	$47.97	54.0
E-TEK	January 17, 2000	$15.0	$97.84	150.1
SDL	July 10, 2000	$41.0	$105.50	333.8
Combined Value of Deals		$58.8		

What Did JDS Uniphase Really Lose?

JDSU set all sorts of records with its reported $51 billion loss for fiscal 2001. But its results, while bad, did not really descend to such abysmal levels, because the company included huge writedowns of acquisitions made with highly overvalued stock. In the end, the losses were closer to $6 billion. Too bad that makes for less interesting headlines.

By Bill Mann (TMF Otter)

August 8, 2001

[Editor's note: This story has been changed since publication to correct an accounting error regarding goodwill amortization charges and tax standing.]

JDSU (NYSE: JDSU) lost $51 billion in fiscal 2001.

Say it with me, now: "$51 billion." That is an amazing amount of money, and it speaks to the craziness that beset valuations in the fiber optic sector in 2000.

But if you look carefully at the components that made up these losses, you will find that the amount JDS Uniphase lost is much, much different than what the headlines say. It's not like it lost $51 billion in cash. The majority of JDS' losses are in a form that will have little effect on its operations. The difference between the two is monumental, and poorly understood.

That's why I took on the quixotic exercise of trying to use financial statements to pin down what JDS Uniphase actually lost in 2001. JDS Uniphase's reported earnings stated that for every dollar of revenue it brought in during the year, it racked up nearly $16 in net loss. Reality paints a story much less grim.

Goodwill hunting

Almost all of these losses are based on write-downs of goodwill—$44.8 billion of goodwill, to be exact. Goodwill is money a company pays for an acquisition above the actual value of the acquisition's assets. Goodwill is treated as a depreciating asset on the books. All of these machinations are accounting conventions, so amortized goodwill otherwise does nothing to a company's cash position.

We can use JDS' July 2000 purchase of SDL as a prime example of an acquisition with heaps of goodwill. When JDS announced the purchase, it offered $41.5 billion in stock at a time when SDL had hard assets of only about $2 billion.

The remaining $39.5 billion is considered goodwill. And here's the kicker: Regardless of the deal's final value— shares of publicly traded companies regularly fluctuate between the time a deal is announced and it closes — goodwill amounts are based upon the date of a deal's announcement. Despite the fact that JDS' stock plummeted during this time, the goodwill amount did not change.

In a period of 12 months JDS Uniphase made three massive purchases: SDL, E-TEK, and Optical Coating Labs. Each of these was an all-stock deal. At the time of announcement, the deals were valued thusly:

Acquisition	Announced	Total Value	JDS Price*
OCLI	Nov. 4, 1999	$2.8B	$47.97
E-TEK	Jan. 17, 2000	$15B	$97.84
SDL	Jul. 10, 2000	$41B	$105.50

*split-adjusted

Exhibit 1   Fool on the Hill

The combined value of the assets JDS Uniphase picked up through these deals was less than $3 billion, so between them its purchased goodwill was $56 billion. Knowing what we do now about the growth projections of the fiber optic industry—actually, at the moment we know NOTHING, which is a large part of the problem facing these companies—it is probably safe to say JDS Uniphase paid too much. (For more on this sector, visit our InDepth: Telecom & Networking area.)

Overpaying with overvalued currency

Ah, but the company didn't use cash. It used stock, which, as of June 30, was valued at $12.50 per stub. If we adjust the purchase price of each of these acquisitions for the change in stock price, the OCLI purchase cost $720 million, E-TEK $1.9 billion, and SDL $4.8 billion—for a total of $7.5 billion. Subtract from this the $3 billion in assets, and JDS' net goodwill purchase adjusted for the change in currency value was $4.5 billion. That's a far cry from $56 billion.

Put that way, it's like offsetting sins. Sure, they paid too much, but at least they paid with grossly overvalued stock. The biggest problem is what this write-down says about the nature of the businesses JDS Uniphase purchased. After all, there is nothing wrong with continuing to take huge amortization charges against earnings until the cows come home. Unless . . .

Unless the purchased companies are worthless. This is the underlying statement whenever there is an asset write-down: The company is saying "this asset is not going to help us in the way we thought it would when we took it on."

If the asset is inventory, or a factory, the write-down is an official way of taking it off the books, because the company does not expect it to yield any returns. Not soon, not ever. Another view is that a company takes a write-down because its book value (total assets minus total liabilities) grows much larger than its market value. In the case of JDS Uniphase, this would make some sense.

I suspect that the truth in this case is a mixture between these two factors: The acquired companies are still expected to produce something, but not as much as initially expected. As such, carrying them on the books at their original purchase value was distortive.

So the $44 billion is actually worth . . .

That's the subtext. As a result, JDS Uniphase, when we adjust the goodwill to current dollar denominations and subtract out hard assets, actually "lost" approximately 86% of its total original investments in those three companies, or $3.8 billion. (The total amount of accounting goodwill was $51 billion, 86% of which is $44.8 billion. If you apply that same proportion to the adjusted purchase price of $4.5 billion, the total written down is $3.8 billion.)

This does not take into account the tax benefits JDS Uniphase will be able to take against its earnings in the form of loss carryforwards—the company can write off past losses against future gains, if any, for what would seem like hundreds of years based on last year's performance—so the actual loss is even less.

If it feels like we are building a Mandlebrot set, well, we are. Models can be nearly infinitely complex. For example, one thing that counts against JDS Uniphase is the opportunity cost of having had a highly valued currency (its stock) that might have, at least partially, been converted into cash through a secondary offering. JDS Uniphase has a nice little war chest of $1.8 billion in cash, but at its heights it could have easily put a few more billion in the bank.

On the other hand, how do you value the fact that JDS Uniphase essentially took out all of its most potent competition through buyouts? What is the future value to JDS Uniphase of not having to worry about what SDL was doing? Good question—and, in an industry that has at least the potential for future explosive growth, not an inconsequential one.

(Continued)

> But in the aim of being roughly right, let's try to total up the real quarterly performance of JDS. We have a write-down we valued at $3.8 billion above. Substitute that amount in for the reported amount—the $44.8 billion discussed previously—and the total 2001 loss is $11.6 billion. Almost exactly half of that amount is in the form of non-cash amortization charges, which the write-down essentially negates. Net those out, and the total loss is about $6 billion. That's horrible, mind you, but $51 billion it ain't.
>
> The big loser in all of this, besides JDS Uniphase shareholders, may be the city of Ottawa, Canadian home of JDS Uniphase as well as **Nortel Networks** (NYSE: NT) and French networker **Alcatel** (NYSE: ALA). Ottawa recently adopted the slogan "Technically Beautiful" to market itself to visitors and investors. But there's not much beautiful about the performance of these three companies over the last year, with JDS' reported loss eclipsing the record set weeks earlier by Nortel.
>
> Late last week, Ottawa dropped the slogan. I suggest a new one: "Hey, they're just accounting losses!"
>
> Fool on!
>
> Bill Mann, TMFOtter on the Fool Discussion Boards

Exhibit 1 (Continued)

The SDL Acquisition

JDSU completed its acquisition of SDL on February 13, 2001. JDSU issued approximately 333.8 million shares of the company's common stock, valued at an average market price of $111.13 per common share.[2] The cost breakdown of the SDL acquisition is as follows (in millions):

Value of securities issued	37,091.9
Assumption of SDL options	4,056.4
Cash consideration	0.2
Total consideration	41,148.5
Estimated transaction costs	44.6
Total purchase cost	**$41,193.1**

The transaction was accounted for using the "purchase method." The notes to the financial statements indicated that it was company policy to amortize goodwill on a straight-line basis over five years.

The allocation of the total purchase cost of SDL is as follows (in millions):

Tangible net assets	617.4
Intangible assets acquired:	
Existing technology	455.4
Core technology	214.2
Trademarks and tradename	46.0
Assembled workforce	47.7
Deferred compensation	203.7
Goodwill	39,228.0
In-process research and development	380.7
Total purchase price	**$41,193.1**

Not reflected in the above figures was the additional compensation, amounting to $300.9 million, paid to certain SDL executives for amending their change of control agreements and signing non-compete agreements with JDSU. Previously, this expense was included as acquisition costs; however, at the fiscal year end, JDSU decided to reclassify the $300-million charge as selling, general and administrative expense during the third quarter of 2001 (see Exhibit 2).

	30-Sep-00	31-Dec-00	31-Mar-01	30-Jun-01	TOTAL
Net sales	786.5	925.1	920.1	601.1	3,232.8
Cost of sales	436.7	449.8	494.2	926.0	2,306.7
Gross profit	**349.8**	**475.3**	**425.9**	**(324.9)**	**926.1**
Operating expenses:					
R&D	62.4	71.2	98.0	94.3	325.9
Selling, general, and administrative	116.2	105.2	440.8	155.4	817.6
Amort. of purchased intangibles	1,107.4	1,104.1	2,120.2	1,055.3	5,387.0
Acquired In-process R&D	8.9	—	383.7	0.6	393.2
Reduction of goodwill & intangibles	—	—	39,777.2	10,307.8	50,085.0
Restructuring charges	—	—	—	264.3	264.3
Total operating expenses	1,294.9	1,281.0	42,819.9	11,877.7	57,273.5
Income (loss) from operations	**(945.1)**	**(805.7)**	**(42,394.0)**	**(12,202.6)**	**(56,347.4)**
Gain on sale of subsidiary	—	—	1,770.2	—	1,770.2
Equity-related write-downs / losses	(41.2)	(52.3)	(759.9)	(30.5)	(883.9)
Interest and other income, net	13.6	12.2	4.6	18.1	48.5
Available-for-sale investments (losses)	—	—	—	(559.1)	(559.1)
Available-for-sale investments (write-downs)	—	—	—	(522.1)	(522.1)
Income (loss) before income taxes	(972.7)	(845.8)	(41,379.1)	(13,296.2)	(56,493.8)
Income tax expense	43.9	49.6	468.8	(934.2)	(371.9)
Net income (loss)	**(1,016.6)**	**(895.4)**	**(41,847.9)**	**(12,362.0)**	**(56,121.9)**
Net income (loss) per share	**$(1.07)**	**$(0.93)**	**$(36.63)**	**$(9.39)**	**$(51.40)**

Exhibit 2   JDS Uniphase Corporation Unaudited Quarterly Results Fiscal 2001 (US$ millions, except share and per share data)

THE DECISION TO REDUCE GOODWILL

In its fourth quarter press release, JDSU explains:

> Fiscal year 2001 began as a period of rapid expansion for JDSU but concluded with a severe industry downturn. . . . Downturns in telecommunications equipment and financial markets have created unique circumstances with regard to the assessment of long-lived assets.

This reversal in fortune for JDSU is mirrored by its stock price.

As mentioned previously, the meltdown of the high-technology sector and the bursting of the

Fiscal 2000/01 Quarter	High	Low
July 1 to September 30, 2000	$135.94	$94.69
October 1 to December 30, 2000	$102.37	$40.94
January 1 to March 31, 2001	$63.88	$17.50
April 1 to June 30, 2001	$28.53	$10.00

Internet "bubble" were phenomena that began around April 2000. During the high-technology

Condensed Consolidated Balance Sheet
(in US$ millions, except share and per share data)

	Interim	FYE 2000
ASSETS	**30-Dec-00** (unaudited)	**30-Jun-00** (audited)
Current assets:		
Cash & cash equivalents	430.1	319.0
Short-term investments	700.6	795.3
Accounts receivable (net)	631.9	381.6
Inventories	493.9	375.4
Other current assets	140.5	101.6
Total current assets	**2,397.0**	**1,972.9**
Property, plant, and equipment, net	930.7	670.7
Intangible assets, including goodwill	20,018.3	22,337.8
Long term investments	893.6	760.9
Other assets	705.6	646.8
TOTAL ASSETS	**24,945.2**	**26,389.1**
LIABILITIES AND EQUITY		
Current liabilities:		
Accounts payable	232.9	195.2
Accrued payroll and related expenses	114.6	98.8
Other current liabilities	331.4	353.2
Total current liabilities	**678.9**	**647.2**
Deferred tax liabilities	926.9	902.1
Other non-current liabilities	21.3	20.2
Long term debt	27.2	41.0
Total liabilities	**1,654.3**	**1,610.5**
Stockholders' equity:		
Common stock and additional paid-in capital	26,340.6	25,900.0
Accumulated deficit and other stockholders' equity	(3,049.7)	(1,122.3)
Total stockholders' equity	**23,290.9**	**24,778.6**
TOTAL LIABILITIES AND STOCKHOLDERS' EQUITY	**24,945.2**	**26,389.1**

Exhibit 2(b)   JDS Uniphase Corporation

boom, many successful companies, such as JDSU, were taking advantage of highly speculative markets and astronomical stock valuations to support aggressive acquisition plans. Acquisitions were an important driver of growth and market dominance for many high-technology companies. With the demise of Internet stocks and technology companies in general, the era of unprecedented growth and merger mania came to a halt. JDSU became one of many companies forced to reassess the value of its past acquisitions. Financial information on JDSU's acquisition of Optical Coating Labs and E-TEK are provided in Exhibit 3 and Exhibit 4, respectively.

On February 4, 2000, JDSU acquired Optical Coating Laboratory Inc. (OCLI), a manufacturer of optical thin film coatings and components used to control and enhance light propagation to achieve specific effects such as reflection, refraction, and absorption and wavelength separation. The transaction was accounted for as a purchase and accordingly, the accompanying financial statements include the results of operations of OCLI subsequent to the acquisition date. The total purchase price of $2,707.5 million included consideration of 54.0 million shares of JDSU common stock, the issuance of options to purchase 6.4 million shares valued at $267.2 million in exchange for OCLI options and direct transaction costs of $8.2 million.

The total purchase cost of OCLI is as follows (in millions):

Value of securities issued	2,432.1
Assumption of options	267.2
Total consideration	2,699.3
Direct transactions costs and expenses	8.2
Total purchase cost	**$2,707.5**

The purchase price allocation was as follows (in millions):

Tangible net assets required	253.2
Intangible assets acquired:	
Developed technology:	
Telecommunications	115.1
Flex products	92.2
Applied photonics	1.0
Information industries	23.9
Proprietary know-how	161.9
Trademark and trade name	38.5
Assembled workforce	14.3
In-process research and development	84.1
Goodwill	1,927.4
Deferred tax liabilities	(4.1)
Total purchase price allocation	**$2,707.5**

Exhibit 3   Acquisition of Optical Coating Laboratory, Inc.[1]

1. "Note 10: Mergers and Acquisitions," JDS Uniphase Corporation Annual Report 2001.

Unfinished Business

When the SDL acquisition was announced on July 10, 2000, JDSU's stock price was trading above $100 per share and continued to climb after the announcement. Upon completion of the merger, JDSU delivered shares valued at $111.13 each to the shareholders of SDL. In just over a year, JDSU's stock price had fallen to $12.50 per share by the end of fiscal year 2001. Moreover, the company's future was not clear. JDSU mentioned in its fourth quarter press release that

On June 30, 2000, JDSU completed the acquisition of E-TEK, a designer and manufacturer of high quality components and modules for fibre-optic systems. The transaction was accounted for as a purchase and accordingly, the accompanying statements of operations include the results of E-TEK subsequent to the acquisition date. The merger agreement provided for the exchange of 2.2 shares of the company's common stock for each common share and outstanding option of E-TEK. The total purchase price of $17,506.4 million included consideration of 150.1 million shares of the company's common stock, which includes 0.8 million exchangeable shares of its subsidiary, JDS Uniphase Canada, Ltd., each of which is exchangeable for one share of its common stock, the issuance of options to purchase 23.2 million shares valued at $2,005.2 million in exchange for E-TEK options, the issuance of 0.5 million common shares valued at $45.5 million in exchange for E-TEK shares to be issued under E-TEK's employee stock purchase plan, $53.9 million of cash, and estimated direct transaction costs of $32.3 million.

The total purchase cost of E-TEK is as follows (in millions):

Value of securities issued	15,369.3
Assumption of options	2,005.4
Cash consideration	53.9
Assumption of employee stock purchase plan	45.5
Total consideration	17,474.1
Direct transactions costs and expenses	32.3
Total purchase cost	**$17,506.4**

The purchase price allocation is as follows (in millions):

Tangible net assets acquired	395.0
Marketable equity investments	950.0

Intangible assets acquired:
Developed technology:
  Existing technology
  Core technology
  Trademark and trade name
  Assembled workforce
	
	248.7
	168.5
	60.4
	10.7

In-process research and development	250.6
Goodwill	15,422.5
Total purchase price allocation	**$17,506.4**

Exhibit 4　　Acquisition of E-TEK Dynamics, Inc.[1]

1. "Note 10: Mergers and Acquisitions," JDS Uniphase Corporation Annual Report 2001.

further deterioration of financial markets and a prolonged slowdown in the telecom sector might result in future write-downs. As Danny Hakim of the *New York Times* noted: ". . . the company is trading at a fifth of its book value, which suggests that the market believes JDS has not gone far enough in revaluing its assets."[3]

NOTES

1. All currency in U.S. dollars.

2. This was the average market price of JDSU's shares around the announcement date: July 10, 2000.

3. Hakim, Danny. "Turnaround Odds on a Fallen Highflier," *New York Times*, New York, NY, Aug. 5, 2001.

5

M&A EXECUTION

T he execution phase is complex, with many moving parts and several checkpoints and hurdles that often cause deals to be terminated in process. While each deal is different, there are some basic timelines and processes that are typical. We discuss these. As well, much of the negotiating in a deal occurs during this phase. Negotiations are complex and include many bargaining elements on which the parties must decide and agree. Because of the needs and desires of each party, it is here that many deals fall apart, especially when the parties cannot agree on certain terms and conditions. Finally, all of the negotiated and agreed-on terms and conditions, as well as other extraneous agreements, must be documented. We discuss several of the most important documents that are used to record the agreement between the parties.

DEAL APPROACHES AND TIMELINES

The deal structure, approach (e.g., hostile versus friendly, tender offer versus negotiated), marketing method (e.g., auction versus one-on-one negotiations), and whether the firm is on the buy-side or sell-side drive the timeline of the deal for the firm. Many elements that affect the timeline are also somewhat out of the hands of the parties, including responses from regulators. However, a "typical" timeline of key steps and events can be constructed for a firm, depending on its role, for several common deal types.

Negotiated Deal

All deals should begin with strategic thinking to determine the appropriate plans for a firm. The most basic mergers and acquisitions (M&A) process after this is to begin initial discussions with potential partners (the other party in the deal). When and if those discussions become serious, the parties typically agree to try to continue talking on a confidential basis (by signing a "confidentiality agreement") and agree to exchange more information. These talks may lead to the signing of a letter of intent, in which the parties agree to try to come to a negotiated agreement. The parties may also agree not to talk to other firms (a *no-shop* or *exclusivity* agreement) and to stop buying or selling each other's stock (a *standstill* agreement), agree not to solicit one another's employees or customers (a *nonsolicitation* agreement), and may agree to penalties (*break-up fees*) on each other if they walk away from the deal. However, each of the former agreements may come a bit later in the process, depending on the deal. The firms conduct due diligence on one another and negotiate the terms and conditions of the deal into a term sheet. That term sheet is then the basis for a definitive agreement, which formally documents the terms and conditions of the deal. Various approvals are sought along the way (typically board approvals), and once a definitive agreement is reached, the deal is publicly announced. External approvals (e.g., stockholder and/or regulatory) are then sought, and if received, the deal can then be closed.

Buy-Side Deal

A firm looking to buy another firm follows the basic process, except that a tactical choice is made concerning how to approach the target(s). We discuss five of these. The buyer may directly approach management and attempt to initial deal talks. This is perhaps the most friendly way to conduct a deal, but often the intention of the buyer is to replace the target management, and so the level of cooperation will vary. Without a formal offer, management has little legal obligation to fully consider (present it to the board or stockholders) such an offer. A second method is a simultaneous board and management approach. This approach ensures that the board is made aware of potential interest, and by choosing which board member(s) is (are) approached, the buyer can help ensure its intentions are constructively handled and conveyed. The approach may lead to less cooperation by management since they may fear that the buyer is going behind their backs. A third approach is a "teddy bear hug," in which the buyer officially discloses to the full board its intentions. If an initial price is stated, depending on the jurisdiction, the board may be forced to respond and/or disclose the offer publicly. This approach is better at ensuring that due consideration is given to the intentions but also may allow the board time to take defensive actions, such as seeking a "white knight" (another potential buyer) or by announcing the potential for a deal, which may affect the trading price of the stock, making it more costly to consider the acquisition. A fourth approach is called a "bear hug," in which the buyer simultaneously approaches the board and the stockholders in a letter. The board is then forced to consider the deal and make a recommendation to stockholders. However, the board can say no, and such a public announcement puts the target into play. A final approach is a tender offer. A tender offer has a specific timeline attached to it and forces a dissenting board to find better alternatives, but it also forces the board to take defensive actions to avoid the deal if it is unhappy with it. In the end, however, this approach gives stockholders the ability to simply accept the deal by tendering their shares.

Sell-Side Deal

After making the strategic decision to sell the firm, the most basic selection is that of the marketing method. A firm may use a traditional auction format whereby it attempts to attract multiple bids according to some fairly well-defined process and timeline. A firm may also use a targeted solicitation approach whereby it markets itself to a chosen list of firms on a somewhat loose timeline. Finally, a firm may conduct a one-on-one solicitation and perhaps include one or just a few critical potential buyers in an attempt to find a buyer. The selection of approach depends on the strategic decision of the firm, as well as the strategic and financial positions of the potential buyers. The entire process, from strategizing to closing the deal, may be as quick as 4 to 5 months. The process begins with an internal phase in which the strategic decisions are made, including the marketing process, valuation and due diligence by the bankers that will conduct the sale, and preparation of a memorandum that will serve as a marketing document for potential buyers. This internal phase may take 1 to 2 months. Then an external phase begins in which potential buyers are contacted and interest is solicited. Potential buyers that express interest are engaged and sign confidentiality agreements, and they are then allowed to begin conducting due diligence and reviewing information about the target. Those potential buyers with interest will then submit (or indicate) interest and perhaps an initial written proposal for a deal. The formal process of finding and engaging a suitable buyer may be as little as a few weeks or several months (there are some firms that are "always" for sale). Negotiations then ensue, after which a definitive agreement is reached, a deal is announced, and the closing is scheduled. The negotiations phase may be a few weeks to a couple of months, but there is a lot of pressure to move quickly because deals can often unravel quickly if not agreed upon in a timely manner. The last phase of waiting until closing may be a few weeks or many months, based on whether the firms need to gain approvals from regulators and/or stockholders.

Tender Offer

Tender offers are used in both friendly and hostile deals. It is quite common in a friendly cross-border deal to use a tender offer. There are advantages to tenders, including that there is a fixed timeline, and the board of the selling firm avoids being held accountable for having negotiated the deal. The stockholder has the right to either tender or withhold, based on the individual's judgment of the facts and the board's recommendation. Perhaps 3 to 4 weeks of preparatory work precede the tender offer commencement. On the tender offer commencement day, a press release is sent, newspaper advertisements are placed, regulatory documents are filed, a 14D-1 (Securities and Exchange Commission [SEC] document, for U.S. deals) is hand-delivered to the target, and an official request for a list of stockholders and mailing lists is made to the target. The target must then make its own regulatory filings and agree to either provide mailing labels and stockholder lists or to mail the tender offer materials to its stockholders. In the United States, the target must then formally state its position on the tender offer in a 14D-9 (SEC) filing with regulators. The Williams Act in the United States requires that the offer remain open for a minimum of 20 New York Stock Exchange business days, roughly 4 calendar weeks, but can remain open longer. However, stockholders have withdrawal rights until the offer expires, and so while tenders may occur, no payment is made to stockholders until expiration. Tender offers may have explicit minimums that allow the buying firm to withdraw the entire tender offer if minimums have not been met. While there are many variations and intricacies on the above, this is the basic process, and it nicely forces action on a prescribed timetable.

ELEMENTS OF THE NEGOTIATIONS

The most important element of the negotiation is the price to be paid, or exchange ratio for the shares to be given. This is perhaps where most of the time and effort is focused and likely the reason most deals fall apart. When the consideration is cash, either a specific amount is offered (e.g., an asset sale in which the buyer does not purchase the stock) or perhaps an amount per share when the stock is purchased. In an exchange offer, when the consideration is noncash, numerous elements define the exchange, including how to define the numbers, averages (e.g., over what number of trading days), and caps and collars around the exchange. Basic exchange agreements are to offer a fixed-dollar amount of shares, a fixed number of shares, or perhaps a fixed percentage of the pro forma entity based on some future-determined share price. The details of specific exchange mechanisms and offers are often complex, require numerous pages of a legal agreement to define, and become more lengthy when earnouts and contingent payments are negotiated as well.

However, other elements of the negotiations are important as well. The tax, legal, and accounting structures to be used must be agreed upon. The parties often agree to indemnify one another to a certain degree and choose a governing law for the agreement (laws differ by state and country, and so this is often critical). As previously discussed, the parties may agree to a standstill and agree to not solicit other potential partners while the discussions are ongoing (*exclusivity*). It is also common to have a break-up fee that penalizes a party for terminating the negotiations without cause. Human resource issues are also important, including the makeup of the management team and board and what they will be paid. Option and pay packages for employees (with emphasis on the executives) are determined, as well as how the compensation, option, health care, and retirement plans for all personnel will change. Certain large stockholders may also receive registration rights (the ability to legally register their shares) and piggy-back rights (the right to sell their shares alongside any subsequent public offerings of stock). The parties also agree to a list of "representations and warranties" in which the parties agree to be penalized if what they have said is later found to be false. While many of the elements of the negotiation are complex and technical, they also include items that bring the negotiations back to daily reality, including what the name of the company will be and where it will locate its headquarters.

DOCUMENTING A DEAL

The amount of documentation produced in a deal can be vast, especially if one includes the contents of the data room in which due diligence documentation is kept. Alongside the core process of executing a deal, much of the attention of the deal team participants is focused on a handful of key documents. We describe some of these here.

Informative Memorandum

Also known as a *descriptive memorandum* or sometimes an *offering memorandum,* this is a memo that is prepared to solicit interest in a particular deal.

Nondisclosures

This is usually one of the first agreements between the parties. They agree not to publicly disclose any nonpublic information about the other party and agree not to disclose the fact that they are in, or ever were in, such discussions until and unless forced by a court of law to do so.

Letter of Intent

The letter of intent (LOI) is a letter in which one party expresses its intention to reach a deal with the other party. Often, many of the major deal terms are expressed in the letters, and a preliminary term sheet may be attached.

Term Sheet

Often also called a *terms sheet,* this is the seemingly ever-changing document that is the focal point at the center of the negotiating table. The bankers, lawyers, and their clients negotiate and decide on all of the critical elements of the negotiated agreement in this document. It is commonly a two-column document with areas of interest on the left (e.g., price, exchange ratio, employee arrangements, deal structure) and the defining verbiage on the right.

Definitive Agreement

This is a formalized version of the term sheet that includes more legal verbiage and explicitly spells out the terms and conditions of the deal. It is also a document that is physically signed by the parties, signifying agreement/acceptance of the terms. It also spells out the rest of the process from that point forward to get to closing.

Fairness Opinion

In a public deal (although also possible in private deals, but this is rare), a board seeks an expert opinion as to the financial fairness of the deal to its stockholders. The board seeks this in the conduct of its fiduciary duties. An investment bank prepares a very detailed document that values the offer and the firm and opines as to the deal fairness. The bank itself is under an explicit agreement with the board, however, that it is opining strictly as to the financial fairness of the deal and nothing else. That is, the bank is not suggesting whether the deal makes strategic or operational sense or that the deal will be met with a positive or negative market reaction.

Proxy Statement

This document is a communication to stockholders. The typical purpose is to inform stockholders of the specifics of the deal, the suitor, and the offer. This is typically the primary information with which the stockholder is asked to vote on the deal. A proxy is also used in a more hostile deal when a suitor is offering a new slate of directors and wishes to gain control in that manner. The proxy is a communication to the stockholders informing them of the proposed directors and their affiliations. Again, the stockholders use this information to make their voting decision.

Other Documents

The documents listed above, except the informative memorandum and fairness opinion, are common to most deals. Numerous other documents are important, but the requirements differ by deal. These include legal and regulatory filings, communications to stockholders, proxy statements, tender offer announcements, and press releases. Each of these can be critical to the success or failure (and many court costs) of a deal.

CASES

CNCP Telecommunications Buyout

The managing director of Lancaster Financial, Inc. must determine how to effectively mediate a potential transaction between the Canadian National Railway (CN) and Canadian Pacific Railway (CP). The transaction involves the purchase by CP of CN's 50% interest in a partnership combining each partnership's telecommunications assets. A key element to be dealt with is the widely divergent opinions as to the value of the partnership held by the two parties. The managing director must develop a negotiation strategy/tactics. The case is best used in a role-playing (negotiations) exercise prior to the class discussion.

Issues: Negotiation, valuation, deal terms

Accura/Flexco Acquisition

The vice president of a venture capital fund is reviewing the due diligence package on a deal that involved financing the merger of two operating companies. He must assess the merits of the deal and prepare a term sheet outlining a proposed financing package for one of the potential investors.

Issues: Due diligence, strategic alternatives

National IR: Catalyst Investments Acquisition of Montreaux

National IR is a large communications consulting firm. The firm is working with a client, Catalyst Investments, in preparation of a hostile takeover bid. A senior consultant with National IR must determine if the acquisition price offer is appropriate, the perceptions of value by shareholder investors, assessment of investor reaction to alternative deal structures, and assessment of the public reaction to acquisition strategies in a politicized environment to create a communication strategy for investors.

Issues: Investor relations, M&A strategy, hostile takeover bid, valuation

CNCP Telecommunications Buyout

Prepared by John Matovich
under the supervision of Professor Robert White

Version: (A) 2002-11-04

Mark Wheaton, managing director of Lancaster Financial Inc., sat in his Toronto office and reflected on tomorrow's meeting between Canadian National Railway Company (CN), owned by the Government of Canada, and Canadian Pacific Ltd. (CP). Tomorrow was September 21, 1988, the start of negotiations between CN and CP regarding the potential purchase by CP of CN's 50 per cent interest in the CNCP Telecommunications Partnership. Lancaster's role was to act as official mediator in the negotiations between two parties who were more familiar acting as competitors than as partners. In addition to having to deal with what might seem to some to be an insurmountable discrepancy in values, the task was all the more formidable given the extremely tight time frame that had been instituted; agreement-in-principle had to be reached within six weeks. As mediator, however, Lancaster had been given an option to extend the timetable by one week if necessary. As the head of Lancaster's team, Mark wondered what process Lancaster should institute in its role as mediator and what steps it could take to help the parties bridge the value gap and negotiate to a successful conclusion.

Lancaster Financial Inc.

Established as a private Canadian-based investment bank in 1986, Lancaster was created and structured to respond to the need for conflict-free advice on various financial matters. Decision-making independence and client confidentiality were assured by virtue of the fact that the company was managed and controlled by its employees who had sole responsibility for its operations.

Lancaster was involved in three areas of investment banking: financial advisory services (which included advice on mergers and acquisitions, fairness opinions and restructurings), principal investment and funds management. Its focus was on Financial Post 500 Canadian companies and it served its clientele from offices in Calgary and Toronto.

From an initial contingent of six founding principals, Lancaster had grown to a total professional staff of 20. With the largest dedicated merger, acquisition and advisory group in Canada, Lancaster's professionals came from backgrounds in investment and commercial banking, taxation, corporate and securities law, accounting, oil and gas, real estate, high technology, manufacturing and government.

In addition to making use of its recognized expertise in valuation, Lancaster's primary role in this exercise was to mediate the discussions and attempt to broker a deal that would be acceptable to all those involved. Clearly, each party felt secure in Lancaster's qualifications and its independence, a trust that had been established through previous assignments undertaken for both CN and CP independently. This, however, also served to "raise the stakes" as far as Lancaster was concerned; anything less than a "win-win" outcome could put in jeopardy future relations with one and possibly two of Lancaster's most important clients.

CNCP Telecommunications (CNCP)

CNCP was formed as a 50/50 partnership between CN's and CP's telecommunications operations in 1980. Financial statements for the company are presented in Exhibits 1 and 2. Both partners had a history of involvement with the telecommunications industry dating back to the construction of telegraph lines alongside their respective railroad rights-of-way in the mid-1800s. By entering into their "Basic Microwave Agreement" in 1961, CN and CP effectively began joint operations of their telecommunications divisions. Several subsequent agreements were concluded in the late 1960s and 1970s with

a view to reducing the duplication of facilities and services. By March 1980, the two parties had agreed to formalize this "pooling agreement" via a partnership structure that would allow them to provide superior telecommunications services to the public at very competitive rates. The combined operations of CN and CP would also allow the partners to be better able to meet increased competition and make effective use of the rapidly changing technology.

	1987	1986	1985	1984	1983
Revenue	316,522	343,757	349,124	338,093	315,014
EXPENSES					
Operating, administration & general	237,351	243,435	247,413	243,842	228,544
Depreciation — CNCP-owned assets Partners' contributed assets	29,514 17,544	30,973 21,253	23,855 25,269	19,924 26,885	16,147 28,606
Debt cost	15,796	16,562	16,469	14,649	16,349
	300,205	312,223	313,006	305,300	289,646
Income before taxes & unusual items	16,317	31,534	36,118	32,793	25,368
Provision for income taxes	8,302	17,559	19,534	16,945	12,862
Income before unusual items	8,015	13,975	16,584	16,298	12,506
Unusual Items*	10,435	—	—	—	—
Net income (loss)	**(2,420)**	**13,975**	**16,584**	**16,298**	**12,506**

Exhibit 1   Statements of Income for Years Ending December 31 ($000s)

*Comprised of an asset write down of $9.96 million and a provision for early retirements and lay offs of $11.5 million. The net tax effect of these items was $11.025 million.

Note that the primary businesses of both CN and CP, namely railroading, caused them to interact more often as competitors than as partners. As such, this agreement represented something of an anomaly to the traditional views that each party held of one another. (There existed considerable mutual distrust and hostility.)

As a national facilities-based telecommunications carrier, CNCP provided a wide range of data,

message and private-line voice services in the competitive segment of the market. A landmark decision in 1979, commonly referred to as Interconnect I, gave CNCP access to local public switched networks in Ontario, Quebec and British Columbia for purposes of data and private voice line transmission. As a result, CNCP was not only the sole provider of Telex services in Canada but also a significant supplier of data and private voice line

	1987	1986	1985	1984	1983
ASSETS					
Current Assets:					
Accounts receivable	33,817	31,322	35,318	38,706	37,234
Prepaid expenses	2,014	3,322	3,229	3,159	2,503
Materials & supplies	1,893	3,383	5,418	7,746	9,134
	37,724	38,027	43,965	49,631	48,871
Fixed Assets	401,661	380,190	372,273	351,567	350,093
Employee loans receivable	2,403	2,671	2,630	2,693	2,961
Deferred pension charges	2,650	—	—	—	—
Deferred unrealized exchange loss	6,392	10,933	14,485	—	—
	450,830	**431,821**	**433,713**	**403,891**	**401,925**
LIABILITIES					
Current Liabilities:					
Accounts payable & accrued liabilities	66,306	54,186	56,928	53,486	43,368
Debt due to Partners	153,493	139,387	145,044	135,292	154,508
Deferred income taxes	27,946	31,667	32,177	31,950	29,035
	247,745	225,240	234,149	220,728	226,911
Partner's Equity					
Partner's equity	195,248	197,668	190,681	183,163	175,014
Foreign currency translation adjustments	7,837	8,913	8,883	—	—
	203,085	206,581	199,564	183,163	175,014
	450,830	**431,821**	**433,713**	**403,891**	**401,925**

Exhibit 2   Balance Sheets as at December 31 ($000s)

transmissions outside the Bell network (Canada's largest public telecommunications carrier).

CNCP was currently undergoing a major transition in its product orientation, primarily as a result of Telex services being displaced by the onset of facsimile technology. Telex revenues, which comprised 44.6 per cent of revenues in 1985, were forecasted to be nil in 1990. By comparison, 21 per cent of 1990 revenues were forecast by management to come from services or products not yet offered.

CANADIAN TELECOMMUNICATIONS INDUSTRY

Regulatory Authorities

The telecommunications industry is heavily regulated in Canada. Telecommunications regulation was predominantly handled through the Federal Railway Act. However, subsequent federal and provincial government statutes introduced regulatory complexities which resulted in a lack of coherence with respect to the federal/ provincial division of authority. Exhibit 3 presents the major telecommunication carriers in Canada and their respective primary regulatory body.

Company	Federal (CRTC)	Provincial	Municipal
* Alberta Government Telephones		X**	
* Bell Canada	X		
* BC Telephone Company	X		
CNCP Telecommunications	X		
Edmonton Telephones			X
* Manitoba Telephone System		X	
* Maritime Telephone & Telegraph Limited		X	
* Newfoundland Telephone Co. Ltd.		X	
Northern Telephone Ltd.		X	
NorthwesTel Inc.	X		
Quebec Téléphone		X	
* Saskatchewan Telecommunications		X	
Telébel Limitée		X	
* Telesat Canada	X		
Terra Nova Telecommunications	X		
* The Island Telephone Company Ltd.		X	
* The New Brunswick Telephone Co. Ltd.		X	
Thunder Bay Telephone System			X

Exhibit 3   Telecommunications Companies and Applicable Regulatory Authorities

*Members of Telecom Canada.

**A Supreme Court of Canada decision is pending and could affirm that AGT is subject to the exclusive legislative authority of Parliament and hence regulation of AGT would be carried out by the CRTC.

The need for a consistent regulatory and policy-making framework had become apparent to all. The federal government had, in preceding years, initiated discussions with its provincial counterparts aimed at solving jurisdictional disputes and arriving at a consistent policy that would apply across the country. On July 22, 1987, the Minister for Communications announced some general principles for a national telecommunications policy with a stated goal of having these guidelines (as amended by public comment) processed into legislation within the next year (see Exhibit 4).

The Proposal

a) New classification scheme:

Carrier Types

Type I   Carriers who own, operate or control network transmission facilities.

Type II   Generally re-sellers of Type I services—proposal would leave Type II's unregulated.

Sub Categories

Type IA   (Telecom Canada Members and NorthwesTel)—own, operate or control facilities crossing provincial or international boundaries and authorized to provide Public Switched Telephone Network ("PSTN") services.

Type IB   (CNCP Telecommunications, Telesat, Teleglobe)—own, operate or control transmission facilities crossing provincial or international boundaries.

Type IC   Local carriers that do not own facilities crossing provincial or international borders.

Type ID   Mobile service carriers.

b) Guidelines for Type I's

   i)   Canadian ownership and control—maximum 20 per cent foreign ownership, no foreign representation on boards of directors.

   ii)   Obligation to serve—IA's must provide service when requested (i.e., to remote areas).

   iii)   Service to be provided on reasonable terms.

   iv)   Interconnection of all Type I's (subject to CRTC terms and conditions—as now)—silent on allowing full interconnect.

   v)   Guaranteed access for Type II's to transmission facilities of Type I's.

   vi)   Common carriers—Type I's cannot control content of messages they carry as Type II's can.

   vii)   Maximization of Canadian facility utilization in routing calls.

   viii) Criteria set for new type I entry: public convenience, necessity.

Exhibit 4   Proposed National Guidelines for the Canadian Telecommunications Industry (as of January, 1988)

Tariff Regulations

Similar to other utilities, telecommunications carriers must receive regulatory approval concerning the rates that they pass on to their customers. The Canadian Radio Television & Telecommunications Commission (CRTC) is the central regulatory body in Canada. The test most commonly applied by the CRTC in setting rates involves the "rate-base rate of return," a complex formula in which costs are normally allocated to various services and returns are examined accordingly. In addition, the CRTC tends to examine the economic justification of a given service, considering factors such as the absolute level of the rate.

Rate regulation was established with a view to making available high-quality, low-cost telephone service to as large a proportion of the general populace as possible. In order to serve this public policy goal of universal telephone service, not necessarily long-distance service, a rate structure had evolved over the years in which the prices associated with various types of service bore little resemblance to the underlying costs. Long distance rates were priced at a premium to their costs to effectively allow for the subsidization of local and rural telephone service, thereby ensuring the affordability of local service to the general public. As a measure of the magnitude of these distortions, a 1985 study by Bell Canada's Engineering Economics Department concluded that it cost Bell $1.93 to generate $1.00 of local service revenue while, contrastingly, it only cost $0.32 to generate $1.00 of long distance revenue.

In 1987, CNCP appeared before the CRTC and argued for de-tariffing of its services. CNCP argued that, for the majority of its services, it was subject to both competitive pressures and CRTC scrutiny. The telephone companies, on the other hand, were subject to a markedly lower level of competition. The CRTC agreed with CNCP and approved the de-tariffing of all its services except for telegram. Bell Canada and BC Telephone subsequently applied for similar de-tariffing but were denied.

CNCP's period of deregulation was relatively brief. Five months after receiving approval, the Federal Court of Appeal granted a stay effectively freezing CNCP's tariffs until it could fully review the challenge to de-tariffing brought forward by the Telecommunications Workers Union (TWU), the main union representing Bell Canada employees. The TWU based its arguments on the contention that the CRTC's jurisdiction did not extend to de-tariffing. As of the date of the case, the situation had not been resolved. The Court's decision was pending and was expected before the end of the year. CNCP had, in the meantime, petitioned the Minister of Communications to draft forbearance legislation which would effectively remove any doubt as to the CRTC's authority to de-tariff rates; the legislation had been drafted but had not yet been put forward in the Canadian Parliament.

System Interconnection

In order to provide communication between the premises of its customers, CNCP required local connections at each end, linking the customer's premises with CNCP's long distance facilities. Such local connections could be accomplished via "dedicated" facilities (i.e., direct cable or radio connections linking a single customer to CNCP's network) or "switched" facilities (i.e., facilities which could link a particular customer with numerous other customers via a connection between CNCP and the local public telephone network). For some time, local public telephone networks were generally used for public telephone service only and private voice and data communication services, whether provided by CNCP or the telephone companies, were in most cases provided via dedicated facilities.

Primarily due to the development of computer technology, demand grew for access to data networks by users who did not have sufficiently large volume requirements to justify a dedicated connection to a data network. Through the widespread use of modems, users were able to access data networks via the local public telephone networks. CNCP's competitive position was markedly impaired in those situations where there were no connections between CNCP and the local telephone networks.

In 1976, CNCP filed an application with the CRTC for an order against Bell Canada to provide the necessary connections to its local telephone networks to enable CNCP to provide direct dial access for its data communications and private voice line services. This order was finally approved in CNCP's favour in 1979 and a similar one was applied to BC Telephone in 1981.

Technological improvements continued to increase the capabilities of the public switched telephone networks to the point where private-line specialized networks were becoming redundant. In an effort to offset this, CNCP filed an application with the CRTC in 1983 requesting access to Bell Canada's and BC Telephone's local networks to enable CNCP to provide a competing long-distance public telephone service.

Following a two-year period, which included a public hearing on this issue, the CRTC denied CNCP's application. Although the commission agreed that competition would lead to lower rates, greater customer choice and an increased rate of technological diffusion, it felt that the application had several important shortcomings (see Exhibit 5). The debate, however, had not been closed by this denial. Two federal-provincial study groups had subsequently been formed to examine issues related to increased competition. Results of the more recent examination, conducted by the Sherman Committee, were due to be presented towards the end of 1988. Speculation was that the report would favour increased long-distance competition.

DEVELOPMENTS IN THE U.S. TELECOMMUNICATIONS INDUSTRY

While the AT&T divestiture decree of 1982 is regarded by many as the most influential decision leading to competition in the telecommunications industry, the roots of increased competition were established by an earlier event. Prior to 1975, carriers such as MCI and Sprint were permitted to compete only in the private-line transmission sector of the market, while AT&T held a monopolistic hold in the long-distance public voice market segment. In 1975, MCI, of its own volition, began to offer a long-distance switched service without the approval of the Federal Communications Commission (FCC). Upon receiving an order from the commission to cease offering the service, MCI took the FCC to court. In 1977, the U.S. District Court of Appeals agreed with MCI and overturned the FCC's ruling, thereby opening the long-distance voice market to competition.

Following this decision, MCI and other companies were able to prosper by taking significant market share from AT&T through price discounting. MCI's revenues grew from less than US$100 million in 1977 to US$1.5 billion in 1983 while its earnings rose from US($0.13) per share to US$0.89 per share over the same period.

However, between 1983 and 1986, several significant regulatory changes occurred that altered the profitability of the long-distance market to AT&T's competitors. The first change occurred in December 1982 when the FCC determined that, if AT&T's competitors were to be allowed equal access to the services of the various local Bell operating companies (BOCs), they should also pay a commensurate amount for this privilege. Prior to this, AT&T's competitors paid extremely low access charges relative to those paid by AT&T due to the inferior service they received; the quality of the call was worse and the customer had to bear the inconvenience of dialling 12 extra digits to place a call. For MCI, this ruling meant that access charges as a percentage of revenue rose from 16 per cent in 1983 to 46 per cent in 1986.

The second major change related to the long-distance rates themselves. For years, the prices for long-distance services had remained well above their underlying costs so that subsidies could be provided to keep the price of local calls below cost. In practice, the BOCs charged AT&T very high rates for interstate access and used these revenues to keep local rates low; AT&T in turn passed these charges on to the consumer. This system worked well while there was a monopoly; as long as rates were high enough to cover revenue requirements, it did not matter how the revenues were distributed between local and long-distance. It became clear to the FCC, however, that this could not be maintained in a competitive environment; rates for switched long-distance access had to move down towards actual cost while rates for local service had to increase.

The equalization of access charges clearly highlighted the underlying economics of the long-distance industry. While it might not necessarily be characterized as a natural monopoly, the industry was certainly dependent upon large economies of scale. MCI, Sprint and the other competitors had previously been profitable due to the large discount that they had received on access charges; once this discount was eliminated, their lack-of-scale weakness was exposed. MCI's profitability dropped to US ($1.67) per share in 1987.

In order to survive, AT&T's competitors maintained their prices below those of AT&T but

29 August 1985
FOR IMMEDIATE RELEASE

Competition in the Provision of
Telecommunications Services and Related Issues
(Telecom Decision CRTC 85-19)

OTTAWA/HULL—The CRTC today announced its decision with respect to competition in the provision of long distance telephone services and a number of other telecommunications services in those parts of Canada served by telecommunications common carriers under federal jurisdiction.

The Commission denied CNCP's application to compete with telephone companies in the provision of long distance telephone service in the areas served by Bell and B.C. Tel.

"The issues raised by the application is whether the long distance telephone market should be opened to competition by CNCP, in the manner proposed by that carrier," according to Mr. André Bureau, Chairman of the CRTC.

"The Commission denied this application. But it would be wrong to interpret the decision as a reflection of the Commission's general position with respect to increased competition in the long distance telephone market. I want to make it clear that the decision was based on the merits of this particular application."

In the same decision, the Commission decided to permit more competition in the provision of various other telecommunications services. In particular, the Commission:

- approved the application of BC Rail to compete with B.C. Tel in the provision of certain private line voice and data services;

- allowed interconnection of private local systems and public non-voice local systems to the facilities of the federally-regulated telecommunications common carriers; and

- allowed resale and sharing of telecommunications services other than long distance public telephone service and primary local telephone service.

- more -

Canadian Radio-television and   Conseil de la radiodiffusion et des
Telecommunications Commission   télécommunications canadiennes   **Canada**

Background of CNCP's Application

On 25 October 1983, CNCP telecommunications applied for authority to allow the interconnection of its facilities with the networks of Bell Canada and B.C. Tel. CNCP's goal was to compete with those two companies in providing long distance telephone services to the general public.

The Commission found that increased competition could yield a number of potential benefits. These include lowered long distance rates, increased customer choice and more rapid introduction and use of new technology.

However, the Commission concluded that it would not be in the public interest to approve the CNCP application, principally for the following reasons:

- Long distance telephone rates are currently priced so as to make a large financial contribution to the cost of providing access to local telephone service. Unless CNCP were to make similar contribution payments, competition could threaten the telephone companies' ability to maintain low basic local service rates.

- If the CNCP application were approved on the basis that it would make contribution payments equal to those of the telephone companies, the financial viability of CNCP's service would be highly doubtful. CNCP would be reduced to offering very limited price discounts for its long distance service and serving a limited number of routes. As a result, a number of the potential benefits of competition would not be realized and the need for regulatory intervention would be increased. Furthermore, quality of service would be threatened, as would the principle of rate averaging.

Exhibit 5   CRTC News Release (Abridged)

reduced the amount of the discount significantly. They also made heavy capital expenditures in their networks to improve the quality of their service, thus enabling them to continue to capture market share from AT&T. The companies also undertook mergers and acquisitions in order to bring about the necessary scale economies sooner. The most prominent of these included MCI's acquisition of SBS, the merger of GTE-Sprint and United Telecom to form US Telecom, and Allnet and Lexitel joining to form ALC.

By 1987, MCI's performance had recovered from these recent regulatory shifts and forecasts were for the company's continued strong growth.

CURRENT SITUATION

As of May 1988, both CN and CP were in agreement that the partnership structure of CNCP no longer met the objectives of the two parties. CN was exploring all of its options with respect to its holding in CNCP, including potential liquidation. The exit clause in the partnership agreement required the consent of both parties in order for either party to sell its interest via public auction.

CP, however, considered the telecommunications venture to be a strategic asset which it felt it could effectively develop. As a result, CP indicated that it would be prepared to purchase CN's interest. The Partnership Agreement included strict terms outlining the rights of first refusal that were accorded to each partner in the event that one party wished to dispose of its interest.

CN was in the process of restructuring (eventual privatization) and needed cash; consequently, CN's primary concern was to maximize the proceeds from the divestiture and, while it was happy to sell its interest to CP, it would only do so for a "fair" price. In this context, a "fair" price was termed to mean a sale price that was at least equivalent to the highest price a third party would be willing to pay in an open and unrestricted market. However, CP had absolutely no desire to participate in a public auction for CN's holding, primarily because it did not want to risk the possible sale of the interest to a third party.

CP also expressed concern about the impact of an auction (and the associated uncertainty therein) on the operations of CNCP.

On July 22, 1988, following several discussions between the group vice-president and the executive vice-president of CN and CP respectively, CP proposed to purchase CN's partnership interest for an implied value of $163.9 million (50 per cent of CNCP). The offer was based on an adjustment to the current estimate of book value to reflect proposed asset writedowns and other restructuring costs, plus an implied premium. CP viewed the offer as a generous one given CNCP's poor earnings record, the change in product mix required to achieve profitability and the uncertain future regulatory environment.

CN, however, felt that CNCP was much more valuable than CP's proposal indicated, although it had not set an asking price. It had engaged an outside consultant who valued future cash flows at $1.1 billion if the company received the license to offer competitive long-distance voice services. The consultant's projections were based on a favourable outcome on its petition to the CRTC occurring in the near term. Under this scenario, CNCP would be able to participate in the long-distance voice market by 1990. It was also envisioned that CNCP would quickly become a significant player in this market, obtaining a projected market share of approximately 16 per cent of the total public long-distance market (in terms of revenues) within five years, post entry.

Lancaster's inclusion in the process was the result of careful monitoring of the situation. Lancaster had determined that an opportunity to structure a deal between the two parties existed and it presented the alternative of having Lancaster mediate the discussions in August.

Lancaster's mandate was split into two Phases. The objective of Phase I was to reach agreement on "price and all other relevant terms and conditions" in the five week period between September 19 to October 24, 1988. Note that this could be extended with each party's agreement for a period of up to one week. The short time frame was imposed because CP thought the mediation was simply a stalling tactic. There was mutual distrust between the two parties as to the sincerity of their stated intentions. Phase II would commence upon the unsuccessful completion of Phase I and established a 10-day period for CN and CP to reach agreement on either a specific transaction or on another resolution mechanism.

The Next Stage

As Mark wondered what he and his team should do over the next several weeks, he recalled the events that had already taken place. In an incredibly short period of two weeks, his team had amassed a significant amount of information in the course of a very intensive due diligence session; see Exhibits 6, 7, 8 and 9. Lancaster had developed a sophisticated understanding of the industry and the major issues involved.

Several questions raced through Mark's mind. Firstly, what rules should Lancaster set out for the mediation in order to clarify its role and the expectations of CN and CP? Secondly, what steps should Lancaster take to bridge the value gap? Finally, the team needed to come up with a definitive strategy and series of steps that would allow them to achieve the most important result in the very short time available: getting the deal done in a manner that would satisfy all of the stakeholders. The meeting location was potentially a significant issue; both parties owned hotels across Canada, and CN's head office was in Toronto and CP's head office was in Montreal.

Selected Financial Statistics (1987)	CNCP	Canadian Companies							
		BCE	BC Tel	MT&T	Bruncor	Newtel	Memotec	Cantel	Rogers
Total Assets (1)	450.9	26,025.0	3,111.7	827.5	919.7	384.7	860.6	111.6	1,032.3
Total Revenues (1)	316.5	14,649.0	1,581.0	359.7	340.9	166.3	346.0	47.3	464.3
Earnings After Tax (1)	8.0	1,374.0	147.0	39.2	35.2	22.0	64.6	(13.9)	(4.5)
Leverage Ratio (2)	0.43	0.48	0.48	0.51	0.62	0.45	0.45	0.74	0.78
Coverage Ratio (3)	2.03	4.30	3.42	3.18	2.87	3.94	5.61	NMF	1.26
Investment Ratio (4)	0.11	0.15	0.08	0.14	0.22	0.12	1.95	0.97	0.09
Beta		0.383	0.314	0.350	0.340	0.380	N/A	NA	1.62
Trading Statistics (1987)									
P/E (5)		9.74 ×	10.50 ×	9.78 ×	10.68 ×	9.28 ×	10.00 ×	NMF	NMF
P/CF (5)		3.38 ×	3.06 ×	3.08 ×	3.51 ×	3.15 ×	3.25 ×	NMF	14.48 ×
P/BV (5)		1.16 ×	1.33 ×	1.29 ×	1.20 ×	1.19 ×	1.48 ×	NMF	31.49 ×
Total Cap/EBIDT (6)		4.31 ×	3.81 ×	3.85 ×	4.59 ×	3.39 ×	3.93 ×	NMF	12.71 ×
Total Cap/EBIT (6)		6.56 ×	6.39 ×	6.36 ×	7.03 ×	5.23 ×	5.11 ×	NMF	25.54 ×
Trading Statistics (1988E)									
P/E (5)		9.32 ×	9.31 ×	8.99 ×	10.68 ×	10.31 ×	10.00 ×	NMF	NMF
P/CF (5)		1.10 ×	1.26 ×	1.22 ×	1.25 ×	1.16 ×	1.32 ×	16.8x	35.44 ×

Selected Financial Statistics (1987)	CNCP	U. S. Companies				
		MCI	AT&T	United Tel	NYNEX	GTE
Total Assets (1)	450.9	5,380.03,9	38,426.0	6,558.4	22,786.3	28,745.2
Total Revenues (1)	316.5	39.085.0	33,598.0	3,064.0	12,084.0	15,4210
Earnings After Tax (1)	8.0	0.61	2,044.0	(50.3)	1,276.5	1,118.7
Leverage Ratio (2)	0.43	1.63	0.26	0.67	0.39	0.54
Coverage Ratio (3)	2.03	0.12	6.01	3.10	4.85	3.09
Investment Ratio (4)	0.11		0.09	0.10	0.11	0.11
Beta			0.58			0.76
Trading Statistics (1987)		68.37 ×				
P/E (5)		10.45 ×	14.07 ×	NMF	10.61 ×	13.28 ×
P/CF (5)		4.30 ×	4.49 ×	10.46 ×	4.11 ×	3.70 ×
P/BV (5)		10.64 ×	1.97 ×	2.90 ×	1.48 ×	1.83 ×
Total Cap/EBIDT (6)		28.85 ×	4.47 ×	8.17 ×	4.32 ×	5.00 ×
Total Cap/EBIT (6)			8.84 ×	19.01 ×	7.88 ×	9.77 ×
Trading Statistics (1988E)		21.77 ×				
P/E (5)		3.59 ×	12.62 ×	24.58 ×	9.95 ×	12.08 ×
P/CF (5)			1.85 ×	2.93 ×	1.39 ×	1.76 ×

Exhibit 6   Comparable Company Statistics ($ millions except ratios)

Sources: Annual reports; Burns Fry report, Statistics on Representative Common Stocks, September 1988; Zacks Corporate Earnings Estimator; CFMRC TSE Equity Securities Database; Valueline.

1. All figures quoted in domestic currencies (i.e., Cdn$ for Canadian companies).
2. Leverage ratio calculated as: (short-term debt + long-term debt) / (short-term debt + long-term debt + net worth)
3. Coverage ratio calculated as: EBIT / net interest
4. Investment ratio calculated as: capital expenditures / gross fixed assets
5. Closing share price as recorded on TSE/NASDAQ/NYSE for October 7, 1988.
6. Total cap calculated as: market value of net worth + book value of long-term debt + book value of short-term debt.

Date	Purchaser	Target	$ millions Total Cost	$ millions Target Sales	$ millions Target Net Income	$ millions Target Assets	$ millions Target Equity	% Acquired	P/E
Aug. 16/85	Private investors	Graphic Scanning Corp.	11.90	151.24	–11.90	N.A.	14.66	5.5	N.A.
Nov. 26/85	Private investors	Millicon Inc.	2.40	0.86	–6.95	N.A.	1.17	8.5	N.A.
Feb. 19/86	Goldman Sachs	Graphic Scanning Corp.	12.90	151.24	–11.90	206.40	14.66	5.1	N.A.
Sep. 29/86	Communications Satellite Corp.	Contel Corp.	2,519.70	2,556.62	239.86	5,074.23	1,327.06	100.0	10.50
Sep. 12/86	Ford Motor Co.	American Network	20.00	66.87	–6.57	35.33	–13.87	28.0	N.A.
Aug. 7/86	AMC Entertainment	TDI Enterprises Inc.	37.70	240.90	–6.96	397.13	168.18	20.4	N.A.
Jun. 17/86	Mercury Warburg Investment Management	Millicom Inc.	5.80	N.A.	97.00	N.A.	98.71	5.1	1.17
Sep. 3/87	MPX Systems Inc.	SouthernNet Inc.	35.30	103.60	3.54	N.A.	38.43	14.2	70.22
Aug. 19/87	Private investors	Int'l Telecharge Inc.	2.80	1.46	–2.71	6.90	–1.28	6.0	N.A.
Mar. 4/88	Moran Asset Mgmt Inc.	American Cellular Network Corp.	6.00	2.57	–3.48	28.12	–9.93	8.6	N.A.
Jul. 11/88	Comcast Corp.	American Cellular Network Corp.	229.84	2.57	–3.48	28.12	–9.93	100.0	N.A.
May 31/88	Private investors	Centel Corp.	2,654.40	1,475.80	157.07	3,014.06	N.A.	94.5	17.88
May 31/88	McCaw Cellular Communications	Cellular Communications Inc.	32.92	34.74	–19.73	N.A.	–14.41	5.7	N.A.
Jul. 11/88	ALLTEL Corp.	Advanced Telecom Co.	41.90	82.66	9.48	N.A.	26.43	14.3	30.84
Jul. 25/88	ALLTEL Corp.	CP National Corp.	285.60	241.21	21.80	470.07	115.05	100.0	13.10

Exhibit 7 Comparable Transactions

Date	Purchaser	Target	% Premium	P/BV	P/Sales	Comments/Description	Status
Aug. 16/85	Private investors	Graphic Scanning Corp.	N.A.	14.76	1.43	Telecommunications service company, involved in cellular telephone, radio, T.V. & data and msg processing	Closed
Nov. 26/85	Private investors	Millicon Inc.	N.A.	24.24	32.99	Develops local area radio networks in one way digital & two way voice & digital communications, operates cellular radio phone systems & one way msg service	Closed
Feb. 19/86	Goldman Sachs	Graphic Scanning Corp.	N.A.	17.25	1.67	Telecommunications service company, involved in cellular telephone, radio, T.V., & specialized data & msg processing	Closed
Sep. 29/86	Communications Satellite Corp.	Contel Corp.	0.46	1.90	0.99	Holding company for local telephone companies in 30 states	Un-successful
Sep. 12/86	Ford Motor Co.	American Network	N.A.	N.A.	1.07	Provides long distance telephone service & radio paging service	Pending
Aug. 7/86	AMC Entertainment	TDI Enterprises Inc.	23.07	1.10	0.77	Formerly Telecom Plus Int'l, designs, installs & services communications for businesses & institutional clients in the U.S. & Puerto Rico, also provides mobile phone service	Closed
Jun. 17/86	Mercury Warburg Investment Mgmt	Millicom Inc.	N.A.	1.15	N.A.	Develops local area radio networks for one way digital & two way voice & digital communications, operates cellular radio telephone systems & one way msg service	Closed

(Continued)

197

Date	Purchaser	Target	% Premium	P/BV	P/Sales	Comments/Description	Status
Sep. 3/87	MPX Systems Inc.	SouthernNet Inc.	N.A.	6.47	2.40	Formerly Tel/Man Inc. provides communications services	Closed
Aug. 19/87	Private investors	Int'l Telecharge Inc.	N.A.	N.A.	31.99	Provides operator assisted long distance phone services as an alternative to AT&T, markets to hotels, motels, hospitals, etc.	Closed
Mar. 4/88	Moran Asset Mgmt Inc.	American Cellular Network Corp.	N.A.	N.A.	27.14	Constructs & operates mobile/portable phone services	Closed
Jul. 11/88	Comcast Corp.	American Cellular Network Corp.	29.03	−23.16	89.40	Constructs & operates mobile/portable phone services	Closed
May 31/88	Private investors	Centel Corp.	44.04	N.A.	1.90	Telecommunications company with interest in telephone, cable & cellular phone business	Pending
May 31/88	McCaw Cellular Communications	Cellular Communications Inc.	2.57	N.A.	16.57	Operates cellular phone systems	Closed
Jul. 11/88	ALLTEL Corp.	Advanced Telecom Co.	0.00	11.06	3.54	Provides long distance phone service to commercial & residential customers	Closed
Jul. 25/88	ALLTEL Corp.	CP National Corp.	30.30	2.48	1.18	Holding company which supplies electric, gas or telephone service	Pending

Exhibit 7 (Continued)

198

	Canada	United States
Bank Rate (Canada) / Discount Rate (United States)	10.56%	6.50%
Government Bonds		
2-year	9.94%	8.39%
5-year	9.87%	8.59%
10-year	9.94%	8.87%
30-year (25-year—Canada)	10.00%	8.95%
T-Bills		
1-month	10.14%	7.10%
3-month	10.33%	7.24%
6-month	10.43%	7.53%
Corporate Bonds		
Bell Canada (2015)	10.84%	
AGT (1997)	10.49%	
Ontario Hydro (2010)	10.68%	
AT&T (2026)		9.70%
Illinois Bell (2004)		9.20%
Average Historical Market Premium (1950-1987 (Canada); 1926-1987 (United States)) [Relative to long-term government bonds]	6.85%	7.43%

	Oct. 5/88	52 Week		% Change 1 Week	% Change 1 Month
		High	Low		
TSE 300	3343	3783	2783	1.80%	1.30%
TSE Telephone Utilities Sub-Index	2488	2909	2267	1.10%	0.53%
S&P 500	271.86	314.52	131.21	1.03%	−1.19%
S&P Telephone Utilities Sub-Index	201.31	204.33	181.25	0.30%	1.88%

Exhibit 8   Financial Market Statistics

Sources: Financial Post; TSE Daily Record; TSE Review; Standard & Poors' Security Owner's Stock Guide; TSE Data Base; Ibbotson and Sinquefeld.

	Estimate	Forecast						Projections			
	1988	1989	1990	1991	1992	1993	1994	1995	1996	1997	1998
Operating Revenues											
Telex	65.0	26.9	0.0	0.0	0.0	0.0	0.0	0.0	0.0	0.0	0.0
Old Products	218.0	239.5	272.2	303.0	333.1	356.6	392.3	431.5	474.6	522.1	574.3
New Products	3.1	40.9	72.9	98.5	135.0	195.5	215.0	236.5	260.2	286.2	314.9
Total Operating Revenue	286.1	307.4	345.1	401.5	468.1	552.1	607.3	668.0	724.8	808.3	889.2
Growth in Operating Revenue (per cent)	(9.5)	7.4	12.3	16.3	16.6	17.9	10.0	10.0	10.0	10.0	10.0
Growth in Operating Revenue (Excluding Telex) (per cent)	8.3	26.9	23.0	16.3	16.6	17.9	10.0	10.0	10.0	10.0	10.0
Earnings Before Interest, Tax and Depreciation	42.8	57.4	90.2	127.5	166.3	217.7	246.0	277.5	312.7	352.2	396.4
Earnings Before Interest and Tax	(5.9)	18.1	41.0	64.8	92.7	139.3	157.0	178.2	203.3	233.1	267.8
Earnings Before Tax	(25.4)	(8.7)	8.3	29.6	55.7	101.0	116.8	136.0	159.8	188.3	220.1
Net Earnings	(83.5)	(5.9)	4.5	16.7	31.5	57.3	66.2	77.1	90.6	106.7	124.8
Net Income	(83.5)	(5.9)	4.6	16.7	31.8	57.2	66.2	77.1	90.6	106.7	124.8
Add:											
Dep'n	48.8	39.3	49.9	62.8	73.6	78.4	89.0	99.3	109.4	119.1	128.6
Deferred Taxes	(46.5)	24.8	15.0	14.2	12.0	16.1	12.6	10.7	8.8	7.1	5.4
Other	(4.7)	(4.5)	(4.5)	(4.6)	(4.7)	(4.7)	(4.7)	(0.7)	(0.6)	(0.6)	(0.6)
Writedown of Assets	103.1	0.0	0.0	0.0	0.0	0.0	0.0	0.0	0.0	0.0	0.0
Cash From Operations	17.2	53.7	65.0	89.1	112.7	147.0	163.1	186.4	208.2	232.3	258.2
Investment Activities:											
Addition to Fixed Assets	(114.0)	(144.3)	(154.4)	(153.1)	(156.4)	(154.2)	(158.8)	(163.6)	(168.5)	(173.6)	(178.8)
Other	(0.7)	(0.1)	(0.3)	0.0	0.1	0.0	(0.1)	0.0	0.0	0.0	0.0
	(97.5)	(90.7)	(89.7)	(64.0)	(43.6)	(7.2)	4.2	22.8	39.7	58.7	79.4
Financing Activities:											
Change in LT Debt	35.1	66.2	54.2	45.7	45.3	40.7	31.7	22.2	26.3	29.3	41.7
Equity Infusion (Dist'n)	36.2	53.2	40.0	21.4	3.5	(28.5)	(34.0)	(43.8)	(63.0)	(85.0)	(95.0)
Change in Working Capital	(26.2)	28.7	4.5	3.1	5.0	5.0	1.9	1.2	3.0	3.0	26.1

Exhibit 9   Forecasted Earnings Information (1) ($ millions)

1. Forecast and projections prepared by an independent consultant advising CN.

2. Forecast information excludes the potential effects on revenues and expenses of a favorable Interconnect II decision.

ACCURA/FLEXCO ACQUISITION

Prepared by Ryan Kovac
under the supervision of Professor James E. Hatch

Version: (A) 2003-07-20

In November 1999, Michael Graham, a vice-president at Working Ventures Canadian Fund, Inc. (WV), was reviewing a due diligence package. The deal involved backing Barry Wood in the acquisition and merger of two operating companies as well as the utilization of the manufacturing platform of the merged companies to expand into the heat sink market via the creation of a new company called Powersink Technologies. The two operating companies were Accura Machining Inc. (Accura) and Flexco Inc. (Flexco), which both manufactured small- to medium-sized metal and plastic components. Graham needed to assess the opportunities and structure a deal in the form of a term sheet that would be acceptable to both Wood and WV's investment committee.

WORKING VENTURES CANADIAN FUND, INC.

Inaugurated in 1990, WV was Canada's first national Labour Sponsored Venture Capital Corporation (LSVCC).[1] WV's mandate was to invest in small- and medium-sized Canadian businesses, for the purpose of creating jobs for Canadians and providing returns to shareholders in this newly formed asset class. By 1999, WV was one of Canada's largest venture capital funds with more than $700 million under management. WV made investments in all sectors of the Canadian economy, but legislation limited its investments to companies with less than $50 million in assets, less than 500 employees and more than 50 per cent of its assets in Canada. No more than $15 million could be invested in any one company.[2] WV typically invested between $500,000 and $5 million in a company, with the

potential for follow-on investments. They funded companies ranging from startups to later-stage entities, with preference towards the latter, and were willing to invest in buyouts. WV usually played the role of an active investor, participating at the board level to influence strategic direction in order to maximize value in its investment, and to control decision-making on major financial issues. WV targeted annualized returns above 25 per cent and was not interested in opportunities with less than this potential. Finally, WV structured its investments with any combination of subordinated debt or preferred shares with an equity kicker, or a direct investment in common shares.

BARRY WOOD

It was proposed to name Wood the chief executive officer (CEO) of the combined entity (the Company). Wood had proven himself as a strong leader and manager, with a knowledge base acquired from working in a senior capacity in both large- and small-business settings, in both Canada and the United States.

Wood's latest entrepreneurial venture was his successful management and exit of M&I Door Systems Ltd. (M&I), a WV portfolio company. Prior to his involvement with M&I, Wood was president and CEO of Resource Plastics Inc. (Resource), the largest independent manufacturer of recycled post-consumer polyethylene plastic films and bottles in North America with 1995 fiscal sales approaching $13 million. Wood left Resource in the spring of 1995, as a result of a dispute with the board of directors. Prior to his employment at Resource, Wood had gained senior management experience in merchant banking and finance, insolvency consulting, computer audit/consulting and general public accounting.

As a result of his success at M&I Door Systems, Wood was asked to become an executive-in-residence[3] (EIR) at WV. Wood had identified both the Accura and Flexco opportunities through personal contacts. He was looking for a platform of companies that, while having good prospects in their own right, could provide the manufacturing base to allow penetration into the thermal dissipation (or heat sink) markets.

Based upon his research of the heat sink market, he had identified the power electronics segment as an under-serviced market opportunity. A separate entity, Powersink Technologies Inc., would be set up as a majority-owned joint venture with Robinson Fin, an American company, which had developed patented and proven cooling fin technology (complex metal components) that greatly improved heat dissipation capabilities. It was expected that Wood would invest a significant portion of his net worth in the Company as part of the transaction.

Accura Machining Inc.

One of the companies to be acquired was Accura, which had been founded by John Bell and Mike Steele in 1989, in Mississauga, Ontario. Each of the founders owned 50 per cent of the company. Accura specialized in the manufacture of metal components for work platforms, medical and analytical instruments, aerospace, electronics and national defense. The company had steady production and a significant backlog of orders. Accura management believed that a significant increase in revenue and improved profit margins over the next three to five years could be attained with the purchase of more machining equipment. Independent research by Wood confirmed that this was a reasonable expectation. Accura's major customers were Skyjack Inc. (Skyjack) and MDS Sciex (Sciex) which together comprised more than 80 per cent of Accura's sales and utilized an equivalent amount of the company's capacity.

Marketing and Sales

While there wasn't a formal marketing plan for Accura, Bell and Steele had built a plant and a profitable book of businesses that matched each other well with respect to equipment utilization and personnel capability. Bell's knowledge of customer needs relative to machining requirements, along with his pricing estimation skills made him an effective salesperson. While Bell had no formal education in selling strategy and tactics, he had effectively used his common sense in generating sales opportunities. Accura sold reliable, quality, intricate small parts, at a competitive price with on-time delivery and strong customer service. From a marketing perspective, Accura had a unique selling proposition of on-time manufacturing of small complex parts.

Accura had used agents in the past, but found that this strategy was not very effective or efficient, so Bell handled the selling responsibility exclusively. Accura did not advertise in trade journals, and there were no government regulations that impacted Accura markets directly. The current backlog of orders was strong, particularly from the Skyjack-Guelph plant (approximately $750,000) and Sciex. Some customers, such as the Skyjack-Georgetown plant, were less profitable. In 1999, Skyjack was uncharacteristically a slow payer as a result of the working capital crunch it had experienced.

Operations

Steele managed plant operations, although Bell usually developed the plant production schedule because of his familiarity with the sales backlog. Steele was a master machinist, having apprenticed for six years before joining Accura. There were two-and-a-half shifts, with three crews reporting to a lead supervisor, as well as several senior operators that worked on their own.

The business operated from an attractive, 10-year-old building in leased space of 15,700 square feet with about 2,000 square feet of office space. There was room to put another five computer numerically controlled (CNC) machines into the existing space. Equipment in the plant was generally quite new and of satisfactory quality. The plant was cleaner than many machine shops but not to the satisfaction of Wood. An expansion to the adjacent space of 8,000 feet (currently used by a company operated by the landlord) was potentially available as well. Alternatively, a move to new premises to combine Accura with Flexco operations one year out when the current lease term expired needed to be assessed.

Bell and Steele always tried to run the plant with 25 per cent excess capacity available to meet customers' emergency requests. With new business now potentially available from Sciex, however, the plant would be in an over-capacity situation. Capital expenditures of $400,000 on CNC equipment for fiscal 2000 would be funded from operations and was expected to provide a cushion. In addition, there was always the option of leasing equipment, as it was standard equipment with good resale demand. It was estimated that CNC capital expenditures of $125,000 were required for every $275,000 of additional annual sales, based on past experience at both Accura and Flexco.

The primary barrier in sales ramp-up was finding staff capable of doing the machining. While many applications involved nothing more than "button-pushing," other applications required significant knowledge and skill. There was no manufacturing engineering capability in the company, which affected the quality of work planning and the complexity of parts that could be effectively made. As a result, Accura was limited in its sales growth with companies such as Sciex. Quality assurance (QA) was adequate, given the company's current size and work complexity, but would be a constraint to growth.

Human Resources

Bell and Steele were capable managers of a business the size of Accura, but they lacked a process orientation. In addition to problems co-existing as managers, during due diligence it became evident that Steele's people-management skills were barely acceptable, and Bell was considered by his staff to be a tyrant. Staff meetings were held, but they were disorganized and unfocused.

Employee training was solely on the job, except when new equipment was acquired and training was provided by the manufacturer. Accura did not provide performance or profit-sharing incentives.

If the transaction was to take place, consideration would have to be given to setting up an employee stock option plan (ESOP). Graham wondered what proportion of the fully diluted shares outstanding should be allocated to such a program. Review of the employee roster indicated there were a number of new employees, largely due to the acquisition of new equipment. Employees rarely received a performance review but wage adjustments were made on an annual basis. Furthermore, there were no job descriptions or guides and a lack of organizational structure (position levels). Employees were non-union.

FLEXCO INC.

The second company to be acquired was Flexco. Flexco, which was founded by George Smith in 1988 and wholly owned by him, serviced the automotive, transportation, aerospace, telecommunications and medical analytical instruments markets. Smith was a master maintenance/mechanic trained in Germany, with more than 25 years of hands-on experience in the machining and manufacturing industry. With his significant machinist/mechanical skills and utilizing the best CNC equipment available, in addition to a skilled labor force, Smith had built his customer base by producing quality components with consistent, on-time deliveries.

Flexco had experienced strong financial performance over the past four years, with the exception in 1999, when planned incremental business with Magna Inc. and Orenda did not materialize when expected. In anticipation of the new business, the company had incurred substantial capital expenditures as well as one-time upfront costs of production set-up, job cost/control and software implementation. Flexco was highly leverage and operating at under-capacity. Therefore, it was a favorable time for Flexco to take on opportunities from Accura.

Flexco's major customers were General Electric's Transport Division (GE) (20 per cent of sales) and Toral Cast, a division of Magna (10 per cent of sales). Flexco also did work for Skyjack and Sciex (10 per cent of sales).

Marketing and Sales

Smith had sought business opportunistically, and, in contrast to Accura, Flexco did many small jobs for a large number of customers. The result was greater diversification of credit risk, but significantly higher production management costs, challenging quality assurance and inefficient cycle times.[4] Compared to Accura, Flexco could manufacture more complex parts, due to its more sophisticated equipment, but it had less versatility than Accura. Like Accura, there was a mix of highly skilled machinists as well as "button-pushers." Flexco had pursued and obtained business in a variety of industries, including aerospace (Orenda), telecommunications, medical/analytical (Sciex) and manufacturing (Magna, Skyjack). The business volumes had increased each year with the GE business experiencing particular growth. There was no significant backlog of contracts currently outstanding.

Flexco used an agent to generate the GE work for which it paid commissions of 10 per cent. The GE work was still reasonably profitable after deducting this commission and factoring in the benefit of the low Canadian dollar. The GE sales were all made to the United States priced in U.S. dollars. Smith had recently terminated his inside sales rep of several years, due to poor performance. Smith and his production manager now handled all responsibilities regarding customers. Flexco did not advertise in trade journals, and there were no government regulations that impacted Flexco markets directly. Customers did not place orders well in advance, though historic monthly order levels followed a clear pattern.

Operations

Tom Jones, a machinist with 25 years of experience, managed plant operations, with Smith helping with specific hands-on work to improve cycle time efficiencies. Flexco operated weekdays around the clock, although afternoon and evening shifts were at 20-per-cent staffing.

The business operated from an attractive building in space leased from Smith's holding company, TML Holdings Limited. Total space was 35,000 square feet with about 3,500 square feet of office space. Currently, 8,000 feet was sub-leased as warehouse space. This space was available on short notice for the relocation of some of the Accura equipment, which could lead to a number of cost saving synergies. The building had been purchased by TML Holdings for $1.5 million in 1998 with mortgage outstanding of $1 million. Equipment in the plant was generally quite new, of excellent quality and well-maintained. There was about $1.5 million debt owing on the equipment, in the form of term loans, as well as a capital lease. The employees were non-union.

POWERSINK TECHNOLOGIES INC. (POWERSINK)

In addition to the acquisition of Accura and Flexco, Wood had encountered an opportunity to manufacture heat-dissipation devices, complex metal components used to protect semi-conductors in telecommunications equipment such as cellular base stations. This involved the machining of aluminum base plates and bonding them to aluminum cooling fin attachments (see Exhibit 1). A heat sink manufacturing company was a dedicated precision machine shop that specialized in the fabrication of extruded aluminum into the variety of shapes that were required to meet the thermal management specifications for a vast array of semiconductors.

In addition to precision machining capabilities, a heat sink manufacturer required marketing and sales knowledge of the complex and diverse electronics industry as well as technical thermal electronics expertise. Existing heat sink companies tried to be specialists in everything from the smallest computer heat sink to the massive

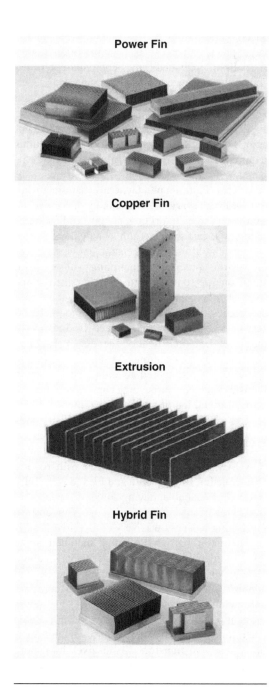

Power Fin

Copper Fin

Extrusion

Hybrid Fin

Exhibit 1   Picture of Heat Dissipation Devices (Heat Sink)

Source: Company files.

thermal management systems of the industrial drives industry. The result of this "Wal-Mart" approach to the industry was that no segment received the detailed, technical support it required in a rapidly changing environment and typically resulted in dismal product delivery performance. Powersink planned to specifically target the power electronics market, including telecommunications equipment, power supplies and motor controls. This $300-million, rapidly growing segment of the market in North America currently had no thermal specialist serving its unique requirements.

THE PROPOSED MANAGEMENT TEAM

Barry Wood was expected to take over as the CEO of the combined Accura/Flexco operation. No chief financial officer (CFO) had been identified but other members of the management team had been identified.

John Bell, Sales Manager

Bell was expected to be retained on a contract basis to ease the transition of the sale. He would assume sales responsibility across both Accura and Flexco. Bell appeared co-operative and willing to work for a few more years, but clearly wanted to cash in on some of his net worth now, as a result of the sale. WV expected he would be useful in assisting Wood in understanding the subtleties of the business and assisting in the transition.

Craig Jerry, Sales Executive

Jerry was to be hired as the successor to Bell as sales manager for Accura/Flexco. Initially, he would assist Bell and acquire thorough knowledge of Accura and Flexco customers and prospects, eventually assuming primary responsibility. Jerry had been a long-term employee of M&I Door, where he had technical sales, product development/improvement and customer trouble-shooting responsibilities. At M&I, Jerry had established excellent customer relations and had demonstrated a good grasp of mechanical and manufacturing issues. He was had studied machining in technical college and brought a creative approach to his work.

George Smith, Director of Logistics & Manufacturing Operations

Smith would initially assist Bell and Jerry in transitioning sales responsibility for Flexco customers to them, before assuming full responsibility for Accura/Flexco operations later in fiscal 2000.

Mike Steele, Manufacturing Manager

It was expected that Steele would work full time for one year to help with the transition in ownership until Smith assumed full manufacturing responsibility.

Doug Swallow, President and Director of Marketing & Sales—Powersink

Swallow, a former director of sales at large heat sink maker, R-Theta, was to be hired to have overall marketing and sales responsibility for Powersink.

David Fast, Manager of Application Engineering, Powersink

Having formerly served in the same position at R-Theta, Fast would assume primary responsibility for customer thermal engineering requirements and the development of Powersink's product offerings.

THE PRECISION MACHINING AND TOOLING MARKET

Each year, this industry produced billions of dollars' worth of precise parts made from a variety of metals and plastics for a range of industries, such as agriculture, automotive and other transport, aerospace, construction, defense, electronics, general manufacturing, medical/analytical and telecommunications. In the automotive industry, large precision-parts makers were often highly specialized, with dedicated, computer-controlled equipment designed to make specific parts at high rates. Aerospace had similar specialization, though volumes were lower than in automotive. Defense applications typically included military armament components. Electronics and telecommunications required a vast array of electro-mechanical components in their assemblies, as did medical/analytical equipment. General manufacturing required such services as machining of parts made from blank stock to drilling, tapping and facing of sand or die-cast sub-assembly components.

Servicing this array of customers was a range of custom precision machining shops, from small one-person shops to medium-sized shops such as Flexco and Accura. Unlike the small companies, shops like Flexco or Accura could service both small and bigger businesses at the level of sophistication necessary to meet big-company expectations. As shops increased in capacity, they appeared to either specialize in industry segments or become captive suppliers to a very limited list of satisfied customers.

The sophisticated end of the industry was now highly automated, with full computer-aided design and computer-aided manufacturing (CAD-CAM) capability and often with robotic parts transfer. Both Accura and Flexco were fully CAD-CAM capable, having some of the latest in CNC machinery and accessories. The custom machining business was very competitive.

The main barriers to entry included some level of machining expertise as well as capital to achieve operational economies of scale and sophistication to be competitive. Furthermore, the greater the complexity of parts, the fewer the competitors. Accura and Flexco represented custom machining businesses of a size and capability ready to transform themselves into more specialized shops either servicing specific industry segments or becoming captive suppliers to a very limited customer list. This would result in improved profitability due to reduced product change-over cycle time, plus lower production, supply chain and QA management costs.

THE THERMAL MANAGEMENT/ HEAT DISSIPATION MARKET

Semiconductors were the heart of the global electronics industry but they could not operate unless they were attached to an aluminum heat sink, a device that dissipated the excessive heat produced by the semiconductor into the ambient air. The $1-billion annual North American market for purchased heat sinks had traditionally been served by a number of companies. Chief among these were companies that attempted to provide a broad range of thermal management products to each and every segment of the electronics market. Most current heat sink manufacturers were concentrating on the high-volume, low-margin microprocessor industry because of its high public profile and volume manufacturing potential. Competition for these smaller heat sinks was high, with low-cost Asian manufacturers representing a real competitive threat.

The MDS Sciex Opportunity

This subsidiary of MDS was the world's leading maker of analytical instrumentation for drug discovery. Sciex was rapidly growing, with recent year-over-year growth of 58 per cent, and Sciex staff indicated that they had a minimum annual growth mandate of 25 per cent.

Sciex was emerging as a significant customer of Accura. Flexco was also an approved supplier to Sciex, currently in the $10,000 to $20,000 range per month and growing. Margins on Sciex business were high for both Accura and Flexco. Sciex had the need for a significant amount of precision machining services, to the point where it had acquired a 49 per cent equity interest in a precision machining company called QLP. Due to unsatisfactory performance by QLP, Sciex had recently exited this relationship. It was estimated that about $9 million of QLP business was now being re-positioned by Sciex.

Sciex expressed an interest in diverting significantly more business to Accura. In return, Sciex would need available capacity to meet spikes in supply requirements, an improvement in pricing, a commitment by the company to supply a technical sales person to support the relationship (which was not included in the Company's projections and would cost about $100,000). A joint effort was also required between Sciex and the Company to improve engineering interactivity (over the Internet) and to reduce product cycle time.

Competition

The largest competitor was Aavid, based in New Hampshire, with heat sink sales of more than US$140 million and consulting engineering sales of more than $40 million. Aavid engaged in all aspects of the thermal management field from stamped and formed board level heat sinks to liquid-cooled chill plates for true power applications.

In spite of its size, Aavid suffered from poor job execution and delivery performance. The company was still vigorously pursuing the microprocessor accounts such as Intel and AMD, to the detriment of business with the power electronics segment. Due to its size, Aavid was a competitor in power electronics, though it was expected its microprocessor focus would be an opportunity for Powersink.

Wakefield was the second largest heat sink manufacturer, boasting sales of US$65 million. Wakefield had suffered serious competitive pressure with its concentration in the microprocessor marketplace, to the point where it nearly entered Chapter 11 protection. Based in Massachusetts, Wakefield was now re-grouping and would again be a competitor.

Thermalloy, estimated to have US$45 million in sales, was recently sold by Bowthorpe International, Inc. to Aavid. Thermalloy had, in the last few years, focused on the microprocessor marketplace, with little effort in power electronics applications.

National Northeast was an aluminum extruder, part of the Mestek conglomerate, who in the past several years attempted to become a true thermal management company. National, based in New Hampshire, sold about $18 million of heat sinks per year. National was not anticipated to be a major competitive threat.

R-Theta, a privately owned Toronto-based company, had grown rapidly in the last six years, with 1998 sales of approximately $20 million. R-Theta had developed the patented Fabfin, a high-ratio fabricated heat sink used in a multitude of power and telecommunications applications. The Fabfin sold primarily in the U.S. market, but R-Theta was the largest Canadian manufacturer of standard heat sinks, with Aavid Canada providing close competition. R-Theta had been seriously weakened by mass defections of staff in the last two years. According to employees that had left the company, these departures occurred because of the poor people skills and lack of leadership skills at R-Theta. During due diligence, Wood had met with the president of R-Theta who had indicated that 15-times-earnings would be his asking price for a sale of R-Theta.

THE PROPOSED DEAL

It would take approximately $7.5 million to purchase all of the shares and assets of both Accura and Flexco, plus an increase in working capital to carry out the strategic plan put forth by Wood.

Part of the funds was to be obtained from an operating line of credit at the bank (not to exceed $2 million) that would be used to finance working capital. This operating line could not exceed 75 per cent of accounts receivable and 50 per cent of inventory. It was believed that the company could qualify for a rate on the operating line of prime plus 0.5 per cent. The prime rate at that time was 6.75 per cent.

In addition it was expected that the company could obtain a bank term loan of up to $1.25 million that would be repaid in equal annual payments over five years. The rate on the term loan was expected to be prime plus 0.85 per cent. The bank loans would require the Company to abide by covenants outlined in Exhibit 2.

It was common to require the vendors to provide a loan known as a vendor take-back (VTB) as part of a sale. It was believed that Bell, Steele and Smith could lend a total of up to $1.2 million, which would bear an interest rate

- Current ratio of 1.2/1 or higher
- Total debt to total tangible net worth ratio of 2.5/1 or higher
- Debt service coverage of 1.5/1 or higher. A lower level of 0.6/1 for fiscal year 2000 will be permitted.
- No payments to be made by the Company to WV or to VTB if such payment places the borrower in default of any of its obligations to the bank.
- General security agreement with full subordination and postponement of claim from WV, Barry Wood, the VTB, and shareholder loans, if applicable.

Exhibit 2   Anticipated Covenants in Bank Loan Agreement

of prime plus 0.5 per cent and would be repaid in three to five years.

Wood had up to $500,000 of personal funds available to put up in the form of any combination of debt and equity. Both WV and Wood wanted to maximize Wood's stake in the new opportunity and they knew that Wood wanted a position of significant influence in the business. Ideally, he would receive 10 per cent to 20 per cent of the common equity, either as direct equity or some form of convertible instrument.

The remainder of the funds was to come from an investment by WV. WV could invest via a debt instrument, straight preferred shares, a convertible instrument or a straight equity investment. WV was looking to exit its investment within five years.

THE EXCEL SPREADSHEET

In order to perform the analysis, Wood had provided a projected income statement and balance sheet in the form of an Excel spreadsheet. This information is provided in Exhibits 3 and 4. One of the key items in the forecast was anticipated sales from the heat sink operation. While Wood was very optimistic about these sales, Graham felt that there was a high degree of risk associated

	1999A	2000F	2001F	2002F	2003F	2004F
Revenue:						
Accura	4,219	5,500	6,188	6,961	7,831	8,810
Flexco	5,290	6,000	6,600	7,260	7,986	8,784
Total Gross Sales	*9,509*	*11,500*	*12,787*	*14,221*	*15,817*	*17,594*
Add: Powersink Technologies	—	*500*	*1,000*	*1,500*	*2,000*	*2,500*
Net Sales	9,509	12,000	13,787	15,721	17,817	20,094
Cost of Goods Sold:						
Materials and Subcontracting		3,332	3,803	4,315	4,873	5,481
Direct wages		3,055	3,508	3,998	4,529	5,106
Factory overhead		1,290	1,382	1,480	1,585	1,697
	5,560	7,678	8,693	9,793	10,986	12,284
Gross Profit	**3,949**	**4,322**	**5,094**	**5,928**	**6,831**	**7,811**
Margin As a % of Net Sales	41.53%	36.02%	36.95%	37.71%	38.34%	38.87%
Operating Expenses:						
Sales and marketing		104	107	109	112	114
General and Administrative		732	783	852	871	891
Powersink startup		1,757	1,266	844	846	849
Total Operating Expenses	**2,673**	**2,593**	**2,156**	**1,805**	**1,829**	**1,854**
Operating Income	**1,276**	**1,730**	**2,938**	**4,123**	**5,001**	**5,957**
Interest Expense (Income)	134	98	76	54	33	11
Depreciation	590	998	963	963	962	960
Less: mgt bonus/vehicles	996	—	—	—	—	—
	1,720	1,095	1,040	1,018	995	971
Income Before Taxes	**553**	**634**	**1,898**	**3,105**	**4,006**	**4,985**
Taxes	221	254	759	1,242	1,603	1,994
Net Income	332	380	1,139	1,863	2,404	2,991
EBITDA- Normalized For Bonuses	**2,272**	**1,730**	**2,938**	**4,123**	**5,001**	**5,957**

Exhibit 3 Pro Forma Income Statement, Consolidated Company, for Fiscal Years Ending November 30 (in $000s)

Note: Numbers are rounded to the nearest dollar.

	Consolidated company for fiscal years ending November 30 (in $000s)					
	1999A	**2000F**	**2001F**	**2002F**	**2003F**	**2004F**
ASSETS	Pro-forma Consolidated					
Current Assets						
Cash	0	0	0	0	0	0
Prepaid expense	47	25	30	35	40	45
Accounts receivable	1,734	2,435	2,746	3,230	3,620	4,193
Inventory	930	663	700	835	886	1,038
Advance to affiliates	—	0	0	0	0	0
Income taxes recoverable	—	0	0	0	0	0
Total Current Assets	2,711	3,123	3,475	4,100	4,546	5,276
Fixed Assets, net	4,963	4,686	4,493	4,542	4,583	4,618
Investment in affiliates	84	84	84	84	84	84
Goodwill	3,411	3,240	3,070	2,908	2,754	2,609
	8,458	8,011	7,647	7,534	7,421	7,311
Total Assets	11,169	11,134	11,123	11,634	11,968	12,587
Liabilities & Shareholders' Equity						
Current liabilities						
Operating line	0	0	0	0	0	0
Accounts payable	458	823	850	890	969	1,056
Income taxes payable	268	0	0	0	0	0
Current Portion- LTD	543	290	290	290	290	290
Total Current Liabilities	1,269	1,113	1,140	1,180	1,259	1,347
Deferred income taxes	366	366	366	366	366	366
Due to shareholder	191	191	191	191	191	191
Existing term loan	1,451	1,161	871	580	290	0
Accura and Flexco vendor take-back	0	0	0	0	0	0
New bank term loan	0	0	0	0	0	0
WV debenture	0	0	0	0	0	0
Barry Wood debenture	0	0	0	0	0	0
WV straight preferred shares	0	0	0	0	0	0
Barry Wood straight preferred shares	0	0	0	0	0	0
	2,007	1,717	1,427	1,137	847	556
Total Liabilities	3,276	2,830	2,567	2,317	2,106	1,903
Shareholders' Equity						
WV convertible debt	0	0	0	0	0	0
Barry Wood convertible debt	0	0	0	0	0	0
WV convertible preferred	0	0	0	0	0	0
Barry Wood convertible preferred	0	0	0	0	0	0
WV new common	0	0	0	0	0	0
Barry Wood new common	0	0	0	0	0	0
Share capital	2	2	2	2	2	2
Retained earnings	0	380	1,520	3,383	5,786	8,778
	2	382	1,522	3,385	5,788	8,780
Required Financing	7,891	7,921	7,034	5,932	4,074	1,904
Total Liabilities & SH Equity	11,169	11,134	11,123	11,634	11,968	12,587
Balance Sheet Error	0	0	0	0	0	0

Exhibit 4   Pro Forma Balance Sheet

Note: Numbers are rounded to the nearest dollar.

with this new venture. He was inclined to structure the deal to provide a reasonable rate of return even if these sales did not materialize. He also noted that the forecasted sales from the combined Accura and Flexco operations could be optimistic and perhaps year-over-year growth could be somewhat lower.

A more detailed spreadsheet including the two financial statements, key assumptions, selected ratios and an internal rate of return (IRR) analysis were prepared for both Wood and WV. This model could be employed as a tool to structure the deal.

THE CHALLENGE

Michael Graham knew that he had to prepare a term sheet that made the case for an investment in this new company. As part of his analysis, he had to identify the key opportunities and risks, provide a deal structure that met the needs of WV and Wood and contained any key clauses

that should be part of any shareholders' agreement. With the foregoing in mind, he set about his task.

NOTES

1. Labour Sponsored Venture Capital Funds were also known as Labour Sponsored Investment Funds (LSIFs).

2. WV was restricted to these criteria at the time of investment, however, WV was able to invest in a limited number of "ineligible" investments, but the money invested in those opportunities would not count toward LSIF pacing requirements legislated by the government.

3. Executives-in-residence were common in venture capital (VC) firms that were looking for experienced operators to help monitor existing investments, "round-out" or become managers of existing portfolio companies and to evaluate potential investments within that EIR's sector expertise.

4. Cycle time refers to the time it takes from the beginning to the end of the manufacturing cycle.

NATIONAL IR: CATALYST INVESTMENTS ACQUISITION OF MONTREAUX

Prepared by Robert Jaques under the supervision of Professor Basil A. Kalymon

Version: (A) 2003-08-13

In March 2001, Peter Block, senior consultant and project lead for National IR, a division of National Public Relations (National), considered his approach to the proposed Catalyst Investments (Catalyst) acquisition of Montreaux. Later in the day, Block would be meeting with Philip Koven, head of the Toronto investor relations division of National. Catalyst had requested assistance with investor and public relations with respect to its planned hostile takeover offer for Montreaux Inc., and Block felt strongly that

National could bring significant skills to the table to help Catalyst sell its deal to investors.

BACKGROUND

Catalyst Investments was a 50-50 joint venture of Aurora Capital Investments Inc. (Aurora) and Frederick Inc. It was incorporated for the sole purpose of making an offer for Montreaux.

Aurora had developed the opinion that Montreaux was being ineffectively managed. The bulk of Montreaux's assets were held in cash. Those investments that were made were mostly in private companies, and the compensation to the top managers was excessive compared both to the value of the business and the value created for minority shareholders. Aurora felt that Montreaux was simply making passive investments, rather than actively creating opportunities from which Montreaux's shareholders could directly benefit. Investments in private companies such as DieMet did not allow Montreaux investors the visibility of their investments, making their company difficult to value. Montreau's sole public investment, Compsol, was in a cyclical industry and seemed to be at the peak of its value at the time of the bid.

Aurora also felt that Montreaux's diverse investments provided no real synergy opportunities, and that the company's share price was suffering from a significant holding company discount, with net book value of close to $8 per share, nearly double the share price.

Catalyst believed that the shares of Montreaux were significantly undervalued, and that a new manager could generate additional value by divesting all or most of the existing businesses and distributing the company's cash to shareholders. Catalyst intended to take over the company with a leveraged bid, and use the excess cash in the company to pay off the debt that would be incurred in the acquisition of Montreaux's shares. Catalyst then intended to sell the assets to realize the value that was currently discounted by the market.

NATIONAL IR

National Public Relations (www.national.ca) was Canada's largest communications consultancy with expertise in corporate communications, public affairs, organizational communications, marketing communications, technology communications and investor relations. Established in Montreal, the firm was first established as the leader in the business and financial market there. The firm also had offices across Canada and in the United States.

The firm provided a wide range of public relations and investor relations (IR) services to clients, including market research, government relations, crisis and issues management, and media relations/training. The IR practice, National IR, had 20 dedicated staff and also used the expertise of over 280 other communications professionals around the country. Client mandates ranged from pre-IPO technology startups to blue chip multinational corporations.

The firm viewed investor relations as critical to a public company's ability to support a strong and stable share price. An effective IR program often meant the difference between an industry-leading stock valuation and merely being one of the pack. An IR program should play a role in reducing the cost of capital, creating a fair market valuation, enhancing the credibility and reputation of an issuer and developing the appropriate shareholder base.

AURORA

Aurora Capital Investments Inc. was a small, private merchant bank with a strong track record for delivering exceptional returns through the leveraged acquisition and stewardship of select corporations. Aurora was formed in 1985 by two partners, both of whom held MBAs, one from Dalhousie University and the other from the University of Western Ontario.

Aurora managed a series of investment funds, with a minimum return target of 25 per cent, and had consistently exceeded this rate of return. As a private merchant bank, investors in Aurora's deals were required to invest a minimum of $250,000 each.

Aurora was usually a lead investor that assembled groups of other investors to buy mostly private companies or to make catalyst investments in smaller firms. When they felt a firm was undervalued, Aurora would take a stake and plan an exit within a relatively short period of time, two to three years. The company had not participated in any hostile bidding situations previous to the Montreaux opportunity. Aurora used the following criteria to identify lucrative, low-risk industries: a historically high level of industry profitability; excellent growth prospects; recession resistance due to necessity-type demand for the industry's products or services; fragmented industry structure conducive to future add-on acquisitions or merger opportunities; and barriers to entry that limited competition from new players. Once an attractive industry was identified, Aurora Capital applied stringent investment criteria to select a well-managed, mid-sized acquisition candidate to serve as a platform for growth in the target industry.

The parameters of investment were dictated by the particular circumstances of each transaction. Due to the exhaustive nature of the research and due diligence that had preceded any transaction, Aurora had a clear perception of the appropriate amount of equity justified by the scope of each individual investment opportunity and was willing to commit the required amount. The partners did their homework; they liked the company and, as a result, there was nothing tentative in their approach to the transaction; when it was deemed appropriate, they also brought in partners, and they had done this successfully in a number of transactions. Partners in portfolio companies included CIBC Wood Gundy Capital, Ontario Teachers' Pension Plan Board, HSBC Capital, and Hospitals of Ontario Pension Plan Board.

Aurora's experienced team then worked with management and carefully selected external specialists to provide the acquired company with the professional and capital resources it needed to rise to the next level. Each acquisition was structured and subsequently managed to maximize long-term value. While all transactions were prudently leveraged to enhance returns, investments with higher volatility were capitalized with greater equity to ensure adequate funding for ongoing growth. With this approach, Aurora Capital had been able to generate outstanding returns and create attractive liquidity events.

Long-term investment was the essence of Aurora Capital's strategy. Philosophically, the company followed in the footsteps of Warren Buffett's idea of selecting industries that have "Mouth-Watering Economics," simply because it is the one investment strategy that had proven to be the best over the course of time. While investments were managed for the long-term, liquidity opportunities, such as IPOs, were provided for investors at the appropriate time. IPOs typically took place when the company required public capital to reach the next stage of growth. Aurora viewed the entry of portfolio companies into the public markets as a normal and necessary event to building the company for the long-term. Once the company had entered the public arena, investors could then determine their own investment horizon for their interest in the company, based on their views of the prospects for the industry and the company's prospects as a platform within it. Aurora's time horizon to providing these liquidity opportunities was from three to seven years.

The proposed acquisition of Montreaux was a departure from Aurora. While the target company was subject to the usual detailed due diligence of Aurora, its status as a holding company to be liquidated was quite different from Aurora's usual "buy and enhance" strategy.

FREDERICK

Frederick Inc. was a private Canadian investment firm dedicated to achieving superior returns through investing in high-quality North American public and private companies. The firm was founded in 1990 by Bob Frederick, former chief executive officer (CEO) of a major investment bank.

Frederick assembled a leading team of partners who would draw upon a distinguished network of advisors in the company's portfolio management. The principals offered a track record of successfully identifying and realizing investment opportunities in both the public and private capital markets.

Frederick focused on companies in the health care, biotechnology and information technology industries with distinctive product advantages, an inspired and experienced management team and a sound strategy for exciting growth. The company assessed entrepreneurs for their vision, ability to attract and retain talented employees, a commitment to the long term and an accountability that stakeholders could depend on.

Frederick looked for companies with the potential to become what we term a platform company—a dominant player in a strategic space able to leverage its leadership position into related areas. Frederick found platform companies to be prolific builders of value.

Frederick invested at various stages of a company's development, and unlike most firms, invested actively in both private and public companies. There was no set rule on investment size. Frederick had invested from as little as $25,000 to seed-fund a project, to close to $10 million in a more mature opportunity.

Though the decision process could last anywhere from several hours to several months, depending on the nature of the opportunity, a time frame of three to six weeks was most common. A company expected to make two or three presentations to the Frederick team as the opportunity was being evaluated. Members of the team who were most involved in the relevant practice area drove the process, but everyone at the firm was exposed to the company during the evaluation. In addition to direct presentations, product demonstrations and a business plan review, considerable weight was placed on reference checks for the company (customers and/or partners) and for the entrepreneurs. Frederick also strongly believed that the investment evaluation process was bi-directional. They were evaluating a potential investment opportunity, and the entrepreneur was evaluating a potential venture partner. Personal chemistry, relevant previous experiences and relationships, and a shared passion for the company vision were all important components of the investment decision, both for the entrepreneur and for Frederick.

As with Aurora, the strategy to "buy and liquidate" was a departure.

Montreaux

Montreaux was formed in 1993 as part of the restructuring of the large Swift family business. The financial unit of the family business had suffered significant losses and was in violation of capitalization requirements for financial firms in Canada. As part of the restructuring, the financial unit was sold to an insurance company, and the remaining assets were spun into Montreaux. At the same time, the family interest was reduced from 80 per cent to 15 per cent, and two principals, David Swift, CEO, and Fred Majors, chief operating officer (COO), negotiated a "profit participation right" clause into the organization's makeup (described in the last paragraph of this section).

Initially, Montreaux consisted of assets in various industries, including real estate, chemicals, and marine transport. In 1999, Montreaux acquired control of a pension consulting firm for $4.5 million, which was sold in 2000 for $4.3 million. In 2000, Montreaux made acquisitions in the broadcasting and telecommunications industries, both of which were minority investments in existing companies. By early 2001, Montreaux consisted of the investments shown in Exhibit 1.

David Swift was well known in Toronto financial circles. When Catalyst approached the brokerages in Toronto, it was discovered that every major house had done business with either Montreaux or Swift directly and therefore would be in conflict if they assisted Catalyst with its bid for Montreaux.

The financial statements of Montreaux are shown in Exhibit 2, 3, and 4. According to the 2000 balance sheet, Montreaux held approximately $140 million of free cash. As of December 31, 2000, Montreaux had 26,106,853 shares outstanding, and its assets consisted primarily of the cash, plus the stakes in Compsol, DieMet, CanMet Media and English Telecom. The total market capitalization as of December 31, 2000, was $103,122,069.

Company	Industry	Interest
Compsol	Environmental/ Chemical	Minority share (44.2%) with control through shareholders agreement to elect majority of board. Company was publicly traded
DieMet	Automotive	Minority share (33.7%) with control through shareholders agreement to elect majority of board. Private Company
CanMet Media	Broadcasting	Minority interest (42.9%). Private company
English Telecom	Telecommunications	Minority interest (21.25%). Private company

Exhibit 1   Montreaux Investments as of 2001

Year	2000	1999	1998
Net Sales	$591,208	$640,588	$585,962
Earnings before undernoted	$62,252	$78,271	$79,087
Interest expense	$(36,391)	$(40,318)	$(41,299)
Depreciation and amortization	$(41,026)	$(40,647)	$(39,048)
Interest, fee, and other income	$14,209	$13,617	$18,944
Gain(loss) on early retirement of debt	$28,842	$—	$(11,235)
Loss on disposition and other costs	$(65,294)	$—	$—
Other restructuring costs	$(11,137)	$—	$—
Dilution gain	$—	$—	$—
Earnings (loss) from continuing operations	$(48,545)	$10,923	$6,449
Income tax (provision) recovery	$(644)	$(3,572)	$(1,875)
Non-controlling interest in loss (earnings)	$17,400	$(2,092)	$5,073
(Loss) earnings from continuing operations	$(31,789)	$5,259	$9,647
Earnings (loss) from discontinued operations	$7,072	$12,883	$66,054
Net (loss) earnings for the year	$(24,717)	$18,142	$75,701
Retained earnings, beginning of year	$158,454	$143,609	$68,816
Adjustment to reflect adoption of new accounting standard for income taxes	$788	$—	$—
Excess of purchase price over stated value of shares purchased for cancellation	$(1,443)	$(3,297)	$(908)
Retained earnings, end of year	$133,082	$158,454	$143,609
(Loss) earnings per share			
Continuing operations	$(1.20)	$0.19	$0.41
Net (loss) earnings	$(0.93)	$0.66	$3.20
Weighted average number of shares	26,504,197	27,557,125	23,691,469

Exhibit 2   Montreaux Income Statements ($000s)

Montreaux Consolidated Balance Sheets			
Year	2000	1999	1998
Assets			
Current assets			
Cash and equivalents	$163,869	$260,130	$211,647
Accounts receivable	$90,085	$91,407	$111,513
Inventories and other	$38,661	$47,799	$69,121
	$292,615	$399,336	$392,281
Property plant and equipment	$262,185	$256,415	$277,597
Other assets	$29,561	$24,134	$24,573
Goodwill, net	$179,164	$180,495	$196,858
Assets of discontinued operations	$—	$2,332	$8,605
Total Assets	$763,525	$862,712	$899,914
Liabilities			
Current liabilities			
Bank indebtedness of consolidated entities	$18,111	$—	$1,595
Accounts payable and accrued liabilities	$104,938	$115,207	$116,133
Current portion of long-term debt and obligations under capital leases of consolidated entities	$17,043	$10,610	$9,819
	$140,092	$125,817	$127,547
Long-term debt of consolidated entities	$296,404	$361,284	$398,242
Other long-term liabilities of consolidated entities	$7,725	$6,908	$61,431
Future income tax liabilities	$16,883	$7,546	$16,724
Non-controlling interests	$96,016	$116,525	$60,062
Liabilities of discontinued operations	$—	$10,377	$8,512
	$557,120	$628,457	$672,518
Shareholders' equity			
Capital stock	$71,631	$74,234	$77,909
Retained earnings	$133,082	$158,454	$143,609
Cumulative translation adjustments	$1,692	$1,567	$5,878
	$206,405	$234,255	$227,396

Exhibit 3   Montreaux Balance Sheets ($000s)

One aspect of Montreaux's organization was a "profit participation right" held by both Swift and Majors. Under this "incentive compensation plan," the two principals were entitled to 10 per cent of the pretax profits of the firm. This plan was eliminated in 2000, and resulted in a one-time payment of $11 million to the affected managers to compensate them for the elimination of the plan. According to the information circulars sent to investors, the CEO and COO had been paid a total of $41 million between 1993 and 2000, including the payout for the elimination of the incentive plan. See Exhibit 5 for more information about the elimination of the plan.

Compsol Inc.

Compsol was a leading provider of outsourced environmental compliance solutions, with a focus on air quality compliance, including entrained solid and liquid emissions. Originally an "orphan division" of a major chemical producer, the company was spun off as a private company to a group controlled by the Swift family. As part of

| | | | Parent | | |
| | Environmental | | Company | Consolidation | Consolidated |
Year: 2000	Services	Manufacturing	and other*	adjustments	Total
Reportable Segments					
Net Sales	$386,728	$183,458	$21,022	$—	$591,208
Earnings from continuing operations	$49,077	$20,302	$(8,186)	$1,059	$62,252
Interest expense	$(20,069)	$(16,165)	$(161)	$4	$(36,391)
Depreciation and amortization	$(27,526)	$(12,369)	$(1,309)	$178	$(41,026)
Interest, fee, and other income	$4,521	$863	$10,066	$(1,241)	$14,209
Gain on early retirement of long term debt	$—	$28,842	$—	$—	$28,842
Loss on disposition and other costs	$(46,709)	$(11,045)	$(7,540)	$—	$(65,294)
Other restructuring costs	$—	$—	$(11,137)	$—	$(11,137)
Income tax recovery	$2,310	$(4,542)	$1,588	$—	$(644)
Non-controlling interest	$21,171	$(3,814)	$43	$—	$17,400
					$—
Earnings from continuing operations	$(17,225)	$2,072	$(16,636)	$—	$(31,789)
					$—
Total assets	$327,965	$259,126	$177,967	$(1,533)	$763,525
					$—
Captial expenditures, net	$16,705	$17,390	$1,737	$—	$35,832

Exhibit 4   Montreaux Segmented Income Statement ($000s)

* Parent company and other amounts include CanMet and English Telecom from their respective dates of acquistion.

the restructuring, it was included in the assets transferred to Montreaux. In 1996, Compsol completed an IPO to raise approximately $61 million through a warrants offering to existing shareholders. At the end of 2000, Compsol's market capitalization was $62.7 million, with 31.35 million shares outstanding. (See Compsol financial statements in Exhibit 6 and 7.)

Compsol was the world's largest provider of traditional flue gas desulphurization systems and services to the electrical power generation industry. The company technology was utilized in 215 units—111 of them outside of North America. This technology was licensed to an exclusive licensee in North America and to 16 licensees outside North America.

Compsol's proprietary advanced technology included a state-of-the-art thermal treatment system, complete with a sophisticated emission control system. The fully automated, high-capacity plant has the ability to treat up to 100,000 tonnes of contaminated soils per year. Compsol believed that this technology delivered the best available efficiency related to capturing SO_2 emissions and minimizing CO_2 production, all at better economics.

Most of Compsol's customers typically operated in the energy industry, principally in electrical power generation and oil refining. They were faced with stricter environmental regulations and the need to reduce costs and improve operating margins. They also recognized outsourcing as an

---

1. **Termination of Incentive Compensation Rights**

Effective March 31, 2000, the Company has recorded the effects of the restructuring of its incentive compensation arrangements with two senior executives, the terms of which included the termination of the executives' rights under the Company's Incentive Compensation Plan (the ICP). The ICP entitled the executives to purchase, at the Company's cost, up to 10 per cent of each of its investments and entitled them to 10 per cent of the Company's cash income. The $11.1 million of restructuring costs represents the cost to the Company, including transaction costs, of terminating the executives' rights under the ICP.

Under the agreement, Montreaux will also pay approximately $9.2 million, including transaction costs, to purchase the executives participation interests in nine existing investments, including Montreaux two principal investments, Compsol Inc. ("Compsol") and DieMet Inc. ("DieMet"). As a result, Montreaux interest in the earnings of Compsol will increase to 41.8 per cent from 38.5 per cent and in DieMet will increase to 34.2 per cent from 31.1 per cent.

In connection with these arrangements, the executives will, subject to certain conditions, use a significant portion of their after-tax proceeds to acquire common shares of the Company in the market.

The payments in respect of this transaction will be made in May 2000.

Exhibit 5   Note Regarding Incentive Compensation

Source: This note appeared in the "Notes to the Consolidated Interim Financial Statements" March 31, 2000 and 1999.

Year	2000	1999	1998
Revenue	$386,728	$429,918	$384,690
Cost of sales and services	$278,217	$307,708	$269,173
Gross Profit	$108,511	$122,210	$115,517
SG&A	$59,428	$63,999	$57,435
Gain on disposal of property, plant and equipment	$(871)	$(43)	$(553)
Depreciation	$18,179	$18,884	$17,046
Earnings from Operations	$31,775	$39,370	$41,589
Loss on disposal of Trade company	$(46,709)	$—	$—
Write-off of deferred charges			$(2,746)
Amortization of deferred foreign exchange	$(1,087)	$(661)	$(1,762)
Amortization of deferred charges	$(1,442)	$(1,563)	$(1,645)
Interest income	$4,225	$2,930	$1,962
Interest expense	$(20,069)	$(20,864)	$(17,916)
Earnings (loss) before income taxes, minority interest and amortization of goodwill	$(33,307)	$19,212	$19,482
Income taxes			
Current	$2,376	$379	$2,575
Future	$(2,261)	$5,390	$4,623
Minority interest	$2,088	$1,800	$1,601
Earnings (loss) before amortization of goodwill	$(35,510)	$11,643	$10,683
Amortization of goodwill	$4,332	$4,657	$4,155
Net earnings (loss)	$(39,842)	$6,986	$6,528
(Loss) earnings per share before goodwill amortization	$(1.13)	$0.37	$0.34
Earnings per share	$(1.27)	$0.22	$0.21

Exhibit 6   Compsol Operating Statements ($000s)

Year	2000	1999	1998
Assets			
Current Assets			
Cash and equivalents	$31,999	$57,918	$39,138
Accounts Receivable	$54,718	$57,609	$71,130
Future tax asset	$—	$3,411	$—
Inventories and Other	$8,221	$13,442	$14,028
Prepaid expenses	$742	$1,464	$4,247
	$95,680	$133,844	$128,543
Property plant and equipment	$127,247	$133,198	$149,313
Deferred charges and other assets, net	$12,092	$11,338	$16,517
Goodwill, net	$82,086	$97,461	$109,275
	$317,105	$375,841	$403,648
Liabilities			
Current liabilities			
Accounts payable	$35,647	$32,145	$43,834
Accrued liabilities	$18,560	$29,152	$26,314
Income taxes payable	$1,773	$4,950	$505
Future tax liability	$189	$—	$—
Current portion of long-term debt	$12,002	$10,103	$9,329
	$68,171	$76,350	$79,982
Long-term debt	$182,274	$186,906	$211,411
Other liabilities	$4,016	$6,197	$9,123
Future tax liability	$12,476	$18,952	$18,019
Minority Interest	$9,221	$7,543	$5,940
	$207,987	$219,598	$244,493
Shareholders' equity			
Capital stock	$57,505	$57,505	$57,505
Retained earnings	$(22,412)	$17,430	$11,233
Cumulative translation adjustments	$5,854	$4,958	$10,435
	$40,947	$79,893	$79,173
	$317,105	$375,841	$403,648

Exhibit 7   Compsol Balance Sheets ($000s)

attractive alternative because it would allow them to focus their resources, including capital, on core activities. Compsol also provided services to the pulp and paper industry and was a leading provider of water treatment chemicals and services in Western Canada.

Compsol's complete outsourcing services covered all aspects of environmental compliance activities, from project risk assessment through to byproduct marketing and distribution expertise.

Industry studies estimated huge capital spending on compliance assets would be required by power generators and oil refiners over the next few years to meet environmental requirements.

Power generation	Estimated that more than $40 billion would have to be spent to bring older coal-fired plants to the same efficiency level required of new ones.

Oil refining   Capital investment of over US$10 billion per year over next five years would be required to meet currently mandated U.S. environmental regulations.

DieMet

DieMet was a leading international manufacturer distributor and supplier in the metal fabrication, metal stamping and injecting mold components used in the tool and die and mold industries. DieMet conducted its operations through four principal operating units: the die set division (die sets), the components division (die set and mold base components) and the fabrications division in North America, and a division in Europe. DieMet was a publicly traded company that was taken private by a group led by Montreaux in 1997.

DieMet's modern manufacturing facilities and highly specialized equipment, including computer automated manufacturing equipment large enough to produce large-scale and complex die sets and mold bases, was one of DieMet's significant competitive advantages relative to most smaller regional manufacturers. DieMet also had broad component manufacturing capabilities which, together with its die set and mold base capabilities, enabled it to be one of the leading full service manufacturers in the die set, mold base and related components industries.

DieMet had produced consistent growth with revenues increasing from $450,000 in 1975 to over $190 million in the 1998 fiscal year. Nearly $90 million was spent on capital expenditures for new plants and modern equipment and $45 million on selected acquisitions to expand capacity and extend the company's product line and geographic reach. The company's manufacturing facilities were state-of-the-art, highly efficient, and had significantly expanded capacity to respond to continuing growth. Exhibit 8 gives DieMet's historical share price leading up to the acquisition by Montreaux.

Month	Price	Volume
Aug-97	Acquired at $8.00	
Jul-97	$7.95	4,820
Jun-97	$7.95	1,760
May-97	$6.70	724
Apr-97	$6.75	461
Mar-97	$6.50	350
Feb-97	$7.45	452
Jan-97	$7.10	671
Dec-96	$6.30	807
Nov-96	$6.60	523
Oct-96	$6.00	530
Sep-96	$5.80	1,890
Aug-96	$5.35	450
Jul-96	$5.05	262
Jun-96	$5.20	400
May-96	$5.85	944
Apr-96	$4.90	758
Mar-96	$5.00	600
Feb-96	$5.00	732
Jan-96	$5.13	426
Dec-95	$5.38	1,150
Nov-95	$5.25	3,710
Oct-95	$6.00	218
Sep-95	$6.13	85
Aug-95	$6.88	541
Jul-95	$6.88	269
Jun-95	$6.00	269
May-95	$6.25	600
Apr-95	$5.88	315
Mar-95	$6.13	120
Feb-95	$6.13	108
Jan-95	$5.75	291

Exhibit 8   Diemet Share Prices Prior to Acquisition by Montreaux

Source: Bloomberg.

Shares outstanding at time of acquisition: 23.1 million

OWNERSHIP OF MONTREAUX

Beginning in February 2001, Catalyst acquired shares in Montreaux and forecast that in late April their company would approach the 10 per cent ownership limit, when it would be required to declare its intentions for Montreaux publicly. See the purchase schedule in Exhibit 9.

At the time, the ownership of Montreaux consisted of approximately eight to 10 institutional investors holding less than half of the stock, with the rest held by retail investors. On a fully diluted basis, Swift held 20 per cent of the stock, including approximately 2.5 million stock options with an average exercise price of $3.15.

VALUATION

Catalyst had prepared valuations for Montreaux that led Williams to believe a bid in the range of $6 to $6.30 per share would allow room for negotiation and still provide a profit to Catalyst. The maximum price that Catalyst was prepared to pay for Montreaux was under $7 per share.

The valuations were based on the public information about Compsol and the historic information about DieMet prior to the takeover. As well, Catalyst had compared Montreaux to other companies in the management and diversified category of the TSE. Selected information about comparable companies is given in Exhibit 10. The historical

Stocks purchased by Catalyst to March 30, 2001		
Date	Number of Shares	Price per share
24-Jan-01	104,800	$3.95
02-Feb-01	200,000	$4.10
05-Feb-01	50,000	$4.45
06-Feb-01	50,000	$4.40
09-Feb-01	23,200	$4.46
15-Feb-01	150,000	$4.70
22-Feb-01	83,900	$4.70
23-Feb-01	29,500	$4.70
27-Feb-01	413,900	$4.98
28-Feb-01	(11,300)	$4.70
30-Mar-01	208,200	$4.88
30-Mar-01	(5,000)	$4.82
Total	1,297,200	

Exhibit 9   Catalyst Share Purchase Schedule

Source: Internal documents.

share prices are given in Exhibits 11 and 12, while selected economic data is given in Exhibit 13.

Company	Net Assets (millions)	P/E	Price/Book	Price/Sales	Price/ Cashflow	Book Value per share	Beta
Montreaux	$206.4	N/A	0.49	0.17	9.3	$7.91	0.43
Brascan	$6,340	11.2	0.91	2.43	8.52	$24.59	0.54
Onex	$19,700	17.16	0.5	0.15	564.8	$12.24	1.18
Compsol	$40.9	14.93	1.54	0.18	2.84	$1.30	0.66
TSE		19.38					

Exhibit 10   Selected Comparable Ratios

Source: Bloomberg, company annual reports.

	Montreaux		Compsol		TSE Index	
	Close	Volume (000)	Close	Volume (000)	Close	Volume (million)
Dec-00	$3.90	282	$2.00	289	8,933.70	2,000
Nov-00	$3.90	1,240	$2.25	71	8,819.90	1,800
Oct-00	$4.25	156	$3.05	73	9,639.60	2,030
Sep-00	$4.10	131	$2.96	314	10,379.00	1,750
Aug-00	$4.05	140	$3.00	150	11,247.90	1,830
Jul-00	$4.60	1,140	$3.00	122	10,406.31	1,520
Jun-00	$4.65	208	$3.30	233	10,195.45	1,910
May-00	$4.75	1,810	$3.65	740	9,251.99	2,170
Apr-00	$4.75	837	$3.35	1,790	9,347.61	1,840
Mar-00	$4.85	1,300	$2.75	614	9,462.39	2,260
Feb-00	$4.90	988	$3.15	105	9,128.99	2,040
Jan-00	$4.35	757	$3.10	145	8,481.11	1,750
Dec-99	$4.64	1,140	$3.20	198	8,415.75	1,510
Nov-99	$4.55	2,760	$2.95	736	7,523.23	1,600
Oct-99	$4.95	107	$3.10	45	7,256.22	1,260
Sep-99	$4.95	183	$3.45	707	6,957.12	1,440
Aug-99	$5.20	342	$3.50	335	6,970.81	1,480
Jul-99	$5.30	692	$3.65	354	7,081.03	1,210
Jun-99	$5.25	1,640	$3.50	3,230	7,010.09	1,380
May-99	$5.65	516	$3.99	325	6,841.80	1,210
Apr-99	$5.80	1,100	$3.65	315	7,014.70	1,580
Mar-99	$5.20	1,010	$4.00	247	6,597.79	1,650
Feb-99	$5.30	630	$4.20	438	6,312.69	1,160
Jan-99	$5.25	748	$4.20	20	6,729.56	1,230
Dec-98	$5.05	1,930	$4.05	520	6,485.94	1,180
Nov-98	$5.00	1,920	$4.30	237	6,343.87	1,330
Oct-98	$5.20	1,380	$5.00	840	6,208.28	1,420
Sep-98	$4.45	456	$4.50	480	5,614.12	1,380
Aug-98	$4.25	400	$5.75	400	5,530.71	1,180
Jul-98	$5.00	601	$7.80	37	6,931.43	1,090
Jun-98	$5.30	1,440	$9.10	638	7,366.89	1,360
May-98	$5.80	823	$8.75	2,450	7,589.78	992
Apr-98	$5.35	255	$7.80	146	7,664.99	1,360

Exhibit 11   Selected Share Prices to December 2000

Source: Bloomberg.

Shares outstanding for Compsol at time of case: 31.5 million.

Daily Closing Share Prices				
Date	Montreaux		Compsol	TSE Index
30-Mar	$4.85	108.4	$2.45	3.0	7,608.0
29-Mar	$4.80	210.8			7,444.8
28-Mar	$4.85	18.4	$2.45	1.5	7,506.5
27-Mar	$4.70	70.0			7,751.3
26-Mar	$4.80	12.0	$2.35	0.3	7,686.6
23-Mar	$4.70	32.5	$2.35	1.2	7,639.8
22-Mar	$4.70	3.5	$2.25	3.0	7,665.7
21-Mar	$4.85	560.0	$2.00	0.2	7,665.5
20-Mar	$4.70	3.4			7,756.5
19-Mar	$4.50	3.0	$2.25	2.6	7,811.1
16-Mar	$4.60	7.1			7,752.2
15-Mar	$4.50	5.0			7,823.1
14-Mar	$4.45	15.6	$2.35	3.5	7,806.9
13-Mar	$4.50	8.6			7,959.5
12-Mar	$4.46	1.2			7,930.3
9-Mar	$4.46	3.6	$2.24	26.6	8,135.5
8-Mar	$4.50	3.1	$2.25	1.5	8,227.6
7-Mar	$4.75	0.3	$2.15	116.2	8,301.8
6-Mar	$4.60	3.7			8,205.6
5-Mar	$4.65	4.3	$2.11	1.0	8,099.3
2-Mar	$4.65	1.7	$2.11	2.3	8,006.9
1-Mar	$4.80	0.3			8,193.8
28-Feb	$4.55	27.7	$2.25	1.6	8,078.7
27-Feb	$4.98	419.0	$2.05	8.0	8,065.7
26-Feb	$4.75	12.1	$2.35	3.7	8,149.8
23-Feb	$4.75	11.3			8,028.8
22-Feb	$4.80	31.8			8,103.8
21-Feb	$4.70	16.4	$2.30	3.1	8,060.8
20-Feb	$4.70	416.0	$2.30	0.4	8,236.7
19-Feb	$4.00	4.2	$2.30	3.4	8,459.7
16-Feb	$4.70	65.9	$2.35	1.6	8,393.2
15-Feb	$4.65	4.4	$2.45	3.0	8,967.3

Daily Closing Share Prices				
Date	Montreaux		Compsol	TSE Index
14-Feb	$4.65	170.6	$2.45	6.7	8,911.5
13-Feb	$4.65	5.2	$2.43	2.5	8,942.1
12-Feb	$4.60	5.7	$2.40	0.1	8,999.9
9-Feb	$4.40	12.1	$2.50	3.0	8,957.6
8-Feb	$4.45	8.4	$2.50	28.0	9,080.7
7-Feb	$4.40	13.9	$2.50	1.0	9,137.6
6-Feb	$4.35	2.5	$2.50	3.0	9,301.4
5-Feb	$4.45	165.0	$2.50	4.2	9,306.1
2-Feb	$4.10	219.5			9,224.1
1-Feb	$4.04	6.4	$2.50	27.6	9,287.7
31-Jan	$4.20	6.7	$2.50	2.1	9,321.9
30-Jan	$4.05	0.6	$2.50	13.8	9,348.4
29-Jan	$4.07	3.0			9,302.2
26-Jan	$4.10	2.1	$2.30	0.4	9,158.2
25-Jan	$4.00	12.2	$2.30	6.0	9,183.4
24-Jan	$4.05	11.8	$2.30	16.0	9,306.2
23-Jan	$4.00	60.0	$2.50	2.5	9,268.8
22-Jan	$4.00	163.9	$2.50	1.0	9,121.0
19-Jan	$3.95	4.4	$2.50	0.8	9,161.1
18-Jan	$3.95	2.9	$2.45	6.9	8,899.1
17-Jan	$3.95	1.5			8,879.4
16-Jan	$3.95	7.2	$2.30	1.0	8,744.0
15-Jan	$4.05	7.9	$2.10	8.8	8,778.5
12-Jan	$3.95	6.7	$2.10	1.9	8,716.4
11-Jan	$3.90	5.9	$2.10	6.4	8,805.4
10-Jan	$3.90	4.5			8,600.8
9-Jan	$3.90	13.8	$2.20	3.1	8,572.0
8-Jan	$3.90	12.7	$2.10	4.1	8,671.7
5-Jan	$3.90	9.5	$2.10	5.4	8,690.2
4-Jan	$3.90	2.6	$2.20	5.0	8,905.7
3-Jan	$4.05	1.8	$2.00	0.6	8,927.8
2-Jan	$4.00	0.4	$2.30	3.1	8,611.5

Exhibit 12   Selected Daily Share Prices—2001

	Canadian Yields (%)	U.S. Yields (%)
T-Bills		
3-month	4.58	4.30
1-year	4.60	4.09
Bonds		
2-years	4.61	4.18
5-years	4.94	4.62
7-years		4.86
10-years	5.32	4.93
30-years	5.70	5.46

Source: US Treasury Web site, Stats Can Web site.

**Average Annual Returns in North American
Capital Markets over the period 1926 to 2000**

	U.S.		Canada	
	Arithmetic Average	Geometric Average	Arithmetic Average	Geometric Average
Long-Term Government Bonds	5.7%	5.3%	6.4%	5.0%
Equities (Market)	13.0%	11.0%	11.8%	10.2%

Source: L. Booth, "Equity Market Risk Premiums in the United States and Canada," *Canadian Investment Review*, Fall, 2001.

Exhibit 13   Selected Interest Rate Data March 2001

Williams prepared a bid at $6.15 per share. See Exhibit 14 for the draft details of the bid. Block realized that the conditional nature of the offer, the low level of initial cash and the fact that, in essence Catalyst was using Montreaux's own money to take it over would represent a communications issue: it would be necessary to convince shareholders to focus on the stated value rather than the makeup of it.

NATIONAL'S INVOLVEMENT

National IR was initially engaged to provide media training to Jim Williams, the president of Catalyst. Catalyst felt that the identity of its takeover target and the position of its CEO in the financial community would create a media event. The company wanted to be prepared to deal with it early.

Catalyst Investments Ltd. Offer to purchase all of the outstanding Class A Common Shares of Montreaux Inc. for $6.15 per Class A Common Share consisting of $1.20 cash and $4.95 principal amount of 7% Series A Short Term Automatically Redeemable Notes of the Offeror plus one Cash Value Right (CVR) of the Offeror having a value of up to $0.10 for each Class A Common Share of Montreaux Inc.

This offer by Catalyst Investments Ltd. to purchase all of the issued and outstanding Class A Common Shares of Montreaux Inc. will be open for acceptance until 5:00 p.m. on June 15, 2001, unless extended or withdrawn.

The offer represents a premium of at least 56% and, depending upon the value of the CVR, of up to 58% over the average closing price of the Shares on the TSE for the 30 trading days ended January 24, 2001, the day that the Offeror began to acquire Shares. The Offer also represents a premium of at least 26% and up to 28% depending on the value of the CVR, over the average closing price of the Shares on the TSE for the 30 trading days ended May 8, 2001, the day prior to the public announcement of the Offer.

The Offer is conditional (unless waived or amended by the Offeror) upon, among other customary conditions, there being validly deposited under the Offer and not withdrawn that number of Shares that, together with Shares held by the Offeror and its affiliates, represents at least 66 2/3% of the outstanding Shares (calculated on a fully diluted basis at the Expiry Time). This and the other conditions to the Offer are described in Section 4 of the Offer, "Conditions of Offer."

As of the date hereof, the Offeror owns in the aggregate 2,824,700 Shares, representing approximately 10.8% of the 26,050,453 Shares outstanding as at April 10, 2001.

The notes and CVRs will not be listed on any stock exchange. The Notes and CVRs will be issued in reliance upon exemptions from the prospectus and registration requirements of Canadian securities legislation and may not be resold by the holder thereof except pursuant to an exemption from such requirements. There is currently no market through which the Notes and CVRs may be sold and none is expected to develop. The Offeror is required to redeem the issued and outstanding Notes for their full face amount plus accrued and unpaid interest as soon as practicable and, in any event, within 35 days following the completion of a Compulsory Acquisition Transaction or Subsequent Acquisition Transaction. The CVRs will be issued as part of and will not be separable from the Notes. The Offeror will redeem the CVRs at the same time as the Notes are redeemed for up to $0.10 per CVR, depending upon the amount of unrestricted cash and marketable securities of HoldCo at such time after deducting HoldCo's obligations. The CVR may be redeemed for less than $0.10 per CVR or may have not value whatsoever.

May 10, 2001.

Exhibit 14   Draft Offer to Purchase

Williams gave a presentation to Block, outlining Catalyst's plans for the takeover. Block arranged for the required media training and began to formulate a strategy for National IR to assist with the overall takeover.

In preparation for his strategy meeting with Koven, Block reflected on his options. First, he felt a need to review the valuation of Montreaux in order to be able to justify the intended bid price with investors. Second, he wanted to identify the issues with the structure of the bid and how to deal with these issues. Next, he wanted to create a communication strategy for the bid itself. This would include the key messages that Catalyst should deliver, as well as the tactics to deliver those messages. Finally, Block wanted to identify steps to convince the shareholders to tender their shares to the offer.

6

M&A—CLOSING THE DEAL

T he process of contemplating and executing mergers and acquisitions (M&A) at a firm can be thought of as a "funnel." A firm may consider dozens or even hundreds of M&A ideas, approaches some subset of those, engages and has serious discussions with even less, and goes down the M&A path with perhaps one. As this funnel gets smaller, so does the risk that each particular deal idea dies. After passing many of the hurdles in execution, effectively, the deal has been negotiated and agreed upon by the parties and is then announced. The announced deal will have an intended closing date some weeks or months later. During this period between announcement and closing, several steps with deal-breaking potential occur, and the impact of deal failure is much greater. Firms at this point have invested time and incurred expenses, have publicly announced the deal and face public and investor relations backlashes if the deal fails, and are possibly subject to hefty deal break-up fees if they cause the deal to fall apart.

CLOSING TIMELINE

The time required to close a transaction varies based on what internal and external approvals are needed, securities filings required, financing that may need to be raised, and any other conditions to closing that were part of the agreement. Taking these known and predicted factors into account, the firms set a proposed closing date. Whether this date is met or not is often out of the hands of the parties but instead is in the hands of regulators or of financing sources or stockholders. To ensure some accountability, however, the parties clearly assign responsibility for each of these tasks and often agree to penalties if they cannot get past certain hurdles on an agreed-upon timeline. During this preclosing period, the firms are also restricted in many ways and are subject to any business conditions that may adversely affect the firm and trigger its inability to close the deal. As such, firms typically prefer to have a short closing period, but since many of the hurdles are outside of their control, this is a tense period. It is important, therefore, to ensure that you negotiate into the deal appropriate incentives and disincentives to ensure the other party remains duly focused on overcoming the obstacles it faces to closing.

HURDLES TO CLOSING

Volitional Choice

During this period, a firm may simply decide that the deal does not make sense or that a better alternative exists. The firm does not know what the public and investor reaction will be to the proposed deal until it is announced. After announcement, the firm has the ability to take into account the market reaction to the deal and can use that to gauge whether to proceed. Because of this, the parties to a deal typically negotiate break-up fees that must be paid by a firm that decides to break a deal, especially for a volitional reason such as this. Because the deal has been announced, other suitors may present offers that, bearing in mind the break-up fees due and the lawsuits that may ensue, appear to be better alternatives.

Material Adverse Changes

The negotiated deal likely includes a list of specific, yet unforeseen, changes and perhaps a blanket material adverse change (MAC) clause that allows a firm to break away from the deal if any of these changes comes to pass before the closing date. These changes might include the loss of key personnel or customers or of any other major change that causes the business to be adversely affected and thus likely of less value to the deal partner. These are commonly changes to the firm that are outside the control of the firm and largely unforeseen at negotiations time.

Negotiated Conditions and Triggers

Similar to MACs, the firms may also have specific, potentially foreseen triggers that are negotiated as conditions to closing the deal. For example, the firm may announce its financial results during the period between announcement and closing. In the negotiated agreement, the firm's financials must exceed some set criteria or else the deal can be cancelled. The firms will likely also agree to further due diligence and perhaps a final due diligence, often called a *bring-down* due diligence, just before the deal closes. If anything is found during these due diligence investigations that is spelled out as a condition to close the deal, the deal may fall apart. Another mechanism is the agreement made by the parties that they not overtly attempt to attract other partners. This differs from receiving an unsolicited bid, which cannot be controlled. However, many lawsuits have ensued based on whether the bid was unsolicited or perhaps that the firm was complicit in attracting new bids. In any case, firms may agree not to shop themselves around but may do so anyway. As a part of these negotiated agreements, however, there are also likely to be financial penalties to the party that breached one of its representations or warranties or was the cause of such a deal-breaking condition. Again, financial disincentives are common here to ensure appropriate alignment of interests.

Financing

Depending on the structure of the deal and how the deal is meant to be financed, a commonly negotiated condition to closing a deal is the ability to obtain financing on reasonable terms. At the time of the negotiation, the acquirer is likely in ongoing dialogue with its bankers about the availability and market costs of financing. However, these discussions may not occur if the deal is done without the aid of bankers. As well, market conditions can be volatile, affecting the cost of capital to finance acquisitions. If the firm is unable to obtain the financing needed before the scheduled closing date, it may have the ability to break the deal.

Internal Approvals

The two most basic internal approvals are at the board and stockholder levels. In the United States, most deals require both the vote of the board and the stockholders. However, a deal may not need the approval of the board. In a proxy battle, the board may reject a deal, but the acquirer is able to use a proxy to have the stockholders directly vote on the deal, which may be approved. Depending on the deal type, the actual "voting" approvals may not be needed. In a hostile deal or where a tender offer is used, the board may not give its approval, and a no stockholder vote is held, but sufficient stockholders may "vote" by tendering their shares that the deal goes through. When a board does not like a deal, it may or may not be required to allow the stockholders to vote on the deal, but these rules vary greatly by country, suggesting that the amount of power and discretion left in the hands of a few board members varies. In a typical deal, both the board and the stockholders must vote. Because of the numerous potential pitfalls before closing, the board will typically authorize the deal just before the scheduled closing. The stockholders' vote required to approve a deal differs in the United States by state, with some states making it more or less difficult to obtain such approval. It is typical to require a majority of at least two thirds of the stockholders.

External Approvals

The two major categories of external steps include securities filings and regulatory approvals. Securities filings are not typically approvals per se but may require that, in the United States, the Securities and Exchange Commission (SEC) rule on (allow) certain exemptions, depending on the compliance method chosen. When the consideration being paid is a security, SEC filings are done. The firm must choose whether to register the securities or not register the securities in reliance on some exemption. Certain types of exemption require hearings with the SEC that can be costly and time-consuming. The alternative is to not register the securities, but unregistered securities will have less value as a form of consideration. When unregistered securities are offered, it is typical to also offer registration rights that allow the recipients to register their stock at some later point. More onerous external approvals are antitrust (Hart-Scott-Rodino [HSR]), industry, and foreign buyer–related (Exon-Florio) approvals that vary greatly by situation. Depending on deal size and industry, no filings may be needed. For HSR, a filing is required along with a sizable filing fee. While on file, the firms must not integrate their operations because there is a possibility the deal may fall apart, and unraveling any combined operations is very difficult. The Federal Trade Commission and Department of Justice then have 30 days to make a "second request" in which they may request additional information to further investigate whether the deal may be anticompetitive. A second request will typically have substantial impacts on the closing dates and may force the proposed partners to divest certain assets before being allowed to close or may make the deal altogether unfeasible. An Exon-Florio review is required when a foreign buyer is involved and when the purchase may have some impact on the security of the nation. Exon-Florio is a U.S. requirement, but similar requirements exist worldwide. Finally, in regulated industries, there may be additional bodies that are required to approve transactions. For example, banking transactions in the United States may also require that notification be made to the Department of the Treasury. As suggested, the level of complexity and difficulty of external approvals varies greatly among deals and must be considered.

CASES

Cemex: The Southdown Offer

Cemex, a cement multinational from Mexico, has become one of the three largest cement companies in the world, through internal growth and a series of global acquisitions over the 1999 to 2000 period. It is a relatively small player in the United States with an insignificant market share. It has had conflicts with the U.S. cement industry over its cement exports to the United States, being the object of a successful antidumping suit brought by the U.S. cement industry before the U.S. International Trade Commission (USITC). One of its key opponents is Southdown, which has testified before the USITC against Cemex. Southdown's chief executive officer is unhappy with his firm's stock price and frustrated by the lack of market recognition despite profitable operations and growth. He is considering selling his company and has talked with Cemex about being acquired. The case allows students to analyze the strategic rationale for an acquisition of Southdown by Cemex and has information to allow students to probe questions of strategic fit and value.

Issues: Antidumping action, cross-border M&A, developing economies

BC Sugar Refinery, Limited

One of the two major sugar refineries in Canada has become embroiled in a takeover battle that pits a flamboyant Vancouver billionaire against the president of Balaclava Enterprises. After BC Sugar Refinery, Limited had all but sealed up the deal with a $15 per share bid, Balaclava Enterprises has now approached the president of Onex Corporation for assistance in raising the ante. Onex's president must evaluate the attractiveness of the industry, the company, and any possible financing alternatives to calculate the value inherent in the transaction. BC Sugar Refinery, Limited's bid will expire on June 26, 1997. However, due to the fact that a large percentage of the shares had already been tendered to the competing bid, Onex's decision must be made within the next few days.

Issues: Deal structuring, financing alternatives, securitization, deal timelines

Antitrust: A Threat to Mergers and Acquisitions?

Both domestic and global environments have become less and less favorable to M&As and more and more likely to scrutinize them and their potential impact on markets and consumers. Obstructionist—or at least impeding—legislation and increasingly wary lawmakers are so common today that it is quite reasonable to ask if antitrust laws and sentiments are really threats to mergers and acquisitions. In this comprehensive article, the authors lay out seven factors that are having an impact on antitrust decisions today. They discuss what corporations hoping to merge or acquire can anticipate from both governments and citizens and what business might do in response.

Issues: Government regulation, antitrust

CEMEX: THE SOUTHDOWN OFFER[1]

Prepared by David Wesley under the supervision of Professor Ravi Sarathy

Copyright © 2003, Northeastern University, College of Business Administration   Version: (A) 2003-03-14

On April 4, 2000, Clarence C. Comer, president and chief executive officer (CEO) of Southdown, Inc. (Southdown), wrote a letter to the company's shareholders, expressing his disappointment with the company's share price:

> Management is pleased with the Company's accomplishments in 1999 and prior years, which have created one of the strongest and most profitable building materials companies in the U.S. . . . . Unfortunately, the stock market has failed to appropriately reflect the value that has been created, or the prospects for further growth.[2] Therefore, Southdown's Board of Directors is exploring and evaluating a number of alternatives. Options include, among other things, a significant share repurchase, expansion through domestic or international acquisitions, or the merger or sale of the Company.[3]

What Comer's letter did not say was that he had already approached Lorenzo Zambrano, president and CEO of Mexico-based Cemex, with an offer to sell Southdown. In fact, Zambrano had just arrived in Houston, Texas, and was scheduled to meet with Comer at Southdown's headquarters the following day.

CEMENT INDUSTRY

Cement was the primary material used in the construction of commercial, industrial and residential infrastructure. Concrete producers, industrial firms and building contractors purchased cement in bulk, while homeowners, gardeners and other small-quantity consumers purchased pre-bagged quantities from commercial distributors.

Fuel was the largest cost in the production of cement, accounting for 50 per cent or more of total variable costs. Therefore, production costs tended to fluctuate in tandem with energy prices. In 1998, the cement industry benefited from lower oil prices which averaged US$11 per barrel for the year. In 1999, however, there was a steady rise in energy costs, and by late summer 2000, oil prices had risen to over $30 per barrel.

Dry-process production was considerably more energy efficient than wet-process production, but required considerably more investment in plant and equipment (see Glossary). In less developed countries, subsidized fuel and insufficient investment in new plant and equipment favored wet-process production.

Cement consumption was cyclical in nature and correlated to population and economic growth (see Tables 1 and 2 for consumption and production trends, respectively; Exhibit 1 provides cement production trends and growth rates). In less developed countries, demand was

Table 1   World Cement Consumption by Region, 2000

Region	%
east Asia	46
southeast Asia	5
southwest Asia	7
Middle East	4
Africa	5
Europe	19
Central America and South America	6
North America	8
Total, 2000 (billion metric tons)	1.650
Total, 1995	1.405
Total, 1990	1.138

Source: Ocean Shipping Consultants, Nov. 2001.

Table 2 World Cement Production and Capacity ('000 of metric tons)

Country	1996	2000
China	490,000	583,190
India	25,000	95,000
United States (includes Puerto Rico)	80,818	89,510
Japan	94,492	81,300
Korea, Republic of (South Korea)	57,334	51,255
Brazil	34,597	39,208
Germany	40,000	38,000
Italy	34,000	36,000
Turkey	32,500	35,825
Russia	27,800	32,400
Thailand	35,000	32,000
Mexico	22,829	31,677
Spain	25,157	30,000
Indonesia	34,000	27,789
France	20,000	20,000
Taiwan	21,537	18,500
Other countries (rounded)	367,280	375,000
World total	1,445,000	1,620,000

Source: US Geological Survey, Mineral Commodity Summaries, 1997 and 2001.

driven by government infrastructure projects and by first-time homeowners who undertook construction themselves. The latter typically purchased pre-bagged cement in small quantities.[4] Cement was a small portion of overall construction costs and there were few available substitutes. As such, sales were more dependent on overall construction levels than price. Large-scale government infrastructure projects, such as highway construction, were even more cyclical than housing starts. The number of government projects depended more on spending policy than cement prices.

Industrialized countries, on the other hand, typically consumed cement in bulk quantities. Even residential users contracted with ready-mix suppliers to undertake building projects. Although long-term demand correlated strongly with economic indicators, day-to-day demand was unpredictable, with approximately half of all ready-mix orders being cancelled on the delivery date, due to unforeseeable circumstances, such as inclement weather.[5]

World cement production amounted to about 1.6 billion tons in 2000. The top 16 countries (in descending order, China, Japan, the United States, India, South Korea, Brazil, Germany, Turkey, Thailand, Italy, Spain, Mexico, Russia, Indonesia and Taiwan) accounted for more than 70 per cent of the world total production.

A low value-to-weight ratio for the transportation of cement favored regionally based mining, production and distribution. The geographic reach of a given plant at an inland location was roughly circular, with the edge of the circle demarcated by the point at which the combined production and transportation costs of deliveries would break even, based on current market prices. Any deliveries outside of this "natural market" would result in a loss to the company. For plants located along railway lines and water-ways, the reach was extended along these corridors, as shipments by sea and rail were more economical than truck-based transportation.

The natural market for cement was not fixed, but fluctuated with changes in market prices and conditions. During periods of high demand, the delivery range tended to shrink as producers found markets closer to production facilities, thereby increasing margins. Under such circumstances, producers charged customers "phantom freight," the difference between the cost of transporting cement and the price actually charged to customers. Since customers paid the same rates, regardless of their distance from the cement plant, customers closer to the plant tended to pay higher phantom freight. In contrast, during periods of lower demand, cement producers needed

Region	1970	1975	1980	1985	1990	1995	Average % Growth 1990-1995	Average % GDP Growth* 1991-1998
China (incl. Hong Kong)	27	47	81	148	211	477	17.7	11.4
Europe	185	194	223	178	196	181	−1.7	1.7
OECD-Pacific	69	83	113	100	126	154	4.1	6.0
Rest of Asia	20	31	49	57	89	130	8.0	5.9
Middle East	19	29	44	75	93	116	4.6	2.9
Latin America	36	52	76	71	82	97	3.4	3.6
Eastern Europe/ former Soviet Union	134	177	190	190	190	96	−12.7	−4.0
North America	76	73	79	81	81	88	1.5	3.0
India	14	16	18	31	49	70	7.3	6.1
Africa	15	20	28	35	38	44	2.7	2.8
World	**594**	**722**	**901**	**965**	**1,156**	**1,453**	**4.7**	**2.5**

Exhibit 1   Cement Production Trends and Average Annual Growth Rates for Major World Regions, 1970 to 1995 (in millions of tons)

Source: Cembureau, 1998.

*Gross domestic product growth rates adapted from: "Global Economic Prospects and the Developing Countries," *International Bank for Reconstruction and Development*, 2000.

to extend their reach in order to find buyers and maximize capacity utilization, thereby offsetting the high fixed costs associated with cement kilns.[6] Under low-demand conditions, producers practiced what was termed "freight absorption," charging less to customers than actual transportation costs.

Despite the high cost of transportation, regionally diversified producers were considered more competitive, as they could shift distribution to areas of higher demand when local demand was depressed. When natural markets of company plants overlapped, production was simply transferred to customers within the higher demand market. Shifting deliveries to higher demand markets allowed geographically diverse producers to maximize plant utilization.

In most countries, the cement industry was highly fragmented with numerous regional and national players. In the 1990s, producers in most countries began to consolidate. Three companies emerged as leading multinational producers, namely Holderbank of Switzerland,[7] Lafarge Group of France[8] and Cemex of Mexico (see Figure 1). All three were engaged in significant acquisitions, especially in less developed

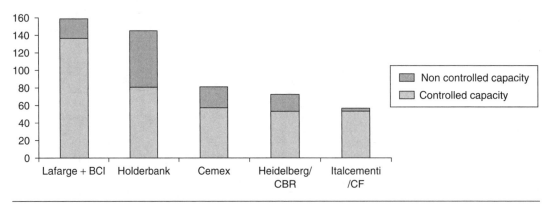

Figure 1   Top Five Cement Producers (millions of metric tons—MMT)

Source: Lafarge Group.

countries where industry growth was expected to outpace industrialized countries (see Table 1).

CEMEX S.A. DE C.V.

Cemex was founded in 1906, in the northern industrial city of Monterrey, Mexico. The company expanded rapidly in the 1970s on the back of Mexico's oil boom, and entered into numerous unrelated industries, such as hotels and chemical plants. In the early 1980s, an economic crisis forced the company to shed unrelated businesses and instead focus on its core product—cement.

In the latter half of the 1980s, Cemex acquired several large Mexican competitors to become the leading cement producer in Mexico. Residential consumers of bagged cement accounted for a large portion of sales in Mexico, where more than half of all homes were constructed by homeowners rather than professional contractors. As a result, bagged cement accounted for approximately 75 per cent of private-sector demand. Unlike most industrialized countries, where cement was considered a commodity product, Cemex had established strong brand loyalty within its home market, based on differences in quality and service. Branded bags of cement were sold through 5,500 regional distributors.[9]

In 1999, Cemex operated 15 plants and 74 distribution centers in Mexico, accounting for 44 per cent of Cemex's total worldwide sales. The company's Tepeaca plant, completed in 1995 at a cost of US$314 million, was the largest and most advanced in North America, with a capacity of 3.2 million tons. Cemex also operated 1,140 ready-mix delivery trucks, which served commercial and government customers. Exports, which accounted for 16 per cent of Mexican revenues, were primarily destined for the United States (47 per cent), the Caribbean (30 per cent), and Central America and South America (23 per cent). (See Exhibit 2.)

Cemex used a variety of energy sources, including oil, natural gas and petcoke,[10] and was often able to shift from one source of fuel to another depending on fluctuations in price. The company had a 20-year energy contract with Pemex, a state-owned oil company, to supply the company with petcoke.

Cemex summarized its mission as follows:

To serve the global building needs of its customers and build value for its stakeholders by becoming the world's most efficient and profitable multinational cement company. Cemex's strategy is to focus on and leverage its core cement and ready-mix concrete franchises in the international markets it serves, primarily concentrate on the world's

	1999	1998	1997	1996	1995	1994	1993
REVENUES	$4,828	$4,315	3,788	3,365	$2,564	$2,101	$2,897
Gross Profit	2,138	1,820	1,467	1,325	1,000	889	1,150
Net Income	973	803	761	977	759	376	522
Cash & Investments	326	407	380	409	355	484	326
Net Plant & Equipment	6,922	6,142	6,006	5,743	4,939	4,093	4,407
Short-term and Long-term Debt	4,371	4,242	4,618	4,769	3,904	3,764	3,550
Stockholders' Equity	5,182	3,887	3,515	3,337	2,878	2,832	3,225
EBITDA	1,791	1,485	1,193	1,087	815	719	914
EBITDA Margin %	37.1	34.4	31.5	32.3	31.8	34.2	31.6
Operating Margin %	29.8	27.3	23.6	23.8	23.9	26.9	24.4

Exhibit 2   Cemex Financial Summary (for years ending December 31) (in millions of dollars, except percentage amounts)

Source: Cemex S.A. de C.V.

most dynamic markets, where the demand for housing, roads and other needed infrastructure is greatest, and maintain high growth by applying free cash flow toward selective investments that further its geographic diversification.[11]

Anti-Dumping

In 1986, Cemex entered into a 20-year joint venture with Southdown, Inc. to market Cemex cement and clinker in the southern United States. The joint venture, known as Sunbelt Cement, paid management fees to Southdown and split the remaining earnings equally between the partners. On September 8, 1989, Cemex purchased Southdown's share of the joint venture and began operating Sunbelt as a subsidiary of Cemex. The properties included distribution terminals, ready-mix plants and a fleet of 360 ready-mix trucks in Texas, California and Arizona. "Southdown

complained that Cemex gradually reduced the joint venture's management fees, and increased its imported cement price in order to squeeze the profits of the joint venture, and therefore of Southdown."[12]

Two and half weeks after the dissolution of the partnership, Southdown filed a dumping suit against Mexican cement producers. The retaliatory action proved successful when the U.S. International Trade Commission imposed anti-dumping duties of 58 per cent on Cemex imports, beginning in 1990. The commission ruled that Mexican producers received unfair subsidies from the Mexican government in the form of lower oil prices, which had resulted in material harm to U.S. producers through the loss of market share. Cemex maintained that U.S. producers, such as Southdown, had been responsible for marketing the cement and, therefore, determined the local market price, which was often higher for

Mexican cement. In fact, U.S. producers relied on imports to supplement their domestic production and actively sought out foreign producers to supply them with additional cement. As a result, when Mexican imports into Florida were all but eliminated in 1991, imports from Venezuela surged 152 per cent, as suppliers sought new sources to meet increasing local demand.[13]

Cemex partially bypassed the anti-dumping action by adding domestic production capacity in 1994 when it purchased the plant in Balcones, Texas from Lafarge for $100 million.[14] At the time, it was considered to be the most advanced cement plant in the United States. By 1999, the Sunbelt Group, which accounted for 11 per cent of total company sales, had one plant with an annual capacity of 910,000 tons, 530 ready-mix trucks, 48 ready-mix concrete plants and 13 cement terminals.

European Expansion

On the wake the anti-dumping ruling in the United States, Cemex decided to look across the Atlantic for further expansion opportunities. In July 1992, Cemex acquired Spain's two largest cement companies for $1.85 billion.[15] The largest, Compañía Valenciana de Cementos, became the holding company for all of Cemex's future international acquisitions. Following the acquisition, Cemex merged its two Spanish subsidiaries, reduced staff, closed all but one of the 19 administrative offices and implemented various technological and operational improvements. By 1999, operating margins had increased to 32.5 per cent, as compared with 6.85 per cent in 1992. Cemex CEO, Lorenzo Zambrano, noted:

> For Spaniards, the idea of a Mexican company coming to Spain and changing top management, 500 years after the conquest of Mexico, was unthinkable. They said a Mexican company couldn't manage in Europe. But we increased our operating margin in Spain by more than three times in three years. We made that company much better than before.[16]

In 1999, Spain represented 15 per cent of Cemex net sales, with more than 72 per cent of company exports destined for the United States.

Cemex Latin America

The company's most significant expansion thrust began later in the 1990s, when Cemex acquired producers in Venezuela (1994), the Dominican Republic (1995), Colombia (1996), the Philippines (1997), Indonesia (1998), Costa Rica (1999), Chile (1999) and Egypt (1999). In almost every case, Cemex initially became a minority shareholder and within one year increased its stake to become the controlling shareholder. Cemex was the largest cement producer in most of these countries and typically owned and operated its own mines, trucks and port facilities (see Table 3). By comparison, Holderbank obtained about 36 per cent of its sales from Europe, 26 per cent from Latin America, 22 per cent from North America, and eight per cent each from Asia-Pacific and Africa-Middle East.

The company's expansion in emerging markets coincided with the Mexican peso crisis of December 1994. In the period preceding the 1994 election, the Mexican government failed to take a number of potentially unpopular fiscal decisions that were needed to maintain the stability of Mexico's economy. Despite the risk of a peso devaluation, the government continued to offer artificially low interest rates. The peso was instead supported through foreign reserves, which fell by more than $7 billion in only one month. In December 1994, the new government announced that it would maintain the previous government's fiscal policy, and investors became concerned about the government's ability to meet its debt obligations. The resulting currency flight to U.S. dollars caused a major devaluation of the peso. This was followed by stock market declines and devaluations across most of Latin America.

Cemex, like most Mexican companies, was severely affected by the peso crisis, as most of the company's dollar-denominated debt was being financed by peso-denominated domestic

Table 3   Cemex Global Operations (as of December 31, 1999)

٩	% of Sales	% of total assets	Prod. Capacity (MMT)	# of plants
Mexico	47.3	42.2	27.2	18
United States	12.2	5.0	1.2	4
Venezuela & Dominican Republic	13.7	11.4	5.0	4
Colombia	3.7	7.2	4.8	5
Central America and the Caribbean	3.6	2.7	2.0	8
Spain	16.6	17.4	10.4	8
Egypt	0.3	5.3	4.0	1
Philippines	2.6	6.8	5.8	3
Indonesia		2.0	5.0[1]	4
Total	**100.0**	**100.0**	**65.4**	**55**

Source: Company files.

1. Total capacity adjusted for 25 per cent of the 20.3 million tons total by Semen Gresik, although Cemex had been given management control for 100 per cent of production.

cash flows. With 50 per cent of company revenues generated from Spanish and other foreign subsidiaries, Cemex, however, turned the crisis to its advantage. Instead of liquidating assets in order to pay off foreign debt obligations, Cemex used overseas cash flows to acquire other Latin American producers at discounted prices.[17]

A few months before the peso crisis hit, Cemex launched its Latin America expansion with the purchase of a majority stake in Vencemos, Venezuela's leading cement producer, for $550 million.[18] The Venezuelan market, which had been dominated by three local producers, all but collapsed following the demise of the Venezuelan banking system, which led to a national economic crisis beginning in 1989. Over the next several years, domestic producers attempted to steal market share from competitors by engaging in predatory pricing. As a result,

Vencemos posted losses of $117 million in 1994. A few months after the Cemex purchase, Lafarge and Holderbank purchased the remaining two Venezuelan producers.[19]

Cemex reorganized the company and refocused efforts on the export market. Within 18 months, Vencemos revenues increased significantly, while margins more than tripled.[20] The company's relatively low energy costs made it the lowest cost producer in the Cemex Group. In 1999, more than half of the company's revenues were derived from exports to the United States and the Caribbean, while Cemex's Venezuelan operations contributed approximately nine per cent to Cemex Group revenues.

The company's next foray into the region came with the purchase of Cementos Nacionales, the leading cement producer in the Dominican Republic. As demand in that country exceeded supply, Cementos Nacionales became a net importer of Cemex cement. In 1999, Cemex was making capital investments in its Dominican operations in order to increase distribution capacity. Net sales represented four per cent of Cemex Group totals. An additional three per cent of net sales came from the company's operations in Panama and Costa Rica, which primarily served the Central American market.

In May 1996, after nearly a year of legal wrangling with local industry groups that wanted to keep the Mexican giant out, Cemex acquired majority stakes in Colombian producers, Cementos Diamante and Cementos Samper, for $600 million. Cemex merged the administration of the two companies and implemented a number of technological and operational upgrades. A protracted civil war, however, prevented the type of economic recovery seen in other parts of Latin America in the late 1990s. Hence, Colombia represented less than four per cent of Cemex net sales in 1999, and had no significant exports.

In 1997, Cemex began to turn its attention to southeast Asia. From the 1960s through to 1997, the "Asian Miracle" produced regional economic growth that was three times greater than Latin America, and resulted in a quadrupling of average real income, while construction, and hence cement consumption, soared in tandem. "Between 1992 and 1997, Thailand alone built nearly three times Britain's total cement capacity."[21]

In 1997, however, the miracle came to an abrupt end, as local markets, beginning with Thailand, collapsed and currencies went into a steep decline against the U.S. dollar. "The crisis stemmed from excessive short-term borrowing that led to economic overheating. Problems were made worse by fixed exchange rates, inadequate financial systems, cronyism, corruption and inadequate political responses."[22] With construction at a standstill, cement consumption all but collapsed in 1997 and 1998.

As with the 1994 to 1995 peso crisis, Cemex saw the economic crisis in southeast Asia as an opportunity for further expansion. Currency devaluations produced dollar-denominated costs well below those of developed countries. Thai cement, which cost only $12 to $15 per ton to produce, could be shipped to the United States for an additional cost of $30 per ton, and sold in the U.S. market for more than $70 dollars per ton.[23] The crisis created a unique opportunity for foreign producers to acquire domestic firms at depressed prices. By 1999, multinational ownership of Asian cement companies had increased to 60 per cent of total regional capacity, up from 20 per cent in 1997.[24]

Cemex began its Asian acquisitions with a 30 per cent interest in Philippine producer Rizal Cement for $93 million. In the wake of the Asia crisis, the Philippines found itself with an installed cement capacity that was more than double domestic consumption, while cement prices fell to an eight-year low. Rizal had two plants with a total capacity 2.8 million tons. In January and February 1999, Cemex increased its stake in Rizal by another 40 per cent for $103 million, while acquiring another Philippine producer, APO Cement, for $400 million.[25] The combined capacity of these two producers provided Cemex with nationwide coverage, including access to that country's major cities. Competition came from Holderbank, Lafarge and Blue Circle, all of which had major operations in the Philippines. In 1999, the company's Philippine operations contributed approximately two per cent to Cemex Group sales.

The next Asian acquisition was Indonesia's Semen Gresik, which represented Cemex's largest installed capacity outside of Mexico at 20.3 million tons per annum.[26] Even though Semen Gresik was an Indonesian state-owned company, the Asian economic crisis threatened its very survival. Cemex was the first foreign company to invest in the cement industry in Indonesia when, in 1998, it purchased 25 per cent of the company for approximately $200 million. As a result, Indonesia's annual cement exports more than quadrupled from less than two million tons in 1997 to more than eight million tons in 1999. Meanwhile, Indonesia remained one of the two largest cement markets in southeast Asia, accounting for 24 per cent of regional consumption.[27]

Cemex's most recent major acquisition came with the $319-million purchase of a 77 per cent interest in Assiut Cement (Assiut), the largest cement producer in Egypt with an installed capacity of four million tons. Due to government-imposed price controls, cement prices in Egypt had not been affected by either the peso crisis or the Asia crisis. Some 95 per cent of Assiut's production was sold in bags to domestic consumers. Cemex planned to increase capacity to five million tons within two years, and build a new 1.5-million-ton capacity plant in southern Egypt.

In 2000, Cemex was investigating investment opportunities in Thailand, Malaysia and India. Jose Domene, president of Cemex's international division boasted, "We can buy any cement company in the world and turn it around."[28] In order to be considered by Cemex as a possible acquisition target, a company had to fit within the following basic criteria:

- Value creation must be principally driven by factors that the company can influence, particularly the application of Cemex's management and turnaround expertise.
- Acquisition must maintain or improve Cemex's financial position.
- The investment must offer superior long-term returns.

In June 2000, Cemex employed 24,000 people worldwide and had an equity market valuation of $5.8 billion. Of the company's 39 majority-owned productions plants, 33 used the more modern dry process. More than 80 per cent of the company's $4.5-billion debt was denominated in U.S. dollars.

Information Systems

In the 1980s, Mexico remained an underdeveloped country with poor transportation and telecommunications infrastructures. As a result, it was impossible for Cemex to provide reliable on-time delivery of cement to construction projects. Average delivery time to work sites was approximately three hours, which irked many

construction companies that had to pay for hundreds of workers to sit idly by while they waited for cement trucks to arrive.[29]

In 1985, Lorenzo Zambrano, a grandson of the company's founder, became president and CEO of Cemex. Zambrano, who held an engineer degree from Instituto Tecnologico y de Estudios Superiores de Monterrey (ITESM), Mexico's leading technical university (the Mexican equivalent to the Massachusetts Institute of Technology or MIT), and an MBA from Stanford, immediately began to implement a technology-centered restructuring of the company. He visited several foreign companies who were leaders in transportation logistics, including Exxon and Federal Express in the United States, borrowing whatever ideas he believed could be adapted to the cement industry.

In order to bypass Mexico's unreliable phone system, in the early 1990s, the company began using global positioning satellites and a digital control center to track orders and co-ordinate deliveries.

> With trucks acting less like trucks and more like fast, switchable packets within a data network, Cemex could quickly dispatch the right one to pick up and deliver a particular grade of cement, reroute trucks when chaotic traffic conditions demanded it, and redirect deliveries from one customer to another as last minute changes were made. Gradually, Cemex reduced the three-hour delivery window to 20 minutes.[30]

Cemex eventually employed its information technology systems throughout its worldwide operations, thereby significantly reducing costs and increasing reliability. By the end of the 1990s, Cemex was the most technologically advanced among its many competitors. Jose Domene explained:

> When we take over new operations, the first thing we do is install a satellite feed so we can incorporate them into our information system. I'm always surprised that our competitors have next to no computers. It means that their headquarters has only last month's operating figures. I can look at last night's at the touch of a button.[31]

In 2000, Cemex introduced an Internet-based strategy known as Cx Networks that would allow customers to place and track orders on the Internet, and which Cemex hoped would eventually save the company approximately $120 million annually.

SOUTHDOWN, INC.

Southdown, Inc. was one of the largest cement producers in the United States, and among the few that remained American-owned (see Table 4). In the early 1970s, most U.S. cement producers were relatively small independent companies. Many ran older inefficient plants that relied heavily on low oil prices to keep variable costs low. An oil crisis in the early 1970s, however, sent costs soaring, which resulted in most U.S. producers being taken over by European companies that had already implemented cost-saving upgrades in their home markets. Toward the close of the 1980s, approximately two-thirds of U.S. cement capacity was in the hands of European cement multinationals.[32]

In 1988, Clarence C. Comer became president and CEO of Southdown. The following year, he became chairman of an ad hoc committee of U.S. cement producers and labor unions that successfully petitioned the U.S. government to impose anti-dumping duties against Cemex and other importers.[33] In 1990, the U.S. International Trade Commission imposed anti-dumping duties of between 40 and 100 per cent against Mexico, Venezuela and Japan. As a result, cement imports declined from 17 per cent in 1989 to eight per cent in 1992.

In 1999, the cement industry in the United States was commodity-driven and very competitive, with numerous national and regional players. Few ready-mix operators had more than 20 mixers or revenues in excess of $3 million, and the country's 5,845 quarries were in the hands of more than 3,800 companies.

Beginning in 1990, the United States entered a period of recession. Cement prices and demand

Table 4 U.S. Cement Industry (1999)

Company Name	Rank	(000 TONS)	% Total
Holnam, Inc.	1	10,699	12.7
Southdown, Inc.	2	10,109	12.0
Lafarge Corporation	3	6,935	8.2
Ash Grove Cement Company	4	5,648	6.7
CBR-HCI Construction Materials	5	5,503	6.5
Blue Circle, Inc.	6	4,386	5.2
Essroc Corporation	7	4,135	4.9
Lone Star Industries	8	3,953	4.7
Texas Industries, Inc.	9	3,399	4.0
California Portland Cement	10	3,317	3.9
Total Top Ten		58,084	68.7
Others		26,409	31.3
Total Industry		**84,493**	**100.0**

Source: Southdown, Inc.

began to decline, and Southdown posted annual losses in excess of $40 million for each of the next three years. To make matters worse, the company's environmental subsidiary, which burned hazardous waste in Southdown's cement kilns, was facing two lawsuits from the U.S. Environmental Protection Agency for exceeding certified feed rates. In 1992, the company began to liquidate its hazardous-waste disposal facilities.

In an effort to reduce costs, the company began to invest heavily in technology, retiring or upgrading inefficient wet plants with newer dry-process technology. Instead of mixing crushed limestone with water before heating, the new process recycled heat from the kiln to a preheating stage, thereby significantly reducing energy consumption. By 1998, approximately 88 per cent of the company's cement clinker was processed using the dry/preheater technology, compared with only 52 per cent for the U.S. industry.[34]

As the United States emerged from the recession of the early 1990s, Southdown once again became profitable. By upgrading its plants, the company was also able to achieve productivity improvements of between 50 and 100 per cent. Ten years after Comer took the helm of Southdown, the company had more than doubled its capacity while maintaining employment levels at just under 4,000 people. In 1999, the company spent $161 million upgrading its main plant in California, making it the largest in the country with a capacity of 3.1 million tons per year.[35]

Southdown operated 12 cement plants with a total clinker capacity of 10 million tons[36] per year (see Table 4 and Figure 3). The company also operated its own mines, where it produced raw material for its cement plants as well as aggregates and specialty mineral products. At the other end of the production cycle, Southdown also operated 616 ready-mix trucks, 66 batch plants and 12 concrete-block plants. Transportation was typically conducted by rail or sea.[37] In addition, the company constructed highway safety devices, such as traffic signals, and had a lawn and garden division that marketed aggregates through retail garden centers.

In recent years Southdown continued to grow revenue while decreasing costs through the implementation of newer technology. The company had also benefited from a technology-led economic boom, which was reflected in high employment levels and increased investment in construction. Additionally, as the U.S. federal government committed significant new funds to upgrade the federal highway system, U.S. demand for cement continued to exceed available supply (see Figure 2). As a result, imports rose from 18 per cent in 1997 to 31 per cent in 1999.

Clarence Comer could not understand why his company's recent successes were not being

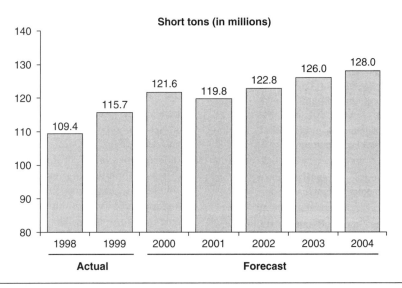

Short tons (in millions)

Figure 2   U.S. Demand Forecast—Portland Cement

Source: Southdown, Inc.

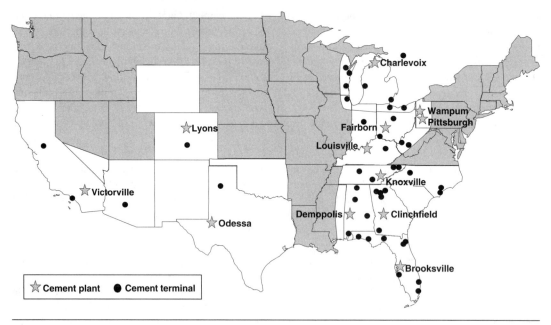

Figure 3   Map of Southdown Operations

Source: Southdown Inc.

translated in higher valuations on the stock market. While his company had more than doubled earnings over the past year and was virtually debt-free, Southdown's shares had declined steadily from $74 per share in mid-1998 to just above $45 per share at the end of 1999 (see Exhibits 3, 4 and 5). Meanwhile, the NASDAQ Composite Index had nearly tripled in value over the same period.

THE SOUTHDOWN OFFER[38]

Throughout the 1990s, Comer met with Lorenzo Zambrano from time to time to discuss anti-dumping litigation, for which Southdown was a plaintiff and Cemex a defendant. In 1999, the two companies discussed the formation of a joint venture to pool ready-mix resources in California, and in 2000 Southdown withdrew its support for the continuation of anti-dumping

tariffs (see Exhibit 6). Comer also expressed an interest in selling Southdown to Cemex, but Zambrano did not at first appear interested.

On April 5, 2000, Zambrano met with Comer at Southdown's Houston headquarters. The purpose of the meeting was to discuss a price at which Zambrano *would* be interested in purchasing Southdown. Zambrano replied that "At a price of approximately $65 per share, Cemex would be interested." That brought the total cost to over $2.5 billion, which would have made it by far the largest purchase ever undertaken by Cemex.[39] Comer, however, believed that Cemex's offer was too low, given the company's performance and growth prospects. It also appeared that the valuation had not given proper consideration to an estimated $60 million in annual cost savings through the integration of Southdown into Cemex's existing U.S. assets.

Toward the close of the summer of 1999, it was clear that the U.S. cement industry would

	1999	1998	1997
REVENUES	$1,271.8	$1,184.7	$1,095.2
Costs and expenses:			
Operating	774.7	717.6	698.3
Depreciation, depletion and amortization	74.6	71.1	64.1
Selling and marketing	29.4	27.8	24.7
General and administrative	65.8	71.4	65.6
Acquisition charge (credit)	(1.5)	75.2	—
Other income, net	(11.0)	(4.8)	(6.7)
	932.0	958.3	846.0
Earnings from continuing operations before interest, income taxes and minority interest	339.8	226.4	249.2
Interest income	4.1	5.9	3.3
Interest expense, net of amounts capitalized	(13.7)	(16.5)	(15.5)
Earnings from continuing operations before income taxes and minority interest	330.2	215.8	237.0
Income tax expense	(112.0)	(86.2)	(78.3)
Earnings from continuing operations before minority interest	218.2	129.6	158.7
Minority interest, net of income taxes	(4.8)	(4.6)	(5.0)
Earnings from continuing operations	213.4	125.0	153.7
Loss from discontinued operations, net of income taxes	(1.0)	(1.6)	—
Extraordinary charge, net of income taxes	(9.2)	—	—
Net earnings	203.2	123.4	153.7
Dividends on preferred stock	—	—	(2.5)
Earnings attributable to common stock	$203.2	$123.4	$151.2

Exhibit 3 Southdown Consolidated Earnings (for years ending December 31) (in millions of dollars, except per share amounts not listed)

Source: Southdown Inc.

not meet forecasted demand. Delays in federal highways projects and unusually wet weather conditions resulted in a moderate decline in Southdown's quarterly revenues. At the same time, costs were rising as energy shortages hit the southern states, leading to an 11 per cent decline in operating margins. Southdown strongly asserted that decline was only temporary. After all, the U.S. economy was still growing at a record pace, and highway infrastructure projects were expected to get back on track in 2001.

	1999	1998
ASSETS		
Current assets:		
Cash and cash equivalents	$21.8	$143.8
Short-term investments		14.8
Accounts and notes receivable, net	129.4	120.0
Inventories	135.4	107.7
Prepaid expenses and other	20.0	18.4
Total current assets	306.6	404.7
Property, plant and equipment, less accumulated depreciation, depletion and amortization	920.3	819.9
Goodwill	134.2	105.5
Other long-term assets	69.6	70.3
	$1,430.7	$1,400.4
LIABILITIES AND SHAREHOLDERS' EQUITY		
Current liabilities:		
Current maturities of long-term debt	$0.4	$0.6
Accounts payable and accrued liabilities	146.8	139.3
Total current liabilities	147.2	139.9
Long-term debt	165.7	167.3
Deferred income taxes	131.1	139.4
Minority interest in consolidated joint venture	35.9	27.7
Long-term portion of postretirement benefit obligation	87.7	91.5
Other long-term liabilities and deferred credits	30.0	30.4
	597.6	596.2
Commitments and contingent liabilities		
Shareholders' equity		
Common stock, $1.25 par value, 200,000,000 shares authorized, 39,987,000 and 35,904,000 shares issued and outstanding, respectively, in 1999 and 39,849,000 and 38,683,000 shares issued and outstanding, respectively, in 1998	50.0	49.8
Capital in excess of par value	376.3	370.6
Reinvested earnings	612.2	431.6
Currency translation adjustment	(1.2)	(1.5)
Treasury stock, at cost	(204.2)	(46.3)
	833.1	804.2
	$1,430.7	$1,400.4

Exhibit 4   Southdown, Inc. Consolidated Balance Sheet (for years ending December 31) (in millions of dollars)

Source: Southdown Inc.

	1999	1998	1997
Operating Activities:			
Earnings from continuing operations	213.4	125.0	153.7
Adjustments to reconcile earnings from continuing operations to cash provided by operating activities:			
Depreciation, depletion and amortization	74.6	71.1	64.1
Deferred income tax expense	1.9	6.2	14.5
Other non-cash charges	0.8	9.7	3.0
Changes in operating assets and liabilities:			
(Increase) decrease in accounts and notes receivable	(4.0)	(11.1)	6.1
Increase in inventories	(22.6)	(10.2)	(1.9)
(Increase) decrease in prepaid expenses and other	(2.6)	2.6	—
Increase in other long-term assets	(4.7)	(11.2)	(6.1)
Increase in accounts payable and accrued liabilities	8.6	33.4	0.5
Decrease in other liabilities and deferred credits	(4.2)	(5.1)	(0.6)
Other adjustments	(1.0)	2.6	4.7
Net cash used in discontinued operations	(1.4)	(0.4)	(1.0)
Net cash provided by operating activities	258.8	212.6	237.0
Investing Activities:			
Additions to property, plant and equipment	(152.4)	(116.4)	(94.6)
Acquisitions, net of cash acquired	(69.4)	(6.0)	(30.2)
Purchase of short-term investments	(14.8)	(18.7)	(6.9)
Maturity of short-term investments	29.6	7.9	14.7
Proceeds from asset sales	16.2	13.9	8.6
Other investing activities	(0.2)	(0.1)	—
Net cash used in investing activities	(191.0)	(119.4)	(108.4)
Financing Activities:			
Additions to long-term debt	122.0	30.0	—
Reductions in long-term debt	(123.6)	(63.6)	(7.2)
Purchase of treasury stock	(159.0)	—	(59.9)
Dividends	(22.6)	(19.4)	(22.9)
Contributions from minority partner	10.0	—	
Distributions to minority partner	(9.3)	(7.0)	(7.8)
Premium on early extinguishment of debt	(11.5)	—	
Other financing activities	4.2	11.7	(2.3)
Net cash used in financing activities	(189.8)	(48.3)	(100.1)
Net increase (decrease) in cash and cash equivalents	(122.0)	44.9	28.5
Cash and cash equivalents at the beginning of the year	143.8	98.9	70.4
Cash and cash equivalents at the end of the year	$21.8	$143.8	$98.9

Exhibit 5   Southdown, Inc. Consolidated Cash Flow (for years ending December 31) (in millions of dollars)

Source: Southdown Inc.

CLARENCE C. COMER
PRESIDENT AND CHIEF EXECUTIVE OFFICER

August 11, 2000

The Honorable Stephen Koplan
Chairman
U. S. International Trade Commission
500 E Street, S.W.
Washington, D.C. 20436

303-TA-21 (Review)

Re: Gray Portland Cement From Japan, Mexico, And Venezuela

DOCKET

Dear Mr. Koplan:

I understand that the Japanese cement producers have stated in their prehearing brief to the Commission that "Southdown publicly opposes continuation of the order" and that "Southdown is now a vocal opponent of continuation of the dumping order."

Southdown has publicly stated only that it decided to withdraw its support from the Committees pursuing the continuation of dumping duties against Japan and other countries. Southdown has not stated to the public that it opposes continuation of the remedies, and the Company has indicated that it would not hesitate to reinitiate proceedings seeking relief from unfair trade practices. Southdown's position in the current reviews is accurately reflected in its responses to the Commission's questionnaires.

Sincerely,

Clarence C. Comer

Clarence C. Comer

Washington2 220642 v1

Southdown, Inc. ▬ 1200 SMITH STREET ▬ SUITE 2400 ▬ HOUSTON, TEXAS 77002 ▬ (713) 650-6200

Exhibit 6 Anti-Dumping Letter

Table 5   Annual Cement Production Capacity ('000 tons)

Plant Location	12/31/96	12/31/99	2001*
Victorville, CA	1,666	2,050	3,100
Charlevoix, MI	1,400	1,540	1,690
Kosmosdale, KY	791	875	1,575
Brooksville, FL	1,304	1,460	1,460
Demopolis, AL	840	990	990
Wampum, PA	720	750	910
Clinchfield, GA	660	835	835
Knoxville, TN	729	830	830
Fairborn, OH	650	750	750
Odessa, TX	538	600	600
Lyons, CO	448	575	575
Pittsburgh, PA	408	408	408
Total Production	**10,154**	**11,663**	**13,723**

Source: Southdown Inc.

*Pro Forma

GLOSSARY OF TERMS

Aggregate: Inert solid bodies such as crushed rock, sand and gravel.

Batch Plant: Equipment used for introducing the ingredients for a batch of concrete materials into the mixer.

Clinker: The material that emerges from the cement kiln after burning. The dark, porous nodules are ground with a small amount of gypsum to produce cement.

Concrete: A hard compact building material formed when a mixture of cement, sand, gravel and water undergoes hydration.

Dry Process: In the manufacture of cement, the process in which the raw materials are ground, conveyed, blended and stored in a dry condition. Exhaust from the kiln is recycled into a pre-heater tower where raw materials are precalcinated. This eliminates the need for adding water.[40]

Kiln: High-temperature oven.

Limestone: Mineral rock of calcium carbonate.

Portland Cement: A commercial product which when mixed with water alone or in combination with sand, stone or similar materials, has the property of combining with water, slowly, to form a hard solid mass. Physically, Portland Cement is a finely pulverized clinker produced by burning mixtures containing lime, iron, alumina and silica at high temperature and indefinite proportions, and then intergrinding gypsum to give the properties desired.

Ready-Mixed Concrete: Concrete manufactured for delivery to a purchaser in a plastic and unhardened state.

Wet Process: In the manufacture of cement, the process in which the raw materials are ground, blended, mixed and pumped while mixed with water; the wet process is chosen where raw materials are extremely wet and sticky, which would make drying before crushing and grinding difficult. This process requires greater energy inputs than dry-processing, in order to evaporate water during production.

NOTES

1. This case has been written on the basis of published sources only. Consequently, the interpretation and perspectives presented in this case are not necessarily those of Cemex or any of its employees.

2. Southdown's share price had reached a high of $74 in 1998, before declining. It had ranged between $45 and $58 in the fourth quarter of 1999, and between $48 and $60 in the first quarter of 2000. Based on 1999 earnings, this gave Southdown a price-earnings ratio of just over 10.

3. "The Year in Review," *Southdown Annual Report*, 1999.

4. Worldwide, Cemex distributed approximately 70 per cent of its cement in bags, compared to five per cent in the United States.

5. "Concrete Solution," *The Industry Standard*, August 28, 2000.

6. H. Dumez, and A. Jeunemaitre, (2000) *Understanding and Regulating the Market at a Time of Globalization*, Saint Martin's Press, New York.

7. Capacity of 90 million tons, 1999 revenues approx. $6.8 billion.

8. Capacity of 64.3 million tons, 1999 revenues approx. $10 billion.

9. Ravi Sarathy, "Cemex(A); Case 1-1: Managing the Global Corporation" in J. De la Torre et al., *Case Studies in Strategy & Management*, Irwin-McGraw Hill, 2001.

10. Petcoke: a petroleum coke made from a solid or fixed carbon substance that remains after the distribution of hydrocarbons in petroleum. It may be used as a fuel source in the production of cement.

11. Cemex 2000 Annual Report.

12. H. Dumez, and A. Jeunemaitre, (2000) *Understanding and Regulating the Market at a Time of Globalization*, Saint Martin's Press, New York.

13. Ibid.

14. "Emerging Multinationals," *The Economist*, May 21, 1994.

15. Ravi Sarathy, "Cemex(A); Case 1-1: Managing the Global Corporation" in J. De la Torre et al., *Case Studies in Strategy & Management*, Irwin-McGraw Hill, 2001.

16. "Well-Built Success," *Industry Week*, May 5, 1997.

17. "Winners? In Mexico?" *Global Finance*, May 1995.

18. "Emerging Multinationals," *The Economist*, May 21, 1994.

19. H. Dumez, and A. Jeunemaitre, (2000) *Understanding and Regulating the Market at a Time of Globalization*, Saint Martin's Press, New York.

20. "Well-Built Success," *Industry Week*, May 5, 1997.

21. "Bagged Cement," *The Economist*, June 19, 1999.

22. Robert Garran, *Tigers Tamed: The End of the Asian Miracle*, University of Hawaii Press, 1998.

23. "Bagged Cement," *The Economist*, June 19, 1999.

24. Ibid.

25. APO's only plant had a capacity of three million tons.

26. The 20.3-million-ton capacity included the Indonesian government share. Cemex, however, had management responsibility for the entire operation, including trading access to Semen Gresik's full production capacity.

27. "Mixing Salsa with Islam," *Latin Trade*, June 2000.

28. "Well-Built Success," *Industry Week*, May 5, 1997.

29. "Concrete Solution," *The Industry Standard*, August 28, 2000.

30. Ibid.

31. "Well-Built Success," *Industry Week*, May 5, 1997.

32. H. Dumez, and A. Jeunemaitre, (2000) *Understanding and Regulating the Market at a Time of Globalization*, Saint Martin's Press, New York.

33. Ibid.

34. Plant Information Summary, *Portland Cement Association*, December 31, 1998. Updated for 1999 and 2000 expansion projects and the Victorville expansion.

35. "Southdown: Concrete Results," *Forbes*, January 10, 2000.

36. Equivalent to 11.7 million tons of cement.

37. Southdown owned two ocean freighters.

38. Adapted from Cena Acquisition Corporation's Offer to Purchase Southdown, Inc., October 5, 2000.

39. At the time, Southdown had a book value of $971.8 million or $27.07 per share.

40. For an interactive tour and description of a dry-process cement plant, see the Portland Cement Association Web site's "Virtual Plant Tour" at www.portcement.org.

BC Sugar Refinery, Limited

*Prepared by Michael Hays and Gillian Pinchin
under the supervision of Professor Robert White*

Version: (A) 2002-09-23

Seth Mersky, vice president of Onex Corporation (Onex), stood looking out of the 49th floor window of his Toronto office on May 30, 1997. Mersky had just been speaking with Stuart Belkin, President of Balaclava Enterprises, who had related the recent events of a prolonged and heated acquisition battle for Vancouver-based BC Sugar Refinery, Limited (BC Sugar). Mersky and Belkin had been friends and business associates for some time as the two had worked together on a number of transactions while Mersky was a senior vice president at the Bank of Nova Scotia.

Mersky had watched the BC Sugar battle with interest since the strategic moves of the two parties had begun to accelerate in February of that year (see Exhibit 1 for a chronology of events). In fact, Mersky had placed a call to Belkin in April, asking if Onex could help Balaclava in its acquisition efforts. At that time, Belkin had declined, believing his offer would be successful. However, the battle seemed to be reaching a conclusion in favor of Belkin's foe, renowned Vancouver take-over artist Jimmy Pattison. BC Sugar's board of directors (of which both Belkin and Pattison were members) had recommended Pattison's offer of $15 per share (on May 29, 1997 Pattison increased his May 20, 1997 bid of $14.75 to $15.00) for 100 per cent of the shares outstanding, over Belkin's offer of the same price per share for 50.1 per cent of the company. Belkin had to withdraw his company's offer due to insufficient shares tendered and it was becoming clear to Belkin that he did not have the appetite to match Pattison single-handedly. As the market began to take the success of Pattison's bid for granted, Belkin made the last-ditch call to Mersky to see what Onex was prepared to offer.

Onex

Onex was a diversified company formed in 1984 and taken public in 1987 to fund growth through acquisitions. Since its formation, Onex had invested close to $900 million in more than 25 companies and generated an average annual pre-tax return on capital in excess of 30 per cent. The company held investments in a diversified group of more than 15 private and public companies, in such industries as airline catering, electronics manufacturing services, automotive components, and food service distribution. While, throughout its autonomous subsidiaries, the company had $11 billion in revenues, $6 billion in assets and 43,000 employees, the holding company itself operated with 14 professional employees, setting financing strategy and evaluating potential acquisition candidates to fuel growth.

Onex used a number of criteria in evaluating acquisition candidates. First, Onex preferred to target companies in strong, stable industries. As Mersky described, "you can make mistakes in a good industry and not go broke, but you can't get away with that in an industry that is unattractive or in decline." The second major criterion in acquisition selection was strong management. As Onex's acquisition strategy was to operate its investments as autonomous subsidiaries, it was imperative that each company was led by a trusted team of managers with a strong record of performance. This was particularly important as Onex did not have a set time horizon like most

1990	In its 100th year, the widely held company adopts a shareholders' rights plan.
1994	Jim Pattison and Stuart Belkin both begin accumulating shares and join the board of directors, along with Pattison associate, Nicholas Geer.
Feb. 18, 1997	At the instigation of Belkin, whose Balaclava Enterprises now owns 19 per cent of the shares, a resolution to strike down the rights plan is put to the general meeting. Shareholders, including Pattison (then at 20 per cent), strike down the plan. Belkin associate, Daniel Pekarsky, joins the board.
March 5	With two quick buys, Pattison raises his BC Sugar stake to 29.5 per cent.
March 12	Belkin offers Pattison $13.80 for his shares.
March 19	Pattison says no; Belkin offers to sell Balaclava shares to Pattison on "reasonable" terms.
March 27	Belkin offers to sell his shares or buy Pattison's for $15 a share. Pattison says he won't pay $15.
April 3	Balaclava increases stake to 20 per cent.
April 9	Pattison offers Belkin $13 a share for Balaclava's BC Sugar shares. Belkin says no.
April 25	Belkin makes a public offer at $15 a share to get 50.1 per cent control.
May 1	Balaclava increases ownership to 20.8 per cent and Canaccord Capital Corp. chairman Peter Brown, a Pattison ally, buys five per cent.
May 4	Committee of BC Sugar advises not to tender to Balaclava.
May 7	Grupo Azucarero Mexico SA buys 1.2 million shares (4.9 per cent) of BC Sugar.
May 9	BC Sugar adopts new short-term poison pill to prevent non-permitted bids while it is shopping the company to other buyers.
May 20	Pattison offers $14.75 cash for all the shares and the board says it will recommend the Pattison bid.
May 29	Pattison increases offer to $15 a share in response to pressure from arbitrageurs who now own most of the stock.
May 30	Belkin withdraws offer because insufficient number of shares were tendered.

Exhibit 1   Chronology of Events

Source: The Financial Post—July 27, 1997.

Leverage Buyout (LBO) funds; instead a rigorous return on investment (ROI) requirement determined if a company was held or divested. Lastly, the company looked for anomalies, or business situations that simply did not make sense. In such situations, Onex was sometimes able to identify and exploit assets that were undervalued due to sub-optimal financial or business structures.

THE JIM PATTISON GROUP

At 68, Jimmy Pattison was one of Canada's best known take-over artists. Based out of Vancouver, Canada, he had parlayed an earlier career as a car salesman into a $3.4 billion (revenue) empire including, among others, car franchises, supermarket chains, magazine distributorships, and Ripley's Believe-It-Or-Not Museums. Pattison often looked at as many as two companies per day in search of acquisition opportunities. Those he was successful in purchasing, he typically kept or took private, growing them to profitable industry leaders using shrewd management teams trained in the "Pattison way," while shrouding operating methods through very limited disclosure. Pattison was a confident man in both his demeanor and business tactics. He rarely lost an acquisition he wanted, particularly on his home turf. With BC Sugar, it seemed that he was again going to be successful.

Pattison began accumulating stock in BC Sugar in 1994 and soon thereafter joined the company's board of directors. By March 1997, Pattison had increased his stake to 29.5 per cent of the outstanding shares and it was clear that he was interested in adding BC Sugar to his growing empire. By April 1997, he was not only embroiled in the BC Sugar acquisition battle, but was also attempting to take private two other large British Columbia companies, Great Pacific Enterprises and Westar Group, with offers outstanding of $106 million and $127 million, respectively. At the time, a president of a Vancouver-based brokerage commented, "It's classic Pattison strategy to increase his shares in a public company, assume full control, then privatize. But he's never finessed three companies at once."

BALACLAVA ENTERPRISES

Stuart Belkin, 39, was the president of Balaclava Enterprises, a family-owned holding company also based in Vancouver. Belkin's family had previous connections with BC Sugar in the 1970s, when two companies that his father had founded were partly owned by the company. Belkin began accumulating stock in BC Sugar in 1994 and joined Pattison on the board of directors. By the time he made his $15 offer for 50.1 per cent of BC Sugar's outstanding shares in April 1997, he already owned 20 per cent of the company.

BC SUGAR REFINERY, LIMITED

In 1890, the Rogers family constructed western Canada's first cane sugar refinery in Vancouver, British Columbia. From there, the company expanded to the production of refined sugar in 1891, importing raw sugar from Asia. By 1997, the Rogers family company had been renamed BC Sugar Refinery, Limited and comprised three wholly owned subsidiaries: Rogers Sugar Limited (Rogers), which operated a cane sugar refinery in Vancouver and a sugar beet factory located in Taber, Alberta; Lantic Sugar Limited (Lantic), which operated sugar cane refineries in Saint John, New Brunswick and Montreal, Quebec; and Refined Sugars, Incorporated (RSI), which operated a cane sugar refinery in Yonkers, New York (see Exhibit 2 for financial statements). Rogers and Lantic combined made BC Sugar the leading refiner, processor, distributor and marketer of sugar products in Canada and the only sugar producer in Western Canada. RSI held an eight per cent market share in the United States.

Rogers primarily met the demands of the British Columbia and prairie markets with the Vancouver facility producing 120,000 tonnes of sugar per year (75 per cent of capacity) and Taber close to 100,000 tonnes per year (near full capacity). While the original Vancouver facility was built in 1890, numerous improvements had been made to the building and processing areas of the plant to maintain them in good condition and to capture modern efficiencies consistent with industry practices. However, Vancouver had recently experienced some disruption in production and cost escalation due to strained labor relations.

Taber was one of the lowest cost sugar-processing facilities in Canada, a result of its proximity to key markets, greater reliance on non-unionized, part-time labor, favorable relations with a relatively small unionized workforce, excellent sugar yields from local beets and a highly efficient production process. This plant was considered one of the brightest jewels in BC Sugar's crown (see Exhibit 3 for Rogers Sugar financial highlights).

SUMMARY FINANCIAL STATEMENTS CONSOLIDATED BALANCE SHEETS ($000)			
	Sept. 30, 1996	Sept. 30, 1995	Sept. 30, 1994
ASSETS			
Current Assets			
Cash	15,293	4,406	592
Accounts Receivable	76,456	74,096	80,321
Inventories	105,267	78,707	87,946
Prepaid Expenses	8,180	7,568	7,208
Deferred Income Taxes	3,598	4,217	6,670
Total Current Assets	208,794	168,634	182,737
Investments and other assets	11,776	11,682	16,464
Fixed Assets, net	134,927	136,084	142,301
Goodwill, net of amortization	140,935	144,948	148,962
Total Assets	**496,432**	**461,348**	**490,464**
Liabilities And Shareholders' Equity			
LIABILITIES			
Current Liabilities			
Bank Loans, secured	5,498	9,330	18,379
Accounts Payable	86,206	60,090	70,581
Current Portion LTD	11,099	9,715	10,289
Total Current Liabilities	102,803	79,135	99,249
Long-Term Debt	118,230	131,236	140,203
Deferred Revenue	35,435	35,029	35,894
Other Liabilities	13,938	9,604	9,071
Deferred Income Taxes	7,726	6,802	3,881
Total Liabilities	**278,132**	**261,806**	**288,298**
Share Capital			
Common Shares	155,613	155,613	155,613
Preferred Shares	—	1,570	1,570
Total Share Capital	155,613	157,183	157,183
Retained Earnings	51,770	32,856	35,355
Foreign Exchange Adjustment	10,917	9,503	9,648
Total Equity	**218,300**	**199,542**	**202,166**
Total Liabilities and Shareholders' Equity	**496,432**	**461,348**	**490,464**
SUMMARY FINANCIAL STATEMENTS CONSOLIDATED STATEMENT OF EARNINGS ($000)[1]			
Revenue	848,554	825,380	790,331
Costs and Expenses			
Cost of Sales	719,445	726,394	684,843
Selling, General and Administration	51,207	44,958	44,426
Depreciation and Amortization	16,464	16,091	16,120

Exhibit 2   Summary Financial Statements

SUMMARY FINANCIAL STATEMENTS
CONSOLIDATED STATEMENT OF EARNINGS
($000)[1]

	Sept. 30, 1996	Sept. 30, 1995	Sept. 30, 1994
Long-Term Debt Interest	15,209	16,362	21,178
Other Interest	343	652	869
Total Costs and Expenses	802,668	804,457	767,436
Earnings Before Non-Recurring Items and Income Taxes	45,886	20,923	22,895
Non-Recurring Items	—	—	17,025
EBT	45,886	20,923	39,920
Income Taxes	17,001	13,435	13,384
Earnings	**28,885**	**7,488**	**26,536**
Shares Outstanding (Class A and Class B)[1]	24,721,914	24,721,914	24,721,914

SUMMARY FINANCIAL STATEMENTS
CONSOLIDATED STATEMENT OF CHANGES IN FINANCIAL POSITION
($000)[234]

	Sept. 30, 1996	Sept. 30, 1995	Sept. 30, 1994
CASH PROVIDED BY (USED FOR)			
Operations			
Cash from continuing operations	45,992	33,325	25,040
Cash from discontinued operations[2]	—	—	9,792
Cash Dividends Paid[3]	(9,971)	(9,967)	(10)
	36,021	**23,358**	**24,865**
Financing			
Net increase (decrease) in LTD	(11,637)	(9,545)	(75,104)
Issue of common shares	—	—	—
Redemption of preferred shares	(1,570)	—	—
	(13,027)	**(9,545)**	**(75,104)**
Investments			
Net Proceeds from sale of investments	—	—	78,223
Additions to fixed assets	(10,188)	(5,810)	(8,795)
Other	2,453	4,500	(7,566)
	(7,753)	**(1,310)**	**61,862**
Increase in Cash[4]	15,079	12,503	6,303
Cash, end of year	9,795	(5,284)	(17,787)

Source: The Financial Post—July 27, 1997.

1. Class A and B shares have equal voting rights, rank equally with respect to dividends and are convertible into one another on a share-for-share basis. As of September 30, 1996, there were 23,813,913 Class A and 908,001 Class B shares outstanding. Class B may elect to receive either cash or stock dividends.
2. Includes a loss incurred with the sale of Kalama Chemicals in 1994 of $5,320,000.
3. The current Class A and B dividends annual rate of $0.40 per share was established with quarterly payment of $0.10 per share on May 25, 1992.
4. Cash is defined as cash less current bank loans.

These financial figures include the accounts of the western Canadian sugar operations of BC Sugar Refinery Limited, which include the cane sugar refinery located in Vancouver, British Columbia and beet sugar processing facilities located in Taber, Alberta.

BALANCE SHEET ($000)	As at September 30, 1996
Cash	10,660
Current Assets	55,078
Total Assets	69,481
Current Liabilities	20,807
Long-Term Debt	30,000
Shareholders' Equity	14,112

INCOME & CASH FLOW STATEMENTS	Year ended September 30, 1996
Revenue	198,414
Gross Margin	50,373
Net Earnings	19,195
Cash Flow from Operations (before changes in working capital)	22,655

Exhibit 3   Rogers Sugar Selected Financial Highlights

The Lantic Facilities had a combined capacity of 465,000 tonnes per year (250,000 in Saint John and 215,000 in Montreal). The plants had been running near capacity and had been implementing some cost reduction initiatives. In 1996, RSI had reported a profit of US$6.1 million (approximately Cdn$9 million), its first profit in several years. RSI had implemented cost reduction programs and market conditions had enabled increased capacity utilization.

THE SUGAR INDUSTRY

Refined sugar had been used extensively for centuries. It was a sweetening agent, a flavor enhancer, a "body" agent, a preservative and a fermentation aid. Refined sugar was derived from either sugar cane or sugar beets, with the finished product being identical in either case.

Demand

Total consumption of sugar in Canada was not cyclical and was expected to grow modestly, slightly higher than population growth. North American per capita consumption of sugar had generally been stable for several decades; however, per capita consumption declined slightly in the 1980s following the introduction of high fructose corn syrup (HFCS). HFCS, a liquid sweetener derived from corn, gained market acceptance as a substitute for liquid sugar in certain applications such as soft drinks. The artificially high price of sugar in the United States also encouraged HCFS production. Artificial sweeteners, which were high intensity non-caloric sweeteners that lacked some of the physical properties of sugar, found applications in certain uses such as diet soft drinks. However, unlike HFCS, artificial sweeteners had, for the most part, created new markets rather than competing with sugar. Even with the introduction of HFCS and artificial sweeteners, by the 1990s, sugar consumption had returned to stability and in 1996 grew by 2.8 per cent.

Raw Materials

While sugar refining appeared to be susceptible to commodity-type swings in input (sugar cane and beet) costs, it was important to note that profitability of Canadian refiners was not materially affected by shifts in the price of commodity inputs. Canadian cane refiners purchased raw cane sugar based on the New York market price, plus ocean freight. A refining margin was added to the raw sugar purchase price to set a base selling price for refined sugar. Rogers' Taber facility, Canada's only sugar beet processor, had established a master agreement with the growers' association that determined the growers' share of revenue and, consequently, the cost of raw material for the Taber operation. The agreement included a formula which set the sugar beet price based on the received selling price of refined sugar.

Competition

While commodity price fluctuations did not cause material profitability issues for refiners, competitive conditions in the refined sugar marketplace had a substantial impact. Key to competitiveness and profitability was achieving low cost production through economies of scale and minimizing transport costs to markets. In 1995, Redpath Sugar Limited (Redpath), BC Sugar's only major domestic competitor, announced a 75 per cent increase of its refining capacity (to 500,000 tonnes per year) and adopted an aggressive pricing strategy to fill this capacity. The price reductions effectively narrowed the spread between the daily refined sugar and raw sugar prices. Reacting to this market move, Lantic entered into a large number of long-term contracts at prices greatly below historical market values. Lantic's margins were put under particular pressure as their two plants (at 250,000 and 215,000 tonnes of capacity) could not compete with Redpath's cost position. While Redpath was expected to reach capacity in the coming year and restore higher price levels, a number of the long-term contracts would remain in place until 1999.

It was unlikely that another major competitor would enter the marketplace in Canada in the short to medium term due to the high capital cost of construction and the existing extra capacity in the marketplace. Other competitors could include, periodically, small regional distributors that sourced refined sugar from either domestic or foreign suppliers. The small distributors would enter and exit the market as dictated by the competitive environment. Imports into Canada, after the anti-dumping regulations were instituted in the early 1990s, were insignificant (less than one per cent of the domestic market).

Trade Regulations

No single external issue impacted the financial success of Canadian sugar refiners more than results from discussions between trade negotiators. In 1995, Revenue Canada initiated a combined anti-dumping and countervailing duty investigation against certain refined sugar imports into Canada. The "dumping complaint" identified refined sugar from the United States, Denmark, the Netherlands, the United Kingdom, and the Republic of Korea. The "subsidy complaint" was directed against the United States and European Union. Revenue Canada completed the preliminary phase of its investigation in mid-1995 and determined that refined sugar originating in, or exported from, all the countries identified had been dumped in Canada. It also found that refined sugar originating in, or exported from, the European Union had been subsidized. These findings were later confirmed by the Canadian International Trade Tribunal, which concluded that dumped and subsidized sugar from the said countries was threatening material injury to the Canadian sugar industry. Duties which reflected estimated margins of dumping and amounts of subsidies were consequently imposed and virtually no dumped or subsidized sugar entered Canada after July 1995.

The duties enabled price recovery in Canada at the expense of restricting access to the corresponding markets. While the duties put in place in 1995 were expected to remain in place until the latter half of 2000, there was the possibility that trade negotiations between NAFTA and the European Union would result in less beneficial legislation. Moreover, the Canadian sugar export issue had been linked to claims that Canada had been blocking U.S. dairy and poultry products by applying protective duties. The U.S. Federal Government had expressed an unwillingness to address access to its market for Canadian sugar until the dairy and poultry issues had been resolved.

Opportunities at BC Sugar

Operational Improvements

Onex had become aware of several BC Sugar projects and initiatives that had been identified but not implemented, that would have reduced costs and increased efficiencies. At a general board meeting in February 1997, the retirement of two long-serving board members coincided with a resolution to strike down the existing shareholders' rights plan. These events opened the way for the takeover battle.

One such project involved a $39.9 million investment in the Taber facility to purchase and install new equipment and processes. The expansion would result in three significant improvements: capacity would be increased to 145,000 tonnes per year; thick juice storage capacity would be built at the intermediate stage to permit further processing at a later date; refined sugar storage costs would be reduced.

Once the expansion was completed, most western production could be moved to the Taber plant to optimize economies of scale and minimize labor relation complications. The Vancouver facility could then be kept as "swing" capacity and, indirectly, as a means to balance the power of the Albertan beet growers. The move to produce at Taber would save an estimated $8.8 million per year.

The Taber plant had a number of strategic advantages. In particular, the location enabled access to a plentiful supply of land suitable to beet production, sugar yields from the local beets were among the highest in North America, and a strong relationship had been established with the beet growers formalized by a five-year revenue-sharing agreement. Moreover, the area had a readily available supply of non-unionized seasonal labor, labor relations were favorable with full-time employees, and Alberta energy costs were among the lowest in North America. All of these factors indicated that the Taber facility would remain a competitive location to produce sugar. Finally, because equipment and processes similar to those used in the Taber upgrade had been implemented successfully in over 300 beet-processing facilities in the United States and Europe over the previous 30 years, Mersky was confident that the projected benefits would be realized.

A project to consolidate Lantic's production into one plant had also been investigated. Both the Montreal and St. John facilities were outdated and there was a compelling argument to bring production under one roof to harness economies of scale. The combined plant would be able to produce 500,000 tonnes per annum with staff equal to that of one of the previous plants. Consulting engineers estimated that the consolidation would cost approximately $60 million and generate $13 million cost savings. It seemed that either location would be effective, and it was feasible that the respective provincial governments would offer incentives to become host to the consolidated plant. The Quebec government had in the past provided grants of approximately 32 per cent of the capital cost for similar projects. Moreover, discussions with the union revealed that they were anxious to keep Lantic as an employer in Quebec. In fact, it was conceivable that a 10-year contract guaranteeing only adjustments for inflation equal to changes in the Consumer Price Index could be negotiated.

Further, each of the BC Sugar subsidiaries maintained completely independent management and administrative infrastructures. Each entity had all levels of functional executives and managers as well as its own separate financial and information systems. The systems were so incompatible, that BC Sugar corporate had to maintain a full-time accounting staff to consolidate subsidiary information. Rogers alone spent $8.5 on management and administrative costs. It was evident that all Canadian assets could be managed out of the Lantic office, as Lantic had more up-to-date systems and controls. The move would save the company $4.5 million in expenses.

With all of the cost savings, Belkin and Mersky speculated that Rogers would be able to generate a consistent cash flow to equity of $38 million and Lantic $25.5 million. These cash flows could also experience some upside if prices recovered from the price war with Redpath.

While Mersky and Belkin loved the Canadian story, they were unsure what value could be realized from the Refined Sugar U.S. assets. While Refined had eight per cent of the U.S. market and had generated net earnings of Cdn$9 million in the previous year, the market was consolidating and successful competition would require a tremendous amount of cash with a potentially mediocre return. Divestiture was an option. Refiners' margins in the United States had been squeezed by the Farm Bill that supported raw cane and beet sugar prices. This situation had led to consolidation as well as sparking the interest of growers' associations in purchasing refining assets. As a consequence, U.S. refineries might sell at multiples as high as 10 times net earnings as compared to a trading multiple of 6.5 times in Canada; the price to cash flow trading multiples were 6.0.

Capital Restructuring

Operational efficiencies aside, it appeared that a restructuring of BC Sugar's capitalization could enhance the value of the assets. The relative stability of BC Sugar's cash flow combined with the industry's limited growth prospects made an Income Trust formation look more advantageous than a stock formation. More specifically, it was conceivable that the markets were undervaluing BC Sugar's assets, believing it was unlikely that retained earnings could be reinvested in the company to generate sufficient returns. The current low interest rate and bond yield environment had fueled income trusts to record valuations. There was a chance that the markets would be receptive to the capitalization of BC Sugar's assets by a yield-based investment which would see all cash flows distributed to the investors.

Creating a BC Sugar Income Fund would involve BC Sugar placing appropriate assets into another operating company, which would then sell its shares to an Income Fund. The Income Fund would then go to the market and place trust units with investors, who would receive ongoing quarterly distributions based on the cash flow of the new operating company. The money from private investors would move up through the structure and would end up compensating BC Sugar for the original operating asset. This structure would differ from a traditional royalty trust, a structure which the public had become familiar

with due to the many resource-based trusts in the marketplace, as it involved an exchange of shares, rather than assets. Valuation of assets for an income trust was determined by the projected cash-on-cash yield. Essentially, the value of assets was calculated by dividing the annual cash available for distribution by the target cash yield. The cash yield incorporated a risk premium over mid- and long-term treasury bonds (see Exhibit 4 for financial market data). A number of income funds had been filed and closed within the previous year. Target yields had ranged from 9.4 per cent for a fund holding a natural gas processing plant asset (units were issued in February 1997) to 15 per cent for a fund deriving revenues from a natural gas wholesaler (units were issued in August 1996). In May 1997, Halifax Container Terminal Income Fund units were issued with a cash yield of 9.7 per cent.

While the income trust market was active and generating high values, some analysts believed these conditions would last less than six months. It was evident that the timing and size of the issue would be critical. To expedite the issue, Onex could issue debentures that would be convertible into trust units at a later date, within three weeks of filing. The two major decisions that would have to be made would be what assets to place in the fund and at what cash yield or valuation.

THE DECISION

Should Onex join forces with Balaclava in a bid for BC Sugar? If so, the Onex team (Seth Mersky, Tom Dea and Mark Hilson) and Stuart Belkin would have to formulate a bidding strategy, a financial plan and a business plan for the operation of BC Sugar post-acquisition. A proposal to Gerry Schwartz, the President and CEO of Onex, would have to made soon if Onex and Balaclava were to present an offer to BC Sugar shareholders before June 27, 1997, the date that Pattison's offer was to expire.

	Toronto Stock Exchange 300 Stock Index	BC Sugar Closing Share Price (BCS.A)	Yield on 91-Day Treasury Bills	Yield on Long-Term Government Bonds	Yield on Long-Term Corporate Bonds
			MONTH-END DATA		
Date					
920331	6,162.76	9.375	7.239	9.28	10.37
920430	6,069.05	9.125	6.719	9.51	10.56
920529	6,143.26	9.625	6.081	9.17	10.22
920630	6,170.05	9.000	5.596	8.87	9.96
920731	6,279.34	9.500	5.170	8.21	9.34
920831	6,221.23	9.750	4.821	8.19	9.31
920930	6,054.57	9.000	7.371	8.53	9.71
921030	6,131.98	8.875	6.055	8.33	9.57
921130	6,052.93	8.625	8.566	8.66	9.90
921231	6,201.72	9.125	7.111	8.54	9.70
930129	6,124.83	9.000	6.560	8.67	9.84
930226	6,406.98	9.875	5.840	8.19	9.37
930331	6,714.88	10.500	5.110	8.27	9.41
930430	7,071.07	10.625	5.340	8.27	9.42
930531	7,271.67	10.125	4.850	8.12	9.17
930630	7,455.35	9.375	4.540	7.96	8.88
930730	7,463.91	9.375	4.160	7.79	8.65
930831	7,798.17	9.750	4.740	7.40	8.37
930930	7,544.63	9.500	4.650	7.55	8.48
931029	8,052.76	10.375	4.380	7.35	8.25
931130	7,926.13	10.000	4.090	7.45	8.32
931231	8,220.23	10.250	3.860	7.12	8.02
940131	8,670.34	10.625	3.632	6.86	7.74
940228	8,436.07	10.500	3.850	7.33	8.13
940331	8,283.08	9.375	5.388	8.25	9.11
940429	8,170.41	9.125	5.818	8.18	9.04
940531	8,301.33	8.875	6.335	8.55	9.40
940630	7,748.33	8.000	6.672	9.29	10.13
940729	8,051.04	7.625	5.794	9.50	10.26
940831	8,393.82	8.500	5.354	8.89	9.70
940930	8,426.82	8.125	5.291	9.04	9.81

Exhibit 4   Financial Market Data

MONTH-END DATA					
Date	Toronto Stock Exchange 300 Stock Index	BC Sugar Closing Share Price (BCS.A)	Yield on 91-Day Treasury Bills	Yield on Long-Term Government Bonds	Yield on Long-Term Corporate Bonds
941031	8,312.82	8.875	5.374	9.29	10.04
941130	7,945.24	8.375	5.789	9.24	10.01
941230	8,205.73	8.125	7.181	9.16	9.95
950131	7,830.41	8.000	7.979	9.41	10.23
950228	8,053.21	8.375	7.768	8.86	9.68
950331	8,451.13	9.500	8.217	8.7	9.48
950428	8,391.47	8.875	7.917	8.44	9.19
950531	8,741.88	9.000	7.394	8.11	8.84
950630	8,923.67	8.125	6.721	8.02	8.76
950731	9,104.07	8.625	6.623	8.5	9.21
950831	8,926.86	8.500	6.338	8.24	8.93
950929	8,977.74	7.875	6.456	8.11	8.77
951031	8,845.80	8.375	5.929	8.11	8.8
951130	9,265.66	8.500	5.816	7.44	8.18
951229	9,397.97	8.625	5.541	7.43	8.12
960131	9,913.64	10.000	5.119	7.35	8.06
960229	9,861.55	10.250	5.18	7.84	8.57
960329	9,964.21	9.625	5.025	7.94	8.58
960430	10,323.89	11.150	4.726	8.07	8.67
960531	10,543.37	10.900	4.645	7.92	8.54
960628	10,167.15	10.750	4.695	7.98	8.58
960731	9,944.05	10.400	4.425	7.86	8.43
960830	10,391.76	10.500	4.033	7.6	8.19
960930	10,716.42	10.900	3.962	7.48	8.04
961031	11,350.62	11.900	3.193	6.81	7.36
961129	12,217.32	11.950	2.69	6.42	6.98
961231	12,061.95	11.750	2.799	6.77	7.35
970131	12,444.13	13.050	2.841	7.07	7.64
970228	12,560.15	13.800	2.858	6.78	7.34
970331	11,961.20	13.150	3.186	6.97	7.53
970430	12,227.41	14.850	3.138	6.97	7.47
970530	13,079.21	14.950	3.005	6.95	7.41

(Continued)

DAILY TRADING DATA FOR BSC.A DECEMBER 30, 1996 THROUGH MAY 30, 1997							
Date	Closing Price	Number of Transactions	Number of Shares Traded	Date	Closing Price	Number of Transactions	Number of Shares Traded
961230	11.950	19	9,910	970317	14.000	66	45,678
961231	11.750	13	9,592	970318	13.750	33	18,350
970102	11.600	15	3,790	970319	13.750	39	24,140
970103	11.700	22	10,740	970320	13.750	29	26,890
970106	11.850	39	8,715	970321	13.750	34	17,701
970107	11.700	27	13,607	970324	13.800	34	16,087
970108	11.550	36	7,473	970325	13.650	47	30,059
970109	11.600	27	9,210	970326	13.750	35	86,568
970110	11.600	50	21,133	970327	13.700	18	8,170
970113	11.400	10	3,400	970331	13.150	36	31,678
970114	11.500	42	19,160	970401	13.250	20	26,800
970115	11.750	61	95,760	970402	13.200	23	21,550
970116	12.000	134	165,712	970403	13.000	18	9,225
970117	12.250	73	198,633	970404	13.050	21	8,660
970120	12.600	105	128,809	970407	13.000	19	4,044
970121	12.550	70	34,195	970408	13.000	15	53,100
970122	12.800	64	48,718	970409	13.250	22	20,112
970123	12.650	56	20,605	970410	13.000	22	60,050
970124	12.550	53	22,648	970411	13.150	15	12,900
970127	12.850	59	41,853	970414	12.850	20	8,640
970128	13.100	87	479,509	970415	12.800	16	3,416
970129	13.050	46	21,265	970416	12.900	21	7,850
970130	13.050	68	83,825	970417	12.750	11	3,779
970131	13.050	71	95,244	970418	12.800	9	3,900
970203	13.000	41	25,116	970421	12.900	15	9,050

Exhibit 4 (Continued)

| | | | | DAILY TRADING DATA FOR BSC.A | | | |
| | | | DECEMBER 30, 1996 THROUGH MAY 30, 1997 | | | | |

Date	Closing Price	Number of Transactions	Number of Shares Traded	Date	Closing Price	Number of Transactions	Number of Shares Traded
970204	13.000	49	16,488	970422	12.900	31	15,950
970205	12.900	51	26,201	970423	12.550	20	8,662
970206	12.900	48	18,636	970424	12.600	16	14,550
970207	12.850	26	11,299	970425	14.950	435	1,278,260
970210	12.700	47	69,527	970428	14.400	373	358,882
970211	12.750	43	30,635	970429	14.500	236	198,602
970212	12.550	23	13,713	970430	14.850	342	539,292
970213	12.800	51	17,397	970501	14.950	300	298,214
970214	12.900	24	6,328	970502	15.000	213	1,350,302
970217	12.750	32	16,277	970505	15.100	160	159,080
970218	12.950	57	23,212	970506	15.200	126	254,733
970219	13.000	292	130,464	970507	15.600	161	128,304
970220	13.350	174	253,355	970508	15.300	81	75,160
970221	14.000	211	133,689	970509	15.350	115	99,783
970224	13.900	140	62,026	970512	15.300	170	775,773
970225	13.600	84	34,470	970513	15.550	181	371,609
970226	13.400	68	45,925	970514	15.450	187	360,738
970227	13.600	70	999,143	970515	15.500	186	448,457
970228	13.800	81	931,648	970516	15.600	74	177,400
970303	13.800	97	56,598	970520	15.100	184	351,367
970304	13.600	60	49,058	970521	14.950	139	205,043
970305	13.800	45	35,320	970522	15.050	78	245,073
970306	13.900	55	44,029	970523	15.000	90	57,971
970307	14.100	126	258,475	970526	14.950	41	33,199
970310	14.150	91	147,142	970527	15.000	87	127,034
970311	14.050	62	45,160	970528	15.000	52	206,192
970312	14.100	43	25,072	970529	15.000	75	1,173,122
970313	14.050	68	64,915	970530	14.950	54	110,470
970314	14.200	108	195,392				

(Continued)

DAILY TRADING DATA FOR BSC.B DECEMBER 30, 1996 THROUGH MAY 30, 1997							
Date	Closing Price	Number of Transactions	Number of Shares Traded	Date	Closing Price	Number of Transactions	Number of Shares Traded
961230	0.000	0	0	970317	0.000	0	0
961231	0.000	0	0	970318	0.000	0	0
970102	0.000	0	0	970319	0.000	0	0
970103	0.000	0	0	970320	0.000	0	0
970106	0.000	0	0	970321	0.000	0	0
970107	0.000	0	0	970324	0.000	0	0
970108	0.000	0	0	970325	0.000	0	0
970109	0.000	0	0	970326	0.000	0	0
970110	0.000	0	0	970327	0.000	0	0
970113	0.000	0	0	970331	0.000	0	0
970114	0.000	0	0	970401	0.000	0	0
970115	0.000	0	0	970402	0.000	0	0
970116	0.000	0	0	970403	0.000	0	0
970117	0.000	0	0	970404	0.000	0	0
970120	0.000	0	0	970407	0.000	0	0
970121	0.000	0	0	970408	0.000	0	0
970122	0.000	0	0	970409	0.000	0	0
970123	0.000	0	0	970410	0.000	0	0
970124	0.000	0	0	970411	0.000	0	0
970127	0.000	0	0	970414	0.000	0	0
970128	0.000	0	0	970415	0.000	0	0
970129	0.000	0	0	970416	0.000	0	0
970130	0.000	0	0	970417	0.000	0	0
970131	0.000	0	0	970418	0.000	0	0
970203	0.000	0	0	970421	0.000	0	0
970204	0.000	0	0	970422	0.000	0	0
970205	0.000	0	0	970423	0.000	0	0

Exhibit 4 (Continued)

| | | | | DAILY TRADING DATA FOR BSC.B | | | |
| | | | | DECEMBER 30, 1996 THROUGH MAY 30, 1997 | | | |
Date	Closing Price	Number of Transactions	Number of Shares Traded	Date	Closing Price	Number of Transactions	Number of Shares Traded
970206	0.000	0	0	970424	0.000	0	0
970207	0.000	0	0	970425	13.000	2	52
970210	0.000	0	0	970428	0.000	0	0
970211	0.000	0	0	970429	0.000	0	0
970212	0.000	0	0	970430	0.000	0	0
970213	0.000	0	0	970501	0.000	0	0
970214	0.000	0	0	970502	14.500	4	1,049
970217	0.000	0	0	970505	0.000	0	0
970218	0.000	0	0	970506	0.000	0	0
970219	12.950	1	10,000	970507	0.000	0	0
970220	13.050	1	2,000	970508	0.000	0	0
970221	13.750	1	2,000	970509	0.000	0	0
970224	13.950	1	3,600	970512	0.000	0	0
970225	13.700	2	5,000	970513	0.000	0	0
970226	0.000	0	0	970514	0.000	0	0
970227	0.000	0	0	970515	0.000	0	0
970228	13.650	1	5,292	970516	0.000	0	0
970303	0.000	0	0	970520	0.000	0	0
970304	0.000	0	0	970521	0.000	0	0
970305	0.000	0	0	970522	0.000	0	0
970306	0.000	0	0	970523	0.000	0	0
970307	0.000	0	0	970526	0.000	0	0
970310	0.000	0	0	970527	0.000	0	0
970311	0.000	0	0	970528	0.000	0	0
970312	0.000	0	0	970529	0.000	0	0
970313	0.000	0	0	970530	0.000	0	0
970314	0.000	0	0				

(Continued)

FINANCIAL MARKET DATA
MAY 30, 1997
(%)

T-Bills:	Latest	Previous Day	Week Ago	Four Weeks Ago
1-month	2.59	2.63	2.62	2.83
3-months	2.93	2.96	2.94	3.00
6-months	3.28	3.33	3.29	3.43
1-year	3.73	3.77	3.27	3.93
Bonds:				
2-year	4.50	4.60	4.55	4.63
5-year	5.70	5.79	5.74	5.74
7-year	6.23	6.32	6.28	6.30
10-year	6.51	6.55	6.53	6.52
30-year	7.23	7.30	7.06	7.08

Source: Financial Post.

Beta (BCS.A) 5-year, monthly data = 1.035

Canadian Equity Market Risk Premiums
January 1950 to December 1996

Estimated Long-Term Canadian Market Risk Premium, Arithmetic Means	= 4.99
Estimated Long-Term Canadian Market Risk Premium, Geometric Means	= 4.24
Estimated Medium-Term Canadian Market Risk Premium, Arithmetic Means	= 4.41
Estimated Medium-Term Canadian Market Risk Premium, Geometric Means	= 3.97
Estimated Short-Term Canadian Market Risk Premium, Arithmetic Means	= 5.81
Estimated Short-Term Canadian Market Risk Premium, Geometric Means	= 4.63

Source: TSE Common Equities CD-ROM Product, 1997.

FINANCIAL MARKET DATA
CANADIAN BOND RATING YIELD SPREADS
ASSUMES A 10-YEAR, CDN$100 MILLION DEBENTURE
MAY 30, 1997
(in basis points)

Investment Grade					
AAA	**AA**	**BB(L)**	**A**	**BBB**	**BBB(L)**
15	20	35	60	70	80

High-yield					
BB(H)	**BB**	**BB(L)**	**B(H)**	**B**	**B(L)**
150	200	250	275	300	400+

Exhibit 4 (Continued)

ANTITRUST: A THREAT TO MERGERS AND ACQUISITIONS?

Prepared by David W. Conklin and Peter H. Pocklington Jr.

July/August 2000

After being a forgotten word for two decades, "antitrust" is again a part of the government's vocabulary.

New York Times, May 21, 2000

In his words quoted above, Kenneth Gilpin was referring to the U.S. government's vocabulary, but governments everywhere are exhibiting a new interest in antitrust. With the current wave of mergers and acquisitions, one question that should be front and centre for an increasing number of companies is this: As you consider further corporate growth, will your plans be able to clear the antitrust hurdles? Adding to the complexity of this question are ongoing changes in the nature and the shape of antitrust hurdles, creating new uncertainties for expansion decisions.

Last year, the Canadian public witnessed merger attempts by several Canadian banks. A focus of concern was a likely decrease in competition among Canada's financial institutions. Canada's Competition Bureau, in reporting on the proposed merger between the Royal Bank of Canada and the Bank of Montreal, predicted that for individuals and small- and medium-sized businesses, the proposed merger would certainly result in a substantial lessening of competition in 104 of 224 local markets and might result in a substantial decrease in competition in another 71 of the local markets. It was not the Competition Bureau but rather elected government officials who had regulatory authority to allow or disallow these mergers. Nevertheless, the Bureau's reports were considered by the Minister of Finance, who subsequently ruled against the proposed bank mergers.

In recent years, antitrust has increasingly become an international issue, with the growing number of international M&As. The European Commission dealing with antitrust recently investigated and turned down the three-way merger proposal, valued at $10.6 billion (U.S.), between Canada's Alcan, France's Pechiney and Switzerland's Algroup. The Commission felt that the proposed merger would unduly limit competition in certain segment of Western Europe's aluminium industry. The Commission counter-proposed that if the trio were to divest certain strategic assets, the merged corporation's ability to control the market would be limited and the chance of the deal being accepted would be greatly enhanced. The parties believed that the price of acceptance was too high and have since decided not to pursue the three-way deal.

Even internal growth may be challenged by antitrust authorities, who confront the paradox that government protection of intellectual property strengthens monopolies. On April 3, 2000, U.S. District Court Judge Thomas Jackson found that Microsoft was guilty of using its "natural monopoly" in a predatory fashion by bundling its Internet browser with its operating system. Hardware makers, having little choice but to offer Windows on their machines, were coerced into accepting Microsoft's bundled browser, making it difficult for rival browsers to compete. A proposed remedy is to impose the opposite of M&As, namely, a break-up of Microsoft into smaller, independent corporations.

An examination of these three industries illustrates the changing nature of antitrust hurdles, and hence the difficulty for management in predicting government decisions. This article argues that most of the forces shaping antitrust are expanding the range of acceptable M&As, and so the time profile of acceptability has become a key determinant in expansion plans. However, public opinion will continue to influence government decisions in many countries, and an increasingly vocal public in concert with media commentaries can introduce a "wild card" to the process. For certain sectors, particularly telecoms, airlines and public utilities, recent trends of privatization and deregulation are creating new market structures where competition may be fragile. In these sectors, in place of the previous sector-specific regulators or government managers, antitrust authorities may sporadically intrude in their efforts to maintain competition.

In the context of rapid changes in industry structures, many countries have recently rewritten their antitrust legislation and regulations, with the result that precedents are few and the implications of new government positions are not yet clear. The practice of collaboration among governments—most notably within the EU—is also at an early stage, adding to uncertainties facing management. Meanwhile, corporations operating in more than one country may face different types of investigations and required undertaking by each set of antitrust authorities. Due diligence in expansion planning will now require that more attention be devoted to the antitrust question.

FORCES IMPACTING ANTITRUST DECISIONS

Traditionally, the Merger Guidelines of some antitrust agencies have referred to what is known as the Hirschman-Herfindahl Index (or HHI). The HHI is a single number: the sum of squares of the market shares of firms in the market. The HHI value of 2,000 has been seen as the upper limit for effective competition. For example, if there are five equal competitors, each with a market share of 20 percent, then the HHI is exactly 2,000. If the HHI for a market is over the 1,800-2,000 range, then market power is regarded as substantial and competition is regarded as weak, and such a market has been a focus for antitrust scrutiny. With four firms, each of which has a market share of 25 percent, then the HHI is 2,500, which is well above the maximum and effective competition has been judged to be weak.

In previous decades the concept of a product and its market was clear cut and precise; an HHI index could be easily calculated or some other market dominance test could be applied; and excessive market power could be readily noted. John Sherman wrote his now-famous antitrust law in 1890 in an attempt to restrict large corporations from limiting competition, on the basis of a philosophy that was relatively easy to understand and apply: "If we will not endure a king as a political power, we should not endure a king over the production, transportation, and sale of any of the necessities of life."

Today, however, many forces are obliterating traditional product boundaries and national markets. At the same time, changes in technologies are reducing entry barriers. Low entry barriers may make a market "contestable" or subject to competition, even if few competitors actually exist. If a firm were to raise prices above a competitive level, it would attract new entrants, and so existing firms will behave as if these new entrants were present. From many points of view, "market dominance" is quickly fading and few corporations can long sustain the "kingship" position that Sherman feared. Yet, for the moment, antitrust agencies may see a dominant position that they believe warrants their involvement.

1. The greater the availability of substitute products, the less the likelihood of antitrust prosecution

The main reason the Standard Oil Company attracted antitrust intervention in the latter part of the 19th and early 20th centuries had to do with a lack of available substitute products. Individuals and industry had no choice but to pay the high prices established by Standard through its ability to limit supply. Today, product boundaries are disappearing due to technological change that creates multi-use goods and services, where a wider set of goods and services competes for the same consumer demand. Consumer preparedness to alter consumption patterns also seems to be increasing, creating an even wider range of substitutes within the marketplace.

Industries in which a variety of substitute products exist will be less able to practise anti-competitive behaviour. A company that attempts to dominate a specific product category through anti-competitive activities may find itself unable to raise prices in spite of its mergers or acquisitions.

The Canadian banks involved in proposed mergers argued that the emergence of Internet banking would provide a viable substitute for the traditional bricks-and-mortar branch system currently in place. This viable substitute, the banks argued, would ensure a reasonable level of competition in those markets that the Bureau believed would be adversely affected by the mergers.

The Competition Bureau's report on the proposed bank mergers used a relatively short two-year time frame to counter the bank's claim that Internet banking will eventually offer the consumer a viable substitute for the bricks-and-mortar branch system. Had the Bureau used a longer time frame, say five to 10 years, the report would probably have come to a much different conclusion. In his letter to the Royal Bank and Bank of Montreal, Konrad von Finckenstein, Commissioner of Competition, noted the following:

"The Banks have argued that Internet banking will significantly reduce barriers to entry and widen the scope of the geographic market by eliminating the need for a costly physical presence. Internet or virtual banking is in a very early stage of development. According to a recent Ernst and Young report, Internet banking is generally viewed by users at this time as a poor substitute for many of the services provided by a branch. As well, security considerations remain a barrier to widespread consumer acceptance and adoption."

2. As international trade and investment barriers are reduced, the likelihood of antitrust prosecution will diminish

Businesses are facing an ongoing decline of trade and investment barriers, and this has the effect of increasing the number of competitors by adding foreign corporations to each product or service market. Geographic regions with open trade policies will, for this reason, be less likely to require aggressive antitrust policies.

An exception to this trend remains with certain industries that are still viewed as nationally imperative and are protected through a variety of barriers. Canada's banking sector illustrates this exception, as noted by von Finckenstein.

"After 10 years, new Canadian banks become subject to the widely-held rule. This means that no shareholder can own more than 10% of any class of shares. This 10% rule, combined with the rules requiring the head office to be located in Canada and the majority of the board of directors to be Canadian residents, effectively eliminates the possibility of foreign entry through the acquisition of an existing Schedule 1 bank."

Von Finckenstein further noted that expansion in the financial services industry in the Canadian market is "impeded by the high cost of gaining new customers due to switching costs and the expectation that branch profitability may not be realized for up to seven years."

The government's use of investment barriers, imposed to "protect" the nation's banks, has artificially limited the level of competition in the industry, which was the primary reason given by the Finance Minister for rejecting the proposed mergers.

The proposed Pechiney-Alcan-Algroup merger also ran into issues surrounding the use of trade barriers. Aluminium producers in eastern and central European countries that are not currently members of the EU were not factored into the Competition Commission's decision in turning down the three-way merger. Had the output from these countries been factored into the effect that the proposed merger would have had on the level of aluminium sheeting competition in the EU countries, the results of the Competition Commission's findings could have been quite different.

3. Recent changes in industry cost structure have reduced the likelihood of antitrust prosecution

For many decades, economies of scale gave corporations a competitive advantage and prevented the entry of competitors. Within this kind of industry structure, the threat of antitrust was important in preventing monopoly pricing. Today, however, in many sectors, recent technological change has created the possibility of low-cost, small-scale production. For example, the market dominance of integrated steel mills has been shattered by the proliferation of mini-mills. As we look to the future, huge hydro complexes will face competition from small-scale gas turbines, and telecom corporations based on traditional copper wire networks will face competition from various types of wireless and cable ventures.

The new economy's emphasis on product differentiation through innovation has created industries that rest, to a greater degree, on human capital. The fixed asset investment needed for many high-tech start-ups is generally low compared with that required by many old-economy manufacturing facilities. The growth of venture capital in many forms has combined with this trend to reduce entry barriers for many new-economy industries. Furthermore, within many economies, the proportion of production that consists of physical goods has diminished, and the proportion that consists of services has increased. For the modern service economy, large-scale economies are less significant and the probability of market dominance is less likely than in the old economy of mass-produced goods.

4. Intellectual property: Increasing international protection raises uncertainty surrounding antitrust issues

Governments throughout the world are enforcing the protection of intellectual property, by giving ownership to patents, trademarks and copyrights in order to reward innovators and thereby encourage more R&D that will ultimately benefit society as a whole. An irony is that this process is purposefully creating and strengthening monopolies.

The World Trade Organization is becoming an increasingly important institution for enforcing intellectual property rights. China's attempt to be granted full WTO membership status has focused attention on the issue of global intellectual property rights. Proponents of China's acceptance into the WTO feel that "the inclusion of China within the framework of multilateral rules and obligations embodied by the WTO is the single best instrument we have to ensure continuing improvement in China's protection of intellectual property, because we know, first hand, that multilateral enforcement through the WTO offers a far more promising method of ensuring continued progress in China's intellectual property environment than does the threat of unilateral retaliation against China" (Robert A. Kapp, President, United States-China Business Council). Yet China may raise antitrust arguments in conjunction with certain products—pharmaceuticals, for example.

The rate of change in the 21st century has increased the importance and focus on innovation. New-economy corporations rely on constant innovation to maintain an advantage over their competitors. Companies will only continue to invest heavily in R&D if they are guaranteed a period of "no competition," where they can earn the required return on their development costs. Patent and copyright laws must be maintained and expanded internationally in an effort to provide the necessary incentive for companies to continue their investments in developing innovative new products.

However, even here, antitrust actions may intrude. In June 1999, Canada's Competition Bureau issued new Guidelines for Intellectual Property in which hypothetical examples illustrated situations in which the Bureau might curtail the exercise of intellectual property rights. These examples included exclusive licensing, foreclosure of complementary products and refusal to license. In some countries, antitrust agencies even possess the right to revoke patents, trademarks or licences.

5. The faster the pace of an industry's change, the less the likelihood of antitrust prosecution

The increasing rate of technological innovation has led to a rapid increase in new-product launches and has led to ongoing changes in industry structures, adding a time dimension to antitrust. Many of these new products can be substituted for older products that in past years had no such competition. Traditional product lines are disappearing, expanding the scope and definition of a product's "market." PalmPilots, with their unique operating systems, now compete directly with personal computers and the Windows operating system. Technological change has also had the effect of blurring product categories. Television sets equipped with "black boxes" can now surf the Internet, adding another product alternative to the standard PC.

It is becoming more difficult to dominate extremely dynamic industries. Microsoft's prosecution is somewhat of an anomaly, as the litigation began in a slower changing high-tech environment while it will surely finish in a rapidly changing environment. Microsoft was able to predict the relative importance of operating systems and software applications over that of the soon-to-be commoditized hardware systems. Microsoft's insight allowed them to license their operating system confidently to a variety of hardware manufacturers, which eventually enabled their operating system to become the standard, forming a natural monopoly. When Microsoft initially used its monopoly power to launch its Internet browser, the Department of Justice may have had just cause to prosecute at that point in time. However, the current environment in the high-tech industry is one of rapid change, and it is becoming much harder for the industry players to predict the future. Microsoft initially underestimated the rate of growth and the emerging importance of the Internet to the high-tech industry, and is now suffering as a result. By the time the final word on the Microsoft case is given, the issue of Windows' dominance is likely to be much less relevant. As Joshua Quittner wrote in *Time:* "The harsh irony—one that Gates and other Microsoft officials are at pains to point out—is that this effort to defenestrate the company comes at a time when the world is moving away from personal computers to large-scale computer networks. And the very thing that Microsoft has a monopoly

on, Windows CE, is struggling for a foothold against the venerable Palm, which controls a Redmondlike 79% of the market for personal digital assistants. And Microsoft's online service, MSN, has fewer than 3 million subscribers vs. 22 million for America Online despite Microsoft's aggressive bundling of it with Windows."

6. Privatization and deregulation

Until recently, certain specific sectors were often owned and operated by governments, or were regulated by agencies dedicated to a particular sector. Throughout the world, privatization and deregulation are rapidly changing the structure of these industries. Telecoms, airlines and various public utilities are undergoing radical transformations—and in many countries it is now the responsibility of the antitrust agency to ensure that the new market is competitive. In the past, many countries had restricted the delivery of health care to organizations owned and operated by the government and/or had imposed clear price regulations on both hospitals and doctors. It is likely that the shift towards greater private-sector activity in health care will bring with it similar antitrust concerns. For participants in these sectors, M&As are particularly problematic.

"Since the 1996 Telecommunications Act became law, U.S. carriers have completed or announced at least 33 deals totalling more than $492 billion [U.S.]. Increasingly, these mergers are creating a new class of vertically integrated super-carriers that offer bundled services worldwide . . . In the end, the impact of mergers on competition boils down to deal-specific details: horizontal or vertical, affected markets, and affected services. Regulators cannot judge if a Regional Bell Operating Companies (RBOC) merger will lessen local competition because there was no competition to begin with. Instead, they ask if the merger would significantly decrease potential competition." (Carolyn Hirschman, *Telephony,* Feb 2000)

Most dramatic, perhaps, is the question of whether WorldCom's $115-billion takeover of Sprint will be blocked in either the U.S. or the EU. It appears that real economies can be attained by the merger, but the resultant dominance in Internet-switching services has raised antitrust concerns, as well as the dominance of the merged corporation in the long-distance market, where with AT&T it may control too large a market share.

7. Public opinion

Increasingly, M&As are attracting media attention and public interest. Inevitably, democratically elected governments will be compelled to pay attention to public opinion in regard to certain expansion proposals. In the case of Canadian bank mergers, the Minister of Finance responded in part to public anxiety in regard to a possible loss of local branches. Huge international mergers raise the spectre of global domination by giant organizations that could collude in ways that might ultimately result in higher consumer prices. Public opinion is becoming more important and more complex as antitrust agencies look towards factors other than economic that involve subjective judgment. The AOL-Time Warner merger illustrates this complexity:

> "As the Federal Trade Commission and the Justice Department prepare to review the AOL-Time Warner merger, commentators are proposing a radical idea: that factors other than economics— for example, the protection of free expression— should be looked at in scrutinizing media deals. Specifically, many media critics would like the antitrust agency to take into account whether media concentration threatens the diversity, independence, and integrity of the American press corps" (Mike Francis, *BusinessWeek,* Feb 2000).

For many corporations, the role of public opinion serves as a "wild card" that may suddenly intrude upon expansion plans.

THE GREY AREA OF MERGING CERTAIN ACTIVITIES

The Internet has become the focus for a wide range of merged activities among corporations that are maintaining distinct corporate structures. Most dramatic, perhaps, has been the decision of Daimler-Chrysler, Ford and General Motors to build an electronic marketplace for trading auto parts, raw materials and components. Whether such collaboration is acceptable from an antitrust perspective remains an important question for many corporations. It is likely that many such collaborations will be examined individually by antitrust authorities.

DUE DILIGENCE

In many countries, antitrust agencies offer pre-merger analyses in which they may suggest whether a proposed merger will likely be acceptable, and whether the divestiture of specific assets would improve the probability of acceptance. For collaborations and strategic alliances of various types, such pre-notification and negotiation will likely form a new component of antitrust activity.

> "Now, instead of using a few broad rules of thumb to test for antitrust, they're digging down into the details of proposed mergers to look for anticompetitive problems. Even if average prices aren't expected to go up in the wake of a deal, for instance, the FTC [Federal Trade Commission] will comb through data to see whether a merger will raise prices for particular groups of consumers. And they're trying to forecast whether a merged company could raise prices excessively in the long run, even if it has no current pricing power." (Dan Carney, *BusinessWeek,* Feb 2000)

For both corporations and antitrust agencies, due diligence has become more time-consuming and expensive. The downside of announcing a merger or acquisition and being compelled later to walk away from the proposal argues in favour of placing antitrust issues near the top of the list in planning for a corporation's expansion.

7

M&A Integration and Value Realization

A fter the announcement and closing of a deal, the heavy lifting begins. Most research on mergers and acquisitions (M&A) finds that it is during the post-merger (*merger* collectively means all forms of deals) phase that most of the value in a deal is created or destroyed. While often called postmerger integration (PMI), this is a misnomer because often the firms themselves are not integrated per se, but rather their operations are linked at some level to gain the synergies proposed. The exception to this is the holding company structure, where certain firms are simply holding companies that own a portfolio of other firms. When an acquisition becomes part of a portfolio like this, it is unlikely to see any integration, except at the capital structure and financing levels. These deals are typically done when a buyer feels a target is undervalued and buys it to somehow realize what it believes is the true value of the firm.

In the more typical case of deals where integration is to occur, the first question concerns to what degree the firms will be integrated. Depending on the strength of and differences between the cultures of the firms, integration may be difficult. Beyond the cultural differences, there may be physical constraints that limit the ability to consolidate non-collocated facilities. However, the fundamental business question concerns which parts of the firms should be integrated to create more value. Many professional service firms have specific practice groups with expertise in the PMI planning and execution. The market for such expertise is enormous in light of the sheer value of M&A that are conducted—and thus the amount of value that has the potential to be created or is at risk of being destroyed. As such, there are numerous methodologies and texts devoted to the practice of PMI. Here, we attempt only to help the reader consider a few basic frameworks in developing a better understanding of how to approach PMI and to realize these sources of value.

WHEN AND HOW TO INTEGRATE

Using a "when" and "how" framework, the management teams must decide what strategic and tactical choices are best for achieving the deal objectives after deal closure.

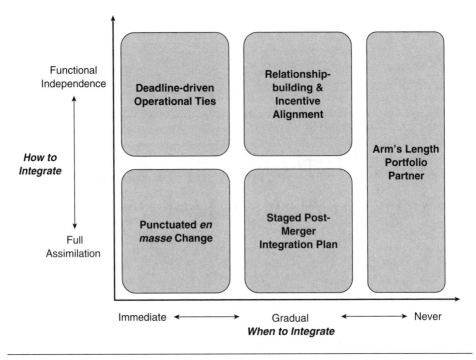

Figure 7.1   Postmerger Integration: When and How

These integration choices are affected by both internal and external forces. Internally, these include the ability of the organizations to tolerate change while remaining productive, as well as the level of cultural and operational similarity between the organizations. These choices may be affected by external forces as well, including the signals they may send to competitors, customers, and investors. The right choices are clearly not obvious, as it is commonly accepted that most deals fail because of poorly planned and executed postdeal integration.

Sources of Value—Synergies

After making the decision that some degree of integration should occur, the question becomes "what" to integrate. One simple framework is to view each of the firms as a value chain, as originally developed by Michael Porter[1] but expanded to include a more detailed view of the firms' operations. The decision then becomes whether each part of the chain should be integrated or left separate between the two firms. As well, you must also decide when and how such integration will occur. To make the integration decisions, we provide a very simple set of decision criteria to complement the strategic intent of the firm, the M&A strategy, and the intended benefits of the deal. Simply, we see that operations should be combined where synergies exist. Assume for a moment the most basic economic model of the firm as revenue minus costs at some level of risk (and thus investment). Simply, a synergy, and thus a decision, should reduce costs, increase revenue, or reduce risk or some combination thereof. While other "strategic" synergies may exist, they will need to affect one of the above at some point, or else the synergy value is perhaps dubious.

Cost Savings

One framework for categorizing cost savings is by type: overhead, indirect, and direct costs. Overhead is the first typical target, and a common form of savings is the reduction of redundant personnel. The most obvious redundancy comes from the duplicated overhead that the two firms supported before the deal. Personnel in overhead-type positions are typically at the highest risk of being affected in the aftermath of a deal. Neither overhead infrastructure alone is typically sufficient to run the combined entity, and so not all overhead personnel are at risk. Indirect cost savings may exist as well, and the firms will look for ways to reduce these, including plants, facilities, assets, information technology (IT) systems, indirect personnel, and all other indirect costs, largely dependent on the nature of the overlap and similarity of the businesses. Finally, direct costs, including line personnel, are also sometime affected but typically only to the extent there was underutilization before the deal. A typical target for cost savings is in the purchase of inputs, raw materials, or any other supplies, due largely to the increased purchasing leverage of the combined entity.

Revenue Enhancement

A simple framework to think about how revenue might be enhanced is to consider an Ansoff product-growth matrix.[2] The two-by-two matrix has "products" on the *x*-axis that are either existing or new and "markets" on the *y*-axis that are either existing or new. The separate firms each had their existing markets (and customers) and sets of product or service offerings. A typical first step in enhancing revenue is to see how the firms can sell their existing products into the other firms' existing markets (new products, existing markets, or existing products into new markets, depending on your perspective). Together, the firms may also have sufficient product- or service-offering breadth to attack altogether new markets, and they may have in the research and development or product development stage new products that can now be rolled out to their combined (larger) customer bases.

Risk Reduction

The riskiness of the cash flows of the firm can actually be reduced, as can the needed capital investment. Cash flows can become less risky because the larger entity has greater purchasing power and thus can perhaps reduce supply risk. The larger entity also has greater leverage and perhaps is a more attractive supplier to its customers because of its broader product offerings, and so it can better ensure its revenue streams by way of longer term customer contracts and less switching risk. Because of its larger size, it likely now has slightly more power than do its competitors to control its pricing in the market and has reduced the pressure that a competitor will compete for its customers. Being a larger firm, it now also enjoys having a greater ability to monitor its competitive environment. Using this knowledge, the firm reduces its competitive uncertainty. Second, the combined firm should need less capital investment to support its operations and infrastructure. More simply, the same cash flows can now be owned by fewer investment dollars. Less capital is now at risk but with the same gross return (cash flow), meaning the return on investment (ROI) actually increases, but risk has declined slightly. This is a situation in which a firm is moving further toward the efficient risk-return frontier by affecting a capital deployment inefficiency. As such, it is possible to create value in M&A, but when at or past an optimal level, scale diseconomies may actually lead to a destruction of value.

Value Realization—Postmerger Integration

The PMI process is perhaps most simply summarized into a three-step process, including the planning, implementation, and then the day-by-day ongoing operations after PMI. To achieve a successful PMI, one must give each of these steps due consideration. The planning process involves evaluation of what the overall strategic goals are for the firm(s) and what the identified synergies are. A common mistake is to plan integration without explicitly linking the entire process to achieving the synergies that were identified. It is critical to identify the synergies, prioritize them, assign accountability to individuals and teams to achieve them, and then put in place appropriate processes to do so. Baseline goals and metrics should be established along with planned checkpoints and oversight processes to ensure that all plans and execution will lead to the realization of the synergies.

Implementation of PMI is an often complex affair requiring a full-time dedicated team to run the process. Often, this team is led or accompanied by external consultants with expertise in PMI. A PMI office is typically established, with direct reporting to the CEO, board, or other appropriate level. The implementation process itself often involves a physical migration of assets, resources, plants, facilities, and so on, alongside the organizational changes and movement of personnel. Of course, PMI also typically involves consolidating IT systems and overhead operations. Again, however, it is critical to prioritize those changes that have the greatest return and minimize the risk of PMI (deal) failure.

The final step in PMI is the transition to day-by-day operations. A firm should both make a clean break from PMI by officially ending it and moving to operations and learn from its successes and mistakes in PMI. PMI can become a never-ending process that actually becomes a part of ongoing overhead in the operations of a firm. This is a mistake. A properly designed PMI will have defined set of tasks and objectives, and once met, PMI is done, and the personnel assigned to the PMI team are redeployed. This sends an important signal to the organization that PMI is over and that the time has come to refocus all efforts on day-by-day work. The second important task is to learn from the process. This learning includes taking what it learns from distinct parts of the two companies and ensuring these best practices are disseminated across the firm. Especially for firms without appropriate internal knowledge-sharing processes, this is a one-time opportunity for knowledge dissemination. As well, for the firm that expects to acquire again, a well-documented process and personnel experienced in PMI will add to its ability to achieve value in future mergers and acquisitions.

PMI—Key Success Factors

There are perhaps hundreds of lists of "key success factors" in PMI that can be used to guide the firm and its focus in the PMI process. They are surely all appropriate to some extent. We point to some of the most critical and most common factors that we have seen lead to successful realization of value, regardless of the extent to which the firms are integrated in PMI.

Leadership

Daily, visible, vocal commitment and involvement from the highest levels of the organization are needed to reduce the anxiety of personnel and to facilitate decisions and participation.

Leadership helps overcome any reluctance to participate in the process—reluctance that is often driven by the fear of losing one's job. From our experience, the employees who participate the most and are the most supportive tend to be the ones least at risk.

Retention

The most critical assets of many businesses are its employees. Often, they are the only assets that walk out the door each night and can easily resign and work for other employers if they are unhappy or their futures are uncertain. As well, the highest performing employees with the most alternative options may be the first to leave, and so retention must be an early focus.

Communications

A PMI plan should include a specific identification of all stakeholder groups, the messages that need to be sent, when (timing and frequency) communications should occur, and by whom. Communications may be one-on-one talks or broadcast, verbal or written, and real-time or passive. The important part is to ensure that stockholders, employees, customers, industry and stock analysts, and other groups receive the appropriate information as, when, and if needed to ensure a successful PMI.

Synergy Focus

As discussed, an explicit focus on these key levers of value must not be forgotten. The synergies, whether cost, strategic, or other, must be explicitly integrated into the objectives of the PMI team and the operational personnel. Too commonly, these synergies are left by the wayside, and integration simply occurs. To the extent that someone is held responsible and rewarded for achieving each objective, as well as empowered to take the steps required to achieve them, the firm will increase its likelihood of achieving the synergies.

Timing

Many point to the "first hundred days" as the most critical stage of PMI. The firm must communicate the right messages and take the right steps quickly and decisively to reduce anxiety and uncertainty, as well as to point the firm and the PMI processes in the right direction. As discussed, there must be a distinct end to the PMI process to ensure the firm gets back to its daily value-creating activities.

One-Time Opportunity

As discussed, PMI may be one of the best opportunities a firm has to make changes and reorient the firm. Firms, just like people, can become entrenched in norms of behavior and process. PMI is a great, perhaps unique, one-time opportunity to break these bad habits and to begin anew. For example, firms can capture and disseminate knowledge and best practices from around the firm, can reorient the firm, and perhaps can set a new pace at which people operate going forward. Leaders who take this opportunity can reset and fix past mistakes and get the firm on a more productive path.

CASES

Information Systems at FirstCaribbean:
Choosing a Standard Operating Environment

The Canadian Imperial Bank of Commerce (CIBC) and Barclays Bank PLC were in advanced negotiations regarding the potential merger of their respective retail, corporate, and offshore banking operations in the Caribbean. Currently, there are four systems in operation in the region. All are carryovers from the premerger operation of the bank. Each of the systems has different pros and cons consisting of degree of fit with the organization strategy, likely impact on organizational culture, and functionality. As part of the effort to standardize practices across the organization, a choice for one standard operating system must be made.

Issues: Postmerger integration, cross-border M&A, systems integration

FirstCaribbean International Bank:
The Marketing and Branding Challenges of a Startup

FirstCaribbean International Bank was the new banking entity created from the combination of the Caribbean operations of two foreign banks, Barclays Bank PLC of the United Kingdom, headquartered in London, England, and CIBC of Canada, headquartered in Toronto, Ontario. A marketing team was formed with the specific responsibility of developing the marketing function and the brand strategy, as well as guiding the branding process of the new entity. The head of the marketing team has a number of concerns: Would geography, history, and commercial practices support or mitigate against a single, centralized marketing strategy for the entire region? What should the new brand be, and how should it be articulated? Should the new brand reflect one or both of the heritage banks, or should the new brand break with the past and reflect a totally new identity? How quickly could the new brand be rolled out?

Issues: Postmerger integration, brand management, brand positioning, market strategy, marketing planning, cross-border M&A

Harmonization of Compensation and
Benefits for FirstCaribbean International Bank

The merger of the Caribbean holdings of Barclays Bank PLC and the CIBC is going ahead, and the reality of integration of very diverse systems and procedures has to be faced. The case deals with understanding the current situation in terms of existing policies and designing policies that would be acceptable to employees from both banks in the organization—FirstCaribbean International Bank—which would be created by the merger. A critical aspect of the merger is the harmonization of compensation and benefits that must be resolved as a matter of priority.

Issues: Postmerger integration, benefits policy, change management, compensation, cross-border M&A

REFERENCES

Michael Porter, Competitive Advantage: *Creating and Sustaining Superior Performance* (New York: The Free Press, 1985).

Igor H. Ansoff, "Strategies for Diversification," *Harvard Business Review,* September–October 1957, 113–24.

INFORMATION SYSTEMS AT FIRSTCARIBBEAN: CHOOSING A STANDARD OPERATING ENVIRONMENT

Prepared by Louis Beaubien and Sonia Mahon

Version: (A) 2005-01-07

On November 1, 2003, Francis Joseph, international development manager at FirstCaribbean International Bank (FirstCaribbean), hung up the phone. The senior vice-president had just told him that a recommendation had to be finalized for the information system that would form the backbone of a standard operating environment for the bank. Joseph's presentation to the executive committee was in one week.

INTRODUCTION

In order to understand the context of Joseph's decision, it is necessary to be aware of how FirstCaribbean came to be one of the premier banks in the Caribbean. It was formed as a merger between the Canadian Imperial Bank of Commerce (CIBC) (total Caribbean assets $4.6 billion)[1] and Barclays Plc. (total Caribbean assets $5.2 billion). Although neither Barclays nor CIBC operated throughout the entire Caribbean, taken together they operated in most of the English-speaking Caribbean (see Exhibit 1). There was a wide diversity among the islands on which FirstCaribbean would operate; populations ranged between 10,000 to more than 2.5 million, and gross domestic product (GDP) per capita ranged from approximately $877 to $24,000 (see Exhibit 2).

Most Caribbean nations are islands (see Exhibit 3), and until the later half of the 20th century most were colonies of European nations. Banks in the region originally operated to facilitate trade with colonial powers and to service their governments and representatives. The majority of financial business operations focused on savings, with some lending and trade financing. Many banks, such as Barclays Plc., were established to finance the production and trade of commodities such as fruit, sugar, rum and petroleum. Although the Caribbean branches of many of these banks were profitable, they were viewed as a small component of the banks' larger global operations.

As the colonial era came to a close, many Caribbean governments nationalized their industries, including banking, in order to gain greater control of their economies. The limitations of state ownership became evident in the 1980s, and many state-owned banks were privatized. The end result was an increase in competition in the financial sector, which was compounded further by the entry of international banks that had previously not been present in the Caribbean, such as CS FirstBoston and Spain's Santander Bank, SA. In order to be more globally competitive, many banks have pursued strategies of organizational alliances or mergers. Mergers, however, can be complicated in the Caribbean because of the many central banks and currencies that must be taken into account.

THE HERITAGE BANKS— CIBC AND BARCLAYS PLC.

CIBC

CIBC had operated in the Caribbean since 1920 and, prior to the merger, employed 1,600 employees at 42 branches and banking centres, serving 350,000 customers. CIBC was the only international bank that operated within the region as an autonomous integrated unit, CIBC West Indies Holdings (CIBC-WIH). In the

Country	CIBC	Barclays Plc.
Anguilla		*
Antigua and Barbuda	*	*
The Bahamas	*	*
Barbados	*	*
Belize		*
British Virgin Islands		*
Cayman Islands	*	*
Dominica		*
Grenada		*
Jamaica	*	
St. Kitts and Nevis		*
St. Lucia	*	*
Netherlands Antilles		*
St. Vincent and the Grenadines	*	*
Turks and Caicos Islands	*	*

Exhibit 1 Distribution of CIBC and Barclays Plc. in the Caribbean

Source: CIBC Economics, World Fact Book, Americas Review 1999—Economic Indicators.

COUNTRY	Population (000s)	GDP/Capita (US$)
Anguilla	10	4,000
Antigua and Barbuda	70	8,419
The Bahamas	280	13,847
Barbados	270	7,750
Belize	230	2,688
British Virgin Islands	20	12,000
Cayman Islands	30	24,000
Dominica	70	3,233
Grenada	100	877
Jamaica	2,570	1,756
St. Kitts and Nevis	40	5,761
St. Lucia	160	3,581
Netherlands Antilles	200	N/A
St. Vincent and the Grenadines	110	N/A
Turks and Caicos Islands	20	6,000

Exhibit 2 Population and Gross Domestic Product in the Caribbean

Source: CIBC Economics, World Fact Book, Americas Review 1999—Economic Indicators.

1990s, a strategic shift occurred in the banking industry that saw organizations focus on a business model of "customer-relationship" banking, rather than a model that relied on "transaction processing." This strategy required a change in business processes and an adaptation of information technology to focus on recording customer profiles (all of an individual's accounts and business with the bank) as single integrated entities within the bank's database, rather than recording and tracking single accounts and the transactions that related only to one given account. The capabilities of an information technology platform were key to realizing this vision.

The system CIBC had chosen was A-SYSTEM. The deployment of this system in 1999 through 2001 had been time-consuming and costly, with a bill of approximately $48 million, however the system offered many solutions to enable the strategy CIBC wished to adopt. The system was implemented in all of the Caribbean operations with the exception of Grand Cayman,

Exhibit 3   Map of Caribbean Region

Source: CIA World Fact Book.

where a similar system, B-SYSTEM was adopted. The B-SYSTEM provided the same customer-centric focus but was more tailored to CIBC's niche market in Grand Cayman.

Barclays Plc.

Barclays Plc. operated in 14 territories prior to the merger, employing 1,531 individuals. The majority of the bank's income was derived from corporate banking (45 per cent) followed by offshore banking (28 per cent) and personal banking (27 per cent). A key strategy that Barclays Plc. had adopted in the Caribbean was focused on operational risk management. As a result, conservative positions were taken in developing business and implementing new capital projects. The information technology that formed the basis of the Barclays network was C-SYSTEM. It was in place in all of the territories in which the bank operated with the exception of two countries, which operated D-SYSTEM.

Unlike the primary system in place at CIBC, C-SYSTEM was not a recent innovation, having been in place for the previous 10 years. C-SYSTEM was not a complex system and lacked the ability to integrate customer data into a single profile. The system was designed specifically for Barclays and modeled the organization's procedures very well. The system was easy to learn, use and deploy.

FirstCaribbean

In the late 1990s, following strategic reviews at both CIBC and Barclays Plc., discussions of a possible merger of their Caribbean operations began between the two banks. What followed was the decision to create a new entity, one that would be a truly *pan*-Caribbean bank. It would be run autonomously, and the heritage banks would retain only a very limited presence at the executive and administrative levels. Both CIBC and Barclays would transfer their assets into a new entity—FirstCaribbean International

Bank—that would be partially owned by each bank (both Barclays and CIBC would own approximately 44 per cent of the new entity), and the remainder would be offered to the public on the four Caribbean stock exchanges (Jamaica, Trinidad, Barbados and the Bahamas).

The new entity was thought to have a truly unique advantage in the market: it was to be the first *regional* bank. The banking industry in the Caribbean was populated either by international banks that operated in one or more territories as units independent of one another, or by a bank from a particular territory such as the Royal Bank of Trinidad and Tobago (RBTT) that operated on one or numerous islands. FirstCaribbean would be the first bank that was regional in origin, orientation and operations. The ability to develop an integrative approach that focused on customer relationships was key to the strategy of FirstCaribbean.

Standard Operations at FirstCaribbean

Francis Joseph's Work Begins

In order for FirstCaribbean to gain from the regional resources of the two powerful banking entities responsible for its genesis, FirstCaribbean had to develop a standard operating environment (SOE) and platform that would integrate its information and operations. Across the territories in which FirstCaribbean had operations, there were four different systems being used. The former CIBC branches were using A-SYSTEM in all instances except for one, where B-SYSTEM was used. Former Barclays Plc. branches were using C-SYSTEM in most branches. Two territories, Cayman Islands and the British West Indies, were using D-SYSTEM.

Joseph knew the standardization of operations was important. The information system that was chosen would have dramatic effect upon the way that FirstCaribbean planned to do business. The new bank had to manage the operations and information systems of both CIBC and Barclays Plc. in

such a way that customer service would not be affected and mandatory financial reporting requirements could be achieved. At the same time, a new information system would have to be adopted in all territories. It was not an option to simply shut down the bank, change the technology, train the staff and then restart the system. Joseph had to find a way to smoothly integrate the new system into the operations of FirstCaribbean.

Aside from technical factors, Joseph was sensitive to the organizational and personnel issues that he would confront. CIBC and Barclays had developed very different cultures over their business history in the Caribbean. Because both organizations operated individual territories as separate units, not only were there disparities between organizational cultures, but also between different territories in the Caribbean. One thing in common for all employees was a degree of uncertainty. What would happen after the merger? Would they still have a job? Would the organization they had come to know suddenly be replaced by a new and unfamiliar one?

Stakeholders within the FirstCaribbean community were concerned with the implications of the implementation. The primary concern of the heritage banks was the speed and quality of the transition. The deployment of the new information system would have to be performed in the requisite time and without too much disturbance to customers or organizational operations. The new management of FirstCaribbean shared these concerns, but was also focused on achieving a system that would be able to serve the bank's strategic focus as well.

There had also been issues of contention between employees. The organizational culture had been very different between Barclays Plc. and CIBC. Barclays' employees were all unionized, and staff remuneration tended to be higher than at CIBC, which as a practice did not have unions in place in any of its divisions worldwide. Throughout the merger process many discussions addressed whether FirstCaribbean would be a unionized organization and the implications for an organization whose management would be largely staffed by former CIBC personnel.

The final decision was that FirstCaribbean would be a unionized organization and would adopt a remuneration schedule similar to Barclays Plc., if not quite as generous.

Another point of contention arose in the efforts to rationalize both organizations' resources that resulted in the overlap and redundancy of the technical infrastructure. Prior to the merger, CIBC operated three data centres in the Caribbean region, and Barclays operated two. Both CIBC and Barclays operated a data centre on Barbados and in the Bahamas (CIBC also operated a centre in Jamaica). As the bank was proceeding with a strategy of regional integration and harmonization of information systems and resources, this distribution of data centres was inefficient.

After a review of the capabilities of the data centres and the legal implications of the territorial locations of the data centres, it was decided that two centres would be necessary, not five. Because of the strict privacy and secrecy laws in place in the Bahamas, the placement of a data centre in this territory was necessary. Barbados seemed the most logical placement for the second data centre, as it had been chosen to be the head office location for FirstCaribbean. In both cases, the technology and office location at the former CIBC centres were superior to the Barclays centres, so these centres would be adopted as the new FirstCaribbean sites. The remaining three data centres would be shut down during the transition.

The union issues and data centre placements were indicative of the many compromises to be made over the course of the merger. The executive team was careful to ensure that both sides (CIBC and Barclays) had a chance to communicate their preferences and concerns. Despite best efforts and intentions on all sides, there were inevitably disagreements and discomfort with some of the executive team's decisions. Any integration or deployment of information systems would have to take these sensitivities into account.

It was important during the merger and integration of the two organizations to maintain a high degree of customer service so as not to cause customers to be concerned, and perhaps withdraw their business. Part of this effort was maintaining employee loyalty and ensuring that employees did not feel alienated or not "part" of the change process. A final concern was that there were four different information systems and accompanying organizational practices in place across the region. Whichever system Joseph chose to adopt, there would be significant training involved.

Joseph had to decide which information system would be the best choice for the new organization. How would he be able to achieve a standard platform that met the needs of the organization, yet would not cause distress amongst the employees? Joseph would have to make his choice and recommendation by the end of the week. He knew that this decision would have a big part of determining whether or not FirstCaribbean was a success.

CHOOSING AN INFORMATION SYSTEM

A-SYSTEM

CIBC made a significant investment in its information systems operations in the Caribbean in 1999 through 2001. Based on a survey of reliability and use in the industry, CIBC decided to implement A-SYSTEM on a global basis. A-SYSTEM was a client/customer-centred information system and handled all internal processes, such as transaction processing and customer profile data records. The success of the system was metred by the fact that many of the processes and workflows that were a part of standard banking operations in the Caribbean region could not be accommodated by A-SYSTEM. A high number of custom components had been applied to the software so that it would fit business processes. The system was the most technologically advanced of the possible choices and would likely require the most training.

While customization seemed like a good approach to have taken, it did have drawbacks. The high costs of the customization were borne in part by the head office of CIBC, as the

Caribbean region depended on the head office for technology support. However, the responsibility would shift to FirstCaribbean following the merger. The arrangement with the A-SYSTEM vendor included upgrades to the newest version of the system for as long as the contract was engaged, but did not include upgrading the custom components. The additional cost of this option was prohibitive to FirstCaribbean. Therefore, if FirstCaribbean were to continue to use the custom system, it would have to choose to not upgrade the core A-SYSTEM components, and risk the possibility that the vendor would no longer support the older version. Alternatively, FirstCaribbean could choose to focus on adopting A-SYSTEM without the customized component and developing new organizational processes that "fit" the system.

Although A-SYSTEM was the most advanced information system and would require intensive training, the investment in additional cost and training time would pay off in a more efficient system. A-SYSTEM operated on a single database and could be managed with central system administration. Further, the system could handle all the information processing that was required by FirstCaribbean—customer retail bank accounts, commercial and corporate accounts, investment and loan accounts. But, perhaps most important, it would allow the integration of all the information.

In looking at A-SYSTEM, Joseph had a great deal to think about. The system offered many advantages in terms of functionality from the bank's point of view. It also offered advantages that Joseph thought would make his life easier—the ability to manage the system from a central location would make it easier to manage both the IT operations and the IT staff.

B-SYSTEM

This system was in place in one former CIBC territory. The local territory purchased the system before the large-scale investment in A-SYSTEM. The system worked well, did not need any particular customization and interfaced well with the A-SYSTEM. Because the system was put into place before A-SYSTEM and posed no outward difficulties in terms of interface and communication of data, head-office managers had allowed the local territory to maintain its use. The system also followed CIBC's current strategy, which focussed on relationship banking.

From an infrastructure point of view, B-SYSTEM operated in a similar fashion to A-SYSTEM. It supported a centralized management of system and data. However, B-SYSTEM had only been used to integrate data and systems across multiple branches within one territory. In past operations, if data were communicated outside of the territory (e.g., for financial reporting purposes) data were consolidated within territory and submitted to central operations. B-SYSTEM had never been used to integrate any data that came from outside the territory, nor used to generate consolidated statements for reporting purposes. Such functionality was of key importance, and Joseph was not sure if B-SYSTEM was up to the task, especially because it did not handle corporate and commercial reporting information as well as A-SYSTEM.

C-SYSTEM

C-SYSTEM was in place in most territories. This system was designed in the United Kingdom for use at Barclays Plc. and was used in the banks operations in all of Caribbean and African territories. While the system was originally designed in the late 1980s, it had gone through several iterations and was built with the knowledge of effective operational procedures within Barclays Plc. As the system was developed specifically for Barclays Plc., future development and maintenance of the system were at the discretion of Barclays' head office. There was no guarantee that if FirstCaribbean continued to use the system, Barclays Plc. would supply any future upgrade or service.

An interesting aspect of C-SYSTEM was the independence of the system, which provided both a major advantage and disadvantage to FirstCaribbean. C-SYSTEM did not operate on a centralized network. Each unit could be customized to the local environment. There was going to be some resistance to any new system, but C-SYSTEM could be customized to each territory, possibly lessening the resistance. There was also a great diversity of infrastructure available in the different territories in which FirstCaribbean would operate. C-SYSTEM would be the most flexible to adapt to a territory with high or low levels of technology.

However, this flexibility and independent nature of the system did not come without costs. Chiefly, the ability of FirstCaribbean to develop its integrated banking strategy would be hampered. The bank would have to either rely on manual integration of many different forms of data (personal customer information, financial information, territorial regulatory information, etc.) or build a customized technology solution to handle all the necessary sorting of data. Joseph was concerned about adding any extra level of integration (human or otherwise), as it increased the possibility of the introduction of errors. On a related note, as the system was not built to be able to consolidate information easily, the ability to perform back-ups was complicated.

C-SYSTEM offered many advantages in terms of cost (not only was it the cheapest, but it was already widely dispersed) and a great deal of flexibility. As it was an account-based system, it was equally able to handle retail, loan, and commercial or corporate account information. Joseph was concerned that it would limit the ability of the bank to execute its customer-driven strategy. He wondered whether the bank needed an integrated system to effect the customer/relationship strategy it advocated or was human action enough? Was he prepared to have to deal with managing two systems, C-SYSTEM and whatever custom solution would be necessary to handle the integration and consolidation of data and information?

D-SYSTEM

D-SYSTEM was in place in two territories that were formerly operated by Barclays.

D-SYSTEM viewed individual customers as unique entities, consistent with strategies of customer-focused banking. D-SYSTEM was therefore more in line with the operational procedures of Barclays Plc. as it operated in Europe, as opposed to procedures in the Caribbean, which operated on an account-based system (i.e., C-SYSTEM).

While D-SYSTEM was an integrated system, its strength was the consolidation of retail and commercial/corporate banking information. It could handle the consolidation of all the information that might relate to a client in terms of current accounts, loans and any accounts that might be tied to commercial or corporate accounts that individuals might control (or businesses they might own). However, the ability to integrate in-depth marketing information or information related to investment accounts was more limited than A-SYSTEM.

D-SYSTEM was designed around a sub-centralized network. In other words, it was designed to integrate and consolidate all the information within a territory and then produce a report on that information. Although there were two territories using D-SYSTEM, they reported all financial information to the Barclay's head office separately. Integration across territories might be possible but had never been tried. Joseph suspected that the system did not have a sufficiently robust information architecture to perform the consolidation tasks the bank found so important.

Unlike other vendors, an opportunity presented itself with D-SYSTEM that had not been presented with other systems. The possibility existed to engage in a co-development effort regarding D-SYSTEM. Rather than simply having the system customized, a new system based on D-SYSTEM might be developed that better suited FirstCaribbean. The advantage was the system could be designed to handle all the requirements the bank might identify. The disadvantage was that no guarantees existed that the system would be delivered on time, would work as promised or would be delivered within budget.

THE DECISION

What should Joseph recommend? While First-Caribbean did not have the resources that its parent organizations possessed, Joseph knew the budget for the integration was not going to be a deciding factor. All the options would essentially have a cost that was proximate to one another and that was within FirstCaribbean's constraints.

If Joseph were going to make a recommendation, it would have to be based on rationale other than cost. Once a decision was made, Joseph would have to decide how to implement his decision.

NOTE

1.   All amounts in US$ unless otherwise specified.

FIRSTCARIBBEAN INTERNATIONAL BANK:
THE MARKETING AND BRANDING CHALLENGES OF A STARTUP

Prepared by Gavin Chen and Derrick Deslandes

Version: (A) 2005-06-09

INTRODUCTION

Francis Lewis was reflecting on the complexity of the task he had just agreed to undertake. He had been offered the job of starting up the FirstCaribbean's Marketing Function and developing the brand strategy for the new Bank. This was a once-in-a-lifetime opportunity. Lewis needed a plan.

FirstCaribbean International Bank was the new banking entity created from the combination of the Caribbean operations of two foreign banks: Barclays Bank plc of the United Kingdom, headquartered in London, and CIBC (formally the Canadian Imperial Bank of Commerce) of Canada, headquartered in Toronto.

MANAGEMENT TEAM
CONCERNS AND CHALLENGES

Lewis and his marketing team had several concerns. First, they had to co-ordinate marketing activities across the 15 countries in which the heritage banks (Barclays and CIBC) competed. This was no easy task. On one hand, these countries shared a single geographic space and had many similar elements of history and heritage. On the other hand, they saw themselves as autonomous countries with different cultures, regulations and business practices. Traditionally, each country's bank management had tactical control over its marketing function, with broad strategic and brand direction being given by their respective head offices. Additionally, Barclays' countries tended to operate as discrete entities, with a relatively high level of local autonomy, and were only loosely co-ordinated by their head office, with little interaction or regional co-ordination.

The marketing team's concerns could be summed up as:

- Would geography, history and commercial practices be supported by or mitigate against a single, centralized marketing strategy for the entire region?
- What should the new brand be, and how should it be articulated?

- Should the new brand reflect one or both of the heritage banks? Or should the new brand break with the past and reflect a totally new identity?
- How quickly could, and should, the new brand be rolled out, in light of everything else happening in the bank, with respect to the merger and the increasing competition in the industry?

FirstCaribbean had already addressed earlier marketing challenges, including selecting a name that communicated the bank's international strength and reach but with a Caribbean identity; and selecting a mark (i.e., trademark) that would convey the new bank's identity (see Exhibit 1).

Selecting the Name and Mark

The name FirstCaribbean was already selected when Lewis came on board. The name *"FirstCaribbean International Bank"* clearly signaled the bank's intentions.

Additionally, the bank needed to develop a mark or symbol that would visually represent the brand. It needed to create a logo that matched the name selected for the bank. Logo and mark research was done co-operatively to ensure a good fit between both.

History of the Process

In the early discussions between the CIBC and Barclays teams, a number of critical decisions were taken. Of great importance was the decision to select a name for the merged entity that was different from that of either parent. This was very important to Barclays, who as a matter of policy would not allow their name to be used on an entity in which they had a minority stake, having had a negative experience in Brazil a few years earlier. This had some risk, as the heritage banks did not want to give customers the impression that they were leaving the Caribbean. Neither did they want customers to believe that the new entity would not have international backing, an important consideration also for regulators and governments.

In January 2001, the heritage banks secretly hired a company called Enterprise IG to guide this process of selecting a new brand name. The project was code named "Project Carnival." Interestingly, heritage bank line managers had no idea that their parent banks commissioned this research. They thought a new competitor was running the project.

The naming process was extensive. Enterprise IG first conducted interviews with senior executives from CIBC (code named Charlie) and Barclays (code named Barry). They then developed functional and image criteria to evaluate all potential names. The functional criterion evaluated names based on viability while the image criterion evaluated names based on effective communication, corporate personality and positioning (see below).

Functional Criteria Distinctive, Memorable, Easy to Read, Easy to Pronounce, Legally Available and Linguistically Appropriate

Image Criteria Financially Secure, International Access, Professional, Relationship-oriented, Connected and Pan-Caribbean

Enterprise IG first generated a list of approximately 500 to 600 names. This list was reviewed and reduced first to 100, then to a short list of 35, then 10, and to a final list of six. Focus groups were conducted in Bahamas, Jamaica, Barbados, and St. Lucia to assess the finalists. The final six names were then linguistically checked for appropriateness across the countries and cultures where FirstCaribbean was expected to operate. This was done in three languages, local English, local Spanish and Creole French.

Two names emerged as clear favorites: *"FirstCaribbean International Bank"* and *"Global Caribbean Bank,"* both with 41 per cent preference. *"Caribbean Atlantic Bank"* had a 20 per cent preference while the others, *"SeaTrust,"* *"Sunward"* and *"Seaward"* all scored less than 11 per cent. No significant regional or island specific variations of name preference were found.

Exhibit 1   The Quest for a Brand Name and Mark   *(Continued)*

The *"FirstCaribbean"* name was legally available in 14 of the 15 countries. However, in Jamaica, a local investment bank had adopted the name First Caribbean Investment and Finance Limited. The bank had to buy the rights to this name from the original owners, reportedly for a sizable sum of money.

The research done by Enterprise IG identified a number of factors in support of the preferred name:

- The research suggested that it was the most appropriate choice in light of the new bank's ability to execute as a regional bank.
- The term *"Global"* raised customer expectations beyond the bank's ability to deliver, given that the bank had no plans to set up offices outside the region.
- The term *"First"* offered a very dynamic marketing platform.
- The name *"FirstCaribbean International Bank"* was the highest scoring name on the following attributes:
  - Serves the entire region
  - Understands local needs
  - Delivers strong customer service
  - Delivers good value for money

Identifying the Right Mark

When Lewis arrived on the scene, the name of the bank had already been selected. Research on an appropriate mark was still ongoing. The Enterprise IG research team first did a number of directional explorations on symbols based on key attributes. Approximately 30 options were created to match the image criteria. This was subsequently reduced to a short list of six to seven options. The short list was further refined to include variations or addition of color. Focus groups on the name-mark combinations were done in four countries: the Bahamas, Barbados, Jamaica and St. Lucia. These four countries were chosen because they represented a good cross-section of First Caribbean markets.

Customers were shown the mark and asked a number of questions. The open-ended questions were used to assess customers' emotional reactions to the each mark, for example—*"What do you like or dislike about this symbol?"*

Respondents were then asked to evaluate each option on a five-point Likert Scale, where 1 = Strongly Disagree and 5 = Strongly Agree. Examples of these questions are:

1. This design suggests a bank that I (or my company) could trust with my money.
2. This design feels appropriate to my country.
3. This design suggests a world-class financial institution.
4. This design makes me feel welcome.
5. This design is appropriate for a bank.
6. This design fits well with the name previously selected.
7. I could envision doing my banking with a bank with this symbol.

Customer responses to these questions were assessed and the responses compared.

Emerging from the regional focus group research, the Enterprise IG team reported that the winning logo was one of the clearest winners that they have ever tested calling the results a slam dunk, based on customer responses. The winning logo was chosen twice as often as the second place logo (45 per cent to 21 per cent) and was the highest scoring logo on five of the seven attributes tested.

Exhibit 1 (Continued)

Barclays' History in the Caribbean

Barclays Bank PLC had provided unbroken service to the Caribbean since May 1837. The early decades of the 19th century saw the establishment of the first joint stock banking companies in England, providing greater resources and security for shareholders and customers. Against this background, and the favorable economic conditions in both England and the West Indies, a group of merchants and bankers in London decided to establish a bank to operate in the West Indies, one of the wealthiest areas of real estate in the world at that time. A Royal Charter to establish this bank with the name the *"Colonial Bank,"* was granted on 1st June 1836. The following May, offices were opened across the Caribbean, commencing in Barbados, Trinidad and British Guiana, and continuing later in 1837 with representation in St Lucia, Grenada, Antigua, Dominica, St. Kitts, St. Vincent, the Danish Virgin Islands and Jamaica.

Throughout much of the 19th century, the Colonial Bank operated as a virtual monopoly in the Caribbean, with the only serious competition being the *West India Bank* in the 1840s. The spread of banking representation across the Caribbean islands provided a degree of resilience to local economic circumstances, and the Colonial Bank proved to be a commercial success. During the ensuing years, the Colonial Bank took on the name of its parent organization, Barclays Bank.

The pace of change became more perceptible from the 1950s, when Englishman George Gilbert Money arrived from Barclays Bank, London. His mandate was to lead the Caribbean region, from the headquarters in Barbados. At that stage, all clerical staff was white, although a few black clerical staff had been engaged in Jamaica and British Honduras (Belize). George Money immediately began hiring suitable people without regard to color, a policy started by Barclays and followed two or three years later by the rest of the region's banks.

This was also the period when the countries of the Caribbean began agitating for independence. This culminated in many being granted independence from England by the end of the 1960s.

Nationalization, political and economic instability in some Caribbean territories, and the negative perceptions of Barclays, due to its previously close ties with the former colonial governments, forced the company to assess its businesses in the region. This assessment led to the sale of the bank's operations in Jamaica, Trinidad and Guyana, the countries ironically with the largest populations, the largest economies and the largest land masses, respectively, but arguably the Caribbean's most unstable countries during the period of the late '60s to the late '70s.

The 1980s saw banks in the Caribbean being computerized, and Barclay's branches changed from the traditional mechanical and electro-mechanical accounting machines to being fully computerized. This period also saw Barclays emerging as the market leader in introducing the first automated banking machines (ABMs) in the Caribbean as well as the provision of credit card services and linking of both to the worldwide credit card network. Despite these successes, the bank recognized weaknesses in its business and began exploring strategies to combat these weaknesses.

At the time of merger, Barclays' Caribbean employed approximately 1,500 staff, serving nearly 400,000 customers: 350,000 retail, 20,000 corporate and small business, and 25,000 off-shore accounts. Retail and corporate banking services were offered in 14 countries and off-shore banking services in five countries: the Bahamas, Barbados, Cayman, British Virgin Islands and Turks and Caicos. Barclays typically had market share of greater than 20 per cent in most of its markets. Barclays' Caribbean and Bahamas regional headquarters was located in Rendezvous, Barbados. Barclays Bank plc, the parent bank of Barclays Caribbean, is an old, large, well-regarded U.K.-headquartered bank, with over 70,000 staff and extensive operation and experience in the United Kingdom, Europe, Africa and the Caribbean.

CIBC's History in the Caribbean

The Canadian Imperial Bank of Commerce (CIBC) established its first branches in the West

Indies in Barbados and Jamaica in 1920. Over the next 60 years, CIBC opened branches in the Bahamas, Trinidad and Tobago, Cuba, St. Vincent, Antigua and St. Lucia.

In 1988, to localize the bank's ownership and to get listed on the stock exchange in Jamaica, CIBC sold 45 per cent of its shares in CIBC Jamaica Limited by way of a public share issue. This pattern was repeated in other countries in the ensuing years. During 1993 to 1997, the bank restructured its operations in response to increasing competition and changing market dynamics. This led to a new regional organization, which positioned the bank to better capitalize on the changes taking place in the region's business environment. As a result, CIBC West Indies Holdings Limited was incorporated, and 30 per cent of this company was sold to the public.

In 1999, a five-year strategic "Vision 2002" meeting was held with the CIBC West Indies management team. This was the first time that regional managers had a chance to meet each other and work together. A year later, in 2002, a revolutionary Service Guarantee Program was launched throughout the region. The rollout of a new regional integrated banking system began in Barbados in April and became operational throughout the West Indies a short time later. To centralize all corporate operations, at the start of the new millennium, the bank opened a new CIBC West Indies Headquarters at Warrens, Barbados.

CIBC Caribbean employed approximately 1,600 staff serving 350,000 retail and commercial clients at 42 branches and centres in the Caribbean. During the last few years, CIBC Canada had reorganized all of its retail and corporate banking operations in the Caribbean under the umbrella of this company. The bank is listed on three regional stock exchanges, in Barbados, Trinidad and Tobago and Jamaica. In addition, two of its subsidiaries, CIBC Bahamas Limited, and CIBC Jamaica Limited, are also listed on their local stock exchanges. The company is headquartered in Barbados. CIBC Canada is one of North America's leading financial institutions as measured by assets, with more than eight million personal banking and business customers worldwide.

Importance of the Caribbean Operations of the Parent Banks

In 2001, immediately prior to the merger, the consolidated financial reports of the separate entities indicated that Barclays' Caribbean operations contributed 2.1 per cent to the parent bank's total assets and 4.3 per cent to its profitability. Similarly, the CIBC's Caribbean operations contributed 2.5 per cent to total assets of the parent bank and six per cent to its profitability.

In 2001, Barclays had total assets of US$248 billion while CIBC had total assets of US$181 billion. The respective portions attributable to the Caribbean asset position were US$5.2 billion for Barclays and US$4.6 billion for CIBC.

Factors Leading to the Merger

Between them, Barclays and CIBC had approximately 250 years of combined banking experience in the region. CIBC had taken halting steps towards *"caribbeanization"* of its ownership structure while banking had held steadfast to its British roots. What factors had driven these two banks into each other arms?

Clearly it was the same factors that had prompted CIBC to restructure its operations over the past 10 years and had caused Barclays to constantly re-examine its strategic options in the Caribbean over the past three decades.

Interestingly, both CIBC and Barclays each had held senior management meetings at around the same time, in 1999, to discuss the way forward for their respective banks. Two years later on July 23, 2001, Barclays and CIBC announced that they were in advanced discussions that were intended to lead to the combination of their retail, corporate and offshore banking operations in the Caribbean, to create an organization that would be named First Caribbean International Bank™. The implementation of which, would be subject to approvals from 15 governments plus the region's regulatory authorities.

Among the factors leading to the merger were that both heritage banks no longer saw the Caribbean as strategic or significantly profitable. In the banks' respective head offices, there were some who felt that the region had become more bother than it was worth. The Caribbean Region was small, distant and unduly complex, with multiple governments and regulatory agencies speaking in a cacophony of voices. The region was relatively poor, with limited growth prospects or upside potential for earning profits. Increasingly, the regulatory requirements by the central banks in their home countries would oblige the heritage banks to devote increased resources to control and compliance. Mitigating the risks to their brands and reputation was expected to further increase their costs.

Thus, on one hand, the heritage banks' assets in the Caribbean were sufficiently significant that they could not easily exit the region, as they would be unlikely to find buyers prepared to pay their asking price. On the other hand, they did not wish to make any further significant investments in the region, nor continue to have their brands exposed. From these considerations, they developed an interesting and innovative strategy—to combine their operations across the region under a new brand name.

The immediate upside was that this would create a larger financial institution, which, it was hoped, would be able to compete more effectively in the region, specifically through the realization of economies of scale and scope, provision of wider choices for consumers throughout the region, and the strengthening of the capital base. Technology and other investments that were not feasible with smaller operations could now be considered. This new bank would be self-contained and would not need to draw on the resources of their respective heritage banks. Reputational risk would be localized as it could be contained to this entity in the region.

Barclays and CIBC hoped this combination would provide benefits and opportunities for customers, staff and the business above those that could be achieved by either heritage bank operation on a stand-alone basis.

Planning for the Merger

To plan and implement the merger, an integration team was created with staff from the heritage banks from their Caribbean operations

and expatriates seconded from their head offices in London and Toronto. After a selection process, PriceWaterhouseCoopers was appointed lead consultant and given the task of leading the planning process.

Radical Restructuring of the New Bank

The implementation team made a radical recommendation regarding the structure for the new bank. They proposed that the new bank should be organizationally structured along "lines of business," as was the evolving practice in the United Kingdom and Canada. This would mean scrapping the old structure of country managers heading banking operations in each territory. This approach was a fundamental departure from how Caribbean banks had been organized for decades. It meant that the senior managers in each country reported "up the line" to their respective executive director in head office, rather than to a country managing director. It was felt that this structure would reduce unnecessary duplication and cost and would speed up implementation. The risk factor? The Caribbean was considered to be a single "market-space" (essentially as one country) in a region that was still fundamentally nationalistic.

The implementation team recommended that the new bank be organized into four strategic business units (SBU) (or lines of business), with each SBU being lead by an executive director:

1. **Retail Banking**—segmented into mass market banking, premier banking and credit card operations

2. **Corporate Banking**—segmented into (small) business banking, commercial and corporate banking

3. **International Banking**—segmented into off-shore personal, premier and corporate banking

4. **Capital Markets**—investment banking serving very large Caribbean companies, multinational companies and governments, all seeking international financing

The team further recommended that the new bank create a strategic support unit (SSU) to provide specialist functional support across the region. This meant setting up a strong centralized head office, containing key support functions, including finance, treasury, human resources, information technology (IT), operations and marketing, with each SSU lead by an executive director.

The proposed structure looked interesting on paper, but it was untried and unproven. At the time of planning, no one could be certain that the system would work as anticipated and that the shift from a more traditional county-based, decentralized structure, to a new head-office driven, centralized structure would be more effective and profitable. Complicating this matter was the question of whether it was better to make these changes immediately on integration or defer them to the future, given the very different organizational cultures and the technical integration yet to come.

The Merger

The merger of the Caribbean operations of Barclays and CIBC brought together a workforce of more than 3,500 staff, operating more than 85 branches in 15 Caribbean countries, with over 750,000 active accounts, total assets of about US$9.5 billion, and a market capitalization of about US$2 billion. By Caribbean standards this was huge, by far the largest merger ever attempted in the region. On the surface, the merger provided the answer to the problems of both heritage banks, who had sat and nervously watched their competitors grow larger, become more aggressive and increasingly more profitable (see Exhibit 2).

- FirstCaribbean International Bank officially opened for business in October 2002.
- Total assets of about US$9 billion and a market capitalization of about US$2.5 billion.
- Approximately 750,000 active accounts, 500,000 customers, 3,500 employees, 85 retail branches, 16 corporate banking centres, five international banking centres and more than 125 ABMs.
- Operating in 15 countries in the Caribbean region, from the Bahamas in the north to Grenada in the south, and Belize in the west to Barbados in the east. FirstCaribbean has operations in: Anguilla, Antigua & Barbuda, the Bahamas, Barbados, Belize, British Virgin Islands, The Cayman Islands, Dominica, Grenada, Jamaica, St. Kitts and Nevis, St. Lucia, St. Maarten, Trinidad, St. Vincent and the Grenadines and Turks and Caicos Islands (15 countries at inception in 2002; entered Trinidad and Tobago in January 2005).
- Regulated by eight central banks and regulatory authorities.
- FirstCaribbean International Bank Limited is traded on the stock exchanges of Barbados, Trinidad and Tobago, and Jamaica. FirstCaribbean International Bank (Jamaica) Limited is traded on the Jamaica Stock Exchange and FirstCaribbean International Bank (Bahamas) Limited is traded on the Bahamas International Stock Exchange.
- FirstCaribbean holds an "A Minus/Stable" credit rating by Standard and Poors—awarded from inception in October 2002.
- FirstCaribbean was structured into four key lines of business:
  1. Retail Banking
  2. Corporate Banking
  3. International Banking
  4. Capital Markets
- FirstCaribbean International Bank is headquartered in Warrens, Barbados.

Exhibit 2   FirstCaribbean Quick Facts

The merger was intended to combine the retail banking, credit cards, corporate banking and offshore banking operations of both heritage banks. Barclays Private Banking and CIBC Wealth Management businesses and their clients were not included in the scope of the discussions and would remain under their respective Barclays and CIBC ownership.

It was hoped that FirstCaribbean International Bank would bring together two complementary and leading financial services businesses in the Caribbean, able to eventually offer customers enhanced products, improved services and extended access to banking services. The merger would establish FirstCaribbean International Bank as a significant Caribbean presence. Hopefully, with greater autonomy than could be previously afforded, the new entity would live up to its name and play a key role in the region.

Under the structure of the proposed transaction, Barclays and CIBC would each own approximately 44 per cent of the ordinary share capital of FirstCaribbean International Bank, with the remainder held publicly. It was the announced intention of CIBC and Barclays to increase the public share holdings of FirstCaribbean from the initial 12 per cent at the time of merger, to up to 20 per cent as soon as was practicable, hopefully within five years after the merger.

The merger of CIBC Caribbean Group and the Barclays Caribbean Banking Operations was expected to create annualised synergies of over US$60 million pre-tax per annum by the end of the first three years of operation following completion of the merge. The intention was that cost savings would be sourced from the combination of operating and processing infrastructure, IT savings, removal of duplicated central costs and branch and office consolidation. Revenue synergies were expected to be sourced from new product and service introductions. Total restructuring and integration costs of more than US$76 million were expected to be incurred as a result of the merge, by the end of the first three years of operation.

MANDATE OF THE NEW EXECUTIVE

In 2000, Michael Mansoor, then president and chief executive officer (CEO) of CIBC West Indies Holdings Limited, said,

> Our goal is to establish FirstCaribbean as a market leader in service, products, ease of access and innovation. With a combined history of more than 225 years of experience in the region, we have a clear understanding of the business and consumer needs in this diverse group of nations. This will be a bank of the Caribbean, for the Caribbean, with connections to the world.

Also in 2000, Charles Middleton, the then Barclays regional director of the Caribbean and Bahamas, said,

> We intend FirstCaribbean to be one of the leading banks in the Caribbean. Its size and diversity should provide our staff with a wide range of career opportunities. It is also the intention to offer staff a share purchase plan that will allow them to participate in the future growth of the company.

The marketing mandate given by FirstCaribbean's new Executive Chairman Michael Mansoor and CEO Charles Pink, who replaced Charles Middleton, had three components. The first was to secure the bank's deposit book. This meant building a brand that would generate trust quickly, to enable the new bank to maintain the deposit levels of the two heritage banks and to keep customers with the new bank through the integration process. If customers became worried about the merger, their first response would probably be to withdraw some or all of their deposits, either voluntarily or through the urgings of competitors. The marketing strategy team was acutely aware of the enormity and uncertainty of replacing two established, well-respected banks with an entirely new—and untried—one. This was no small task.

The second component was to build a brand that would attract the right kind of borrower. There are always individuals and businesses in the wider market who wish to borrow. The problem is that many of these borrowers or the projects for which they seek financing have risk profiles that are unattractive. All banks try to attract and keep borrowers that have a high probability of repaying their loans, on the terms agreed. Borrowers with attractive projects know they are in a strong negotiation position and that they have choices. A bank's reputation and brand has particular relevance to them. Given that the future is uncertain—borrowers very much wish to select a bank that will work and stay with them for the long haul, through thick and thin—because any long-term financed venture has uncertainty. For customers, the interest rate (price) is important; however, once the bank has a competitive rate (and not necessarily the lowest rate), the degree to which they believe they can rely on their bank, the relationship they have with their bank manager and their overall customer service experience become key criteria in making a selection decision and staying with a chosen bank.

The third component was to grow the bank's loan book. This meant immediately launching retail advertising campaigns to attract business, even as the retail banking and corporate banking lines of business (divisions) were being reorganized under new leadership. The new marketing team's task was to ensure that the FirstCaribbean name was positively implanted in the mind of every citizen in every country in which the bank operated. In marketing terms, FirstCaribbean needed to get top of mind awareness and become the customers' first choice.

THE IMPORTANCE OF BRANDING IN BANKING

The key goal of every commercial organization is to generate significant profits. To do this in a competitive market, the company must attract, win and keep customers. Unfortunately, competition drives commoditization. The organization must continually try to improve its sales and margins. The creation of a strong brand enables the company to differentiate itself from its competition and to sell more effectively (see Exhibit 3).

In service-based organizations, brands take on an even more critical role, given the intangible nature of the products sold. In banking, branding is critical in building and maintaining the customer's confidence in the organization. Given that the core business of any bank is to first establish itself as a deposit-taking institution, such trust is necessary to assure customers that the financial institution is a place worthy of their confidence and that will provide safekeeping for

---

Why bother to brand? Because a strong brand . . . makes selling easier and more profitable. Brands provide the following benefits:

1. DISTINCTIVENESS—Positive differentiation versus competitors.

2. EMOTIONAL BONDING—Imprints in customers' hearts and minds.

3. PERSONALITY & CHARACTER—Becomes an icon.

4. CREDIBILITY—Reassures. Engenders confidence and dependability.

5. PREFERENCE & HABIT—Builds loyalty and share.

6. VALUE PRICING—Provides customers with value-for-money assurance and earns the business a better margin.

7. LEVERAGE—Preference. Customer acquisition and retention.

Exhibit 3   Summary of Reasons for Making a Brand Investment

their money and, in some cases, their life savings. To engender this confidence, a bank must build a reputation that encourages depositors to place their money with it; and hopefully become lifelong customers. If a bank does not succeed at this, it will not accumulate the necessary asset base to lend effectively.

For many Caribbean banks, the majority of their profits came from their lending activities. If the bank's brand and reputation were weak, the cost of raising money would become more expensive. The consequence was that the bank would be unable to offer competitive lending rates, or it would have to operate on a slimmer margin. In either case, it would cause the bank to have a lower level of profitability versus its competitors. Business can be quite Darwinian. The marketplace will ultimately punish companies if they are perceived as weak.

New banks and new bank brands have a particular challenge. They have a high risk of potential failure amd customers and the wider market may not accept them. Like a newborn, the first few years can be crucial.

BUSINESS CHALLENGES

In 2002, when the new entity was attempting to work out its brand strategy, there were three contextual issues that were influencing the business. These raised real challenges in developing a brand and marketing strategy:

The first issue was that, for the previous three to four years, both heritage banks had cut spending to practically zero. The first two years (1998 to 2000) consisted of the merger negotiations and the next two years (2000 to 2002) of due diligence, as each heritage bank assessed the value of the other. Both banks had stopped investing in promoting, advertising or developing their brands, products and services. Consequently, sales turnover started to decline and was further eroded by competitive attacks.

The second issue was that competitors, sensing that CIBC and Barclays were distracted

with the merger, started aggressively poaching their better customers. Consequently, First-Caribbean's loan book first went flat and then started to decline as it lost market share. At this critical juncture, the new bank needed an advertising, promotions and sales strategy that could reverse this trend and kick-start loans growth (see Exhibit 4).

The third factor was that the merger was becoming more expensive than originally anticipated. Consequently, budgets for a number of important and previously planned initiatives, including branding and communications, were continually being cut/trimmed. There was a real fear among the marketing team members that marketing funding to launch the new brand was being cut to dangerously low levels. They feared they might exhaust their budget before the new brand took root and the team got the brand to where it needed to be. The analogy used by Lewis was that of a missile on a launch pad. They had enough funding to fuel the launch, but they risked not having enough to get the project into the required "orbit." If funding was exhausted before they achieved "marketing orbit," the new brand could crash and burn around them. This was no small concern. Brand building takes time; it yields incremental results and requires long-term investment. Companies have to be prepared to make a significant commitment of time and resources in order to have any reasonable chance of success.

BUILDING INTERNAL SUPPORT AND THE MARKETING FUNCTION

For decades, banks in the region treated their operations in each country as separate entities with little cross-border co-ordination. Marketing was generally localized. The head office gave directions to each senior country manager, who was simply required to follow the instructions. Management structures were traditional, conservative and hierarchical. For many years this was the standard practice, with all competing entities

---

Banking in the Caribbean Region

A range of international banks (primarily of British and Canadian heritage) competes with a few regional banks and some local banks in serving each of the Caribbean countries. Financial institutions generally offer seamless local operations. In the larger countries, commercial banks also compete with merchant banks, investment houses, credit unions and building societies. The majority of both the international and regional banks are multi-product/ multi-service institutions offering a full range of competitive products. In short, Caribbean financial institutions operate and behave much like their counterparts elsewhere.

In the Caribbean, regulatory authorities frown on the idea of cross-border movement of capital, as being potentially inimical to their national interests. Many countries continue to have foreign exchange controls and regulations. Cross-border banking is difficult because of differing regulations and controls imposed by each Caribbean country's Central Bank. The challenge lies with the multiplicity of regulatory authorities seeking to control banking activities. There are some eight different Central banks and regulatory authorities that operate in the framework of their national interests and laws, with minimal regional co-operation. The matter is further compounded as different accounting standards and practices are used, although, increasingly, most practices are consistent with the Internationally Accepted Accounting Standards.

Some Caribbean states, namely the Bahamas, the Eastern Caribbean States, Barbados and the Cayman Islands, have thriving offshore banking sectors specializing in asset management for high net worth individuals.

Exhibit 4   Banking in the Caribbean Region

Note: Further information on Caribbean Banking can be found in Ivey #9B05M015—"Note on Banking in the Caribbean."

---

doing the same thing. However, with the evolution of the financial markets in the Caribbean, strong indigenous commercial banks and other non-commercial financial institutions were emerging with a focus that looked beyond their country's borders, seeking regional investment and growth opportunities.

The recognition of the importance of marketing as a critical tool of success seemed to be finally reaching the banking sector, but progress was slow. Many senior bankers, who had spent their entire career with a single bank, actively resisted it. In many banks, the head of retail banking typically had responsibility for marketing (such as it was practised). How would this person react when this authority was transferred? Bankers tend to be rather conservative and change happens slowly in the industry. Lewis was a newcomer to the banking industry. Would he be able to gain the acceptance and respect of his colleagues? Would they allow him and his team to quickly do what they thought was

necessary? Would they give the marketing team their support? Before joining the banking industry, Lewis had been warned that the internal politics in banks could be quite fearsome and vicious.

Over the years, a significant number of the senior management of both banks was non-Caribbean expatriates, seconded from their respective heritage bank. These persons often brought useful specialist skills and current, first-world experience. However, their perspectives, frames of reference and expectations reflected a different culture, which was sometimes out of sync with how things are done in the region. There was always a risk in bringing in an expatriate—some senior managers acculturated effectively into the region and others poorly. Their typical tour of duty was about three years, making it difficult for them to have a lasting impact. Also, because their next (home country) posting was dependent on their success in their current posting, expatriate managers were often short term in their business focus.

Given this history, the new FirstCaribbean CEO (himself an expatriate seconded from Barclays) insisted that the FirstCaribbean marketing and human resource departments be staffed by Caribbean professionals as far as possible and be headed by experienced Caribbean nationals. He felt that with a Caribbean marketing team, the new bank would be better able to understand and respond to the needs of Caribbean customers. Lewis was fully supportive of this strategy, but as he reflected on the task of recruiting, he needed to find competent, experienced marketers in a hurry. This was easier said than done because the market for experienced Caribbean professionals, especially in the field of marketing, was weak at best.

Over the years, Barclays and CIBC had paid little attention to their Caribbean marketing function. Barclays tended to treat each Caribbean country as a separate market (and business entity) and allowed each country a significant degree of local autonomy. Each country manager reported separately to the head office. There was limited effort to capitalize on synergies or co-ordinate activities.

CIBC started with a similar organizational structure to Barclays. However, in the mid-1990s, it restructured and started merging country operations into a single centralized entity. CIBC standardized marketing and promotional activities to provide greater control and to generate marketing efficiencies and cost savings. The danger posed by a centralized strategy was that it could be slow or unresponsive to individual country needs and market variations. Experience in some companies had demonstrated that centralized head offices sometimes implemented marketing programs without fully assessing their relevance to the cultural proclivities and business practices of each country.

The FirstCaribbean integration team proposed taking the CIBC's business model even further. They believed that a decentralized structure was inherently complex, unwieldy and slow. Also, complexity increases costs. They saw benefits, not only in terms of efficiency of the marketing functions, but also in terms of the speed with which decisions could be made and implemented.

A requirement of the brand building process was the creation a dedicated, professional marketing team. This team would centralize the marketing function and co-ordinate the implementation of marketing strategy across the 15 countries. It had to operate seamlessly to build, guide and promote the new brand.

However, there was great instability within the marketing department itself. At this time, Lewis was also trying to create a new marketing function, with staff being hired and new policies and procedures being developed. Thus, the marketing team that was to do the brand building work was just being newly recruited. Lewis tried to use consultants as a short-term measure, but this proved unsatisfactory. Although he anticipated that it might take a year to find the staff he wanted, Lewis had an immediate need to act quickly. His newly recruited staff was largely untried. They were now becoming familiar with their roles and had not yet learned how to work as a team. Creating a marketing team under these circumstances was no small challenge.

POSITIONING, DIFFERENTIATION AND THE BRAND VALUES

Given the similarities of the products and services offered by banks, it was critical for Lewis's team to position and differentiate the new bank (see Exhibit 5).

Critical to the new bank's success was the importance of being customer focused: listening to customers, understanding their financial needs and partnering with them to provide advice, service and financial solutions. The bank sought to promote itself as a professional business partner helping customers achieve their financial goals, guiding them to make the right choices and, in the process, demonstrating that the new bank had the customers' interests at heart.

At the heart of the FirstCaribbean Brand were five key values (or brand muscles). These were to

Vision Statement

To create the Caribbean's No. 1 financial services institution:

- First for customers: Customer First
- First for Employees: Employer of Choice
- First for Shareholders: Including Employees
- First for the Caribbean: Caribbean Centric

Mission Statement

FirstCaribbean International Bank will be the bank of first choice for customers and employees in the Caribbean, ranking first for service and first for innovation in the eyes of all.

Heritage Statement

FirstCaribbean International Bank is an associated company of Barclays Bank Plc and CIBC.

Brand Promise

Caribbean Pride. International Strength. Your Financial Partner.

Organizational Values (CRICKET)

Customer   We are committed to exceeding customer expectations across all the unique regional markets we serve.

Respect   We instill respect in our organization due to a commitment to openness, diversity and integrity.

Innovation   We are the market leader in a competitive environment, through constant innovation and agility.

Caribbean   We are the true Caribbean bank, committed to finding solutions and opportunities that help our customers, our people and our region to grow.

Knowledge   We bring the knowledge of thousands to benefit every customer, by sharing information and fostering a learning organization.

Excellence   We commit to excellence by raising the standards of performance and delivery.

Teamwork   We are a team working together toward a common goal, bringing out our best as individuals and as a group.

Brand Values (CRISP)

Caribbean Commitment   We provide products and services that cater to the Caribbean. Our commitment is to community, nation and region.

Respect   We listen in order to understand your financial needs; you can trust us to give you superior service and complete confidentiality.

International Standards   We will lead in integrity, quality and innovation, providing international reach and recognition.

Strength   We are strong, built solid on the foundation of two world class banks, establishing security, reliability and opportunity.

Partnership   We help you to achieve your financial goals by providing added value and sustained professional support.

Exhibit 5   Vision, Mission and Organizational Brand Values

be foundations of the new brand and were to be used to position the bank to build customer loyalty and market share. These values were identified following extensive research across the region during the pre-merger period. These brand values defined the character and personality of the new bank. An acronym of these values spells CRISP:

Caribbean Commitment	We BELONG. This region is our home. We will use our unique knowledge, understanding and skills to meet the region's banking needs. We provide products and services that cater to the Caribbean.
Respect	We LISTEN. We shall always act with confidentiality and care, to provide genuine, relevant and trusted service.
International Standards	We aim to be the BENCHMARK BANK for product development and service quality. We will lead in integrity and innovation, providing international reach and recognition. We shall be among the best the Caribbean offers the world.
Strength	Security, reliability and confidence are our HERITAGE and our PROMISE. We are strong and shall continue to build on our legacy and the solid foundation of our two world-class parent banks, providing the reliability, safety and security customers expect.
Partnership	We shall foster MUTUALLY BENEFICIAL RELATIONSHIPS to help customers make the right choices and achieve their financial goals by providing added-value and sustained professional support.

These brand values were forged into the FirstCaribbean Brand Promise or tag line *"Caribbean Pride. International Strength. Your Financial Partner."*

This tagline or slogan would appear every time the FirstCaribbean logo was used.

The vision of the new bank was to be first in everything it did, *"First for Customers, first for Employees, first for Service, and Innovation, in the eyes of all."* The new bank was committed to being the Caribbean's No. 1 financial service institution.

THE CHALLENGE—BRAND CREDIBILITY AND RATE OF ROLL-OUT

The marketing team was apprehensive about brand credibility. In every customer encounter, there is an opportunity to positively influence customer perceptions. If service were poor, there would be customer disappointment and anger. The team feared that during the 18-month technical integration period, there was a high risk of disruptions and poor customer service. The team was uncertain as to how quickly the new bank could get up to speed. How should they appropriately shape customer expectations?

Lewis's marketing team could not be sure of the customer impact of integration. An integration of this scope and complexity had never been attempted before in the region. There were no models that could be referred to. While the integration team did its best to create a robust merger plan, no one could be sure that this plan would work as anticipated or that there would not be unintended consequences.

Another related challenge was to determine what brand promise(s) could credibly be made. Quite a bit of work had been done in defining the brand values and brand promise. These were largely aspirational; they would not be "real" for some time. The new marketing team had to be careful in shaping customer, regulator and staff expectations, and not to make or suggest promises they could not keep. If they got this wrong, all the work done on the brand up to that point could all be wasted, and instead of the emergence of a strong, attractive and well-respected brand, the new brand could be stillborn.

The marketing team was unsure of how to proceed in the face of these uncertainties. On many occasions, the members discussed the idea of how fast they could (and should), "cook" the brand—"microwave versus slow simmer." A key implementation consideration was how to co-ordinate the integration and branding processes so as to ensure the long-term success of the merger. Customers had many expectations, but these expectations would not be fully realized until some time in the future. During the 18 to 24 months of integration, the new bank would have to freeze all product development. This made it difficult to respond to customer requirements. This also meant that Internet and telephone banking, refurbished branches, new branches or ABMs, better trained staff, more effective systems, etc. all had to wait and for the technical integration to be completed.

CONCLUSION

Market research indicated that the perceptions of the customers of both heritage banks were mixed. Their brands had strength and they were admired for their continuity and reliability. However, many mass-market customers considered the heritage banks to be foreign/colonial, unfriendly, predatory and often unresponsive. Premier, corporate and international customers were generally more pleased. Negative perceptions were a potential problem and had to

be addressed. The integration task was to merge the two banks into a positive, stable bank and not merely create a larger, inefficient and uncaring entity.

Lewis's team had to assure the Caribbean public and FirstCaribbean customers that the merger and transformation would be successful. The marketing team had to create a new identity, drawing on the positives of the old heritage brands while trying to leave behind any negatives that existed. The new brand had to carry over the strong history and tradition of its parent brands, while being promoted on its own terms, independent of its progenitors. All of this had to be done without giving the impression that the heritage banks were abandoning the region. The task required not only transforming customers' perceptions but also maintaining the goodwill of the regional governments and the regulatory agencies as well.

Additionally, the marketing team had to figure out how to get employees and their unions to buy into the new brand, given that they would be required to implement it and live its values. This was critical, given that ultimately it was the staff members who had to communicate the new brand to customers. If the team could not get staff buy-in, then communicating the brand to the general public would be difficult, if not impossible.

Lewis's marketing team wondered whether the staff would rise to the challenge, given the restructuring going on across the bank and the uncertainty regarding future employment. Would staff be prepared to leave their heritage bank culture and adopt a new one? Would staff see this as a merger of equals or as an acquisition of one heritage bank by the other?

Lewis knew that this would be one of the most challenging undertakings in his professional life. The question was where to start.

Harmonization of Compensation and Benefits for FirstCaribbean International Bank

Prepared by Edward Corbin and Betty Jane Punnett

Version: (A) 2004-12-15

Introduction

The head of the Integration Team had met with the head and team members of the Human Resources Transition (HRT) team, and emphasized the need to ensure a smooth transition from the heritage banks' human resources (HR) policies to the integrated policies. The transition and integration of HR were perhaps more complex than the teams had originally recognized. Now that the merger of the Caribbean holdings of Barclays Bank Plc. and the Canadian Imperial Bank of Commerce (CIBC) was going ahead, the integration of very diverse systems and procedures had to be faced. The first step was to meet with the respective HR representatives in each of the heritage banks to understand the current situation, in terms of existing policies. The task would then be to design a policy that would be acceptable to employees from both banks in the new organization, FirstCaribbean International Bank, that would be created by the merger. A critical aspect of the merger was the harmonization of compensation and benefits, which had to be resolved as a matter of priority.

Background

FirstCaribbean International Bank was to be created by a merger between Barclays Bank Plc. (Caribbean) and CIBC (West Indies Holdings Ltd.). In the merger, these two banks were known as the heritage banks. Barclays Bank had operated in the English-speaking Caribbean for 150 years. CIBC also had a long history in the

region, having opened its first offices in the 1920s. Both banks were well established and well respected in the region. Neither, however, held a dominant position, and their Caribbean operations were both a relatively small portion of their global operations and, strategically, less important than the offices in regions such as the Far East. Although the heritage banks were profitable in the Caribbean, each envisioned substantial investment as necessary to ensure continued profitability and increased competitive advantage. Against this background, the two banks had independently decided to seek alternatives to their current mode of operations. The outcome was a decision to merge their Caribbean operations into a new entity to be called FirstCaribbean International Bank. The merger was seen as creating a more effective organization, based on operational synergies and improved service.

Prior to achieving regulatory approval, the directors of Barclays Bank Plc. and CIBC (West Indies Holdings Ltd.) began discussions related to the creation of a strategic alliance between the two international banks. This strategy was a response to competitive pressures, global trends to create economies of scale and the desire to create an institution that could be internationally competitive. FirstCaribbean International Bank was to be created with its headquarters in Barbados. Barbados is a tiny island set in the east of the Caribbean archipelago, with a population of approximately 275,000 people, a democratic government system, a steadily growing economy and a reputation for being one of the most developed of the developing countries in the region and in the world.

Barclays Bank Plc. (Caribbean) was a branch of Barclays International and operated in 14 countries across the region. It employed approximately 1,534 people in 45 branches. Barclay's strengths were its strong regional heritage, established offshore and international business, credit card expertise and established corporate relationships. Barclays Caribbean banking operations had a net income of US$72.6 million, and total assets were US$5.2 billion for the year ended December 31, 2001.

CIBC operated in eight countries across the region and employed approximately 1,639 staff. CIBC operated 42 branches in the Caribbean, was perceived as a leader in product innovation, had an emerging capital markets business and had one of the best technology platforms in the region. CIBC's Caribbean operations showed net income of US$67.8 million, and total assets were US$4.6 billion for the year ended October 31, 2001.

With the merger, the FirstCaribbean International Bank would become the largest single full-service bank in the English-speaking Caribbean with an asset base of US$10 billion, 3,000 employees and operations in 15 countries. The vision of the merged bank was "to create the Caribbean's number one financial services institution: first for customers and first for employees." A key vision was to be perceived as one of the employers of choice within the financial services sector in the region.

Before the merger talks formally began, the directors and chief executive officers (CEOs) from both heritage banks held high-level discussions related to due diligence; this process took approximately two years to complete. By early 2002, the decision to merge had been reached, and an initial assessment of the steps needed to accomplish the merger had been made. The two heritage banks had set up an Integration Team made up of representatives from each bank, to oversee the merger process. The Integration Team was to allow for a merger that would be accomplished efficiently and effectively, while allowing existing staff to continue with business as usual—i.e., normal banking activities—so that current customers could carry on business

with little or no interruption. The merger was to be accomplished so that it would be seamless from the customers' point of view.

The Integration Team had established a number of work-groups to achieve this objective. These work-groups focused on the major operational areas affected by the merger. A key factor was the integration of human resources, and the HRT team-group was established with a senior human resource practitioner from Barclays International as its leader. The objectives for the HRT as its leader to ensure that employees from both banks were treated equitably and to accomplish a transition from two separate, and entirely different, bank structures, to a new, integrated structure, with as little disruption as possible to "business as usual."

THE CHALLENGE

The challenge for the HRT was to examine the current policies and practices in each of the heritage banks, consider and evaluate options for moving from two systems to one, and make recommendations to the Integration Team. Recommendations needed to be within the cost parameters of the integration process and the early principles of the evolving culture. The senior executives and the integration team had to give their formal approval before the recommendations could move forward. Consideration would also have to be given to the unions that represented the interests of the workers. Moreover, shareholders in the heritage banks, as well as prospective shareholders in the FirstCaribbean International Bank, needed to be satisfied that the merger was in their best financial interest. An additional challenge was that all governments and regulatory bodies needed, either directly or indirectly, to establish their own comfort levels, regarding the merger and its impact on the human resources.

Strategies for human resource integration needed to take into account employees at all levels of the organization. Strategies needed to encompass options for selecting staff for the integrated bank, dealing with redundancies, establishing training and development programs, and harmonizing pay and benefits. Complicating all of this, FirstCaribbean International Bank would be operating in 15 different countries, and each country had its own legislation and regulations regarding HR practices, including different pay scales. A further complication was that employees were local, regional or extra-regional, and each group had its special expectations and requirements. Local employees are those who work in their home country (i.e., Barbadians working in Barbados), regional are employees from within the Caribbean region (i.e., Trinidadians working in St. Vincent and the Grenadines), and extra-regional are persons from outside of the region (i.e., Canadians working in Jamaica, in this case, typically people from Canada or the United Kingdom assigned in one of the Caribbean countries).

Worthy of note were the daily minimum wages for four Caribbean countries: BDS\$158 (Barbados); J\$800 (Jamaica); ECC\$100 (St. Kitts) and GYD\$1,422 (Guyana). Note the variation in exchange rates: US\$1 = BDS2; US\$1 = J50; US\$1 = ECC 2.7; US\$1 = GYD196.

Prior to the merger, Barclays and CIBC in the Caribbean had substantially different corporate cultures and HR practices:

- In Barclays, the culture of a "job for life" with all the attendant cultural influences, was evident, whereas in CIBC this seemed less the case.
- CIBC was more noted for product innovation than Barclays.
- CIBC had a single and more integrated information technology (IT) platform called an Integrated Central Banking System (ICBS), whereas Barclays had a non-integrated multiplatform system.
- Barclays had a more generous compensation and benefits package than CIBC.
- CIBC had a more defined and operational performance management system (PMS), which linked rewards to performance throughout the business, whereas Barclays' pay regimen was driven much more by its industrial relations environment.

- CIBC was perceived to have a more aggressive approach to business development in the region.
- Barclays was a branch of Barclays International (United Kingdom), as opposed to CIBC Holdings Ltd., which was a separate legal entity.
- Barclays' business was significantly unionized, whereas CIBC was largely non-unionized.

These corporate cultures had to be integrated along with the more basic HR policies and practices.

THE COMPENSATION AND BENEFITS HARMONIZATION TEAM

One of the most important tasks in the HRT strategy was harmonization of pay and benefits. As a result of this being a specialty area, a Compensation and Benefits Harmonization Team (CompBen) was established as a "work stream" of the HRT. Two expatriates, who were compensation and benefits experts from the United Kingdom, headed this CompBen Team. They created a full team of eight members, which included two local senior HR representatives, one each from CIBC and Barclays. The intention was to ensure that there was equal representation from both heritage banks and there was local input and representation regarding compensation and benefits systems.

A strategy used by the HR transition team, supported by the executive team, anchored its harmonization process in a Framework Agreement, which had been achieved between the bank and the trade unions. The overriding principle was that all employees in the new bank would not be disadvantaged as a result of the harmonization process. In the design work done by the CompBen team, there was no explicit consultation with the trade unions. The output of that team was, however, subject to consultation with the trade unions as part of the implementation process.

The CompBen Team had to consider the existing offerings from the two heritage banks.

Their mandate was to consider the facts relating to compensation and benefits, undertake critical analysis and make the most informed decisions leading to harmonization. This process had to be completed in time for first official day of the new bank, FirstCaribbean International Bank, hence, time was of the essence and teams had to be action-oriented.

THE SUMMARY FACTS

The CompBen Team had to overcome some internal challenges. Cultural differences between the U.K. experts/consultants and the legal experts resulted in tensions, as both sides brought different perspectives to the issues being discussed. The team was able to compile a summary of core facts pertaining to both heritage banks to aid their decision-making. The team also faced intense time pressures because of the deadline for delivering results, and they had to constantly weigh financial implications and costs against human resource issues, some of which were emotional and cultural in nature.

Some facts are highlighted as follows:

- CIBC had wider pay scales than Barclays: CIBC pay scales were 75 per cent to 125 per cent and Barclays' pay scales were 75 per cent to 110 per cent for clerical and 85 per cent to 110 per cent for managers.
- 58 per cent of CIBC managers and 32 per cent of CIBC clerical staff were paid below the minimum of Barclays' range.
- Neither Barclays nor CIBC was leading-edge in its approach to using salary benchmark data, although CIBC had the better system of the two.

Only 19 CIBC employees (eight clerical, 11 management) were paid more than the maximum of the Barclays range (see Exhibit 1).

- Barclays had a flat profit-share plan for all employees with a generic link to business performance and a performance-related pay scheme for managerial employees.

- All CIBC staff participated in a bonus scheme with a maximum bonus target potential up to 10 per cent or 42 per cent of base salary. Staff could benefit from a bonus payment as low as 10 per cent of base salary, to as high as 42 per cent of base salary, depending on their employee level, the performance of their branch and their individual performance (see Exhibit 2).
- The car benefit at CIBC commenced at a more senior level than at Barclays, but was more generous.
- More Barclays' managers than CIBC managers benefited from the car loan scheme.
- Cars were awarded at an employee level of MG6 at Barclays, and at Barclays, employees qualified for a car at one equivalent grade higher at level 7.

The number of staff who received cars, the associated costs and the maximum purchased value are shown in Exhibit 3.

THE COMPENSATION SURVEY

The initial meetings of the harmonization team included critical analysis of official documents related to the different pay structures within both banks. A compensation survey was conducted and statistics were generated to form a picture of the major tasks facing the team (see Exhibit 4).

The team found that although CIBC employed seven per cent more staff than Barclays, Barclays' total payroll cost was 25 per cent higher. The higher average salary (compensation plus benefits) at Barclays was reflected in Barclays' higher average cost per employee: $39,559, compared with CIBC's average cost of $29,481 per employee.

At Barclays, there was a culture of paying profit share without any direct link to performance, whereas at CIBC, there was a clear pay-performance link. This finding provided an additional challenge for harmonization of compensation and benefits, as absolute numbers would not necessarily provide the best means for interpreting fairness and equity. The situation was further complicated by the fact that Barclays

Salary Grades and Associated Job Classifications				
Barclays	**No. In Grade**	**CIBC**	**No. In Grade**	**Classification**
Non-clerical		Grade 1	60	Non-clerical
Grade 1	528	Grade 2	574	Clerical
Grade 2	402	Grade 3	365	Clerical
Grade 3	298	Grade 4	275	Supervisory
Grade 4	149	Grade 5	120	Supervisory
MG 6	32	Grade 6	121	Junior Management
MG 5	53	Grade 7	82	Middle Management
MG 4	44	Grade 8	31	Middle Management
MG 3	13	Grade 9	6	Senior Management
MG 2	7	Grade 10	4	Senior Management
MG 1	3	Grade 11 – Exec. Mgt.	0	Executive
SX Directors	2		1	Executive

Exhibit 1   Grade Map: Barclays Versus CIBC

Source: Company files.

Barclays Employee Level	Barclays (%)	CIBC Employee Level	CIBC Bonus Range %	FirstCaribbean Employee Level
	(a) Performance Pay			
1	0 - 12	1	0 - 10	0 - 15
2	0 - 12	2	0 - 10	
3	0 - 12	3	0 - 10	
4	0 - 12	4	0 - 16	
		5	0 - 16	
	(b) Profit Share Schemes			
MG6	0 - 24.5	6	0 - 20	0 - 30
MG5	0 - 24.5	7	0 - 24	
MG4	0 - 24.5	8	0 - 30	
MG3	0 - 24.5	9	0 - 42	
MG2	0 - 24.5	9	0 - 42	

Exhibit 2   Bonus Payment Schedule

Barclays Grade	Number of Employees	Purchase Limit	Compensation Cost	CIBC Level	Number of Employees	Purchase Limit	Compensation Cost
MG6	32	28,000	896,000	Level 6	121	Do not receive company car benefit	
MG5	53	28,000	1,480,000	Level 7	82	35,000	2,870,000
MG4	44	28,000	1,232,000	Level 8	31	57,500	1,782,500
MG3	13	33,000	429,000	Level 9	6	57,500	345,000
MG2	7	50,000	350,000	Level 9	6	57,500	345,000
MG1	3	60,000	180,000	Level 10	4	57,500	230,000

Exhibit 3   Car Benefits Scheme

Description	CIBC	Barclays	Difference	Comments
Total Compensation	$41,071,150	$51,480,386	$10,409,236	Barclays 25.34% higher payroll costs, attributed to higher (0.9%) statutory benefits and 3.69% higher non-statutory benefit costs.
Head Count	1,639	1,531	108	CIBC = 7.05% more employees
Average Cost per Employee	25,058.85	33,625.34	8,651.49	Average salaries higher and benefits package more generous at Barclays.
Bonuses	5.83% of total salary payments	10.34% of total salary payments	4.51%	More generous staff incentive plan at Barclays. Plan offered to everyone except entry level.
Staff Benefits as % of Total Cash Compensation	11.56%	15.69%	4.13%	Barclays had a more generous bonus payment scheme and vacation leave entitlement, especially at management grades.
Staff Benefits Statutory/Total Cash Compensation	2.77%	3.69%	.92%	Requirements and rates vary from location to location. Variation less than 1%.
Staff Benefits Non-Statutory/ Total Compensation	8.79%	11.48%	2.69%	More generous benefits provided for staff at Barclays.

Exhibit 4   Comparison of Employee Information Barclays/CIBC (in US$)

Source: Barclays/CIBC Compensation and Benefits Team document. Figures have been modified for purposes of confidentiality.

paid a total bonus of 10.34 per cent compared to CIBC's 5.83 per cent of total salaries. The compensation team members knew that the culture of receiving bonus payments without the performance link was entrenched in Barclays, and it was not likely that the employees would give up this system easily or willingly.

HUMAN RESOURCE MANAGEMENT ISSUES

The HRT needed to balance the costs and benefits of various options in order to make a recommendation to the Integration Team. The key internal stakeholders were the heritage banks, First Caribbean International Bank's executive and the employees. External stakeholders were the union, customers and shareholders, including the local governments. Satisfying all of these stakeholders would not be easy. The recommendations needed to be pragmatic from a profit perspective, but also needed to take into consideration employee morale and customer satisfaction.

Barclays staff enjoyed an advantage because their salaries and benefits packages were more generous than those at CIBC. Employment contracts would have clearly outlined these terms of employment, and changing these conditions by reducing salaries or benefits would have negative effects. The new bank did not want to begin with negative industrial relations or low satisfaction among employees. There were also signs of disquiet among staff when the merger was announced, as rumors spread about the future of the staff of both heritage banks. Of particular concern were the trade unions' responses to the very sensitive issues associated with compensation and benefits.

THE TRADE UNION FACTOR

Trade unions were entrenched in most of the islands where the heritage banks operated, and union officials were beginning to exert their influence. This response was considered normal since compensation and benefits are always two of the most contentious issues between employers and employees, and with the merger, significant changes were expected in these areas. While Barclays was already unionized when formal merger discussions began, CIBC became unionized during the process.

The banks did not want to begin new operations under the cloak of industrial unrest. In a very competitive environment with the presence of other established international banks, such as the Bank of Nova Scotia and the Royal Bank of Canada, the board of directors did not want to jeopardize the goodwill the two heritage banks had created over the years. This sentiment was particularly relevant to retaining commercial clients, whose confidence in the new bank would be critical from day one.

THE OPTIONS FROM THE COMPBEN TEAM

The Compensation and Benefits Team, through the HRT, was considering a number of options.

Option 1

A proposal for full harmonization whereby all CIBC staff moved from their existing positions to equivalent positions in the Barclays range. Harmonization would ensure that their comparative ratio was maintained when they moved to a higher scale. Under this plan, Barclays staff would not receive salary increases.

Option 2

In this option, the Barclays salary scales would be revised to fit within the existing CIBC salary scales.

Option 3

This was a more complex option, which involved moving all CIBC staff, including managers, to the minimum of the Barclays range and "rippling" both Barclays and CIBC staff who fell within 75 per cent to 85 per cent of the maximum salary. All CIBC staff who currently earned below the Barclays minimum would move to the Barclays minimum, protecting some of the differential for those clerical staff positioned just below the minimum (the "ripple" effect).

For example, both CIBC and Barclays clerical employees' (who were positioned between 75 per cent and 85 per cent of the maximum pay range) salaries would increase between one per cent and three per cent according to the individual's position in the range. The increases would be adjusted in order to protect the original differential and to ensure that no one "leapfrogged" their colleagues, which could

happen if a flat increase were given across the 75 per cent to 85 per cent range.

DECISION TIME

The CompBen team weighed the options after careful analysis of all the facts accumulated over the eight weeks of intense meetings. They had to send their recommendations to the HR transition team through the HR integration team. The CompBen team asked "what is the best option for FirstCaribbean International Bank when it begins operations on its initial day as the new bank?" The team leaders knew that their advice would have to be analysed by the HR transition team members, before going to the executive for final approval.

8

M&A Avoidance and Alternatives

Firms that are the target of mergers and acquisitions (M&A) may wish to avoid doing a deal, while firms considering M&A have numerous alternatives available to them. There may be good strategic reasons that a firm wishes not to be acquired and so uses one of the defensive tactics available to it. When a firm wants to do a deal, after its strategic decision to do a deal, it must decide what type of deal to do. While some of these are discussed in the structuring chapter, there exist numerous other options beyond a straight merger or acquisition. Depending on the situation and strategic intent and whether the firm is on the sell- or buy-side, these other options may make more sense.

Defensive Tactics

The topic of defenses to M&A is common in the daily business news when unwelcome M&A suitors attempt deals. One of the critical concerns in enacting such defenses is the seemingly obvious conflict with the board's fiduciary duties. A defense is a structural or legal impediment to another firm being able to conduct a successful takeover. Part of the inherent market value of any firm is the premium likely to be paid and the likelihood of takeover—called the *takeover premium*. By enacting defenses, the board is taking away, or at least reducing, this portion of the stock value. Therein lies the potential for conflict. However, a board has substantial legal discretion in suggesting that such defenses are superior alternatives to a deal, by relying on the business judgment rule, as long as they do not breach any other fiduciary duty. In fact, a plaintiff unhappy with such a board decision has the burden of proof in demonstrating gross negligence on the part of the board in such a case. This is a high burden, and one well defined (and redefined) in the courts. As such, these defenses are commonly implemented both before any deal is proposed as well as when specific takeover attempts are made. We review several of the most common defenses.

Charter and Bylaw Provisions

The legal documents for a firm can specify long board tenures and staggered elections (thus thwarting a proxy fight for board seats) or can disallow the removal of a board member except for cause (legally doing something wrong). These documents can also establish the voting mechanisms (e.g., noncumulative voting and supermajority requirement) that make obtaining a vote more difficult. The easiest mechanism is the choice of location of incorporation since takeover laws and defenses differ by locale.

Shareholder Rights Plans

Called a "poison pill," this gives stockholders the right to buy subsidized stock, making a deal less attractive to a potential buyer because of the likely dilution. Two common types are a *flip-in* or a *flip-over.* A flip-in allows current stockholders to buy discounted shares of the target if an acquirer buys more than some set percentage of the firm. A flip-over allows stockholders to buy subsidized shares of the acquirer (subsidized by the target) at perhaps 50% of the market value, resulting in a substantial dilution of the acquiring entity.

White Squire

A board can sell or issue shares to another entity, commonly a financial investor, or to an employee stock ownership plan (ESOP). This new set of shares outstanding makes it more expensive to acquire the firm, more difficult to gain control because the shares are in "friendly" hands, and more difficult to win a proxy vote.

Defensive Sale or Acquisition

A target can find another potential bidder, a "white knight," that takes either a substantial or controlling interest in the target. The existence of the white knight, typically with deep pockets, keeps a potential hostile acquirer away because of the added cost and difficulty of gaining control. A target firm can also make an acquisition of its own that makes it less attractive to the potential suitor. The acquisition can be made in a business that makes sense for the target, but not for the hostile suitor, and can make the acquisition in a leveraged manner (lots of debt) that makes it unattractive to the suitor. The target can make other restructuring-related moves that may also make it less attractive, such as to sell key assets or recapitalize the firm (e.g., with high leverage).

Litigation

Although not a long-term solution, a target can sue the suitor for any number of reasons and can tie up the deal in court while other defenses are enacted. It may take time to find a white knight or to find a suitable acquisition to make. However, this can be a costly path to take, especially if the grounds for the suit are frivolous.

Key Employee Contracts/Golden Parachutes

The executives and key personnel of a firm can be granted generous severance packages that are triggered in a change-of-control transaction. By doing so, the firm creates a liability that makes it more costly to acquire.

ALTERNATIVES TO M&A

Both buy-side and sell-side firms have more options available to them to put in place a deal that both may make more strategic sense and may be a better fit with the resource limitations and capabilities of the firm. We break these into three categories. First, cooperative mechanisms are deals that can be done between two or more firms that allow them to cooperate in some way. These include joint ventures, cross-shareholdings, alliances, licensing, franchising, and other forms. Second, ownership change mechanisms are deals in which you change what you own and how you own it. These include split-offs, spin-offs, subsidiary–initial public offerings (IPOs), and tracking stock issuances. Finally, there are ownership change mechanisms in which you simply change how the firm is owned but do not change what you own. Here, we include management buyouts (LBOs by management), share repurchases, and recapitalizations. While many other mechanisms exist, we have chosen to cover these as they are some of the more common ones.

Joint Ventures

Two or more firms contribute assets, cash, and/or personnel into a new, jointly held entity. Through the joint venture, the parties cooperate in some way, and the benefits flow back to the parent entities. The upside of these deals is that the parent entities are not affected or restructured and that the two firms can still cooperate. The downside is that partial ownership can result in a lack of understanding as to which party is responsible for managing and growing the venture. As well, over time, the justification for the original venture and the benefits back to the firms may change, making the joint venture mode less desirable.

Cross-Shareholdings

While the two firms do not merge or acquire one another, each can take an equity stake in the other. This enhances the incentive for the two firms to cooperate with one another because the value of their stake will increase as the other firm succeeds.

Alliances

An alliance is a legal agreement between the parties to cooperate in some way through its existing entities. The parties may agree to go to market together and jointly offer products or services (as a more complete offering) or may share in other ways, such as in product development, in which the parties make their products work together seamlessly.

Licensing

A firm may allow another to sell its product or to relabel and sell as its own brand a product or service (e.g., DSL Internet lines) offering. Licensing is also common with technical inputs to products, such as software code. For example, it is common to license software code and then use it in your own firm's products. These deals benefit from the lack of investment or commitment required but can create channel conflicts in which other customers or potential partners are excluded from using your products.

Franchising

As is common in the fast-food and many retail industries, owner-operators use the brand and central operations of a franchisor but are separately owned firms. This mechanism may be used when M&A will not work, because ownership restrictions exist in a certain jurisdiction, or when internal investment capital is insufficient to fund growth or growth by M&A.

Split-Off

As an alternative to selling an entire firm, perhaps only a part of the firm should be separated. In a split-off, current stockholders are given the option to exchange some of their shares for shares in the new, separate entity. The exchange is typically tax free and requires that the parent exchange at least 80% of the ownership in the entity. Stockholders can choose whether to participate. This method ensures that the owners of the stock are interested in owning it (they opt in), but there may be insufficient interest among the existing stockholder base to fully distribute the stock.

Spin-Off

A spin-off is similar to a split-off, with the same 80% rule and tax-free status, but the shares are exchanged to all stockholders regardless of their interest in the shares. As such, the shares are distributed pro rata to the existing stockholders. This is a sure way of ensuring that the shares are distributed but also may put the stock into the hands of disinterested owners, who then sell the stock in the open market.

Subsidiary-IPO

Instead of selling the stock internally, a firm can create a separate, 100% owned subsidiary and conduct a public offering for some portion of its shares. This method subjects the firm to the sometimes grueling and costly initial public offering process and may result in tax liability for certain portions of the proceeds. However, this does put the stock into the hands of willing and interested investors and allows the new entity to raise its own operating capital.

Tracking Stock

A firm can offer "letter" stock or a tracking stock that has no ownership per se but separately represents some division or subsidiary. It allows investors to participate in the earnings and growth of a particular set of assets or business, without owning the larger entity. As such, it attracts investors interested in the "pure-play," specific assets, but the owners of this stock actually have no legal ownership of the underlying firm or assets. As such, these stocks tend to trade at a discount.

Management Buyout

As an alternative to selling the firm to an outside group, the management group may lead the buyout. A management buyout (MBO) typically requires that the management group borrow money to finance the deal, and so it is similar to a leveraged buyout, but the management team is the investor, to the extent that they can afford to invest. When additional capital is required (typically), they turn to a private investor group that provides the equity capital required. The firm's cash flows and assets are then leveraged, and debt is used to buy out the existing stockholder base. These deals give an inside management team great incentives to work hard and be loyal to their firm because their wealth is directly tied to it.

Share Repurchases

In lieu of investing in another firm, a firm may choose to invest its cash in its own stock. As well, a stock buyback plan can be used to consolidate the ownership base of a firm. A consolidated ownership base may make a firm easier to acquire because an acquirer can then gain a controlling position by having to convince fewer stockholders to sell their shares. However, this also may send a negative signal to the market. While the new interest in the shares suggests that insiders feel the stock to be a good value, it also signals to the market that the management team has run out of good investment ideas and sees no other ways to invest and grow the firm.

Recapitalization

This can be done either in preparation for the sale of a firm or in contemplation of making an acquisition. Recapitalizing a firm means replacing some or all of the current stock and debt holdings with a new set of stock and/or debt. The new capital structure may allow the firm more flexibility to raise additional acquisition-related financing, give the firm more flexibility to cleanly combine its stock with that of another firm, or may make it easier (or harder) for another firm to make a successful bid, depending on the goals of the firm. While each of the above mechanisms is used in a specific situation, a recapitalization may be done simply clean up a complex capital structure or to open more options to the firm to pursue its strategic goals.

CASES

Blue Jay Energy & Chemical Corporation

Eagle Corp. has made a tender offer for a further 15% of the shares of Blue Jay Energy. The price is well below what some feel is the real value of the shares. The focus of the case is on strategies to close a potential value gap in the context of a hostile takeover bid. The primary alternatives are to rely on a poison pill, spin-off, and a leveraged recapitalization. The case illustrates the use of the financial markets (synthetic white knight) to negotiate a deal.

Issues: Leverage, financial strategy, restructuring, white knight defense, hostile M&A

IPC Corporation, Singapore

The CEO of a Singapore-based computer company, with successful operations in Europe and Asia, was contemplating whether to pursue growth opportunities in the United States. The company had to decide between developing its own subsidiary; acquiring a small mail-order company based in Austin, Texas; or not entering the U.S. market at this time. If the acquisition option was pursued, there were challenges regarding fixing an appropriate value for the company, as well as integrating the U.S. subsidiary into its own global network.

Issues: Market entry mode choice, alternatives to M&A, growth strategy, international business

ATS Inc.

Ontario Teachers' Pension Plan Board's Merchant Banking Group (MBG) looked through an information memorandum on ATS Inc. (ATS). The senior management members of ATS were interested in acquiring certain noncore assets of its parent company, Aer Lingus PLC, of Dublin, Ireland. Aer Lingus made its investment in ATS following a policy of diversification from its inherently cyclical core business of air transportation. However, the board of directors of Aer Lingus had recently determined that Aer Lingus should focus primarily on its core European businesses. Consequently, Aer Lingus had agreed to sell its shares of ATS to the management and employees of ATS pursuant to a binding letter of intent being executed. The focus of the case is whether the MBG should participate in the deal and, if so, on what terms.

Issues: Alternatives to M&A, capital investment, M&A strategy, merchant banking

---

BLUE JAY ENERGY & CHEMICAL CORPORATION

Prepared by Andrew dePass and Mike Hill under the supervision of Professor Robert W. White

On February 4, 1988, the Blue Jay Energy & Chemical Corporation's (Blue Jay) President was faced with the most critical decision of his short and highly successful tenure as President and CEO. Only four days had passed since Blue Jay had learned of Calgary-based Eagle Corp.'s $14 per share tender offer for 13 million Blue Jay shares which, if successful, would raise Eagle's voting interest in Blue Jay from 9.7 per cent to 25 per cent. While Eagle's offer represented a 13 per cent premium over Blue Jay's current trading price, Blue Jay's president considered the bid "grossly inadequate" based upon his belief that despite Blue Jay's outstanding recent performance, the company's stock was undervalued on the market. This opinion was supported by the findings of Blue Jay's financial advisor who had estimated Blue Jay's net asset value to be 60 to 85 per cent higher than its trading price. With Eagle's tender offer set to take place on the Toronto, Montreal and Vancouver stock exchanges on February 22, 1988, Blue Jay's President had little time to devise a defense plan.

Given the undervalued state of Blue Jay stock and the logical strategic fit between the two companies, it was clear that Eagle's offer represented the beginning of a hostile takeover attempt. Blue Jay's financial advisor had provided Blue Jay's President with several viable alternatives which would serve to protect shareholder interests by realizing the full value of the firm. It was now up to Blue Jay's President to decide which alternative would best respond to the Eagle threat.

COMPANY BACKGROUND

Blue Jay was an integrated petrochemical and petroleum company with an established multinational presence in the production of primary, intermediate and related downstream petrochemicals through Bluebird Limited (wholly owned subsidiary), while maintaining significant operations in the oil, gas and sulphur industries in Canada through Starling Energy Limited (wholly owned subsidiary). An illustration of Blue Jay's corporate organization can be seen in Exhibit 1.

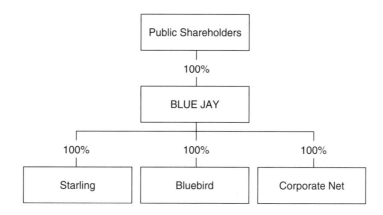

Exhibit 1   Corporate Organization

Blue Jay was established in 1971 as the investment arm of the federal government. Through the years, Blue Jay's diverse portfolio came to include interests in petrochemicals, oil and gas, office and industrial automation, venture capital, fishery products and mining. The result of this amalgamation of business interests was a corporate debt level which peaked in 1982 at $4.5 billion and a consistently poor reputation among investors as reflected in the company's stock performance.

When Blue Jay's President joined the company in 1986, he brought with him a new strategic outlook for Blue Jay:

> The strategy we adopted in mid-1986 was to refocus the Company on two core businesses—petrochemicals and petroleum—and sell the rest.

The divestiture of non-contributing assets combined with buoyant prices for the company's petrochemical commodities resulted in an impressive revitalization of the company's financial position. By the end of 1987, Blue Jay had reduced its debt by over $2 billion and had seen dramatic improvements in cash flow and earnings relative to 1986. In 1987, Blue Jay's consolidated revenue and net income were $2.868 billion and $178.1 million, respectively, whereas in 1986, revenue was $2.604 billion with a net loss of $353.8 million. This turnaround earned rave reviews from analysts who referred to Blue Jay's management as "one of the best management teams in the country."

BLUE JAY'S CORE BUSINESSES

Bluebird

Bluebird was an international petrochemical company engaged in the manufacture and sale of basic petrochemicals as well as intermediate and downstream petrochemicals including synthetic rubbers and plastics. It operated through three major divisions: the Basic Petrochemicals

Division (BPD), the Global Rubber Division (GRD) and the Plastics Division (PD).

BPD operated a major petrochemical plant in Corunna, Ontario, where it produced ethylene, propylene and butadiene. It also operated a styrene production facility at Sarnia, Ontario. BPD was the second largest Canadian producer of ethylene and styrene and the largest Canadian supplier of propylene. Forty per cent of the division's output was consumed by other Blue Jay divisions and a substantial portion of the remaining ethylene production was sold to DuPont Canada and Eagle under long-term contracts.

Bluebird, through its GRD, was the largest producer of synthetic rubber in the world. It manufactured both specialty and general-purpose rubbers, with a business strategy aimed at increasing production of high margin specialty products. GRD was the world's leading producer of bromobutyl rubber, a high margin product used in radial tires, and the leading producer of nitrile rubber. In general purpose rubbers, GRD was the world's second largest producer of polybutadiene rubber, a commodity product used in tire treads.

Bluebird's PD was a major supplier of polystyrene resin in North America, with a 15 per cent market share. This business was based principally on the former U.S. polystyrene operations of the Monsanto Company, acquired in 1986.

In addition to strong cash flow generation ($265 million in 1987 on sales of $2.4 billion), which was expected to continue as commodity prices remain high, and a tax pool in excess of $1 billion, Blue Jay's petrochemical division also had a tradition of research excellence and product development. Its R&D staff exceeded 400 persons and its budget was among the highest in Canada. As well, the division was well-positioned in an increasingly global chemical industry with plants in five countries.

Starling Energy Ltd.

Starling was a major Canadian producer of oil, gas and sulphur and was involved primarily in the exploration for and the production and marketing of conventional crude oil, natural gas liquids, natural gas and sulphur in Western Canada. Starling was one of the top 15 crude oil producers in Canada and marketed a portion of its production of crude oil and natural gas to Bluebird for use in the production of petrochemicals. Starling was also Canada's second largest producer and the largest supplier and marketer of sulphur.

In 1987, the operations of Starling were affected by the continued weakness in the world's sulphur market that resulted in reduced selling prices and volumes sold during the year. In addition, Starling substantially reduced the level of its expenditures on oil and natural gas exploration and development. However, Starling had an excellent year in expanding its asset base, replacing all of its 1987 production of oil and natural gas through successful exploration programs and enhanced recovery efforts. As well, Starling made further progress in improving its long-term financial position by reducing its debt by $397 million in 1987. In 1987, Starling's revenues and net income were $173.8 million and $15.8 million, respectively. This compares favourably to 1986 figures when revenues were $159.1 million with a net loss of $377.7 million.

A complete summary of the financial performance of Blue Jay and its component business units can be found in Exhibits 2, 3 and 4.

EAGLE CORPORATION OF ALBERTA

Eagle was a major Canadian energy corporation whose operations were conducted primarily in Canada and whose products and services were marketed on a worldwide basis. Eagle's companies, which employed over 7,100 people, were active in petrochemicals, gas transportation and marketing, petroleum, manufacturing and consulting, and research.

Eagle's bid to purchase 13 million shares of Blue Jay came several months after Eagle had initiated discussions with Blue Jay to investigate the possibility of acquiring Blue Jay's petrochemical divisions. Such an acquisition,

	1987	1986	1985
Revenue	$2,868.5	$2,604.7	$2,935.8
Expenses			
Cost & expenses before the undernoted	2,131.6	1,979.0	2,213.1
Depreciation, depletion & amortization	280.0	313.2	280.0
Write-down of property, plant & equipment	—	304.7	—
Interest on long term debt	231.8	312.2	299.7
Other interest	12.4	2.6	31.7
	2,655.8	2,911.7	2,824.5
Income (loss) before the following	212.7	(307.0)	111.3
Income taxes	(76.2)	80.9	(35.2)
Minority interest	(17.2)	(10.6)	(18.3)
Income (loss) from operations	119.3	(236.7)	57.8
Equity in earnings of discontinued operations	0.7	(70.9)	(25.8)
Non-recurring items	107.5	10.8	127.2
Net income (loss)	227.5	(296.8)	159.2
Preferred share dividends	(49.4)	(57.0)	(53.1)
Net income (loss) applicable to common shares	$178.1	$(353.8)	$106.1
Per common share			
Income (loss) from operations	$1.33	$(7.73)	$0.13
Net income (loss)	$3.39	$(9.31)	$2.86

Exhibit 2   Consolidated Statement of Income for Years Ending December 31 ($ millions)

according to Eagle's chairman, would "make us very strong in the free trade arena," since Blue Jay was one of the few Canadian chemical companies with a multinational presence. Eagle's 1986 and 1987 financial statements can be found in Exhibits 5 and 6.

BLUE JAY'S NET ASSET VALUE

Blue Jay's relationship with its financial advisor dates back to 1986 when the advisor was retained by Blue Jay to aid in the company's divestiture program. It was at this time that the advisor's analysis identified the extent to which Blue Jay's shares were underpriced. According to the financial advisor's valuation, Blue Jay's

common shares still remained significantly undervalued despite the operating improvements and strong relative share price performance that were achieved in 1986 and 1987. This valuation provided trading values for Bluebird and Starling as separate entities, based on the trading levels of comparable companies, and indicated that Blue Jay's net asset value exceeded its recent share price by approximately 60 to 85 per cent (see Exhibit 7). Thus, Blue Jay as a holding company was trading at a substantial discount to the sum of its parts. Such undervaluation clearly made the company an attractive candidate for restructuring in order to realize the value of the company's underlying assets. More importantly though, this undervaluation made Blue Jay an excellent takeover candidate.

	1987	1986	1985
Assets			
Current Assets			
Cash and short term investments	$54.1	$165.5	$70.1
Accounts receivable	510.6	521.7	699.5
Inventories	377.5	359.8	469.0
Other current assets	16.1	11.9	10.0
	958.3	1,058.9	1,249.1
Long Term Investments	245.1	658.8	997.5
Property, Plant & Equipment	3,998.7	4,065.0	4,362.3
Other Assets	243.8	458.9	514.9
	$5,445.9	$6,241.6	$7,123.8
Liabilities			
Current Liabilities			
Short term loans	$165.7	$162.1	$ 306.3
Accounts payable and accrued liabilities	452.8	368.8	410.4
Long term debt due within one year	144.0	105.4	142.7
	762.5	636.3	859.4
Long Term Debt	2,624.5	3,750.7	3,883.3
Deferred Income Taxes	396.0	254.8	314.9
Interests of Minority Shareholders	268.9	495.3	590.5
	4,051.9	5,137.1	5,648.1
Shareholders' Equity			
Capital Stock			
Preferred	628.5	721.2	765.3
Common	586.8	381.2	352.5
Retained Earnings	178.7	2.1	357.9
	1,394.0	1,104.5	1,475.7
Total Liabilities and Shareholders' Equity	$5,445.9	$6,241.6	$7,123.8

Exhibit 3   Consolidated Balance Sheet, as at December 31 ($ millions)

Bluebird

Blue Jay's financial advisor estimated that the fully distributed trading value of Blue Jay's petrochemical assets was $900 million to $1,050 million, based on a 6.5 to 7.5 P/E multiple. This multiple reflected the trading levels of comparable companies in the industry, and projected a 1988 net income of $140 million. The trading multiple, which was actually lower than industry comparables, had been adjusted by the advisor to reflect the company's relatively high financial leverage and to recognize that the company's 1988 forecasts were based on the expectation of unusually high commodity prices. Exhibit 8 shows market and financial statistics of comparable chemical companies.

Starling

Oil companies generally trade on their projected cash flow from operations, rather than

	1987	1986	1985	1984	1983
BLUE JAY CO.					
Revenues	$2,868.5	$2,604.7	$2,935.8	$2,790.3	$2,591.5
Total Assets	5,445.9	6,241.6	7,123.8	7,188.3	6,409.7
Total long term debt and redeemable					
preferred shares	3,665.3	5,054.8	5,348.3	5,484.2	5,331.8
Free cash flow from operations	378.0	186.3	228.8	164.3	102.1
Net income (loss)	227.5	(296.8)	159.2	56.2	(48.7)
Per common share	3.39	(9.31)	2.86	0.29	(2.51)
Fully diluted	2.64	(9.31)	1.99	0.29	(2.51)
BLUEBIRD CO.					
Revenues	$2,464.0	$2,047.6	$2,193.6	$2,218.4	$2,112.3
Total Assets	2,369.9	2,386.3	2,431.2	2,368.4	2,308.7
Total long term debt and redeemable					
preferred shares	1,287.3	1,637.7	1,572.1	1,365.2	1,331.3
Free cash flow from operations	301.5	89.8	17.4	26.4	11.5
Net income	167.4	18.6	(10.2)	26.3	9.0
Contribution to Blue Jay net income (loss)	172.4	13.0	(17.0)	19.2	2.1
STARLING CO.					
Revenues	$452.0	$556.6	$766.5	$628.7	$547.0
Total assets	2,922.5	3,278.2	3,748.7	3,458.3	3,180.5
Total long term debt	1,918.7	2,316.0	2,353.5	2,360.0	2,215.2
Free cash flow from operations	119.3	176.3	312.9	181.3	133.1
Net income (loss)					
Before write-down	15.8	(22.2)	85.4	26.1	21.1
Write-down of assets	—	(355.5)	—	—	—
Contribution to Blue Jay net income (loss)					
Before write-down	(17.8)	(10.7)	94.7	30.7	15.7
Write-down of property, plant and equipment	—	(218.0)	—	—	—

Exhibit 4   Summary of Operations by Division for Years Ending December 31 ($ millions, except per share amounts)

estimated earnings. Therefore, the financial advisor's estimated fully distributed trading value for Starling of $450 million to $550 million was based on a 3 to 4 multiple of 1988 projected cash flow from operations (implied by the trading levels of comparable companies; see Exhibit 9). Due to Starling's high degree of leverage, the company's common shares, in effect, represented a leveraged play on the possibility of higher oil prices. In this way, Starling's shares had a significant element of warrant value.

As well, the advisor believed that the acquisition value of Starling would be significantly lower than its trading value due to limitations on the universe of potential purchasers imposed by the Investment Canada regulation concerning the oil and gas industry. In addition, the large amount of debt that a purchaser would be required to assume would also negatively affect any acquisition price. It was the opinion of the financial advisor that these impediments to achieving full value for Starling's assets were exacerbated by the fact that Starling was part

	December 31	
	1987	**1986**
Assets		
Current Assets		
Cash and short term deposits	$74,207	$48,407
Funds on deposit	—	138,050
Receivables	405,449	300,428
Inventories	117,354	110,441
Asset held for sale	—	358,998
Prepaid expenses	8,004	6,931
	605,014	963,255
Long Term Investments	768,308	505,318
Plant Property and Equipment	4,455,908	4,282,265
Less accumulated depreciation and depletion	1,227,425	1,064,734
	3,228,483	3,217,531
Other Assets	83,943	76,848
Total	$4,685,748	$4,762,952
Liabilities and Common Shareholders' Equity		
Current Liabilities		
Bank loans	$72,163	$76,986
16 1/4% Unsecured debentures	—	138,050
Accounts payable and accrued liabilities	342,879	312,361
Income taxes payable	4,044	6,022
Dividends payable	29,813	35,186
Long term debt instalments due within one year	76,290	69,884
	525,189	638,489
Long Term Debt	2,358,941	2,390,999
Deferred Income Taxes	103,532	53,583
Deferred Gain	52,879	57,535
Interest of Others in Subsidiaries	13,502	146,731
Preferred Shares— Redeemable	328,908	826,908
Convertible Debentures	150,000	—
Common Shareholders' Equity	1,152,797	648,707
Total	$4,685,748	$4,762,952

Exhibit 5   Eagle Co. Consolidated Balance Sheet ($000)

of a larger holding company. Therefore, the highest value for Starling was thought to be in the public market. However, "maintenance of ownership" debt covenants required Blue Jay to own more than 50 per cent of Starling's common shares.

POSSIBLE REASONS FOR UNDERVALUATION

A number of Canadian research analysts had proposed reasons for Blue Jay's undervaluation:

> A troubled history has led to numerous disappointments and market scepticism towards pronouncements of a recovery.
>
> *Canadian Research*

> In the past, Blue Jay has traded at the large discount to net asset value due to (a) a diverse and complex conglomerate (i.e., 'Holding Company Discount'), (b) a large corporate debt load, (c) subsidiaries had difficult industry conditions (Starling).
>
> *Canadian Research*

> The company deserves a new group of analysts as an integrated oil or chemical company and a market revaluation to the earnings multiples such companies now receive.
>
> *First Marathon*

> The stock has been hit in the past by low commodity prices, high interest rates and a strong U.S. dollar. All these factors are now positive.
>
> *First Marathon*

Another possible reason for the undervaluation was simply that the market had not yet fully recognized the substantial improvement in Blue Jay's financial performance.

In addition, while oil companies generally trade on their projected cash flow from operations, chemical companies tend to trade on their

	Year ended December 31		
	1987	**1986**	**1985**
Revenue	$2,322,438	$2,680,966	$3,347,236
Operating Costs and Expenses			
Operating expenses	1,603,20	1,819,347	2,288,419
Depreciation and depletion	178,071	292,544	310,180
Petroleum and gas revenue tax	—	(25,620)	52,903
Loss on foreign currency translation	12,968	21,474	22,162
	1,794,240	2,107,745	2,673,664
Operating Income	528,198	573,221	673,572
Other Income (Deductions)			
Interest expense	(242,729)	(284,292)	(315,915)
Allowance for funds used during construction	2,501	3,480	3,171
Equity in earnings (losses) of affiliates	12,789	(15,204)	(7,235)
Loss on investments	(18,146)	(30,125)	—
Miscellaneous income and other (deductions)	(13,410)	(14,312)	1,921
	(258,995)	(340,453)	(318,058)
Income Before Income Taxes, Interest of Others in Income of Subsidiaries and Extraordinary Items	269,203	232,768	355,514
Income Taxes	(74,341)	(61,614)	(155,892)
Interest of Others in Income of Subsidiaries	(15,732)	(63,157)	(65,511)
Income Before Extraordinary Items	179,130	107,997	134,111
Extraordinary Items	—	(7,800)	(216,522)
Net Income (Loss)	179,130	100,197	(82,411)
Less Preferred Share Dividend Entitlement	49,296	84,071	85,511
Net Income (Loss) to Common Shareholders	$129,834	$16,136	$(167,922)
Average Common Shares Outstanding (Thousands)	185,321	134,655	128,087
Net Income (Loss) Per Common Share			
Before extraordinary items			
Basic	$0.70	$0.18	$0.38
Fully diluted	$0.67	$0.17	$0.38
After extraordinary items			
Basic	$0.70	$0.12	$(1.31)
Fully diluted	$0.67	$0.12	$(1.31)

Exhibit 6   Eagle Co. Consolidated Statement of Income ($000, except for share data)

projected earnings. Starling has strong cash flow but negative net income. To the extent that Blue Jay tends to be valued on its earnings, the $450 million to $550 million estimated trading value of Starling may not even be reflected in its parent's (Blue Jay) market valuation.

ALTERNATIVE RESPONSES TO EAGLE'S TENDER BID

Blue Jay and its advisors had devised a number of alternative plans to increase shareholder value

	Amount	Per Share
Bluebird[a]	$900 – 1,050	$11.17 – 13.04
Starling	450 – 550	5.59 – 6.83
Cash from Latex Sale[b]	370	4.59
Corporate, Net[c]	(125)	(1.55)
Illustrative Net Asset Value	$1.595 – 1.845	$19.80 – 22.91
Current Trading Value[d]	$997	$12.38

Exhibit 7   Blue Jay Net Asset Valuation: Risks and Opportunities

a. Assuming the conversion of the $300 million of 1980 Preferred Shares and 80.55 million shares outstanding.
b. Assumes $55 million of the $425 million net proceeds from the sale of the Latex business are used to pay down Bluebird debt.
c. Assumes that corporate assets equal corporate liabilities.
d. Share price as of 1/29/88 times 80.55 million shares outstanding.

by realizing the full value of Blue Jay's assets, when Eagle announced its tender bid. Given the estimated value of the company (see Exhibit 7), it was clear that Blue Jay's President could not recommend Eagle's $14 tender offer as being in the shareholders' best interests.

Blue Jay's President, officers and investment bankers reviewed a wide range of alternatives to induce shareholders to reject Eagle's bid as inadequate and to increase Blue Jay's value in the marketplace. Blue Jay had several options: do nothing and rely on federal government ownership restrictions to prevent Eagle from eventually gaining control; request its investment bank to search for a "white knight" to thwart Eagle's bid; try to increase shareholder value (push Blue Jay's stock price over the Eagle bid) by a spin-off plan; or increase shareholder value by a recapitalization plan.

Do Nothing

Blue Jay possessed an inherent "poison pill." Upon selling Blue Jay to the private sector, the Canadian government restricted the voting ownership in Blue Jay by a single shareholder to 25 per cent. If this restriction was breached, the Blue Jay board had the right to remove the holder's rights and the entitlement to dividends.

Thus, effectively, transfer of the ownership of Blue Jay could occur only through an asset sale, approved by the Blue Jay board.

While this by-law would make complete acquisition of Blue Jay by Eagle or anyone else difficult without a long fight with both Blue Jay and the federal government, Blue Jay's President did not eagerly support this alternative. Relying on the poison pill did nothing to generate value for his shareholders and did not release the true value of the firm as estimated by Blue Jay's investment bankers.

White Knight

Blue Jay's President, with the advice of the investment bank, could provide shareholders with an alternative offer by seeking a white knight—a fair and friendly competing tender offer. A friendly white knight that agreed with the valuation could enter the arena with a tender bid higher than Eagle's, thereby thwarting Eagle's "hostile" takeover attempt.

Although the extent of Blue Jay's undervaluation seemed to make the search for a white knight easy, no obvious white knight existed. Selling Blue Jay as one piece would not be easy. Blue Jay consisted of many diverse businesses. Bluebird (PetroChemicals) was a highly

	MARKET VALUE ($mm)	P/E MULTIPLE			PRICE/ CASH FLOW		MKT CAP/ EBDIT	PRICE/ BOOK	PRICE/ NET PP&E	TOTAL/ DEBT ADJUSTED BOOK CAP[5]	TOTAL/ DEBT CURRENT MARKET CAP[6]	CURRENT DIVIDEND YIELD[7]	MOODY'S/ S&P RATINGS[14]
		LTM	1987 (E)[2]	1988 (E)[2]	LTM	1987 (E)[3]							
CONGLOMERATES													
Dow Chemical	16,281	20.1 ×	17.5 ×	14.3 ×	9.0 ×	8.1 ×	8.2 ×	3.0 ×	3.0 ×	43.5%	20.2%	2.6%	A2/A
Du Pont	27,688	17.9	15.9	13.7	6.1	5.6	6.0	2.0	1.8	28.5%	16.4%	2.8%	Aa1/AA
Monsanto	6,465	14.3	14.1	12.2	6.1	5.8	5.3	1.6	2.2	35.6%	25.3%	3.4%	A1/A
Olin Corp.	1,238	17.0	16.0	12.8	6.1	5.7	6.5	1.6	1.7	36.7%	26.0%	3.1%	NR/NR
Average		17.3 ×	15.9 ×	13.2 ×	6.8 ×	6.3 ×	6.5 ×	2.1 ×	2.2 ×	36.1%	22.0%	3.0%	
INTERMEDIATES													
Rohm & Haas	3,285	20.9 ×	17.6 ×	15.1 ×	14.7 ×	12.8 ×	10.0 ×	3.2 ×	5.1 ×	27.4%	10.7%	1.7%	A1/A
Reichhold	301	16.0	16.5	12.5	9.1	8.9	6.2	1.5	1.5	37.0%	28.4%	2.0%	Baa3/NR
Dexter	638	17.1	16.6	14.6	8.9	8.5	8.4	2.4	3.7	37.5%	20.1%	2.3%	A2/A
Ethyl Corp.	3,751	19.8	19.3	16.8	12.4	11.9	9.6	4.1	6.3	36.0%	12.1%	1.3%	A2/BBB+
Witco	935	14.2	13.2	12.0	7.4	6.9	6.5	2.0	2.5	34.1%	20.9%	2.7%	A2/A
Average		17.6 ×	16.7 ×	14.2 ×	10.5 ×	9.8 ×	8.1 ×	2.6 ×	3.8 ×	34.4%	18.4%	2.0%	
BASIC PETROCHEMICALS													
National Distillers	2,130	19.8 ×	17.7 ×	12.5 ×	10.7 ×	9.7 ×	12.8 ×	2.0 ×	1.5 ×	52.6%	35.3%	3.3%	Baa2/BBB
Himount[15]	2,922	30.0	16.3	13.7	16.8	11.2	13.6	6.5	7.7	21.0%	3.9%	0.4%	NR/NR
Aristech	741	15.2	12.6	9.9	9.0	8.5	6.0	2.3	2.6	15.6%	7.5%	0.6%	NR/NR
Average		21.7 ×	15.5 ×	12.0 ×	12.1 ×	9.8 ×	10.8 ×	3.6 ×	3.9 ×	29.7%	15.6%	1.4%	
LEVERAGED FIRMS													
Union Carbide	3,799	24.0 ×	12.8 ×	9.7 ×	4.3 ×	3.6 ×	6.2 ×	3.5 ×	0.9 ×	78.3%	50.7%	5.0%	Baa3/BB+
FMC[11]	1,745	11.5	18.9	13.7	4.2	4.7	2.3	NM	1.3	136.9%	50.3%	0.0%	Ba2/BB
Vista[12]	495	12.2	14.3	10.7	5.1	5.2	5.0	4.0	1.8	65.3%	31.9%	0.0%	NR/NR
Georgia Gulf	500	12.4	11.8	N/A	6.8	6.4	5.7	6.4	4.2	56.5%	16.9%	0.0%	NR/NR
Average		15.0 ×	14.5 ×	11.4 ×	5.1 ×	5.0 ×	4.8 ×	4.6 ×	2.0 ×	84.2%	37.4%	5.0%	

Exhibit 8   Market and Financial Statistics of Selected Chemical Companies (1) (US$, except Canadian firms)

(Continued)

	MARKET VALUE ($mm)	P/E MULTIPLE			PRICE/ CASH FLOW		MKT CAP/ EBDIT	PRICE/ BOOK	PRICE/ NET PP&E	TOTAL/ DEBT ADJUSTED BOOK CAP[5]	TOTAL/ DEBT CURRENT MARKET CAP[6]	CURRENT DIVIDEND YIELD[7]	MOODY'S/ S&P RATINGS[14]
		LTM	1987 (E)[2]	1988 (E)[2]	LTM	1987 (E)[3]							
CANADIAN FIRMS[8,9]													
Celanese Canada	297	16.5 ×	14.1 ×	12.5 ×	5.6 ×	5.1 ×	5.4 ×	2.0 ×	2.5 ×	0.0%	0.0%	4.6%	NR/NR
C-I-L	404	26.9	23.0	21.3	6.4	5.9	5.6	0.7	0.7	32.4%	39.1%	1.4%	A+(low)/A
DuPont Canada[4]	902	15.0	13.5	11.8	7.4	4.5	6.1	2.6	3.0	34.2%	16.8%	1.1%	A/BBB(high)
Union Carbide Canada	344	21.5	18.0	14.3	6.6	6.0	8.0	1.1	1.3	44.7%	41.8%	1.2%	A(low)/BBB
Eagle	1,308	24.2	15.9	11.7	2.3	2.0	4.9	0.9	0.4	65.7%	68.3%	4.6%	A(low)/ BBB(high)
Average		20.8 ×	16.9 ×	14.3 ×	5.7 ×	4.7 ×	6.0 ×	1.5 ×	1.6 ×	35.4%	33.2%	2.6%	
INDICES													
S&P Chemicals[10]	65,982	18.5 ×	16.0 ×										
TSE 300[16]	111,068	21.0	20.8										
S&P 400[13]	1,740,077	23.1	19.6	17.5									

Exhibit 8 (Continued)

1. All multiples are based on closing prices on 6/16/87, current shares outstanding, and financial data for the latest twelve months ended 3/31/87, except where noted.
2. IBES earnings estimate as of 5/14/87.
3. Estimated 1987 Cash Flow based on IBES earnings estimate and seven per cent growth of 1986 Non-cash items.
4. Adjusted for two-for-one stock split effective 5/15/87.
5. Sum of long term debt, short term debt and minority interest divided by the sum of long term debt, short term debt, minority interest shareholders' equity (including preferred stock).
6. Sum of long-term debt, short term debt and minority interest divided by current market capitalization (market value plus total debt).
7. Dividend Yield from RT-Quotes as of 6/11/87.
8. Data in Canadian dollars.
9. 1989 Earnings and Cash Flow multiples based on the average of earnings estimates by Midland Doherty and Richardson Greenshields.
10. Index multiples based on LTM earnings ended 3/31/87 from S&P Analyst Handbook, April 1987, and closing price on 6/16/87.
11. FMC underwent major recapitalization in 1986 and completed 5.667 to 1 stock split on 5/28/86.
12. Fiscal year ending 9/30.
13. Based on IBES earnings estimates as of 5/14/87.
14. Canadian credit ratings by CBRS/DBRS.
15. Fiscal year ending 10/31.
16. Based on Canadian Corporate Earnings Forecasts as of 5/12/87.

Exhibit 9   Market and Financial Statistics for Selected Oil Companies (1) (data through 3/31/87)

	MARKET VALUE ($mm)	P/E MULTIPLE LTM	P/E MULTIPLE 1987 (E)[2]	P/E MULTIPLE 1988 (E)[3]	PRICE/CASH FLOW LTM	PRICE/CASH FLOW 1987 (E)[4]	MKT CAP/EBDIT	PRICE/BOOK	PRICE/NET PP&E	TOTAL/DEBT ADJUSTED BOOK CAP[5]	TOTAL/DEBT CURRENT MARKET CAP[6]	CURRENT DIVIDEND YIELD[7]	MOODY'S/S&P RATINGS[8]
CANADIAN INTEGRATED OILS (w/Chemicals)[2]													
Imperial Oil	11,294	24.6×	18.0×	15.2×	10.6×	6.3×	6.3×	2.2×	1.9×	16.5%	8.3%	2.3%	Aa2/AA+
Shell Oil	3,445	17.8	25.3	20.3	4.7	7.4	5.7	1.3	1.0	23.7%	19.7%	1.5%	A1/AA
Texaco Canada	4,319	15.8	12.6	9.4	10.0	8.1	6.7	1.8	2.2	3.5%	2.0%	3.4%	A++/AA
Ultramar (7)	1,511	NM	—	—	2.9	—	7.1	1.0	0.6	56.6%	55.7%	8.3%	NR/NR
Average		19.4×	18.6×	15.0×	7.0×	7.3×	6.5×	1.6×	1.4×	25.1%	21.4%	3.9%	
US INTEGRATED OILS[9]													
Amoco	22,317	33.0×	20.6×	16.6×	6.5×	5.5×	6.0×	2.0×	1.2×	25.1%	14.6%	3.8%	Aaa/AAA
Amerada Hess	3,065	14.1	13.5	11.5	5.1	4.8	5.1	1.4	0.9	36.8%	30.1%	0.4%	Ba3/B
Phillips Petroleum	3,767	20.4	22.6	13.1	3.4	3.3	4.2	2.3	0.4	78.9%	62.2%	3.6%	Ba1/BB
Unocal	4,539	27.2	23.5	16.7	3.0	2.7	5.6	2.6	0.6	74.8%	53.1%	2.6%	Baa3/NR
Kerr-McGee	1,753	83.1	31.0	21.1	4.2	3.6	5.8	1.3	0.8	37.6%	31.6%	3.0%	A3/A
Average		23.7×	22.2×	15.8×	4.4×	4.0×	5.4×	1.9×	0.8×	50.6%	38.3%	2.7%	
CAN. EXPLOR. & PROD[2]													
Pan Canadian Petroleum	4,122	28.7×	21.2×	15.5×	13.4×	10.8×	10.3×	3.2×	2.2×	6.3%	2.1%	1.7%	A++/AA
Alberta Energy	1,084	19.2	24.4	15.2	5.2	5.4	7.3	2.0	0.6	59.3%	42.0%	1.4%	A(l)/BBB(h)
Norcen Energy	689	12.4	17.8	10.3	3.1	5.6	5.8	1.1	0.4				
Canadian Occidental[10]	1,261	28.1	21.9	16.1	6.5	5.8	6.9	1.9	1.1	23.3%	13.8%	1.7%	A_/A
BP Canada	1,052	67.9	26.9	13.3	12.1	3.7	18.6	2.4	2.6	22.2%	10.7%	1.1%	NR/NR
Average		22.1×	22.4×	14.1×	8.1×	6.3×	7.6×	2.1×	1.4×	35.2%	26.0%	1.6%	
STARLING CO.	704	NM	NM	NM	4.8×	5.3×	9.6×	1.4×	0.3×	81.8%	76.1%	1.1%	NR/NR

1. All multiples based on closing prices on 6/16/87, current shares outstanding, and financial data for the latest 12 months ended 3/31/87.
2. Data in Canadian dollars, except where noted.
3. IBES earnings estimates as of 5/14/87.
4. Estimated by Canadian Corporate Earnings Forecasts as of 5/12/87.
5. Sum of long term debt, short term debt and minority interest divided by the sum of long term debt, short term debt, minority interest shareholders' equity (including preferred stock).
6. Sum of long-term debt, short-term debt and minority interest divided by current market capitalization (market value plus total debt).
7. Data through 12/31/86.
8. Ratings for Texaco Canada and all Canadian E & P companies are by CBRS and DBRS.
9. Data in U.S. dollars.
10. Adjusted to normalize $431.2 million writedown in 1987.

attractive acquisition candidate. However, the highly leveraged Starling was far less attractive. In addition, restrictions by Investment Canada on the sale of Canadian Oil & Gas interests (Starling) added to the potential difficulty. Blue Jay's President and investment bank were confident that a white knight could eventually be found; the problem was one of timing. Blue Jay was not sure if an acceptable white knight could be found and in place before the February 22 deadline.

Spin-Off Alternative

The spin-off alternative was designed by Blue Jay's investment bank to create value for Blue Jay shareholders by making Bluebird (PetroChemicals) and Starling separate publicly traded companies, thereby reducing the "holding company" discount. Bluebird would trade on the basis of its projected net income, which would not be reduced by consolidation with Starling's losses. On the other hand, Starling would trade on the basis of its projected cash flow.

In the spin-off alternative, Blue Jay would distribute its Bluebird (PetroChemicals) shares directly to its shareholders, leaving Starling as its remaining asset. The alternative form of spin-off (i.e., distributing Starling) was made impossible because of Starling debt covenants that required that Blue Jay retain control. The spin-off would also involve a series of cash transfers within the company. Prior to the spin-off, $55 million of the $425 million of proceeds from the sale of Blue Jay's latex business (sold to BASF as part of Blue Jay's earlier divestiture program) would be used to pay down Bluebird's long term debt, while the remaining $370 million would be dividended up to Blue Jay.

In addition, some of Blue Jay's corporate obligations would need to be eliminated, since Starling's projected cash flows would be insufficient to service such obligations. Therefore, $125 million of 1983 Preferred Shares (Blue Jay) would be tendered for retirement with $135 million of the $370 million dividended up to Blue Jay. In addition, $300 million of Blue Jay's 1980

Preferred Shares would be called for conversion into additional Blue Jay shares.

The remaining $235 million of net proceeds from the sale of the latex business would be distributed to Blue Jay's shareholders as a special one-time cash payment. Blue Jay's investment banker's total estimated initial value for this alternative was $16 to $20 per share. Exhibit 10 shows the transaction diagram for the spin-off alternative. Exhibit 11 provides a pro forma financial impact of the transaction.

The Recapitalization (Recap) Alternative

The recap alternative was designed to create value for Blue Jay's shareholders by making Starling a publicly traded company, and by highlighting the substantial debt capacity of Bluebird. Blue Jay would be viewed as a highly leveraged petrochemical company with a significant investment in the oil company. Such recapitalized companies tend to trade primarily on the basis of cash flow rather than earnings.

Under the recap, Blue Jay would distribute to shareholders the following:

- Forty-nine per cent of its shares in Starling, this percentage being limited by Starling debt covenants that require Blue Jay to retain control of Starling (one share of Starling per Blue Jay share).
- A one-time cash payment of $370 million, funded by the $425 million of net proceeds from the sale of Blue Jay's Latex business.
- Proceeds from $130 million of Floating Rate Notes, with a five-year maturity.
- Proceeds from $240 million of zero coupon preferred shares (i.e., deferred preferreds) of Blue Jay. This preferred stock, due in 1993, was intended to further leverage Blue Jay's common stock without requiring cash payments for the first five years.

According to the analysis of Blue Jay's investment banker, the total value of this recapitalization to Blue Jay shareholders would fall between $17 and $20.50 per share. Exhibit 12 shows a transaction diagram for the recapitalization alternative.

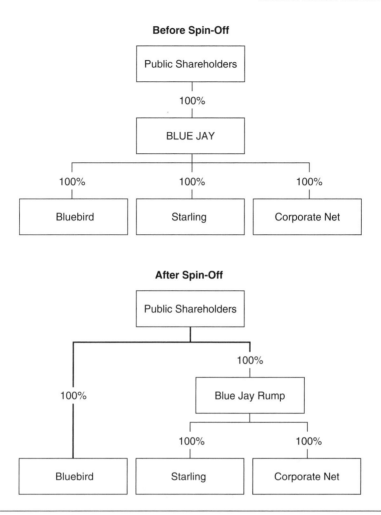

Exhibit 10   Transaction Diagram for Spin-Off Alternative

Exhibit 13 presents the pro forma financial impact of the alternative.

THE DECISION

As Blue Jay's President examined his alternatives in the face of Eagle's $14 tender offer for 25 per cent of Blue Jay, he knew that he had only a day or two to choose the most appropriate one.

Blue Jay's President was convinced of Blue Jay's true value and was determined to realize that value for Blue Jay's shareholders. However, he was concerned that the Canadian marketplace might be slow to react to either the spin-off or recapitalization alternatives. While Blue Jay's investment bank had successfully executed several of these complex restructurings in the United States, Blue Jay would be the first Canadian firm to restructure in this manner.

	Actual 11/30/87	Adjust 11/30/87		Blue Jay Rump		Pro Forma 11/30/87 Bluebird	
		Amount	%	Amount	%	Amount	%
Long Term Debt	$2,717	$2,717	58%	$2,042(3)	77%	$693(8)	41%
Minority Interest	450	268(1)	0	0	0	268	16
1980 Preferred	300	300	6	0(4)	0	0	0
1983 Preferred	125	125	3	0(5)	0	0	0
1985 Preferred	205	205	4	0(6)	0	205	12
Common Equity	789	1,069(2)	23	596(7)	23	540(9)	31
Total Capitalization	$4,586	$4,684	100%	$2,638	100%	$1,706	100%
Coupon Bearing Securities/Capitalization(10)	83%	77%	—	77%	—	68%	—

Exhibit 11   Pro Forma Financial Impact of Transaction Spin-Off Alternative (Cdn$ millions)

1. Adjusted for the defeasance of $281 million Bluebird Third Preferred Shares.
2. Adjusted for $280 million net gain on the sale of the Latex business. Does not adjust for any gain on defeasance of Third Preferred.
3. Equal to Starling Debt and Corporate Debt before transaction.
4. Assumed to be converted into common.
5. Assumed to be repaid with Latex proceeds.
6. May actually exist on balance sheet but would be offset by matching asset.
7. Equal to Adjusted Common Equity plus $300 million additional equity from conversion of 1980 Preferred Shares, minus Cash Dividend; where Bluebird basis equals $630 million reported basis, plus $280 million gain, minus $370 million dividend; and cash dividend equals $233 million. Assumed no taxes incurred in transaction.
8. Equal to Bluebird long term debt minus $55 million assumed to be repaid.
9. Equity equals basis as calculated in Note 7.
10. Coupon Bearing Securities includes Long Term Debt, Minority Interest, and all Preferred Shares.

Before Recapitalization

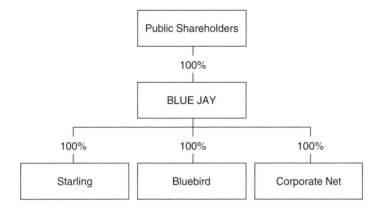

After Recapitalization

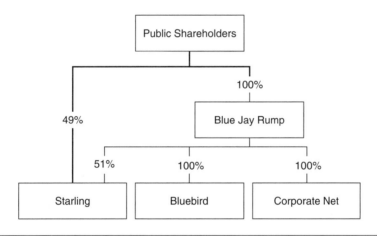

Exhibit 12   Transaction Diagram for Recapitalization Alternative

	Actual 11/30/87	Adjust 11/30/87		Blue Jay Rump[3]		Pro Forma 11/30/87 Bluebird	
		Amount	%	Amount	%	Amount	%
Total Debt	$2,717	$2,717	58%	$2,662[4]	58%	$2,662	58%
New Senior Note	0	0	0	130	3	130	3
Minority Interest	450	268[1]	6	573[5]	13	573	12
Deferred Preferred Security	0	0	0	240	5	240	5
1980 Preferred	300	300	6	0[6]	0	0	0
1983 Preferred	125	125	3	125	3	125	3
1985 Preferred	205	205	4	205	4	205	4
Common Equity	789	1,069[2]	23	629[7]	14	700	15
Total Capitalization	$4,586	$4,684	100%	$4,564	100%	$4,635	100%
Coupon Bearing Securities/Capitalization[8]	83%	77%	—	86%	—	85%	—

Exhibit 13   Pro Forma Financial Impact of Transaction Recapitalization Alternative (Cdn$ millions)

1. Adjusted for the defeasance of $271 million Bluebird Third Preferred Shares.
2. Adjusted for $280 million net gain on the sale of the Latex business.
3. Assumes that Starling will be consolidated on financial statements.
4. Adjusted for $55 million of debt paid down with proceeds of Latex sale.
5. Adjusted for $305 million of Starling Minority Interest (49 per cent of $621.6 million basis).
6. Assumed to be converted into common.
7. Equal to Adjusted Common Equity plus $300 million from conversion of 1980 Preferred Shares, minus $370 million Cash distribution, $240 million Warrant distribution, and $130 million Senior Note Distribution.
8. Coupon Bearing Securities includes Long Term Debt, Minority Interest, Notes, Warrant Security and all Preferred Shares.

IPC CORPORATION, SINGAPORE

*Prepared by Charles Dhanaraj under the supervision of
Professors Paul Beamish and Chow Hou Wee*

In the first week of December 1992, Patrick Ngiam,[1] Chairman and CEO of IPC Corporation, Singapore, was considering the company's strategy for the North American market. He had to give his final decision to the Board of Directors scheduled to meet that day. Leading among the options was a proposal to acquire a computer mail order business, Austin Computer Systems Ltd., based in Austin, Texas. An offer had to be finalized within that week. Patrick did not want to rule out the other option of developing IPC's own subsidiary in the United States. The board was also scheduled to review the company's plans to list the company on the Singapore Stock Exchange in the next six months.

COMPANY HISTORY

IPC was incorporated on May 8, 1985 under the name of "Essex Electric Pte. Ltd." to manufacture and market personal computers (PCs). Patrick Ngiam, along with his brother Benjamin Ngiam, started the company soon after completing their degrees in Electrical Engineering at the University of Essex. IPC adopted its present name in March 1991, to symbolize "intelligent personal computers," and much later "integrated processors and communications." The company's initial focus was on manufacturing printed circuit boards for multinational companies. Later, it diversified into board assembly on a contract manufacturing basis. After researching the European markets, Essex introduced its own IPC line of PCs in 1985. Since the initial launch of its first IBM-compatible PC, the IPC XT, the company had grown aggressively. An overview

of the major milestones of IPC is shown in Exhibit 1.

The financial performance of the company was considered impressive, with a strong and steady growth in sales volume and profitability. Sales in 1992 were estimated at S$275 million and the profit after tax was estimated to be about S$42 million (See Exhibit 2).

PRODUCTS

IPC's product lines were broadly grouped into three product groups: general purpose computers (GPC), consumer computing products (CCP) and application specific products (ASP). The GPC group comprised desktop PCs including the IPC Dynasty series, and sales of semi-knocked-down kits to other PC assemblers, both locally and abroad, who assembled and sold the PCs under their own private brands. The CCP group included the portable PCs (notebook and laptop computers) of which the IPC Porta series computers were the dominant products. The ASP group comprised primarily the point-of-sale (POS) terminals for chain stores, specialty stores, supermarkets, general retail stores, and the hospitality industry. Contract manufacturing of POS terminals for other overseas manufacturers was included under this category. Besides these product groups, the company also carried out trading and distribution of computer related components, parts and sub-systems of other manufacturers. The overall contribution of these product groups to the company's sales and profitability is shown in Exhibit 3.

Year	Major Events
1985	— Incorporated in Singapore as Essex Electric Ltd. — Launched its first 8088 (XT) computer
1986	— First R&D department was set up in Singapore. — Entered the European market, appointing its first distributors in The Netherlands and Sweden.
1987	— Appointed Systec S.A. (currently known as IPC France) as distributor in France.
1988	— Launched the IPC Point-of-Sale terminal.
1989	— Launched its first portable PC, the IPC Portadesk 386SX. — Awarded pioneer status by the Economic Development Board (EDB) with a five-year tax-free holiday. (This was further extended by another three years in 1993 to December 31 1996.)
1990	— Incorporated IPC Europa GmbH in Germany. Invested in a highly integrated and automated computer assembly and burn-in production facility at a cost of approximately S$1.1 million in October.
1991	— Introduced its first notebook and also its first RISC-based multi-processor server. Change of corporate name to IPC Corporation (Pte.) Ltd., together with a change of a new IPC logo.
1992	— Set up IPC Austria GmbH to penetrate the Austrian, Central and East European market. — Established a China marketing office in Beijing to tap the Chinese market. — Plans initiated for the public offering of the company.

Exhibit 1   IPC Corporation—Milestones 1985–1992

	1988	1989	1990[2]	1990a	1991	1992
Turnover	30,119	54,947	67,676	54,012	183,567	274,496
Operating Profit	246	922	6,412	6,988	14,381	42,573
Profit after tax & extraordinary items	174	860	6,390	6,953	13,028	41,526
Fixed Assets	195	849	1,160	2,041	3,492	11,124
Current Assets	6,626	9,637	15,706	18,456	25,554	99,852
Current Liabilities	6,468	9,125	9,135	10,040	13,879	53,069
Long-term Liabilities	31	179	220	505	188	115
Net Tangible Assets	322	1,182	7,972	14,929	27,458	49,384

Exhibit 2   Financial Highlights 1988–1992 (all figures in thousands Singapore Dollars)[1]

1. Average exchange rates for Singapore Dollars (units per US$) were 2.00 in 1988, 1.94 in 1989, 1.90 in 1990, 1.74 in 1991 and 1.63 in 1992.
2. The financial year changed from July-June to January-December in 1991. Figures for the six months ending on December 31, 1990 are given separately under column titled 1990a. This applies to Exhibits 2, 3, and 4.

	1988	1989	1990	1990a	1991	1992
Sales Contribution						
GPC	100.0	100.0	86.6	83.2	82.6	76.0
CCP	—	—	0.2	1.4	2.9	8.9
ASP	—	—	13.2	15.4	10.4	8.9
Distribution	—	—	—	—	4.1	6.2
Profit Contribution						
GPC	100.0	100.0	60.0	68.5	55.9	69.3
CCP	—	—	0.2	1.1	4.3	8.5
ASP	—	—	39.8	30.4	38.8	21.2

Exhibit 3   IPC Corporation—Product Group Analysis (as % of total)

OPERATIONS MANAGEMENT

IPC had close control over the management of its operations. Realizing that computer-related products had a relatively high rate of obsolescence compared with other durable goods, the company followed a policy of minimal inventory. IPC's strategic alliances with its vendors played an important role in the maintenance of its inventory policy. In order to have an optimal level of inventory of parts and components, IPC worked with vendors to replenish its stocks on a weekly basis for most of its high value items. IPC also implemented a well-managed system of coordinating its sales, purchasing and production functions whereby orders for high value items were made only when orders were received from its customers, in a manner similar to the "just-in-time" concept. The production department would then schedule its operations so that assembly could commence the moment the required parts and components were received from IPC's vendors. IPC salvaged obsolete stocks by selling them to less industrialized countries and sometimes converting them into service parts/components.

THE GLOBALIZATION PROGRAM

Since inception, the Ngiams had placed a strong emphasis on international markets rather than the domestic market. Singapore had a number of computer manufacturers: multinational companies such as IBM, Digital, Hewlett-Packard, and Compaq, as well as local companies such as GES (Datamini), and Aztech. There were also strong niche players such as Creative Technology which focused exclusively on the multimedia components (sound cards, etc.) market. Patrick recalled the beginning of the company:

> Singapore is a very small country and the domestic market is very small. We are not a protectionist country and the competition is very stiff. If you want to compete, you need economies of scale and the only way we could get that is to go beyond our local market. We need to go beyond Asia even. So we had to look to either the United States or Europe. We chose Europe to begin with.

> We knew right from the beginning that we had to have a broader market to survive. In the mid-1980s, Asia was not the most attractive market for the IT products. The market was fairly small, and the "big boys" had a strong hold.

The European Market

IPC entered Europe first by appointing distributors in The Netherlands and Sweden in 1986. Later it appointed Systec S.A. as a distributor in France. With excellent progress in partnership, Systec S.A. was renamed IPC France. Plans were underway in 1992 to acquire 50 per cent of the French company and position IPC France as the European headquarters for IPC's products.

IPC introduced the IPC POS terminal and a new 386SX desktop PC to the European market in March 1989, and also started to mass produce the IPC POS terminals in April 1989. In describing the reason for IPC choosing Europe as the first market for these products, Patrick said:

> Europe, to a large extent, resembles Asia with a number of small countries each with its own language and culture and unique business environment. Most of the larger countries have 60 to 65 million people, large enough to create their own industry but not big enough when the industry is maturing. So you can go in and be profitable but you need to expand beyond any given market.
>
> The United States is a homogenous, consumer-oriented market, and highly competitive. So you need to have either a "fantastic" product, no matter how small you are, to cater to a specific niche, or you need to have a sizable organization to compete. Our product at that time was just "an alternative product" to IBM PC and so our advantage did not lie in going to the United States.

Acceptance of IPC's products continued to grow in Europe, and in October 1989, a survey conducted by Datapro and published in *01 Informatique,* a French magazine, ranked IPC second among all commonly used PCs in France. Acceptance of IPC's products in Europe was given a further boost when IPC was placed in the No. 2 position, ahead of established brands such as Dell and Hewlett Packard, in terms of overall user satisfaction in a survey of approximately 1,800 French PC users, 65 per cent of whom were technical professionals. IPC was rated the highest in terms of price/performance ratio, and was rated highly for its before and after sales service, proving the effectiveness of IPC France as IPC's distributor in France.

To further expand and consolidate its distribution network in Europe, IPC set up a wholly owned subsidiary, IPC Austria, in June 1992 to cater to the Austrian and Central and East European markets. Essex Electric Holdings, B.V., the Netherlands also wholly owned, and its wholly owned subsidiary Essex Electric B.V., were set up in September 1992 to cater to the Dutch market. A 51 per cent owned joint-venture, IPC Czechoslovakia, was likewise set up in the Czech Republic in September 1992. European revenues went from S$17 million in 1988 to S$112 million in 1992. Patrick Ngiam, in commenting on IPC's success in the European market, noted:

> We entered Europe at the time when the Taiwanese were offering a lot of cheap products for they needed to get a critical mass for their PC industry. We believed we had a strong business concept and a clear strategy for gaining market leadership and we went around talking to a number of potential partners in Europe to build our business and we found partners who shared our vision for the long term. Unlike the short-term philosophy of our Taiwanese competitors we focused on cultivating the brand name. We were able to achieve a strong product differentiation which helped us to earn premium prices. We were able to invest the profits in manufacturing facilities to upgrade the quality even further. That has been our strategy all through and that probably was a reason for our success in the global market. Our partners liked to do business with us for they saw something of a unique value we were bringing to the market place.

Asia Pacific Market

IPC also prepared itself for aggressive growth in Asia after having successfully established itself in Europe. In June 1991, IPC Malaysia was incorporated as a wholly owned subsidiary of IPC Singapore to distribute IPC products in Malaysia. The lifetime warranty concept was introduced in Singapore to build up a high-quality image for IPC's products. Between December 1991 and January 1992, IPC also invested in three of its resellers in Singapore, the IPC Centres. In January 1992, IPC was awarded the 1991 Enterprise Award of the Business Times-DHL Singapore Business Awards for its success in penetrating overseas markets for computer products. IPC was awarded the Singapore Design Award 1992 at the Third International Design

Forum for the IPC Porta-PC 386SLP3 notebook which was introduced later that year.

IPC decided to make a concerted effort to penetrate the Chinese market in 1991, and set up a Beijing representative office in 1992 and carried out an aggressive marketing campaign through a series of advertisements in several major Chinese newspapers and computer journals to promote its products. To further build IPC's name, a seminar was organized in Zhuhai in late 1992 for major resellers throughout the main cities of China, together with some of IPC's major vendors. The total Asia Pacific sales grew from S$12 million in 1988 to S$140 million in 1992.

The North American Market

IPC's initial entry into the North American market came when the company participated in the Comdex Fall '88 exhibition in the United States in October 1988, and launched the prototype of the IPC POS terminal. The IPC point-of-sale (POS) terminal utilized integrated open architecture which combined the transaction

speed of electronic cash registers ("ECR") with the data processing capability of a computer. In April 1989, seeing the interest of the American consumers, IPC set up IPC America, a wholly-owned subsidiary located in Delaware. The small sales office employed three sales people and was mainly responsible for the sales and distribution of the POS terminals throughout the United States. Despite significant efforts, the North American sales were not as strong as expected (see Exhibit 4). Established brands such as NCR and AT&T had a strong hold on the POS market, and had superior products in the market.

ACQUISITION OPPORTUNITY
AND CORPORATE OBJECTIVES

Patrick, despite the strong growth in Asia and the success in Europe, continued to investigate opportunities for a significant presence in the United States. In 1990, he even suggested to

	1988	1989	1990	1990a	1991	1992
Singapore	23.5	20.8	13.3	19.3	27.8	25.6
Other ASEAN countries	1.0	0.6	4.0	10.4	7.9	5.0
China, Hong Kong, Taiwan	3.6	1.9	2.3	0.4	12.1	16.3
Japan & Korea	—	—	0.4	0.8	0.5	0.8
Other Asia Pacific	11.7	17.6	5.5	4.2	3.6	1.9
France	25.2	31.5	30.3	25.6	13.9	25.9
Other European Countries	30.8	26.0	39.9	33.6	28.4	18.5
North America	0.1	0.5	1.7	3.2	2.2	3.2
Middle East	2.2	0.3	1.6	2.1	2.8	2.2
South Africa	1.9	0.8	1.0	0.4	0.8	0.6
Total	100.0	100.0	100.0	100.0	100.0	100.0

Exhibit 4   Geographic Distribution of Sales (percentage of total sales)

his board that the company should seriously consider moving the company's headquarters to the United States. Despite an interest in the U.S. market, there was a lot of resistance to such a move from the board.

Board of Directors

IPC Corporation was a family-controlled company. The board of directors was fully made up of family members. Patrick Ngiam, 38 years old, was the central figure as the Chairman and Chief Executive Officer of the company, with his brother Benjamin Ngiam (36) supporting him closely in the marketing and operations area. Benjamin was also responsible for the day-to-day operations as the Managing Director of the company. Ms. Lauw Hui Kian, Patrick's spouse, was the Administration and Finance Director, and Patrick's two other younger brothers, Bernard (32) and Alfred (29), were in charge of the sales/marketing and engineering areas, respectively. With the company's rapid growth and increasing opportunities around the globe, the company decided to go for a public listing of 20 per cent of its equity in 1993.

The company was hoping to raise about S$150 million through the initial public offering, part of which would be used for financing the working capital requirements and the rest of which would be used for accelerating the company's growth through acquisitions. The overall mission of the company was to become a S$5 billion company by the year 2000 AD. The North American market was of great interest to the company. Patrick summarized his position as follows:

> The United States is a tough market to crack. But we look at it as a "land of technology," where many of the innovations originate. Being in the United States would help us to be at the leading edge in terms of technology. I wanted a direct link to what is happening.

> Despite the tough competition and the large number of players, the market is also large and we want to take advantage of that. We really would like to have one third of our revenues come from the United States.

> In the IT industry, it is never too late to enter a market. Maybe, you can be "too early" an entry . . .

The U.S. market (including Canada) was indeed the largest market for PC sales (see Exhibit 5) and showed a continued growth. Many Asian companies were entering the U.S.

Region	1991	1992	1993 (Expected)	Average Growth Rate (%)
Western Europe	17.517	18.872	17.999	2%
United States and Canada	26.666	28.262	32.502	10%
Japan	4.586	4.750	5.885	13%
Asia Pacific	4.573	5.219	7.052	24%
Rest of World	4.236	6.991	10.255	56%
Total	57.579	64.095	73.694	13%

Exhibit 5   Worldwide PC Market (revenues in billions of US$)

Source: Dataquest.

market to enhance their product image as well as to take advantage of the large market and the latest technology.

Market Entry Options

After almost two years, just at the time when the company was reconsidering its options for the United States, it was informed of the availability of a computer mail-order business, Austin Computer Systems Ltd., in Austin, Texas. Austin Computer Systems Ltd. seemed to present the ideal fit with what Patrick had been looking for in an acquisition: a small company, with established technology, and distribution channels, and skilled manpower.

Some of the board members had suggested developing IPC's own subsidiary, either by using its existing unit, IPC America, or by starting a new venture in the Bay area (California) in the United States. With aggressive marketing such a unit could contribute substantially to the company's sales within three to five years. Patrick had gathered some information on the status of the PC industry in the United States, as well as the details of Austin.

THE PC INDUSTRY IN THE UNITED STATES

The PC industry had evolved rapidly since the invention of the microprocessor in the early 1970s. It was estimated that in 1992, about 35 per cent of U.S. households had a computer at home. The computer industry, which encompassed a broad range of activities, was approaching the US$300 billion mark or about five per cent of the GNP, and the estimates for the year 2000 were at US$700 billion. PC products comprising desktops, laptops and notebooks were about one-tenth of the total industry. High growth was the norm in the computer industry. Even though the overall industry was growing at 10 per cent per

year, there were segments such as the workstation and notebook computer segments which were growing 50 to 100 per cent per year. Companies such as Compaq were pursuing aggressive strategies to outdo the industry leaders such as IBM. Most of the top global players in the industry were U.S. multinational companies (see Exhibit 6).

	Revenues (US$ bil.)	Group Share (%)
IBM	5.25	29.2
Apple	4.38	24.4
NEC	2.04	11.4
Compaq	1.68	9.3
Olivetti	1.17	6.5
Groupe Bull	0.91	5.1
Commodore	0.74	4.1
Packard Bell	0.70	3.9
Tandy	0.58	3.2
Dell	0.40	2.2
DEC	0.12	0.7

Exhibit 6   Top Ten Players in the Global Desktop PC Market (1991)

Source: Dataquest.

Mail Order Business

The mail-order business was a growing segment within the computer industry. In 1992, mail-order computers accounted for an estimated 14 per cent of the US$29 billion-a-year market for personal computers and peripherals in the United States (see Exhibit 7). According to a Chicago-based catalog consultant, computer suppliers led the mail-order business in sales

	1992	1995 (forecast)
Traditional resellers	47.0%	27.0%
Mass merchandisers	12.0	25.0
VARs/systems integrators	20.0	25.0
Mail-order/direct marketers	14.0	13.0
Computer Superstores	3.0	10.0

Exhibit 7   PC Sales by Channel Distribution in the United States

Source: Market Share Reporter.

growth. The attractions of mail order were quite powerful and primarily due to the price. Mail-order operators did not have the expense of running stores, and their huge volumes guaranteed some of the best prices from the component manufacturers on whom they relied. As a result, prices could run 30 per cent below the list price on store-marketed major brands. For customers of reputable dealers, helpful salespeople, fast deliveries, and a policy of hassle-free returns were as much a part of the attraction of mail order as low price. For example, Dell Computer Corp., one of the pioneers in the computer mail-order business, recorded US$546 million in sales in 1990 and also topped J.D. Power & Associates' first PC customer satisfaction survey in the same year.

Dell Computer Corp. symbolized the best of the mail-order business. Sales in 1992 were expected to be near US$2 billion. Earnings during the previous 12 quarters had never dipped below five per cent. Dell contended that the company had the most efficient and effective means of distributing and supporting PCs. Since Dell Computer sold almost all of its products directly, it could maintain lower prices by eliminating dealer and distributor profit margins. User problems were resolved over the telephone or through

Xerox Corp., which was contracted to provide field service. Other leading competitors were Gateway, which was aggressively expanding in the mail-order business, and some small companies such as Austin Computer Systems Ltd., and Zeos International Inc.

AUSTIN COMPUTER SYSTEMS

Austin Computer Systems Ltd. (ACS) was one of the smaller companies in the mail order business but with a good reputation for customer service and brand recognition. The company was started by Robert Diwan in 1984, when he moved to the United States from Saudi Arabia. Diwan was born in Lebanon, and graduated from the American University of Beirut with a degree in business administration. Prior to starting Austin, Diwan was the financial controller of Midmac in Saudi Arabia.

Initially, the company focused on retailing personal computers as a reseller of IBM compatibles and peripherals. In 1987, when IBM introduced the PS model with a closed architecture, the market for add-ons slowed down. Diwan saw the phenomenal success of Dell in the mail-order business, and took to the direct channel, manufacturing PCs and selling them direct nationwide. From the beginning, Diwan focused on superior marketing to keep customers informed and also satisfied. Initial efforts were directed at a direct marketing campaign with magazine advertisements and an 800 number access. In 1988, ACS worked out a strategic agreement with General Electric for on-site service. Under the agreement, GE service units would provide the physical front to Austin's customers distributed throughout the United States. Diwan focused on customer service and offering technologically up-to-date products. Between 1989 and 1992, Austin received five "editor's choices"[2] from *PC Magazine*. Under Diwan's leadership, the company sales grew from US$2 million in 1984 to projected sales of US$65 million in 1992.

In 1989, Diwan started a subsidiary, Austin Applications, Inc., to focus on software development. Most of the software development efforts were addressed to the needs of ACS but Diwan saw that the software could be successfully marketed to other companies. By 1992, Austin Applications had developed software packages such as StoreKeeper, Contact Manager, Dental Keeper, Medical Keeper, and PC Tracker. While the copyright for StoreKeeper was registered, the rest had yet to be registered for copyrights. In 1990, Diwan started a subsidiary in England, Austin U.K. Ltd., which was to serve as a European hub to market the computers to Europe and Asia. The company had signed a number of distribution agreements with overseas suppliers in South America and the Middle East, as shown in Exhibit 8.

Advertising and Promotion

With an aggressive advertising campaign and timely product introductions, Austin had quickly captured local media attention. The customer base was slowly expanded to include small and medium businesses, and government clients. Advertising expenses were typically in the range of eight to 12 per cent of sales. Austin was ranked as one of the top 100 business markets in America by *Business Marketing* magazine in 1991 as well as 1992 (see Exhibit 9). The accumulated advertising expenses of the company over the past five years amounted to US$11.7 million. Austin participated regularly in the COMDEX/Fall trade shows, and other PC shows promoted by government and local bodies.

Year Signed	Name of the company and Location	Type of Agreement	Remarks, if any
1991	Oman Computer Co., Oman	Exclusive	
1992	Desktop Equipment & Solutions, Lebanon	Exclusive	
1992	Riad Computer Center, Syria	Non-exclusive	
1992	Riad Computer Center, Jordan	Non-exclusive	
1992	G. Kallenos Infosystems Ltd., Cyprus	Exclusive	
1992	Compu Rent & Services, Egypt	Exclusive	
1991	Computer Data Networks, U.A.E.	Non-exclusive	Expired but can be renewed
1992	Computer Data Networks, Kuwait	Non-exclusive	Expired but can be renewed
1991	Procom S.R.L., Bolivia	Exclusive	
1992	Safari Co. Ltd., Saudi Arabia	Exclusive	Validity of contract currently being disputed due to payment problems
1991	Factum Sistemas S.A. de C.V., Mexico	Exclusive	

Exhibit 8   Austin Computer Systems, Inc. Overseas Distribution Agreements

	1991 Ad Spending (US$ mil.)	1991 Ranking	1992 Ad Spending (US$ mil.)	1992 Ranking
AT&T Co.	35.486	1	39.318	4
Hewlett-Packard Co.	32.182	2	41.322	2
IBM Corp.	31.027	3	50.447	1
Dell Computer Corp.	18.318	10	19.943	13
Compaq Computer Corp.	14.512	13	26.563	9
Apple Computer Inc.	12.710	15	13.537	19
Gateway 2000	12.549	16	21.175	11
CompuAdd Corp.	8.519	30	10.092	29
Advanced Logic Research Inc.	5.096	58	3.233	92
Austin Computer System	4.417	69	3.654	81
Corel Systems Corp.	4.387	72	7.197	44
Advanced Micro Devices Inc.	3.695	89	5.112	61

Exhibit 9   Marketing Expenses of Selected Firms in "Top 100" List

Source: Business Marketing.

Customer Service

In addition to the promotion efforts, ACS also provided a number of pre-sales and post-sales services. ACS' PC-Tracking system let customers track the status of their order by permitting them to tap into ACS' production and shipping files via their own computers and a modem. Electronic bulletin boards for customers also became a standard channel for addressing customer queries, where round-the-clock customer support via telephone lines was not feasible. The sales divisions were organized to cater to specific industry segments, including Fortune 1000 companies; small-and-medium companies; individual end-users; retail outlets; federal and Texas state government and education bodies; value-added resellers; international interests; and networking. Austin had major corporate clients such as Exxon and Houston Light & Power which were based in Texas. It also sold a significant proportion of its PCs through mail-order by advertising in various U.S. computer magazines and had a widely dispersed customer base throughout the United States.

Manufacturing

Austin had a leased manufacturing facility and had the equipment to assemble and test desktops and notebooks. Most of the assembly was done manually and tested manually. Given the low volume at which it was operating, it did not want to invest in automation. A simple database of materials was used to control and monitor the materials flow. Often raw materials annual forecasts were provided by the product engineers and, based on the forecast, purchase orders were released. For most purchase orders (overseas), annual requirements were mandatory to get the supply of parts. When the forecast was not made properly, as was often the case, the company had to contend with a huge build-up of inventory.

The Problems at Austin

Austin's growth over the years was quite impressive but the profitability of the company was continuously being eroded. The stiff competition in the PC market put the low-volume players under extreme pressure. Compaq had stepped up its marketing campaign, introducing the Prolinea line, kick-starting a price war in 1992, and continuing to market aggressively. Dell was responding by introducing the Dimension line, offering a good price/performance ratio. Service demands from customers were going up and with the liberal provision in the sales agreements, the company had no control over the returns of defective products.

The company had problems with some of its vendors. Most of the components were procured from Taiwan and other parts of Asia. The delivery wait was over two months and the payment terms were often strict. Added to this, the company had to contend with quality problems in some of the components. In terms of key components such as microprocessor chips and memory, Austin, owing to its low volume, had very little power in negotiating with suppliers such as Intel for getting its computer chips. Large competitors like Compaq and Dell were able to strike much better procurement agreements with Intel, Microsoft and other vendors. Diwan believed that a merger with a bigger company was essential for survival.

Organization Structure

Robert Diwan was a hands-on manager and had a very simple management structure (shown

in Exhibit 10). Mike Zamora, President of the company, had been with the company for a number of years and had the full confidence of Diwan. While Diwan focused on strategy and marketing, Mike focused on operations and accounting. Mike also had close contacts with the corporate customers and was a strength when it came to corporate accounts. The Director of Operations was generally responsible for manufacturing, purchasing, quality and shipping and reported to Mike. Rich Jacobson, an engineer by training, was in charge of the finances. In 1992, Austin had 185 employees. Personnel turnover was generally high in Austin, given the large number of high-technology companies within the region.

Diwan did not plan to quit the business scene but he was prepared to resign his executive positions to pave the way for new management. Indications were that he would not be willing to report to another CEO, if IPC decided to appoint one. If IPC decided to acquire ACS, Patrick had to resolve this management issue. With most of the Singapore managers actively involved in the initial public offering planned for 1993, Patrick did not see the possibility of any of the top managers being sent to the U.S. subsidiary.

David Scull

As Patrick was brooding over the alternatives, he remembered one of his American acquaintances whom he had met in one of the business conferences. David Judson Scull (40) was then working as Executive Director, Asia Pacific Sales, with Seagate Technology (Singapore) Pte. Ltd., an American disk-drive manufacturer with manufacturing operations in Singapore. Seagate was also one of the large multinational corporations in Singapore and had an excellent reputation for marketing and management. Between 1977 and 1983, Dave had worked in Indonesia with two different U.S. MNCs, as Logistics Manager, and in an Indonesian oil company as District Manager. Later he worked for another U.S. MNC in Malaysia and China as Manager of

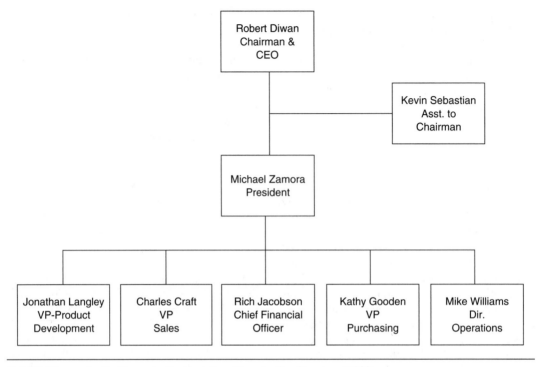

Exhibit 10   Austin Computer Systems, Inc. Organization Structure (1992)

Operations until 1987, when he joined Seagate as Sales Manager, and was subsequently promoted to Executive Director.

Dave had shown an enthusiastic interest in joining IPC to further its American operations. Patrick considered this a good opportunity to get him to join IPC. He could assign him to head the U.S. operations, and give him a broad mandate to accomplish the company's goal of becoming a S$3 billion company by 1997, with one third of the revenues coming from the U.S. operations. Patrick sensed that Dave was very confident of accomplishing these goals. Dave could be hired under the IPC Corporation umbrella, and assigned as the Head of the U.S. operations, and he could be charged with the implementation of IPC's plans in the United States. One of the

critical issues in such an arrangement was to decide how to design the compensation package for him.

Acquisition Decision

Patrick had to find a way to evaluate the fair market value of Austin. The company was privately held and managed by Diwan for all practical purposes. Patrick had met with Diwan just a week earlier where they had discussed the computer market in general and Austin's business in particular. The discussion also centered around the need to compete head on against Dell and Gateway.

IPC had received Austin's financial statements for the years 1990 and 1991 with projected figures

	Dec. 31, 1990	Dec. 31, 1991	Dec. 31, 1992 (Projected)
Product Sales	39,011	40,832	59,446[1]
Cost of Product Sales	29,380	29,995	46,981
Gross Profit	9,631	10,837	12,465
Selling & Admin Expenses	7,759	9,798	12,333
Other Income (expenses)			
Interest expense	(175)	(249)	(395)
Interest income	64	45	35
Credit line charges	(259)	(200)	(441)
Total other income (expenses)	370	(404)	(801)
Income (loss) before taxes	1,502	635	(669)
Income tax	0	26	0
Net income (loss) after tax	1,502	609	(669)
Net income (loss) after adjustment[2]	—	—	(3,200)

Exhibit 11   Austin Computer Systems Inc. Consolidated Income Statement (figures in thousands US$)

1. Original product sales projection of US$65 million was adjusted downward based on past trends to include possible returns which are typical of a mail-order business.
2. Obsolete inventory may call for a write-off about US$1 to US$2 million. Given the nature of the computer industry, an exact analysis may be required before finalizing the exact value of the write-off. Some customers' bills have been outstanding. Up to US$1.2 million may have to be written off as bad debt. A conservative estimate of final adjusted loss is shown in the statement.

for 1992 (Exhibits 11 and 12). The auditors' provision for future losses was very alarming. Evaluating the company in order to assess a fair market price was turning out to be a complex job. Diwan had mentioned that he had rejected an offer to sell the company for US$10 million in 1991. There were some indications that Diwan would be prepared to sell the company for US$5 million cash, given the difficulties he was facing in 1992. Although it seemed like a bargain, Patrick wondered if the acquisition of Austin was the best option to enter the North American market.

	Dec. 31, 1990	Dec. 31, 1991	Dec. 31, 1992
Assets			
Current Assets:			
Cash and cash equivalents	969	653	568
Trade accounts receivable	3,470	4,767	5,055
Receivable from affiliates	395	745	747
Inventory	1,877	2,961	3,520
Other assets	79	379	169
Total current assets	6,790	9,506	10,059
Property and equipment	461	499	579
Others	8	8	13
Total Assets	7,259	10,013	10,651
Liabilities and Stockholders' Equity			
Current Liabilities:			
Accounts Payable	3,981	6,306	7,850
Accrued liabilities	2,502	1,281	2,792
Notes payable (N/P)	0	850	1,650
N/P to shareholder	40	406	405
Total current liabilities	6,523	8,843	12,697
Capital lease obligation	0	8	4
Total liabilities	6,523	8,851	12,701
Stockholders' equity:			
Common stock	26	26	26
Prior years' earnings	(51)	710	1,135
Dividends to shareholder	(740)	(185)	(50)
Current year earnings	1,502	610	(3,161)
Total stockholders' equity	736	1,161	(2,050)
Total liabilities and stockholders' equity	7,259	10,013	10,651

Exhibit 12 Austin Computer Systems, Inc. Consolidated Balance Sheet (figures in thousands US$)

NOTES

1. The surname is pronounced "Niam."

2. In the PC business, "editor's choice" had a lot of positive impact on customer perception of the quality and reliability of the product.

ATS Inc.

*Prepared by Brian Ginsler and Nicole Piscione
under the supervision of Professor Robert White*

Version: (A) 2002-09-26

Michael Lay, Portfolio Manager, and Dean Metcalf, Assistant Portfolio Manager, Ontario Teachers' Pension Plan Board's (OTPPB) Merchant Banking Group (MBG), looked through Orenda Capital Corporation's information memorandum on their client, ATS Inc. (ATS). The senior management of ATS were interested in acquiring certain non-core assets of its parent company Aer Lingus plc, of Dublin, Ireland (see Exhibit 1 for corporate structure and ownership).

ATS was founded in 1978 by Klaus Woerner and was a North American leader in the design and manufacture of state-of-the-art factory automation systems. Woerner,

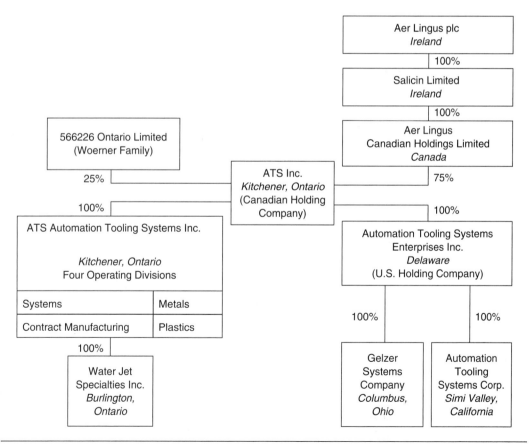

Exhibit 1   Corporate Structure and Ownership

Chief Executive Officer, had been the driving force in developing the company from its start up in 1978 to its present size. While Woerner was principally responsible for ATS's expansion and growth, he had attracted a team of talented colleagues to support his efforts (see Exhibit 2). For a general history of ATS see Exhibit 3.

Aer Lingus made its investment in ATS in 1985 following a policy of diversification from its inherently cyclical core business of air transportation. However, the board of directors of Aer Lingus had recently determined that Aer Lingus should focus primarily on its core European businesses. Consequently, Aer Lingus had agreed to sell its shares of ATS to the management and employees of ATS pursuant to a binding letter of intent executed on March 11, 1992.

THE ONTARIO TEACHERS' PENSION PLAN BOARD

OTPPB was established in 1990 as an independent corporation to administer the benefits and to

Klaus Woerner President and CEO	Age 51. He held a degree in mechanical engineering from Ryerson Polytechnical, as well as being a qualified tool and die maker. Founded the business in 1978. Previous experience in manufacturing engineering in automotive and other industries while at Litton Industries, Ford Motor Company and Electrolux.
Roger Awad Sales Manager	Age 48. He held a degree in engineering technology from St. Clair College. He had been at ATS for nine years. Over 20 years experience in manufacturing equipment sales and process engineering including time with competitors of ATS, as well as Chrysler and General Motors.
Ron Jutrus Chief Financial Officer	Age 36. He was a business graduate (Hons. BBA) from Sir Wilfrid Laurier University and a chartered accountant. Six years with ATS. Prior experience in public accounting, consulting, data processing and financing with Peat Marwick Thorne.
Jeff Wilson General Manager, Kitchener Systems	Age 36. He was a professional engineer with a degree in mechanical engineering from the University of Waterloo. Seven years with ATS. Previous experience General Motors and Bendix.
Joseph Moreno General Manager, Gelzer Systems Co.	Age 44. He was a graduate electrical engineer from the navy with 22 years experience at Gelzer in manufacturing and engineering roles.
Jeff Palser General Manager, Plastics Division	Age 47. He graduated from a technical school in the United Kingdom. He had been at ATS for two years. He had over 20 years experience in a variety of positions relating to the manufacture and sale of moulded plastic products.
Robin Porter General Manager, Metals Division	Age 37. He graduated from a technical school in the United Kingdom and commenced employment at ATS in 1991. Previous experience included management and technical positions with manufacturers of component parts for automotive assemblies.
John Heald Manager, Contract Manufacturing	Age 37. He completed apprenticeship in tool and die manufacturing at George Brown College and held a diploma in industrial and manufacturing engineering from Humber College. He commenced employment at ATS in 1991. His previous experience included production management at ITT Automotive.

Exhibit 2   Management Profiles, as of March 11, 1992

Year	
1978	• ATS was founded by Klaus Woerner as a small special purpose machine and die shop employing four people. The company was profitable in its first year.
1979	• The company began to explore the possible use of microcomputers in automated assembly system applications, which were just starting to appear in the market.
1982	• ATS was awarded a $1.2 million order from Control Data for an electronic component forming and printed circuit board ("PCB") assembly machine. • A relationship, which developed with Northern Telecom, led to the company's first application of robotics using an IBM industrial robot to insert relays into telephone circuit boards.
1983	• ATS pioneered the application of machine vision technology that allows a computer to analyse a picture taken with a camera, input the data automatically into its program and adjust the action of the physical machine (i.e., robot) accordingly (within certain programmed limitations).
1985	• Klaus Woerner, in partnership with David Bunker, launched Automation Specialties in Burlington to manufacture vibratory bowl feeders, a key automation component that was in demand regionally. Automation Specialties was incorporated as 139898 Canada Inc. • The company grew to over $9.0 million in revenue. Continuing rapid growth during this period placed financial pressures on ATS. To obtain the necessary additional capital to finance ATS's rapid expansion, discussions were held with a number of possible investors to strengthen the equity base. Eventually, an agreement was reached in September 1985 under which Aer Lingus plc acquired 75 per cent of the voting stock and provided a needed working capital injection of $2.0 million. This investment provided ATS with the financial flexibility to pursue larger and more diverse opportunities. For Aer Lingus, ATS represented a diversifying portfolio investment. Aer Lingus' involvement has always been restricted to board-level input. The transaction also resulted in Automation Specialties becoming a wholly owned ATS subsidiary.
1986	• ATS started to aggressively promote its capability in the United States market. These efforts were quickly successful in obtaining project orders from major United States-based customers such as Rockwell, Delco, Westinghouse and Hughes Aircraft. • The decision was made to look at developing a stronger United States presence by establishing a manufacturing facility in that country, in order to serve the growing customer base in the aerospace and electronics industries.
1987	• ATS Corp., a stand-alone satellite systems integration facility located in Simi Valley, California, was launched in February 1987, by acquiring certain assets and the management of a small company called Advance Automation. • Additional space was leased close to the main Alpine Road plant to handle increasing volumes.
1988	• Backlogs surged from United States customers and the Kitchener plant was expanded by 40,000 square feet to provide the necessary space. • The Metals Division was launched to supply precision turned OEM parts to the auto industry on a long-term single source agreement. • The Plastics Division was launched to complement the Metals Division.
1989	• In June 1989, ATS reorganized itself to create a new parent company, ATS Inc., and acquired Gelzer Systems Company, a respected competitor located in Columbus, Ohio, which had been in business for over 20 years.

Exhibit 3   General History   *(Continued)*

Year	
	• The Metals Division became profitable and a strategic decision was made to seek additional customers to broaden the customer base. • ATS customers requested the company to supply products to European plants.
1990	• Volumes in the Metals Division turned soft as the automotive market entered a downturn. Losses were triggered as capital and preproduction expenditures related to new Ford wiper component preproduction increased. The situation was complicated by Ford's request that actual capacity be doubled as compared to plan, in order for ATS to become the single source supplier ahead of schedule. • ATS was awarded the Canada Export Award by the Canadian Department of External Affairs. • The recession deepened and ATS reported its first loss ever primarily as a result of losses incurred in the OEM business and poorer than expected results in systems operations.
1991	• Major cost reduction and restructuring programs were put in place in early 1991, which significantly reduced operating expenses, to help the company absorb the continuing costs of establishing the Parts Divisions and the reduced volumes due to the recession. • Contract manufacturing activities were launched in the last quarter of the fiscal year. • Management decided to divest of the Burlington operations during the last quarter—1990 and 1991 results are restated to present the Burlington company as a discontinued operation. • Losses experienced in the Parts Divisions along with inventory write downs to reflect weakened market conditions. • The company engaged Ingersoll Engineers Consultants to assist management to develop a renewed corporate strategy focussed on a management by objectives philosophy.
1992	• Parts Divisions became profitable in spite of the continuing recession and being in a start-up phase. • On March 11, 1992, a binding letter of intent providing for the purchase of Aer Lingus' ownership position by a management-led group was agreed to.

Exhibit 3 (Continued)

manage the investments of the pension plan for over 200,000 Ontario teachers. The MBG, formed in 1991, consisted of four individuals working as part of the investment division of the corporation. The MBG was formed "to invest in companies seeking to capitalize on value-added strategic opportunities."[1] At its inception in 1990, OTPPB had liabilities of $22 billion and a pensioner population of just under 40,000. As at April 1992, OTPPB was faced with an approximate $3.6 billion deficiency in assets (investable funds).[2]

As a financial partner, the MBG was interested in assisting Canadian businesses meet their long-term objectives. In order to select its investment portfolio, the MBG looked for Canadian companies with a strong management team, significant management financial commitment, value-added products and/or services, market share leaders, sustainable competitive advantage in attractive and growing niche markets, and stable or growing operating cash flows.[3]

ATS INC.

ATS had established a leading market position in systems integration, a high growth industry. The company supplied turnkey factory automation systems for communications, appliances, computers, automotive and defense related businesses. In addition, the company was an original equipment manufacturer (OEM) and supplier of precision turned parts, plastic mouldings and electrical components to several fast growing niches within the automotive and telecommunication industries.

ATS's 1991 revenues were $58.83 million, and its revenues for the six months ended March 31, 1992, were $36.35 million. Aer Lingus plc, the controlling shareholder, had ATS adopt a March 31 year-end to bring the ATS fiscal year-end into alignment with its own March fiscal year-end.

ATS served its customers out of its Kitchener, Ontario, plant as well as plants in Columbus, Ohio, and Simi Valley, California. ATS also owned and operated Water Jet Specialties Ltd. of Burlington, Ontario. ATS was in the process of divesting of this operation in the belief that the products and services were not a strategic fit with its core systems integration and OEM parts manufacturing businesses.

ATS sales had grown at a compound annual rate of nearly 23 per cent over the past five years. ATS had projected earnings before interest and taxes (EBIT) of $10.63 million on sales of $72.71 million for the fiscal year ending March 31, 1993. See Exhibit 4 for historical financial statements. ATS had taken steps to expand its operations by following its clients to European and Far East markets (see Exhibit 5) and was awarded the "Canada Export Award" in 1990 by the Export Development Corporation.

ATS Automation Tooling Systems Inc. Products and Services

ATS Automation Tooling Systems Inc., located in Kitchener, Ontario, was comprised of a systems group and an original equipment manufacturing (OEM) group.

Factory Automation Systems Business

ATS Automation Tooling Systems Inc. systems division undertook complete turnkey contracts including conceptual and detailed designs, machining and assembly, development and application of computer software controls plus field service and training of customer personnel. ATS also supported customers in their product developmental efforts. ATS Automation Tooling Systems Inc.'s 1991 sales for the systems business were $28.88 million, down from $40.06 million in 1990. However, for the six months ended March 31, 1992, sales were $28.11 million. Historically, over 75 per cent of ATS Automation Tooling Systems Inc.'s factory automation business was sold into the United States. Customers included many of the largest North American corporations. Contracts had been secured from manufacturers in communications, appliances, computers, automotive and defense-related businesses.

OEM Parts Manufacturing

This business operated under three separate divisions located in Kitchener, Ontario. For OEM divisional operating income information, see Exhibit 6.

Precision Turned Metal Parts. Launched in 1988, this division had grown to sales volumes in 1991 of over $6 million. ATS Automation Tooling Systems Inc. was now approaching capacity at this location, which would necessitate a move to larger premises and require capital expenditures to support additional volumes. The primary focus for this division was niche markets within the automotive sector. For example, ATS had a strong presence in the fast growing anti-lock brake (ABS) market. The majority of its metals business was under long-term, single sourced customer purchase orders. The plant had recently been awarded the Ford "Q1" quality status, the highest quality rating Ford awarded to its suppliers.

Engineered Plastic Injection Moulded Parts. Also launched in 1988, the Plastics Division had a difficult start resulting from the loss of a major, high-volume order. Therefore, it did not record a profit during its first four years. It recorded 1991 sales of $3.9 million. Its primary focus was on insert moulding of highly engineered parts. While primarily dependent on automotive business, ATS

	1987	1988	1989	1990	1991	1992 Annualized
Sales	23.74	31.65	58.10	60.65	58.83	72.71
Cost of Sales	18.89	22.49	43.27	47.35	46.22	52.37
Gross Margin	4.85	9.16	14.83	13.30	12.61	20.34
Gen. & Admin.	2.19	5.27	6.40	6.30	5.95	6.54
R&D Expenses	0.39	0.99	1.06	1.52	1.19	0.34
Deprec. & Amort.	0.42	0.63	1.57	2.24	2.51	2.83
Total	3.00	6.89	9.03	10.06	9.65	9.71
EBIT	1.85	2.27	5.80	3.24	2.96	10.63
Interest: Senior Debt	0.67	0.94	2.26	4.01	3.18	2.33
Interest: Sub. Debt	0.00	0.00	0.00	0.00	0.00	0.00
Other	0.00	0.64	0.09	0.69	0.42	0.57
Pre-Tax Income	1.18	0.69	3.45	(1.46)	(0.64)	7.73
Taxes	0.71	0.23	1.43	(0.55)	(0.13)	3.09
Net Income From Ops	0.47	0.46	2.02	(0.91)	(0.51)	4.64
Earnings from Discontinued Ops	0.16	0.00	0.30	0.17	(0.07)	(0.50)
Net Income	0.63	0.46	2.32	(0.74)	(0.58)	4.14
Current Assets						
Accts. Receivable	5.39	7.98	8.02	10.96	12.49	12.31
Contracts In Progress	3.83	4.97	21.85	16.71	7.36	9.14
Other Inventory	0.81	1.22	2.17	5.87	5.51	5.30
Pre-Paid Expenses	0.07	0.08	0.38	0.50	0.55	0.64
Taxes Recoverable, Other	0.00	1.13	0.96	1.63	0.16	0.00
Total Current Assets	10.10	15.38	33.38	35.67	26.07	27.39
Property, Plant, Equip.	4.82	13.91	21.22	26.24	29.23	30.21
Less Accum. Deprec.	1.02	1.74	3.26	4.97	7.37	9.10
Net PPE	3.80	12.17	17.96	21.27	21.86	21.11
Investment In Discontinued Operations	0.47	0.56	0.72	0.87	0.79	0.73
Investment in tax credits	0.09	0.11	0.17	0.14	1.69	1.69
Goodwill	0.07	0.07	2.37	2.21	1.99	1.92
Total Assets	14.55	28.29	54.60	60.14	52.41	52.86
Current Liabilities						
Bank Indebtedness	1.85	5.21	10.41	15.45	10.16	9.11
Accounts payable	4.14	3.37	7.67	7.27	7.29	6.77
Current Portion of LTD	0.46	1.13	4.37	3.11	3.58	4.39
Taxes Payable & other	0.22	(0.06)	1.26	0.11	0.43	1.50
Total Current	6.67	9.65	23.71	25.94	21.46	21.77
Long-Term Debt	5.17	8.86	12.24	16.17	14.34	11.49
Deferred Income Taxes	0.49	1.26	2.24	1.53	0.61	1.10
Acquisition financing						
Senior Term Loan						
Subordinated Notes						
Total Liabilities	12.33	19.77	38.19	43.64	36.41	34.36
Capital Stock	1.20	9.43	15.15	16.10	16.33	15.38
Retained Earnings	1.02	(0.94)	1.33	0.58	0.01	3.10
Foreign Exchange Transaction	0.00	0.03	(0.06)	(0.18)	(0.34)	0.02
Total Equity	2.22	8.53	16.42	16.50	16.00	18.50
Total Liabilities and Equity	14.55	28.29	54.61	60.14	52.41	52.86

Exhibit 4   Summary Income Statement (Cdn$ millions)

	Canada	United States	Other
Systems Engineering	13%	75%	12%
Plastics	95%	5%	—
Metals	64%	325%	4%
Contract Manufacturing	100%	—	—

Exhibit 5   Segmented Revenue Profile by Division, Fiscal Year Ended September 1991

Automation Tooling Systems Inc. also had some clients in the telecommunication, computers and appliance industries.

Contract Manufacturing. Launched in 1991, this business consisted of producing, on a contract basis, high volume electrical mechanical components for automotive customers. ATS Automation Tooling Systems Inc.'s contract sales in 1991 were $1.1 million.

Historical Fiscal Results for 1990

ATS experienced its first loss in the amount of $0.74 million. The loss resulted from the costs of

	ATS Metals Division			ATS Plastics Division			ATS Contract Manufacturing Budget FY March 1993
	6 Months March 1992	FYE Sept. 1991	FYE Sept. 1990	6 Months March 1992	FYE Sept. 1991	FYE Sept. 1990	
SALES REVENUE	8,942	6,109	2,351	5,513	3,900	2,413	4,618
Variable Expenses							
Raw Materials	1,394	1,517	385	2,635	1,607	1,296	2,921
Labor	658	690	241	750	665	570	302
Consumables	727	501	181	117	47	35	66
Subcontracting	398	146	16	512	352	40	—
Repairs and Maintenance	368	329	119	320	149	154	—
Inventory Charges	313	198	145	(416)	110	(149)	—
Other	—	—	—	—	—	—	18
TOTAL VARIABLE EXPENSES	3,858	3,381	1,087	3,918	2,930	1,946	3,307
VARIABLE CONTRIBUTION	5,084	2,728	1,264	1,595	970	466	1,311
Labor	1,223	1,037	450	400	385	265	87
Premises & Equipment	665	415	176	233	239	134	160
Depreciation	1,054	954	593	249	361	351	453
Gen. & Admin. Expenses	350	280	541	302	306	365	173
TOTAL FIXED EXPENSES	3,292	2,686	1,760	1,184	1,291	1,115	873
OPERATING INCOME	1,792	42	(496)	411	(321)	(648)	438

Exhibit 6   ATS Automation Tooling Systems Inc., Original Equipment Manufacturing Divisional Statement of Operations (Cdn$, in thousands)

Note: Six-month period ending March 1992 has been annualized.
Contract Manufacturing analysis is based on 1993 budget.

substantial expansion on a number of fronts while the core business started to experience the effects of the recessionary slowdown. As well, the receipt of large orders from the Ford Motor Company, which did not provide ATS with progress billings to fund the construction costs, increased working capital needs during the period. The increased debt burden required to meet these needs created financial pressure at a time when interest rates increased significantly.

Volumes in the parts division decreased as a result of reduced demand in the automotive sector. This reduced the base earnings performance, especially in the metals division. Heavy capital expenditure obligations combined with reduced operating results placed a strain on the company's cash flow. Furthermore, Aer Lingus plc was suffering significantly as a result of the downturn in the world airline industry and was not in a position to inject further funds.

Historical Fiscal Results for 1991

This was a year in which the company focused on restructuring and strengthening its operations. It launched the Contract Manufacturing business in the last quarter, which generated some additional cash flow for the group. Gross profit margins were down significantly due to the strength of the Canadian dollar relative to the U.S. dollar, which depressed prices, see Exhibit 7.

Historical Fiscal Results for Six Months Ended March 31, 1992

The systems division showed strong performance and order activity was quite strong. The formation of long-term "strategic alliances" in which ATS worked closely with customers from product design through systems construction, strengthened customer ties and increased

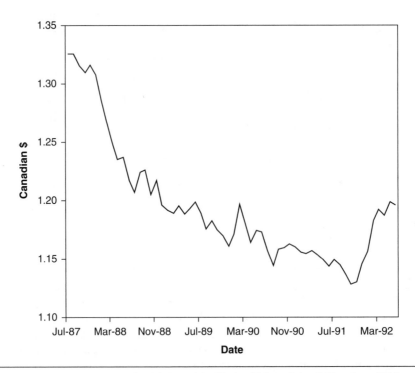

Exhibit 7   Foreign Exchange (Cdn$/US$) Monthly Closing Values, July 1987 to June 1992

the backlogs to levels where capacity constraints were a issue of concern. The parts division had become profitable in the face of the continuing recession and the emergence of the division from its start-up phases.

INDUSTRY

Systems Integration (Automation)

The approximate size of the custom automation systems market (excluding captive business) was $700 million and was growing at a 10 per cent to 15 per cent rate per annum. The market was fragmented as it was populated by a large number of small and medium sized companies, most of which were privately owned. No one company had a dominant position. Companies with sales in excess of $60 million were few. The largest industrial automation and machine tool company in North America was Giddings & Lewis Inc., which acquired its larger rival Cross & Trecker Corp. on October 31, 1991. This brought its consolidated sales to approximately US$670 million, with sales of US$100 million earned from its Integrated Automated Division (see Exhibit 8). Giddings & Lewis was publicly listed on NASDAQ (GDIL) with a stock price of US$40 representing a multiple of 20 times price to earnings. Another major player, with sales over US$60 million per year, was Universal Instruments Corp., located in Binghamton, New York. It had a good reputation in, and was primarily focused on, high-speed printed circuit board assembly. A significant offshore competitor was Hirata of Japan, which boasted excellent customer service and delivery. The other industry players were smaller in size as compared to the aforementioned companies.

The emergence of the automation industry was driven by a number of factors. Reduced trade barriers and the corresponding trend for manufacturers to compete on a global scale reinforced the need to produce on a rapid, consistent basis, products with improved quality and reliability, while at the same time, reducing the cost

of doing so. As well, during the 1980s, the costs of labor increased faster than productivity gains in developed countries. While some companies tried relocating to lower labor cost centers, many others had turned to automation as a solution to this problem. These trends were expected to continue and in fact accelerate during the 1990s. In addition, the older age of many North American plants relative to European or Asian competitors suggested the likelihood and the necessity for significant capital expenditures by North American manufacturers in the 1990s to modernize their assembly operations. New technology in manufacturing applications was accelerating and, therefore, increasing the potential for future systems integration growth. For example, in the electronics industry, including computer and telecommunication sectors, the tolerances related to circuit board assembly were reducing to levels where human assembly was no longer practical. Automation could also benefit pharmaceutical, packaging and food processing companies that often required sterile processes within their operations, which were labor intensive and difficult without automation.

OEM Parts Manufacturing

The OEM parts manufacturing industry was highly competitive and difficult to measure. For example, the automotive parts business was of the order of several billions of dollars with many thousands of suppliers throughout North America.[4] A competitive advantage in this industry was facilitated by close proximity to major automotive plants.

The OEM industries faced challenges ahead due to the cyclical nature of the automotive market and the fact that recent sales of new vehicles were showing weakness from the levels of the mid- to late-1980s. Further, manufacturers in the automobile industry were increasingly attempting to outsource, within strict quality guidelines. As a growing industry, new players emerged out of a desire to earn greater revenue from their existing knowledge base and to complement their existing services to their clients.

	1987	1988	1989	1990	1991	G&L Avg. 1987-1991	ATS Avg. 1987-1992
Sales	125.23	168.94	233.11	242.96	326.61		
Cost of sales	90.25	124.39	167.14	173.50	241.48		
Gross Margins	34.98	44.46	65.97	69.47	85.13		
Cost as % of sales	72.10%	73.60%	71.70%	71.40%	73.90%	72.50%	75.60%
SG&A	29.09	30.57	35.03	39.31	46.93		
SG&A/Sales	23.23%	18.09%	15.03%	16.18%	14.37%	17.40%	11.10%
Depreciation	15.47	5.59	6.13	6.57	7.46		
Depreciation/Sales	12.35%	3.31%	2.63%	2.70%	2.28%	4.70%	3.10%
EBIT	(9.57)	8.40	24.81	23.58	30.74		
EBIT/Sales	−7.65%	4.97%	10.64%	9.71%	9.41%	5.40%	8.30%
Net Income	(9.57)	8.40	17.71	19.27	21.04		
Profitability							
Debt/Equity	0.04	0.04	0.03	0.00	0.23		
ROE	−6.08%	8.93%	17.38%	16.31%	10.35%		

Valuation of Gidding & Lewis

	1989 IP Valuation	Current Value
P/E Multiple: 1989 Actual	8.5	21.00
Market to Book Multiple	1.4	3.75
EBIT Multiple	6.1	18.71

Exhibit 8   Giddings & Lewis Inc., Income Statement Comparison With ATS (US$ millions)

THE PROPOSED DEAL

Klaus Woerner, ATS management and employees, along with other investors (collectively the Investor Group) would establish a company (New ATS), which would acquire the shares and assume the liabilities of ATS. The total funds required for the transaction would be approximately $41.27 million (see Exhibit 9 for pro forma financial requirements as at June 30, 1992, and Exhibit 10 for proposed terms of financing).

New ATS was seeking a working capital operating line of credit of $7.0 million and an $18.0 million senior term loan, to be secured by the company's current and fixed assets. The new ATS would assume the existing $3.04 million term loan. In addition, $6.5 million of subordinated notes and $9.23 million of common equity of New ATS, representing 60.0 per cent ownership, would be offered to investors in the form of non-separable investment units totaling $15.73 million. Woerner agreed to reinvest $4.77 million

	Cdn$ in Millions	Per Cent of Total Capital
Working Capital Loan (cash)	(0.77)	(1.9%)
Senior Term Loan	18.00	43.6%
Existing Term Loan	3.04	7.4%
Subordinated Notes	6.50	15.7%
Common Equity	14.50	35.1%
Total Capitalization	41.27	100.0%

Exhibit 9   New ATS Inc. Pro Forma Capital Structure, as at June 30, 1992

ownership position back into the company, with another $500,000 coming from almost 100 managers and employees of ATS (see Exhibit 11 for Woerner's memo to ATS employees).

This transaction was expected to close on June 30, 1992. Lay and Metcalf predicted that the North American economy would show only a minor gradual improvement and that the annual inflation rate would be three per cent (see Exhibit 12 for financial market data). ATS expected to spend approximately $3.0 million per annum on capital expenditures. ATS predicted that the sale of the Burlington division would net $1.0 million. Also, ATS predicted a sale of the 80 Alpine Road facility in Kitchener for pre-tax proceeds of $3.3 million in fiscal 1994. The blended interest rate on the senior credit facilities was estimated to annually average 10 per cent over the next eight years. The senior debt borrowings would be primarily denominated in U.S. dollars and the coupon on the subordinated notes was assumed to be 13.5 per cent. In accordance with ATS's accounting policy, research and development expenditures were expensed as incurred.

THE DECISION

The MBG was a new initiative of OTPPB. Any decision made would affect its credibility and potential for future investments. Lay and Metcalf had to ensure that the total investment would meet OTPPB's investment criteria: to outperform the TSE 300 Total Return Index by at least 200 basis points, see Exhibit 13; long-term investments (three to six years); and to achieve an internal rate of return greater than 20 per cent for long-term investments (three to six years); and to continue the growth of the MBG's investment portfolio. The investment decision would have to consider whether a financial partner should be involved. If Lay and Metcalf decided not to involve another partner, they would have the difficult task of convincing George Engman, head of the Merchant Banking Group, why ATS should be the first independent deal the MBG would perform. In addition, they would have to decide whether this investment would involve equity, subordinated debt, or a combination of the two. The deal-closing date was set at June 30, 1992, to coincide with the end of ATS's first quarter of fiscal 1993.

Before Lay and Metcalf presented their ideas to Engman, they felt that a number of questions had to be considered. Why was ATS for sale? What did Aer Lingus know that they didn't? Should MBG make a counter proposal? What would become of ATS if Woerner was no longer involved? Would the capital expenditures required compromise the financial stability of ATS? Could OTPPB handle this deal if no other players were interested? What would OTPPB's exit strategy be? Was there a window of opportunity for an initial public offering within the investment horizon or would Woerner ever consider selling an ATS division to another party? Finally, should Lay and Metcalf go to Young Ichiban for sushi that day?

A. SENIOR DEBT	
(i) Working Capital Line of Credit Facility	
Borrower:	New ATS.
Facility:	Operating line for demand loans and/or letters of credit.
Total Commitment:	Cdn$7.0 million.
Anticipated Initial Draw Down:	None at closing.
Use of Proceeds:	The proceeds will be used by the company to finance future working capital requirements.
Borrowing Base Formula:	Lesser of (i) the total commitment or (ii) the aggregate of 85 per cent of accounts receivable, 80 per cent of contracts in progress and 50 per cent of inventory. To be co-ordinated with term facility below.
Interest Rate:	Calculated daily and payable monthly in arrears, initially at the rate in relation to prime or bankers' acceptances.
Security:	Fixed and floating charge on all assets subject to prior charges on Ohio facility in favor of the Government of the State of Ohio *et al.*
(ii) Line of Non-revolving Term Loans:	
Borrower:	New ATS.
Facility:	Cdn$18.0 million.
Currency:	Available in both Canadian and U.S. dollars.
Use of Proceeds:	To refinance existing permanent bank borrowings.
Borrowing Base:	To be co-ordinated with working capital facility but in general, 50 per cent loan to value against fixed assets.
Interest Rate:	Floating and fixed rate options.
Commitment Fee:	To be arranged.
Term:	5 years.
Amortization:	7.5 years.
Repayment:	18 months repayment holiday, thereafter $1.5 million semi-annually.
Security:	Fixed and floating charge on all assets subject to prior charges on Ohio facility in favor of the Government of the State of Ohio *et al.*
Covenants:	To be arranged.

Exhibit 10   New ATS Inc. Proposed Terms of Financing, as at June 30, 1992

B. INVESTMENT UNITS: SUBORDINATED NOTES AND COMMON SHARES

(i) Subordinated Notes:

Issuer:	New ATS.
Amount:	Cdn$6.5 million.
Instrument:	Subordinated Notes.
Purpose:	To finance the purchase of Aer Lingus plc's 75 per cent common share ownership position in ATS.
Maturity:	6 years.
Rate:	13.5 per cent per annum calculated daily and payable quarterly in arrears.
Commitment Fee:	To be arranged.
Subordination:	Payments of principal and interest on the Notes shall be subordinated to all senior debt under a standard subordination agreement.
Repayment:	No principal repayments until the end of the 18th month following the draw down date. Subject to maintenance of senior debt covenants, on the 18th month following closing and annually thereafter, the company shall repay the principal in the amount of $1.3 million.
Prepayment:	The company may repay the Subordinated Notes without penalty at any time following 18 months after closing.
Covenants:	To be discussed, but in any event, to be no more restrictive than senior covenants.

(ii) Common Shares:

Issuer:	New ATS.
Amount:	Cdn$9.23 million. An additional estimated $5.27 million will be invested by ATS management and employees.
Instrument:	Common shares.
Ownership:	The amount being offered (i.e., $9.23 million) represents a 60 per cent fully diluted ownership interest in New ATS.
Dividends:	None unless dividend policy is changed by unanimous resolution of New ATS's board of directors.
Other:	Shareholders' agreement to be entered into with normal course provisions including: • restrictions on the sale and transfer of shares; • anti-dilution protection; • piggyback rights; and • board of directors representation.

Automation Tooling Systems

ATS Inc.   80 Alpine Road   Kitchener, Ontario   N2E 1A1   Tel: (519) 744-4400

MEMO

From :   Klaus Woerner   March 11, 1992

To: Employees

RE: Employee buyout of Aer Lingus

I am extremely pleased to report that yesterday, we successfully negotiated what we consider to be a very fair and reasonable price for the purchase of all the shares of ATS held by Aer Lingus.   The purchase is only conditional upon our raising the necessary funding.   Our investment advisors who assisted us in the negotiations are confident that they can raise the necessary financing in order to close the purchase and sale agreement on schedule.

The closing is scheduled for the end of June and we are now moving quickly into the financing stages of the buyout. The first step will be to finalize our proposed financing structure and finish our "offering documents".   We will be working on this over the next two weeks.

Upon completion, those of you who have stated their desire to participate will be provided with a copy of the documents once you have signed and returned a confidentiality agreement which will be made available to you. The confidentiality agreement is required by the terms of our agreement with Aer Lingus and it is intended to ensure that people do not improperly release our sensitive information to unauthorized people. In addition, we will be looking at alternative financing arrangements for the employees so that the employees can finalize their investments by the closing date.

I know that many of you have questions.   We will be setting up a number of meetings with interested employees to deal with these as soon as practical. I expect that this will include meetings with our legal counsel and investment advisors who can address many issues which we are not as knowledgeable about or where we expect them to help us. You will be advised as to the time and location.

I am extremely excited about this opportunity.   I know that those of you who have already joined me in the buyout, share this enthusiasm for the future of our company.   Others may also wish to join us in the next while and I will address this in due course with the employee group.

Sincerely,

Klaus Woerner

Kitchener, Ontario   Columbus, Ohio   Simi Valley, California   Burlington, Ontario

Exhibit 11   Woerner's Memo to Employees

Term	March 11, 1992	Previous Day	Week Ago	Four Weeks Ago
2 Year	8.34	8.26	7.89	7.29
5 Year	8.81	8.87	8.18	7.88
7 Year	8.85	8.87	8.58	8.23
10 Year	8.88	8.98	8.62	8.37
25 Year	9.34	9.32	9.16	9.06

**Historical Canadian Common Equity Market Premiums
for period: December 1950 through December 1991**

Arithmetic Mean Spread Over Long Government Bonds	5.458%
Geometric Mean Spread Over Long Government Bonds	4.606%

Average Industry Betas

OEM Automobile	1.00
Automobile Parts	0.95
Computers	1.20
Semiconductor	1.50

Exhibit 12   Financial Market Data, Canadian Government Bond Yields (%)

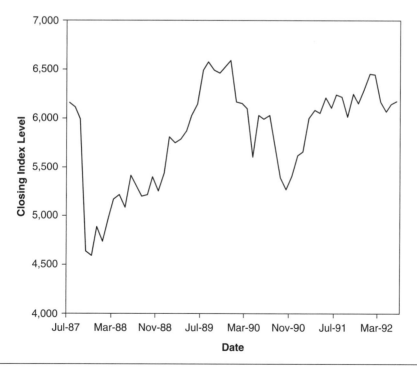

Exhibit 13   TSE 300 Total Return Index, Monthly Closing Values, July 1987 to June 1992

NOTES

1. Ontario Teachers' Pension Plan Board, "Merchant Banking Group Brochure," 1998.

2. As of December 31, 1998, Ontario Teachers' Pension Plan Board's total fund assets wcrc in excess of $59 billion.

3. Ontario Teachers' Pension Plan Board, "Merchant Banking Group Brochure," 1998.

4. Orenda Corporate Finance Ltd., "ATS Information Memorandum," April 1992.

9

AFTER THE MERGER

Recoveries and Exits

As discussed, most mergers and acquisitions (M&A) research finds that most M&A deals do not create value. While those studies often use different measures of "value" and vary in "for whom" they measure such value, the fact remains that many deals do go wrong. The causes for such failure are often complex and largely dependent on the "for whom" question. That is, one firm's failure, for example, overpayment, is another firm's success—premium received for the stock price. Regardless of perspective, we can often break down the sources of common failures to either a predeal or postdeal cause. Following the framework of Horovitz,[1] the most basic causes of failure are either the wrong decision being made or the inability to fulfill the decision. Within each of these phases, there are several potential reasons deals fail.

Quite simply, a firm may make a strategic choice that is inconsistent with its best interest, regardless of whether the poor choice is intentional (i.e., driven by some dubious justification) or an error in judgment. A second frequent cause is an inadequate assessment of the potential partner. This may come from mistakenly choosing a partner to fit an appropriate strategy or in selecting an appropriate partner but by valuing the firm incorrectly. Closely linked to this is that inadequate due diligence may lead the firm to not uncover elements of the partner that do not measure up to expectations. As well, the deal itself may have been done on inappropriate grounds—one of the dubious reasons for mergers discussed in Chapter 2. The dubious justification allowed the deal to get through the deal-screening and approval processes—likely the driver behind one of the other causes listed above. Finally, using our three-stage deal approach—strategize, execute, realize— the firm may have poorly executed the deal. Execution is complex and requires many highly technical tactical decisions be made. Managers or advisors without appropriate experience or expertise may lead the deal into a suboptimal outcome.

INABILITY TO FULFILL

Once a deal is done, even if for the right reasons and executed flawlessly, there are numerous pitfalls in the realization phase that can cause a deal to fail. The simplest is a bad or missing postmerger integration (PMI) plan. The PMI plan should be based on realizing the synergies and/or achieving some set of intended outcomes for the firm. To the extent that the plan does not focus on the value drivers, does so inadequately, is unrealistic to implement, has the wrong team running it, or any of a host of other reasons, the plan may be a plan for failure. To complement that, the plan itself may be poorly executed, even if it is the appropriate plan. This may come from either not following the plan or that other contingencies have changed, and the plan itself becomes inappropriate. As such, the plans may need to have some flexibility built into them to adapt to then-current needs. A third set of causes of failure may come from the actions of those leading the PMI. The PMI team may simply not take sufficient action or may make mistakes in executing the plan. Without a specific set of objectives tied to the incentives of the individuals involved, these people may simply not do what they are meant to do because they are focused on other activities. Political processes may also intervene and stop these PMI personnel from being able to accomplish what they had planned to do. Finally, time-related causes commonly are identified as reasons for failure. The "first 100 days" are critical to gaining momentum in putting the organization on the right change track. Time is critical, and it is important to match types and amounts of changes to the timing. Too much change, too soon, is as dangerous as too little, too late. The organization, the people, the processes, and resources all need to be ready and sufficiently aligned to accept change but also may need some change forced on them to gain momentum and reduce uncertainty and anxiety.

WHEN MERGERS FAIL

When a deal has failed, the basic choice is whether to fix the problem or exit the deal. The first question to ask is whether the problem is fixable. A management team facing this must consider the cause or causes, and any collateral damage may have occurred. That is, while the problem may be fixable, such a fix may only be a temporary fix, and it is the cause itself that must be remedied. As well, a deal failure may trigger other issues, such as the departure of key personnel, negative momentum in sales growth, or a ruinous attitude or morale among the staff. A second consideration is getting the management team and board to make the fix or exit decision and to commit to it. A psychological issue that can come into play is that of "escalation of commitment."[2] This phenomenon explains the behavior of individuals who increasingly become committed to a prior decision regardless of evidence that the decision was wrong. This is particularly relevant in M&A because managers may become committed to a deal because of the likely personal repercussions of admitting a mistake in having done a deal and committed the resources of the stockholders to it. The right choice for the firm is to treat sunk costs as spent and to make a new decision based solely on the best choice given all known information at that point in time. That decision may be to fix the problem or to exit the deal.

FIXING DEALS

When the choice has been made to fix the deal, as stated, it is important to get to the root cause of the failure. For example, failure may be shown by an inability to integrate operations on a set timeline. However, the cause may not be bad planning but underlying cultural differences that have hampered internal cooperation. A basic problem-solving approach in diagnosing the problem and creating a new plan might include the use of an objective third party or oversight board to study the underlying causes of the failure and to set out a new plan. The group should likely include multiple stakeholders to ensure adequate information input and buy-in going forward. The team should also explore what collateral damage has occurred with stakeholder groups, including customers, employees, and so on. Regardless of whether the problems occurred during PMI or long after, a tactical plan can be put into action to remedy it.

A key concern in fixing the problems in postdeal firms is that two or more formerly separate organizations have been forced to integrate to some extent. In doing so, many organizational changes, such as expanded or contracted roles and responsibilities, cause political problems and infighting. The situation may lead to an inability to cooperate using solely internal teams. In these situations, it is common to bring in an external party to examine the problems and to facilitate the implementation of a solution. Certain consultancies specifically offer expertise in PMI integration and focus on getting teams to cooperate. However, because it is outsiders that are driving change, there may be a lack of long-lasting internal commitment. As such, there are also benefits to solving the problems using internal personnel. Incentives can be aligned to get people to begin working together to solve problems together. When the teams solve the problems together, more commitment may be possible. However, these same teams may lack the objectivity needed to diagnose problems. In the end, these competing issues all need to be addressed.

ALTERNATIVES TO FIXING IT—EXITING

If the decision is made to exit, the deal cannot usually be simply reversed once in motion. The decision to exit may be based on changes in market conditions that no longer make the deal a viable component of the firm or may be driven by some underlying reasons that caused the deal to fail. The underlying drivers of the decision are likely linked to one or more stakeholders who may also present the best option for exiting the business. If the deal itself simply no longer makes competitive sense based on a strategic change either in the business or its environment, selling the firm may be a better option. We discuss some of the most common exits.

External Sale

When the strategic rationale for the deal no longer exists, this may be the best option. The firm may elect to use one of the sell-side options discussed in Chapter 8 and market the target to new owners.

Internal Sale

When no obvious external buyer is apparent, or when the part of the driving force that is causing the issues between the firms is a strong but uncooperative management team in the target, an internal sale may make sense. An internal sale would be structured as a management buyout, perhaps with financing agreement between the firm and its new owner-managers.

Partial Sale

When no obvious external buyer is apparent, but when it is important to maintain some strategic linkage or partial ownership to the target, some of the other options discussed in Chapter 8 may make sense. The target itself can be placed under its own separate management that has operational links to the parent firm. However, to reduce the amount of capital invested in the target, a subsidiary-IPO, spin-off, or split-off may be used to reduce the ownership yet maintain some linkage to the firm.

Closure

Although managers will be very reluctant to do so, the best option may simply be to break up and close the business. The business itself will surely have assets and resources that are marketable and have some value in a sale, even if in a fire sale. This path entails admitting to the public and to the stockholders that the M&A deal has been a severe failure, and so it is a difficult choice from a public and investor relations perspective. However, when the target is a financial drain and is using valuable management time and resources, the best strategic choice may be to view the deal as a sunk cost and move on.

CASES

DaimlerChrysler: Post-Merger News

Daimler-Benz AG, a large automobile manufacturer in Europe, and the Chrysler Corporation, one of the Big Three automakers in North America, have merged to create DaimlerChrysler. On the surface, everything seemed to be going as planned. In reality, all was not well. Organizational changes, conflicting information, and doubts about the future structure of the company resulted in the departure of numerous Chrysler employees, including many mid-level managers and engineers. While initially amalgamated into Daimler, the Chrysler Group ended up as one of three separate automotive divisions. In 2001, DaimlerChrysler recorded a $1.2 billion loss in operating profit (before one-time effects). Estimates for 2002 called for a break-even result, but the company was facing a $9 billion lawsuit filed by the fifth largest shareholder, who claimed that Daimler had deceived investors by touting the venture as a merger of equals.

Issues: Postmerger outcomes, lawsuits, dissident shareholders, investor relations

Gillette's Energy Drain (A): The Acquisition of Duracell

In 1996, Gillette acquired Duracell batteries for $7.3 billion in stock. The purchase was met with optimism not only by Gillette's senior management and its highly visible director, Warren Buffett, but also by Wall Street analysts. The case highlights the numerous challenges that Gillette has encountered since its acquisition of Duracell. Despite the initial enthusiasm, Duracell has proven to be a drain on Gillette's earnings and has cost Michael Hawley, James Kilt's predecessor as CEO, his job after only 18 months in the position—in large part for his inability to turn around the financial hemorrhaging at the Duracell division. The key strategy questions revolve around what can be done to turn around the battery business to help it achieve the potential for Gillette that everyone had assumed it possessed.

Issues: Postmerger integration, synergy realization, strategy implementation, corporate strategy, competition, executive turnover

Call-Net Enterprises Inc. (A)

Call-Net Enterprises Inc. is a publicly owned telecommunications company offering phone, data, and online services. After years of successful growth, Call-Net participated in an unfriendly takeover costing $1.8 billion, and its capital expenditures were higher than ever, leading to a significant net loss for the year. In addition, their stock prices were falling. Crescendo Investment, along with some of Call-Net's major shareholders, called a special shareholders meeting to request the removal of six of the nine board directors. The company's board of directors is faced with planning their strategy for the upcoming shareholders meeting and with making some long-term plans for the company.

Issues: M&A outcomes, corporate governance, board of directors, synergy realization, postmerger integration

REFERENCES

1. J. Horovitz, "Pitfalls in M&A Activity," in *Managing Complex Mergers: Financial Times Management,* ed. P. Morosini and U. Steger, 116–34 (Mahwah, NJ: Prentice Hall, 2004).
2. B. M. Staw, "Knee-Deep in the Big Muddy: A Study of Escalating Commitment to a Chosen Course of Action," *Organizational Behavior and Human Decision Processes* 16 (1976): 27–44.

DAIMLERCHRYSLER: POST-MERGER NEWS[1]

Prepared by Doug Airey, Andy Gepp, Cathy Harris and Yves Menard under the supervision of Professor Pratima Bansal

Version: (A) 2003-09-09

SETTING THE STAGE

In May 1998, when Daimler-Benz and Chrysler announced that they would merge to create DaimlerChrysler, the following statement was issued:

We believe that the merger of Chrysler Corporation and Daimler-Benz AG to form DaimlerChrysler is an historical step that will offer Daimler-Benz shareholders exciting perspectives. In addition to participating in the growth of two very profitable automobile companies, the merger offers the opportunity to benefit from the additional earnings potential that we believe will be generated by the merged activities of the new company.

We have already identified opportunities to increase sales, to create new markets for Daimler-Chrysler, to reduce purchasing costs and to realize economies of scale. We are well-positioned to capitalize on these opportunities to increase the earnings power of DaimlerChrysler AG. In the short term, we see synergies of $1.4 billion that we expect to more than double in the medium term. Even beyond that, given the creativity and inventiveness of our teams, we expect to be able to identify substantial additional benefits as the integration process accelerates.

The challenge that faces us, of course, as we move toward merger completion is to meld two strong, dynamic companies into one that can keep growing and evolving without missing a beat. To do that, we must blend not only our management and our operations, but we must blend our cultures and work styles.[2]

1998

To facilitate the merger, Robert Eaton, Chrysler's chairman and chief executive officer, formed "The Dream Team." Its members included Robert Lutz, Thomas Stallkamp, Francois Castaing, James Holden, Thomas Gale and Dennis Pawley (see Exhibit 1). They were responsible for returning Chrysler to profitability during the early '90s after its second brush with bankruptcy in 12 years. Prior to the public announcement of the

Robert Eaton	Chairman, CEO and Dream Team creator
Robert Lutz	Vice-chairman
Thomas Stallkamp	President (as of January 1998)
Francois Castaing	Executive Vice-president International Operations
James Holden	Executive Vice-president of Sales and Marketing
Thomas Gale	Executive Vice-president of Product and Design
Dennis Pawley	Executive Vice-president of Manufacturing

Exhibit 1   Chrysler's Senior Management— The Dream Team

merger, two of the members of the Dream Team, Francois Castaing and Robert Lutz, resigned. While executives of the Big Three often moved around, the loss of two of the seven top Chrysler executives signaled dissent.

In November 1998, DaimlerChrysler announced the positions for its two-tiered board system: the supervisory board and the board of management. The supervisory board was similar to a board of directors; however, it consisted of an equal number of representatives from labor organizations and outside corporate directors. The supervisory board was responsible for appointing the board of management and approving all major company decisions. Appointments to the 20-member supervisory board consisted of 14 Europeans and six Americans (see Exhibit 2).

The board of management was made up of the company chairman and the heads of the operating and functional divisions. It was responsible for executing company strategy. Of the 18 positions on the board, 10 were allotted to Daimler executives and eight to Chrysler executives. Its members included Juergen Schrempp and Robert Eaton who were co-chairmen of the board (see Exhibit 3). The four remaining members of the Dream Team were also appointed to the new board of management.

Not only did there appear to be unrest among top executives, there also appeared to be some discontent elsewhere in the organizations. At the Paris auto show in late November 1998, Mercedes-Benz (M-B) engineers frequented the Chrysler booth and mocked the quality and technology of Chrysler's cars. Schrempp forced the critics to leave the show and apologize to Chrysler executives. Schrempp explained that the engineers were "old-fashioned and unwilling to admit that Mercedes has anything to learn from Chrysler."[3]

Dennis Pawley had joined Chrysler in 1989 and was credited with the implementation of its lean manufacturing system, quality improvement, warranty cost reductions and millions in savings. On December 4, 1998, Pawley announced that he would retire as of January 31,

Member	Position	Background
Hilmar Kopper	Chairman*	European
Karl Feuerstein	Deputy Chairman/ German Labor	European
Stephen Yokich	US Labor**	American
Willi Boehm	German Labor	European
Erich Klemm	German Labor	European
Helmut Lense	German Labor	European
Herbert Schiller	German Labor	European
Peter Schoenfelder	German Labor	European
Rudolf Kuda	German Labor	European
Bernhard Wurl	German Labor	European
Manfred Gobels	Corporate member	European
Manfred Schneider	Corporate member	European
John Browne	Corporate member	European
Bernhard Walter	Corporate member	European
Mark Wossner	Corporate member	European
Robert Allen	Corporate member	American
Richard Thoman	Corporate member	American
Robert Lanigan	Corporate member	American
Peter Magowan	Corporate member	American
Lynton Wilson	Corporate member	American

Exhibit 2   DaimlerChrysler's 20-Member Supervisory Board, November 1998

Source: "DaimlerChrysler Appoints New Supervisor, Management Boards," *Dow Jones Business News,* December 16, 1998.

*Also chairman of supervisory board of Deutsch Bank, Europe's largest bank and DaimlerBenz's largest shareholder.

**President United Auto Workers

1999. He stressed that his departure had nothing to do with the merger:

> Let me put one thing to rest right now—this move has nothing whatsoever to do with the merger of Daimler-Benz and Chrysler Corporation. I believe there is incredible opportunity and potential, both professionally for individuals and for the combined business enterprise, in the new DaimlerChrysler.[4]

Pawley was the first Dream Team and board of management member to leave postmerger. Ten days later, Gary Henson, an American, was appointed senior vice-president of manufacturing; however, no board of management replacement was ever named.

Despite the fairly equitable composition of the board of management, integration efforts were marred by bickering between the Americans and Germans. Differences in management styles, processes, cultures and work styles fuelled a growing chasm between the two. When Chrysler executives voiced their reluctance to use weekends to fly in or out for weekday meetings, a Stuttgart manager suggested that the Germans were much more dedicated to their work than their American counterparts. One correspondent described the cultural differences as follows: "If the Dream Team was a rock 'n' roll band, Daimler was a methodical orchestra conducted by Schrempp."[5]

1999

By March 1999, many Chrysler mid-level managers and engineers had departed. In spite of this, DaimlerChrysler claimed that the integration process was proceeding on schedule. Even though strict guidelines segregated the Daimler and Chrysler brands, synergies were expected from joint administrative functions, market research, vehicle and spare parts logistics, and wholesale operations. As a testament to this approach, excess capacity at the plant in Graz, Austria, which manufactured Jeep Cherokees, was expected to produce the Mercedes Benz

Member	Company	Responsibilities	Changes	BoM Position
Juergen Schrempp	Daimler	Co-chairman		
Robert Eaton*	Chrysler	Co-chairman	Retired 03/31/00	Removed
Manfred Gentz	Daimler	CFO		
Thomas Stallkamp**	Chrysler	President of DC AG	Quit 09/24/99	
James Holden**	Chrysler	S&M in North America + Chrysler brand mgt	Fired 11/17/00	Removed
Dieter Zetsche	Daimler	S&M in non American + M-B brand mgt	President/CEO Chrysler Group, 11/00	See 2001 BoM
Theodor Cunningham	Chrysler	S&M in Latin America	Gave up BoM position 09/99	Removed
Eckhard Cordes	Daimler	Corporate Development & Management		
Thomas Gale**	Chrysler	Strategy, Design and Operations, Chrysler brands	Retired end 2000	Removed
Thomas Sidlik	Chrysler	Procurement Chrysler brands + Jeep Operations		
Gary Valade	Chrysler	Global procurement & supply		
Juergen Hubbert	Daimler	DB passenger cars		
Kurt Lauk	Daimler	Commercial vehicles	Succeeded by Dieter Zetsche 09/99	See 2001 BoM
Manfred Bischoff	Daimler	Aerospace and non-automotive operations		
Klaus-Dieter Voehringer	Daimler	Research & technology		
Klaus Mangold	Daimler	Services		
Heiner Tropitzsch	Daimler	Human resources & labor relations Daimler	Retired 09/99	
Dennis Pawley**	Chrysler	Production & Labor Relations	Retired 01/31/99	Removed

Exhibit 3   DaimlerChrysler Board of Management—18 Members: 10 Daimler, 9 Chrysler Executives, November 1998.

Source: "DaimlerChrysler Appoints New Supervisory, Management Boards," *Dow Jones Business News*, December 16, 1998.

*Dream Team Creator
**Dream Team Member

Note: Those listed in bold face font were on the Board in 2001.

Member	Company	Responsibilities
Juergen Schrempp	Daimler	Chairman
Manfred Gentz	Daimler	Finance & Controlling/HR
Dieter Zetsche	Daimler	President & CEO Chrysler Group
Eckhard Cordes	Daimler	Corporate Development & IT Management
Thomas Sidlik	Chrysler	Procurement & Supply Chrysler Group & Jeep
Gary Valade	Chrysler	Global Procurement & Supply
Juergen Hubbert	Daimler	Passenger cars M-B/Smart
Manfred Bischoff	Daimler	Aerospace & Industrial Non-Automotive
Klaus-Dieter Voehringer	Daimler	Research & Technology
Klaus Mangold	Daimler	President & CEO DB InterServices
Gunther Fleig	Daimler	HR & Labour Relations Director
Rudiger Grube	Daimler	Corporate Development (Deputy Board Member)
Wolfgang Bernhard	Daimler	COO Chrysler Group (Deputy Board Member)

DaimlerChrysler Board of Management, 13 Member Board: 11 Daimler, 2 Chrysler Executives, December 2001

Source: "DaimlerChrysler AG," Hoover's Company Profiles, April 23, 2002.

M-class sports utility vehicle. Using the Graz facility would deflect the need to build new facilities, saving DaimlerChrysler millions of dollars. In addition, the implementation of an integrated control system for financial performance measurements was expected to yield faster, more accurate reporting of divisional results. Further, all purchasing functions, from supplier selection to logistics, previously executed by each of Daimler's units, were combined under Gary Valade, executive vice-president of global procurement and supply in Auburn Hills, Michigan, at Chrysler's headquarters. In an effort to facilitate these transitions, DaimlerChrysler implemented a variety of exchange programs designed to increase executive and employee understanding of the cultural differences between the companies and their respective countries.

Despite the original three-year time line, on September 24, only 10 months after the merger, DaimlerChrysler declared that the integration program had been completed successfully. Further, in an effort to improve accountability and facilitate the decision-making process, DaimlerChrysler announced that it would streamline the board of management. The restructuring was intended to "reflect the global nature of the business, enable a greater focus on markets, accelerate decision-making and deliver greater shareholder value."[6]

The new board of management was reduced from 17 to 14 members. Two of the three positions that were cut belonged to Chrysler executives. Thomas Stallkamp, named president of DaimlerChrysler at the time of the merger and revered as Chrysler's "spiritual leader" in charge of the integration process, was "let go." Theodor Cunningham, executive vice-president of sales and marketing in Latin America, "stepped down" to focus on distribution and brand development as executive vice-president of global sales and marketing for DaimlerChrysler Corporation (DCC), the new designation for the American arm of DaimlerChrysler. Kurt Lauk, executive vice-president of commercial vehicles, left the company and was succeeded by Dieter Zetsche. Zetsche already held a position on the board of management and had close ties to Schrempp. The position of president at DaimlerChrysler was eliminated, and James Holden, marketing chief, was named president of DCC. The streamlined board consisted of nine executives from Daimler and five from Chrysler (see Exhibit 3). The changing shareholder structure of DaimlerChrysler shared mirrored this trend (see Exhibit 4).

In October, further restructuring took place. To replace the sales and marketing positions that were eliminated from the board of management, the Sales and Marketing Council was created to develop and ensure consistent brand policy and increase customer focus. More importantly, the automotive business was broken into three distinct brand divisions: M-B/Smart, headed by Juergen Hubbert; Chrysler Group, headed by James Holden; and Commercial Vehicles, headed by Dieter Zetsche. All three were board of management members. The new structure increased the autonomy of the U.S. unit and gave managers more decision-making powers. In effect, it re-created the old Chrysler Corporation. The Chairman's Integration Council (CIC) and the post merger integration (PMI) teams, set up at the beginning of the merger and headed by Stallkamp, were disbanded. Further integration initiatives were allocated to the divisional levels. In addition, the Automotive Council was formed and headed by Thomas Gale. The purpose of the Automotive Council was to drive product integration and ensure the sharing of innovation, knowledge, technologies and ideas. Executives from all three divisions served on the Automotive Council and shared responsibility for finding ways to combine operations, architecture, componentry, and platforms.

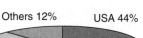

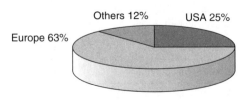

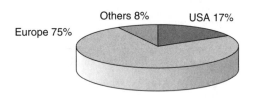

Exhibit 4   DaimlerChrysler Shareholder Structure, November 1998 to December 2001

The move to three autonomous units served to soothe the growing tensions between the partners. "These companies always underestimate the level of cultural difficulties," said David E. Cole, director of the University of Michigan's Center for the Study of Automotive Transportation. "They always say 'we'll deal with it up front,' but they never do."[7] Holden stressed that "separate automotive divisions should not be misconstrued as a retreat from integration."[8] He did not believe that morale was a critical issue and emphasized the need for effective communication. However, he did confess that, "I think we lost a little bit of our ability to communicate regularly and informally with our troops."[9]

In reaction to the changes, one U.S.-based auto investor stated, "If you wanted to look at it from the bullish spin, you might say that Schrempp will get everyone playing his way. He is creating his own team." On a darker note, "He just wants his loyalists there, regardless of their track record."[10] The further departure of highly regarded Chrysler executives and the imposed changes also accelerated the decline of morale in Auburn Hills.

This bad news arrived just prior to the good news. For the nine-month period ending September 30, net income and revenues had increased 12 per cent. Operating profit, adjusted for one-time effects, improved 15 per cent. The results were higher than expected.

In November, Thomas Gale voiced his expectations for potential synergies for Daimler-Chrysler in components that would "swamp everything else." He believed analysts were looking too much to platform mergers to reap synergies. While platform synergies can yield significant savings, the DaimlerChrysler merger did not intend to capture synergies from platform amalgamation. Mercedes-Benz models were rear-wheel drive, and most Chrysler models were front-wheel drive making combined platforms technically impossible. Instead, synergies were expected to be realized in melding components. According to Gale, "The platform is really about how we bend the sheet metal. The real expense is in the pieces of the car. If we can share suspension or transmission components, even if they're going into different end-products, the savings are huge."[11] Gale, aware of rumors that their German partners were choking Chrysler's creativity and fast time to market, accused the press of "National Enquirer Speculation"[12] regarding the merger.

By the end of 1999, industry volume was falling and Chrysler introduced few new products. The redesigned 2000 minivan was still in the works and, when completed, was not as innovative as the 1999 model. Prior to the 2000 minivan debut, Chrysler continued to pump out the old minivans, forcing dealers to load on rebates and incentives to clear the excess stock. The more innovative 1999 model and its reduced price tag ate into sales of the 2000 model.

Typical of Chrysler's "shoot then aim" approach, product decisions continued to be made without thorough analysis. Nonetheless, the target of $1.4 billion in synergies in the first year of the merger was realized and came primarily from combining purchasing and back office operations. Overall, 1999 ended with a 14 per cent gain in annual revenues, a 19 per cent gain in net income and a 5.8 per cent increase in the number of employees (see Exhibit 5). On a per share basis, annual earnings rose from $5.62 to $6.25 (see Exhibit 6). Critical analysts were quick to attribute the increases to merger synergies—the very synergies that they complained were not being realized over the first year of the merger.

Meanwhile, Schrempp was frustrated with the falling stock price despite good financial performance (see Exhibits 7 and 8). One executive commented, "Schrempp has gone through all these heroic efforts to put great numbers on the board, and the stock market yawns."[13] Schrempp believed that the technology stock boom was diverting investment from industrial sectors and that investor concerns of a possible economic slowdown might be playing a role in DaimlerChrysler's poor stock performance (see Exhibit 7).

2000

On January 26, 2000, Dream Team creator Bob Eaton announced his retirement, effective March 31. At the time of the merger announcement in 1998, Eaton had indicated that his role was transitional and would last a maximum of three years.

By July, the economic boom was waning. Consumers, fearful of a recession, postponed large purchases. The effect on the car market was a 15 per cent drop in sales. While Chrysler's operating revenues increased 17 per cent, operating profits and DaimlerChrysler's share price fell. Some models were reaching the end of their life cycle, and heavy incentive programs were being used to clear stock. This increased marketing costs and eroded profits. Schrempp

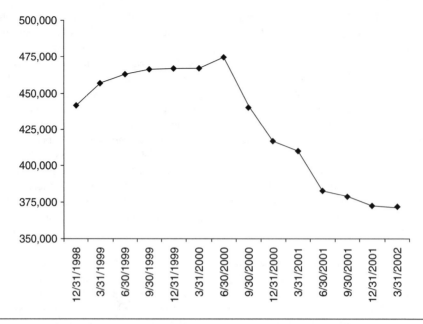

Exhibit 5   DaimlerChrysler Employee Numbers, December 31, 1998 to March 31, 2002

	1999	2000	2001
Revenues	151.0	152.4	136.1
Operating Profit	11.1	9.2	(1.2)
Operating Profit (adjusted*)	10.4	4.9	1.2
Net Income	5.8	7.4	(0.6)
Net Income (adjusted*)	6.3	3.3	0.7
EPS	5.77	7.39	(0.59)
EPS (adjusted*)	6.25	3.26	0.65

Exhibit 6   DaimlerChrysler Key Financial Indicators, 1999 to 2001 (US$ billions)

*Excluding one-time effects

maintained that profits would rise by year end from the sale of non-automotive businesses. He also announced three cost savings programs: to cut overhead in Stuttgart and Auburn Hills by 25 per cent and to eliminate 5,000 to 5,500 jobs; Strategic Cost Optimization through Process Efficiencies (SCOPE), with expected savings of $6 billion (though he failed to outline how these savings would come about); and to make the Smart brand profitable by reducing fixed costs by 45 per cent in three years.

In August, Schrempp announced he would no longer disclose information on merger synergies because the two companies were now one. This did not go over well with industry analysts who saw the move as shirking on the follow-up as to why the merger made sense in the first place. According to Christian Breitsprecher, an auto analyst at Deutsche Bank, "DaimlerChrysler's unwillingness to break out synergies creates the impression that they're not coming through at the anticipated rate."[14] Problems were also escalating

DAIMLERCHRYSLER (DCX) SHARE PRICE—NOVEMBER 1998 TO APRIL 2002

DAIMLERCHRYSLER (DCX) SHARE PRICE VERSUS NASDAQ, DJIA AND S&P 500
November 1998 to April 2002

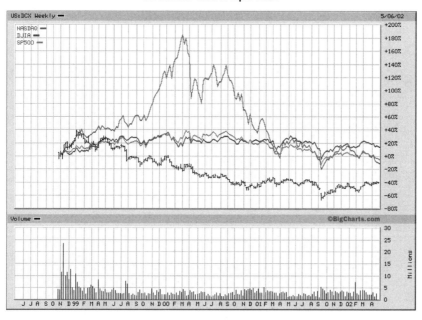

Exhibit 7   DaimlerChrysler (DCX) Share Price   *(Continued)*

DAIMLERCHRYSLER (DCX) SHARE PRICE VERSUS FORD (F) AND GENERAL MOTORS (GM)
(November 1998 to April 2002)

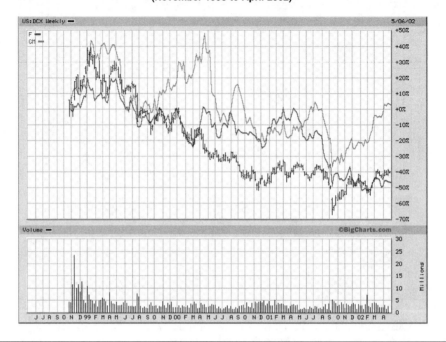

Exhibit 7 (Continued)　　　DaimlerChrysler (DCX) Share Price, November 1998 to April 2002

Source: www.BigCharts.com, June 2002.

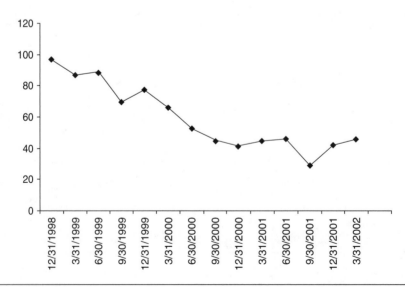

Exhibit 8　　　DaimlerChrysler Quarterly Market Capitalization, December 31, 1998 to March 31, 2002
(US$ billions)

with DaimlerChrysler's Pacific Rim partners. Earlier in the year, DaimlerChrysler had purchased a 37 per cent stake in Japan's Mitsubishi Motors for $2.2 billion and a 10 per cent stake in South Korea's Hyundai Motors for $470 million. Mitsubishi was losing money at an alarming rate and Hyundai was plagued by family feuds. Each of these deals caused DaimlerChrysler share prices to fall further.

North American auto sales continued to decline. Despite decreasing demand, Holden ran Chrysler's production at 113 per cent capacity. The rationale was that sales are booked when vehicles are sold to dealers, not consumers. In effect, Holden was only delaying inevitable cutbacks. Dealers became inundated with vehicles, necessitating heavy incentives to clear them and driving up marketing costs. By year-end, $1.8 billion had been lost in the last half of the year alone.

On Sept 29, Thomas Gale, the second-last Dream Team member, announced that he would retire at year-end after 33 years with Chrysler. However, he agreed to continue in an advisory role for two years.

By October, the Chrysler Group recorded a third-quarter operating loss of $512 million. EPS hit $0.33, down 75 per cent from the previous year. In contrast, General Motor's (GM) EPS was up 22 per cent on the year, while Ford's remained the same. Ford's lack of improvement could be directly attributed to its Firestone tire recall (see Exhibit 7). Without consulting Schrempp, Holden announced plans to idle seven plants as sales were expected to slow even further. He attributed the problems to "money drain from incentives, a poorly executed launch of the new minivan and the bottom falling out of the economy."[15]

It was at this time that Schrempp, in an interview published by the London *Financial Times,* confessed that the "merger of equals" was "never intended to be any such thing." According to him,

The structure we have now with Chrysler [as a stand-alone division] was always the structure I wanted. We had to go a round-about way, but it had to be done for psychological reasons. If I had gone and said Chrysler would be a division, everybody on their side would have said, "There is no way we'll do a deal." But it's precisely what I wanted to do.

According to Paul Eisenstein, head of The Detroit Bureau, "He's essentially told employees 'never trust what I say.' Among the media, it just confirmed what we all came to cynically realize."[16]

Because of his habit of implementing radical changes without consulting DaimlerChrysler, Holden, the last Dream Team member, was terminated on November 17. His departure eliminated yet another board of management position, reducing the total members to 13. Holden was replaced by Dieter Zetsche, who subsequently moved to Auburn Hills. At the same time, Wolfgang Bernhard, a close associate of Zetsche's, was named chief operating officer of Chrysler Group. On November 20th, his first day in the United States, Zetsche demanded the resignation of three executives closely associated with Holden: Theodor Cunningham, executive vice-president of sales; Kathleen Oswald, chief administrative officer of Chrysler Group and highest ranking woman; and Antonio Cervone, vice-president of communications. According to U.S. and German executives, "At least 24 German managers will be dispatched to Auburn Hills to implement Zetsche's restructuring plans."[17] No specifics were given about how the Chrysler unit would be restructured, but Zetsche promised that dramatic, painful steps would be taken. In response, shares hit a new all-time low of $37.90.

The news fuelled Chrysler employees' fears of job cuts, product development cost cuts and assembly plant closures. Schrempp (who, in a rare move, attended the Auburn Hills meeting) and Zetsche did little to allay their fears. Schrempp emphasized that staffing levels were too high: "We've got a 14 per cent (U.S.) market share, and we're staffed for 20 per cent. We will have a plan by early December."[18] Schrempp also apologized three times for his comments reported in the London *Financial Times* regarding his ever-existing intention to make Chrysler a division of DaimlerChrysler, not a partner. "I am the one to blame and I apologize to you. I do stand behind the structure, but I'm sorry if I offended anyone." When asked about the post-merger brain drain from Chrysler, Schrempp had this to say, "Someone asked me whether, if I could turn things back, is there somebody I would really have liked to keep? I mentioned one name, just to be polite. But generally speaking, I'm very happy the way it went."[19]

After Holden's dismissal, news leaked that the $7.5 billion Chrysler bank account was empty. Rumors spread that Daimler had used the money to purchase the shares in Mitsubishi and Hyundai. Then, on November 27, Kirk Kerkorian, DaimlerChrysler's third-largest shareholder, filed a federal $9 billion lawsuit against DaimlerChrysler accusing German management of lying to shareholders about the deal being a "merger of equals." At the time of the merger, Kerkorian was the single largest shareholder of Chrysler stock with 14 per cent ownership. Kerkorian argued that he never would have voted in favor of the deal had the truth been known.

While Phase 1 synergies of $1.4 billion were realized in the first year, Phase 2 technology sharing efforts were problematic. On the Daimler side, concerns focused on the possibility that using Mercedes parts in Chrysler products would damage Mercedes' luxury image. On the Chrysler side, Mercedes technology was sometimes rejected because the U.S. market was highly price-sensitive and would be unwilling to pay higher prices for luxury features.

2001

In January, 2001, two and a half years after the merger was announced, the press was still speculating on the cultural issues associated with the merger. At the Detroit International Auto Show, a Canadian correspondent commented: "The Germans were collected at the front of the hall, the Americans at the rear. Never the twain shall meet. The Germans talked to the Germans and the Americans talked to the Americans."[20]

The next month, Schrempp launched the Executive Automotive Committee (EAC) to focus on cross-divisional matters and a companywide strategic overhaul. The EAC was headed by Juergen Hubbert and Juergen Schrempp. Schrempp announced that, "Not everything succeeded as we would wish to have seen. A few things have not worked out and a few things have taken longer."[21] Zetsche also instituted a three-year, $3.9 billion turnaround plan which included cutting 26,000 jobs (see Exhibit 5), reducing material costs by 15 per cent, sweeping changes to senior management at Chrysler Group, closing six American car plants and eliminating shifts. Revised profit estimates called for a loss of $2 billion to $2.4 billion in 2001, break even in 2002 and $2 billion profit in 2003. By the end of the first quarter, losses reached $2.7 billion, the biggest lost in German business history.

By May 2001, Chrysler cut its Western European market share target for 2005 from five per cent to 1.2 per cent. Accessing the European market was one of the benefits that DaimlerChrysler had hoped to derive from the merger; however, market share had reached only 0.7 per cent. Schrempp dispatched a German team to Auburn Hills to scale back Chrysler and decrease costs. By early 2002, overachievement on the cost-cutting side offset the failure to improve revenues. Losses for 2001 came in at $1.9 billion, slightly below the projection made in February 2001. Overall operating profit for DaimlerChrysler, after adjustments, was $1.2 billion, well below the $4.8 billion to $5.6 billion target set at the beginning of the turnaround plan (see Exhibit 6).

In an effort to return the Chrysler unit to profitability, DaimlerChrysler's 2002 strategy included ongoing, fixed manufacturing and material cost reductions. In 2001, 19,500 employees and 1,000 contractual workers were cut, and the plan for 2002 included cutting another 3,500. Non-product spending was targeted to be cut by 58 per cent. Meanwhile, the Executive Automotive Committee was working towards corporate integration and was analysing products, powertrains and components to find commonalities. Of 45 projects identified, 19 were already being implemented.

2002

In March 2002, a Delaware federal judge denied DaimlerChrysler's request to dismiss Kirk Kerkorian's lawsuit on eight out of nine of the security law violations. The go-ahead was given for Kerkorian's lawyers to question Daimler-Chrysler executives and examine confidential documents relating to the merger. Only the ninth count, alleging conspiracy, was dismissed. Schrempp responded by saying, "[Daimler-Chrysler] continues to believe that all claims in these cases are without merit and intends to defend against them vigorously."[22] The decision set the stage for the discovery phase to begin; however, the case was expected to take years to resolve.

Perhaps Morton Pierce, head of the merger group at Dewey Ballantine LLP, had it right when he stated,

> In some sense the easiest thing about a merger is negotiating it and signing the deal. The hardest thing is putting it together and making it work after you've consummated the deal. You've got two different cultures, and if you're talking about different countries, you're talking not only about two different corporate cultures, but two different real cultures. It takes a lot of work to make that work.[23]

NOTES

1. This case has been written on the basis of published sources only. Consequently, the interpretation and perspectives presented in this case are not necessarily those of DaimlerChrysler or any of its employees.

2. DaimlerChrysler AG.

3. "Schrempp Silences Chrysler Critics," Automotive Industries, 12/01/98.

4. "Dennis K. Pawley, DaimlerChrysler Executive Vice-president of Manufacturing Retires," DaimlerChrysler AG, 12/04/98.

5. Ted Evanoff, "Clash with Daimler Leaves Once-inventive, Cash-fat Chrysler Struggling," The Knight Ridder Tribune Business News, 04/15/01.

6. "DaimlerChrysler Streamlines its Management Board," DaimlerChrysler AG, 09/24/99.

7. Joann Muller, "The One-Year Itch At DaimlerChrysler Its Reorganization May Not Be Enough To Bridge Culture Clashes," Business Week, 11/15/99.

8. Ralph Kisiel, "D/C turns 1: Bigger . . . but Better?," Automotive News, 11/15/99.

9. Ibid.

10. Joann Muller, Kathleen Kerwin and Jack Ewing, "Man With a Plan: DaimlerChrysler's CEO Forcing Out Key U.S. Execs—At What Cost?," Business Week, 10/04/1999.

11. "Chrysler Executive Sees Merger Synergies Increasing," Dow Jones News Service, 11/01/99.

12. Ibid.

13. Doron Levin Column, Detroit Free Press, 02/29/00.

14. Christine Tierney, Matt Karnitschnig and Joann Muller, "Defiant Daimler," Business Week, 08/07/2000.

15. Alisa Priddle, "Chrysler Confounding Critics," Ward's Auto World, Volume 37, #12, 12/01/01.

16. John Frank, "Managing Mergers," PR Week US, 11/27/00.

17. Bill Vlasic and Daniel Howes, "3 More Top Execs Go; 24 Germans to Arrive," The Detroit News, 11/21/00.

18. Ibid.

19. "Titans of the Global Economy: Juergen Schrempp–A DaimlerChrysler Perspective," The Globalist, 12/06/00.

20. Eric Reguly, "Daimler, Chrysler Still a Culture Clash," The Globe and Mail, 01/30/01.

21. Russell Hotten and Matthew Fletcher, "Daimler and Chrysler: A Marriage in Crisis," The Mail on Sunday, 03/04/01.

22. "Judge Rejects Automaker's Request to Dismiss Tracinda Lawsuit," AP Business News, 03/22/02.

23. Morton Pierce quote from interview on Capital Ideas, 01/05/99, Transcript #99010504FN-L07.

GILLETTE'S ENERGY DRAIN (A): THE ACQUISITION OF DURACELL[1]

Prepared by Professor Frank C. Schultz and Michael T. McCune

Version: (A) 2005-01-25

It was February of 2001, and James Kilt, newly elected chief executive officer (CEO) of Gillette, was preparing for his first strategy session with Gillette's board of directors. Kilt pondered what actions to propose in order to satisfy the board, as well as investors, that he had an effective turnaround plan for Gillette's Duracell division.

Kilt, 52, had been the president and CEO of Nabisco just one week previously and was widely credited with dramatically increasing its performance. Gillette's board, which included investor Warren Buffett, hired Kilt to take charge of a company that "had gone nowhere for four years."[2] Gillette's stock price, at $34, had fallen 45 per cent since its high in 1999.

Kilt's biggest challenge in the strategy session, which was just two weeks away, was to lay out a plan for Duracell. Gillette had originally acquired Duracell in September of 1996 for $7.3 billion in stock. Gillette's earnings had been growing at 17 per cent annually for the six years prior to the acquisition. "People are going to be surprised by how well we do," stated then CEO, Alfred M. Zeien in regard to the acquisition, "[Duracell will] make the next five years [at Gillette] even better than the last five."[3]

THE GILLETTE COMPANY[4]

When King C. Gillette founded the Safety Razor Company in 1901 in a small office located over a fish store in Boston, he sold only 58 razors and 168 blades in his first three years of operation. One century later, the company that still carries his name totalled more than $9.2 billion in revenues in 2000. During those 100 years, Gillette became one of the most recognizable name brands from the United States to Europe to the Far East. Even as early as 1926, King C. Gillette

said of the safety razor that he invented, "There is no other article for individual use so universally known or widely distributed."

Gillette has introduced a number of new razor shaving systems during the last 30 years, beginning with the Trac II shaving system in 1971 and followed by a new system in 1977 known as the Gillette Atra. Between 1977 and 1988, new disposable razors with pivoting heads and twin blades were introduced along with an updated version of the original Trac II razor. Then, in 1990, the company introduced the Sensor shaving system and followed its release several years later with the Sensor Excel and the Sensor for Women. In 1998, Gillette brought another new shaving system to the market—the Mach3 razor. In 2001, the Mach3 and the Sensor were the top two shaving systems in the United States.

During its first 100 years, Gillette diversified its businesses to include more than razors. At the beginning of 2001, the Gillette Company comprised four distinct business segments: personal-grooming products, small appliances, oral care products and portable power.

The personal grooming segment included men's and women's razors, shaving creams and lotions, and deodorants. In this segment, Gillette operated under the name brands of Gillette, Right Guard, Soft & Dri and Dry Idea. In 2000, Gillette ranked fifth in personal care manufacturers. It has been the world leader in shaving products over the last century, holding a 77.2 per cent market share in the razor blade refill market and 52.4 per cent market share in the disposable razor market. Gillette had become the world's second largest deodorant producer, behind Proctor and Gamble. In 2000, personal grooming products generated $4.385 billion in revenues. This segment also accounted for $1.42 billion of Gillette's operating margin (see Exhibits 1 and 2

	2000	1999	1998	1997
Assets				
Current Assets				
Cash and cash equivalents	$62	$80	$102	$105
Receivables, less allowances	2,506	2,527	2,943	2,522
Inventories	1,162	1,392	1,595	1,500
Deferred income taxes	566	309	517	320
Other current assets	386	1,489	283	243
Total Current Assets	**4,682**	**5,797**	**5,440**	**4,690**
Property, plants, and equipment, net of accumulated depreciation	3,550	3,467	3,472	3,104
Intangible assets, less accumulated amortization	1,574	1,897	2,448	2,423
Other Assets	596	625	542	647
Total Assets	**$10,402**	**$11,786**	**$11,902**	**$10,864**
Liabilities and Stockholders' Equity				
Current Liabilities				
Loans payable	$2,195	$1,440	$981	$552
Current portion of long-term debt	631	358	9	9
Accounts payable and accrued liabilities	2,346	2,149	2,170	1,794
Income taxes	299	233	318	286
Total Current Liabilities	**5,471**	**4,180**	**3,478**	**2,641**
Long-term debt	1,650	2,931	2,256	1,476
Deferred income taxes	450	423	411	359
Other long-term liabilities	767	795	898	1,101
Minority interest	41	38	39	39
Contingent redemption value of common stock put options	99	359	277	407
Total Liabilities	**8,478**	**8,726**	**7,359**	**6,023**
Stockholders' Equity				
8.0% cumulative series C ESOP convertible preferred, without par value	—	85	90	93
Unearned ESOP compensation	—	(4)	(10)	(17)
Common stock, par value $1 per share	1,365	1,364	1,358	1,353
Additional paid-in capital	973	748	621	309
Retained earnings	5,853	6,147	5,529	5,021
Accumulated other comprehensive Income				
Foreign currency translation	(1,280)	(1,031)	(826)	(790)
Pension adjustment	(34)	(30)	(47)	(20)
Treasury stock	(4,953)	(4,219)	(2,172)	(1,108)
Total Stockholders' Equity	**1,924**	**3,060**	**4,543**	**4,841**
Total Liabilities and Stockholders' Equity	**$10,402**	**$11,786**	**$11,902**	**$10,864**

Exhibit 1   Gillette Company Financial Statements, Balance Sheet (for years ending December 31) (in US$ millions)

Source: Company files.

	2000	1999	1998
Net sales	$9,295	$9,154	$9,200
Cost of sales	3,384	3,392	3,499
Gross profit	**5,911**	**5,762**	**5,701**
Selling, general and administrative expenses	3,827	3,675	3,485
Restructuring and asset impairment charges	572	—	440
Profit from operations	**1,512**	**2,087**	**1,776**
Nonoperating charges (income)			
Interest income	—	—	—
Interest expense	223	136	94
Other charges - net	6	46	34
	224	175	120
Income from continuing operations before income taxes	1,288	1,912	1,656
Income taxes	467	664	583
Loss on disposal of discontinued operations, net of tax	(428)	—	—
Income (loss) from discontinued operations, net of tax	(1)	12	8
Net Income	**$392**	**$1,260**	**$1,081**
Net income (loss) per common share, basic			
Continuing operations	$0.78	$1.14	$0.95
Disposal of discontinued operations	(0.41)	—	—
Discontinued operations	—	0.01	0.01
Net Income	**$0.37**	**$1.15**	**$0.96**
Net income (loss) per common share, assuming full dilution			
Continuing operations	$0.77	$1.13	$0.94
Disposal of discontinued operations	(0.40)	—	—
Discontinued operations	—	0.01	0.01
Net Income	**$0.37**	**$1.14**	**$0.95**
Weighted average number of common shares outstanding			
Basic	1,054	1,089	1,117
Assuming full dilution	1,063	1,111	1,144

Exhibit 2   Gillette Company Financial Statements, Income Statements (for years ending December 31) (in US$ millions)

Source: Company files.

for Gillette Company's balance sheets and income statements; Exhibit 3 for the stock price performance of Gillette, ticker symbol "G").

In the area of small appliances, Braun became part of the company in 1964. Some products that carried the Braun logo were electric razors, coffee makers and hair dryers. In 2000, Braun held 16 per cent of the men's electronic shaver market and ranked fifth in the production of coffee makers. This segment produced total revenues of $1.65 billion in 2000 and an operating margin of $218 million.

Gillette was also involved in the oral hygiene market since its acquisition of Oral-B laboratories in 1994. Oral B and Braun combined their capabilities to create the best selling powered toothbrush, the Braun Oral-B 3D. In 2000, Oral-B generated $676 million in revenues for Gillette, along with a $75 million profit margin.

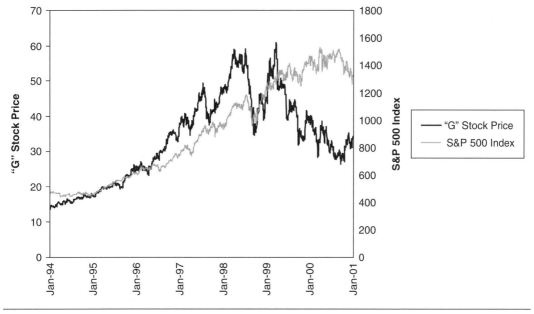

Exhibit 3   Stock Price of Gillette Company (G), Compared to S&P 500 Index

In the portable power segment, the company acquired Duracell, the United States' leading producer of alkaline batteries, in 1996. In 2000, Duracell accounted for $2.6 billion of Gillette's total revenues and $439 million of its total operating margin.

Gillette also had a stationery division during a large portion of its history, mainly consisting of Paper Mate, which manufactured pens and other similar items. Gillette sold this division to Newell Rubbermaid for a loss of $428 million in 2000.

THE ACQUISITION OF DURACELL

During the later half of the 20th century, the Gillette Company diversified into a number of businesses. Its acquisitions ranged from Paper Mate to Braun to Oral-B. During the 1990s, it was rumored that Gillette was seeking another product line that would fit well within its current worldwide distribution network and would offer significant market growth. In September of 1996, Gillette announced the purchase of the Duracell Corporation for $7.3 billion in stock. The purchase was overwhelmingly approved by Gillette stockholders at an annual meeting in December of the same year. The acquisition was highly regarded in the investing community as well with investment analyst Connie Maneaty, who stated, "This is a brilliant deal for Gillette. The opportunity to take two global franchises like Gillette razors and Duracell batteries comes along so infrequently."[5]

Before its acquisition by Gillette, Duracell had been the leading producer of alkaline batteries in the United States. Between 1991 and 1996, the company had experienced consistent growth in revenues of about eight per cent per year and had increased total revenues by 46 per cent during that time frame. The company also increased operating margins by more than 75 per cent. At the time, 20 per cent of Duracell's sales were outside of the United States. In 1996, 37 per cent of Gillette's revenues came from the United States; 32 per cent from Western Europe; 11 per cent from Latin America; and 20 per cent from other global areas.

The Gillette Company was known for its solid relationships with vendors around the world, especially drug stores and retailers. Analyst Amy Low said at the time of the merger, "There's a perfect fit between the two companies in terms of channels of distribution."[6] Gillette was determined to make a smooth transition for Duracell and its employees. Charles R. Perrin, the chairman and CEO of Duracell at the time of the acquisition, was offered a job at Gillette as head of Duracell operations. Gillette also offered generous departure terms for any Duracell employee whose job would be eliminated because of the combination. At the time of the acquisition, the restructuring of Duracell was estimated to result in cost savings of $80 million to $120 million per year.

BATTERIES AND THE BATTERY INDUSTRY

A battery is simply an electrochemical container of stored energy that is used on demand. The use of batteries can be traced back to as early as the late 18th century when Alessandro Volta began to experiment with zinc and silver plates. He would create what would become the world's first dry battery, in which solid metals interacted with each other to create a chemical reaction. Soon after, Georges Leclanche developed the first working battery, which was widely used in the telegraph system. His "wet cell" battery, which used a liquid substance to create a chemical reaction, was contained in a porous pot and was the prelude to what would become the zinc-carbon battery. Since then, most batteries used in today's society are dry cell batteries including the familiar alkaline battery that, as an industry, generated $2.6 billion in U.S. domestic sales in 2000.

Batteries can generally be divided into two separate categories: primary and secondary. It is important to note that these categorizations do not necessarily refer to a battery's use in a device. Instead, they mainly refer to the battery's ability to be recharged. Primary batteries could not easily be recharged so they were made for one-time use; once the battery had discharged its energy, it was discarded. On the other hand, secondary batteries were those that could be recharged multiple times over the course of their life. Primary and secondary batteries each offered their own advantages and disadvantages. Primary batteries tended to hold their charge for longer amounts of time and were less expensive than secondary batteries. However, secondary batteries had a higher energy density and were more usable in extreme temperatures. The difference between these batteries often came down to their applications.

Primary batteries mainly consisted of alkaline and zinc-carbon cells. Companies such as Duracell and Energizer concentrated on the disposable market because they believed that consumers were more apt to want a convenient, no hassle, portable power source. Alkaline batteries became the standard in the United States due to the fact that they lasted six times longer than the outdated zinc-carbon. However, in countries outside the United States, zinc-carbon batteries still held a majority of the market share. Conversion to alkaline outside the United States was much slower than originally expected, and hindered international sales of some U.S. battery companies. For example, in India, alkaline batteries made up only three per cent of the battery market compared to 70 per cent in developed countries. This has been attributed to tough economic conditions and the high cost of building new battery manufacturing facilities capable of handling the production of alkaline batteries.

The secondary battery market also had a variety of different types of batteries. This battery market consisted of lead-acid, nickel-containing (NiCd and NiMH), and lithium-ion batteries. Lead-acid batteries were most commonly found in automobiles and other transportation uses. Nickel-containing and lithium-ion batteries were used in electronic consumer products that utilized a rechargeable battery. Lithium batteries have increased in popularity for high drain devices such as laptop computers and cellular phones due to their high energy density and weight. However, most other rechargeable consumer products used a nickel-containing secondary battery.

Batteries also came in a variety of sizes and shapes. The International Electrotechnical Commission was responsible for creating standardized numbers for the different sizes of batteries; these numbers incorporated both a battery's size and electrochemical makeup. These standardization codes differed from those often printed on a manufacturer's packaging. Although the American National Standards Institute's designations for batteries officially no longer existed, they were still used by manufacturers for battery labelling in relation to their size. For alkaline batteries, the most popular sizes that were available on the market were AAA, AA, C, D and 9-Volt. The AA size accounted for almost half of all alkaline battery sales. (Exhibit 4 shows dollar sales volume by battery size in 2000). Other primary battery types in use today included miniature batteries used for hearing-aids and electronic watches.

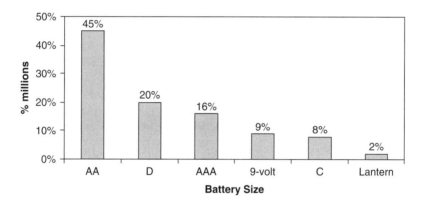

Exhibit 4   Sales by Battery Size in 2000 (in US$)

Source: Market Share Reporter.

It was estimated by industry experts that about 75 per cent of all alkaline battery sales were a result of impulse purchases.[7] Batteries ranked as 25th in sales in the top 200 products of general merchandise/health and beauty aids for retailers. The distribution of alkaline batteries occurred through three main channels in the United States: supermarkets, drug stores and discounters. These retailers often marketed alkaline batteries at impulse buying locations such as the checkout lane and then complemented those with other displays in separate departments. An unidentified director of marketing services of a battery supplier has said, "It's critical for manufacturers to assist merchants in effectively maximizing their retail floors. Providing merchandising and display avenues that enable retailers to market the high impulse nature of batteries would be a useful step."[8] As a result, battery manufacturers have tried to meet the diverse needs of the retailers by providing different displays and other tools such as clip-strips, which are small hangers attached on the end of a grocery or merchandise aisle, to place batteries in limited spaces.

In 2000, discounters were responsible for 52.5 per cent of total dollar sales of alkaline batteries (see Exhibit 5). This figure has increased steadily during the previous four years from 48.7 per cent in 1996. Drug stores and supermarkets were the other two main suppliers for alkaline batteries in the market place. They held 23.8 per cent and 23.7 per cent of total dollar alkaline sales in 2000, respectively.

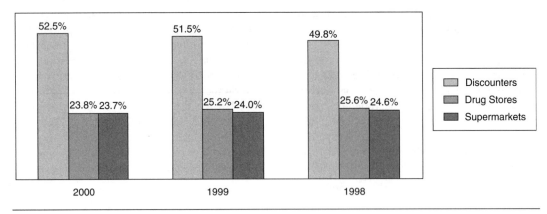

Exhibit 5   Sales by Retailer Type (in US$)

Source: AC Neilson data reported in mass market retail.

ALKALINE BATTERY
INDUSTRY COMPETITORS

The alkaline battery industry had three main manufacturers: Duracell, Energizer and Rayovac (see Exhibit 6). While Energizer and Duracell had been competing for many years, Rayovac was a relatively new force in the industry. In 1996, these three companies combined to total $4.8 billion in revenues and operating margins of $832 million. Since then, revenues have increased by seven per cent to $5.2 billion and operating margins have decreased by three per cent to $807 million in 2000. In the context of the two main brands, Duracell and Energizer, revenues increased 1.3 per cent during those four years, and operating margins dropped by more than 10 per cent. The only company to experience growth in both revenues and operating margins from 1996 to 2000 was Rayovac.

Energizer Holdings Incorporated

Energizer Holdings Incorporated was the world leader in the manufacturing of dry cell batteries, selling more than six billion batteries each year. The company's wide variety of products included alkaline, carbon zinc, miniatures and rechargeable batteries as well as flashlights. Energizer currently produced two general brands of batteries: Energizer and Eveready.

Energizer Holdings Inc., which had been its own publicly traded company, was acquired by Ralston-Purina in 1986. At that time, battery products were separated into two divisions by brand. Zinc carbon batteries were sold under the Eveready brand, while Energizer became the major brand for the company in the alkaline market. In 2000, Ralston Purina completed a spin-off of its battery segment, and Energizer Holdings became a publicly traded company again.

In the alkaline market, Energizer had two major brands, the original Energizer battery and the more recent release of the Energizer e^2. The e^2 was launched in 2000 as a power source for more "high tech" devices such as digital cameras, CD players and cellular phones. While the original e^2 was available only in smaller sizes, both brands soon become available in AA, AAA, C and D sizes. Energizer also manufactured rechargeable batteries for electronic devices as well as watch and hearing aid batteries. In 1997, Energizer held a 36.5 per cent market share of all alkaline battery sales. Since, then market share has dropped to just below 30 per cent in 2000. In 1994, the company generated $2.1 billion in revenues and an operating margin of $312 million.

	Year	Revenues	Operating Margin	Operating Margin	Growth-Revenues	Growth-Operating Margin
Duracell						
	1995	$2,079	$409	19.67%		
	1996	$2,251	$450	19.99%	8.27%	10.02%
	1997	$2,478	$526	21.23%	10.08%	16.89%
	1998	$2,576	$597	23.18%	3.95%	13.50%
	1999	$2,726	$606	22.23%	5.82%	1.51%
	2000	$2,577	$439	17.04%	−5.47%	−27.56%
Energizer						
	1995	$2,168	$345	15.89%		
	1996	$2,184	$352	16.10%	0.70%	2.00%
	1997	$2,178	$342	15.70%	−0.26%	−2.73%
	1998	$2,071	$324	15.62%	−4.90%	−5.38%
	1999	$2,000	$275	13.76%	−3.44%	−14.93%
	2000	$1,914	$279	14.58%	−4.30%	1.38%
Rayovac						
	1995	$415	$32	7.60%		
	1996	$423	$30	7.16%	1.93%	−3.97%
	1997	$432	$35	7.99%	2.13%	14.03%
	1998	$496	$41	8.18%	14.75%	17.44%
	1999	$564	$54	9.51%	13.84%	32.29%
	2000	$704	$89	12.69%	24.74%	66.54%

Exhibit 6   Comparative Financial and Trend Data

Source: Company files.

In 2000, the company reported $1.9 billion in revenues and an operating margin of $279 million. In the four years between 1997 and 2000, Energizer's revenues decreased, every year, and operating margins decreased three of the four years.

The Rayovac Corporation

The Rayovac Corporation was originally founded in 1903 as the French Battery Company in Madison, Wisconsin. Rayovac still had its world headquarters in that location and had grown to 3,300 employees. Significant growth was catalyzed by Thomas H. Lee's decision to purchase Rayovac in 1996 and to take it public. In 1997, an initial offering was made at $14 per share on the New York Stock Exchange. This was followed by a major facelift to the company's packaging and marketing practices.

Rayovac's main brand of disposable alkaline battery was the Rayovac Maximum. It was comparable to the products of Duracell and Energizer, but cost approximately 15 per cent less. Rayovac also engaged in the rechargeable battery market, selling NiMH and rechargeable alkaline batteries for consumer use. In the year 2000, Rayovac's revenues increased by 25 per cent and its operating margin was 66 per cent higher than that of 1999. Since its initial offering, Rayovac has had 16 straight quarters of increased growth in revenues. Before becoming a public company, revenues for the company were approximately $400 million a year. In 2000, Rayovac generated more than $700 million in revenues. During that same time period, Rayovac increased its total market share of alkaline batteries from 10 per cent to 12 per cent.

Other Competitors

During the 1990s, electronics manufacturers also began to enter the battery market. Sony was the largest supplier of secondary batteries to original equipment manufacturers (OEMs) and was also involved with the alkaline market. Sony's Stamina line of alkaline batteries was test-marketed in several areas. Sony claimed that these batteries performed better in the company's electronic devices. Kodak also promoted this type of concept with camera batteries. Another large electronics producer, Panasonic, produced consumer-orientated secondary batteries and was slowly entering the alkaline market. Other smaller producers of alkaline batteries included RCA, Gold Peak and the more recent brand, Star Struck. Major retailers and supermarkets also began selling their own private label brands of batteries. However, these batteries were often manufactured by outside companies, including Duracell and Energizer, and then sold under the private label brand. In 1997, the total market share of brands outside of Duracell, Energizer and Rayovac totalled 11.7 per cent. In 2000, their market share had increased to 13.3 per cent and generated $350 million in revenues.

COMPETITIVE DYNAMICS IN THE
ALKALINE BATTERY INDUSTRY

In May of 1997, Gillette announced restructuring plans at Duracell with an estimated charge of $283 million and anticipated layoffs of 1,700 jobs. A year later, Gillette made its first competitive move with its new battery business. At the same time as it was introducing its new Mach3 razor technology, Gillette made its first upgrade to Duracell's offerings. The "Duracell Ultra" was rolled out in May of 1998 in the AA and AAA sizes and featured 50 per cent longer life on "high-drain" devices such as digital cameras and portable CD players. Ultra did not replace Duracell's original "Copper Top" line, but instead the two brands were allowed to co-exist on retailer shelves. As it had regularly done with shaver technology upgrades, Ultra was priced at a 20 per cent premium over the older technology. In January of 1997, Gillette fired the long-time advertising agency associated with Duracell (Ogilvy & Mather) and hired BBDO (Gillette's advertising agency) to assist with the $60 million launch of the Duracell Ultra. The campaign promoted "More Power, More Life" (see Exhibit 7).

Duracell, however, was not the only player to upgrade its alkaline battery technology. Two smaller players, Sony and Panasonic had previously entered the market in the hope of leveraging their reputation in consumer electronics. Sony, which had never been a significant player in the alkaline segment but had long been involved in the development of battery technology—including the initial development and commercialization of the lithium ion rechargeable battery—introduced its Stamina line in AA size in February of 1997. Its introduction was supported by television, radio and concert sponsorships and used the message "So the beat goes on." Panasonic followed two months later with the Panasonic Plus alkaline in AA size for high drain devices, which it claimed was better than the industry leader. Like Sony, Panasonic was a highly recognized brand in consumer electronics and offered a full range of batteries including carbon zinc and lithium ion.

Rayovac also beat its two larger counterparts to the punch with its alkaline upgrade. It replaced its existing battery with the Rayovac "Maximum" in August 1997. The new battery was priced 20 per cent below Duracell and Energizer levels. Prior to the introduction of Maximum, Rayovac had employed basketball

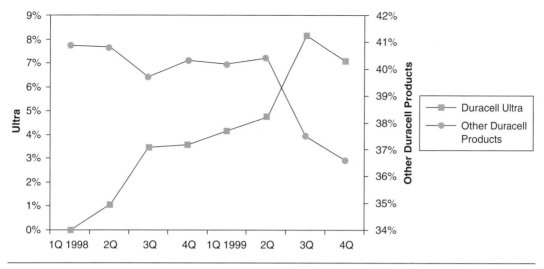

Exhibit 7   Market Share of Duracell Products (in US$)

Source: Market Share Reporter.

great Michael Jordan to promote its rechargeable line of batteries, Renewal. With the launch of Maximum, Rayovac spent $25 million on a new advertising campaign with the Chicago Bulls star and the tagline "Maximum Power, Maximum Value." An additional $30 million was spent one year later on the "Duracell Challenge," in which customers would receive their money back if Rayovac Maximum did not outlast Duracell and Energizer (see Exhibit 8).

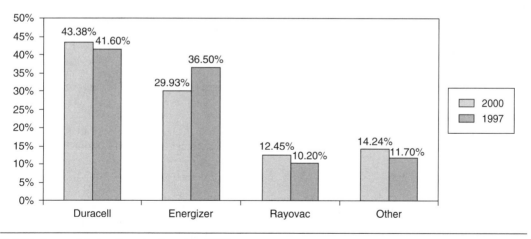

Exhibit 8   Market Share by Brand (in US$)

Source: Market Share Reporter.

Energizer, which had previously upgraded its AA and AAA batteries in August and November of 1997, announced in May of 1998 that it would come out with a new "Energizer Advanced Formula" battery in AA, AAA, C, D and 9-volt sizes. In contrast to Gillette's targeting of its upgraded offering, Energizer indicated that Advanced Formula was not designed exclusively for high drain devices but instead incorporated more active ingredients and patented resistors that made them applicable for all devices. According to Energizer internal testing and independent research, Advanced Formula could last 60 per cent longer than ordinary alkaline batteries and nine per cent longer than Duracell Ultra. A $150 million worldwide (US$70 million) advertising campaign employing the Energizer Bunny was used to help launch the product upgrade. In contrast to the launch of Ultra, Advanced Formula was introduced at the same price point as its previous alkaline, which it now replaced.[9] As one analyst pointed out: "It's a classic example of two rivals trying to one-up each other. Duracell's going to have to reassess its strategy now."[10]

In February of 1999, Duracell announced the introduction in June of a "new" Ultra with a 20 per cent improvement in performance over the original Ultra and now available in C, D and 9-volt sizes as well. Duracell research showed that the new Ultra lasted up to 80 per cent longer in digital cameras, 60 per cent longer in flash cameras, 80 per cent longer in mobile phones, two hours longer in super boom boxes and up to three hours longer in halogen torches. The new Ultra also had an extended shelf life of seven years, up from the previous five, and was promoted with a $140 million advertising spend. According to A. Bruce Cleverly, senior vice-president, business management and business development, stated:

> Duracell intends to continue delivering technological innovation that electronic device manufacturers can capitalize on as they design the next generation of high-tech devices. Offering this superior performing line of high-tech batteries will only fuel the growth potential of the high-tech device base, particularly as it expands to include power-hungry devices, which use all of the Duracell Ultra battery sizes.[11]

Just three months after the announcement of the new Ultra, Duracell took the competitive battle to the courtroom, charging Energizer with false advertising claims. A judge ordered the ads removed, claiming that the ads raised "serious questions as to the accuracy." Energizer's parent, Ralston-Purina complied. This was not the first time, however, that competitors in the battery industry had met in court. In August of 1998, Rayovac had filed a lawsuit to bar a former engineer from working for Duracell. In April of 1999, Rayovac sued Gillette, alleging patent infringement over hearing aid battery technology. Gillette ultimately prevailed with the judge nullifying Rayovac's patents.

In September of 1999, Gillette announced a round of layoffs and a restructuring. Gillette cut 4,700 jobs and shut down 14 plants, saving $200 million. Gillette indicated that the move was brought on by slumping sales in Asian and Latin American markets.

The series of technology upgrades and escalating performance claims by the major battery manufacturers caught the eye of the independent consumer testing organization that publishes *Consumer Reports*. In December of 1999, it published its findings on the relative superiority of the various brands, and concluded:

> The moral on battery shopping is simple: buy by price. Most of the time, the cheaper brand will work as well as costlier ones, whether they're powering portable stereos, toys, wall clocks or flashlights. Don't be put off by store brands; the ones we tested are as good as the big names for most bread and butter uses. . . . Sales and bulk packs can also save you money on many brands, big and small.

Consumer reports also commented that the "look" of many of the store brands (the dimples and indentations) matched those of the major brands. When asked about the potential connections between the store brands and the major manufacturers, an Energizer spokeswoman commented, "The relationship we might have with retailers is proprietary."[12]

The next competitive battery technology upgrade came in February of 2000 when Energizer introduced a "super premium" line of batteries named e^2 Titanium. The product launched in June of 2000 and this time was meant as a line extension rather than a replacement to its Advanced Formula brand. The $100 million introduction of e^2 Titanium did not employ the Energizer Bunny, which was to remain associated with Advanced Formula only, but it did encourage customers to "take power to the next level." According to Energizer, e^2 could, in some cases, last twice as long as normal alkalines and 78 per cent longer than regular batteries in regular cameras and 240 per cent longer than regular batteries in digital cameras. e^2 was priced at approximately a 32 per cent premium to Advanced Formula and four per cent to six per cent higher than Ultra. In that same month, Energizer targeted the lower end of the market by introducing a value priced Eveready alkaline battery.

In the same month that Energizer announced e^2 Titanium, Duracell announced its third generation of Ultra. Ultra with M3 technology would be introduced in September of 2000. M3 technology was "Packed with Power," and offered "More Fuel, More Efficiency and More Power." "More Fuel" as inactive ingredients were removed and more active ingredients added, "More Efficiency" due to reformulated ingredients that facilitated electron flow and "More Power" from patented and patent pending technologies that extended life and enhanced performance. A $70 million advertising campaign was used. Ultra with M3 technology arrived on store shelves with redesigned packaging but no increase in price.

Just prior to Kilts arrival at the beginning of 2001, Gillette attended to its traditional Copper Top line by announcing a new Duracell Plus that would be available in June of 2001. A $100 million advertising campaign touted that the improved "Copper & Black" technologies were designed to "Deliver Longer-Lasting Performance," marking the first change to the traditional Copper and Black line in nine years.

THE BOARD OF DIRECTORS MEETING

As Kilt considered the strategic options available to Duracell, he couldn't help but remember that his predecessor, Michael Hawley, had been fired after only 18 months as CEO, due in large part to an inability to reverse the trends at Duracell. It was apparent that, despite the initial optimism expressed by the company and the accolades from the investment community, Duracell had become a drain on Gillette's performance and had brought to an end Gillette's impressive earnings growth history. While selling off Duracell was certainly an option, would the board be willing to accept the implicit acknowledgement that the acquisition had been ill-advised? Were there other options, short of divesture, that Kilt could recommend to the board in two weeks that would turn Duracell around and return the Gillette Company to its former reputation as a dependable financial performer?

NOTES

1. This case has been written on the basis of published sources only. Consequently, the interpretation and perspectives presented in this case are not necessarily those of Gillette or any of its employees.

2. Banc of America Securities analyst William Steele.

3. "Can Gillette Regain its Voltage?" *Business Week*, October 16, 2000, p. 102.

4. Portions of this section adapted from the Gillette Company website: www.gillette.com.

5. William M. Bulkely, "Duracell Pact Gives Gillette an Added Source of Power—Purchase of Battery Maker for $7.3 billion Promises Distribution Advantages" *Wall Street Journal*. September 13, 1996, A3.

6. Ibid.

7. Mass Market Retailers (MMR), September 20, 1999.

8. Quoted in MMR, September 20,1999.

9. Energizer had raised the price of its alkaline lineup four per cent in April of 1998.

10. Tony Vento, Edward Jones analyst quoted in "Energizer Steps up Battle of the Battery; Its Long-Life Formula Follows Duracell's," *St Louis Post Dispatch*, May 27, 1998.

11. "Duracell Successfully Establishes High-Tech Alkaline Battery Segment," *PR Newswire*, November 2, 1999.

12. The case authors traced the patent numbers found on selected store brands to the major battery manufacturers.

CALL-NET ENTERPRISES INC. (A)

Prepared by Gail Robertson under the supervision of Professor Larry Tapp

Copyright © 2000, Ivey Management Services   Version: (A) 2001-06-26

On August 4, 1999, Call-Net Enterprises Inc. (Call-Net) was in turmoil. Crescendo Investments LLC (Crescendo) and some of the major institutional shareholders, together representing approximately 13.3 per cent of outstanding common shares of the company, presented Call-Net with a requisition for a special meeting of common shareholders. The purpose of this special meeting was to call for and consider the removal of six of Call-Net's nine members of the board of directors, including the removal of president and chief executive officer (CEO), Juri Koor, from both the board of directors and from his position as president and CEO of Call-Net. Crescendo planned to replace the six directors with nominees proposed in the requisition, and to appoint a president and chief financial officer (CFO) who was sympathetic to their purpose, which was to break up the company and sell off the assets. This requisition was also signed by shareholders holding approximately 25 per cent of the outstanding Class B non-voting shares, making this requisition a top priority at Call-Net. The meeting was scheduled for October 14, 1999.

On August 26, an independent committee of the board of directors was established, with Larry Tapp, chairman of the board appointed to chair this committee. The mandate of the committee was to:

- Actively pursue the sale of the corporation in whole or in part;
- Supervise any negotiations with third-party offerors;
- Oversee the preparation of the management proxy circular for the October 14 special meeting; and
- Consider value-maximizing alternatives for Call-Net shareholders.

The independent committee had less than two months to determine the best course of action for Call-Net and to recommend a strategy and plan of action to the board of directors prior to the special meeting.

CALL-NET ENTERPRISES INC. (CALL-NET)

Call-Net, incorporated in 1986, was described in 1999 by management as "a publicly owned Canadian telecommunications company offering local and long-distance voice, data and online services across Canada principally through its wholly owned subsidiary Sprint Canada Inc., one of Canada's leading national communications solutions companies."

Call-Net was based in Toronto, Ontario, with 2,600 employees operating out of 17 locations across Canada, as well as operating an extensive national network and operations in the United States and the United Kingdom. By the end of 1999, Call-Net was expected to be providing data, Internet, local and long-distance communications services to 90,000 business and one million Canadian households. Call-Net had a 16 per cent market share in the Canadian long-distance services market, a 25 per cent market share of small- and medium-sized business long-distance market and a seven per cent share of the data services market (see Exhibit 1 for product portfolio).

Call-Net's long-distance services, data services and local services markets were highly competitive. Key competitors provided similar services to those of Call-Net from a significantly greater resource base. Consolidations had been the hallmark of this industry in the past few years. Key competitors were:

- AT&T Canada—Metronet purchased Rogers Telecom Inc. in June of 1998, and agreed to merge with AT&T Canada to form a publicly

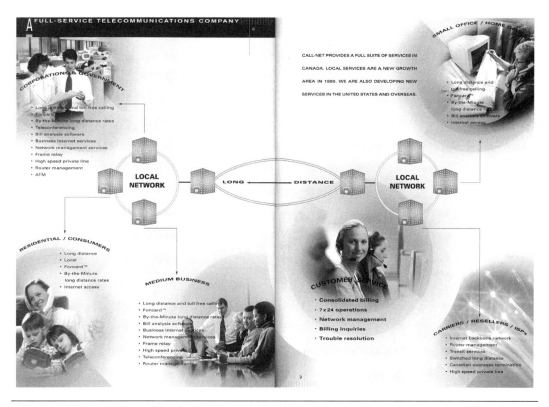

Exhibit 1   Product Portfolio

listed company in which AT&T Corp. had a substantial voting and equity interest.

- Bell Canada—competed internationally through the formation of Bell Nexia and investments in Aliant and Manitoba Telephone and competed nationally in the business segment of long-distance and data services markets. BCE Inc. entered a strategic partnership with Ameritech Corporation, with Ameritech acquiring a 20 per cent minority interest in Bell Canada from BCE Inc. Bell Canada still had the lion's share of the market, but competition had made major inroads recently, especially in the long-distance services market.
- BCTEL Telus—Telus Corp. and BC Telecom Inc. merged in January 1999, and formed a partnership with GTE Inc. to compete across Canada.

Revenues at Call-Net had grown annually since its incorporation thirteen years ago, with the greatest growth occurring since 1994, when long distance was opened to full competition. Call-Net management projected ending 1999 with an estimated five per cent increase in revenue over 1998. However, intense competition and price-cutting in the industry was expected to have an increasingly negative impact on the bottom line. The net loss for 1999 was expected to be considerably more than the $236 million loss in 1998 (see Exhibit 2 for 1998 financial statements and Exhibit 3 for 1999 Q3 financial statements).

Call-Net common shares were traded on the Toronto and Montreal stock exchanges (CN) and Class B non-voting shares were listed on the Montreal and Toronto stock exchanges (CN.B) and on the Nasdaq Stock Market (CNEBF). The Call-Net stock price for CN shares had fallen from Cdn$11.50 per share at year-end 1998 to Cdn$7.50 by August, 1999 (see Exhibit 4).

CONSOLIDATED BALANCE SHEETS

As at December 31 (million of Canadian dollars)	1998	1997
ASSETS		
Cash and short-term investments	189.3	558.4
Accounts receivable	235.1	141.9
Total current assets	424.4	700.3
Capital assets [note 3]	953.1	242.6
Other assets [note 4]	1,496.8	110.6
Total assets	2,874.3	1,053.5
LIABILITIES AND SHAREHOLDERS' EQUITY		
Bank indebtedness [note 5]	41.8	—
Accounts payable and accrued liabilities	515.4	198.0
Total current liabilities	557.2	198.0
Long-term debt [note 6]	1,332.7	564.9
Contingencies [note 10]		
Shareholders' equity		
Capital stock [note 7]		
Common Shares, unlimited authorized	124.8	124.8
Class B Non-Voting Shares, unlimited authorized	862.4	151.3
Class C Non-Voting Shares, unlimited authorized	347.8	128.4
Deficit	(350.6)	(113.9)
Total shareholders' equity	984.4	290.6
Total liabilities and shareholders' equity	2,874.3	1,053.5

See accompaying notes

On behalf of the Board:

Robert Crockford

Director

Alan R. Abraham

Director

Exhibit 2   Financial Statements 1998

CONSOLIDATED STATEMENTS OF OPERATIONS AND DEFICIT

Years ended December 31 (millions of Canadian dollars, except per share amounts)	1998	1997	1996
Revenues	1,227.6	920.9	712.6
Carrier charges	787.7	505.7	444.7
Gross profit	439.9	415.2	267.9
Operating costs	380.2	324.7	224.8
Integration costs [note 2]	81.7	—	—
Earnings (loss) before interest, taxes, depreciation and amortization	(22.0)	90.5	43.1
Depreciation and amortization	(111.7)	(46.6)	(33.2)
Operating income (loss)	(133.7)	43.9	9.9
Interest on long-term debt	(99.9)	(40.0)	(26.1)
Interest and investment income (expense)	(1.8)	12.4	9.1
Income taxes	(1.3)	—	—
Net income (loss) for the year	(236.7)	16.3	(7.1)
Deficit, beginning of year	(113.9)	(130.2)	(123.1)
Deficit, end of year	(350.6)	(113.9)	(130.2)
Earnings (loss) per share [note 12]	(3.32)	0.31	(0.14)

See accompanying notes

CONSOLIDATED STATEMENTS OF CASH FLOWS

Years ended December 31 (millions of Canadian dollars)	1998	1997	1996
OPERATING ACTIVITIES			
Net income (loss) for the year	(236.7)	16.3	(7.1)
Add operating items not requiring cash:			
Depreciation and amortization	111.7	46.6	33.2
Interest on long-term debt	79.1	36.5	25.5
Foreign exchange loss on refinancing	16.3	—	—
Cash flow from operations before changes in non-cash working capital	(29.6)	99.4	51.6
Changes in non-cash working capital balances related to operations:			
Accounts receivable	69.9	(22.2)	(27.0)
Accounts payable and accrued liabilities [note 3]	(114.4)	61.5	26.0
	(44.5)	39.3	(1.0)
Cash provided by (used in) operating activities	(74.1)	138.7	50.6
INVESTING ACTIVITIES			
Investment in fONOROLA Inc. [note 2]	(1,510.1)	—	—
Acquisition of capital assets	(346.7)	(104.3)	(59.7)
Proceeds on disposal of capital assets	113.8	—	—
Investment in Microcell Telecommunications Inc. [note 4]	—	—	(7.8)
Other	3.9	(0.1)	0.3
Cash used in investing activities	(1,739.1)	(104.4)	(67.2)

(Continued)

CONSOLIDATED STATEMENTS OF CASH FLOWS

Years ended December 31 (millions of Canadian dollars)	1998	1997	1996
FINANCING ACTIVITIES			
Issue of capital stock	930.5	21.3	10.6
Issue of long-term debt	686.9	343.4	—
Repayment of long-term debt	—	—	(3.5)
Increase in bank indebtedness	41.8	—	—
Repayment of fONOROLA Inc. high yield notes	(198.0)	—	—
Debt issue costs	(17.1)	(10.7)	—
Cash provided by financing activities	1,444.1	354.0	7.1
Net increase (decrease) in cash during the year	(369.1)	388.3	(9.5)
Cash and short-term investments, beginning of year	558.4	170.1	179.6
Cash and short-term investments, end of year	189.3	558.4	170.1

See accompanying notes

Statements of Operations			
	1998	**1997**	**1996**
Net income (loss) based on Canadian GAAP	(236.7)	16.3	(7.1)
Integration costs capitalized	26.3	—	—
Deferred foreign exchange losses	(12.2)	—	—
Capitalized interest	8.4	—	—
Net income (loss) based on U.S. GAAP	(214.2)	16.3	(7.1)
Unrealized gains (losses) on other assets available for sale	(1.6)	21.7	—
Comprehensive income (loss) based on U.S. GAAP	(215.8)	38.0	(7.1)

U.S. GAAP does not recognize the disclosure of a subtotal of the amount of earnings before interest, taxes and depreciation and amortization in the consolidated statements of operations and deficit.

Earnings (Loss) Per Share			
	1998	**1997**	**1996**
Net income (loss) – basic and diluted	(3.00)	0.31	(0.14)

Statements of Cash Flows			
	1998	**1997**	**1996**
Cash provided by (used in) operating activities	(74.1)	138.7	50.6
Cash used in investing activities	(799.0)	(209.4)	(24.6)
Cash provided by financing activities	550.6	354.0	7.1
Net increase (decrease) in cash	(322.5)	283.3	33.1
Cash and cash equivalents, beginning of year	393.7	110.4	77.3
Cash and cash equivalents, end of year	71.2	393.7	110.4

U.S. GAAP does not recognize the disclosure of a subtotal of the amount of funds provided by operations before changes in non-cash working capital items in the statements of cash flows.

U.S. GAAP excludes non-cash transactions from the statements of cash flows, including acquisitions for share consideration and the conversion of liabilities to equity.

Exhibit 2 (Continued)

ADDITIONAL FINANCIAL INFORMATION

Historical Review	1998	1997	1996	1995	1994	1993
Statement of Operations ($MM)						
Revenue	1,227.6	920.9	712.6	457.5	176.3	133.9
Gross Margin	35.8%	45.1%	37.6%	34.0%	29.0%	33.7%
EBITDA	(22.0)	90.5	43.1	(15.7)	(31.1)	8.8
Net Income (loss)	(236.7)	16.3	(7.1)	(64.7)	(55.4)	(3.1)
Earnings (loss) Per Share	(3.32)	0.31	(0.14)	(1.58)	(1.62)	(0.16)
Balance Sheet ($MM)						
Working Capital	(132.8)	502.3	155.6	165.1	144.4	94.0
Total Asssets	2,874.3	1,053.5	575.5	524.8	400.0	254.8
Long-term Debt	1,332.7	564.9	186.0	168.1	140.9	10.8
Shareholders' Equity	984.4	290.6	253.0	249.5	204.3	222.9

1998 Quarterly Review	First Quarter		Second Quarter		Third Quarter		Fourth Quarter	
(Unaudited)	1998	1997	1998	1997	1998	1997	1998	1997
Statement of Operations ($MM)								
Revenue	258.1	207.7	258.5	224.5	358.8	236.6	352.2	252.2
Gross Margin	42.1%	43.3%	42.1%	44.0%	31.2%	46.3%	31.4%	46.4%
EBITDA	23.2	20.2	(59.0)	25.7	10.9	24.0	2.9	20.6
Net Income (loss)	3.2	4.6	(84.7)	9.5	(76.1)	4.9	(79.1)	(2.8)
Earnings (loss) Per Share	0.06	0.09	(1.57)	0.18	(0.91)	0.09	(0.90)	(0.05)
Balance Sheet ($MM)								
Working Capital	507.5	168.4	69.3	178.2	121.9	541.1	(132.8)	502.3
Total Assets	1,048.6	615.2	2,829.6	619.6	2,755.1	1,014.5	2,874.3	1,053.5
Long-term Debt	577.5	192.5	1,349.5	199.3	1,304.3	553.0	1,332.7	564.9
Shareholders' Equity	294.3	259.2	884.4	269.4	1,063.6	289.8	984.4	290.6

Stock Information	First Quarter		Second Quarter		Third Quarter		Fourth Quarter	
	Common	Class B	Common	Class B	Common	Class B	Common	Class B
1998 share price ($) and trading volume								
High	28.00	28.00	28.75	28.75	28.35	28.00	15.50	15.00
Low	17.50	18.00	21.50	21.85	10.00	9.85	9.25	9.25
Close	25.50	25.50	26.00	25.00	10.50	10.50	14.00	13.75
Volume (000s)	5,998	6,103	4,414	14,779	5,284	23,037	3,674	17,721
1997 share price ($) and trading volume								
High	21.50	22.00	24.25	23.00	28.75	28.75	29.75	29.75
Low	17.50	16.25	18.75	18.50	23.25	22.50	20.50	20.80
Close	21.50	22.00	23.25	22.50	27.35	27.25	22.45	22.45
Volume (000s)	2,215	2,796	2,926	6,078	2,475	3,509	3,011	2,527

Source: Company files.

OPERATING HIGHLIGHTS

	Quarter Ended		
(Unaudited)	Sept. 30,1999	June 30,1999	Sept. 30,1998
Billed Minutes (millions)	2,085	2,001	2,080
The Most™ Online Access Points	42	42	17
Residential Internet Customers (in thousands)	180	167	123
Local Access Cities in Service	3	1	0
Central Office Collocations	62	37	0
Addressable Local Access Lines (in thousands)	2,442	511	0
Local Access Lines Installed or Ordered	25,600	9,100	0
Installed	*17,600*	*7,725*	*0*
Order backlog	*8,000*	*1,375*	*0*
Fiber Route Miles–North America	16,200	16,200	14,700
Canada	*7,200*	*7,200*	*6,100*
United States	*9,000*	*9,000*	*8,600*
Number of Customers (in thousands)			
Residential	1,035	1,054	1,280
Business	87	88	87
Percentage of Customers "Bundled"	13%	12%	7%
Average Revenue per Customer (per month)			
Business	$647	$659	$765
Residential	$34	$35	$39

CONSOLIDATED STATEMENTS OF INCOME (LOSS)

	Quarter Ended			Nine Months Ended	
(Unaudited) (millions of Canadian dollars, except per share amounts)	Sept. 30, 1999	June 30, 1999	March 31, 1999	Sept. 30, 1999	Sept. 30, 1998
Revenues	$307.9	$323.2	$340.7	$971.8	$875.4
Carrier charges	202.4	214.3	239.2	655.9	546.0
Gross profit	105.5	108.9	101.5	315.9	329.4
Operating costs	(117.5)	(99.2)	(91.1)	(307.8)	(272.6)
Other expense	(10.0)	—	—	(10.0)	(81.7)
Earnings (loss) before interest, taxes, depreciation and amortization	(22.0)	9.7	10.4	(1.9)	(24.9)
Depreciation and amortization	(53.8)	(50.0)	(46.4)	(150.2)	(66.6)
Interest on long-term debt	(48.6)	(44.1)	(32.7)	(125.4)	(64.0)
Interest and other income (expense)	4.2	7.9	3.0	15.1	(2.1)
Costs on redemption of long-term debt	—	(48.2)	—	(48.2)	—
Income taxes	(0.1)	(0.3)	—	(0.4)	—
Net loss for the period	$(120.3)	$(125.0)	$(65.7)	$(311.0)	(157.6)
Weighted average number of shares (in millions)	90.4	90.3	90.3	90.3	65.1
Loss per share	$(1.33)	$(1.38)	$(0.73)	$(3.44)	$(2.42)

Results of the third quarter of 1999 include advisory costs and other expenses of $10.0 million as a result of the Company's Special Shareholders' Meeting. [1998–Results of the second quarter included a charge of $81.7 million in connection with the acquisition of fONOROLA Inc.]

Exhibit 3   Financial Statements Q3 1999

CONSOLIDATED BALANCE SHEETS

As at Sept. 30 (Unaudited) (millions of Canadian dollars)	Sept. 30, 1999	Sept. 30, 1998
ASSETS		
Cash and cash equivalents	$357.3	$261.3
Short-term investments	122.4	24.7
Other current assets	249.6	223.1
Current assets	729.3	509.1
Capital assets	1,072.2	874.4
Other assets	1,440.6	1,371.6
Total assets	$3,242.1	$2,755.1
LIABILITIES AND SHAREHOLDERS' EQUITY		
Current liabilities	$430.1	$387.2
Long-term debt	2,137.4	1,304.3
Shareholders' equity	674.6	1,063.6
Total liabilities and shareholders' equity	$3,242.1	$2,755.1

CONSOLIDATED STATEMENTS OF CASH FLOW

(Unaudited) (millions of Canadian dollars)	Quarter Ended			Nine Months Ended	
	Sept. 30, 1999	June 30, 1999	Mar. 31, 1999	Sept. 30, 1999	Sept. 30, 1998
OPERATING ACTIVITIES					
Net loss for the period	$(120.3)	$(125.0)	$(65.7)	$(311.0)	$(157.6)
Add operating items not requiring cash					
Depreciation and amortization	53.8	50.0	46.4	150.2	66.6
Interest on long-term debt	26.2	27.4	27.8	81.4	47.1
Loss on disposal of capital assets	0.5	—	—	0.5	—
Foreign exchange loss on refinancing	—	—	—	—	16.3
Writedown of other assets on redemption of long-term debt	—	17.3	—	17.3	—
Cash flow from (used in) operations before working capital changes	(39.8)	(30.3)	8.5	(61.6)	(27.6)
Changes in non-cash working capital balances related to operations	43.5	(74.4)	49.4	18.5	147.7
Cash provided by (used in) operating activities	3.7	(104.7)	57.9	(43.1)	120.1
INVESTING ACTIVITIES					
Acquisition of capital assets	(123.2)	(133.0)	(179.5)	(435.7)	(142.6)
Disposal of capital assets	20.9	41.8	51.9	114.6	—
Investment in fONOROLA Inc. (net of cash acquired of $287.8 and capital stock issued of $674.1)	—	—	—	—	(839.0)
Investment in Cybersurf	(12.0)	—	—	(12.0)	—
Other	—	—	—	—	(13.5)
Cash used in investing activities	(114.3)	(91.2)	(127.6)	(333.1)	(995.1)
FINANCING ACTIVITIES					
Decrease in bank indebtedness	—	(39.6)	(2.2)	(41.8)	—
Issue of capital stock	0.5	—	0.7	1.2	256.3
Issue of long-term debt	—	985.8	—	985.8	686.9
Repayment of long-term debt	—	(258.7)	—	(258.7)	(200.6)
Debt issue costs	(0.4)	(23.8)	—	(24.2)	—
Cash provided by (used in) financing activities	0.1	663.7	(1.5)	662.3	742.6
Net increase (decrease) in cash and cash equivalents during the period	(110.5)	467.8	(71.2)	286.1	(132.4)
Cash and cash equivalents, at beginning of period	467.8	—	71.2	71.2	393.7
Cash and cash equivalents, at end of period	$357.3	$467.8	$—	$357.3	$261.3

The comparative consolidated statements of cash flows and balance sheets have been restated to disclose changes in cash and cash equivalents and to exclude certain non-cash investing and financing transactions as required by the new accounting recommendations of the Canadian Institute of Chartered Accountants. Cash equivalents comparise only highly liquid investments with original maturities of less than 90 days.

Source: Company files.

Charts

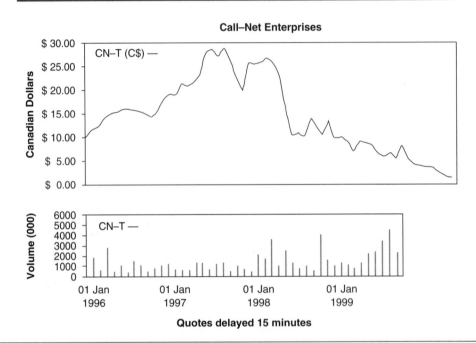

Exhibit 4   Stock Price January 1996 to September 1999

Source: Globeinvestor.com; November 2000.

Call-Net had been investing heavily in infrastructure for the future. Call-Net had purchased *f*onorola on June 27, 1998 in an unfriendly takeover bid, at a cost of $1.8 billion. *f*onorola was a leading facilities-based alternative provider of switched-voice long distance and data services. The *f*onorola acquisition allowed Call-Net to increase sales and customer service resources and gave Call-Net a national fibreoptic network, which they completed in April of 1999. The *f*onorola acquisition also gave Call-Net an entry into the United States where Call-Net expected to complete a fibreoptic network by the end of 1999. There was a downside to this acquisition however. Many in Sprint and the investment community at large believed that Call-Net had overpaid for *f*onorola shares.

Capital spending in 1999 was higher than ever, with the total expenditures expected to be more than $200 million higher than the $347 million spent in 1998. Management projected the cost of completing Call-Net's national fibreoptic network at $179 million and the cost of launching local services at $132 million in 1999.

Crescendo's belief that Call-Net had overpaid for the acquisition of *f*onorola and that the Call-Net stock was undervalued, a belief shared by the institutional shareholders, had precipitated the call for the special meeting.

CALL-NET MANAGEMENT AND BOARD OF DIRECTORS

Juri Koor—president and chief executive officer. Koor had more than 25 years experience in the data processing, manufacturing, financial services and telecommunications industries in Canada, the United States and overseas. He had been at the helm of Call-Net since 1991.

Board Members

- Hon. Alan R. Abraham, C.M., C.D., Halifax, Nova Scotia—lieutenant-governor of Nova Scotia;
- Jeffery Barnes—partner, Fraser Milner, Toronto, Ontario—Fraser Milner was the law firm for Call-Net, but was also Koor's personal law firm;
- Robert Crockford—president, The Valley City Manufacturing Company, Dundas, Ontario—Crockford's company manufactured custom wooden cabinetry and he was one of the first investors in Call-Net;
- Patrick N. Smith—vice-president, System Integration and Technology Planning Sprint Corp., Kansas City, Missouri;
- Peter Y. Tanaka—partner, Strathshore Financial Inc., Toronto—Tanaka was the former assistant deputy minister for Strategic Investments for the Ontario Government;
- Lawrence Tapp—dean, Richard Ivey School of Business, The University of Western Ontario, London, Ontario—Tapp had owned and operated a number of private companies and, aside from Crockford, was the only person on the board of directors with any operating experience;
- Thomas Weigman—senior vice-president, Consumer Market Strategy and Communications, Sprint Corporation, Kansas City, Missouri; and
- Lauren Wright—vice-president and general manager, Long Distance International Operations, Sprint Corp., Kansas City, Missouri.

The Crescendo proposal involved the replacement of members of the board of directors. The directors who were considered acceptable to Crescendo were three Sprint representatives (at that time, Smith, Weigman and Wright).

Chief Financial Officer

Vince Salvati—senior vice-president and chief financial officer. Salvati was formerly an executive officer at AT&T in the United States and chief financial officer of Bell Canada. He joined Call-Net in 1998 with more than 28 years of financial experience, more that half of which was spent in the communications industry. All of Salvati's experience had come from the inside management; he had no experience in public office or treasury.

The Independent Committee

The independent committee of the board of directors was formed on August 26, 1999; Tapp was appointed chairman of the independent committee.

The independent committee began its task by meeting with major institutional shareholders and with management from Sprint (a 25 per cent shareholder). From these meetings, they learned the following:

- There was no trust for the president and chief executive officer, Koor;
- There was no trust for the chief financial officer, Salvati. They felt he had provided incorrect forecasts and had thus lost credibility;
- Major shareholders wanted both Koor and Salvati terminated;
- Major shareholders believed that Call-Net had overpaid for *f*onorola;
- Major shareholders believed the stock was undervalued; and
- Major shareholders believed that the only alternative was to sell off the Call-Net assets.

The independent committee then began exploring options, from selling the company in its entirety to selling off portions of the company.

CALL-NET FOR SALE

A summary of the steps taken from August 1999 to October 14, 1999 were as follows:

September 1999

- The board of directors formed the independent committee and appointed Tapp as chairman of the independent committee.

- The independent committee selected Scotia McLeod to be their advisors and began to assist with the process of meeting with select shareholders.
- Members of the independent committee met with representatives from Sprint and with some of the major institutional shareholders to collect information which would help them to determine the best course of action for Call-Net.
- The board of directors separated the roles of president-CEO and chairman of the board. Tapp was appointed chairman of the board.
- Sprint had made an offer to Call-Net and on September 29, the independent committee informed Sprint that the offer for a technology deal which would have cemented the brand position was unacceptable to the board of directors.
- The independent committee began to explore other sale options, but attracted no firm acceptable offers.
- On September 30, the board of directors passed a resolution to appoint insider Kevin Bennis to the position of executive vice-president and chief operating officer of Call-Net Enterprises Inc. It was clear to the board that Koor was a liability and they needed a strong leader in a position to move up as needed.
- The board of directors began to develop the mandate for a special committee that would continue to pursue the possible sale of the company.

October 6, 1999

- The independent committee updated the board of directors on their activities. The committee reported that the general comments from major shareholders were that the actions surrounding the Canadian-focused business plan were seen as positive; however, investors continued to express concern over the company's operating performance and management, and the overall relationship with Sprint.
- Koor and Salvati reported to the board that bondholders were more favorably disposed towards management than to the shareholder proposal and that there was a reasonable probability that the Crescendo request for a waiver of rights from the bondholders would fail.

THE DECISION

The Call-Net board had every reason to believe that Crescendo, as part of the unfriendly takeover bid, would propose their own slate of senior management and board members for Call-Net at this meeting, knowing that their candidates for these positions would support an immediate selling off of Call-Net's assets. The board of Call-Net was committed to stopping the Crescendo bid.

The board of directors of Call-Net, upon recommendation of the independent committee, had to make a decision that would determine the future of the company. The board had to decide how to approach their meeting with Crescendo and the major shareholders on October 14.

10

CROSS-BORDER M&A

W ith the total volume and amount of mergers and acquisitions (M&A) across the world in trillions of U.S. dollars per year, cross-border deals represent roughly one third of all deals in the U.S. market and more in many lesser developed countries in the world. Interestingly, in the United States and Canada, while more cross-border deals involve buying firms outside North America, roughly 40% of the deals done involve the acquisition of firms by parties outside North America.[1] While domestic-only and cross-border deals are similar, being cross-border adds numerous complexities and issues that are unique and challenging. However, the rewards can be commensurate.

Numerous decisions are made before the decision to conduct a cross-border M&A (CBMA) deal. We often see one of two paths that management teams go down in getting to this decision. Firms commonly either make a "mode"-initiated choice or a "location"-initiated choice. Based on the mode choice, the firm may then end up in a CBMA deal. As well, based on the choice to internationalize (regardless of mode), the firm may end up in the same situation.

Critical choices in CBMA include the choice of entry mode and the country to which a firm might go. The modes discussed in Chapter 8 detail some of the more common deal types in addition to straight M&A. Joint ventures are particularly common when entering new countries because the foreign partner has local knowledge and capabilities. The one mechanism not discussed yet is that of greenfield entry. As an alternative to a cooperative mode, certain firms simply establish operations in a foreign country and grow from there. Here, we focus on the unique nature of doing deals with existing foreign entities.

Using our three-step deal framework—strategize, execute, realize—we can point out some of the unique facets of CBMA. However, across these phases, a few overarching complexities should be considered. The cultural differences between the firms and the countries can create both difficulties and opportunities. The cultural differences make communications and operational integration more difficult, but the existence of those differences may also raise initial awareness that all parties should be cognizant of the differences and to plan for them. Because of the added complexity, more advisors are required to deal with the numerous tax and legal jurisdictions and to handle the added regulatory

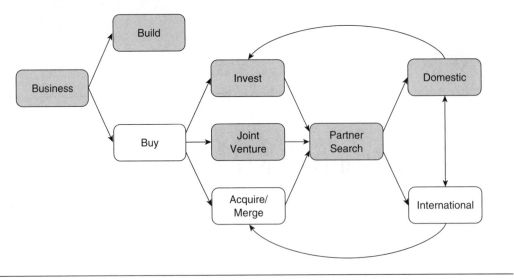

Figure 10.1   Path 1: Mode-Initiated CBMA

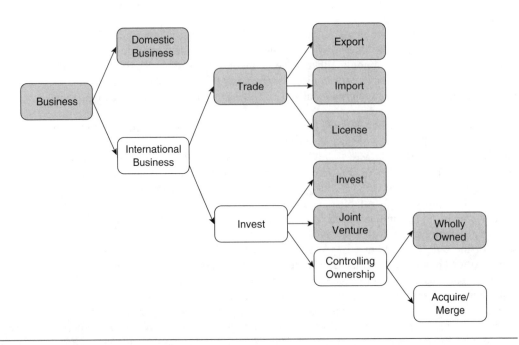

Figure 10.2   Path 2: Location-Initiated CBMA

processes. As well, maintaining confidentiality may be more difficult when more advisors are involved, more people are involved, and because different cultures may treat their confidentiality obligations differently. While these complexities cut across the phases, there are also some stage-specific considerations that are important.

CBMA—Strategize

The decision to do CBMA involves both the decision to do a deal with a nondomestic partner and the choice of the mode. The firm needs to bear in mind both its own strategic needs and the constraints and opportunities posed by any mode-country choice. For firms contemplating CBMA, we review several critical considerations.

Selection of Country, Mode, Partner

Regardless of the order of selection of the country target and mode, each selection must be both by itself and as a set of selections. A firm must choose from among the countries in the world where it wishes to do business. This is a strategic decision, perhaps based on lowering its production costs or on opening new growth markets. The choice of mode is also a strategic choice, based both on its internal resources and experience, but is also related to the choice of country, as ownership restrictions and norms of deal type exist by country. Within a country-mode choice context, a set of potential partners must be screened and a deal candidate found. However, the order of these choices is by no means country, mode, partner and instead is quite likely to be partner, then mode, based on where the partner country is. In any case, all three decisions must be made.

Country Restrictions

In choosing the country or the mode within the country choice, certain other considerations are important. Certain countries place restrictions on the foreign ownership of domestic firms, assets, and real property. In addition, operating in those countries may be difficult based on the difficultly of getting travel visas for personnel to move freely between the firm's locations. Even more difficult may be gaining semipermanent working visas to enable personnel to take on longer term expatriate assignments. As well, the legal environments differ around the globe, making protection of intellectual property more or less difficult. In more unstable legal environments where property rights protection laws differ, this may extend to greater risk that foreign courts or governments may actually appropriate firm assets. Finally, exchange restrictions can be a burden in ongoing operations, as certain foreign countries without freely traded and floating currencies may restrict the repatriation of profits.

Country Rules

The choice of country must also include the business rules and taxation risks and opportunities. Tax rules and treatments differ tremendously by country. These include the treatment of capital gains, branch taxes (when the firm is treated as a branch plant of a foreign owner), the ability to carry forward or back net operating losses, and accounting rules for the treatment of inventory, among others. The tax and accounting rules in the country may severely limit the ability for certain deals to make financial sense or change the choice of mode to maximize any tax benefits and mitigate risks.

Country and Firm Cultures

The different cultures of both the two countries and the two firms must be considered when the intention is to integrate the firms at some level. While international cultural differences are commonly anticipated, the firms themselves may differ from country norms, making things either easier or more difficult. Another element of cultural difference involves the leadership and governance norms (beyond the legalities of governance). These elements of culture may affect every element of both accomplishing a deal and operating the entity going forward.

Exiting Is Hard

When a CBMA decision is made, a firm should also consider its options for exiting. Such a future exit may be for either planned reasons or as a method to recover from a failed integration or poorly performing operations. The market of potential buyers for a failed foreign deal may be small and thus illiquid, making an exit more difficult. Certain foreign governments may also impose restrictions on the sale of the firm, as well as make the proceeds from the sale more difficult to repatriate. The bottom line is, a firm should build into its contingency plans that exiting may be difficult, time-consuming, and costly.

CBMA—EXECUTE

The execution of a CBMA deal follows roughly the same process as a domestic deal, but with added complexities and steps in each subprocess. We provide a framework of pitfalls that are common in CBMA.

Valuation

In valuing a foreign firm, the analyst must account for several different elements that can change the valuation. The cost of capital may differ, both as a result of how the deal is to be financed and the growth and riskiness of the assets and cash flows in that location. The valuation needs also to incorporate the exchange rate uncertainty in valuing the cash flows, under the assumption that repatriation or international trade is the goal. The firm thus must also consider whether and how to hedge any such risk.

Negotiations

CBMA negotiations are more complex because they include additional negotiated elements and must differently negotiate others. For example, the consideration to be paid must also include exchange rate fluctuations, choice of payment terms and currencies, and who will bear the costs of exchange costs. While firms normally agree on a choice of governing law, this decision must be made within the allowable bounds of their existing jurisdictions, and they may choose different governing laws for different portions of the agreement.

Deal Structure

The allowable tax, accounting, and legal structures for the deal differ by country, as do the benefits and risks involved in each choice. Because of this, the choices made may be limited or the parties forced to make certain structural decisions based both on what the laws allow and what the best business choices may be.

Due Diligence

The due diligence process is made tougher because cultural differences exist in the opaqueness at both the individual and firm levels. It may simply be difficult to get the appropriate information needed to thoroughly examine the other firm. Different countries require different levels of reporting and record keeping, exacerbating the ability to evaluate a firm. At the individual level, there may be different norms of honesty and fair dealing that make due diligence more or less difficult.

Internal Approvals

Each country has its own laws regarding stockholder and board voting requirements for the approval of different deal types and perhaps specific to cross-border deals. That said, if approvals are not certain, the ability to do hostile deals also varies, and thus alternative options may not be as plentiful.

External Approvals

For various philosophical and political reasons, countries around the world differ in their willingness to allow foreign buyers and sellers to do deals with their domestic firms. As such, CBMA deals may face additional scrutiny and will need to gain approvals from additional regulatory bodies. Because regulatory bodies from each country may battle for jurisdiction, these processes may be unclear. Of course, the filing and disclosure requirements, as well as the process timelines, differ by country, making this a potentially onerous process.

CBMA—Realize

As with domestic deals, managers running CBMA deals must then make appropriate decisions and take appropriate steps to realize the projected value in the deal. However, as with the other steps, cross-border deals face additional complexities in the realization phase that make them more difficult.

Whether to Integrate

The first choice is whether to integrate. Based on the cultural and legal obstacles, this decision may not be obvious. Of course, the two firms may be located numerous time zones and thousands of miles away, and so it is unlikely that the firms will close either location and consolidate operations. More likely, the firms will integrate certain operations (see the value chain concept in Chapter 7) and perhaps do personnel exchanges to facilitate learning and communications.

What to Integrate

As above, because travel may be daunting, certain operations may not be overly costly or complex to integrate. Because the firms serve different markets, there may be no need to integrate sales and marketing forces. However, it is likely that some processes within the firms are integrated at some level to gain any synergies foreseen. The complexity comes from finding what to integrate and how such integration can add value to the combined firms beyond the additional costs of running an integrated operation.

Postmerger Integration Complexities

Finally, the process of integrating the firms may be more difficult both in the postmerger phase and during ongoing operations. After the deal, communications to and among the numerous additional stakeholder groups must be done and perhaps with tailored messages. The retention of employees will vary based on differing tolerances for ambiguity during the change phases. Labor laws differ by region and may make it more complex to fire personnel to achieve postmerger integration (PMI) goals. Of course, the integration of accounting and financial systems may force additional and changed accounting procedures to comply with the reporting requirements in the reporting country. Internal systems will need to allow for the determination of appropriate transfer pricing mechanisms that are both agreeable and compliant with tax and trade authorities. The integration of systems across the firm is also made more difficult by the potential existence of multiple languages in use for systems and of different operating systems, hardware, and software. Finally, the issues of management control may be made more difficult when the firms are not collocated. Although a new management team (firm) may "own" and be "in charge," without local presence on the ground, local management may revert to running its own operations as before. As such, reporting arrangements and the definitions of job responsibilities and authorities must be made explicitly clear and reinforced with the physical presence of management to ensure the firms operate as planned going forward.

CASES

Bombardier Transportation and the Adtranz Acquisition

Bombardier Transportation, one of the world's largest manufacturers of passenger rail cars, has successfully negotiated the purchase of Adtranz, a large European manufacturer of rail equipment. The newly appointed chief executive officer has been brought in to manage the acquisition. The new CEO faces many challenges, including decisions about the pace of integration, location of headquarters, organization structure, personnel retention, and personal management style. Students may use this case to discuss postacquisition strategy and how fast companies should move to integrate acquisitions.

Issues: Cross-border M&A, postmerger integration, retention, management in a global environment, leadership

Vincor and the New World of Wine

Vincor International, Inc. was Canada's largest wine company and North America's fourth largest in 2002. The company had decided to internationalize and, as the first step, had entered the United States through two acquisitions. The company's chief executive officer felt that to be among the top 10 wineries in the world, Vincor needed to look beyond the region. To the end, he was considering the acquisition of an Australian company, Goundrey Wines. He must analyze the strategic rationale for the acquisition of Goundrey as well as probe questions of strategic fit and value.

Issues: Market entry alternatives, cross-border M&A, growth strategy, internationalization

NOTE

1. Thomson Financial Securities Data Corporation (SDC) database, 2005.

BOMBARDIER TRANSPORTATION AND THE ADTRANZ ACQUISITION

Prepared by David Barrett
under the supervision of Professor Allen Morrison

Version: (A) 2004-06-15

On January 10, 2001, it had been one month only since Pierre Lortie was appointed president and chief operating officer of St. Bruno, Quebec-based Bombardier Transportation (BT).[1] BT was one of three major operating groups of Montreal, Canada-based Bombardier Inc. (BBD) and, with 2000 revenues amounting to Cdn$3.45 billion, it was one of the world's largest manufacturers of passenger rail cars. In an effort to expand BT's presence in the global rail equipment industry, executives at BBD had recently completed a successful negotiation for the acquisition of Adtranz from DaimlerChrysler for US$725 million. At approximately twice the size of BT, Adtranz (headquartered in Berlin, Germany) would not only expand BT's revenues and geographic scope but would significantly increase its competencies in propulsion systems and train controls and would complete its product portfolio. However, before the deal could close, BT required, among others, the regulatory approval of the European Commission (EC). Lortie was well aware that the EC process could be long and protracted.

Although Lortie had not been directly involved in the acquisition decision or negotiations, he was a supporter of the merger efforts. As he assumed his new responsibilities, Lortie began a thorough review of the work accomplished and the planning efforts undertaken to ensure an efficient integration of the two entities. As part of this process, he undertook a series of one-to-one meetings with members of his senior management team. The meetings were designed to measure the strengths and weaknesses of his key managers, but also to discuss the strategic and operational priorities.

BT was structured into five geographically-based operating units—North America, Atlantic Europe, Continental Europe, Mexico and China—and one market/functional unit, Total Transit Systems—which focused on turnkey projects. In contrast, Adtranz was organized around product segments (i.e., high speed trains, cars, subway trams) and functions (i.e., bogies, drives, car bodies) making its structure and allocation of responsibilities quite foreign to Bombardier. Although each business complemented the other nicely and constituted a good strategic fit, the organizational structures were incompatible. Even though, BT's management team in Europe had not been involved in the discussions and reviews with Adtranz that had preceded and immediately followed the deal, they were keenly aware of the organizational issues and eager to establish their position as soon as the nod could be given to proceed with the takeover.

On January 10, 2001, Lortie had just finished his first in-depth meeting with Rick Dobbelaere, vice-president of operations of Bombardier Transportation, Atlantic Europe. Dobbelaere had come prepared with questions about how BT and the senior management team would set priorities during the interim period while awaiting EC approval. He presented these to Lortie in question form:

> Do we sit and await approval from the EC before taking steps towards the potential integration of Adtranz? Should we focus our planning on ways to improve the product quality and reliability of Adtranz equipment with existing customers? Should we start to institute personnel changes within BT in anticipation of the merger, and if so, at what pace? Do we focus on top-line revenue growth or start to immediately focus on bottom-line cost cutting?

Dobbelaere was highly respected, not only within the Atlantic Europe division but throughout Bombardier, and Lortie was aware that his concerns and questions were shared by others, particularly in Continental Europe.[2] But Lortie realized that he faced additional issues, including concerns over BT's ongoing operating performance. As Bombardier expected EC approval of the acquisition within a matter of weeks, Lortie and his team had little time to waste.

BOMBARDIER COMPANY HISTORY

The Early Years

In 1921, at the age of 19, Joseph-Armand Bombardier opened a garage in Valcourt, Quebec, where he earned his living as a mechanic. Early in his life he looked for a solution to the problem of traveling the snow-covered roads near his village, which kept many people isolated during the long winter months. Over a 10-year period, Bombardier used his garage to develop multiple prototypes of a vehicle that would make winter travel easier. In 1936, he submitted his B7 prototype, the precursor to today's snowmobile, for patent approval. This seven-seat passenger model sported a revolutionary rear-wheel drive and suspension system, both major innovations at that time.

After receiving an initial 20 orders, Bombardier assembled a work crew of friends and family to manufacture the B7s. Customers included country doctors, veterinarians, telephone companies and foresters. By 1940, Bombardier had built a modern factory in his village that had an annual capacity of 200 units. In 1942, Bombardier incorporated his business as L'Auto-Neige Bombardier Limitee (ANB). Shortly thereafter the company began to receive orders from the Canadian government for specialized all-track vehicles for use by the armed forces efforts during the Second World War. Between 1942 and 1946, ANB produced over 1,900 tracked vehicles for the Canadian armed forces. Although not a profitable venture, the war-time manufacturing experience allowed Bombardier to refine his manufacturing process and develop competence in government relations.

The 1950s saw technological advances in lighter engines, improved tracking and high-performance synthetic rubber. In 1959, Bombardier achieved his lifelong dream when ANB introduced a one-passenger snowmobile. At an original price of Cdn$900, the Ski-Doo sported five-foot wooden skis, a coil spring suspension system and could travel at speeds of up to 25 miles per hour (mph). Sales increased from 225 units in 1959 to 2,500 units in 1962 and 8,000 units in 1964. Joseph-Armand Bombardier died in 1964, leaving a Cdn$10 million company to his son, Germain.

In 1966, Germain Bombardier passed on the presidency to his 27-year-old brother-in-law, Laurent Beaudoin, and in 1967, the company name was changed to Bombardier Limited. In 1969, the company went public with the intention of utilizing the funds to vertically integrate and increase its manufacturing capability. BBD grew as the market for snowmobiles rapidly expanded in the late 1960s and early 1970s. The North American snowmobile market grew from 60,000 units to 495,000 units in the period between 1966 and 1972, and BBD captured one-third of this market. Between 1966 and 1972, BBD's sales soared from Cdn$20 million to Cdn$180 million while profits rose from Cdn$2 million to Cdn$12 million. Under Beaudoin's leadership, the company pushed into the lucrative U.S. market, unveiled new products and utilized aggressive marketing initiatives to drive the business. In 1970, the company completed the acquisition of Austrian-based Lohnerwerke GmbH. Lohnerwerke's subsidiary, Rotax, was a key supplier of engines for Bombardier Ski-Doo snowmobiles and also a tramway manufacturer. This provided BBD with its first entry, albeit involuntarily, into the rail business. The energy crisis of the mid-1970s put the brakes on the snowmobile industry, and when the dust settled, the largest of the six remaining manufacturers was BBD.

Bombardier Begins to Diversify

Laurent Beaudoin, the chief executive of Bombardier, realized that in order to reduce cyclical risks and ensure its long-term survival, the company needed to diversify into other products beyond snowmobiles. To bolster sagging snowmobile sales, Beaudoin began to seek out opportunities for BBD within a more broadly defined transportation industry. In the late 1960s and early 1970s, BBD made several strategic acquisitions.

Transportation

In 1974, snowmobiles represented 90 per cent of BBD revenues. By securing a Cdn$118 million contract (US$99.14 million) with the city of Montreal to supply the local transit authority with 423 subway cars, BBD had made its first major move to diversify its revenues away from its predominant snowmobile business. Using rubber-wheeled cars licensed from the supplier

to the Paris subway system, BBD's work won positive reviews from Montreal commuters. Further contracts followed, including supplying 36 self-propelled commuter rail cars to Chicago in 1977, 21 locomotives and 50 rail cars to Via Rail Canada in 1978, 117 commuter cars to New Jersey Transit Corporation in 1980, 180 subway cars to Mexico City in 1982, and 825 subway cars to the City of New York, also in 1982.

The mid-1980s was a turbulent time in the rail transportation industry, and BT looked to capitalize on industry uncertainty by purchasing companies at low prices and growing its market share through these acquisitions. Pullman Technology was acquired in 1987, Transit America in 1988, and controlling interests in rail equipment companies in France and Belgium in 1988. In the early 1990s, BT also acquired Concarril (Mexico's top rail manufacturer) as well as UTDC in Canada. These acquisitions and investments established BT as one of the leading suppliers of rail cars and cemented its international reputation.

Aerospace

In 1973, BBD commenced diversification into the aerospace business with the acquisition of a controlling interest in Heroux Limited of Longueuil, Quebec. Heroux designed, manufactured and repaired aeronautical and industrial components at its two Canadian plants. In 1986, following an international bidding contest, BBD acquired struggling Canadair from the Canadian government at a total cash and share price of Cdn$293 million. By applying aggressive marketing tactics, cost-cutting measures and tight controls, BBD was quickly able to turn operations around. Subsequent acquisitions of Short Brother PLC (an aircraft producer in Northern Ireland) in 1990, Learjet Corporation in 1990 and a controlling stake in de Havilland in 1992 and the remaining interest in 1997 firmly entrenched BBD in the civil aircraft industry. During the 1990s, BBD introduced a series of new planes including the Lear 60, the Challenger 600-3A, the Challenger 604 and the Lear 45. BBD delivered its first Canadair Regional Jet in

1992 and its first Global Express business jet in 1999, the CRJ 700 (75 seat jet) in 2001.

Corporate Balance

By the early 1990s, BBD had diversified to the point where snowmobile sales represented less than 15 per cent of the company's revenues. BBD still controlled 50 per cent of the Canadian market and 25 per cent of the U.S. market for snowmobiles, but BBD had clearly established itself as a diversified company. By 1992, sales had increased to US$3.43 billion and profits to US$104 million. While, in many cases, the companies acquired by Bombardier were in poor shape, observers noted that the majority of Beaudoin's deals and acquisitions had been turned around and were making money.

Different operating groups at BBD took centre stage at different times during the 1990s (see Exhibit 1). In 1994, the recreational products group seemed to surge forward, fuelled by increased snowmobile sales and sales of Sea-Doo watercraft, first introduced in 1968. Profits from this group represented 37 per cent of the company's profits and made the recreational products group central to the company's success. The mid-1990s saw a boom in the aerospace group as both regional and business jet sales took off with the expanding economy. Many observers credited Bombardier with creating an entirely new commuter jet segment as the result of product innovation. Aerospace group sales grew from 1996 levels of US$3.16 billion to 2000 levels of US$7.79 billion. In 2000, the aerospace group represented 66 per cent of the company's revenues and 85 per cent of its profits.

BT continued to grow during this period as well. BT was awarded a prestigious contract to produce specialized rail cars for the huge Eurotunnel engineering project. In early 1995, Waggonfabrik Talbot KG of Germany was acquired for $130 million cash. In late 1997, BT acquired DWA Deutsche Waggonbau GmbH of Berlin for Cdn$518 million (approximately US$359.52 million) and thus doubled its train and subway car manufacturing capacity in Europe. In December of that year, BT secured a US$1.18 billion contract with Virgin Rail Group of Great Britain to supply 78 diesel/electric multiple units and rail cars. In November 1999, the company entered into a joint venture to construct a manufacturing facility in China and to subsequently build 300 inter-city mass transit railcars for the Chinese Ministry of Railways (see Exhibit 2).

Bombardier Growth Philosophy

BBD sought acquisition opportunities that allowed it to add value to the business through the application of its existing competencies. Acquisitions were typically not viewed solely as financial plays but as a way for BBD to complement or strengthen its existing businesses. BBD prided itself on thoroughly evaluating target companies so that pay-back was not reliant on the divestiture of some aspect of the acquired business. In negotiations, BBD had also shown that it was not afraid to walk away from a deal if it meant overpaying for a business. But once a deal was completed, BBD had a reputation for being patient in the integration of the acquired company.

In addition to a strong track record of integrating acquisitions, BBD had strengths in product costing and tendering. It also had extensive experience in product assembly. Whether aircraft, recreational products or rail cars, most products made by BBD were assembled as opposed to manufactured. Utilizing external suppliers and adopting just-in-time delivery methods resulted in substantially reduced inventory levels, throughput time and assets. BBD sought ways to control product technology and design, assembly and distribution while outsourcing other non-core functions.

When taking over a business, BBD tried to eliminate waste and turn around underperforming assets by applying tried and tested management approaches over time as opposed to rushing to replace existing methods. This approach to acquisitions had garnered strong employee support over the years as workers realized that BBD would invest in new products and thus protect jobs. When BBD entered the aerospace industry through acquisitions, it did not replace existing

Fiscal Year*	Overall	Transportation	Aerospace	Recreational Products	Capital	Other
2001e	16,101	3,043	10,562	1,687	1,033	(224)
2000	13,619	3,446	8,126	1,473	739	(165)
1999	11,500	2,966	6,444	1,628	571	(109)
1998	8,509	1,679	4,621	1,633	245	332
1997	7,976	1,597	4,011	1,866	162	341
1996	7,123	1,575	3,309	1,641	140	459
1995	5,943	1,310	2,981	1,111	112	430
1994	4,769	1,312	2,243	791	97	323
1993	4,448	1,238	2,228	556	58	367
1992	3,059	726	1,519	391	56	366

Profits Before Taxes—Segmented by Division

Fiscal Year*	Overall	Transportation	Aerospace	Recreational Products	Capital	Other
2001e	1,428	121	1,237	86	(15)	—
2000	1,124	174	904	18	28	—
1999	827	148	682	(46)	43	—
1998	627	85	462	1	64	16
1997	606	63	270	212	47	14
1996	461	100	150	174	42	(6)
1995	346	66	141	117	22	(1)
1994	207	(24)	137	76	14	4
1993	151	(73)	181	29	7	7
1992	121	4	137	(9)	(12)	2

Revenue—Segmented by Region

Fiscal Year*	Overall	Canada	Europe	United States	Asia	Other
2001e	16,101	1,241	4,757	8,592	471	1,040
2000	13,619	1,013	4,362	7,139	327	779
1999	11,500	900	4,049	5,497	259	796
1998	8,509	962	2,260	3,964	760	563
1997	7,976	949	2,342	3,712	605	367
1996	7,123	4,504	1,779	841	—	—
1995	5,943	3,619	1,536	789	—	—
1994	4,769	2,696	1,431	642	—	—
1993	4,448	2,335	1,675	438	—	—
1992	3,059	1,331	1,373	355	—	—

Exhibit 1 Bombardier Revenue and Profit History, 1992 to 2001 (Cdn$ million)

Source: Company files.
e - estimate
*fiscal year end January 31. As a result, 2001 data essentially covers results from 2000.

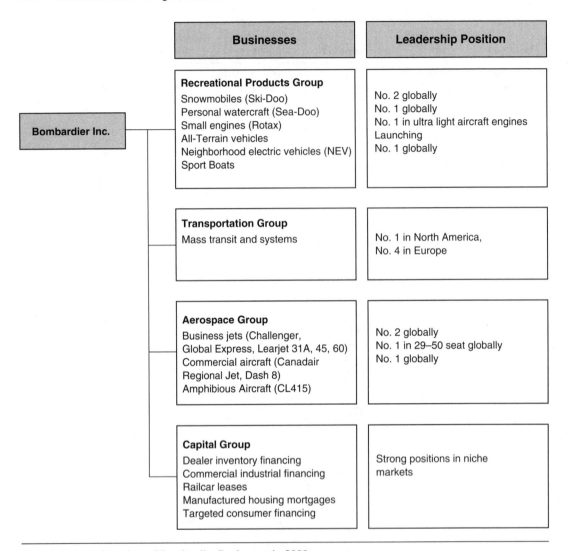

Businesses	Leadership Position
Recreational Products Group Snowmobiles (Ski-Doo) Personal watercraft (Sea-Doo) Small engines (Rotax) All-Terrain vehicles Neighborhood electric vehicles (NEV) Sport Boats	No. 2 globally No. 1 globally No. 1 in ultra light aircraft engines Launching No. 1 globally
Transportation Group Mass transit and systems	No. 1 in North America, No. 4 in Europe
Aerospace Group Business jets (Challenger, Global Express, Learjet 31A, 45, 60) Commercial aircraft (Canadair Regional Jet, Dash 8) Amphibious Aircraft (CL415)	No. 2 globally No. 1 in 29–50 seat globally No. 1 globally
Capital Group Dealer inventory financing Commercial industrial financing Railcar leases Manufactured housing mortgages Targeted consumer financing	Strong positions in niche markets

Bombardier Inc.

Exhibit 2   Overview of Bombardier Businesses in 2000

Source: Adapted from McKinsey Quarterly, 1997, Volume 2.

staff. Instead, it used personnel from BT to teach successful approaches and manufacturing methods developed elsewhere in the organization. Transfers were not all one way; aerospace also shared its best practices in engineering management. With a commitment to excellence in assembly, inventory and management control, the aerospace group and BT were both able to make significant gains in productivity and product quality.

Despite the similarities in operating strategy, BBD's businesses differed in important ways. Bombardier's rail business was counter-cyclical versus other businesses in the company. An event, such as an energy crisis, would affect the rail industry differently than recreation or aerospace. Also, technology and product development were somewhat different across the businesses. In recreational and aerospace products, a Ski-Doo or business jet was developed for the market in general while in rail, each customer had unique requirements and demanded tailor-made products. Generic rail cars simply did not exist. Customer demand varied according to a wide range of factors, including car size, weight, number of doors, propulsion system and so on. Other variables included the materials being used (steel versus aluminum), the type of car being produced (tramway, subway, inter-city or high-speed rail) and the infrastructure interface (track width).

BT was well regarded for its competencies in assembling rail cars, but it had no in-house expertise in propulsion systems, locomotives and switching and communications gear. Mark Cooper, vice-president of supply management of the inter-city trains for Adtranz, commented on Bombardier's reputation:

> Overall, Bombardier had a good level of credibility in the market place, despite being the smallest of the four rail manufacturers and rail service providers. It was seen to be one of the most effective in terms of its ability to deliver contracts and to manage and govern itself.

The Global Rail Transportation Industry

In 2001, the railway transportation industry could be divided into six distinct segments: services, propulsion and controls, total transit systems, rail control solutions, rolling stock and fixed installations. Bombardier was absent from the last segment which it considered as non-strategic and quite distinct in nature from the others.

1. Services included the planning and implementation of high quality production and maintenance programs for both new and existing systems. Services also included the development of long-term process improvements to both systems operation and rolling stock maintenance.

2. Propulsion and Controls provided the diesel and electric motors, traction drives and control systems for trains.

3. Total Transit Systems provided a process through which manufacturers developed and supplied complete transportation systems and services. Working in partnership with local civil contractors and suppliers, manufacturers designed, integrated, installed and delivered a broad range of technologies—from large-scale urban transit systems to airport people-movers.

4. Rail Control Solutions were required to operate safe and efficient railways. Customers needed effective and "fail-safe" rail control and signaling equipment and systems.

5. Rolling Stock included subway cars, locomotives, inter-city/regional trains, high speed trains, tram cars and light rail.

6. Fixed Installations referred to the building of rail infrastructure.

Public Policy and the Role of Governments in Regulating the Industry

The role of transportation and, with it, the attitudes and values of the public and government differed considerably from country to country and from continent to continent. Differences in public policy affected travel behaviors in a major way. While the cost of raw fuel amongst developed nations varied only marginally, fuel taxation levels differed by up to 800 per cent. As a result, public policy decisions affected not only the demand for fuel but also the demand for public transportation as an alternative to the automobile. Because of lower gasoline taxes and the promotion of automobile travel in the United States, public transport ridership was three to nine times lower there than in European countries.

Most industry analysts believed that European policies promoting reductions in congestion, pollution abatement, urban development, traffic safety and energy conservation would continue and that support for public transportation systems would continue for the foreseeable future. The question was whether the United States would embrace European norms as congestion increased in that country. The combination of greater geographic distances, car-friendly culture, efficient and large air travel system and aversion to government subsidies convinced many that U.S. rail policy would take a great many years to significantly change in a direction that supported an increase in rail transportation usage and investment.

Government regulations significantly affected industry structure in one other important way. Because U.S. passenger trains frequently shared tracks with freight trains, the government mandated that U.S. passenger rail cars be reinforced and strengthened in order to sustain collisions without collapsing with the ensuring high casualties that would result. As a result, U.S. trains were substantially heavier than European trains and were uncompetitive and poorly adapted to markets outside North America. European Union standards were widely embraced by governments and customers throughout the world, particularly in emerging economies such as China and India.

Infrastructure Model

A common perception in both Europe and the United States was that the rail industry, as a whole, was best designed to operate as a monopoly. High sunk costs, low marginal costs and demands for managerial co-ordination perpetuated this opinion. However, the emerging approach in the European Union (EU) was to separate the high-speed train industry and subject its component parts to competition. Although the potential technical, economic and social gains associated with this approach were perceived as exceptional, the process was often complicated by different national visions of how the industry should be divided between public and private ownership. Most countries opted to retain state ownership of infrastructure with the creation of a state agency to manage it. However, rolling stock companies were slowly becoming privatized. In 1998, the United Kingdom became

the first country in the EU to totally privatize its rail system, including both infrastructure and rolling stock (see Exhibit 3).

The U.K. model of privately owned infrastructure and rolling stock had its troubles. The government was forced to operate the infrastructure element of the system when Railtrack, the private company it selected to manage the vast U.K. rail infrastructure (nearly 23,000 miles of track and 2,500 stations), went bankrupt in October 2001. Also, some in the United Kingdom worried about safety risks associated with spreading accountability across multiple for-profit companies. Conversely, the French model of public-owned, train operator had been a tremendous success. As one industry observer remarked,

> France was operating state-of-the-art 300 km/h trains on a new network of rail lines dedicated to fast passenger service, and making money doing it. Britain was operating 1960s technology, 200 km/h trains on the nation's undependable and failing 19th century freight/passenger network, and losing money.[3]

Despite the success of the publicly operated French system, the EU was not designed to promote monopolistic, country-centred railroad companies. As a result, the U.K. model of privatized rolling stock and state-operated infrastructure more closely fit the cultural and social paradigm emerging in the EU and was thus being adopted cautiously and to differing degrees throughout the EU. During the latter half of the 1990s, public sector funding gradually shifted from supporting nationally subsidized rail systems to include more significant involvement from local municipal governments and the private sector. The belief was that by shifting to private ownership of rolling stock, the railway industry would eventually emulate the automobile or air transport models. Airlines worked with governments to secure terminals and immediate air space and runways, while operating and maintaining their own or leased airplanes. In effect, the airlines rented the infrastructure. Many believed that rail companies should operate in a similar fashion.

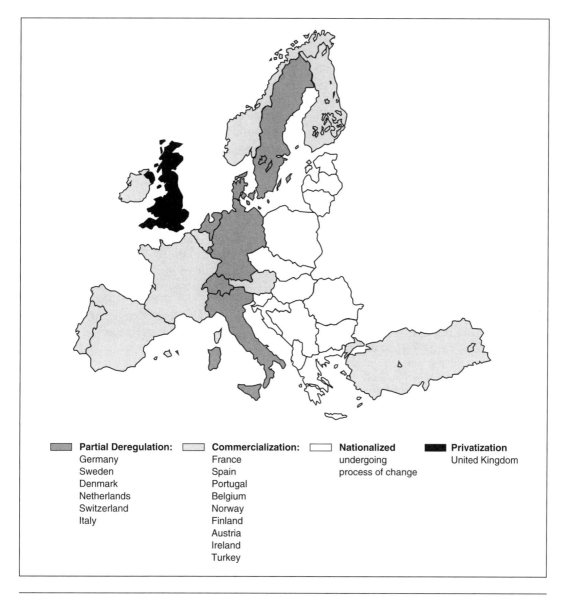

Exhibit 3   Growing Privatization of the European Union Rail Industry

Source: Company files.

High-speed Trains

By the early 2000s, the European Commission continued to rank the development of a European-wide high-speed train infrastructure as its highest investment priority in transportation infrastructure. The Community of European Railways (COER), a continent-wide association of railway companies, asserted that high-speed rail services were especially appropriate for the 200 kilometre to 300 kilometre distances between heavily populated urban centres. Most of Europe fit this profile with mobility increasing as the prospects of a single European market progressed. But for Europe to fully benefit from the one market model, decisions in infrastructure policy required a European, and not a nationalistic, approach. However, many predicted that the tendency for governments to protect national producers would be detrimental to the continent-wide objectives for many years to come.

Customers

The privatization of many national railways had changed the financing arrangements and customer base within the European rail car industry. In the past, manufacturers like BT sold directly to government operated railroads. However, with the privatization of rolling stock operations increasing in Europe, leasing arrangements were now available to operators. In the United Kingdom, equipment manufacturers sold to one of three large rail equipment leasing companies (ROSCO) owned by one of three large British banks (Bank of Scotland, HSBC or Abbey National Bank) which then leased the new rolling stock to the train operators. This lease-versus-purchase option reduced up-front costs for rolling stock operators and significantly decreased their overall capital requirements. It also put a premium on standardized trains—necessary to protect residual values. This, in turn, significantly reduced the incentives to purchase rolling stock from within a rail operators' home country.

In countries with private rail operators, revenues were generated through ticket sales and government subsidies while expenses were incurred through infrastructure franchise fees, day-to-day train maintenance, fuel and labor costs and leasing expenses. Since leasing costs on old, existing stock were much cheaper than on new equipment, operators preferred to delay purchases for as long as possible. When equipment was ordered, rail operators would sometimes seek additional delays by complaining that delivered equipment suffered from low reliability, which prevented it from meeting defined service standards the operators had committed to achieve in order to gain the

concession from the government to operate the train service. This, in turn, caused manufacturers to incur late delivery charges and inventory costs as rail cars piled up in shipping yards awaiting minor repairs or adjustments. Many observers believed that these dysfunctional practices would be repeated in other European nations as they evolved to private operating models.

DAIMLERCHRYSLER AND ADTRANZ HISTORY

Although the roots of Chrysler go back to 1920 in the United States, the history of Daimler-Benz dates to the 1880s in Germany and to the efforts of two inventive engineers—Gottlieb Daimler and Carl Benz. After a series of initiatives, Daimler-Benz was officially incorporated in 1926 and began producing cars under the Mercedes Benz brand.

By the 1980s, competition in the global automobile market had increased dramatically, and Daimler-Benz was looking to diversify its business. Between February 1985 and February 1986, the company acquired three conglomerates[4] for a combined US$ 1.11 billion. The cash expenditures of these 1985/86 acquisitions put a strain on its balance sheet, and by mid-1993, Daimler-Benz reported its first loss since the Second World War. In 1994, operations recovered somewhat with the company showing US$750 million in profits. But in 1995, the company's fortunes sagged again as it reported a loss of US$4 billion—the largest in German industrial history.

In 1995, Daimler-Benz's chief executive officer (CEO), Edvard Reuter, was forced to resign and was replaced by the aerospace division head, Jurgen Schrempp. One of Schrempp's first moves as CEO was the acquisition of 50 per cent of the rail division of Swedish-Swiss ABB Asea Brown Boveri Ltd. in exchange for US$900 million cash from Daimler-Benz. This joint venture formed the new ABB Daimler-Benz Transportation (Adtranz). Adtranz would become the largest rail service provider in the world with annual sales of US$4.5 billion.

By the mid-1990s, Robert Eaton had assumed the position of CEO at Chrysler at a time when the economic conditions in the automobile industry included an excess manufacturing capacity and an Asian economic crisis. Industry analysts were projecting an annualized global overcapacity of 18.2 million vehicles by the early 2000s. It came as no surprise that both Eaton and Schrempp were seeking partners due to the inevitable consolidation within the industry.

DaimlerChrysler AG was formed in November of 1998 when Daimler-Benz and Chrysler merged in a US$37 billion deal. In 1998, the newly formed company had revenues of US$130 billion, factories in 34 countries and sales of 4.4 million vehicles making it the fifth largest automobile manufacturer in the world. In 1999, Daimler-Chrysler acquired the remaining 50 per cent of Adtranz from ABB for US$472 million.

ADTRANZ

Although the name Adtranz dates back only as far as 1995, the multiple production facilities that comprised the company date back to the 19th century. By the time of the DaimlerChrysler merger, the rail business in Europe had narrowed to four primary players: Alstom (France), Siemens (Germany), Adtranz and Bombardier. Unlike Altsom and Siemens, which had strong single country affiliations, Adtranz facilities and staff were a collection of multiple companies in multiple countries across the continent. Many of these companies also had a history of unstable ownership. For example, since 1989, the Adtranz facility in Derby, England, had experienced the following ownership changes: 100 per cent British Rail Engineering, then 40 per cent ABB, 40 per cent Trafalgar Rail and 20 per cent employee ownership, then 100 per cent ABB, then 50 per cent Daimler Chrysler and 50 per cent ABB and finally 100 per cent DaimlerChrysler. Each new ownership group brought its own philosophies to manufacturing, sales, contract tendering, personnel, etc. Mark Cooper commented on the cultural challenges in Adtranz:

I don't think that Adtranz has had enough time to fully develop its own culture. Every two years there seems to have been a change of ownership, a change in structure, a change in values, and a change in processes. So under those circumstances you don't get a good sense of who you are.

In the late 1990s, Adtranz represented less than three per cent of DaimlerChrysler's revenues. Revenues of US$3.3 billion were recorded at Adtranz in 1999, and in 2000, after years of continual losses, Adtranz reported its first year of break-even results. Although Adtranz revenues were up over 15 per cent in 2000, the annual revenue growth over the previous four years averaged only 4.5 per cent. Given the complexity of the business and its peripheral role in DaimlerChrysler's overall strategy, many observers believed DaimlerChrysler would eventually divest its rail business.

Production Challenges

Although DaimlerChrysler's assembly process and knock-down capabilities had been introduced, Adtranz's reputation for producing high quality products was poor. In particular, Adtranz was having quality, reliability and certification problems with its core Electrostar and Turbostar model trains designed for the U.K. market (see Exhibit 4). In 2000, the Electrostar model had only eight trains in service as customers were refusing to accept this train. Reliability was achieved under the terms of the contract.[5] The Turbostar had 279 trains in service, but only 86.5 per cent were available for operation. Reliability was also not achieved under the terms of the contract. Deciphering the causes of these reliability problems was a challenge for BT managers. Neil Harvey, director of public affairs at BT, provided one common interpretation:

In terms of the reputation of Adtranz's products and its overall reputation as a company, many believed there was a certain amount of mismanagement. In particular, some felt that too many contracts were being bought, and there was often very poor follow-through on products, production and subsequent support.

Intercity Transport

Electrostar* Electric Multiple Unit, Class 375/377

United Kingdom

Bombardier Transportation is responsible for supplying 182 Class 375/377 Electrostar* trains to the UK Govia owned rail operator, South Central Ltd. These state of the art, air-conditioned electric trains are either three or four cars in length. Each vehicle has two wide sliding powered doors per side capable of handling the passenger densities and flows required by busy urban and sub-urban services.

The trains operate at speeds up to 160 km/h on suburban services south of London. 15 of the 4-car trainsets are dual voltage capable of both 25 kV AC 50 Hz overhead and 750 V DC third rail operation. The remaining 167 electric trainsets in 3 and 4-car formations are single DC voltage only.

Particular attention has been paid to the provision of a high degree of reliability, safety and maintainability whilst ensuring low whole life costs.

The Class 375/377 Electrostar trains have a high level of passenger comfort with a very quiet interior environment and are fully compliant with the requirements of the Disability Discrimination Act. A modern passenger information system linked to the Global Positioning System relays messages in both visual and audible form. Each car will be fitted with a closed-circuit television surveillance system for enhanced internal security, allowing the driver to view car interiors whilst the train is stationary.

BOMBARDIER
TRANSPORTATION

Exhibit 4   Bombardier's Electrostar

Source: Company files.

In addition, Adtranz's customer support function and its initial contract bidding processes were viewed by some as inadequate. Many at BBD believed that Bombardier's structured governance system, manufacturing controls and proven bidding systems would be excellent complements to Adtranz.

A STRATEGIC ACQUISITION FOR BOMBARDIER

Despite awareness that certain management practices needed adjustment, BBD viewed the acquisition of Adtranz as a smart strategic move for several reasons. Europe is the nexus of technological advances in the industry. Asia and South America primarily utilized European engineering concepts and had a history of failing to develop new technologies on their own. North American trains were too heavy and, hence, more expensive and costly to operate compared to the refinements in other world markets and therefore not competitive. Also, the green movement and strong government support signaled long-term growth in the demand for rail transportation in Europe.

Not only did BBD find the European rail market attractive, but it was increasingly interested in balancing the revenue streams produced by its various groups. Strengthening the company's rail business was viewed as an important move to counter-balance Bombardier's growing, but cyclical, aerospace group. Dr. Yvan Allaire, executive vice-president at BBD, explained this strategic perspective: "Bombardier's value for shareholders is as a premium diversified company, not as an aerospace company."

Although margins were often lower in rail, (in 2000, margins for the aerospace group were 11 per cent—more than twice that of the transportation group) the industry benefited from the traditional business practice of advance and progress payments from customers. These payments translated to a low level of net utilized assets and very positive cash flow, contingent on a growing backlog of orders. These cash flows provided BBD with capital that was utilized throughout the company. Allaire explained this possibility:

> Transportation is a huge cash generator. While the margins are low, cash is large in this business. In fact, we have traditionally financed a large part of the investment in the aerospace sector from cash coming from transportation. A lot of people don't understand this.

Although low-margin businesses traditionally had profit levels driven by cost control, in the rail transportation industry, variability and project management performance were additional key drivers. For example, penalty charges for late delivery of each car generally amounted to 10 per cent of the value of such car. In comparison, period costs in sales, general and administration (SG&A) accounted for six per cent of expenses. Preliminary investigation by BT managers indicated that repair and late delivery charges amounted to nearly 20 per cent of Adtranz's expenses. By applying BT's production and cost control systems, it was thought that acquiring Adtranz would provide substantial upside potential to raise profits.

Finally, BT had a strong reputation for its expertise in subway, trams and light rail cars. Adtranz had expertise in propulsion systems, high-speed and inter-city cars and signaling systems. While the acquisition would clearly strengthen Bombardier's global reach, it would also bring needed technology and product expertise to the electrical locomotive, high-speed train, propulsion, and train control/ communications. Closing this gap was becoming an imperative in Europe. For instance, in 2000, Bombardier was precluded to bid on the largest order ever awarded in the United Kingdom because Siemens, Alstom and Adtranz had refused to sell the propulsion system to them. In addition, Adtranz—at over twice the size of BT—would add $2.7 billion in backlog to maintenance and services while providing more service facilities for customers in the European marketplace.

The Acquisition

Financial analysts had anticipated that Daimler-Chrysler would seek a sales price of 25 per cent to 30 per cent of 1999 revenues of US$3.3 billion. However, ongoing problems in Daimler-Chrysler's automobile business may have hastened their unloading of the non-core asset. Although Alstom and Siemens were BBD's main competitors in the rail industry, neither competed to acquire Adtranz in part because of the beliefs that the European Commission would probably not approve of the merger due to their current strong positions in several market segments.

On August 4, 2000, BBD announced its intention to buy Adtranz for US$715 million. In its negotiations with DaimlerChrysler, BBD agreed to pay the purchase price in two installments of cash—one at closing and one six months later. Under the deal, Bombardier also agreed to the assumption of certain debt. For the deal to proceed, regulatory approval was notably required in both the EU and the United States. Given the complimentary operations of both companies in the United States (mechanical versus propulsion), U.S. approval was never a significant issue. However, matters were different in Europe where it was initially estimated that the approval process would take between four and six months.

In negotiating the deal, DaimlerChrysler insisted on a limited due diligence process. In response, it was determined that any disagreement between the asset valuation done by BBD and the value given by DaimlerChrysler would lead to adjustments in a manner agreed upon; however, if adjustments exceeded a given amount, BBD could claim that there had been a material adverse change. This disagreement would then be submitted to an independent arbitrator for adjustment. Allaire commented on the limited due diligence process:

> It was certainly the first time that Bombardier agreed to go into an acquisition without first doing full due diligence. DaimlerChrysler basically said, "Look, have your people do an initial review and don't worry about the rest—we'll give you an equity guarantee. Adjustments will have to be made to the price if the provisions already taken in our books are not sufficient.

DaimlerChrysler had good reasons for wanting to limit the due diligence process. A new management team had just been put in place and was supposedly making progress streamlining Adtranz's operations. It was a natural concern that the management team would be seriously demoralized if Bombardier was invited in, only to later walk away from the transaction. And, secondly, Adtranz had serious worries about opening their books to a direct competitor. For Bombardier to come in and examine their pricing, cost structure, contracts and so on would have been off-limits under EU competition rules governing mergers and acquisitions.

Negotiations With the European Commission

With the negotiations complete, BBD then applied to the EC for regulatory approval. Since 1990, the system for monitoring merger transactions in Europe has been governed by the Merger Regulation Committee of the European Commission. The Merger Regulation Committee eliminated the need for companies to seek approval for certain large-scale mergers in all European countries separately and ensured that all such merger requests received equal treatment. The control of mergers and acquisitions was one of the pillars of the EU's competition policy. When companies combined through a merger, acquisition, or creation of a joint venture, this generally had a positive impact on markets: firms became more efficient, competition intensified and the final consumer benefited from higher quality goods at lower prices. However, mergers that created or strengthened a dominant market position were prohibited in order to prevent abuses. A firm was in a dominant position when it was able to act on the market without having to account for the reactions of its competitors, suppliers or customers. A firm in a dominant position could, for example, increase its prices above those of its competitors without fearing any significant loss of sales.

In order to merge competing companies in Europe, the approval of the EC's merger task force was required. A review was comprised of two phases. Phase 1 involved a preliminary review, although full approval could be granted at this stage. Should Phase 1 identify potential competitive issues or conflicts associated with the proposed merger, a deeper investigation proceeded to Phase 2. This second phase could take months or years to complete as the depth and breadth of the investigation increased.

While many mergers were ultimately approved by the EC merger task force, this was in no way guaranteed. During the prior year, Alcan's proposed purchase of Pechiney was turned down by the task force. And GE's proposed acquisition of Honeywell was facing growing opposition. With this track record, some feared that the EC might have a bias against North American companies buying European businesses.

BBD utilized a negotiation strategy that it hoped would prove successful in gaining regulatory approval. It identified potentially contentious issues in advance and developed tactics to minimize disagreement. In order to comply with the likely EC demands, BBD volunteered to divest non-strategic transportation assets in Germany and to extend for several years a series of supply contracts with smaller companies based in Austria and Germany. BBD was the main customer for these small suppliers and, with the acquisition of Adtranz, technologies previously purchased from these companies could now be manufactured within the newly assembled Bombardier/Adtranz. The few years of continued sales to BBD allowed these small companies to transition into new industries or to find new customers.

On a separate matter, BBD realized that the market share of the combined companies might be an issue for certain product segments in certain countries and so tried to shape the focus of the merger task force to the European market

in total and not to any specific country. Primary geographical areas of concern were Germany, Austria and the United Kingdom. The German market was a key area with annual sales over US$1.8 billion; in Germany, Bombardier/Adtranz would have had a 50 per cent share. Concessions were made to ensure that a third competitor (Stadler) was allowed to strengthen its position in the German regional train market. Allaire, who led the negotiating team at the EC, commented on the efforts to win regulatory approval.

> You always have to make concessions—that's part of the deal over there. You don't get through the EC review process without some concessions unless you are buying something totally unrelated. But if there is any relatedness, the acquiring party must come up with concessions that will make the transaction acceptable.

For BBD, the preliminary result of the negotiation was not a Phase 1 approval, but a shortened Phase 2 process because issues were identified in Phase 1 and solutions were already designed. BBD believed, in March 2001, that Phase 2 would conclude within a month or so of further negotiations. While BBD was pleased with the results of its efforts to this point, the company had no firm guarantees that the transaction would be approved, or if approved, under what final conditions and timelines.

PIERRE LORTIE

A graduate of Université Laval (Canada) and Université de Louvain (Belgium), Pierre Lortie was both an engineer and an economist by training. He also received an MBA with honors from the University of Chicago. Prior to taking over BT, Lortie had been president and chief operating officer of Bombardier Capital (2000–2001). He had also been president and chief operating officer of Bombardier International (1998–2000), president of Bombardier Aerospace, Regional Aircraft (1993–1998), and president of Bombardier Capital Group (1990–1993). Before joining Bombardier in 1990, Lortie had been chairman, chief executive officer and president of Provigo Inc.—a major, Quebec-based retailer (1985–1989)—and president and chief executive officer of the Montreal Stock Exchange (1981–1985).

Over the years, Lortie had developed a reputation within BBD as a turnaround expert. His movements throughout BBD corresponded with the transformation of under-performing businesses into market leaders within a few years of his taking the helm. His philosophy included a combination of approaches: strong and decisive leadership, hands-on management, good relationships with existing personnel and the development of pride within those on the team. He also believed in the importance of rapidly achieving small, visible wins in order to build the support necessary to make subsequent larger changes. Lortie summarized his approach:

> You have to figure out the business model and focus everything on the key factors. You also have to work with the people . . . making sure they are focusing on what has to be done . . . helping them, coaching them and removing roadblocks. You should never forget that people like successes and being on the winning team.

Lortie recognized that his style and methods of change management were in some ways different than approaches taken by others in turnaround situations. Although aware of the need to streamline costs, he did not follow the traditional approach of implementing massive, short-term, cost-cutting tactics as an initial step in the turnaround plan. Instead, he focused first on creating a healthy operating environment through the implementation of reporting and governance systems aimed at monitoring key metrics and assessing current and potential success. His main objective was to ensure a balance between cost reduction or restructuring initiatives and revenue growth. He strongly held the view that balance was necessary because halting growth would hurt the market performance of a company far more than would a failure to rapidly reduce costs.

In promoting change, he not only engaged and empowered people at all levels, he also sought to create the trust and credibility necessary for a leader to implement further, more difficult changes that may be required based on assessment of the metrics. Lortie commented on the rationale behind his move to BT:

> My job at Bombardier has been to turn around operations that were not doing well. This is what I did at Bombardier Capital and Regional Aircraft. When Bob Brown (CEO of BBD) asked me to take over the job at transportation, he was concerned that there were difficulties in the current transportation group and high expectations involving the Adtranz merger. He felt that the magnitude of the task of stitching together the two organizations and rapidly delivering acceptable performance required someone who had a track record. There was some concern that I had not been at Bombardier Capital long enough to complete the restructuring process I had set in motion. But Adtranz was going to be Bombardier's biggest acquisition ever and getting it right seemed to be more important than keeping me at Capital.

Determining a Course of Action

While Lortie was a veteran of Bombardier and had participated in the strategic plan and budget reviews of the group over the years, he admitted knowing relatively little about Bombardier Transportation operations, per se. But he was convinced that the process for building and operating trains was not dissimilar to commercial aircraft. Many of the key success factors were thought to be the same. Beyond this core belief, Lortie faced an overwhelming number of decisions. He summarized the long list.

> What was the best way for us to leverage the potentially increased size of Bombardier Transportation? Should we take a top line approach to results or a bottom line approach? How can we tailor the integration to balance revenue and cost initiatives? How do we reconcile the fundamentally incompatible organizational structures, particularly in Europe? How do we go about designing the "best" organizational

structure under the circumstances? How should we proceed to approve new bids (those arising in the first few weeks and longer term) and ensure they are profit-making propositions? How should we develop and instill a project management culture in an organization that has no such tradition (or lost it)? How do we get management focused on the operations, on "getting it right," avoid finger pointing at former Adtranz management, create a climate conducive to teamwork while conducting a thorough due diligence of all Adtranz contracts and operations? How and when should Bombardier integrate its manufacturing philosophies into the existing Adtranz operations? What should Bombardier do to minimize tensions and maximize teamwork with personnel changes imminently on the horizon? How should those personnel changes be made? Who, in the management ranks of Adtranz and BT, should I keep and who should I replace and how should I go about the process of making these decisions? Should the headquarters of the merged companies be located in St. Bruno, Quebec, Berlin or a more neutral city like Brussels, Paris or London? And finally, what kind of style should I use in leading the organization forward? How directive should I be versus participative in making decisions?

NOTES

1. St. Bruno was located on the south shore of the St. Lawrence River, in the suburbs of Montreal.

2. BT Continental Europe was based in Berlin and included six manufacturing facilities in Germany and one each in Austria and the Czech Republic.

3. Andersen, Svein and Eliassen, Kjell (2001), *Making Policy in Europe*, London, Sage, p. 72.

4. Daimler owned 50 per cent of Motoren-und Turbinen-Union (a manufacturer of aircraft engines and diesel motors for tanks and ships) and bought the remaining 50 per cent for $160 million. Daimler purchased 65.6 per cent of Dornier (a privately held manufacturer of spacecraft systems, commuter planes and medical equipment) for $130 million. Daimler additionally purchased control of AEG (a high-technology manufacturer of electronic equipment, such as turbines, robotics, data processing and household products) for $820 million.

5. Reliability is measured as the total distance travelled by the rail car between breakdowns. The total performance of all rail cars is then averaged together to get the mean reliability number as a factor of distance travelled by each train model. This is then measured in subsequent periods to evaluate performance and reliability levels going forward.

VINCOR AND THE NEW WORLD OF WINE

Prepared by Nikhil Celly under the supervision of Professor W. Beamish

       Version: (A) 2005-11-07

On September 16, 2002, Donald Triggs, chief executive officer (CEO) of Vincor International Inc. (Vincor) was preparing for the board meeting to discuss the possible acquisition of Goundrey Wines, Australia. Vincor had embarked upon a strategic internationalization plan in 2000, acquiring R.H Phillips and Hogue in the United States. Although Vincor was the largest wine company in Canada and the fourth largest in North America, Triggs felt that to be a major player, Vincor had to look beyond the region. The acquisition of Goundrey Wines in Australia would be the first

step. Convincing the board would be difficult, as the United States was a close and attractive market where Vincor had already spent more than US$100 million on acquisitions. In contrast, Australia was very far away.

THE GLOBAL WINE INDUSTRY

Wine-producing countries were classified as either New World producers or Old World producers.

Country	Wine Production* (million litres)	Share of World Production (%)
France	5,330	19.9
Italy	5,090	19.0
Spain	3,050	11.4
United States	1,980	7.4
Argentina	1,580	5.9
Australia	1,020	3.8
Germany	900	3.4
Portugal	770	2.9
South Africa	650	2.4
Chile	570	2.1
World	27,491	

Exhibit 1   Top 10 Producers of Wine in the World 2001

Source: G. Dutruc-Rosset, Extract of the Report on World Vitiviniculture, June 24, 2002.

*Does not include juice and musts (the expressed juice of fruit and especially grapes before and during fermentation; also the pulp and skins of the crushed grapes).

Note: 1 litre = 0.26 gallons; each case contains 12,750 mil bottles = 9 litres.

Some of the largest New World producers were the United States, Australia, Chile and Argentina. The largest of the Old World producers were France, Italy and Spain (see Exhibit 1). The world's top 10 wine exporters accounted for more than 90 per cent of the value of international wine trade. Of those top 10, half were in western Europe, and the other half were New World suppliers, led by Australia (see Exhibit 2).

France

France had been a longtime world leader in the production of wine, due to historical and

Country	Wine Production* (million litres)	Share of World Exports (%)
Italy	1,830	26.5
France	1,580	22.9
Spain	990	14.4
Australia	380	5.5
Chile	310	4.5
United States	300	4.3
Germany	240	3.5
Portugal	200	2.9
South Africa	180	2.6
Moldavia	160	2.3
World	6,897	

Exhibit 2   Top 10 Exporters of Wine in the World, 2001

Source: G. Dutruc-Rosset, Extract of the Report on World Vitiviniculture, June 24, 2002.

cultural factors. France was the top producer of wine in the world (see Exhibit 1). The French had developed the vins d'appellation d'origine contrôlée (AOC) system centuries ago to ensure that the quality of wine stayed high. There were many regions in which quality grapes could be grown in France. Some of their better known appellations were Bordeaux, Burgundy and Champagne. France was the second largest exporter of wine (see Exhibit 2).

Italy

Italy, like France, also had a very old and established wine industry that relied on the appellation method to control the quality. Italy was the second largest producer of wine in the world (see Exhibit 1) and the largest exporter (see Exhibit 2).

Australia

Grape vines were first introduced to Australia in 1788. The wine "industry" was born in the 1860s when European immigrants added the skilled workforce necessary to develop the commercial infrastructure. The Australian wine industry grew after 1960 with the development of innovative techniques to make higher quality wine while keeping costs down. Australia was the sixth largest producer of wine in the world (see Exhibit 1). Australia had 5.5 per cent of the total export market and was ranked fourth in the world for its export volume (see Exhibit 2).

Chile

The first vines were introduced to Chile in the 16th century. Due to political and economic instability, the wine industry was not able to develop and take on a global perspective until 1979 when Chile began to focus on the exporting of natural resources to strengthen its economy. Despite being only the 10th largest producer, Chile had 4.5 per cent of the total export market and was ranked fifth in the world (see Exhibit 2).

Argentina

Argentina had a long history of making wine. However, the quality of the wine from Argentina was never as high, due to the small area of land that was capable of producing high quality grapes. Argentina was the fifth largest producer of wine in the world (see Exhibit 1), but did not feature in the top 10 exporters of wine.

All of the countries, with the exception of Argentina, were capable of shipping brands that could compete at a wide range of price points. The French wines typically were capable of competing in the higher price classes, and could retail for more than US$100 per bottle.

MAJOR WORLD MARKETS

After a 2.2 per cent gain in 2001, the global wine market was estimated to have increased another 1.2

per cent in 2002 to 2.55 billion cases, according to *The Global Drinks Market: Impact Databank Review and Forecast 2001 Report*. Wine consumption was projected to expand by 120 million cases by 2010. Most of the growth was expected to come from major wine-consuming nations, such as the United States, United Kingdom, Australia and South Africa, as well from less developed wine markets, such as China and Russia.

Wine imports were highly concentrated. The 10 top importing countries accounted for all but 14 per cent of the value of global imports in the late-1980s. In 2001, half the value of all imports were purchased by the three biggest importers: the United Kingdom (19 per cent), the United States (16 per cent) and Germany (14 per cent).

France and Italy were the number one and two countries in the world for per capita consumption (see Exhibit 3). However, the consumption rate in France was relatively stagnant, while Italy was

Country	Wine Consumption (millions litres)	Share of World Consumption (%)
France	3,370	15.4
Italy	3,050	13.9
United States	2,133	9.7
Germany	1,966	9.0
Spain	1,400	6.4
Argentina	1,204	5.5
United Kingdom	1,010	4.6
China	580	2.6
Russia	550	2.5
Romania	470	2.1
World	21,892	

Exhibit 3 Top 10 Wine Consuming Nations, 2001

Source: G. Dutruc-Rosset, Extract of the Report on World Vitiviniculture, June 24, 2002.

showing a decrease. Italy, unlike France, had a very small market for imported wines. The import market sizes for France and Italy were respectively 13.4 per cent and 2.8 per cent in 2001, based on volume.

The United Kingdom's wine market was considered to be the "crucible" for the global wine market (Wine Market Report, May 2000). The United Kingdom had very small domestic wine production and good relationships with many of the wine-producing countries in the world. This coupled with the long history of wine consumption, resulted in an open and competitive market. The United Kingdom was ranked number seven for consumption in 2001 with a trend of increasing consumption. The United Kingdom wine market was dominated by Old World country imports, however New World imports had grown as Australian wines replaced French wines as the number one import (see Figure 1).

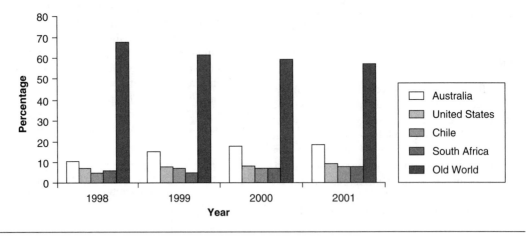

Figure 1   United Kingdom Wine Market Share

Source: Company files.

Other Countries

In 2001, Canada was ranked number 30 in the world for per capita consumption with an increasing trend. Japan had seen a steady increase in the size of its imported wine market. Asia presented a great opportunity for wine producers around the world because it had populous markets that had yet to be tapped.

THE U.S. WINE INDUSTRY

The international image of the U.S. wine industry until the mid 1970s was that of a low quality jug wine producer. This changed in 1976 during a blind wine-tasting contest in France where California wines from Napa Valley beat out several well-established European wines for the top honors. From that time forward, there has been a focus on developing high quality wines that could compete in the international market from the northern California appellations, such as Napa Valley and Sonoma County. The United States was the fourth largest producer of wine (1.98 billion litres) in 2001 (see Exhibit 1), with California wines accounting for 90 per cent of production volume. There were more than 3,000 wineries in all 50 states. The nation's top wine-producing states were California, New York, Washington and Oregon.

The United States saw huge gains in the total volume and value of its wine exports, increasing from US$85 million in 1988 to US$548 million in 2002. The major markets for U.S wines included the United Kingdom, Canada and Japan. Together they represented 66 per cent of the total export market value for the United States (see Exhibit 4).

The United States was the third largest wine market in the world, consuming 2.13 billion litres a year in 2001. It was also one of the biggest untapped wine markets in the world;

Country Ranking by 2002 Dollar Value	Value ($000)	Volume (litres 000)
United Kingdom	188,895	95,446
Canada	92,571	50,348
Japan	81,199	32,342
Netherlands	53,201	26,388
Belgium	18,791	10,884
France	13,326	5,943
Germany	11,818	8,634
Ireland	10,153	5,380
Switzerland	7,199	3,914
Denmark	5,710	3,933
Mexico	5,001	3,705
Taiwan	4,868	2,736
South Korea	3,865	2,439
China	3,370	2,537
Singapore	3,002	1,822
Sweden	2,782	1,145
Hong Kong	2,393	1,140

Exhibit 4   U.S. Wine Exports, Top Countries (By Dollar Value in 2002)

Source: Wine Institute and Ivie International using data from U.S. Dept. of Commerce, USA Trade Online. History revised. Numbers may not total exactly due to rounding.

seven per cent of the U.S. population accounted for 86 per cent of the country's wine consumption. The total wine market in the United States in 2001 was $21.1 billion with an average growth rate of six per cent since 1994. Of this, approximately $10 billion were sales of New World wines.

While California wines dominated the domestic market (67 per cent market share) due to the ideal growing conditions and favorable marketing and branding actions taken by some of California's larger wineries, imports were on the rise. The United States had one of the most open markets in the world for wine, with low barriers to entry for imports. Imports represented 530 million litres for a 25 per cent share of the market. By 2002, wine imports grew by 18 per cent (see Figures 2 and 3).

Wine was the most popular alcoholic beverage in the United States after beer, which accounted for 67 per cent of all alcohol consumed. The table wine category represented 90 per cent of all wine by volume, dessert wine was six per cent and sparkling wine accounted for four per cent. U.S.-produced table wine held an 83 per cent share of the volume and 78 per cent of the value. Premium wine ($7 and more per 750 ml bottle) sales increased eight per cent over 2001, accounting for 30 per cent of the volume but a sizeable 62 per cent of winery revenues. Everyday value-priced wines selling for less than $7 per bottle grew about 1.5 per cent by volume. This segment represented 70 per cent of all California table wine shipments and 38 per cent of the value.

The United States wine industry was fragmented with the largest producer E. & J. Gallo, supplying 30 per cent and no other producer supplying more than 15 per cent by volume in 2002.

In the United States, a law mandated the implementation of a three-tier distribution system. The wine producers were required to sell to a wholesaler, who then sold to an established customer base of grocery stores, liquor stores, hotels and restaurants. Wineries were capable of using a two-tier distribution system, which allowed wineries to sell directly to the customers through gift shops located at the winery. The role

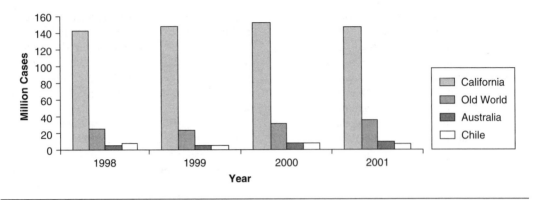

Figure 2   United States Wine Markets 1998 to 2001

Source: Company files.

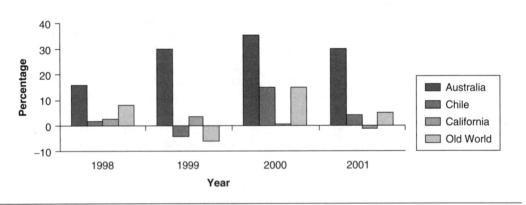

Figure 3   United States Wine Market Growth Rates

Source: Company files.

of the distribution channel was growing and taking on greater strategic importance as the trend towards international and domestic consolidation grew.

THE CANADIAN WINE INDUSTRY

Canadians had been making wine for more than two centuries, but Canada's modern day success in the production of high quality vinifera-based wines went back only a quarter century. The signing of the North American Free Trade Agreement in 1988, together with a ruling under the General Agreement on Tariffs and Trade (GATT) required Canada to abandon the protection it offered its wine industry. While many producers felt threatened, many more responded by reaffirming their belief in their capacity to produce premium wines, and redoubled their efforts to prove it. New vineyards were planted with only the finest varieties of grapes:

Chardonnay, Riesling, Sauvignon Blanc, Pinot Gris, Gewürztraminer, Pinot Noir, Cabernet Sauvignon, Merlot and others.

During 1988, the Vintners Quality Alliance (VQA) was launched in Ontario, culminating six years of voluntary initiatives by the leaders of Ontario's wine industry. This group set the standards, to which they agreed to comply, to elevate the quality of Canadian wines and provide quality assurances to the consumer. British Columbia adopted similar high standards in 1990, under the VQA mark.

The 1990s was a decade of rapid growth. The number of commercial wineries grew from about 30 in 1990 to more than 100 by the end of the decade, and consumers began to recognize the value represented by wines bearing the VQA medallion. Canadian vintners continued to demonstrate that fine grape varieties in cooler growing conditions could possess complex flavors, delicate yet persistent aromas, tightly focused structure and longer aging potential than their counterparts in warmer growing regions of the world.

In Canada, despite increasing import competition, sales of Canadian quality wines were increasing as consumers moved up the quality and price scale (see Figure 4).

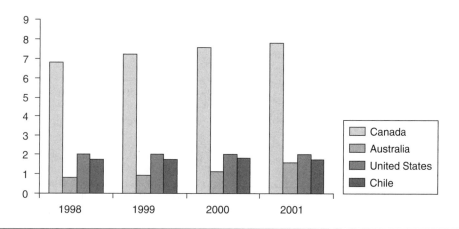

Figure 4   The Canadian Wine Market

Source: Company files.

Canadian quality wines began to capture both domestic and international recognition not only in sales but also by garnering an impressive list of significant wine awards, beginning in 1991 when Inniskillin won the Grand Prix d'Honneur for its 1989 icewine at the prestigious VinExpo, in Bordeaux, France. New access for Canadian wines, especially icewine, in the European market, and expanding market opportunities in the United States and Asia were giving Canadian wines greater market exposure.

THE AUSTRALIAN WINE INDUSTRY

The Australian wine industry was structured to be able to deliver large quantities of high quality branded wine to the world's major markets, at costs less than many of their Old World and New World competitors. Since Australia had a very limited domestic market (population of only 17 million), the wineries realized that if the industry was to continue to grow it would have to do so internationally.

As a result, Australian wineries had gained, and were expected to continue to gain, market share. Growth had been in exports as well as domestic sales (see Exhibits 5 and 6). Australia had recently overtaken France as the largest exporter to the United Kingdom, where seven of the top 10 wine brands were Australian. Exports to North America had grown at 27 per cent by volume in 2001. Consumption of Australian wine in Canada was up 24 per cent and in the United States consumption was up 35 per cent. The growth trends were expected to continue. Export growth had been driven by sales of premium red wine which accounted for 53 per cent of Australia's wine exports.

Domestic wine consumption had grown from 296 million litres in 1991 to 398 million litres in 2001, an annual growth rate of four per cent. The Australian domestic market was relatively unregulated compared to North America, although alcohol taxes were high (42 per cent). Wineries were allowed to have their own retail outlets and sell directly to retailers or on-premise customers. The 7,500 licensed liquor retail outlets accounted for 56 per cent of wine sales while

	Million Litres	AUD$ Million
United Kingdom	183	762
United States	78	457
Canada	17	106
New Zealand	23	83
Germany	13	55
Other	61	301
All Markets	375	1,764

Exhibit 6   Australia—Top Export Markets, 2001

Source: Company files.

	1998 to 1999	2000 to 2001
Wineries (number)	1,150	1,318
Hectares under vine	122,915	148,275
Wine grape production	793	1,035
Wine consumption	373	398
Wine exports million litres AUD$ million	216 $991	339 $1,614
Wine imports million litres AUD$ million	24 $114	13 $92

Exhibit 5   Australia Wineries

Source: Company files.

the 28,000 licensed on-premise outlets accounted for 44 per cent of wine sales.

Although there were 1,300 wineries in Australia, the industry was the most concentrated of any major wine region, with 80 per cent of production being accounted for by four players: Southcorp Wine, Beringer Blass, BRL Hardy and Orlando Wyndham. The large wineries had their own sales forces, as well as warehouses in the major markets.

Southcorp Wines was Australia's largest winery and vineyard owner, with sales of AUD$1.5 billion. Beringer Blass was owned by the Fosters Group and had wine revenues of approximately AUD$800 million (seven million cases). The purchase of Beringer (for AUD$2.6 billion) provided the company with significant growth and U.S. market access.

BRL Hardy had revenues of more than AUD$700 million. The company had several top brands and a very strong U.K. market position. A recent joint venture in the United States with Constellation brands had improved their United States market access. Orlando Wyndham was owned by Pernod Ricard, a French publicly traded spirits company.

TRENDS IN THE GLOBAL WINE INDUSTRY

Wine was unique among alcoholic beverages in that its top 25 brands represented only seven per cent of the global market. In 2002, Martini vermouth was the world's most widely distributed wine, while Gallo's E. & J. Wine Cellars was the largest-selling brand, at 25 million cases annually, with most of those sales in the United States.

Globally, vermouth and other fortified wines were projected to continue their long-term decline, but this would be more than offset by expected growth in table wines, which accounted for more than 90 per cent of total wine consumption. The hottest sales category was Australian wines, with brands such as Rosemount Estate, Jacob's Creek and Lindemans showing double-digit growth rates.

The North American market was expected to exhibit annual growth rates of three per cent. There were positive demographics with the 20 to 39 age group having a per capita consumption at 7.9 litres and the 40+ age group having a per capita of 14.0 litres. The ongoing trends were a shift in consumer preference to red wines and premium wines (see Exhibit 7, 8).

The global wine market was consolidating in terms of its retail, wholesale and production

	Retail Price	% By Volume	F'02 Trend*	% By Sales
Jug	<$3	36%	–4%	12%
Premium	$3 - $7	36%	–2%	27%
Super Premium	$7 - $15	18%	8%	28%
Ultra Premium	>$15	10%	3%	33%

Exhibit 8   The U.S. Market for California Wine, Fiscal 2002

Source: Company files.

*Total U.S. table wine market +1%; imports +9%; states other than California +4%

operations. One key to success seemed to be distribution and marketing. Globalization was also altering the structure of firms both within the wine industry and among those distributing and retailing wine. Rapid growth in supermarkets and in concentration among distributors was driving wine companies into mergers and acquisitions to better meet the needs of those buyers and their customers. Since information about the various niches and the distribution networks in foreign markets was expensive to acquire, new alliances between wine companies were being explored with a view to capitalizing on their complementarities in such knowledge.

Recent examples of such alliances included the purchase by the owner of Mildara Blass (Fosters Brewing Group) of Napa Valley–based Beringer, the alliance between Southcorp/ Rosemount and California's Mondavi, BRL Hardy's joint venture with the second largest U.S. wine company, Constellation Brands (to operate as Pacific West Partners) and the purchase by New Zealand's biggest wine firm (Montana) of the country's second largest winery (Corbans). See Exhibit 9 for the 10 largest wine companies worldwide.

	Retail Price	% By Volume	Trend	% By Sales
Popular	< $7	33%	–5%	20%
Premium	$7 - $10	35%	5%	30%
Super Premium	$10 - $15	24%	19%	33%
Ultra Premium	$15 - $20	6%	31%	15%
Specialty	>$20	2%	45%	6%

Exhibit 7   The Wine Market—Canada, Fiscal 2002

Source: Company files.

Company	Country	Wine sales ($million)
E. & J. Gallo Winery	United States	1,500
Foster's Group	Australia	818
Seagram	Canada	800
Constellation Brands	United States	712
Southcorp	Australia	662
Castel Freres	France	625
Diageo	Britain	590
Henkell & Sonlein	Germany	528
Robert Mondavi	United States	506

Exhibit 9   Top 10 Wine Companies and Sales in 2002 (US$)

Source: Direction des Etudes/Centre Français du Commerce Exterieur.

Note: Excludes France's LVMH, which earned more than 75 per cent of its $1.6 billion in wine sales from champagne.

VINCOR INTERNATIONAL INC.

Vincor International Inc. (Vincor) was formed as a combination of a number of Canadian wineries: Barnes Wines, Brights Wines, Cartier Wines, Inniskillin Wines and Dumont over the period from 1989 to 1996. Vincor began operations in 1989 with a management buyout of Ridout Wines (Ridout) from John Labatt Ltd. The Ridout management team, led by Allan Jackson, Peter Graigner and John Hall, sought out Donald Triggs to lead the purchase and become CEO. They raised more than Cdn$2 million in equity, largely from personal finances, and borrowed $25 million to buy out Ridout. The new company was renamed Cartier Wines and Beverages.

Vincor had grown in three stages to become Canada's largest wine company in 2002. The first stage of growth had been a leveraged buyout (LBO) in turbulent times 1989 to 1995, followed by a period of consolidation and rationalization, building Canada's Wine Company (1990 to 2000). The third stage of growth was Building an International Wine Company (2000 onwards).

The first stage had seen the formation of Vincor and wine company acquisitions. From 1995 to 2000, Vincor acquired eight wineries, integrated its sales, marketing, production and accounting and merged two wine kit companies. This lead to economies of scale and a 21 per cent market share in 2000.

During this period, Vincor developed Canada's first premium wine brands: Jackson-Triggs, Inniskillin and Sawmill Creek. The Canadian wine market had seen a shift from popular (less than $7 retail price) to premium ($7 to $10 retail price), leading Vincor to start focusing on the premium and super premium ($10 to $15 retail price) segments. They developed vineyards and re-capitalized wineries to support premium growth. Product coverage was also achieved in the growing ultra premium ($15 to $20 retail price) and specialty (more than $20 retail price) segments. The year 2000 saw Vincor at a strategic crossroad. Triggs recalled:

We were faced with three options. We could choose to be a cash cow by further developing our dominant Canadian position. A second option was to develop a diversified Canadian beverage conglomerate. A third option was to expand to the United States and perhaps beyond.

We went for option 3. The move was driven by opportunities as well as threats. In terms of opportunities, the global trend was one of strong growth and premiumisation. There was an industry consolidation favoring global brands. The market was fragmented with the largest player only having one per cent market share. The markets for New World wine were growing. The dynamics in the U.S. market were highly profitable with very high profit margins. We were already #5 in North America and #22 globally.

On the risk side, wine was an agricultural industry and as such susceptible to changing weather conditions. A diversified portfolio in terms of production and markets would only be an asset.

Triggs and Vincor decided to go international. The company's mission statement was drafted to reflect the new strategic plan:

> To become one of the world's top-10 wine companies, producing Vincor-owned New World, premium branded wines, which are marketed and sold through Vincor-controlled sales and distribution systems in all major premium wine consuming regions.

Where Were the Big Markets?

According to Triggs:

> The United States was the largest market with New World wine sales of $10 billion followed by the United Kingdom and Australia at $3.7 billion each. Canada and the rest of Europe were next at $700 million. Japan was the sixth largest with sales of about $500 million. To be a New World market player, Vincor needed to be in five to six markets.

In 2002, the company's strategy was formulated for each region. In Canada, the aim was to build share in premium segments, to develop export capability and to generate cash and improve return on capital employed. In the United States, Vincor decided to focus on portfolio migration to high-end super-premium, enhancement of sales capability, product innovation and a shift to consumer marketing. Vincor's international strategy was to develop new geographic markets for core brands, specifically for icewine, a signature product for Canada that had attained world recognition. It was a luxury product in terms of pricing and margins and one of the top-five wine brands in select Asian duty-free stores. The U.S. launch was in F'01 in 1,850 high-end restaurants. By 2002, Inniskillin was being sold in 3,300 premium restaurants across the United States. The European launch of Inniskillin was slated for F'02.

U.S. Acquisitions

R.H. Phillips

On October 5, 2000, Vincor acquired R.H. Phillips, a leading California estate winery, which produced a range of super premium wines. The aggregate purchase price, including acquisition costs, was US$56.7 million. In addition, R.H. Phillips' debt of US$33.8 million was assumed and refinanced by the company. The Phillips acquisition and the refinancing of the assumed debt were funded entirely through borrowing from the company's senior lender.

R.H. Phillips was established in 1981 by John and Karl Giguiere. It was located in the Dunnigan Hills Viticultural Region near the wine regions of Napa and Sonoma. R.H. Phillips specialized in the production of super premium wines, marketing its products under the brands R.H. Phillips, Toasted Head, EXP and Kempton Clark. Its wines were sold throughout the United States and in several other countries, including Canada. In 2001, its brands generated sales revenues of approximately US$25 million for Vincor. Its wines were distributed across the United States by a network of 13 sales executives, distributors and brokers.

The Phillips acquisition established a presence for Vincor in the U.S. wine market, in addition to adding strong brands, which were well-positioned in the super premium category, one of the fastest growing segments of the wine market. With its national network of distributors and sales professionals, R.H. Phillips provided a platform for future acquisitions in the United States (such as the Hogue acquisition), while also facilitating the marketing of Vincor's products in the United States.

The Hogue Cellars

On September 1, 2001, Vincor acquired Hogue Cellars for US$36.3 million. Hogue was the second largest wine producer in Washington state, well-known for its super premium wine. Hogue was a family controlled and family operated winery founded in 1982 by Mike and Gary Hogue.

The Washington state wine industry had emerged as the second largest producer of premium wines in the United States, after California. Hogue produced red varietals, including Cabernet Sauvignon, Merlot and Syrah, as well as white varietals, including Chardonnay, Sauvignon Blanc, Riesling and Pinot Gris. In 2001, sales of Hogue-produced premium wine were 415,400 cases. In addition to its owned brands, Hogue was the U.S. agent for Kim Crawford wines of New Zealand and Heritage Road wines from Brian McGuigan wines of Australia.

The Hogue acquisition added 11 sales people nationally and immediately increased Vincor's annual U.S. sales volume to more than one million cases and its annual U.S. revenues to more than US$60 million.

INTEGRATION WITH R.H. PHILLIPS

Vincor's management believed that Hogue was an excellent complement to the R.H. Phillips portfolio, as Hogue was primarily a super premium brand, with approximately 88 per cent of its volume in the super premium category. The strength of the Hogue product range lay in different varietals from the R.H. Phillips range. Different appellations greatly reduced portfolio overlap, as the character and taste of the wines were clearly distinct. Given the price and quality positioning of both businesses, customers were similar and opportunity existed to improve the efficiency and effectiveness of the sales force, while simultaneously developing incremental sales for all brands in the combined portfolio. Vincor incurred expenses of US$4 million from the integration of Hogue and R.H. Phillips and from transaction costs related to the Hogue acquisition. It was management's objective that the integration of Hogue and R.H. Phillips would result in the realization of annual synergies of US$2.8 million.

VINCOR IN 2002

In 2002, Vincor was Canada's largest producer and marketer of wines with leading brands in all segments of the market in Canada. Vincor had a 22 per cent market share and sales of Cdn$376.6

million (see Exhibit 11 for Financials). Andrés Wines Ltd., the second largest winery in Canada, had approximately an 11 per cent market share. Vincor was North America's fourth largest wine producer in terms of volume and the world's 22nd largest wine producer in terms of revenue.

The company had wineries in British Columbia, Ontario, Quebec, New Brunswick, California and Washington state, marketing wines produced from grapes grown in the Niagara Peninsula of Ontario, the Okanagan Valley of British Columbia, the Dunnigan Hills of California, the Columbia Valley of Washington state and other countries. The company's California and Washington wines were available throughout the United States and in parts of Canada. (see Exhibit 10 for Corporate Structure).

Canada's government liquor distribution systems and the company's 165-store Wine Rack chain of retail stores sold Vincor's well-known and industry-leading brands: Inniskillin,

Subsidiary	Jurisdiction of Incorporation
Hawthorne Mountain Vineyards (2000) Ltd	Canada
The Hogue Cellars, Ltd	Washington
Inniskillin Wines Inc.	Ontario
Inniskillin Okanagan Vineyards Inc	British Columbia
R.H. Phillips, Inc	California
Spagnol's Wine & Beer Making Supplies Ltd	Canada
Sumac Ridge Estate Winery (2000) Ltd.	Canada
Vincor (Quebec) Inc	Quebec

Exhibit 10   Vincor's Significant Legal Subsidiaries 2001 (all wholly owned)

Source: Company files.

| | F'98 | F'99 | F'00 | F'01 | F'02 | Average Annual Growth | |
						F'01-02	F'98-02
Revenue	206.4	253.2	268.2	294.9	376.6	27.7%	17.7%
EBITDA	28.1	35.0	37.9	49.5	70.5	42.4%	26.1%
% Revenue	13.6%	13.8%	14.1%	16.8%	18.7%		
Net Income	10.8	11.7	13.3	14.3	26.9	40.1%	25.6%
Avg.Capital Empl'd	145.5	191.6	222.1	310.4	468.2		
ROCE (EBIT)	14.5%	13.8 %	12.7%	13.1%	12.5%		
Funds Employed							
Receivables	30.4	33.3	35.7	37.4	55.1		
Inventory	65.1	83.1	70.7	125.9	175.6		
Working Capital	57.8	73.3	67.9	111.9	184.9		
Net Fixed Assets	45.2	60.0	73.3	165.9	178.8		
Other Assets	59.8	87.1	82.7	133.4	161.5		
Funds Employed	162.8	220.4	223.9	411.2	525.2		
Turnover	1.2 ×	1.1 ×	1.2 ×	.7 ×	.7 ×		
Financing							
Debt (net)	50.9	92.5	80.5	254.5	110.1		
Deferred Tax	9.6	12.1	14.1	11.4	18.3		
Equity*	102.3	115.8	129.3	145.3	396.8		
Financing	162.8	220.4	223.9	411.2	525.2		

Exhibit 11   Vincor Consolidated Financials (1998 to 2002) (Cdn$ millions)

Source: Company files.

Note: EBITDA — Earnings Before Interest, Taxes, Depreciation and Amortization

*Increased in 2002 due to the fact two equity issues were completed that year.

Jackson-Triggs, Sumac Ridge, Hawthorne Mountain, R.H. Phillips, Toasted Head, Hogue, Sawmill Creek, Notre Vin Maison, Entre-Lacs, L'Ambiance, Caballero de Chile, Bellini, Spumante Bambino, President Canadian Champagne, Okanagan Vineyards, Salmon Harbor and other table, sparkling and fortified wines, Vex and the Canada Cooler brands of coolers, and the Growers and Vibe brands of cider.

In the United States, R.H. Phillips, Toasted Head, EXP, Kempton Clark and Hogue wine brands were distributed through a national network of more than 127 distributors, supported by eight brokers and 40 sales managers. The company's icewines were sold in the United States through a dedicated team of sales managers and internationally, primarily through the duty-free

distribution channel. The company had seven employees outside of Canada engaged full-time in the sale of icewine.

Vincor's portfolio had evolved as per Table 1.

Table 1   Evolution of Vincor's Portfolio—Table Wine

	F'95 % By Vol	% by $	F'02 % By Vol	% by $
Popular	83	80	47	28
Premium	17	20	53	72

Source: Company files.

The company's objectives in 2002 were to obtain a top quartile return on capital employed (ROCE) of 16 per cent to 20 per cent and to achieve sales of Cdn$1 billion and an earnings per share (EPS) increase of more than 15 per cent. At the time these objectives were to be met as per Table 2.

	1999	2000	2001
Sales (000)	16,280	21,509	20,942
EBITDA	3,102	6,014	3,548
EBITDA % Sales	19.1%	28.0%	16.9%

Exhibit 12   Goundrey Financials (for years ending June 30), AUD$ (000s)

Source: Company files.

Table 2   Company Sales Objectives (Cdn$ milllions)

	Current	5 Years
Canada	300	400
United States	100	200
Icewine	15	50
Acquisitions	0	350
Total	415	1,000

Source: Company files.

GOUNDREY WINES PTY. LTD.

Goundrey Wines was one of the pioneer winery operations in Western Australia. The Goundrey family had established the vineyard in 1972, and the first vintage was produced in 1976. By 1995, the business had grown to approximately 17,000 cases in annual sales and was sold to Perth businessman Jack Bendat. Bendat expanded both the vineyards and the winery to reach 2002 sales levels of 250,000 cases annually and revenues of AUD$25 million. Goundrey was one of the largest wineries in Western Australia selling under two labels, Goundrey and Fox River (see Exhibit 12 for Financials).

Bendat was 77 years old, and health and family concerns had resulted in his recent decision to sell the business. Vincor believed it would be able to purchase the assets of Goundrey for AUD$46 million plus working capital at close (estimated at AUD$16.5 million) plus transaction costs of AUD$2 million for an enterprise value of AUD$64.5 million.

The majority of the Goundrey brand volume (85 per cent) was sold in the AUD$15 to AUD$30 super premium segment of the Australian market. The ultra premium segment ($30 to $50) accounted for seven per cent of sales and the premium ($10 to $15) for the remaining eight per cent. The company's sales were almost entirely in the domestic market with three per cent export sales. When asked what was Goundrey's export strategy, Bendat said, "I answer the phone."

Goundrey employed its own sales force in Queensland and New South Wales, with a total of 13 sales reps and four sales managers in two states. In other states, Goundrey had appointed distributors. In all regions, Goundrey was the most important winery for the distributor. Goundrey had tighter control of its distribution capability in Australia than most of its competitors. Goundrey consumption was running at more than 26 per cent year over year growth versus 2001.

Located 350 km south of Perth, the winery could process 3,500 tonnes of grapes. The winery also had its own bottling capability, enabling it to support an export business where each export market has different labeling requirements.

Triggs felt the Goundrey acquisition would be an important strategic move for Vincor. He saw several major advantages. First, the acquisition would be a significant step in achieving Vincor's strategy of converting from a North American to a global player. The Australian wine industry had captured market share in the world's new wine markets and was poised to continue to do so. Second, the Western Australia region had an established reputation for super and ultra-premium wines. Although the grape harvest was a mere four per cent of the Australian total, more than 25 per cent of Australia's super-premium wines were sourced from that state. Third, the company had developed its own sales force in Queensland and New South Wales. Triggs wanted the proposal to go through.

APPENDIX

Additional Cases Available From Ivey Publishing

CQUAY Technologies Corp. *(Case 9B04M068)*

Alternative for Chapters 2, 3, 4, 5
Issues: Strategy, valuation, sell-side M&A, governance

CQUAY Technologies Corp. was a privately held Canadian software company with offices in Toronto, Calgary, and Washington, D.C. CQUAY marketed a patented location intelligence engine called Common Ground. The company's technology was designed for an emerging, multi-billion-dollar segment of the spatial information management market. A year earlier, the board had asked the chief executive officer to shape the company into an acquisition target over the next 18 to 24 months. A year later, there were no imminent acquisition discussions, and recent customer traction and the sales pipeline seemed to merit raising growth capital instead of following the acquisition-focused plan. The CEO wanted to keep his stockholders and board happy by executing the plan they had given him but did not want to jeopardize possible customer growth. If he refocused the plan, he feared it might change acquisition opportunities. Without further contracts, the existing cash would sustain the company for only another 6 to 8 months. The CEO thought the most likely outcome was to sell the company, but he needed to make the company more attractive. He planned to present options and a recommendation to the board of directors later that month.

Deloitte & Touche: Integrating Arthur Andersen *(Case 9B04C004)*

Alternative for Chapter 7
Issues: Postmerger integration

In 2002, approximately 1,000 Arthur Andersen employees joined Deloitte & Touche, effectively creating the largest professional services organization in Canada. The combined entity employed 6,600 people and represented annual billings of over $1 billion. A cochair for the national integration team was faced with a huge challenge: to develop a company-wide plan to create support materials to aid the Deloitte staff in integrating the

Andersen staff in the organization. The integration process was monitored through a monthly survey and would be used by the team to benchmark unit to unit over time and to take remedial action at specific stages if the integration goals were not attained. The most recent survey indicated that Deloitte employees felt that in the company's haste to finalize the deal with Andersen, it was forgetting about its own employees. Some within the Deloitte organization did not understand the amount of attention given to Andersen employees, whom they viewed as "damaged goods." The cochair and integration team must determine the best way to deal with the feedback and the cultural differences that are surfacing.

Amtelecom Group, Inc. *(Case 9B04N014)*

Alternative for Chapters 1, 2, 3, 4, 8
Issues: Governance, M&A strategy, M&A approach, valuation, alternatives
The chief executive officer of Amtelecom Group, Inc. (AGI) must make a recommendation to the board of directors regarding the best way to sell its Amtelecom Communications subsidiary. AGI owns and operates ICS Courier, a national fixed-route courier business and Amtelecom Communications, a regional telecommunications, cable television, and Internet business. Amtelecom Communication's capital requirements are not being satisfied because cash is being diverted to ICS Courier to cover its losses. As well, AGI's stock has been performing poorly. To alleviate these problems, the board has decided to sell off Amtelecom Communications. The three sales alternatives being considered are selling to a strategic buyer, initial public offering (IPO) via a common share offering, and IPO via an income trust offering. This case can be used to teach students about valuation in a strategic setting and provides an opportunity to apply sum-of-parts valuation to value a diversified firm, apply discounted cash flow, conduct a transactions analysis to determine the stand-alone value of a firm, and gain a basic understanding of income trusts.

CIBC-Barclays: Accounting for Their Merger *(Case 9B04B022)*

Alternative for Chapters 4, 7
Issues: Accounting in M&A
The Canadian Imperial Bank of Commerce (CIBC) and Barclays Bank PLC have signed an agreement to combine their retail, corporate, and offshore banking operations in the Caribbean to create FirstCaribbean International Bank. In principle, it appeared that both parties were agreeing to a combination of their assets to form a new entity, in which case a new holding company could be constituted to absorb the assets being merged. Alternately, as Barclays's interest in the merger was substantially greater than that of CIBC, the transaction could be construed as an outright purchase of the CIBC interests by Barclays. The problem with this second approach, however, was that Barclays Caribbean presently had no separate legal form in the region.

China Minmetals Corporation and Noranda, Inc. *(Case 9B06M013)*

Alternative for Chapters 4, 6, 8, 10
Issues: Cross-border M&A, politics, governmental influence/regulation

The proposed takeover of Noranda, Inc. (one of the biggest mineral players in the world) by the Chinese state-owned enterprise, China Minmetals Corporation, was cause for Canadian government concern as it required some understanding about the workings and objectives of state-owned enterprises. There was particular concern about the labor issues and human rights violations in China, as well as the possible impact of these on the proposed takeover. Equally important, Canada ran a substantial risk of sending the wrong message to the People's Republic of China if it was to block such a takeover and, in some respects, to be seen as shutting its doors to one of the world's largest and most powerful emerging economies.

Tsingtao Brewery Co. Ltd. (A) *(Case 9B05M063)*

Alternative for Chapters 2, 7, 9
Issues: Postmerger integration, M&A strategy
Tsingtao Brewery Co. Ltd., the most famous Chinese beer producer, was surpassed by Yanjing Beer in the mid-1990s due to its inefficient operation system and fierce competition from home and overseas competitors. From 1994 to 2002, Tsingtao Brewery took over 47 small- and medium-sized companies and regained its dominant position in the beer industry. However, the quick expansion incurred many problems such as the bottleneck of the capital and managerial pool, cultural conflicts, multiple brands, low profitability, and other ailments of being such a big company. In July 2001, Peng Zuoyi suddenly died of a heart attack, and Jin Zhiguo succeeded as general manager. Facing the challenging situation, Jin made the decision to transform the business strategy of Tsingtao Brewery from "growing large to become powerful" to "growing powerful to become large," which focuses on postacquisition integration.

Arla and MD Foods: The Merger Decision (A) *(Case 9B04M076)*

Alternative for Chapters 1, 2, 6, 7, 8, 10
Issues: M&A strategy, approvals, cross-border M&A, integration
The managing director of MD Foods of Denmark and the president of Arla of Sweden, both cooperatives, were contemplating whether their companies should merge to create Europe's largest dairy company. Arla and MD Foods wished to continue the success of their joint ventures in a much closer relationship but wondered if their owners (the milk-producing farmers in each country) would approve the merger. In addition, the two companies were different in size, organizational structure, organizational culture, monetary currency used, and language spoken. Finally, a cross-border merger of two cooperatives was unprecedented throughout the world. The supplement "Arla and MD Food: The Merger Decision (B)" *(Case 9B05M013)* describes the merger decision.

Gillette's Energy Drain (B): Energizer's Acquisition of Schick *(Case 9B05M027)*

Alternative for Chapters 2, 7, 9
Issues: M&A strategy, implementation, integration
This is a supplement to "Gillette's Energy Drain (A): The Acquisition of Duracell" *(Case 9B05M026)*. Highlighted is Energizer's acquisition of Schick. Gillette was just

dabbling in batteries, but its source of profits had always been in razors and blades. Now, that business is under direct threat by Energizer, with its acquisition of Schick. This supplement provides an excellent example of multipoint competition and raises the following question: Should Gillette have anticipated that the acquisition of a battery company would ultimately put razor profits at risk?

VF Corp: Acquiring the Iconic Skateboard Footwear Brand VANS (Case 9B06N008)

Alternative for Chapters 2, 3, 4
Issues: Valuation, stock consideration
The chief financial officer of VF Outdoor Americas—a division of the world's largest apparel company, VF Corporation—must decide on the financial viability of purchasing the skateboard VANS lifestyle brand. In his decision, the chief financial officer needs to develop an offer of what VF should pay for VANS and prove to the parent company that the acquisition will be accretive to earnings per share.

Worldcom, Inc.: What Went Wrong? (Case 9B05M043)

Alternative for Chapters 2, 7, 9
Issues: M&A strategy, integration, recovery, exits
Accounting fraud issues have taken center stage whenever there is a discussion about the bankruptcy of Worldcom. However, Worldcom's performance was in turmoil even before the fraud issues surfaced. The fundamental strategic, management, and industry issues that catalyzed the culture allowing fraudulent behavior that led to the bankruptcy of the company are discussed.

Rayovac Corporation: International Growth and Diversification Through Acquisitions (Case 9B06M025)

Alternative for Chapters 2, 10
Issues: M&A strategy, globalization, cross-border M&A
The Rayovac case discusses the company's bold and risky acquisitions strategy as it diversifies into personal care and grooming, lawn and garden care, insecticides, and pet foods. The company assumes it can successfully manage diverse product categories across diverse geographic markets in which it has limited experience. Success will depend on how well the acquired companies are integrated and managed under Rayovac's supervision. Increasingly, it will also depend on external conditions beyond Rayovac's control, such as macroeconomic conditions and foreign exchange fluctuations. Students should be able to analyze the case from the point of view of international business and strategy and perform a financial analysis of potential future returns using different assumptions for sales growth and margins of the various businesses acquired.

HSBC—The Bital Acquisition (Case 9B04N012)

Alternative for Chapters 3, 5, 7
Issues: M&A strategy, brand positioning, multinational, cross-cultural management

HSBC is one of the largest and most global financial institutions in the world. The company has identified Bital, Mexico's fourth largest bank, as a potential acquisition target. Negotiations have come down to the wire, and the controlling Mexican shareholders are trying to get HSBC to raise its offer. Is it worth it? HSBC must decide on both strategic and short-term financial criteria under some degree of uncertainty, as illuminated by a due diligence process. The HSBC executive who has handled the acquisition at a local level—and would be chief executive officer of HSBC Mexico should the deal go ahead—is assessing the pros and cons of the acquisition and must also identify the priorities that he and his team would have to address, including culture change issues, rebranding Bital as HSBC Mexico, personnel issues, and maintaining the continuity of the business.

Rogers Communications, Inc.—
Maclean Hunter Limited *(Case 9A96B046)*

Alternative for Chapters 1, 3, 4, 5
Issues: Board of directors, valuation, deal execution
Ted Rogers, president and CEO of Rogers Communications (RCI), announced that a strategic merger was being sought with Maclean Hunter Limited (MHL). Over the course of the past several weeks, a private company controlled by Mr. Rogers had purchased a block of stock representing approximately 8% of the shares held by the public. The focus of the case is to formulate a presentation to RCI's board of directors, which discusses the price, strategy, and terms of a planned offer to acquire all remaining MHL shares.

ABOUT THE EDITORS

Kevin K. Boeh is currently a Ph.D. candidate and instructor at the Richard Ivey School of Business, University of Western Ontario. His doctoral research combines the disciplines of strategy and finance and focuses on mergers and acquisitions, initial public offerings, the role of investment bankers and consultants, international business, and corporate strategy. He is also an experienced Wall Street investment banker and management consultant. He has completed more than 100 M&A and IPO transactions consisting of over U.S.$5 billion in M&A transactions and over U.S.$5 billion in capital raised for both public and private companies. Boeh formerly served as Vice President, Group Head at investment bank Robertson Stephens and as the Head of the Strategic Development Group. Previously, he was with the consulting practices of both A. T. Kearney and Accenture, where he provided strategic advisory services to management teams and boards. He has completed extensive international work with clients in the United States, Canada, France, Germany, Israel, Japan, the United Kingdom, and Australia. He has been a frequent keynote speaker at conferences and events and has authored numerous research articles and white papers. Boeh serves on the boards of directors of two companies and helps direct a merchant banking fund. He received his M.B.A., Finance and Strategy, from UCLA—The Anderson School and an undergraduate degree in Economics from The Colorado College.

Paul W. Beamish holds the Canada Research Chair in International Business at the Ivey Business School, University of Western Ontario. He is the author or coauthor of 44 books and more than 100 articles or contributed chapters. He has received best research awards from the Academy of Management, the Academy of International Business (AIB), and the Administrative Sciences Association of Canada (ASAC). In 1997 and 2003, he was recognized in the *Journal of International Management* as one of the top three contributors worldwide to the international strategic management literature in the previous decade. He served as Editor-in-Chief of the *Journal of International Business Studies* (*JIBS*) from 1993–1997 and is a Fellow of the Academy of International Business. At Ivey, he has responsibility for Ivey Publishing, the distributor of Ivey's case collection. From 1999–2004, he served as Associate Dean Research.

Beamish has authored nearly 100 case studies, primarily in the international management area. These have appeared in *Asian Case Research Journal, Case Research Journal,* and more than 70 books. His cases have been consistently among Ivey's top external sellers. He is past recipient of best case writing awards from the European Foundation for

Management Development, ASAC, and AIB. He is the editor of a series of cases on the merger and integration of the regional operations of CIBC and Barclays to form FirstCaribbean International Bank. His M&A-related journal articles have appeared in *JIBS, Organization Studies,* and *Management International Review.*

Before entering academia, Beamish worked for the Procter and Gamble Company of Canada, where he had direct experience with the acquisition and integration of Victory Soya Mills.